THE LIBRARY OF LIVING CATHOLIC THOUGHT

(Under the direction of The Faculty of the Bellarmine School of Theology of Loyola University)

Toward Understanding
Saint Thomas

TOWARD UNDERSTANDING SAINT THOMAS

M.–D. CHENU, O.P.

Translated with Authorized Corrections
and Bibliographical Additions

by

A.–M. Landry, O.P.

and

D. Hughes, O.P.

HENRY REGNERY COMPANY
Chicago

Nihil obstat quominus imprimatur:
  L.–B. Geiger, O.P.
  L.–M. Régis, O.P.

Imprimi potest:
  Thomas M. Rondeau, O.P.
    Provincial of the Canadian Dominican Province
      October 22, 1963

Imprimatur:
  Bishop Paul Grégoire
    Montreal, Quebec, Canada
      October 22, 1963

This translation is from the French original, *Introduction à l'étude de Saint Thomas d'Aquin*. Montreal, Institut d'études médiévales— Paris, librairie philosophique J. Vrin, 1950.

Manufactured in the United States of America
Library of Congress Catalog Card No. 64–14598

Contents

Part One

LIFEWORK OF SAINT THOMAS

Contents

Part Two

WORKS OF SAINT THOMAS

Contents

Contents

Toward Understanding
Saint Thomas

Presentation

In spite of so many assurances on the part of my friends, I cannot altogether escape a feeling of uneasiness in presenting this book to the public. Not that I judge it to be superfluous, because, even with the excellent introductions that have already been written, I believe that it is original. Nor do I consider it a hasty piece of work, since it was first the object of continuous teaching for a period of over twenty years. Yet, an introduction of the present sort can be written only as an outline, and such an outline is necessarily lacking in the living quality that came from word-of-mouth communication and in the spiritual or textual experiences that were its constant support. It was, then, a matter of introducing my students, of "having them make an entrance", into the majestic—and disconcerting—edifice of Saint Thomas's writings which were to be, for years to come, a part of their basic text matter, both in philosophy and theology. Encountering my students on such a subject was not without its element of enthusiasm, while at the same time I wanted it to be painstakingly and soberly faithful to history and its objective rules. How, then, was I to preserve in a book the warmth that had accompanied an initiation conceived in such cordiality and the simplicity that excluded any show of pedantry? For, an initiation such a task had turned out to be, rather than an introduction.

What finally brought me to make up my mind was the memory of the glowing eagerness of my students, both at Le Saulchoir and at the Institut d'études médiévales of Ottawa (now of Montreal), who, having to open the pages of Saint Thomas at the very start of their studies, followed my modest courses and drew a decisive measure of help from them. Yet, these elementary lectures, revised and readied for print, have now taken on a character of compactness that may be discouraging to any reader who is not an "initiate." The latter, on the other hand, is no longer in need of a guide. This equivocal state of affairs, however, is probably the lot of every introduction to all great

1

works, whether they deal with thought or with art, since one does not gain entrance into a great work without first making a survey of its component parts.

The entrance into the thought-system of Saint Thomas proposed here, is none other than the milieu in which it was borne and worked out. This milieu, to be sure, was a spiritual one—it was that of the Gospel-spirited Mendicants and that of the discoverers of Aristotle— but it was also one in which the institutions of the age, its universities, literary achievements, and community life itself were essential components of a single reality. This whole book is based on the conviction that the works of a genius and the human soil in which these works implanted themselves and bore fruits—even beyond the promise of that human soil—are closely interdependent in their individual realizations and truth. Consequently we cannot understand them in any other way. There is no dividing gulf between the truth that the mind lays hold of and the conditions under which it is thought out. On the contrary, they are constantly meshing together to the mutual advantage of both. These conditions, therefore, understood within the homogeneity of history as well as in the eternal selfsameness of truth, are efficacious means of making one's approach to truth. To be sure, I am, with Carlyle, a believer in the primacy and irreducible character of personal genius. Saint Thomas is perhaps the most striking example of this. At the same time, however, it is a known fact that the human being, in the precise measure of his genius, is solidly one with his community, that is, with the social conditions of the human groups within which he is implanted.

While progressing from chapter to chapter in this book and as he discovers the social components underlying the thought, work, sources, and methods of Saint Thomas, the reader will, I am quite confident, find himself gaining insight into his interior life. To witness the birth of a master theologian and to watch him at work in an age when theologians and theology were not set apart from the world and its conditions, outlook, techniques, and culture, is a grand spectacle to behold! It is, moreover, a lesson to anyone who is acquainted with theology's later state of exile and her vain watchfulness at maintaining her rights. It is hardly necessary to add that the coherence between truth and the conditions of its realization does not mean that truth is of only relative value, as some have blunderingly inferred. Truth is no less true because it was set forth in a temporal setting.

In the case of written works, it is through the analysis of their literary forms that one discovers the communion between a system of thought and its social environment, from which, as it happens, the system draws its own styling of concepts and language. Pushing to the very bottom this analysis of the literary forms of thought has, I believe, turned out to be extremely fruitful. Therein, moreover, lies the unity of my work which I want to be something else than a mere collection of very learned data on the chronology and genuineness of Saint Thomas's writings. A commentary on Aristotle, a commentary on the Bible, a *quodlibet*, a *summa*, these are not shapeless vessels which pure reason can use indifferently. Rather, they have their own laws and their own spiritual bearing. Augustine wrote "confessions," and Dionysius moved onward through symbols. Saint Thomas, professor at the University of Paris, taught, held disputes, wrote commentaries. The diversity of literary genres is precisely one of the factors indicating the creative vitality of this medieval university which was then in full flight—a vitality making itself felt even in theology, thereupon become a science, that indispensable organ in a Christian order.

The detailed results of biographical, chronological, and critical research, then, I shall leave to the array of books in which these data have already been collected in order to avoid encumbering an undertaking that I mean to confine to the very interior of the mind of Saint Thomas as he was actually developing and building up his works. We have been left without any confidential indications from him, but it is my hope that through successive approaches we shall have acquired imperceptibly a familiarity—at once enlightening and fruitful—with his magnificent thought. In which case, we shall be in a position to understand better the objects of his thinking.

I have also given up the idea of furnishing a complete bibliography at the end of each chapter. The *Bulletin thomiste* will adequately answer needs on this point. I have preferred to limit myself to a number of indications to be considered only as starting-points for future personal work. In advancing the latter, I here again find myself in the presence of my former students who would pick up the trail opened up in the classroom and pursue, in full-length texts, the experiences that their first reading contacts had provided. Each chapter, then, will be brought to a close with a number of "Research Suggestions" designed to sharpen the appetite of the reader and to give me the pleasure of prolonging with him the friendly talks that we are about to begin.

Translators' Note

Without interrupting any longer than necessary Father Chenu's "friendly talks" with the reader, a statement of the purpose and procedure of the translators seems appropriate.

Father Chenu's "superb introduction" (1) has in the original the rugged expressiveness and style of a most competent thinker and scholar, as well as the power and vitality of a convincing preacher. Fidelity to his thought, and so far as possible to his style, has been accepted by the translators as their primary obligation both to the author and his readers. The almost equally pressing need for felicitous readability has not been neglected, but it is admittedly subordinate.

In carrying out their work, the translators have adhered to a code of production, wherein techniques and devices were standardized so far as possible. Attention is drawn to the five following points:

1. No positions of the author have been changed save in one instance in which, at his own request, his text has been abandoned and replaced by that of the German edition of the work (2). New bibliographical materials have been added, however, in the spirit of the author's own practice as described in his Presentation above. Research subsequent to 1950 has provided the occasion for most of the additions, and existing English translations of works referred to in the book have been pointed out. On the whole, the additional data have been provided with the prime thought of helping especially the English speaking reader who is less familiar with foreign language books (3).

---

1) K. STRECKER, *Introduction to Medieval Latin*, English trans. and rev. by R. B. PALMER, Berlin, 1957, p. 104, note 11.

2) See ch. IX, 282, note a.

3) The adequate tool for the history, works, sources, and doctrine of Saint Thomas is the *Bulletin thomiste* (Le Saulchoir, 1924 . . .) to which the author refers in his Presentation. For abundant references to studies, texts, periodicals, collections on the Middle Ages in general, and on Saint Thomas in particular, the reader may also consult the following: P. MANDONNET et J. DESTREZ, *Bibliog-*

2. All quotations, Latin, French, or otherwise, have been carried over into English by the translators themselves. For the benefit of the student wishing to do more reading in a quoted work, references to other existing English translations have usually been supplied. Modern language quotations have been given only in English. Latin quotations included in the French text have been relegated to the footnotes, and those already in the footnotes are given only in English. Technical Latin and Greek words and phrases have been maintained within the text; they are translated once, either the first time they appear in the book, or in the passage where explanations about them are given. Two lists of them with the pages upon which they appear have been provided at the end of the book. Titles of works referred to have generally been maintained in their original language, in accordance with the author's practice.

3. Footnotes are indicated by numbers and letters. Numbers identify notes of the original French edition, sometimes given precision for reference purposes. Additions to them have been bracketed, as was also done in the case of a small number of precisions added to the text. Letters indicate either Latin quotations brought down from the text to the footnotes, or completely new notes supplied by the translators. From chapter VI onward, Latin editions of the authentic works of Saint Thomas have been indicated. References are to the two latest complete editions of his works—Parma and Vivès—to the incomplete Leonine critical edition, and to other more available texts, critical or otherwise. Most of the existing English translations have also been indicated.

4. Abbreviations have been abundantly used throughout. Three lists of them are provided at the end of the book. The table of *sigla* has been worked out in order to provide the student with as complete as possible information concerning the work that is referred to, and also to supply a helpful array of sources which he may consult for further personal research. In view of the trend to publishing within collections and series, such a list is far from being superfluous. Most of the periodicals, collections of texts and studies, and editions used in the work have been included—even paperbacks find their place in it, since paperbacks too have become an indispensable tool for the student,

---

raphie thomiste, 2d ed., rev. with additions, by M.-D. CHENU, in *BibTh*, I (1960); V. J. BOURKE, *Thomistic Bibliography 1920–1940*, Suppl to *MS*, XXI (1945); P. WYSER, *Thomas von Aquin*, in *BESP*, XIII/XIV (1950); F. VAN STEENBERGHEN, *Philosophie des Mittelalters*, in *BESP*, XVII (1950); V. J. BOURKE, *Introduction to the Works of St. Thomas Aquinas*, Reprint from *S. Thomae Aquinatis Opera Omnia*, vol. I, New York, Musurgia Publishers, 1948, pp. iii–xxiv; K. STRECKER, *Introduction to Medieval Latin*, English trans. and rev. by R. B. PALMER, Berlin, 1957, especially pages 90–111. Part of the bibliographical material concerning periodicals, collections, and editions pointed out in the preceding is also given at the end of the present work. See below, pp. 350–366.

and oftentimes the only available means of access to otherwise out of print books. For the reader's convenience, this list of *sigla* has been basically reproduced inside the covers of the book.—The third list is that of abbreviations of the titles of all of Saint Thomas's works that have been specifically referred to in the book, together with the pages upon which these references appear.

5. The list of proper names of the original has been done over to include the names of any author, translator, and editor not previously named. No subject index has been provided since the work is one that should be meditated upon rather than referred to.

To the *Institut d'études médiévales* of Montreal where the present translation was done, and to its librarians for generously providing facilities and free access to all materials and instrumentation that have made the present work possible, a unique debt of gratitude is due.

The guiding principle for both Father Chenu and his translators into English has been admirably summarized and expressed by E. Gilson: "These pages, the density and richness of information of which defy analysis, are, from the first to the last, a fervent offering. One cannot give to another ready-made truth, but rather the means of making its conquest. Father Chenu tells the student: This is what Saint Thomas did; go and do the same. Those who will do so after Father Chenu will owe him the happy result of having been introduced to the study of the true, real, and ever-alive Saint Thomas Aquinas" (4).

D. HUGHES, O.P.   A.-M. LANDRY, O.P.
Institute of Mediaeval Studies   *Institut d'études médiévales*
Toronto   Montreal

Montreal, 1963

---

4) From E. Gilson's review of the French original: *Introduction à l'étude de saint Thomas d'Aquin*, in *PIEM*, XI (1950), reprinted without change in 1954. See *BT*, VIII (1947–1953), 10.

Part One
Lifework of Saint Thomas

Chapter I

The Work in Its Milieu

I. BIOGRAPHICAL NOTE

1224-5
Roccasecca
(in Aquino)

Saint Thomas was born near Aquino, in southern Italy, in the fortified castle of Roccasecca, either at the end of 1224 or at the beginning of 1225. This was the time when Honorius III (1216–1227) was good-temperedly maintaining, in both Church and State, the prestige that his predecessor, Innocent III, had won for the Papacy. It was also the time when Frederick II (1215–1250), at the helm of the Holy Roman Empire then extending from Germany to Sicily, was temporarily at peace with the Church through the pact of San Germano (1230). In France, Louis IX, still a child, was just about to start his long reign, at the very moment when the tide of the drama-packed crusade against Raymond VII of Toulouse and the Albigensians was turning in favor of the Capetian royalty. The Moors, despite their defeat at the hands of the Crusaders at Las Navas in 1212, were solidly entrenched in the Spanish Kingdom of Granada and still laying siege to the Christian world. In fact, the founding of the Latin Kingdom of Jerusalem only served to make more acutely felt the haunting shadows of Islam. Farther away, the Tartars kept on pressing, thus making clear the power and human resources of the Asiatic continent. The Christian order, which had been molded in the pattern of the geography and culture of the Roman Empire, had thought of itself as embracing all mankind and as the achievement of the "City of God" on earth. Now, Christians were becoming conscious of the facts that faith had touched only a part of the human race and that there existed a whole world containing tremendous secular resources.

Landulf of Aquino, feudal lord, was entangled in local rivalries as well as in the political struggles of the Empire. Close by him was the

11

powerful abbey of Monte Cassino, lying right on the boundaries of the Church States and the Kingdom of Sicily. Here, in 1230, he brought his youngest son, Thomas, and offered him as an oblate. This move, at once religious and self-interested in character, recalls to mind the social surroundings and cultural climate in which, according to feudal traditions, the lad was to grow up. Meanwhile, the struggle between Pope and Emperor had resumed, more violent than ever, and when Frederick II invaded Italy, Thomas had to leave the Benedictine abbey (1239). Whereupon he was sent to the schools of Naples to begin, in the faculty of arts, a university life that would stop short only at his death. After five years spent there, and seven more of philosophy and theology at Paris and Cologne in the university *studia* [houses of study] of the Friar Preachers, he began a teaching career that was to unfold without break or distraction.

It is plain that Thomas's joining the Preachers—in spite of the violent opposition of his family (1244)—was, together with the religious orientation of his soul, the factor that fashioned all his activity, considered not only from an outward point of view but, especially, from that of doctrine and motivation. This activity had a homogeneousness whose total constancy we shall faithfully observe as a clearcut trait of his life.

In the fall of 1245, Thomas came to Paris to the convent of Saint James, then the most prominent scholastic center of the Order, situated right at the heart of the University. He was enrolled as a student of Albert the Great who was then a professor in the faculty of theology. During the summer of 1248, he left Paris to go with Master Albert who was to take charge of the new *studium generale* [general house of studies] founded at Cologne by the Order. He remained there until 1252, when he came back to Paris to teach and thus prepare himself for his Masterate in Sacred Theology.

The University, at this time, was the scene of a bitter struggle, due precisely to the rivalries between the seculars and religious. A strike, decided by the professors and that was to be rather long-lived, added to the effervescence. After having commented first on the Bible (1252–1254), then on the *Sentences* of Peter Lombard (1254–1256), Thomas received, as these incidents were taking place at the beginning of 1256, his *licentia docendi* [license to teach] at the instance of Pope Alexander IV who wrote about Thomas in terms of no uncertain praise. Now a master, he went on teaching until June, 1259, in one of the two Dominican schools incorporated with the University. Returning to Italy, he taught at the papal curia, first in Anagni (1259–1261), then in Orvieto (1261–1265). From there, he went to the convent of Santa Sabina in Rome (1265–1267), whence he was recalled by Clement IV to work at the papal curia in Viterbo (1267–November, 1268).

In the meantime, battling had started all over again at the University of Paris. The battleground was not one of corporate rights alone but one of doctrine as well, because the spread of Aristotelianism had provoked an intellectual and moral crisis that was becoming daily more acute. Saint Thomas, whose own position had been called into debate, but whose accrediting had grown to considerable proportions, was hurriedly called back to Paris. The years that followed his return, from 1268 until Easter of 1272, were to be of an almost unbelievable fruitfulness. It was undoubtedly in answer to a request made by King Charles of Anjou, who was anxious to revive the University of Naples, that Thomas returned to the latter city and became head of the faculty of theology (1272). Invited by Pope Gregory X to take part in the forthcoming Council of Lyons, he set out on his journey in January, 1274, but he died on March 7, at the Cistercian abbey of Fossanova.

The biography of Saint Thomas, as will readily be seen, is one of extreme simplicity. In carrying out a career completely organized around the university mode of life, he made a few journeys which took him to Paris, the papal curia, Paris again, and Naples. One would be mistaken, however, in judging his life to be merely the quiet existence of a professional person completely absorbed by his teaching and seemingly untouched by the social and political affairs of his day. The great events in his silent existence grew out of his presence at the heart of the University. The drama that went on in his mind and in his religious life, and on which the fate of Christian thought hung in the balance, had its causes and produced its effects right at the University—a university, it is true, in which all the ingredients of a civilization in full bloom were massed together, to which, moreover, Christian faith had, deliberately and authoritatively, committed its doctrine and spirit. It is, then, right at the University that Saint Thomas found, not only the technical conditions for drawing up his work, not only the polemic occasions for turning it out, but also the enveloping and penetrating spiritual milieu needed for it. It is within the homogeneous contexts supplied by this milieu that it is possible today to discover the historical intelligibility of his work, just as they supplied the climate for its fruitfulness at the time that it was born. It is not unimportant that, in the days of Saint Louis and of Frederick II, Saint Thomas should arrive at Paris at a time:

when, in a new society just entered upon a communal era, it was in the corporate university body that intellectual eagerness and curiosity were concentrated and were to introduce Aristotle and ancient reason to Christian thought;

when the cathedral of Notre Dame of Paris was being completed and the *Romance of the Rose* written;

13

when, after the battle of Bouvines wherein the Holy Roman Empire and its feudal hierarchy were jointly defeated (1214), Europe was entering on a new era in which it would cease to be a theocratic entity;

when the Moslems were hemming in the Western world by their military successes and seducing it by their science and philosophy;

when, finally, merchants and missionaries were pushing their way into the region of Cathay and discovering the world's dimensions and the variety of its civilizations.

Neither is it unimportant that Saint Thomas should join the Friar Preachers in the Christian world of Innocent III and that he should find in the midst of this new religious family, at the most opportune time, an Albert the Great to be his master (a).

II. THE NEW SCHOOLS

The University, with its own structure and spirit, had just sprung up in the city schools, leaving the monastic schools, tied up as they were with feudal conservatism, to their intellectual routine. Indeed, centres of culture and teaching had been the subject of a spiritual and geographical shift of capital importance that was brought about through the economic and social evolution that was making over the face of the Western world (b). Feudal institutions were crumbling, weighed down by a structure that was no longer in keeping with the conditions and needs of human society. A widening of commercial enterprise, an increase in the circulation of money, the reopening of the Mediterranean to ship traffic, improved technical devices, a specialization of craftmen's skills, a rapid increase in population—all had been factors toward the gradual development of urban centres. In them, a new class of matured people had won for itself a whole series of freedoms—personal, civic, and agrarian—with all this taking place outside the old domanial economy that entailed the serfdom of the individual and the denial of the individual's right to associate. The exercise of authority was now no longer tied up with possession of the soil, any more than were the economic standards of the day. The crop of new elites was formed independently of the landed aristocracy; it was now a world of give and take that saw artisans and traders taking their chances, for labor was now seen as a means of getting ahead and no longer as an inferior function. Along with the factors that had brought it into existence, the old order was doomed to decay. Under

a) For bibliographical data on the life of Saint Thomas, see the Research Suggestions below, 78.

b) On the new economic and social conditions, see the Research Suggestions and bibliography given below, 69–71.

that regime, social security and stability for the individual had been assured through the binding of man to man by means of the principle of "homage" which created a personal dependency both summary and advantageous, and was hallowed by an oath of allegiance. The new regime discarded private contracts of allegiance in favor of collective charters, thus ensuring the precedence of the common good over private interests and guaranteeing the *jura et libertates* [rights and freedoms] of all. Having secured their freedom, the Communes were not a mere association of individuals; on the contrary, they represented collective entities that held sway over the life of the individual in all its manifestations. They were persons, in the juridic sense of the word, and truly the subjects of rights.

While the passage from the feudal state to the Commune was taking place during the course of the XIIth century, men had progressively been acquiring independence in their thinking, along with a sense of personal responsibility, an urge to pursue new ventures on their own, and also that nimbleness of mind enabling man to cope with the unforeseen problems arising in a newly opened world. The city schools, now filled with students affected by the spirit of the age, carried over in their intellectual standards and their organization of studies the same aspirations that the corporations and municipal governments were embodying in the social life and organization of the cities. Simply looking at things from the outside, the fact alone that schoolmen now enjoyed the privileges of free association and of an elective system is enough to show how far the university colleges had gotten away from the old monastic schools with their restriction to the enclosure of their domain, with their commitment to a class of people that knew no traveling, with their abbatial rule based on paternalism, monastic schools, in short, that were closely dependent upon that majestic feudal system on which monastic life had laid its earthly foundations.

Thomas Aquinas belonged by birth to a prominent feudal dynasty, and family traditions would have had him a monk in the most powerful abbey of his day—Monte Cassino—where he actually passed the first period of his youth. Yet, thanks to the freedom he had won when he was battling to follow his own religious calling, Thomas entered in a pathway that would lead him to the most restless and the most representative of the city schools, lying right at the heart of the new society, the University of Paris.

It cannot, of course, be said without qualification that studies in the XIIIth century monasteries were in a state of decay. In fact, if many a masterpiece had come out of their literary workshops, many were still to come forth that would leave the products of the schools in their dust. Yet, the finest achievements, whether of a personal or local character, cannot conceal the fact that, as the century rolled along, and as the new social and cultural movement gained ground, the monastic schools were outclassed as institutions. A decidedly different type of people were now coming to the schools of Paris, Bologna, Oxford, and Cologne. First of all, they arrived in numbers that quickly overflowed the cathedral cloisters, taking over for themselves a city quarter that was to be their own and where they ruled, even in the streets that soon rang with their noisy clatter. These new students were the type that Abelard had to cope with, and no longer those Anselm had known in his monastic schoolroom. Further, the new schools automatically linked up in a "university" of studies, which, in turn, became one of the corporate societies of the new city, patterned upon the guilds. The University was now a collective entity with juridic status, able to carry on business in the name of the teaching profession, and thus raised to hold the rank of "office" in the city. It had the right to arrange its life as suited its purposes, even to the point of having its own police force, so long as it did not encroach upon the rights of the larger collective body (c). Since its prime interest lay in cultural and intellectual values, and rightly conscious of its universal dignity, it even tended to extend its influence beyond the jurisdiction of the city or to offer advice in matters politic. Teachers and students alike enjoyed a "status" (1) that was enhanced not only by the *jura et libertates* pertaining to it, but also by a moral, and soon, a political prestige, the latter working either to the advantage or the disadvantage of higher learning.

From the rue du Fouarre to the abbey of Sainte-Genevieve, the schools lined up, nearly covering the ridge along the rue Saint-Jacques where Albert the Great and Thomas Aquinas would soon have a school of their own, open to all comers, and formally accepted as part of the University body in whose rights and scholastic programs and public demonstrations it would share. Into these schools came pouring a population eager to learn, no longer regarding knowledge as a propaedeutic to monastic life but as a road to culture and an indispensable tool for carving out a career. The faculty of arts worked itself up to a position of autonomy that was both intellectual and administrative. The doctors and lawyers introduced their cycles of

---

c) See P. KIBRE, *Scholarly Privileges in the Middle Ages. The Rights, Privileges, and Immunities, of Scholars and Universities at Bologna, Padua, Paris, and Oxford*, in *MAAP*, LXXII (1962).

1) Give to the word *status* the full meaning it had in the medieval vocabulary. See G. DE LAGARDE, *La naissance de l'esprit laïque au déclin du moyen âge*, Vol. I: *Bilan du XIIIe siècle*; ch. VIII: *Le régime des estats*, 3rd ed., Paris–Louvain, 1956, pp. 99–125.

studies. Professors and students formed themselves into corporations in order to protect their rights and to secure their privileges (a). Rivalries and personal ambitions were soon to install themselves in their midst. There were also unsuspected problems that the financial requirements of schooling were to raise and which the establishment of the colleges attempted to solve. As best as could be, copies of books were multiplied by methods unknown in the old *scriptoria;* and the very make-up of the manuscripts is revealing of the needs and habits of this intellectual democracy (2).

It was a far cry, now, from the monastic schools where the teaching personnel, inspired only by the love of God, and without haste, or personal ambition, or care for the morrow, prepared the young monk for the reading of the Bible and taking part in the divine service. Even Citeaux that had recently done so much to restore monastic life to its magnificent lustre, broke off from this new world. It built its abbeys far from the cities, sent its monks back to manual labor, and reduced its program of studies to the practice of spiritual reading, condemning dialectic and all other forms of secular learning. And when the Order of Saint Benedict of a later date will attempt to inject new life in its studies, it will have to seek support from outside the cloister, and by a significant redress of things, it will actually found a "college" close to the Parisian schools (3). To the new Orders, the mendicant Minors

---

a) See G. POST, *Parisian Masters as a Corporation, 1200–1246,* in *Spec,* IX (1934), 421–445.

2) It was to ensure under these new conditions the multiplying and the correction of texts, and to regulate as well the relations between copyists, correctors, bookdealers, masters and students, that the practice of composing *exemplaria* [copies] controlled by the University and reproduced part by part, was inaugurated. See J. DESTREZ, *La "pecia" dans les manuscripts du moyen âge,* in *RSPT,* XIII (1924), 182–197; *La "pecia" dans les manuscrits universitaires du XIIIe et du XIVe siècle,* Paris, 1935. [For further information on the medieval manuscripts, copyists, etc., see R. STEELE, *The* pecia, in *TBS,* 1930, pp. 230–234; J. DESTREZ, *Etudes critiques sur les oeuvres de saint Thomas d'Aquin d'après la tradition manuscrite,* in *BibTh,* XVIII (1933), 5–31; C. A. ROBSON, *The* Pecia *of the Twelfth-Century Paris School,* in *DSt,* II (1949), 267–279; G. FINK–ERRERA, *Jean Destrez et son oeuvre: La Pecia dans les manuscrits universitaires du XIIIe et du XIVe siècles,* in *Script,* XI (1957), 264–280; J. DESTREZ (+) et G. FINK–ERRERA, *Des manuscrits apparemment datés,* in *Script,* XII (1958), 56–93; A. DONDAINE, *Secrétaires de saint Thomas,* Rome, 1956; G. FINK–ERRERA, *De l'edition universitaire,* in *L'homme et son destin* (APCIPM, 1960), 221–228; and for a good over-all view on matters pertaining to books in the Middle Ages, see J. W. THOMPSON, *The Medieval Library,* in *UCSLS,* 1939, Part IV: *The Making and Care of Books in the Middle Ages,* 594–661.]

3) In 1260. See *ChUP,* I, 410 n. 361. P. AUGER, in *Le collège de Cluny,* Paris, 1916, has a very superficial moralism replace the evolution of institutions when he attributes the tardiness of this foundation to the preoccupation of saving the young monks from a perverting contact with the student milieux of the University of Paris. Let him read the letter Peter of Celle, abbot of Saint Remy, wrote to John of Salisbury (1164) on the character of the new school, in which

and Preachers, was to fall the lot and policy of being at hand, at the heart of the new civilization, and of ensuring a holy reaction to its intellectual intoxication or its moral disorders. Faced with this new civilization on the rise, it was important that the Church be rid of its outmoded feudal framework. Francis of Assisi and Thomas Aquinas were the two poles around which this new Christian world revolved (a).

III. THE UNIVERSITIES

The university, in point of fact, the original creation of the new order, was also a product of Christianity, perhaps the most meaningful thing, in the way of foundations, that this new Christian order could show. So much is this true that it is somewhat difficult for us today to picture a university completely stamped with an ecclesiastical character in which all resources, ranging from such matters as the conduct of its physical existence and the enactment of its police laws to the level of the highest inspirations of all its personnel, from doctors of medicine to professors of grammar, were dependent on a regime of clerics.

The historian who has seen a university of this sort taking shape in the bosom and as a result of the efforts of the Church is not surprised to see it find its material and moral environment subsequently supplied by that same Church. At the same time he is prepared to leave unquestioned the fact that the statutes regulating university teaching arose from the most varying circumstances. The condemnation of Aristotle was an act of a doctrinal order. Yet, a number of statutes of an administrative nature authorized and soon ordered Aristotle to be read. Faced with facts such as these, the historian will come to expect

the master is not paid, in which one is not thwarted by disputation, in which every question is answered and every reason understood, the happy school of Christ, far removed from the deceiving seductions of Paris. See J. LECLERCQ, *Les études universitaires dans l'Ordre de Cluny*, in *MB*, 351–371. [The Latin text of Peter of Celle's letter will be found in *ChUP*, I, 24. The English text of the passage here summarized is given by L. THORNDIKE, *University Records and Life in the Middle Ages*, in *RCSS*, XXXVIII (1944), p. 19, note 2.—The reader will find therein the English translation of a number of the passages of the *ChUP* which Fr. Chenu quotes or to which he refers in the present work. As stated above (2), however, the translators have given their own version of Fr. Chenu's quotations of documents and authors.]

It was in 1245 that Stephen of Lexington, abbot of Citeaux, took the initiative of founding at Paris a college (of the Bernardines, as it was called) for his monks. Coming after Citeaux's long-lasting powerlessness in the face of the new culture, the foundation was warmly approved by Innocent IV whose text is very savorous to read. See *ChUP*, I, 175 n. 133; and the references gathered by A. WILMART, in *RAM*, X (1929), 370, note.

a) For readings on the new schools and the universities, see the references given in the Research suggestions, 71–72.

an intermingling of the two orders and to understand that therein the
way was cleared for the Medievals to give full play to their intellectual
freedom and studiousness and for Saint Thomas to set forth his own
interpretation of Aristotelian doctrines. It will not astonish him to see
the papal legate fixing the hours of courses and laying down the rules
for the conferring of degrees for the faculty of arts at Paris and the
faculty of medicine at Montpellier. Nor will he think it strange to
behold Archbishop Kilwardby dogmatizing at Oxford on matters of
grammar! And it was through pressure from Rome that Thomas
Aquinas, after the painful incidents of 1252–1256, was admitted
among the masters of Paris (4). There, in the midst of it all, the
Papacy was right at home. To say the least, one has a false view of
history, who accuses it of "hand-forcing tactics," when, in many instances, it was the Papacy that created the new foundations, such as
at Toulouse, Siena, and Piacenza, and when, at any event, it was the
Papacy that favored the right of association and brought about the
freeing of institutions from the local conservatism of the old cathedral
schools.

Intellectual corporation of the city, the university was at the same
time an official body of the Church, with its own proper "office," and
with rights and liberties that it enjoyed pursuant to charters granted
by authority of the collective Christianity it meant to serve. The
Roman policy of exemption, which had already been in use for two
centuries in favor of the religious Orders, was now happily applied
to this university government. It teamed up completely and fruitfully
with the increase in exchanges and with the constant coming and
going of people, which gave an international flavor to the pursuit of
knowledge just as they did to commercial enterprises. The ease with
which the newly-founded religious Orders could move about as well
as their centralized mode of government, fitted in perfectly with the
evolution that society and the Church were undergoing. Thus also
it came to be that the Preachers and the Minors spontaneously
became the builders of the new teaching regime whose progress and
inspirations were due to the initiative of the Church.

Under the leadership of the Englishman, Alexander of Hales, the
German, Albert the Great, and the Italians, Bonaventure and Thomas
Aquinas, Paris was to become the intellectual capital of the Christian
world. The work of Saint Thomas is inconceivable apart from this
universalism wherein it takes on its fully meaningful relief just as it
originally received from it its component materials (5). It is no mere
coincidence that Brother Thomas was sent to Paris and that he en-

4) See *ChUP*, I, 307, n. 270.
5) See E. GILSON, *Albert le Grand et l'Université de Paris*, in *VInt*, XXII (May
25, 1933), 9–28.

tered upon his teaching career there; rather one is led to see him in Paris as a result of some sort of determinism brought about at once by the laws of his Order, the directive action of the Church, and the very evolution of society.

Quite obviously, it was the faculty of theology that formed the soul of the University and that supplied the *raison d'être* of the Church's jurisdiction. Here, again, was something new: that a body of authorized professors, invested with a *licentia docendi* should be given in the Church charge and authority of expounding the revealed truths of faith. To be sure, both in theology and catechesis, there had always been masters acting as adjuncts to the episcopal order. But here it was a question of professors, of a school of men who were professionals in their work, whose energies were devoted to developing a science, and whose juridical status depended on the corporation and was not, properly speaking, a function of the hierarchy. Theirs was an intermediary status that was to remain non-existent in the Eastern Church—just as the latter remained unfamiliar with scholasticism, at least in the larger reaches of that form of knowledge. In the field of sacred doctrine, the "doctor in theology," or the *magistri* [masters] as they were collectively called, made up a sort of new department in which the teaching of the truths of faith expressly enlisted the services of natural reason or of its philosophy in order to bring into being an organized science, a scholastic theology. Any bettering of teaching methods was recorded within the growth of the educational institutions. The *magistri* were officially regarded as qualified to discourse on matters of faith and doctrine. Once a question had been disputed, theirs was the office of "determining" a solution that was then accepted as carrying authority (6). They were not *auctoritates* [authorities] in the same decisive sense that the magisterium of the Church is an authority, since neither their position in the hierarchy nor the subject matter of their proper work would admit of such a ranking, but nevertheless, they did form a true theological "source," for the School did exist in the Church, with its proper place beneath that of the Fathers in the realm of the faith. Saint Thomas, Albert the Great, Bonaventure, were "doctors of the Church."

---

6) Thus, after the question had been disputed, the master gave his own determination of it (see below, ch. IX [and ch. II]); thus especially the masters as a body or through their common consensus solved controversies, particularly in those cases where faith was building itself up into a theological science. A typical case in point is that in which eight of Peter Lombard's positions were, with great respect for the "Master" of the *Sentences, communiter reprobatae a magistris parisiensibus* [disapproved in common by the Parisian masters]. *ChUP*, I, 270, n. 194. See M.–D. CHENU, Authentica et Magistralia. *Deux lieux théologiques aux XIIe-XIIIe siècles,* in *DTF,* XXVIII (1925), 257–285 [republished in *La théologie au XIIe siècle,* ch. XV: Les *Magistri. La "science" théologique,* in *EPM,* XLV (1957), 323–350].

All the foregoing serves to establish beforehand the proper setting of the masters' endeavors and even to forecast the literary form in which their work would be molded. Theirs would be a type of teaching having its own techniques, formularies, ceremonial, its own particular audience and sort of sequestration that even the finest kind of pedagogy is unable to eliminate entirely. For theology started the process of being detached from the pastoral office. There lay a tremendous risk in such an occurrence; yet, such a hazard was in the nature of things, and in line with the laws of the progression of the mind. Genius and sanctity, or more plainly, the faith of the theologian will prevail over the craft, but the craft will remain a perfectly normal tool, and the medieval university will perfect its use to the point of refinement. And in the closely-knit techniques of this craft the work of Saint Thomas is a masterpiece. One needs only recall to mind the *Contra Gentiles* in any of its chapters, or again the *Itinerarium* of Saint Bonaventure, to become convinced that the most refined of spiritual values could be fittingly incarnate in this kind of style.

For all these reasons, then, one can readily understand why the professors of the faculty of theology should have established close relations with those of the faculty of arts, the two forming a single *universitas magistrorum* [university of masters]. The men who taught theology had passed through the arts course before entering upon their theological studies, and the University regulations stipulated that they should receive this preliminary formation. This co-dwelling was soon to raise problems about the exact limitations of their respective fields in the very proportion that the old framework of the seven arts—always a pliant tool in Bible reading—was giving way under the pressure exercised by a philosophy in the process of growth and whose claims no longer allowed for its being fenced in by dialectic. As we shall see, the pivotal point in this critical period of growth was furnished by the entrance of Aristotle on the scene, but right away we may foresee the budding of the coming crisis in the autonomy that the faculty of arts was gaining for itself. It is on institutional grounds, then, that conflicts were to arise, and this served only to give a greater depth and permanence to their bitterness. Between the masters of the two faculties, oppositions sprang up; and yet alliances were also made, to which the very set-up of the University gave sharp meaning despite misunderstandings and compromises. Saint Thomas proved himself a rugged foe of the Averroist Siger of Brabant, leader of the minority group in an unruly and divided faculty of arts. Yet he enjoyed an extraordinary prestige with the personnel of the arts department. In fact, at his death, they wrote to the Preachers a most warm letter—even today we are deeply touched on reading it—in which they begged to have his last writings as well as the honor of preserving at Paris the mortal remains of the master, "so good a cleric, so kind a father, so outstanding a doctor" (7).

If we keep harking back to Paris, it is not only because Saint Thomas won such high standing there, but also because its University was effectively the prototype of the other new schools. It was a truly adequate product of the new society and the spiritual site of the renaissance. This renaissance was, of course, a widespread phenomenon that aroused the same enthusiasm wherever it put in an appearance. Step by step, it made steady progress. The second third of the XIIIth century witnessed the laying, at a surprisingly fast rhythm, of new foundations, whether ecclesiastical, seignorial, or communal. These establishments were not merely the offspring of superficial emulation; they resulted rather from the unrestrainable drive of the new elite creating the organisms that would provide for their development and culture. The situation was all the more meaningful in view of the fact that during the XIIth century even the most definite measures decreed by those in highest authority had practically come to nought, in the "arts" as well as in theology. Where, moreover, some outstanding success had been achieved, it had remained local and passing in character.

At the period of which we speak, and for some time previous, however, Bologna was a worthy rival of Paris. Its corporate set-up and manner of administration were somewhat different from those of the French University. Yet, in its own proper sphere and in its own way, it was in perfect harmony with the commonly prevailing effervescence. The law city, it brought to light the *Pandectes* and made extensive use of the *Digest*. Irnerius was its shining light, just as Abelard was the shining light of Paris; and the *Decretals* of Gratian played the same role in its schools as the *Sentences* of the Lombard at Paris. At the very time that Albert the Great was teaching how to read Aristotle at Paris, Frederick II was enlisting at Bologna the specialists of Roman law in the service of his new Empire. Rome, in fact, showed as much distrust against these imperial law-experts as she did against the rationalistic philosophy of the Parisian Averroists.

Padua, mothered by the University of Bologna from which it broke off in 1222 and warmly supported by the commune, was modeled on its *alma mater*. Among all the foundations of northern Italy, it is of special interest to us, because it was the center in which Albert the Great, while receiving his early formation, discovered his Dominican

7) ". . . tanti clerici, tanti patris, tanti doctoris." *ChUP*, I, 504, n. 447 [Foster ed., 154.]

vocation and unearthed the first elements that were to feed his extraordinary and precocious curiosity.

At just about the same time (1224), Naples was founded in princely style by Frederick II to be a counter-action to Bologna, grown too independent to suit the imperial taste. For a long time, it remained in a state of stagnancy. Yet, through its location in the Kingdom of the two Sicilies on one of the lanes of traffic between the East and the West and midway between Islam and Christendom, it was to furnish support to the political and scholarly aims of the Emperor. In particular, it was the scene in which the translations of the Arabian authors were undertaken, with Michael Scot, who was favorite court philosopher between the years 1228 and 1235, supplying the greatest share in the effort—as witness his translations of Averroes (8). We know that Peter of Ireland was there too and that, around the years 1240–1244, he was instructor to the young Thomas Aquinas (9). It was, however, only under Angevine rule that the foundation was to take on university stature, and Saint Thomas, at the time, was summoned to organize the faculty of theology. This was in October, 1272, after Charles I had invited both masters and students of Paris to come share, as in a copious meal, in the teaching of the restored university, where, as Charles put it, nature and city made up a setting of the richest kind (10).

Paris, however, still remained, in the words of the masters who had asked for the return of the body of Saint Thomas, "the noblest of all university cities" (11). During the second half of the XIIIth century, some decentralization became necessary, but at the time that Saint Thomas taught there, the effects of such a process had not as yet affected the supremacy of the French university as a leader at either the spiritual or the institutional level, at least so far as philosophy and theology were concerned. From as far back as the last third of the XIIth century, Paris had acted in the role of counselor to princes and prelates alike. Thus, in 1169, Henry II of England had offered to submit his quarrel with Thomas à Becket to the assembled masters of Paris (12). From this time on, in fact, to quote an expression used by

---

8) See R. DE VAUX, *La première entrée d'Averroès chez les Latins,* in *RSPT,* XXII (1933), 193–245, especially 196–210.

9) See M. GRABMANN, *Magister Petrus von Hibernia, der Jugendlehrer des heiligen Thomas von Aquin,* in *MAG,* I (1926), 249–265.

10) See *ChUP,* I, 501, n. 443.

11) ". . . omnium studiorum nobilissima civitas." *Ibid.,* 504, n. 447 [Foster ed., 154.]

12) See *ibid,* Introd., 23 n. 21: ". . . ready to stand by the judgment of the curia of his Lord the King of the Franks, or by the judgement of the Gaulish Church, or of the scholars of Paris" (Letter of Thomas à Becket to the Archbishop of Sens).

the Pope, it was the oven in which the intellectual bread of the Latin world was baked. Elsewhere, it was a case of feeding milk to sucklings, but here it was strong nutriment for strong minds (13). In its accumulated resources, in its teaching personnel, in its recruitment from various nations (a), in its professional and teaching organization, in its scholarly traditions, in the quality of its methods, in its curiosity of spirit, in its creative inspiration, the University of Paris was the intellectual center of Christendom, the domain par excellence of high culture, "the city of philosophers" (14), the new Athens (15). From the spiritual and institutional standpoints, it is impossible to conceive Saint Thomas outside of Paris. Viterbo, Rome, Naples were merely so many episodes in his intellectual life as in his teaching career. Paris was his natural home.

IV. THE RENAISSANCE

The genesis of the institutions of learning brings us to that intellectual movement which brought them to life and in which they

---

13) In the same vein, GEOFFROI OF VINSAUF, *Poetria nova*, 1010–1012 (ed. by E. FARAL, *Les arts poétiques du XIIe et du XIIIe siècles*, in BEHE, 238 (1924), 228): "Dispensing in the arts, Paris nourishes the strong with loaves of bread; Educating babes in the cradle, Orleans feeds them with the milk of authors."

a) On the "nations" at Paris, see P. KIBRE, *The Nations in the Mediaeval Universities*, in MAAP, XLIX (1948), ch. III; A. L. GABRIEL, *English Masters and Students in Paris during the XIIth Century*, in AnP, XXV, 1–2 (1949); IDEM, *Skara House at the Mediaeval University of Paris*, in TSHME, IX (1960); L. J. DALY, *The Medieval University 1200–1400*, New York, 1961, 48–63. See also the references on the universities given in the Research Suggestions below, 71–72.

14) ". . . civitas philosophorum." ALBERT THE GREAT.

15) It is, indeed, at Paris that the *transitus hellenismi ad Christianismum* [the passage from Hellenism to Christianity] was achieved. At the end of the XIIIth century, Thomas of Ireland, O.P., will set down (without forgetting his own country) the theme of this symbolic history of culture in the following manner: "The Blessed Dionysius . . . came to Paris so that he might make of this city the mother of studies after the pattern of Athens. Like Athens, the city of Paris is divided into three parts. One is that of the merchants, the laborers, and the common people; it is called the Town at large (*magna villa*). Another is that of the noblemen in which are located the king's court and the cathedral church; it is called the City. The third is that of the students and of the colleges; it is called the University. Studies were first transferred from Greece to Rome, then from Rome to Paris during Charlemagne's time, around the year 800, and the school had four founders: Rhabanus, Claudius, Alcuin, master of King Charles, and John surnamed the Scot who, however, was born in Ireland, Ireland being greater Scotland. The said John was one of the four commentators upon the Blessed Dionysius, the latter's books having been commented upon four times: by John the Scot, John the Saracene, Maxim, and Hugh of Saint Victor." *De tribus sensibus S. Scripturae*. Ms. *Paris Nat. 15966* (quoted in HLF, XXX, 406). On the theme of this *translatio studii* [transfer of study] spoken about throughout the entire Middle Ages, see E. GILSON, *L'humanisme médiéval*, in *Les idées et les lettres*, Paris, 1932, 132–185.

found the deeper cause of their emergence just as did the type of man then in the process of new birth. For it is really a "renaissance" that we are witnessing here, with the discovery of Aristotle and the assimilation of Greek reason by Christian theology as of the high points in the procedure.

It is important, even at the risk of falling into verbal paradox, that XIIIth century scholasticism, in which Saint Thomas proved himself to be the master, be placed in its true perspective. Scholasticism originated at the very heart of an authentic rebirth, the first effort of which had been furnished at the time of the Carolingian renaissance, the later stage of which is known under the name of the XVIth century Renaissance. Each stage had its own privileged area within which its eagerness bore fruitful results. In each one also, there were flaws and setbacks that were to provoke the reactions of its successor. The most profound of disagreements between the modern and medieval revivals, however, should not blind us to the fact that the movement of rebirth was one throughout. The breaches that did appear show how delicate a task it was to achieve balance for such a rebirth in a Christian organism; they do not prove the movement to have been congenitally incoherent. In point of fact, Saint Thomas is the theologian who, by his very work, was to define the laws and conditions of its equilibrium since, with his metaphysics of nature, he established the status of human reason in a Christian regime of thought. It cannot be said that this achievement was in the nature of a simple parenthetical pause in the history of the influence of the ancient world or in the evolution of the human mind.

During the first revival, the discovery of the ancient culture, though still rudimentary, had acted on the minds of men as a kind of lure and source of inspiration. The spell of Rome, of an idealized and chimerical Rome, gives the key to the secret grandeur of Charlemagne's "Holy Empire." Underlying the most novel political problems was the mystical vision of resurrecting the Roman Empire with its universal political ideal. Clustered around this myth of a new Rome, are to be found the elements of the Carolingian renaissance: the classical culture of Alcuin, the organization of the teaching discipline, and the relish for beautiful script. In spite of their weaknesses, the aspirations of this revival did open the doors of history on the era of the Middle Ages, after the Moslems had decisively upset the old geographical and political equilibrium of the world. It was at this time that, in the field of sacred doctrine, the rules of grammar applied to Scripture, began sowing the seeds of an incipient rationalism that was soon to be dangerously duplicated, when dialectic, another of the arts of the *trivium,* was similarly applied to the same contents of Christian revelation.

On the other hand, if, during the Quattrocento, the enticement of Antiquity animated the whole field of culture, not excluding political science and philosophic speculation, it is plainly within the twofold domain of letters and plastic arts that the great Renaissance scored its victory and lasting grandeur. The very word humanism remains forever stamped by these specialties, while at the same time, it crystallizes a conception of nature with which the Christian cannot easily accommodate himself. The Catholic reform movement of the time set up a ferocious resistance to the ascendency of the pagan ideals. Savonarola battled to save Florence from the Medici. Cajetan struggled against the Paduan brand of Aristotelianism. And if the Dominican William Petit collaborated at Paris with Lefèvre d'Etaples, his contemporary John Reuchlin was condemned at Cologne by the Inquisition.

Located between these two crossroads of history, the XIIth and XIIIth centuries do not destroy the homogeneous unfolding of the whole renaissance movement, although they do bear witness to a shift in the balance of the whole. It was within the boundaries of this second revival that the Schoolmen really found the medium needed for their labors. Luther was not laboring under a delusion when he anathematized at once the School and Aristotle. The entrance of the Stagirite into the University of Paris in the XIIIth century and the revival of Roman law at Bologna in the XIIth are the two hinges around which the "renaissance" of the period revolved. The fact that Christianity made a success of it is no reason to misjudge it under a scholasticism such as the Humanists have masked it. The use of "ancient themes" in the romances of the period, the cult of Virgil the prophet, the frequent resort to the ancient "authors," the popularity of Ovid, the whole mess of immoral works that were condemned with Aristotle in 1277—all these factors are proof that even the letters of the period fed on the Ancients. The success enjoyed by dialectic and the newly-found treasures of Greek and Arabic science, however, overwhelmed the rise of this medieval humanism. This would seem to justify the criticisms raised against it by the men of the Quattrocento. Still, it would be well to determine at what points the criticisms can be applied, so as to leave to the Middle Ages, in the history of Western civilization, its own interior movement and the meaning of its forward progress. For, only on this condition shall we be able to understand its philosophy of nature and its theology of grace (16).

16) This historical perspective evidently implies that critique is applied to the summary category: *Middle Ages,* as well as to the "classic" anti-medieval concept: *Renaissance* (Burckhardt). Without making one's own J. NORDSTRÖM'S excessive reaction (in his *Moyen âge et Renaissance,* trans. from the Swedish, Paris, 1933), one must revise these schemas, taking as points of departure the works of Pirenne, Haskins, Dawson, and Gilson [See the bibliography in the

Here, then, in effect, were the two sides of one and the same drama that Christianity had to face as it came in contact with the newly recovered legacy of the Ancients: on the one hand, the growth of Aristotelian rationalism, on the other, the restoration, in its law and in its spirit, by the jurists of Frederick II, of the pagan Roman Empire, under the emblems of the Holy Roman Empire. Both aspects of that legacy had the same grandeur, but both offered the same threats. The acts and doctrinal pronouncements of the popes show that they were acutely aware of both the grandeur and the menace. Within the parallel facets of this drama, the work of Saint Thomas and of his confreres found its historical and spiritual dimensions.

If, therefore, it is true that we are dealing here with a process of reconquering and of exploiting the capital of the ancient civilization, both the men involved and the works that they produced will have one feature in common, whether the scene of their activity be the palace of Charlemagne, the University of Paris, or the Florence of the Medici: their genius reveals itself within the art of imitation, for imitation actually is one of the poles of the axis around which every rebirth revolves. Eye and imagination, speculative thought, instrumentation and techniques, all benefit, in the effort needed to grasp and reproduce reality, from the wealth and models that the Ancients handed down. These old treasures and models, put to their best use by those men endowed with personal creative power, are treated with the deepest reverence, and their authority has the force of law. As canons of the word or as norms of thought, they express principles that have value beyond all measure of time. In this respect, Ariosto does not rank below Alcuin, and Ronsard aligned himself with Horace, just as Siger of Brabant did with the Philosopher.

Imitation, however, does carry within itself the seeds of a burdensome dullness. For instance, the formalism that was to develop among the Schoolmen is, at its own level, of the same type as the servility shown by the grammarians and the men of letters of both the XIIth and XVth centuries. In either case, "the following of the formula clogs up the movements of life. Indeed, at the end, the precepts of the Ancients that had originally been a proclamation of the rights of truth, are now turned against truth herself" (17). Should one wish

Research Suggestions for this section, 72–73]. On the other hand, historians of letters as well as historians of the spiritual life, sociologists, and philosophers, agree in placing the great cleft marked by the XIIth century, "one of the most profound that ever marked the evolution of European societies" (M. BLOCH), as the time when "the religion of the new times" began (A. WILMART).

17 E. FARAL, *Les arts poétiques du XIIe et du XIIIe siècles*, in *BEHE*, 238 (1924), 79.

to discover whether, in the sphere of the pure and ever free creativeness of the mind or in that of the every day teaching procedure, any measure of protection can be found against this type of decaying process, his search will bring results more easily within the School than among the Humanists. The exacting demands of the mind had here gradually brought into being a technique called the "reverential exposition" for the handling of these ancient "authorities." This technique was to be shamelessly used, and the Quattrocento philologers were to find cause for scandal in it. It is a fact, as we shall see, that Saint Thomas and his contemporaries did make a constant use of it, but they employed it on the strict principle that, for the philosopher, rational investigation, however risky, was to take precedence over the acceptance of authorities and the cult of the Ancients. As Saint Thomas put it: "The study of philosophy is not done in order to know what men have thought, but rather to know how truth herself stands" (18).

The divergence between the medieval renaissance and that of the Humanists is on this point profound. It is necessary that we study how this difference came about and how it made for a different handling of texts, for we are here hitting upon the core of the paradox that saw a revival movement giving birth to a scholastic way of thinking and teaching. It is actually in this context that Saint Thomas was to find both a key to his Aristotelianism and a measure for it. His case is indeed only one among other cases of men of the Middle Ages in their attitude with regard to Antiquity. However impressive it may seem, it only serves to disclose, at the level of thought, the spirit that was common to the whole medieval renaissance movement itself.

The fact is that a movement of returning to the Ancients can stem from two types of inquisitiveness, which, if not always separate, are quite different from one another. In the one case, the Ancients are cultivated for their own sake and with the express purpose of recapturing for ourselves by dint of patient research their former greatness, their views, their beauty. Treated this way, their writings become an object of admiration, with philology acting as its tool. The human sympathy that we find here in their favor does not exist apart from a certain aristocratic distinction, indeed from an archaeological opulence. Erasmus, independent of the role he played in reviving the Gospel, is the master example of this sort of restoration.

Then there is the other case in which the ancient culture is brought back to live in a climate different from the one in which it first thrived. Even if some measure of historical accuracy be sacrificed in

---

18) " . . . studium philosophiae non est ad hoc quod sciatur quid homines senserint, sed qualiter se habeat veritas rerum." *In I De coelo,* lect. 22; Marietti ed., 109, n. 228.

the process, the old is made to live anew in what is truthfully a re-birth, with processes of spiritual assimilation going on in the new organism that enable it to absorb without loss every crumb of the old. As a result, a synthesis takes shape, and provided genius takes a hand in the matter, imitation, under the driving power of creative inventiveness, is freed from the drag of its own weight.

> This kind of humanism is quite different from the historical humanism of the past which is characteristic of the Renaissance. Rather, it is a humanism of the present; or, if one prefers, of the intransient. When Erasmus turns to consider the philosophy of the Medievals, he no longer discerns in it the philosophy of the Greeks, any more than he recognizes as genuine Latin, the language in which it is expressed. He is right. Plato, Aristotle, Cicero, and Seneca are no longer there in the garb they wore in the days of their earthly existence. Yet he is wrong, because it is really they who are there, as people still living and who, by the fact of their living, change. Indeed, it is even because they are not as yet dead that they are so hardly recognizable. What Albert the Great or Saint Thomas asked of these Ancients was not so much to tell them what they had formerly been in Greece or in Rome, but rather what they were still capable of becoming, what they themselves would have become, if they had lived in Christian territory, in the XIIIth century. But what am I saying? They do exist then and there; they survive. The historian who meets them in those surroundings is constantly torn between the admiration of the depth with which the thinkers of the Middle Ages understand them, on the one hand; and, on the other, the disquietude that an archaeologist might feel were the low relief he was studying suddenly to turn into a living and changing thing. Take away Plato and Aristotle, and what will be left of the medieval philosophy? But just as the Alexander portrayed in the *Chansons de geste* is a Charlemagne who leads his barons on to battle, so, and in a much deeper sense, Plato and Aristotle live on in Bonaventure and Aquinas, because they have adopted the latters' faith and principles (19).

Under conditions of this sort, it is just as summary an over-simplification to label Saint Thomas an Aristotelian as it is to call the Cistercian mystic Aelred of Rievaulx a Ciceronian because the latter was delighted to transfer the whole substance of the old Roman's *De Amicitia* to his own *De Spirituali Amicitia* (a). New wine in old skins! This is a fact that the historian must remember when he discovers the innumerable Aristotelian threads that run through the warp and woof of the *Summa Theologiae;* a fact, too, that the Thomist philosopher must not lose sight of when he reads the commentaries of Saint Thomas on Aristotle's *De Anima* or on his *Meta-*

---

19) E. GILSON, *Le moyen âge et le naturalisme antique,* in AHDLMA, VII (1932), 35.

a) On this work, see the materials given in Dom A. HOSTE, Bibliotheca Aelrediana. *A Survey of the Manuscripts, Old Catalogues, Editions and Studies concerning St. Aelred of Rievaulx,* in InPat, II (1962), 63–73.

physics. For it is in the latter properly medieval genre that we find the precise and subtle point at which two purposes met: first, that of reading Aristotle aright; and yet second, that of reaching, beyond Aristotle, the goal of philosophical truth. This is particularly true in the case of Saint Thomas.

A renaissance of this sort, however, is not merely a restoration of Antiquity. Even granted that the return to the Ancients is more than a secondary element in the process, it still is neither the adequate cause nor the most telling sign of such a cultural rebirth. There is need for a soul in the body of rich materials thus restored to the light of day. More than that, the restoration itself is only the first effect to flow from the wants of that soul, for it is within her bosom that the glad event of the old being born anew takes place. For a long time perhaps, the newly discovered sources were accessible, but over the same length of time, unable to bear fruit, due to the absence of the spirit that had not yet moved over the waters. Let that spirit move, and it is a new world that is enthusiastically uncovered from under the old forms, with man in the midst of it all and revealed to himself for his own regeneration. Florence in the XVth century is a case in point, admirable and simple, of this sort of spectacle. But something akin to it is sketched out in the aspirations of the XIIth century clerics, as well as in the dreaming of Charlemagne's counselors. We have previously noted from the very survey of the economic conditions of the times the unprecedented fervor with which the new generations were stirred up, and the youthful spirit of independence that gave origin to the rise of the universities. We shall soon see to what lengths of mystical excess the evangelism of the times— the movement that gave a religious prop to the work of regeneration —was sometimes brought.

It is enough, at this point, to grant the fact that, on the vast and far-flung front of culture—from the practice of beautiful literary style to the contemplation of metaphysical truth, from the development of the plastic arts to the discovery of new methods of scientific experiment—this reawakening was not uniform in nature, neither in its recapture of the old treasures nor in the spiritual initiative that it aroused. In some instances, entire fields remained inert, their doors held shut by some simple turn of fate; while in others, the incoercible power of some creative genius burst, in a single stroke, past the slow pace set by imitation. And if we pass on from the world of forms and belles-lettres to the world of thought, we meet with the most confusing turns of chance, as witness, for example, the fact that while all the works of Aristotle were recovered by the Middle Ages, the texts of

Plato remained buried in oblivion. Such strokes of fortune make for all the more instability in the lines of demarcation of culture, a domain in which, all things considered, the spirit often shows disregard for apparently the most crying of needs. If it be true that in the XIIIth century Siger of Brabant had at his disposal every textual source he needed to restore, in its most undiluted form, the naturalism of Greek thought, it is equally true, by contrast, that in the IXth century Scotus Erigena had built up, with a faulty text of Dionysius as his starting point, a splendid Platonic world.

If, therefore, the two component parts of every renaissance are such as we have stated, our attention is now drawn to finding out just what Saint Thomas harvested from the inheritance of Antiquity, but also in what way his genius transformed the Aristotelian man [without detriment to the latter's original structure], just as grace perfects nature without violence to its original structure. Rarely, in the history of thought, is there to be found a more beautiful case in which the inspirations of a creative mind contended with the most sincere practice of imitation.

V. THE ENTRANCE OF ARISTOTLE

By the time that Saint Thomas had arrived in Paris, at the middle of the XIIIth century, the literature of Antiquity no longer lured the minds as it had done not so long before. Ovid, it is true, continued to serve as a source for a few works on the art of love, and Priscian was still law unto the grammarians. Yet, the fact that Statius was placed on equal footing with Virgil and that Quintilian's *Institutio* could show nothing better, in the way of progeny, than certain miserable *artes dictaminis* [arts of composition] (b) is enough for one to presume that, after a brief show of life during the XIIth century, the age of belles-lettres was cut short. Good taste had fled the scene to be replaced by dry formalism. Peter of Blois had long since railed against the decay. Out of the bosom of Antiquity, philosophic reason had just been revealed, and the promises that it gave were so dazzling that even the staunchest Christians were either thrown off balance or deeply disturbed. It was the rise of Aristotelianism, a sensational

---

b) See L. J. PAETOW, *The Arts Course at Medieval Universities with Special Reference to Grammar and Rhetoric*, in *The University Studies* (University of Illinois, Urbana, Ill.), III, 7 (1910), who writes: "In its earliest and widest sense *dictamen* signified the art of composition, both in prose and poetry. As a rule, three kinds of composition were distinguished, metric verse, rhythmic verse, and prose. At all times such exercises in composition, especially in verse, had formed a part of grammatical and rhetorical instruction, but in an age when few could write at all the practical value of the *dictamen prosaicum*, which consisted mainly in writing letters and documents, soon asserted itself" (70–71). See also J. DE GHELLINCK, *L'essor de la littérature latine au XIIe siècle*, II, in *ML–SH*, V (1946), 54–68.

event in the rediscovery of Antiquity, that was to be the determining factor, both material and spiritual, of the development of the work of Saint Thomas.

Aristotle had already been for some time a living figure in the Christian world, but his was a particular image, that of the logician par excellence. The general esteem in which he was held as a technician was not without the element of distrust that the spiritual-minded invariably feel for those who use their wits in discussing words and concepts (20). So long as only the *Categories* and the *Perihermeneias* had been read—this was actively done with some measure of continuance only from the time of the XIth century, and then with the help of the writings of Boethius (21)—Christian appreciation of the *manducator verborum* [word eater] remained within discreet bounds. Abelard with his intemperate lucidity, however, fostered suspicious with the result that theologians set up an opposition. While their resistance makes us see how tight a hold dialectics had taken on the minds of scholars, it also makes us feel the balance and quality of mind of those masters who, like John of Salisbury, greeted the recovery of the *Analytics* and *Topics* as the finding of an admirable art of thinking. Aristotle began to be called the philosopher par excellence (22).

At this time, as a matter of fact, the Stagirite was already putting in his appearance as a natural scientist and a philosopher of nature. By way of Sicily, but particularly by way of Toledo, the Greco-Oriental world was being revealed to the West. Through the numerous translations of ancient works, philosophic as well as Christian, an intense inquisitiveness was being awakened (a). Taking first rank in the interest thus manifesting itself, were those sciences concerned with physics, biology, and astronomy. The latter were otherwise increased in their recovered capital through the share furnished by the

---

20) See J. DE GHELLINCK, *Quelques appréciations de la dialectique d'Aristote durant les conflits trinitaires du IVe siècle*, in RHE, XXVI (1930), 5–42; A.-J. FESTUGIÈRE, *Aristote dans la littérature grecque chrétienne jusqu'à Théodoret*, Excursus in *L'idéal religieux des Grecs et l'Evangile*, 2d ed., in EB, 1932, 220–262.

21) See A. VAN DE VYVER, *Les étapes du développement philosophique du haut moyen âge*, in RBPH, VIII (1929), 425–452.

22) JOHN OF SALISBURY, *Metalogicon*, lib. II, c. 16; Webb ed., 90; P. L., 199, 873 C; McGarry ed., 110. See M. GRABMANN, *Aristoteles im Werturteil des Mittelalters*, in MAG, II (1936), 63–102; [also, *Aristoteles im zwoelften Jahrhundert*, in MSt, XII (1950), 123–162]. And already quite some time ago J. DE LAUNOY, *De varia Aristotelis fortuna in Academia Parisiensi*, in *Opera omnia*, IV, Paris 1732, 175 ff.

a) See J. T. MUCKLE, *Greek Works translated directly into Latin before 1350* in MSt, IV (1942), 33–42; V (1943), 102–114; S. D. WINGATE, *The Mediaeval Latin Versions of the Aristotelian Scientific Corpus, with Special Reference to the Biological Works*, London, 1931; and the bibliographies in the works referred to in the Research Suggestions on the entrance of Aristotle, below, 73–75; see also ch. VI dealing with Saint Thomas's commentaries on Aristotle.

Arabs, at the very moment when the knights of the Reconquista were bringing back to the troubadours echoes of the poetry of Islam. So it would seem to have been nature, more than reason, that Aristotle first revealed to the minds of the West. In fact, it was the medical men who gave him his initial welcome, and Daniel of Morley counselled those of his friends who wanted to study science to go to Spain rather than to the schools of Paris where everything was stiffened by dialectics and verbalism. In the opinion of the English naturalist Alexander Neckam, to recommend Aristotle made no more sense than to bolster with a lantern the brightness of the sun. With data that were on the whole somewhat on the disparate side, Alfred of Sareshel, also an Englishman, built up a biological philosophy of man. In 1210, it was the *libri de naturali philosophia* [books on natural philosophy] that were banned. Again in 1229, with the idea of luring clients to their newly opened university, the masters of Toulouse published this enticing announcement: "Here, those who wish to make a searching study into the bosom of nature, will be able to hear lectures on the books on nature that have been proscribed at Paris" (23). Finally, among the entire works of the Aristotelian encyclopedia, Albert the Great will show special appreciation for the riches contained in the treatises on animals (24).

In minds that were now on the alert for new knowledge, it was to a two-edged curiosity that the Aristotelian conception of nature was to give rise. On the one hand, running counter to the appealing, but idealistic tendencies that laid stress on the spirit—an outlook encouraged by the Augustinian tradition of thought—man's attention now focused on the world of matter and sense, on the study of life and its laws, on the phenomena of generation. The results revealed in this appeal to experience appeared wonderful when compared to the wretched contents of the lapidaries and bestiaries. On the other hand, and bolstering the value of this appeal to experience, there was a feeling of anticipation concerning the resources of intelligibility contained in a notion of nature defined as an internal principle in every being and a cause sufficient to explain all of its operations without recourse to super-natural influences or symbolic interpretations bringing about a dissevering of the unity of knowledge. In brief, what now appeared was a world that was *real*, a world *capable of being understood*. A mother-science of physics was begotten, and from it

23) "Libros naturales qui fuerunt Parisius prohibiti poterunt illic audire qui volunt nature sinum medullitus perscrutari." *ChUP*, I, 131, n. 72. [On the University of Toulouse, see C. E. SMITH, *The University of Toulouse in the Middle Ages. Its Origins and Growth to 1500 A.D.*, Milwaukee, 1958].

24) See A. BIRKENMAJER, *Le rôle joué par les médecins et les naturalistes dans la réception d'Aristote aux XIIe et XIIIe siècles.* Extract from *La Pologne au VIe Congrès international des sciences historiques*, Oslo, 1928, Warsaw, 1930.

were to spring forth all the other particular sciences dealing with nature, starting with a science of man, the science of that being whose nature was free, yet bound up with the world system that surrounded him. The thrill that men felt in discovering such a conception of nature in Aristotle points to something more than a passing renaissance. It confirms the fact that an element of capital importance had been definitely added to the scholastic system of thought which was then in its formative process. Realism, both ontological and epistemological, was this element that the new physics carried within itself. Henceforth, the very notion of science was linked up with the knowledge of existent objects.

The acceptance, however, of Aristotle's philosophy of nature confirmed a certain absence of interest in the mathematical disciplines. True, a place had been kept for them, both at Toledo, in the Arabic science taught there, and at Chartres, where they were part of a Platonism with which their destiny seems to have been tied up in the minds of philosophers. Although the Aristotelian ordering of the sciences does fix a place for mathematics, it does not, however, lend itself easily to its development. This serious deficiency was to weigh heavily on scholasticism. In fact, the day would come when, having shut itself up in the confines of its Aristotelian science, scholasticism would openly reject, along with its excesses, the most lawful ideals of mathematical analysis, thus closing the door on a new world of thought and drawing up its own condemnation in the bargain!

Finally, along with Aristotle's philosophy and by virtue of the latter's very confidence in the essential understandableness of the world, a conceptual rationalism began to assert itself more and more. As a result, logic was given its true status, that of a simple tool, and a safeguard was thus provided, for the masters at least, against the pitfalls of the formalism into which the first generations of Paris university people had fallen. On the other hand, this rationalism bore the seeds of an intellectualism somewhat short in its outlook, thus threatening to restrict the permanent power of invention of the human mind as well as the sense of mystery. The latter tendency was reinforced by the techniques adopted in academic exercises, and from the first decades of the XIIIth century on, it found expression in the particular machinery of the dialectics of scholasticism as well as in the academic style so characteristic of it. The humanism of a John of Salisbury, the lyrical qualities shown by the Victorines, not to mention the rhetoric of a Hildebert of Lavardin, had disappeared. From this background was born, with its shortcomings as well as its qualities, the language of the School, the very language used by Saint Thomas.

In the new Aristotle, however, it was not simply a question of human qualities and human weaknesses such as have just been touched upon. The Christian world set up an opposition against him because he was the source of other perils, and their seriousness should not be concealed under the pretext that today the Stagirite not only has freedom of the city but also holds a position of advantage in Christian thought. Indeed, to pass over these dangers would precisely be to misjudge in advance the role that Saint Thomas played in the spiritual revolution taking place in the West.

Save for a few exceptions that were accidental in character, Christian tradition had spontaneously sustained itself with Platonic philosophy. In a religious tradition of this nature, it was already a delicate task to turn from the Platonic way of thinking to follow Aristotle on the roads opened up by his philosophy. As a matter of fact, even before it could be revealed that the two systems were incompatible, it was impossible that a breaking off from ideas that were solidly entrenched be accomplished without incidents of one sort or another. It, moreover, was apparent that the world of Aristotle was itself irreconcilable with the Christian way of conceiving the universe, man, and God. In Aristotle, there was no mention of creation. His world was an eternal one, delivered over to the clutches of determinism, without a provident God knowing anything about the world's contingencies. His man was a being bound up with matter, subject like it to corruption, a man whose moral perfection did not involve religious values. The face of Aristotle's philosophy was turned earthward. In fact, by its denial of the exemplary ideas, it had cut off the very road that could lead to God and had obliged the light of reason to retire within itself. Aristotelian science was playing against Christian wisdom.

Coming into contact with this self-sufficiency of reason, the soul of Christendom reacted immediately with shock, as though it were faced with the lust of the spirit that had brought about original sin (25). Saint Bonaventure soon made himself the mouthpiece of the ensuing resistance, in the scientific and irrefragable opposition that he directed against Siger of Brabant and Thomas Aquinas. Resistance, however, had been in the air as early as 1210. Under one form or another and coming from all quarters of the Church hierarchy, it manifested itself at successive dates, in 1215, 1225, 1231, 1245, and as late as 1263, when William of Moerbeke and Thomas Aquinas, then working together at the Roman court under the sympathetic eyes of Urban IV, were occupied with their studies of Aristotle: the one with a translation of the Stagirite, the other with a commentary on his text.

---

25) "The spirit of Christ does not reign where the spirit of Aristotle dominates", in the words of ABSALON OF SAINT VICTOR (+ 1203), *Sermo 4; P.L.*, 211, 37 D.

The point about the resistance is that it showed the difficulty that any one must encounter who tries to set a nature autonomous in her order within the framework of a Christian universe (26).

At a rather early date, however, scholars had become conscious, not only of the scientific riches to be found in the Aristotelian encyclopedia, but also of the undeniable human value of his thought. As early as 1231 some effort had been made at a compromise. Gregory IX had charged three Parisian masters with the task of making corrections on the books that were forbidden, "so that the useful would not be spoiled by the useless" (a). From 1230 to 1240, roughly speaking the program of studies included large sections of Aristotle's text, particularly of the *Ethica Vetus et Nova* (27). True, the *Libri Naturales* were still not offered except in very summary form, but around 1244 Albert the Great was commenting on them by the page at the faculty of theology, and at the same time, Roger Bacon was doing a series of questions based on the same books at the faculty of arts. In England, Robert Grosseteste, a former chancellor of the University of Oxford and now the Bishop of Lincoln, a scholar with immense prestige in the world of religion and thought, and, in fact, a man with a keenly alert mind, undertook, between 1242 and 1247, to make a complete translation of both the *Nicomachean Ethics* and of some of its Greek commentators (28). Finally, the barriers were let down completely at Paris. In 1252, the year when Saint Thomas began teaching his doctrine, already conditioned by a deliberate and decisive choice for Aristotelian teaching, the Stagirite's *De Anima* was listed among texts to be used in the English nation section of the faculty of arts. In 1255, the whole of the Aristotelian corpus was placed on the curriculum. As will be seen, the masters had won over for themselves a complete cycle of philosophy teaching that went far beyond the pro-

---

26) See M. GRABMANN, *I divieti ecclesiastici di Aristotele sotto Innocenzo III e Gregorio IX*, in *MHP*, V, fasc. I (1941): *I papi del duecento e l'aristotelismo*.
  a) ". . . ne utile per inutile vitietur". *ChUP*, I, 143, n. 87.
  27) See the program discovered and published by M. GRABMANN, *Eine für Examinazwecke obgefasste Quaestionensammlung der Pariser Artistenfakultät aus der ersten Hälfte des 13 Jahrhunderts*, in *MAG*, II (1936), 182–199 [analysed by F. VAN STEENBERGHEN, *Siger de Brabant*, t. II, in *LPB*, XIII (1944), 415–420].
  28) GROSSETESTE, however, is without illusion, and he loses his temper against those who, through a violent exegesis of texts, would make a Christian out of Aristotle. "Let them not, therefore, deceive themselves and vainly work themselves into a sweat so as to make a Catholic out of Aristotle, lest they be needlessly consuming their time and the powers of their minds, and that by making Aristotle a Catholic they make heretics of themselves." Quotation from his commentary on the *Hexaemeron* in *Assisi ms. 172*, fol. 198v, published by E. LONGPRÉ, *Thomas d'York et Mathieu d'Aquasparta. Textes inédits sur le problème de la création*, in *AHDLMA*, I (1926), 270, note. [On Robert Grosseteste, see the various studies presented in *RGSB*, ed. D. A. Callus in 1955, and the latter's *The* Summa theologiae *of Robert Grosseteste*, in *SMH*, 180–208.]

paedeutics of the seven arts and of the ancient dialectic. In itself, this was enough to raise, within the institutional organization, the problem of a philosophy that was now set free from the superintendence of the theologians. The stage was set for Averroes.

When Aristotle arrived in Paris, he did not come alone, nor was the doctrine brought in under his name simon-pure, so that the problem raised by his entrance into Western thought became even more complex. Already in ancient works, and even more so in the Syrian and Arabic literature, a philosophic syncretism had injected within the corpus of Aristotle's writings elements that were heterogeneous to it and that seemed to justify, even from a textual basis, the new orientations that philosophy and religion were taking. As early as the XIIth century, an Arabic patchwork text of the *Enneads* had been translated into Latin under the title of *Theologia Aristotelis*. Another book, the *Liber Aristotelis de Expositione Bonitatis Purae* (otherwise known as the *Liber de Causis*), done into Latin by Gerard of Cremona, was making the rounds at the same time. In an almost word-for-word reproduction, it was the vehicle of some of the theses of Proclus's *Elementatio Theologica* which had, at an earlier date, been carried over into first the Syrian and then into the Arabian tongues. Albert the Great was to draw support from the *Liber de Causis* in his attempt to superimpose a Platonic metaphysics on Aristotle's appeal-to-experience philosophy. Around 1270, the Averrorists of Paris thought they were borrowing from Aristotle the reprehensible doctrine of emanation that they were teaching. It was only toward the end of his career, and after William of Moerbeke had made a direct translation of the *Elementatio,* that Saint Thomas identified therein the *Liber de Causis.*

More remarkable, however, and leading to a greater compromising of Aristotle's doctrine was the fact that, along with his works, the abundant yield of Arabian speculation, particularly that present in the works of Avicenna, was poured into the West through the translators at Toledo. It amounted to the Christians facing a block of philosophical writings in which the authentic Aristotle was shrouded, so to speak, in the folds of Arabian philosophy. The fact was given public notice in 1210 when the first alarm was sounded and it was decreed that "neither Aristotle's books, *nor the commentaries thereon,* are to be read" (a). It was precisely against this compounded mass and the errors it contained that William of Auvergne hurled his denunciations when he spoke of "Aristotle and his followers" (b). The

---

a) "Nec libri Aristotelis, *nec commenta* legantur". *ChUP*, I, 70, n. 11.
b) "Aristoteles et sequaces ejus."

De Causis Primis et Secundis was ample witness of the seductions and dangers deriving from that sort of philosophic syncretism in which, to one's bewilderment, Augustine and Dionysius were used to enfold Arabian emanationism, a task they were ill-equipped to perform.

There was to be a second stage in which the Arabian influence would make itself felt, and this time it would be in the line of an authentic Aristotelianism. Averroes, in fact, made his appearance to swell the torrent of literature on the Stagirite's philosophy at the time when the latter's moral writings were beginning to be actively circulated (due to the efforts of Robert Grosseteste). His works were translated around 1230 at the court of Frederick II (29), to a large extent by Michael Scot who dedicated his version of the *De Coelo*—and this is a significant coincidence—to Stephen of Provins, one of the three Parisian masters to whom had been allotted the task of expurgating Aristotle. His thought did not sink into the consciousness of scholars immediately following upon their contact with his text, true; but, all in all, the crisis came to a head soon enough. Even though Albert the Great was not too well acquainted with him when he was teaching at Paris between 1240 and 1248, and even when he wrote his *De Unitate Intellectus* in 1256, the Arab nevertheless was singled out and denounced during the decade that followed and that witnessed the writing of that master document—the *Contra Gentiles*. It was only with the appearance of Siger of Brabant, however, and from 1266 on, that the quality of his exegesis and the wholly rational bent of his thought were to win over disciples to his cause in the faculty of arts. This was to be the most drastic episode and the critical point in the restoration of Aristotle's philosophy. Christian doctrine was then threatened, not so much perhaps by the particular errors about the unity of the intellect or the eternity of the world, as by the very tendency to philosophism that the masters in the arts department started to brandish. Saint Thomas found himself wedged in between the Augustinian tradition of thought, now more emphatic than ever in its criticism of Aristotle, and the Commentator with his interpretation of the Stagirite. In order to make distinctions where they were called for, Thomas availed himself of those of the Greek commentators that he could then lay his hands on: Simplicius, Philoponus, and Themistius. Even though he speaks of Averroes as of one "who was not so much a Peripatetic, as a depraver of the Peripatetic

---

29) In this spiritual geography, notice the role played by Frederick II. See M. GRABMANN, *Kaiser Friedrich II und sein Verhältnis zur aristotelischen und arabischen Philosophie*, in MAG, II (1936), 103–107; A. DE STEFANO, *La cultura della corte di Frederico II*, Palermo, 1938.

philosophy" (a), in one of those rare passages in which we feel him giving vent to angry displeasure, the fact remains that he constantly had the works of the Arab at his elbow when he was doing his own commentary on the Philosopher. It is indispensable that this be kept in mind if one would judge in detail his Aristotelianism. What followed is well known. Saint Thomas was discredited in the condemnations of 1270 and 1277, and his endeavors dismissed. The fact is, moreover, that, judging from the violence of the conflict that took place at the time, any attempt at concealing the real issue at stake must be disallowed, for Aristotelianism did breed rationalism with all of its consequences. How, then, can we explain that Saint Thomas took upon himself the task of having Christian thought assimilate such an Aristotelianism?

VI. THE ORDER OF FRIAR PREACHERS

It was in the Order of Friar Preachers that Saint Thomas found the resources he needed to enter upon such a task. Indeed, it would be more accurate to say it was due to his being a Friar Preacher that he developed that clear-sighted and courageous mastery with which he brought the task to completion. Looking at the Dominican Order, which was then such a novelty in its style of religious life, we come to detect, in its most secret implications, the hunger for regeneration that was making itself felt upon the minds and souls of men at that time.

"The founding of the Order of Friar Preachers," Father Mandonnet relates,

> was very closely bound up with the general needs that were making themselves felt in the Christian world at the start of the XIIIth century. Having brought religious life to a new stage of development, the Church of Rome decided to make use of it in order to solve some of the urgent problems with which she was confronted. Until then, the monks, vowed to live out their lives in their own monastery, were dedicated to the work of their personal sanctification by laboring on the soil, and by reciting the divine office in choir. The canons regular, too, were so set up that their lives were very close to that of the monastic regime. Neither of these groups could be used in a ministry that demanded, above all, a Church militia that was both well-lettered and actually in contact with the social life of the times. The Preachers, with their new type of vocation and a mode of organization that was also new, were the answer to the needs of the new age (30).

---

a) ". . . qui non tam fuit Peripateticus, quam philosophiae peripateticae depravator." *De unit. int.*, c. 2; *Opusc. philos.*, Marietti ed., 76, n. 214.

30) P. MANDONNET, *Saint Dominique. L'idée, l'homme et l'oeuvre*, II, Paris 1938, 83.

But if the Dominican form of religious life thus fitted the wants of a new age, the reason was that, along with its Franciscan sister, it was the new age's most beautiful fruit then ripening under the action of the grace of God. We have already mentioned the sort of aspirations that were then stirring up a world just emerging from a decaying feudal system (a). The thirst for knowledge, the relish for freedom, the very earnest, even sometimes intemperate, pursuit of material and spiritual wealth—all these things were embodied in the restless, but industrious, urban classes recently liberated from the passive kind of life that people had lived as serfs. The old institutions in the Church, both secular and regular, remained entangled in their ancient forms and unable to understand this new generation of people and to secure for them, in orderly fashion, those human and religious conditions necessary for their hard-won freedoms. So far is this true that even the most justifiable of proceedings undertaken by the new generation were not unmixed with some sentiment of anti-clericalism. The clear and far-seeing vision of Innocent III procured a happy solution when he opened the way to the founding of new bodies of religious: brotherhoods of men, who would engage in preaching, but whose evangelical poverty would preserve them against the seductions of the new economic order at the same time that it freed them from the dead weight of the feudal system The zeal of these brotherhoods turned the earthly initiatives of their contemporaries to the service of a state of life which, up to that time, was unknown. The Friars Minor and the Preachers were the first models of their kind of religious life. If we look into their origins, their recruiting, their clientele, their elective mode of government, their juridic adaptability, their freedom for apostolic travels, if, in a word, we observe the sort of sensational novelty that they presented within the religious mode of life, we find that it was precisely their institutional organization that furnished the connatural environment within which the social, cultural, and spiritual effervesence of the age found both fulfillment and balance (31). With them, the monastery moved from the lonely

---

a) See above, 14–15.

31) In order to measure better that institutional revolution which took place within the religious state, let one witness the reaction of a monk of a highly tempered stamp and of great lucidity of mind, who was stupified by the sudden prestige of the new teams to whom the Lateran Council had attempted to close the route: ". . . that, spurning the instructions of the most blessed Benedict and those of the magnificent Augustine, and going against the legislation enacted by the council held under Innocent III of glorious memory, so many literate men have suddenly flocked to unheard of Orders." *Ex Matthei Parisiensis cronicis majoribus,* ad annum 1244, in *MGH–SS,* XXVIII (1888), 247–248 [partly trans. by J. A. GILES, *Matthew Paris's English History from the Year 1235 to 1237,* 3 vols., London, 1852–1854; Latin text also ed. by H. R. Giles, 7 vols., in *RBMAS,* LVII (1872–1884)].

reaches of the valleys into the center of the large cities. This was more than a symbol.

To measure the depth of this communion of feeling between the new Orders and the world in which they worked, one has only to note how the Friars were greeted in all circles, especially at the University, typical foundation of the times, where intellectual emancipation was geared to mesh with social emancipation. With a keen insight into the needs of the Christian world, under which lay a deep understanding of the aspirations that moved the men of his day, Saint Dominic sent off his first disciples to the schools and chose to open the convents of his Order in university cities. At Paris, the Friars were received with effectual sympathy, both by the masters and the commune. The University, in fact, was to become a nursery of recruits to the Order, even before the chairs they occupied there were officially incorporated (32). The convent-college of Saint James, the keystone of a compact hierarchy of schools, was both expression and sanction of the trust that the Christian world had in the intellectual rebirth which was then in progress. Albert the Great and Thomas Aquinas were to find in it the soil in which their thought could take root, through the organic balance of a contemplative life and the state of free receptivity which this same contemplative principle secures for the scientific fitting out of the mind.

Let Aristotle come to Paris, and he will find at Saint James the place par excellence to make himself heard. He will not meet with a school of clerics who would attempt an expurgated edition of his works, as was ordered to be done in 1231, but rather with a company of men endowed with the intellectual and religious greatness of mind that will guarantee, under the light of faith, the renewal of his thought from the inside—the only kind of renewal that is tolerable to any philosopher. Thus, when the adoption of Aristotle into the

---

32) On May 3, 1221, master John of Barastre, professor at the University, transferred, as a gracious gift to the Friar Preachers, the land and buildings that he possessed at the summit of Mount Saint Genevieve, at the place called Saint James, "facing Saint Stephen on the right, between the two contiguous doors leading out of the city." At the same date, the University itself "spontaneously and freely" granted to the same religious the rights and concessions it held on the same grounds. And "in witness of reverence and gratefulness, because they hold the place itself from the University as from a mistress and patron, those Brothers will accept us and our successors as confreres in a general and perpetual participation of their prayers and good deeds."
The entrance into the Order in 1230 of John of Saint Giles, former professor of medicine at Montpellier and now regent of theology at Paris as successor to John of Barastre, introduced the Dominican school within the University body in a decisive manner. These events would have been of no consequence had they not translated into facts that a preestablished communion of spirit existed in the aspirations and institutions of the new civilization. See *ChUP*, I, 99 ff., nn. 42, 43, 44 and ff.

Christian family took place, it came as a master stroke of a theology thoroughly at home in its own faith, and not as the mere consequence of a reasoned choice between rival philosophies.

Moreover, when Saint Thomas came to Paris, he found at Saint James not only proper surroundings that were congenial for his work, but also, in these very surroundings, a man who, by his thinking, had blazed a pioneer trial, and by his writings, had cleared the premises. The man was Albert of Cologne, who, as far back as 1245, when master and pupil met for the first time, already enjoyed a prestige at once extensive and debated. His purpose, and he took no pains to keep it a secret, was to make Aristotle understandable to the Latins. In his own words: "What I want to do is to make the different parts —physics, metaphysics, and mathematics—intelligible to the Latins" (33). He followed out his proposal both in paraphrases of the Aristotelian texts and in disputed questions in which he could be more personal. His *Summa de Creaturis* was undoubtedly the fruit of the latter effort. Approximately between 1240 and 1248, while some urged him on and others blamed him, Albert brought forth into the schools of Paris, where one was not yet allowed to teach Aristotle officially, five commentaries of the latter's works in the field of natural philosophy. The *Physics* headed the list that also included the *De Anima*. His lectures, and perhaps their publication too, created such a sensation that Albert, to Roger Bacon's great scandal, came to be quoted on an equal footing with the other recognized authorities. The precautions he took to present himself as no more than an interpreter, as well as the spirited way he replied to his detractors, only serve to underline the boldness of his enterprise (34). Yet it was a boldness

33) "Nostra intentio est omnes dictas partes [physicam, metaphysicam, mathematicam] facere Latinis intelligibiles." *In Phys.*, lib. I, tr. 1, c. 1, in *AMOO*, III (1890), 2.

34) Here is Bacon's highly colored testimony: "It is now thought by the common student, and by many who are thought to be very wise, and although they are deceived, by many good men, that philosophy has now been given to the Latins. Composed in the Latin tongue, it has been done up and made popular at Paris in my time. And the author of it is cited as an authority. For just as Aristotle, Avicenna, and Averroes are quoted in the schools, so is he. He is still living, moreover, and he has enjoyed in his life an authority that no other man has ever had in doctrinal matters, for Christ did not reach this point, since even He, during His life, incurred reprobation as well as His doctrine." *Opus tertium*, c. IX, in *RBO*, I (1859), 30.

Texts are numerous as concerns Albert's violent reactions against foes of his undertaking. "Some know-nots want by every means to impugn the use of philosophy, and, to a higher degree than elsewhere, among the Preachers where there is no one to resist them. They are like brute animals in their blasphemy of things of which they are ignorant." *In Epistola Dionysii*, ep. VII, §2, in *AMOO*, XIV (1891), 910 B. ". . . and I say this on account of certain lazy men who, looking for solace for their laziness, look for nothing else in writings but for something to criticize. And since such men are lying in the torpor of their laziness, for fear of being judged to be alone in their torpor, they try to

aware of what this implied insofar as method is concerned, since Albert openly vindicated the independent character of the various lines of research according to the laws that are proper to each branch of knowledge. "In matters of faith and morals, one should follow Augustine rather than any philosopher when both are in disagreement. But if it were a matter of medicine, then I would follow Galen or Hippocratus; and if the question is one of speaking about the natures of things, follow Aristotle rather, or somebody else who is an expert on natures of things" (35). Moreover, a reflexion made at the beginning of his commentary on the *Posterior Analytics* shows to what a many-sided vision of the intelligibility of the world and of the progress of knowledge his mind was open: "Not all the demonstrative sciences have been established. On the contrary, several are still waiting to be discovered" (a). Albert was the first, at the time of reason's first emancipation in the West, "to define the status of the sciences in the Christian world" (36).

The chroniclers have preserved the record of the loving and trustful understanding that existed right from the start between Master Albert and his pupil: first at Paris, from 1245 to 1248; then at Cologne, from 1248 to 1252. It was during the latter period that Saint Thomas made a transcript of the questions on the *Ethics* discussed by his professor. This harmony that marked the relations of the two men was to remain to the end. It is enough to recall in what a state of emotion Albert hastened off to Paris in 1277 to uphold the recently condemned good name and writings of Saint Thomas. Yet, certain doctrinal differences between master and pupil appeared either in their conclusions or in the general inspiration of their work. It was, in fact, Albert's ambition to fit in the spiritualistic tendencies of the Platonic philosophy with the experimentalism of Aristotle, and this goal took root in a temperament and a feeling for philosophy and

---

cast blemish on the chosen ones. Their likes have killed Socrates, had Plato flee Athens for the Academy, and by their machinations have compelled even Aristotle to leave. . . . What the liver is in the body, they are in the common body of study. In every body there is bile which, when it passes into the state of vapor, sours off the whole body; so too in study there are some very sour and bilious men who turn all others to sourness and allow them no search of truth in the sweetness of companionship." *In Polit.*, lib. VIII, c. 6, in *AMOO*, VIII (1891), 803–804.

35) ". . . Augustino in his quae sunt de fide et moribus plusquam philosophis credendum est, si dissentiunt. Sed si de medicina loqueretur, plus ego crederem Galeno, vel Hippocrati: et si de naturis rerum loquatur, crede Aristoteli plus vel alii experto in rerum naturis". *In II Sent.*, d. XIII, a. 2, ad obj., in *AMOO*, XXVII (1894), 247. Of Augustine he says: "He did not know natures well." *In Phys.*, lib. III, tr. 3, c. 4, in *AMOO*, III (1890), 312.

a) ". . . scientiae demonstrativae non omnes factae sunt, sed plures restant adhuc inveniendae." *In Post. An.*, lib. I, tr. I, c. 1, in *AMOO*, II (1890), 3.

36) F. VAN STEENBERGHEN, *Siger de Brabant*, vol. II, in *LPB*, XIII (1942), 476.

theology that were quite different from those of Saint Thomas. As a result, it is hard to measure what amount of influence Albert exercised on the development of Saint Thomas's doctrine. In any case, it is at a higher spiritual level that communion is established between such men, as the fate of their enterprise bears witness.

The part taken by Albert in the life of studies among the Preachers set a standard of philosophic work and a scientific disposition of mind that sanctioned the Order's native position within the university movement and the cultural growth then in progress. For the Preachers, organization and doctrine were thus consolidated. From the very start of his teaching career, Thomas was carried along by the grace proper to his Order, which, in turn, saw itself truly represented in his person.

VII. THE RETURN TO THE GOSPEL

From what has just been said, one may infer that it was not the entrance of Aristotle that was the decisive factor in the molding of the thought of Saint Thomas any more than the rebirth of Antiquity provided the elements from which the theology of the XIIIth century was shaped. This renaissance was only one of the factors in a renovating process whose vital impulse took its rise from religious yearning, and whose ideal, among the Mendicants, was nothing short of a return to the original way of life of the Church. In the Christian world of the XIIIth century, the rebirth incorporated itself with the ideals of life as set forth in the Gospel.

That renascent and evangelical movements should thus merge should not be cause for surprise since even in times when everything points to a distressing displacement in the order of values, we nevertheless find examples in which a renaissance and a return to the Gospel succeed in working hand in hand. Of this, the period of XVIth century humanism furnishes cases in point. If renaissance implies imitation and restoration of Antiquity, this, however, as we have seen, occurred within an awakening of the spirit—that great upsurge of social, literary, philosophic, and religious forces sweeping with them the generations of the end of the XIIth century. It is time for us to examine through what means the genius of Saint Thomas, inheriting the treasures of Antiquity, wrought a transformation of the Aristotelian man [without destroying the latter's essence], just as grace renovates human nature without doing violence to its original structure.

In the shaping of the restoration movement of that time, the Church indeed had had its share. Despite the presence of institutions that were paralyzed by the weight of the old feudal privileges and riches, the Church had nurtured earnest men who, from time to time,

44

had cried out their exasperation against the compromising acts and vices of the clergy. The reformers, from Peter Damian's time on, were not satisfied to play a purely negative role. They tried to make reform possible, and with this end in mind, they strove to present anew, for clerics and layfolk alike, the ideals of the pristine Church. The program they would restore was the program of "apostolic life" itself, with its community form of existence, its itinerant preaching, its teaching of the masses based on the testimony of exemplary living, and its candid type of brotherhood. In their hands, the texts of the Gospels recovered the forcefulness of their meaning, acting as the leaven of a regeneration that soon overflowed the bounds of canonical reform and acted as a stimulant to the masses of the people themselves. The "poor of Christ" and journeyman preachers sprang up on all sides, to the extent that, without any attempt at browbeating, Innocent III had to act to keep the movements in check.

It was a difficult task to bring such movements to a point of stability within the framework of the existing institutions, especially when the motives that inspired the first workers lost their original purity and when social and moral demands brought the Communes of the people into conflict with the ancient society, and even sometimes with the Church. But if many of these movements degenerated into revolutionary and heterodox sects, others achieved their proper balance within the Church. In Francis of Assisi, a man of his age if ever there was one, the new spirit was embodied in holiness, while Dominic, *vir evangelicus* [the Gospel man] (37), founded an *Ordo Praedicatorum* [Order of Preachers], in which the old form of religious life was transformed along the lines of the constitutional set-up of the Communes and corporations. In it, moreover, every amount of rational inquisitiveness will be practised under the guidance of the light of faith. Joachim of Fiore had gone astray in his apocalyptic dream of a Christian world that was to be made over anew, and after him the spiritualistically-minded jeopardized the work of reform then in progress. Yet, he was a ringing echo of the aspirations of his time, and he had rightly anticipated the coming of an "order of preachers" and announced that the world would witness a magnificent outpouring of the spirit. When William of Saint Amour started hurling denunciations against the Mendicants for being the promoters of a new Christianity, his was not a simple quarrel stirred up by his conservative tendencies (38).

---

37) This is the descriptive title given to him by JORDAN OF SAXONY, his successor and biographer. See *Libellus de principiis ordinis praedicatorum*, n. 104; Scheeben ed., in *MOFPH*, XVI, 2 (1935), 75.

38) See M.–D. CHENU, *Réformes de structure en Chrétienté*, in *EH*, V (1946), 85–98.

It is not our intent to restate here Thode's paradoxical statements bearing on Saint Francis as a forerunner of the Renaissance (39). There is no denying, however, that, with the whirlpool of currents marking these times, it was one and the same atmosphere that enfolded the *renovatio* [renovation] taking place in the fields of culture, science, thought, and religion. In Saint Thomas, the Friar Preacher, inspiration rooted in the Gospel became the soul of a theology stocked with the wisdom of the Ancients. As we said before (a), Francis of Assisi and Thomas Aquinas were the two poles around which the Christian world of that day revolved. This is literally true. Notwithstanding the most serious disagreements that arose, even in doctrinal matters, between their fraternal Orders, the two men cannot be set up in opposition to one another, and we refuse to do so, because it was a same age that bore them.

This Gospel-inspired spirit effectively sustained and nourished theology in full flight. Once more, we must point to the fact that it was not the rediscovery of the Aristotelian texts that brought about the rise of the life-giving sap, but rather the reawakening of a faith that fed on sacred texts. Thus, while regular courses on the *Physics* of Aristotle were offered at Saint James from 1240 on, the convent was also extremely busy, under the guiding hand of Hugh of Saint Cher, with the great task of compiling the *Correctoria* of the Bible (b). This was an important undertaking. Although their ambition to try to achieve a revision of the corrupted Vulgate by appeal to the original texts could not succeed, the undertaking itself gives an idea of the almost unbelievable dash with which these young theologians were impelled. Yet even more than that, the same enterprise was actually begun over and over, and by different groups in both the Dominican and Franciscan Orders, the latter, however, preferring to confine themselves to the more modest method of simply correcting the version of Saint Jerome. The same Hugh of Saint Cher also directed the composition of a word-concordance of the Bible. The first of its kind, it was based on the principle of interpreting the meaning of terms by appeal to texts and contexts. Albert the Great was among the first to make an assiduous use of it.

What interests us more than the actual results of these ventures, however, is the spirit that animated the men who undertook them, their taste for quenching their thirst at original sources, and also their anxious faith-inspired search for appropriate tools. At this point,

---

39) However, did not a historian of art, little suspect of theologism, but sensitive to spiritual affinities, recently speak of Francis of Assisi as of one "to whom must be ascribed all the secret movements which in the end provoked the Italian Renaissance"? E. FAURE, *Introduction à l'art italien*, in *AA*, XIX (1938), 6.

a) See above, 18.

b) See below, ch. VII, 240–241.

we cannot fail to recall similar undertakings that took place when a later movement of return to the Gospel was in progress. One has only to think of the *Complutenses* that were worked out at Alcala; or of the *Quintuplex Psalterium* that Lefèvre d'Etaples brought out at Paris. Those previous efforts, at any rate, are a significant witness to the existence of a theological method at a time when the technical study of the Scriptures was at the base of sacred teaching and held first place in the esteem of the students as well as in the rules that governed teaching.

From this point of view, more credit than is usually allowed ought to be given to Peter Comestor's *Historia Scholastica* for the role it played and the repute in which it was held during the Middle Ages. In the teaching program of the day, alongside the unconnected glosses on the Scriptures and the systematization found in Peter Lombard's *Sentences,* Comestor's work was the representative of "Sacred History" with its own resources that were being deliberately sought after ever since Andrew of Saint Victor's day. The *magister in theologia* [master in theology] still remained a *magister in sacra pagina* [master in the sacred page]. Within such a tradition, the work of Saint Thomas found spiritual and scientific balance (40).

This movement back to original sources also extended to the writings of the Fathers. Enough will be said later about the kind of screen with which the triumph of dialectics eventually masked the reading of the patristic texts simply to bring out for the present the fact that, at this particular time, men were curious about them and labored over them with the result that their actual value in theology was revealed anew.

Along with the copies of the works of the Ancients that were so often transcribed at that time (41), our libraries also preserve the *originalia* [originals] of the writings of Ambrose, Augustine, Jerome, Gregory, Chrysostom, and John Damascene; that is, complete texts, over and above the anthologies and books of maxims, copied out and put into service. To make the "originals" more serviceable, *tabulae* [tables] and *capitulationes* [compendia] were compiled. It was in this fashion that Robert Kilwardby put into circulation the texts of Augustine that would otherwise have been quite unmanageable due to their

---

40) See M.-D. CHENU, *Le réveil évangélique,* in *La théologie au XIIe siècle* (EPM, XLV, 1957), ch. XI. On the study of the Bible, see B. SMALLEY, *The Study of the Bible in the Middle Ages,* 2d rev. ed., Oxford, 1952; C. SPICQ, *Esquisse d'une histoire de l'exégèse au moyen âge,* in *BibTh,* XXVI (1944). See below, ch. VII.

41) "In how many cases did the discovery of Latin Antiquity by the Renaissance consist in discovering the manuscripts which the Middle Ages had copied and corrected, so that our humanists might then discover them?" E. GILSON, *Héloïse et Abélard,* Paris, 1938, 244 [English trans. by L. K. SHOOK: *Heloise and Abelard,* in *AApap,* XXXVIII (1960)].

massiveness (42). While no effort was being spared to get Aristotle done into Latin, Dionysius had no cause for envy. During the very same period, Grosseteste, who was devoting himself to that translation, also translated into Latin several Greek works of the early Christian period, ranging from the letters of Saint Ignatius to the *De fide orthodoxa* of Saint John Damascene (a). He composed, moreover, a concordance of the Fathers. It would seem quite certain that around the year 1200 a number of strong theological currents, later on to be checked by the success of Peter Lombard's *Sentences* at the Lateran Council of 1215, had already based their effort on an appeal to original sources among the Greek doctors (43).

Not everybody, to be sure, made the bad-humored demands for pure texts and for the role of philosophy in sacred doctrine that Roger Bacon insisted upon. Yet Saint Thomas himself, who turned to William of Moerbeke for help in controlling the Aristotelian versions at his disposal, was disturbed at the faultiness in the patristic texts he was using. As the old Chronicler tells us, he would have gladly given all the wonders of Paris for a copy of Chrysostom's commentary on Saint Matthew (44).

As in the Catholic reform of the XVIth century, the common people were seeking an answer to their hungering piety in the strong meat of doctrine that the clergy of the old regime were no longer supplying. In the liturgy, the theatre, the various forms of art, they found the nourishment that they were prepared to assimilate. The layfolk, lean-

---

42) See A. CALLUS, *The* Tabulae super Originalia Patrum *of Kilwardby*, in *SMM*, 243–270 [and *New Manuscripts of Kilwardby's* Tabulae super Originalia Patrum, in *DSt*, II (1949), 38–45].

This *tabulae* literature, it is true, also fostered the temptation of neglecting the *originalia*. See J. DE GHELLINCK, *Patristique et argument de tradition au bas moyen âge*, in *Aus der Geisteswelt des Mittelalters* (*BGPTM*, Suppl., III, 1, 1935), p. 423, with the long documentary note. [On Kilwardby, see E.M.F. SOMMER–SECKENDORFF, *Studies in the Life of Robert Kilwardby, O.P.*, in *IHP–DH*, VIII (1937).]

a) See above, note 28.

43) The theological syncretism of the years 1180–1210, during which elements having their source in the Greek doctors were introduced provoking great restlessness, has not yet been cleared up. See M.–H. VICAIRE, *Les Porrétains et l'avicennisme avant 1215*, in *RSPT*, XXVI (1937), 449–482. See below in this chapter: *The Augustinian Tradition*. [New light has been thrown on the question, however, in A. DONDAINE, *Ecrits de la petite école porrétaine*, in *CAG*, 1962. See also the articles of N. M. HARING, *The Case of Gilbert de la Porrée Bishop of Poitiers (1142–1154)*, in *MSt*, XIII (1951), 1–40, and *The Porretans and the Greek Fathers*, in *MSt*, XXIV (1962), 181–209.]

44) [See below, ch. VII, note 23.]—"The latest studies on the Greek documentation of Saint Thomas reveal, on the contrary, that the Angelic Doctor had recourse to a comprehensive use of the thought of the Greek Fathers which he read in translation. This exception was worthwhile calling to attention." J. DE GHELLINCK, *loc. cit.*, 423. [For more data on the question, see G. GEENEN, *Saint Thomas et les Pères*, in the article *Thomas d'Aquin* of the *DTC*, XV (1946), col. 738–761.]

ing on the new religious Orders for support of their apostolic-minded piety, reached the level of meditation of the mysteries through the repeated recitation of the *Ave*, through the chaplet of Our Lady's joys, or through the stories of miraculous events. New forms of devotion to the Passion of Our Lord and his Eucharistic Presence began to blossom in associations and brotherhoods. Saint Thomas's office of the Blessed Sacrament came as the keystone both of a devout movement of the Christian peoples and of an abundant literature of hymns and sequences. Even in the missionary expansion of Christendom with its aura of chivalry, we find a reminder of the Gospel's progressive surge in the pristine Church, as well as the stirring up of problems for theological consideration—problems of spiritual conquest that the arms of the Christian kings were definitely unable to achieve. Whoever it was that Saint Thomas intended primarily to reach in his *Contra Gentiles,* he wrote the work at the very time when schools for the study of the Arabic tongue were being founded by both the Dominicans and Franciscans. Finally, this evangelical movement of the day was not even lacking in bold programs of reform. One of these, set up by Humbert of Romans, as a matter of fact, came out of the convent of Saint James. It was submitted officially to the Council of Lyons in 1274. So well set up was this program that the Protestants of the XVIIth century did not hesitate to publish it as proof that their claims were justly founded (45).

If, then, theology armed itself with all the accoutrement of a scientific knowledge; if, moreover, it adopted Aristotelian reason into its own service, the motive was primarily that it was carried forward by the exacting demands of a faith wanting to organize itself scientifically and wanting to satisfy the aspirations of the souls in these new circumstances. This was a hearty achievement, but it was soon to be menaced by the outlook of the nominalists with their irreducible dualism between a naked faith and a critical system of knowledge. Masters of the Paris of 1250 were aware of the magnificence of such an undertaking, since they knew well the dangers that threatened its equilibrium and protested vigorously against "those who use procedures in theology that are proper only to philosophy, and then turn around and employ methods in logic that are proper only to theology" (a). Cardinal Ximenès later on did not found a university at Alcala "in order to aid the progress of humanism, but rather, to under-

---

45) HUMBERT OF ROMANS, *Opusculum tripartitum de tractandis in concilio Lugdunensi,* in *Fasciculus rerum expetendarum et fugiendarum,* Brown ed., II (Appendix), London, 1690, 185–228. The edition was probably done from P. CRABB, *Concilia,* t. II, Cologne, 1551.

a) ". . . quandoquidem logici theologice et theologi philosophice in suis disputationibus . . . procedentes." Letter of ODO, legate of Innocent IV, to the University of Paris, Dec. 21, 1247, in *ChUP,* I, 207, n. 176.

take, with the help of the ancient belles-lettres which were such admirable tools of culture and mental enlargement, a lasting restoration
and renovation of his deficient clergy" (46). In like manner,
the university schools at Saint James really aspired to further
their ideal of an apostolic life and doctrine by welcoming Aristotle or Cicero and by enlisting Greek wisdom into the service of the Gospel. The *Secunda Pars* of Saint Thomas's *Summa
theologiae* is a true spiritual theology (as one would say nowadays) and not a mere variation on the themes of the *Nicomachean Ethics.* Yet, Aristotle really lives once more in its pages.
As Erasmus clearly saw, without Christian scholasticism Greek
thought would have perished long ago: "If Aristotle is well known in
our schools, it is not due to himself but to the Christians: for he also
would have perished had he not been joined to Christ" (47). Or, to
use Boutroux's expression: Christian philosophy is Aristotle's most
beautiful achievement.

VIII. THE AUGUSTINIAN TRADITION

It would not be wide of the mark to compare the role played in
theological circles by a good number of the works of the Greek Christian doctors brought into circulation among the Latins at the end of
the XIIth century with the influence exercised over philosophical
speculation by the arrival of Aristotle during the same period. The two
cases testify to the existence of the same factor of inquisitiveness
which helped in bringing about a renaissance common to both fields
and nourished in both cases by researches undertaken in Greater
Greece as well as by voyages to Constantinople. This is not the place
to gather together the resources born out of such undertakings. Judging by the way that the West passionately seized upon certain elements unknown in its own tradition of thought, however, it would
seem that this contribution from the East stirred up some rather
violent countertendencies in the controversies of the day (48). In any

---

46 L. FEBVRE, *Annales d'histoire sociale*, 1939, 33.

47) "Nam quod Aristoteles hodie celebris est in scholis, non suis debet, sed
Christianis: periisset et ille, nisi Christo fuisset admixtus." *Letter to Henry VIII,*
Allen ed., V, 319. PICO DELLA MIRANDOLA had already said: "Without Thomas,
Aristotle would be mute". See E. GILSON, *Le moyen âge et le naturalisme
antique,* in *AHDLMA*, VII (1932), 36.

48) The penetration of the Pseudo–Dionysian themes was evidently the most
fertile in incidents. Yet, the opposition between the Greeks and the Latins had
become generalized and hardened as early as the middle of the XIIth century,
as witness this reflexion of WILLIAM OF MALMESBURY concerning Scotus Erigena:
". . . However, let it be forgiven him in those respects in which he deviates from
the line of thought of the Latins, while he is keeping his eyes keenly fixed on
the Greeks. That is why, as it were, he has been thought a heretic." *De gestis*

case, what came out of the Orient represented a precious capital not only because of the documentary data it supplied, but also because of the loads of spiritual riches it carried for meditation of the mysteries and of the original perspectives it offered for building a science of theology.

For example, we may note: the principle of method adopted by the Greek-loving followers of Gilbert of la Porrée according to which concepts must be submitted to a *translatio* [carrying over] "from the plane of natural reason to theology" (a), the Dionysian critical analysis of the divine names (perpetuated by Scotus Erigena) (b), the utilization of the *theoria* [contemplation] of the Ancients for the understanding of the creative nature of God's knowledge, the theme of emanation from God and of return to Him in the development of the Christian economy, the integration of broad views on the cosmos with a theology that tended at times towards overmuch psychologizing, the inspiration derived from a Trinitarian speculation that was very "personalistic" in its outlook. All these Greek elements, without mentioning a number of other Greek doctrines that made Christology and the theology of the sacraments all the richer, were well suited to leaven the somewhat ponderous dough contained in the *Books of Sentences* of the Latins. Yet, on the very eve of Saint Thomas's entrance into academic affairs at Paris, there occurred the great incident of 1241. At that time, the Parisian masters condemned several propositions inspired by a neo-Platonism of Dionysian vintage, and undoubtedly many Dominican professors at Saint James were implicated (49). The incident shows the presence of some bouts of fever in the process of assimilating those magnificent but delicate themes.

Whatever amount of inquisitiveness the recovery of Greek theology may have stirred up and howsoever fruitful it may have been, the fact remains, however, that, during the period that saw it gradually developing into the scholastic system, the doctrine of the Latin masters was dominated in its principles, spirit, and structure by the theology of Saint Augustine—the Doctor par excellence of the Latin Church and, "after the apostles, the greatest amongst teachers of the

---

pontificum Anglorum, P.L., 179, 1652 D [WILLELMI MALMESBIRIENSIS MONACHI De gestis pontificum Anglorum libri quinque, ed. from the autograph ms. by N.E.S.A. Hamilton, in *RBMAS*, LII (1870), 393].

a) ". . . a facultate naturali ad theologiam."

b) On Erigena's part in bringing Dionysius to the Latins, see M. CAPPUYNS, *Jean Scot Erigène: sa vie, son oeuvre, sa pensée*, in *UCL*, ser. II, XXVI (1933), 150–161; 216–221. The text of his translation will be found in *Dion*, I (1937). See below, ch. VI, 229.

49) See *ChUP*, I, 170, f., n. 128. See M.–D. CHENU, *Le dernier avatar de la théologie orientale en Occident au XIIIe siécle*, in *Mélanges A. Pelzer (UL-RTHP*, 3d ser., fasc. XXVI, 1947), 159–181.

churches" (50). The work of Peter Lombard alone would be token
enough of the truth of this fact. His *Liber Sententiarum* was a modest but clever compilation of Augustinian thoughts and texts—from
which, however, the barbs had been eliminated—with the result that
they were pressed into service to the benefit of a classical theology.
The *Book of Sentences* became the manual universally used and the
basic matter being taught in the universities (51). The unheard of
success it enjoyed at the Lateran council of 1215 served to determine
once and for all the school tradition that would exist within the framework of Western theology and would bar any rival attempts seeking
to reinforce their positions with help from the Greek doctors (52).

One could call to attention the fact, it is true, that there was a
marked difference between the strictly theological Augustinianism of
the Lombard and that other form of it which, when faced with the
menacing impact of Aristotelianism, fortified itself with a metaphysics
and psychology nonetheless consistent with Augustine's authentic line
of thinking. It was precisely the latter form of Augustinianism that
Saint Thomas was to encounter at Paris. But this important evolution,
which was linked with the growth of scholasticism, in no wise de-
tracted from Augustine's authority. While Saint Bonaventure, for example, was flatly stating that his master's positions could in no way
be changed (53), Saint Thomas himself, in those very passages where
he admits that Augustine was influenced by the opinions of the
Platonists, was most careful not to take exception to his texts, and he
respectfully applied to them the procedure of reverential exposition.
By this time, too, thanks to the *capitulatio* of Robert Kilwardby (54),

50) ". . . maximus post apostolos ecclesiarum instructor." The description is
from PETER THE VENERABLE's *Epistola ad sanctum Bernardum*, P.L., 182, 405.

51) See F. CAVALLERA, S. *Augustin et le Livre des Sentences de Pierre Lombard*, in *AP*, VII (1930), 438–451.

52) "We, however, leaning on the sacred Council's approval, believe and con-
fess with Peter the Lombard that . . ." Such is the Council's solemn formula
(*Denz*, 201, n. 432), by means of which the attacks of the Porretans and of
Joachim of Fiore were dismissed. See J. DE GHELLINCK, *Pierre Lombard. IV—
Luttes autour du Livre des Sentences*, in *DTC*, XII (1933), col. 2003–2011.

In that long resistance of Latin theology to a contribution of elements
coming from alien sources, was there not, linked up in one unique reaction of
defense, an implicit conjoining of the condemnation of 1210, which rejected
David of Dinant, Amaury of Bène, the books of Aristotle, and of the triumph
of the Augustinian "conservatives" of the Lateran? It was the same Lateran
Council that attempted to oppose the new apostolic teams which, in their return
to the Gospel, were liquidating some of the obsolete forms with their solidarity
on an antiquated regime.

53) "And it is quite absurd to say this [that Augustine was mistaken] about
so great a Father and the most authentic Doctor among all the expositors of
Sacred Scripture." *Quaestio disputata de scientia Christi*, q. IV, c., in *BOO*, V
(1891), 23.

54) See above, 47. On this diffusion of the works of Augustine, see A. WIL-
MART, *La tradition des grands ouvrages de S. Augustin*, in *Studi Agostiniani*

the works of Augustine were being more assiduously read in their
original form—at least the more important of them (55). All this
would seem to have refreshed and enlarged the knowledge that
theologians had of them. In any case, his writings continued to be the
basic collection upon which the university libraries were built, just as
they had been in the monastic libraries. The book-dealers at Paris
always carried large sections of them on their lists of books whose
price was fixed by the University.

But the prestige of Augustine does not appear as having been
wholly due to the continuous and somewhat ancient veneration paid
him. It is our opinion that it also fed on the new enthusiasms aroused
by the evangelical movement which, as we have already seen (a),
brought about a transformation of the Christian world during that
period. All reforms in the course of the Church's history, it
has been said, were stirred up and supported through the influence
of Augustine. Such was the case in the XIIIth century. For it was not
as the result of an improvisation relating to their institutional form
that many of the new religious groups seeking to restore the "apostolic life" turned to the rule of Augustine (56)—the Dominicans, we
know, did just this. Rather should we say that their choice was bound
up with a resurgence of the great Doctor's own spirit within the
aspirations and mentality of the day.

The fact is that in the West the name of Augustine stood for the
highest and the purest type of Christianity, just as his spirit represented what was the most religious in the basic sense of that term.
This outstanding prerogative enjoyed by a doctor, in the Church, displayed all its value at precisely this time in history when human
reason, howsoever legitimately, sought to enlarge its boundaries by
conquering for itself a new understanding of the world. It was not a
matter of simply achieving balance by compromise between faith
and reason, but an irrefragable need of spiritual unity. Later on, in
the XVIth century, many theologians fell into the sin of believing that

---

(*MA*, II, 1931), 267–315. One of the factors in Augustine's control over the
XIIth century was the work of the canonist Yves of Chartres (+ 1115) who, in
his *Decretum*—an especially theological work, it is true, by comparison with his
Panormia—supplied 425 texts of Augustine, whereas Burchard's collection which
he was exploiting contained only 60 (communicated by the Rev. Tarré).

55) Since one came into contact with certain minor works only by means of
the quotations supplied by the florilegia. The *De utilitate credendi* is quoted
eleven times by Saint Bonaventure, but, except in one case, it is always the same
sentence that is quoted.

a) See above, 44 ff.

56) See P. MANDONNET, *Saint Dominique. L'idée, l'homme et l'oeuvre*, Paris,
1937, II, 167–202: *La règle de saint Augustin, maîtresse de vie apostolique.*
[See the text of *The Rule of Saint Augustine*, in Latin and English, in ROBERT
OF BRIDLINGTON, *The Bridlington Dialogue . . .*, trans. and ed. by a religious of
C.S.M.V. London, 1960, xviii–xxiv.]

they had to renounce Augustine in order to better open their minds to an understanding of the man of that Renaissance. Actually, this was a catastrophe, for it appears that Augustine was, at times, abandoned to Luther or to Jansen. Saint Thomas, during the medieval renaissance, rejected certain of the neo-Platonic sources of Augustine and still remained the latter's faithful disciple, both in theological doctrine and in the quality of his spirituality (57).

On later pages, we shall often have occasion enough to show the importance of the Aristotelian tenets of Saint Thomas and how decisive they were in the development of his very theology, and even of his spirituality. Let us first describe at this point the capital inherited from Augustine and outside of which it is impossible to conceive a Saint Thomas—a capital moreover, that was the peaceful joint-possession of all the masters of the XIIIth century, supplying the homogeneous milieu within which the scholastic system of the Medievals took shape.

The Christian quality of this joint inheritance from Augustine was very pure. In fact, Augustine's point of departure was not a philosophy at all, either of the world or of man. It was a concrete economy of human beings engaged in a destiny that saw them born under the burden of a sin but ransomed by a God Who was made flesh and suffered to save them and Who was the principle of a healing grace meted out to them according to the choice of His free love. It is true that Augustine had discovered himself as he was reading the *Enneads*, but his theology came, not from his reading of Plotinus, but from his conversion. From that event the whole Augustinian system, both in its speculative and moral aspects, was to live on in Christian thought and unceasingly be reborn. Due to these facts, it became possible for later theology together with Saint Thomas, to give body to the abstract consideration of human nature and to metaphysical essences. In point of fact, the concrete and quasi-experimental study of the *states* of man, beginning with his state as *viator* [way-farer], brought into its own service every form of analysis. As a result the study of man was placed within the unfolding of history and of its sacred series of hap-

---

57) It seems that the questions *De veritate* (1256–1259) were inspired and nourished by Saint Thomas's first personal and deep-reaching encounter with Augustine. They must be read, not as a demolition of Augustine, but rather as an absorption, within another type of noetic analysis, of his very rich experience.

No doubt it was the repeated reading, one prolonged beyond the florilegia, of the *De praedestinatione sanctorum* and of the *De dono perseverantiae*, which led Saint Thomas to discovering the historical existence of semi-pelagianism, and thus to underscoring with much greater emphasis, from the *Contra Gentiles* onward, God's initiative in the preparation for grace. See H. BOUILLARD, *Conversion et grâce chez S. Thomas d'Aquin. Etude historique*, in ESJLF–Th, I (1944), 91–122: *Découverte du semi-pélagianisme*.

penings (58). Thus, in the *Ia Pars* of Saint Thomas's *Summa*, the treatise on man begins with an Aristotelian-inspired analysis of human nature (questions 75–89), but it includes, immediately following, the study of the "condition" of the first man before the fall (questions 90–102), an aspect one could hardly expect to find in Aristotle's treatise περί ψυχῆς [*On the soul*]. Within the moral analysis of sin, moreover, Saint Thomas introduces as an essential, if novel, chapter a study of that mysterious original sin which he sees as the major and permanent cause of man's later condition. Such developments are not simply material additions; rather, they involve the transposition of the entire conception of man within new perspectives.

In a similar way, there is a primacy of religious intuitiveness in Augustine's conception of God. Augustine, to be sure, did not neglect to seek in God the efficient cause of the world, but he took particular delight in studying the exemplary ideas. In such a course of inquiry so openly responsive to inspirations proceeding from the Platonic theme of participation, he was led to an acute perception of the mysterious conjunction of the transcendence of God and His intimate presence in the heart of things. In this instance, contemplation took precedence over rational explanation. It was less a matter of explaining the cosmos than of recognizing traces of the presence of God within it. The great themes of *vestigia* [vestiges] and *imago Dei* [image of God] were to find their place in the most scientific of medieval cosmologies, and only in the days of late scholasticism were they to be dropped. What we have here is the lofty soaring of an intellectual outlook in which the sense of mystery was both the condition and the criterion in getting hold of truth. This outlook settled upon a separation between functions in knowledge, with the supreme intelligibles reached by a higher reason (*ratio superior*) and science turned over to a lesser reason (*ratio inferior*), each *ratio* then having its own range of operations and even its own objects. Saint Thomas bent all his efforts to reabsorb this dualistic teaching within his own system. In order to guarantee the oneness of the human mind, which is reason and mystery all in one, he harmonized with the theory of demonstration the method and doctrine of analogy, by means of which he was able to extol the transcendence of God and to provide for a preservation of the deepest reaches of the human mind.

By means of his perspective, Augustine was led to see created beings less in their own proper consistency than in their representative value. The dichotomy of *res et signa* [things and signs], in which

---

58) For their theoretical formulations on man as well as in their concrete embodiments of him, the Medievals took their inspiration from the most dramatic and the most subjective passages of Augustine's autobiography.

all objects of knowledge were ranged, lay at the base of his whole methodology. Later on, it became hardly more than an artificial framework kept as a heading in the *Sentences* of Peter Lombard and of all his commentators, including Saint Thomas. Yet, this division, admittedly inadequate as a ground of classification for natural sciences, served to retain an atmosphere of symbolism from which even the most rationalistic of the Aristotelians were unable to escape. In the writings of Saint Thomas, this symbolism never explicitly took shape as a conscious and systematic theory as it did in the *Itinerarium mentis* of Saint Bonaventure. Nevertheless, it penetrated first his commentaries on the Scriptures and again his autonomous works. In the latter it safeguarded around the notion of "science" all those resources of intelligibility of a religious nature in which, paradoxically, the Aristotelian theory of the sensible adjoined the mystagogy of Dionysius. It was only with Descartes' age that theology finally closed its frontiers on symbolic tendencies, leaving their use to the "mystics" alone. The men of the Middle Ages lived in an Augustinian world. This fact will have to be observed at that very moment when we shall come to discover in the advent of "nature" and of "reason" the historical significance of Thomism (59).

If, therefore, the world is ultimately intelligible only in its relation to God, whether this relation be real or symbolic, the behavior of men, in parallel fashion, has value only through and within this framework of reference. For Augustine, morality cannot be conceived apart from religion. If the urge for happiness which is behind moral striving does not have God for its object, it becomes the source of all sorts of perversion. The rational eudemonism in Saint Thomas and the entire Aristotelian architecture of the *IIa Pars* of his *Summa* must be completely integrated with Augustine's dynamic mode of thinking in which the ultimate end dominates as a pervasive religious tenet, and in which the theological order, acting as a magnetic pole, frees all asceticism from a system of morals shut in upon itself.

It was not, therefore, as a result of purely supernaturalistic views that Augustine proclaimed the sovereignty of God and the absolute gratuitousness of grace—even in the preparatory stages of its reception. Rather, his position rested on his general views of the relation of creatures, including the free rational creature, to their God: a God who was at once, for his creatures, the *causa essendi* [cause of their being], the *ratio intelligendi* [principle of their understanding], and the *ordo vivendi* [norm of their living]. Medieval Augustinianism gave body to this teaching of Augustine and to his spiritual insights,

---

59) The expression is GILSON's. See the title of ch. IV of *Etudes de philosophie médiévale*, in *PFLUS*, III (1921), 76.

a "scholastic" body, through a metaphysics of divine causality and a philosophy of nature. This was perhaps the most beautiful synthetic piece of work achieved by medieval thought. In any case, it is the most salient feature that stands out in the works of the XIIIth century masters just as it is their commonly shared good, even when, as in the case of Saint Thomas, they separated, in their psychological explanations, the theory of illumination (wherein God is a *ratio intelligendi*) from the theory of grace.

Finally, we shall not be departing from religious values if we take up that other part of the Augustinian capital, namely: the sense he had of the reality of the spirit—*Noverim te, noverim me* [That I may know Thee, that I may know myself]. From Augustine, in fact, proceeded the never-ending interest shown by later thinkers and mystics in the problem of the soul's self-knowledge. The Greeks had stirred up man's inquisitiveness in regard to the world of nature. The Doctor of Christendom, on the other hand, opened it up to the world of the spirit. A number of systems, very different in their contexture, sprang forth from the latter inquisitiveness. In each one was guaranteed the transcendence of spirit, and among the spiritual beings, of the human soul which, while a nature, has that characteristic proper to it among natures that it is immediately present to itself. While not knowing itself as a thing, the soul does know itself "as an active subject whose spontaneity always remains beyond the grasp of the knowledge that it has of itself". Augustine's theory of the *mens* [mind] as the image of God became the basis of the soaring mystical thoughts of the Victorines and of Saint Thomas's theoretic psychology as well. This means, in effect, that the νοῦς [intellect] could no longer be contained within the scope and materials of Aristotle's περί ψυχῆς. All the afore-mentioned constituted a unique climate which the naturalism of Aristotle could not deteriorate and in which it took on a further dimension.

Such were the foundations upon which the Medievals built their science of man, as regards both his noetic processes and the principles of his moral life. Whatever greatly differing philosophies, or even theologies, might be built up, they all included an extoling of the following precious assets: that contemplation takes first place over all else, that wisdom is the source of man's happiness, that his intelligence is possessed with dynamic powers. No matter how voluntaristic some of the systems turned out to be, they nevertheless respected this Augustinian intellectualism.

There is no cause for surprise, then, if looking into the fields of technique and pedagogy, we discover that Augustine was considered by all, not merely as a master, but as *the* master of Christian culture. To the latter he supplied framework and methods, materials and inspirations. One might say that he was the forerunner of even its shortcomings. The Latin civilization of the Middle Ages, truly a Christian product, was born out of Augustine: the convert rhetorician who was unfamiliar with the sciences, the grammarian who was given to allegorical exegesis, the dialectician who, not without subtleness, found in his practice of dialectics remarkable resources for the formation of the mind and for its deepest religious pondering (60). Finally, and most important of all, at the summit of this Christian culture, he set the place of theology, that wisdom to which philosophy and the seven arts were made to serve as handmaids, but which also, within the realm of faith and under its guiding light, became a science, an *intellectus fidei* [understanding of faith] provided with all the resources of human reason and wide open to every object of its inquisitiveness. If Saint Thomas reabsorbed the Platonic dualism that the followers of Augustine maintained in their concepts of wisdom and science, he nevertheless did so in such a manner as to give fulfillment to the most deep-rooted of Augustine's religious and intellectual aspirations (61).

IX. SCHOLASTICISM

But is it not something of a paradox that Augustine should have become the father of scholasticism or, at any rate, that Augustinianism, whose spiritual dynamism and literary procedures seem to oppose to such an extent any attempt at systematization, could have taken body in the scholastic system with its depersonalizing techniques and its didactic forms? The problem is a thorny, if interesting one. Yet it is within the heart of this problem that we shall ultimately come to recognize the spiritual balance of the Christian XIIIth century, that we shall also come to understand, in its genesis and properties, the Augustinian affiliation of Saint Thomas the Aristotelian.

To convince ourselves of the difficulty of putting Augustine into a

---

60) For this lofty perspective, one should not omit consulting the work of H. I. MARROU, *Saint Augustin et la fin de la culture antique*, 2d rev. ed., in *BEFAR*, CXLV (1949), in which precisely Augustine is presented as the heir of the ancient and the forebearer of the medieval culture.

61) To be sure, in this evoking of the Augustinian inheritance of scholasticism, it is not our contention that we are solving the problem of the Augustine–Thomas relations in which, furthermore, there are so many other problems blending. The worst solution would be to imagine that there is a common core of truths around which would be organized different constructions, the resulting contributions of each "system." In those very passages in which Thomas and Augustine are in agreement and meet, they are different, and each element of their thoughts carries the stamp of their originality. One will find a good guide on this question in E. GILSON's *Réflexions sur la controverse S. Thomas–S. Augustine*, in *Mélanges Mandonnet*, I (*BibTh*, XIII, 1930), 371–383. It is in this sense that we acknowledge Father Cayré to be right in the repeated representations he makes in his various works on the philosophy of Saint Augustine.

system, it is enough to recollect the tragic outcome of the efforts of Jansen and his followers. It is not only that Jansenism fell a prey to heresy. It so happened that, by a bitter derision of fate, its teachings and conclusions wound up at the end as flat contradictions of what Augustine had held. On the other hand, the opponents of Jansenism (I am thinking here of Saint Alphonsus of Liguori and of a few others), instead of snatching from him his ill-used treasures, fell into a moralizing that emptied Augustinian *sapientia* [wisdom] of its theological intellectualism and spiritual unity. Actually, the latter were only building up a scholasticism devoid of Augustine, while the former, with their preoccupations touching upon the archaic, were impeaching scholasticism in the name of Augustine. Saint Thomas, by contrast, had been a true scholastic who was genuinely reared in Augustine.

Scholasticism is almost always the word used, whether with eulogizing or disparaging intent, to qualify medieval thought, in theology as well as in philosophy, and even in law and the other fields of instruction. But what does the word stand for?

Invariably, at first contact with a scholastic text, a modern reader cannot get away from the impression that he has just entered into a strange world. Even if he is familiar with the Latin language, he is baffled by any of the following: the machinery through which the author conveys his thought; the line of argument that he follows throughout; his parcelling out of his subject matter; his monotonous repeating of formulas; his ever-recurring use of divisions, subdivisions, and distinctions; the distressing impersonality of his style. Faced with this sort of situation, the modern student finds himself in a state of bewilderment which he does not easily overcome and which serves to conceal, at the outset of his study, the extreme variety of the individuals and generations that made up the Middle Ages. So true is this that he may overlook the fact that "scholasticism" is peopled with men such as Anselm and Ockham, Abelard and Richard of Saint Victor, and again that scholasticism housed the learned humanism of John of Salisbury, the Ciceronian style of Peter of Blois, the flowing rhetoric of William of Auvergne, the harmonious use of symbols of Bonaventure, the petulance of Roger Bacon, and so on. Only on the condition that one takes into account this multiple diversity which reveals an exceptional intensity of life and warns one beforehand that any attempt at defining scholasticism will be tinted with relativeness, should one agree to talk about it and to define its way of going about its business. It is necessary, however, that a description be attempted of that mental regime of medieval man, since it was within this regime, that Saint Thomas's most personal intellectual and literary endeavors entered the record.

It is quite true that the style in which the Schoolman wrote and thought sacrificed everything to technique and that the latter's austerity stripped it of any of the resources of art. Or perhaps it would be truer to say that, in his style, the Schoolman fashioned for himself a special rhetoric, in which imagery, comparison, figure of speech, symbolism, were immediately conceptualized without any catering to sensible diversion (a). Any figure of speech was reduced to an example or turned into an allegory, both processes in which reason crudely exploits the imaginative faculty to the detriment of its very productiveness. Hence the abstract character of the scholastic style which is all taken up with classifications, divisions, distinctions, formal oppositions, all media that favor precision in thought and in the art of discussion. Even the medieval writer of history, who could be expected to be restive with analytical processes, seemed to take delight in them. In his chronicle, Raoul Glaber establishes a series of worked-out relations between the four evangelists, the four elements, the four cardinal virtues, the four faculties of the soul, the four rivers flowing from Eden, the four ages of the earth. Glaber endeavored, through classification and allegorical analyses, to express the hidden kinships between the objects of reality. In the speculative disciplines, authors acted in the same way, but in accordance with the laws of their proper objects. Thinking was a "craft," the governing principles of which were fixed down to the last detail.

To start with, there were the rules of grammar. Unlike today, the first of the seven arts was not relegated to the position of a remote preparation for culture. Rather, it was looked upon as an abiding soil, even for cultivating theology, with speculative grammar, moreover, almost promoted to the dignity of a philosophical discipline. Medieval scholasticism remained based upon grammar, and its attention to language was intentionally pushed to the extreme. Note that it was not only the *nominales* [nominalists]—of whatever allegiance they happened to be in either the XIIth or the XIVth century—who followed the practice. It was present even in treatises dealing with the most substantial of philosophical and theological problems (b). There was a grammar of the "divine names" underlying the scholastic metaphysics of analogy, and in Saint Thomas as well as in others of his day, the treatise on Trinity contains whole questions devoted to the critical study of abstract and concrete names. Even more, it is the whole plot of the philosophical enterprise which places trust in the correspondence between the laws of language and the laws of thought and leans for support on the study of signification. The movement started with Abelard but was kept alive for two centuries by specula-

---

a) See below, ch. V, 169–172.
b) See M.–D. CHENU, *La théologie au XIIe siécle*, in *EPM*, XLV (1957), 90–107, ch. IV: *Grammaire et théologie*.

tions on words and their properties and went so far as the nominalistic theory of *suppositio* [supposition]. Through the treatises entitled *De modis significandi* [On the modes of signification], was assembled a foundation for the highest of speculations. As a result, the literal and literary interpretation of authors and of their texts gradually disappeared from teaching, to be replaced by a logical type of exegesis. Quite plainly, verbalism could be the disastrous outcome of such a procedure. This menace, however, does not impair the high quality and good services of the discipline itself.

The rigidness of external forms was accentuated even more by the academic tradition within which scholasticism developed. *Scolasticus* [scholastic] definitely kept, even in its ideological meanings, the root connotation it derived from the word *scola* [school]. The Schoolmen were professors. They had the professor's typical traits and limitations; they had his scientific qualities. Whereas the Fathers of the Church and the writers of the early Middle Ages were occupied with a pastoral ministry in which a popular type of teaching and the realities of every day life imposed upon their writings, both a variety of literary forms and working conditions that were more concrete and exciting, the clerical teachers and university masters spoke to a special type of listeners and were conditioned in their work by the demands of their professional techniques. "Theology is the first great technique of the Christian world" (62). Even their sermons, witness those of Saint Thomas, were scholastic. The Church herself called the greatest among them her "Doctors," and no longer her "Fathers" (a). The age of science had begun, even for the contents of the faith.

Thinking is a craft. Along with grammar, but to a greater degree, dialectic was to become the tool suited to the thinking of the Schoolmen. This is their second trait: they were dialecticians. Yet the word "dialectician" is equivocal, even from the point of view of its history, covering, as it does the *rationes necessariae* [necessary reasons] of Saint Anselm (b) and the *Sic et non* of Abelard, the handling of the mystical theme of love by Richard of Saint Victor and the nominalism of Ockham, the controversies of Berengar of Tours and the dynamic

---

62) J. MARITAIN, *Distinguer pour unir ou Les degrés du savoir*, 4th ed., Paris, 1946, 583 [trans. in English under the title: *Distinguish to Unite or The Degrees of Knowledge*, under the supervision of G. B. PHELAN, New York, 1959, 294].

a) See G. LE BRAS, *"Velut splendor Firmamenti"*: le Docteur dans le droit de l'Eglise médiévale, in *Mélanges E. Gilson* (*EPM*, special vol., 1959), 375–388.

b) On Saint Anselm's *rationes necessariae* to which the author refers a number of times, see A. M. JACQUIN, Les *"rationes necessariae" de S. Anselme*, in *Mélanges Mandonnet*, II (*BibTh*, XIV, 1930), 67–78; C. OTTAVIANO, Le *rationes necessariae in S. Anselmo*, in *Sophia*, I (1933), 91 ff.; C. VAGAGGINI, *La hantise des "rationes necessariae" de saint Anselme dans la théologie des processions trinitaires de saint Thomas*, in *SB*, I (1959), 103–139.

qualities of Bonaventure's *Itinerarium Mentis in Deum,* the angelic soaring of Aquinas and the subtleties of a Duns Scotus. No modern has condemned with greater show of truth or in more pitiless terms the dangers of dialectics than a XIIth century John of Salisbury. Yet, at the time when the second part of Aristotle's *Organon* was being brought to light, it was this same exquisitely cultured John who set up a paean of praise of all the wonderful fruitfulness of logic, proclaiming that without the *Topics,* the art of disputing is profitless (63). Dialectic, however, had one common denominator: it was an art practiced by all, and by all held in high esteem.

In point of fact, dialectic was first of all an art, an *ars sermocinalis* [art of the word], a part of the *trivium* concerned with the expressions of thought as distinguished from the *quadrivium* with its *artes reales* [arts of the real] whose objects were things. Even when the *Analytics* of Aristotle, with their theory of demonstration, put in their appearance, followed by the *De anima* with its psychological explanation of the processes of abstraction, dialectic held its place as an art—the art of forging and utilizing the tools of discussion, of either convincing or confounding an adversary. Dialectic was a technique universal in its scope. It was indifferent, after a fashion, to the subject matter to which it was applied, and it delighted in playing for its own sake the game of *pro et contra* [pro and con] in which negation is one of the moments serving to build up a response forcing the mind to give its assent. Hence, to raise a question in dialectical form, or to pose what was called the *problema dialecticum* [dialectical problem], was valuable for the very form in which it was cast. Even where, spontaneously, one would have no thought for disputing, it was still the practice to raise the problem "for the sake of the form" (a "pro forma" practice, if ever there was one). We shall see in later pages the technical power of such a procedure to bring about an evolution in literary genre and to build up a body of doctrines (a). Still and all, it was a technique, and formalism was an imminent danger as tending to breed verbiage, "garrulous loquacity," as Giraud of Barri put it (64). That result was avoided only where dialectic remained applied to objects that are real and fruitful for the mind—including, first and foremost, the type of object that is religious in nature. Otherwise, in the words of John of Salisbury's diagnosis, ". . . logic, if left to it-

---

63) See JOHN OF SALISBURY, *Metalogicon,* lib. III, c. 5–10; Webb ed., 139 ff.; *P.L.,* 199, 902 ff.; McGarry ed., 170 ff.

a) See below, ch. II.

64) GIRALDUS OF BARRI, *Speculum ecclesiae,* in GCO, IV (1873), 7, note: ". . . Students nowadays working in the *trivium* . . . are in a hurry for their quick transfer to the study of logic and to what seems to be garrulous loquacity, *[garrulae loquacitatis apparentiam]* and this to the end of appearing sharp and knowing."

self, lies bloodless and sterile, and it does not fecundate the soul to bear the fruits of philosophy, if it does not conceive from another source" (65). Thus, when and where scholastic philosophy came to take its own particular problems as its proper object, it became a philosophy feeding upon philosophy rather than one feeding upon reality.

Notwithstanding the afore-mentioned, dialectic supplies science with a formidably powerful instrument for critical investigation and the mind with an excellent form of exercise, in the measure that, remaining a method of discussion, it does not try to moult its dress into that of a universal method overriding the objects of every other discipline. Dialectic, moreover, weaves itself naturally into the processes, indeed, as it were, into the very tissues of the intellect. With medieval Schoolmen of Anselm's and Eckhart's caliber, it supplied rigorous logic to even the loftiest of religious elevations, giving the lie to our false modern idea that there is opposition between mysticism and scholasticism. In Saint Thomas, a sharp awareness of the relativeness of methods, together with his psychological realism, held down to its role as a tool, especially in *sacra doctrina* [sacred doctrine], theology, the formalism of dialectic. In the course of the XVIth century, Capponi della Porrecta presented the *Summa* in syllogistic formularies. His clapping of his master's text into the armor of dialectic was an act of treason against his master—and against theology! (66).

The factor, however, that was to intensify the use of dialectic and to give to the scholastic endeavor its specific feature, was the application of it to the understanding of texts. The latter were either single treatises chosen as matter for commentaries or a selection of texts serving as the basis and proof of some speculative construct. Therein lies what we believe to be, both in theology and in philosophy, the decisive trait of the scholastic system's mental and literary structure. It aimed at building a rational form of thinking, consciously and voluntarily working from texts it held to be authoritative. Here again, however, care must be taken against too summary and too uniform a diagnosis, since, in the actual handling of texts as well as in their evaluation, there were differences that reached even the state of equivocation. Saint Thomas did not treat a text of Aristotle as if it were a text of Scripture. Yet the procedure of working from a text was a general one, whatever the form it actually took. Scholasticism itself was to come to an end on the day when the method of authority

---

65) ". . . dialectica, si sola fuerit, jacet exsanguis et sterilis, nec ad fructum philosophie fecundat animam, si aliunde non concipit." JOHN OF SALISBURY, *Metalogicon*, lib. II, c. 10; Webb ed., 83; P.L., 199, 869 B; McGarry ed., 100.

66) S. CAPPONI DELLA PORRECTA, *Elucidationes formales in Summam theologicam S. Thomae*, 5 vols., Venice, 1588.

was completely thrown overboard as a result of violent reaction against it.

We have just used the phrase *method of authority,* but it needs an immediate explanation. Let us first resolutely cast aside the simplistic interpretation according to which scholasticism abusively transferred the method proper to theology into the field of the rational disciplines —from grammar all the way up to metaphysics. Scholasticism, in this view, would have applied to the latter the submissive acceptance and rules that the human mind has to observe when it is dealing with the word of God. We are not questioning here the fact that in this or that author there is a contamination of this sort, in a civilization in which the sense of the sacred saturated and made everything holy, from the oath sworn by the serf to the workings of the mind itself. In the afore-mentioned, however, there is neither the expression of a true cause nor of a general practice. Saint Thomas bent every effort at extricating the laws proper to human reason, as well as the methodological autonomy of the sciences, while applying an ontology to nature and to grace. Even the Augustinian Bonaventure cannot be said to have confused philosophy and theology.

The scholasticism of the Medievals cannot, moreover, be defined as a system intent upon subordinating intellectual life to religious life and building up a speculative system with the essential objective of bringing philosophy into immediate harmony with Christian dogma— or with Moslem dogma, if one were speaking of Moslem scholasticism. Yes, the men of the Middle Ages did pursue a particular scientific ideal, a conception of the world, according to which the resources of all the various sciences together would be committed to a superior and unique wisdom. Think what one may about this dream, just as one may think what one may about the dream of political unity, the fact remains that the design to build up a system of thought respecting as an integral part the religious problem or even a posited revelation, is not an attitude exclusive to the system of the Schoolmen. Any num-ber of other philosophies, some deistic, some mystical, some simply rationalistic, share in this sort of preoccupation. Spinoza, for one, was certainly not a Schoolman; Leibnitz, for another, made wide the room for religious speculation. On the other hand, Origen and Augustine both professed to work out Christian dogma with the help of their respective philosophic resources; yet, they were not Scholastics.

If the Schoolmen chose to labor over texts and to practice a method of authority, the reason will be found in the internal unfolding of medieval civilization and of the means at its disposal to carry out its task. We have seen how, in the medieval West, the successive stages involved in the cultural growth of the era were ruled by the progres-sive, yet unco-ordinated, discovery of the literary, scientific, and esthetic riches of ancient Greece and Rome (a). The IXth century, the XIIth and XIIIth centuries, and the Quattrocento, despite shifts in balance and interruptions, were the historical centers in this recovery. The one feature common to all these resurrections, these re-naissances, was naive curiosity aroused in the minds of men by the new treasures offered to their appetites. Imitation of the Ancients, their childlike or deliberate enchantment, now became the foundation of the new culture and, in the schools, the guiding principle of academic activity. The general run of people grew dull under the weight of imitation, but a number of men, creative geniuses, held high sway over it by the inalienable force of their personalities. Yet both the former and the latter had one thing in common—their techniques. In grammar, rhetoric, science, law, and philosophy, the *auctores* [authors] were the permanent source of speculation. Even the most novel inspirations were keen to clothe themselves with their accredited standing. We shall have occasion to see the kind of treatment these *auctores* were gradually subjected to, through the sifting process of dialectical critique, from Abelard's *Sic et Non* to the *expositio reverentialis* [reverential exposition] so widely practiced by Saint Thomas (b). One can already foresee how great a relativeness we shall have to record in our survey of this treatment. Yet we are already in a position to conclude that, in such cultural wrappings, the "commentary" was the literary prototype in which all intellectual effort was to be bedded (c). The past, philosophical or otherwise, will have become part of current thought, through the exposition of "authentic" texts, even after the literature of questions and disputes will have swarmed over the literal commentary. In the literary whole of Saint Thomas's works, the first and essential portion is made up of commentaries: on the Lombard, on Aristotle, on Boethius, on Dionysius. In the more personal of his works, just as in those of all other Schoolmen, each step forward is adorned with some text known to be authoritative. Hence arises the disconcerting effect on the modern eye of the textual machinery with whose help medieval thought unfolds itself. It is always a risky business to get one's science from books (or to give oneself up to the routine of imitation). The history of scholasticism (of the Renaissance as well) and of its later decay bears this out. Nevertheless the clumsiness of later scholasticism does not lessen the value of its first discoveries, arising as they did from the Schoolmen's unsophisticated trustfulness and their power of inventiveness.

Curiously paradoxical as it may seem, the scholastic method of

a) See above, 24 ff.
b) See below, ch. IV, 144–149.
c) See below, ch. II, 80–85.

authority was allied, in fact, to an extreme confidence in the power of reason. If testimony for this were required, one would need only point out the Schoolmen's use and abuse of dialectic and of its dissecting method. Today, those who reproach them for their parrotting of authorities are the very ones to take them to task, a few moments later, for their intemperate use of reason. The problem is that of faith and reason. Let us drop the clichés with which XIXth century apologetics has cluttered our minds. In the Middle Ages, the matter of balance between them was completely different and was defined not from a peevish partitioning of their sovereign domains but rather from the observant bringing together of their resources and methods, both in philosophy and in theology.

A type of scholasticism will arise in which the roles of faith and reason will be reversed and confused. Everyone knows the famous passage in which Father André, the biographer of Malebranche, describes his young friend's reaction of shock when he came in contact with the teaching methods of the day:

> Since he had the habit of reflection from his earliest years, this is what he found bizarre in the methods then prevalent in the schools. In philosophy, where everything must be within the province of reason, he was asked to feed himself on the authority of Aristotle; in theology, on the other hand, where the authority of God must be the sole prop, he was invited to feed on reasons, or rather, on the reasonings of reason, which, as a rule, are anything but reasonable. And there he stood, disgusted once again with the School (67).

We share this disgust. At the same time, however, we expressly deny that Saint Thomas (like Anselm, Bonaventure, and others) had any solidarity whatsoever with this "baroque" kind of scholasticism.

Among all, Saint Thomas was the master who gave reason its due and who vigorously marked off in the life of the mind the boundaries between authority and reason. All medieval Schoolmen were motivated by a confidence in reason, which the thrusts of the enemies of dialectic—from Peter Damian to Saint Bernard—were unable to unsettle. As early as the XIth century, Berengar of Tours, after recalling the nice things that Augustine had said in praise of dialectical practice, continued:

> It is surely a sign of a great heart to have recourse to dialectic in all things, because to make appeal to it, is to appeal to reason. Consequently, since man is made in the image of God because of his reason, he who does not have recourse to reason relinquishes his own dignity and is unable to restore himself, from day to day, in the image of God (68).

67) ANDRÉ, s. j., *Vie du R.P. Malebranche, prêtre de l'Oratoire, avec l'histoire de ses ouvrages*, Paris, 1886.

68) "Maximi plane cordis est per omnia ad dialecticam confugere, quia confugere ad eam ad rationem est confugere, quo qui non confugit, cum secundum

That surely is an expression of human and Christian nobleness of spirit which will later become fully conscious of its intellectual scope within a metaphysics of nature. Medieval humanism is the expression of this true naturalism. Once again Aristotle was at home in the Christian world.

To the foregoing, finally, add the power of creativeness. For anyone unable to penetrate the arcana of medieval pedagogy, it should be sufficient to accept for a fact that the peoples of that age had the spirit of the young. The men who built the cathedrals could hardly become bogged down in the writing of commentaries. They built *summas*. As we have already said (a), imitation of the Ancients did not snuff out inspiration, especially religious inspiration. The medieval rebirth and the Gospel movement were creative movements, within the *renovatio temporis* [renovation of the day] of which Francis of Assisi and Thomas of Aquino became the masters. The word "tradition" had not yet become weighted down with meanings consequent upon the Protestant controversies nor by the appearance of philosophies whose model is found in de Bonald. Whatever fideistic movements arose during the era simply served to mar the features of the medieval countenance. Whether the Medievals did little thinking about their own dynamic qualities, and whether they were wanting in historical sense, at times they had astonishingly strong foresights about the progressive elements that tend to stir up the successive generations of humanity. ". . . We shall never discover truth if we content ourselves with what has already been discovered. . . . Those who wrote before us were not our lords but our guides. Truth is evident to all, but man has not yet taken possession of it." These are the words of Guibert of Tournai, a modest Franciscan of the XIVth century, in his treatise *On the method of learning* (69). John of Salisbury had already said, ". . . finding comes after seeking, and no one displeased with study can harvest the fruit of science" (70). Everyone knows the admirable formula in which Bernard, master of the younger generations of students at the school of Chartres, united tradition with progress.

---

rationem sit factus ad imaginem dei, suum honorem reliquit, nec potest renovari de die in diem ad imaginem dei." BERENGAR OF TOURS, *De sacra cena*, Vischer ed., 1834, 100 [*Berengarii Turonensis De sacra coena adversus Lanfrancum*, W. H. Beekenkamp ed., in *KHS*, II (1941), 47].

a) See above, 28 ff.

69) . . . Nec unquam veritas invenietur, si contenti fuerimus inventis. . . . Qui ante nos scripserunt, non domini nostri sed duces fuerunt. Veritas patet omnibus, nondum est occupata." GUIBERT OF TOURNAI, O.F.M., *De modo addiscendi*, A. De Poorter ed., in *RNSP*, XXIV (1922), 195–228. See 226.

70) ". . . inquisitioni succedit inventio, nec apprehendit scientie fructum, cui querendi displicet studium." JOHN OF SALISBURY, *Metalogicon*, lib. II, c. 13; Webb ed., 85; *P.L.*, 199, 870 D; McGarry ed., 104. See IDEM, *De septem septenis*, sect. I; *P.L.*, 199, 947 C.

"Bernard of Chartres used to say that we are like dwarfs sitting on the shoulders of giants, so as to see more and farther than they do, not as a result of our own sharpness of vision or bodily height, but because we are carried aloft and elevated on their gigantic stature" (71). When it turned its back on such axioms, scholasticism, however magnificent its bodily structure, simply died.

Saint Thomas was a scholastic philosopher, not, indeed, because he maintained a certain number of theses that were the stock-in-trade of a *philosophia perennis* [perennial philosophy] nor because he endeavored to bring faith and reason into a working harmony. Rather he was such because, past master in the reading of the Ancients— Aristotle, Dionysius (Oh that he would have known Plato!)—he made all the intellectual treasures of the Ancients his own, exploiting them with the resources of dialectics. Yet Aristotle's logic and psychology kept him from falling into the pit of vain pettyfogging. He shaped into the forms and words common in his day the most personal of his thoughts, even to the extent of giving a mistaken impression to an inexperienced reader. His *Disputed Questions* testify that the scholastic style is capable of fullness in literary development and forms. His much more stripped-down *Summa,* on the other hand, offers the masterpiece in the genre characteristic of the School—the "summa" or systematic encyclopedia of any given science.

Saint Thomas was above all a scholastic theologian. Let us expel the idea, modern in its origin and still plaguing us today, that there was an opposition between scholastic and positive theology. Controversy against Protestantism, and later against rationalism, has brought about, as a result of the demands of polemic, a dislocation of that internal unity of theological knowledge within which Saint Thomas and his contemporaries labored—I was going to say, breathed. Saint Thomas was a master of theology, he commented upon Scripture. This doctrinal exegesis represented not only the teaching required by his office but the ground from which all vital force arose into his science. Sometimes, as was the fashion in his day, the citations from the Bible with which his writings are sown are no more than ornamental. Yet the very pith of his work was scriptural, and his theology had at its roots the Gospel movement of his day, just as it did the renaissance movement of which it was one of the effects. By facing the very demands put before him by this candid and hearty faith, Saint Thomas sought out faith's intelligibility. By discerning within the contents of

71) "Dicebat Bernardus Carnotensis nos esse quasi nanos gigantium humeris insidentes, ut possimus plura eis et remotiora videre, non utique proprii visus acumine aut eminentia corporis, sed quia in altum subvehimur et extollimur magnitudine gigantea." JOHN OF SALISBURY, *Metalogicon,* lib. III, c. 4; Webb ed., 136; *P.L.,* 199, 900 C; McGarry ed., 167. [See R. KLIBANSKY, *Standing on the Shoulders of Giants,* in *Isis,* XXVI (1936), 147–149.]

revelation an internal and objective hierarchy of truths and of their reasons for being so, he was able somehow to reconstruct in his own mind and in its own rational form the knowledge that God has of Himself and of His works. It was under the very pressure of the *auditus fidei* [hearing of faith] (the scientific state of which is now called positive theology) that the *intellectus fidei* [understanding of faith] (the scientific state of which is now called speculative theology) began and developed. Whence followed the perfect stature and spiritual richness of theology. Its fountain-head was, according to the various levels of this understanding of revelation, the trust that faith placed in the resources of human reason, extending from dialectic to metaphysics. Herein is the characteristic proper to scholastic theology, the abiding richness of the Thomistic system, the lovely fruit of the only renaissance that succeeded in the Western Christian world.

X. RESEARCH SUGGESTIONS

1. THE HUMAN ENVIRONMENT.—It cannot be a matter here for the student to undertake the study of general history, the framework and causes of which we could only outline. It is, however, indispensable to do some essential readings on the economico-social conditions of the civilization of which Saint Thomas was to be one of the high lights. It is very Thomistic to observe, in the consubstantial union of its body and soul, in what manner human society acts and reacts from the standpoint of its spiritual comportment. One may read, therefore, H. PIRENNE, *Medieval Cities. Their Origins and the Revival of Trade*, trans. F. D. HALSEY, 2d ed., Princeton, 1949; the original ed. redone in French: *Les villes du moyen âge. Essai d'histoire économique et sociale*, Bruxelles, 1927 [and republished in *Les villes et les institutions urbaines*, 6th ed., Paris–Bruxelles, 1939, I, 303–431. See also his *Histoire économique de l'occident médiéval*, Paris–Bruges, 1951.— The reader will find ample materials and bibliography on the subject in *The Cambridge Economic History of Europe*, the first three vols. of which deal with the Middle Ages: Vol. I, *The Agrarian Life of the Middle Ages*, ed. J. H. CLAPHAM and E. POWER, Cambridge, 1942; Vol. II, *Trade and Industry in the Middle Ages*, ed. M. M. POSTAN, and E. E. RICH, Cambridge, 1952; Vol. III, *Economic Organization and Policies in the Middle Ages*, ed. M. M. POSTAN, E. E. RICH, and E. MIL-LER, Cambridge, 1963. See also, J. THOMPSON, *Economic and Social History of the Middle Ages (300–1300)*, and *Economic and Social History of Europe in the later Middle Ages (1300–1530)*, in TCHS, 1928 and 1931].

On the communal movement, in France for instance, see A. LUCHAIRE, *Les Communes françaises à l'époque des Capétiens directs*, Paris, 1890, a 2d ed. of which was prepared with Introduction and Bibliography by L. HALPHEN, Paris, 1911; and C. PETIT-DUTAILLIS, *Les Communes françaises. Caractère et évolution des origines au XVIIIe siècle*, in *EvH*, XLIV (1947). [On all that precedes, the reader will find a list of selected titles available in English and in foreign languages in J. H. MUNDY and P. RIESENBERG, *The Medieval Town*, in *AB*, XXX (1958), 185–187.]

On the feudal system, see M. BLOCH, *La société féodale. La formation des liens de dépendance*, in *EvH*, XXXIV (1939); F. L. GANSHOF, *Qu'est-ce que la féodalité?*, 2d ed., in *CLeb*, 5th ser., LIII (1947) [English ed.: *Feudalism*, in *TB/1058*.—See C. STEPHENSON, *Mediaeval Feudalism*, in *GSB*, 1956, with the *Suggested readings*, pp. 109–111].

On corporations, see the first chapters of E. COORNAERT, *Les corporations en France avant 1789*, 5th ed., Paris, 1941.

On the structures of society, of bodies and of states, on the coherence between institutions and doctrines, see the remarkable chapters of G. DE LAGARDE in the 4th vol. of the series of his works on *La naissance de l'esprit laïque au déclin du moyen âge*, Paris, 1942 [Vols. IV–VI of this edition have been completely recast in Vols. IV and V of the new edition. Vol. IV: *Guillaume d'Ockham: Défense de l'Empire* was published Paris-Bruxelles, 1962; Vol. V: *Guillaume d'Ockham: Critique des structures ecclésiales* is forthcoming]. Observe the "reactionary" character of the opposition set up by the Feudals against the doctrinal and methodological, as well as against the economic and political novelties.

Among the works on general history, in France, see L. HALPHEN, *L'essor de l'Europe*, in *PEC*, VI (1932); H. PIRENNE, G. COHEN, H. FOCILLON, *La civilisation occidentale au moyen âge du XIe au milieu du XVe siècle*, in *HGMA*, VIII (1941) [trans. I. E. CLEGG, *Economic and Social History of Medieval Europe*, New York, 1937. Also H. PIRENNE, *A History of Europe from the Invasions to the XVIth Century*, trans. B. MIALL, from the French of the 8th ed. (Paris-Brussels, 1936), New York, 1939.]; J. CALMETTE, *Le monde féodal*, new ed., in *Clio*, IV (1951), and *L'élaboration du monde moderne*, 3d ed., in *Clio*, V (1949). More restricted in scope, G. SCHNÜRER, *Kirche und Kultur im Mittelalter*, t. II, Paderborn, 1929, trans. in French: *L'Eglise et la civilisation au moyen âge*, t. II, Paris, 1935. For a general bibliography, with historical summaries heading the various periods of it, see L. J. PAETOW, *A Guide to the Study of Medieval History*, revised ed. prepared under the auspices of the Mediaeval Academy of America, by D. C. MUNRO and G. C. BOYCE, New York, 1931 [reprinted, New York, 1959.—To supplement Paetow from 1931 on, see L. HALPHEN, *Initiation aux études d'histoire du moyen âge*, 3d ed., revised to 1952 by Y. RENOUARD, Paris, 1952, containing titles of the best writings in English on the Middle Ages. For the latest titles, see *Progress*

of Medieval and Renaissance Studies in the United States and Canada,
annual publication under the direction of s. HARRISON THOMSON,
Boulder, 1923, and *Cumulative Book Index,* New York, E. H. Wilson,
1912. For works on general history in English, see *The Cambridge
Medieval History,* 7 vols. with abundant bibliography, London-New
York, 1911–1936; *Studies in Medieval History,* ed. G. Barraclough, 9
vols., Oxford, 1938–1956; *The Oxford History of England,* ed. G. N.
Clark, Oxford, 1934 . . .; Vol. III: *From Domesday Book to Magna
Carta* (1089–1216) by A. L. POOLE, 1951, and Vol. IV: *The Thirteenth
Century* (1216–1307) by F. M. POWICKE, 1953, supply ample biblio-
graphical material].

2. THE SCHOOLS.—See C. H. HASKINS, *The Renaissance of the Twelfth
Century,* Cambridge (Mass.), 1928, ch. II: *Intellectual Centers,* and
ch. XII: *The Beginnings of Universities* [reprint in *MerB,* M 49 (6th
printing, 1961)]; see especially, G. PARÉ, A. BRUNET, P. TREMBLAY,
La Renaissance du XIIe siècle. Les écoles et l'enseignement, in *PIEM,*
III (1933). A compilation of notes will be found in E. LESNE, *Les
écoles de la fin du VIIIe siècle à la fin du XIIe,* in *Histoire de la
propriété ecclésiastique en France,* t. V (*MTPFCL,* L. 1940). [See
also the two articles of F. VAN STEENBERGHEN, *Réflexions sur l'organisation des études au moyen âge,* in *MLull,* 1954, 29–44, and
*L'organisation des études au moyen âge et ses répercussions sur le
mouvement philosophique,* in *RPL,* LII (1954), 572–592.]

For the general history of the universities, see H. RASHDALL, *The
Universities of Europe in the Middle Ages,* Oxford, 1895, completely
revised by H. E. CRASTER and F. M. POWICKE, 3 vols., Oxford, 1936.
There is a good over-all view in S. D'IRSAY, *Histoire des universités
françaises et étrangères des origines à nos jours,* t. I: *Moyen âge et
Renaissance,* Paris, 1933, and an excellent ch.: *L'enseignement et les
universités,* by C. THOUZELLIER, in *La chrétienté romaine (1198–1274)*
(*FM,* X, 1950), 341–386. See also P. DELHAYE, *L'organisation
scolaire au XIIe siècle,* in *Trad,* V (1947), 211–258; G. POST, *Parisian
Masters as a Corporation, 1200–1246,* in *Spec,* IX (1934), 421–445;
V. BELTRAN DE HEREDIA, *La formacion intelectual del clero en España
durante los siglos XII, XIII y XIV,* in *REF,* VI (1946), 313–357. [For
a more complete and up to date list of suggested readings in English
on this question of schools and universities, the reader is referred to
C. H. HASKINS, *The Rise of Universities,* re-edited by T. E. Mommsen
in *GSB,* 1957, Bibliographical note, 95–104, and to the works referred
to above 16, note c; 24, note a; and 33, note 23.]

The most fruitful kind of work is to familiarize oneself at length
with the texts of the *ChUP,* I (1889). The introduction and notes give
their perspective and meaning to these texts. Use also the selection of
texts and the notices in L. THORNDIKE, *University Records and Life in*

the Middle Ages, New York, 1944. Although their interest is not as immediate for our purpose, one may equally consult the texts that concern the University of Bologna; see F. EHRLE, *I più antichi statuti della facoltà teologica di Bologna*, in *UBM*, I (1932); G. ZACCAGNINI, *La vita dei maestri e degli scolari nello studio di Bologna*, Genoa, 1926 [for the other mediaeval universities, see the Bibliographical note referred to above in HASKINS' *The Rise of Universities*, 96–98].

Suggestions for practical exercises. Establish a geography of the schools in its main evolutions. Draw a map of Paris as a university milieu in the XIIIth century. Study how, within the differing frameworks of the monastic and of the urban schools, theology was to evolve from a "monastic" theology to a scholastic theology, as techniques, structures, mentalities crisscrossed in a Christian world undergoing such rapid transformation. The Benedictine humanism, as it has been called, confirms by its defiances the outclassing of its schools as institutions. See J. LECLERCQ, *L'humanisme bénédictin du VIIIe au XIIe siècle*, in *Analecta monastica*, 1st ser. (*StA*, XX, 1948), 1–20. Bring out the points where the corporative and the intellectual emancipation meet with one another.

3. THE RENAISSANCE.—On the concept of renaissance in the "classical" antimedieval sense, see, in the wake of MICHELET, *Histoire de France au XVIe siècle*, t. VIII: *La Renaissance*, Paris, 1855, G. VOIGT, *Die Wiederbelebung des classischen Altertums*, Berlin, 1859, a third ed. of it by M. LEHNHARDT in 1893, the first volume of it trans. into French: *Pétrarque, Boccace et les débuts de l'humanisme en Italie*, Paris, 1894; J. BURCKHARDT, *Die Kultur der Renaissance in Italien*, Stuttgart, 1860, an 18th ed. of it by W. GOETZ, 1928, a French trans. of it from the 2d ed.: *La civilisation de la Renaissance en Italie*, Paris, 1885 [English trans. by S. G. C. MIDDLEMORE, *The Civilization of the Renaissance in Italy. An Essay*. Introd. by H. HOLBORN, in *MLWBB*, XXXII (1954)]. In reaction against this concept, see among others J. NORDSTRÖM, *Moyan âge et Renaissance* [Trans. from the Swedish; see above, note 16], Paris, 1933. And the reaction against the "liberal myth" concerning the Renaissance is still going on. [On this debate, see W. K. FERGUSON, *The Renaissance in Historical Thought*, Boston, 1948, and the bibliography therein supplied.]

On the "medieval" renaissance, besides the works of Haskins and Paré mentioned above, see especially the studies of E. GILSON, and in particular: *Le moyen âge et le naturalisme antique*, in *AHDLMA*, VII (1932), 5–37; *Humanisme médiéval et Renaissance*, in *Les idées et les lettres*, Paris, 1932; *Héloïse et Abélard. Etudes sur le moyen âge et l'humanisme*, Paris, 1938, a 2d rev. ed. in 1948 [trans. L. K. SHOOK: *Heloise and Abelard*, in *AApap*, XXXVIII (1960)]; and more generally, *L'esprit de la philosophie médiévale*, 2d rev. ed. in *EPM*,

XXXIII (1944) [trans. from the 1st ed. by A. H. C. DOWNES: *The Spirit of Mediaeval Philosophy*, New York, 1940]. See, moreover, P. VIGNAUX, *La pensée au moyen âge*, in *CAC*, 207 (1938) [revised and re-edited: *Philosophie au moyen âge*, in *CAC*, 323 (1958), trans. E. C. HALL: *Philosophy in the Middle Ages. An Introduction*, in *MerB*, 1959]; and in the *Encyclopedia Britannica*, 11th ed., Cambridge, 1911, the two articles *Middle Ages* (J. T. SHOTWELL) and *Renaissance* (J. A. SYMONDS). [The subject is still giving rise to many and various studies. See, among others: E. PANOFSKY, *Renaissance and Renascences*, in *KR*, VI (1944), 201–234; E. FARAL, *L'humanisme et la pensée médiévale*, in *Pensée humaniste*, Paris, 1950, 5–12; U. T. HOLMES, *The Idea of a Twelfth Century Renaissance*, in *Spec*, XXVI (1951), 643–651; E. M. SANFORD, *The Twelfth Century, Renaissance or Proto-Renaissance?*, in *Spec*, XXVI (1951), 635–641; M.-D. CHENU, *La théologie au XIIe siècle*, in *EPM*, XLV (1957): *La nature et l'homme. La Renaissance du XIIe siècle*, 19–51, and *Conscience de l'histoire et théologie*, 62–89; G. SARTON, *The Appreciation of Ancient and Medieval Science during the Renaissance (1450–1600)*, Philadelphia, 1955.]

It will be good practice to meditate upon the ambivalence of those concepts by means of which an effort is made to seize the spiritual and cultural forces at work in a *renovatio temporis*: renaissance, reform, return to the sources, penchant for antiqueness, and so forth. Meditate, for instance, upon the *restitutio bonarum litterarum* [restoring of fine letters] of the XIIth century which began through the revival of Quintilian's rhetoric. In what sense do we speak today of a medieval "Humanism"? What are its traits, in art, in philosophy, in cultural achievement, in Christian thinking? To penetrate within the perspective of the various fields of literature, J. DE GHELLINCK, *L'essor de la littérature latine au XIIe siècle*, in *ML-SH*, IV-V (1946), supplies perfect notices and bibliographies. There are copious materials and penetrating intelligibility in E. R. CURTIUS, *Europäische Literatur und lateinische Mittelalter*, Bern, 1948 [a 2d ed. in 1953; trans. into English by W. TRASK: *European Literature and the Latin Middle Ages*, in *BolS*, XXXVI (1953)], and for a very stimulating monograph, see G. PARÉ, *Les idées et les lettres au XIIIe siècle. Le Roman de la Rose*, Montreal, 1947.

Observe throughout all that precedes, as against the notion of a medieval economy conceived as a whole, the great cleft marked by the XIIth century, "one of the most profound that ever marked the evolution of the European societies" (M. BLOCH).

4. THE ENTRANCE OF ARISTOTLE.—See P. MANDONNET, *Siger de Brabant et l'averroïsme latin au XIIIe siècle*, in *LPB*, VI–VII (1908, 1911); F. VAN STEENBERGHEN, *Siger de Brabant d'après ses oeuvres inédites*, t. II: *Siger dans l'histoire de l'aristotélisme*, in *LPB*, XIII

(1942). [Ch. II of the latter work was published without the notes and a number of developments under the title: *Aristote en Occident. Les origines de l'aristotélisme parisien*, in *EP*, I (1946); the latter work, brought up to date by the author who also added three more chapters taken mainly from his own contribution to *Le mouvement doctrinal du IXe au XIVe siècle* by A. FOREST, F. VAN STEENBERGHEN, M. DE GANDILLAC, in *FM*, XIII (1951), 177–328, was translated by L. JOHNSTON and published under the title: *Aristotle in the West. The Origins of Latin Aristotelianism*, Louvain, 1955; the same author has discussed the matter further in his *The Philosophical Movement in the Thirteenth Century* (Belfast Lectures, 1953), Edinburgh, 1955.] See also D. A. CALLUS, *Introduction of Aristotelian Learning to Oxford*, in *PBA*, XXIX (1943); the numerous monographs by M. GRABMANN (the results of his studies and the results of similar monographs can be followed, in connection with our own perspective, in the bibliography of the *BT*, since 1924); P. DUHEM, *Le système du monde. Histoire des doctrines cosmologiques de Platon à Copernic*, t. IV, new printing, Paris, 1954; C. HASKINS, *Studies in the History of Mediaeval Science*, 2d ed., Cambridge (Mass.), 1927; and the excellent over-all view of A. PELZER, in M. DE WULF, *Histoire de la philosophie médiévale*, 6th ed., Vol. II, Louvain-Paris, 1936 [trans. E. C. MESSENGER, *History of Mediaeval Philosophy*, 3d ed., 2 vols., New York-London, 1952].

It is important: (1) to locate the rise of Aristotelianism within the revival as a whole of ancient culture, letters, neo-Platonic philosophy, and Roman law; (2) to avoid being satisfied with a classification of such categories as *logica vetus, logica nova, naturalia,* and the like; one should rather attempt to discern the ambient atmosphere and the effervescence created by the inheritance the components of which were successively put into circulation; (3) to relive, echoing in our own contemporary sensitiveness, the shock that was then experienced by theology when confronted with those *profanae novitates* [profane novelties]. As practical exercises, the student may: sketch the stages of the entrance of Aristotle, where it took place, what was brought in, the factors of its diffusion, its success; measure the role of Boethius, which varied according to periods and objects; extract from the texts of John of Salisbury (*Metalogicon*) the features of one of those stages; by means of a special investigation, bring oneself to feel the rapid multiplying of the Arabo-Latin and Greco-Latin versions (the work being done on the *Aristoteles latinus* [see below, ch. VI, note 27], the monographs of Grabmann, and other similar sources); gather evidence of the reaction provoked by the rise of Aristotelianism and of the new theology during the first half of the XIIIth century; analyse in particular the stirring adjuration which Gregory IX addressed to the University of Paris in 1228 (*ChUP*, I, 114–115), as well as the texts of Roger Bacon and of Albert the Great.

One of the elements essential to the knowledge of the cultural and philosophical development of the XIIIth century is the restoration of the "presence" within it of the Arab world. The researches on Latin Averroism and Latin Avicennism are far from having borne all their results, especially as regards the study of Saint Thomas. See E. LÉVI-PROVENÇAL, *La civilisation arabe en Espagne,* in *IHA,* I (1948); U. MONNERET DE VILLARD, *Lo studio dell'Islam in Europa nel XII e nel XIII secolo,* in *StT,* CX (1944); G. THÉRY, *Tolède grande ville de la renaissance médiévale,* Oran, 1944. At the philosophical and theological level, L. GARDET and M. M. ANAWATI, *Introduction à la théologie musulmane. Essai de théologie comparée,* in *EPM,* XXXVII (1948). For a general bibliography, see P. J. DE MENASCE, *Arabische Philosophie,* in *BESP,* VI (1948). As an example of a monograph in which the Arabic doctrines (Avicenna in the case) are taken into consideration with effective results, see A. FOREST, *La structure métaphysique du concret selon saint Thomas d'Aquin,* in *EPM,* XIV (1931). [To the preceding bibliography on the entrance of Aristotle may be added the following which deal with one or another of the topics and suggestions mentioned: G. THÉRY, *Notes indicatrices pour s'orienter dans l'étude des traductions médiévales,* in *Mélanges J. Maréchal,* II (*ML-SP,* XXXII, 1950), 297–315; F. PELZER, *Neuer Forschungen über die Aristoteles-Übersetzungen des 12. und 13. Jahrhunderts. Eine kritische Übersicht,* in *Greg,* XXX (1949), 46–77; L. MINIO-PALUELLO, *Jacobus Venetus Graecus, Canonist and Interpreter of Aristotle,* in *Trad,* VIII (1952), 265–304; J. D. PEARSON, *Index Islamicus 1906–1955: A Catalogue of Articles on Islamic Subjects in Periodicals and other Collective Publications* compiled by J. D. Pearson with the assistance of J. F. Ashton, Cambridge, 1958; M.-TH. D'ALVERNY, *Notes sur les traductions médiévales d'Avicenne,* in *AHDLMA,* XIX (1952), 337–358; B. H. ZEDLER, *St. Thomas, Interpreter of Avicenna,* in *MS,* XXXIII (1955–56), 1–18; IDEM, *Saint Thomas and Avicenna in* De potentia Dei, in *Trad,* VI (1948), 105–159; A. LOBATO, *Avicena y Santo Tomas. Presencia del filosofo arabe en las primeras obras de Aquinatense,* in *EstF,* IV (1955), 45–80; V (1956), 83–130].

5. EVANGELISM AND THE FRIAR PREACHERS.—On the evangelical movements of the XIIth century and the birth of the mendicant Orders, see H. GRUNDMANN, *Religiöse Bewegungen im Mittelalter,* Berlin, 1935. Read a good biography of Saint Francis, and, above all, for the present purpose, P. MANDONNET, *Saint Dominique. L'idée, l'homme et l'oeuvre;* t. I: *Etapes,* augmenté de notes et d'études critiques par M. H. VICAIRE; t. II: *Perspectives,* augmenté de notes et d'études critiques par M. H. VICAIRE et R. LADNER; Paris, 1938 [Trans. into Eng-

lish by M. B. LARKIN: *Saint Dominic and his work*, St. Louis-London, 1944.—See also, M. H. VICAIRE, *Saint Dominique de Caleruega d'après les documents du XIIIe siècle*, Paris, 1955; IDEM, *Histoire de saint Dominique*, 2 vols., Paris, 1957; M.-D. CHENU, *Moines, clercs, laïcs. Au carrefour de la vie évangélique*, in *RHE*, XLIX (1954), 59–89; M. H. VICAIRE, *Fondation, approbation, confirmation de l'Ordre des Prêcheurs*, in *RHE*, XLVII (1952), 123–141; 586–603; D. KNOWLES, *The Religious Orders in England*, Vol. I, Cambridge, 1950, pp. 146 ff.—The reader will find an extensive bibliography of the primary and secondary sources of early Dominican history, in W. A. HINNE-BUSCH, *The Early English Friars Preachers*, in *IHP–DH*, XIV (1951), xvii–xl. See also G. R. GALBRAITH, *The Constitutions of the Dominican Order 1216 to 1360, PUMHS*, XLIV (1925).] On the study of Scripture, see below, ch. VII.

Practical exercises. Study how the Church's constitutional law evolved under the prodding of the evangelical reawakening: in what way the Gospel-inspired *vita apostolica* [apostolic life] and the pastoral issuing from it, influenced theology. Look into the foundation of the convent and college of Saint James at Paris, symbolically located at the initial point of that "route" to Compostella which expanded the reaches of intelligence and of charity. Look into the biography and the works of Albert the Great prior to his episcopacy; his intellectual temperament.

6. SAINT AUGUSTINE IN THE MIDDLE AGES.—Concerning the rooting of the Middle Ages in Augustine—and here it is less a question of knowing him in himself than in his destiny in the West—read H. I. MARROU, *Saint Augustin et la fin de la culture antique*, 2d ed., in *BEFAR*, CXLV (1949). Compare the Augustinianism of the *Soliloquia* and of the mystics of the XIIth century. Examine Augustine's passing into tradition: how his own experience, after having made use of the traditional resources of Latin rhetoric, imposed itself as an authority, the result being the founding of a tradition. Compare Augustine and the "Augustinianisms," at both the philosophical and theological levels. Look into "Augustinianism and the technical differentiations of Christian thought" (Title of a section of ch. VII: *De la sagesse augustinienne*, in J. MARITAIN, *Distinguer pour unir ou Les degrés du savoir*, 4th ed., Paris, 1946, 577–613 [291–309 in the English ed., quoted above, note 62]).

Look into Augustine's diffusion and standing. Gather the reflexions of Saint Thomas on his inspirations and mentality (for instance: "Augustinus loquitur de natura humana non secundum quod consideratur in esse naturali, sed secundum quod ordinatur ad beatitudinem" [Augustine is speaking of human nature, not according as it is considered in its natural being, but according as it is ordered to beatitude]. *De spirit. creat.*, a. 8, ad lum). Analyse the texts wherein Saint Thomas undertakes a "reverential exegesis" of Augustine [see below, ch. V]. Use for this G. VON HERTLING, *Augustinuszitate bei Thomas von Aquin*, in SBAW, *philos.-philol. Klasse*, 1914, IV, 535–602.

Of the doctrinal elements involved in the conflict between Saint Thomas and the Augustinian school, there is a good resumé and a bibliography of the numerous works done on them, in L. GILLON, *Signification historique de la théologie de saint Thomas*, in the article, *Thomas d'Aquin*, in DTC, XV, I (1946), col. 651–693.

[For other expositions and bibliography on Augustine and Augustinianism, the reader is referred to the articles *Augustin* and *Augustinisme*, both in DTC, I (1909), by E. PORTALIÉ. The first of these is available in English: *A guide to the Thought of Saint Augustine*, trans. R. J. BASTIAN, in LLCT, 1960. Also E. GILSON, *Introduction à l'étude de saint Augustin*, in EPM, XI (1943); trans. L.E.M. LYNCH: *The Christian Philosophy of Saint Augustine*, New York, 1960.]

7. SCHOLASTICISM.—Besides the work of G. PARÉ referred to above, see H.-D. SIMONIN, *Qu'est-ce que la scolastique?* in VInt, X (Feb. 10, 1931), 234–242; M.-D. CHENU, *L'équilibre de la scolastique médiévale*, in RSPT, XXIX (1940), 304–312. [See the just remark of E. GILSON about the "essence" of scholasticism, in his *History of Christian Philosophy in the Middle Ages*, in RHLL, 1955, 249. For an over-all view of the philosophical and theological thought contained under the word, see *ibid.*, Parts Six-Ten in particular. On the scholastic method: M. GRABMANN, *Geschichte der scholastischen Methode, nach den gedruckten und ungedruckten Quellen dargestellt*, 2 vols., new ed., Berlin, 1956. On personalities and problems, J. PIEPER, *Scholasticism. Personalities and Problems of Medieval Philosophy*, trans. from the German by R. and C. WINSTON, in PanB, 1960. The reader may also consult other good histories of medieval philosophy, such as those written by M. DE WULF (referred to above), and F. COPLESTON, *A History of Philosophy;* vol. II: *Mediaeval Philosophy. Augustine to Scotus*, London, 1950; reprint in ImB, D135a and D135b (1962). For a survey, see G. LEFF, *Medieval Thought from Saint Augustine to Ockham*, in PB, A424 (1958), and on the evolution of medieval thought, D. KNOWLES, *The Evolution of Medieval Thought*, London, 1962.]

Retrace the evolution of the word, both in the medieval Latin, and in the modern historical ideologies (up to and including the word "neo-scholastic"). Observe the diversity of the temperaments which make up that culture called scholastic. Take notice of the fact that this epithet is used equivocally as it is applied in turn to philosophy and theology. Analyse the role played by dialectic in the scholastic system of thought, and prior to this, the meanings and uses of the

Latin word [*dialectica*]. The *quaestio*, especially in its finished form of a *quaestio disputata*, is decidedly the procedure of thought arrived at by medieval scholasticism, and the literary genre characteristic of it. See below, ch. II.

8. BIOGRAPHY OF SAINT THOMAS.—Having pursued the foregoing various temporal and spiritual attempts of acceding to Saint Thomas, give to his biography its proper context, body, and living features. On the question of its chronological bases, the divergences of which it is not our task to settle here, see P. MANDONNET, *Thomas d'Aquin novice prêcheur*, in RT, VII (1924), 243–267, 370–390, 529–547; VIII (1925), 3–24, 222–249, 396–416, 489–533 (the contents of this study by far exceed in interest what its title suggests); by the same, *Thomas d'Aquin lecteur à la Curie romaine*, in XTh, III (1923), 9–40; A. WALZ, *Chronotaxis vitae et operum S. Thomae*, in Ang. XVI (1939), 463–473; IDEM, *San Tomaso d'Aquino*, Roma, 1945. Excellent doctrinal portraits of Saint Thomas exist, but not a good "biography." [Reviewing the *Thomas von Aquin* (Basel, 1953) of A. WALZ, F. VAN STEENBERGHEN qualified it as "the most exact biography" of Saint Thomas existing today (in RPL, LIII (1955), 312). The new French ed. of this work: *Saint Thomas d'Aquin*, adaptation française par P. NOVARINA, in PM, V (1962), is more than a translation from the German, but rather a synthesis of Walz's historical works on the subject. The latest in bibliography is therein included. The Italian original quoted above was trans. in English by F. S. BULLOUGH: *Saint Thomas Aquinas: a Biographical Study*, Westminster (Md.), 1951. For the biographical documents, see K. FOSTER, *The Life of Saint Thomas Aquinas. Biographical Documents*, trans. and ed. with Introd., London–Baltimore, 1959.]

Chapter II

Works of Saint Thomas and their Literary Forms

I. THOUGHT AND LITERARY FORM

After a presentation in general outline of the broad cultural contexts of the life-work of Saint Thomas, it may seem that it is taking things from too far afield to begin a study of his works from an examination of their literary forms. In the very measure that they are works of the mind and the expression of a philosophy and of a wisdom, do they not lie beyond the reaches of any craft? Are they not free in their means of expression? Are they not like something detached and standing at a lofty distance away from stylistic artifice and convention?

In point of fact, however, such thinking is illusory and fundamentally a psychological error about the way even the most pure type of thinking is bound up with the modest tool of language and its processes. Embodied in language, a system of thought may only thus be grasped, that is, within the very formulae it has adopted and within the structures with which it has fitted itself out. The forms and structures of language are not neutral or interchangeable garments that must, as quickly as possible, be put aside. They are the permanent support of thought, so that by examining the forms in which a mind is dressed, one has a good chance of discovering its very inner workings. As a matter of fact, even in its general features, literary form is bound up with the way a mind goes about its thinking. Plato wrote dialogues, and with him, the myth-form was a tool of expression intimately bound up with his most profound intuitions. It was a tool, so to speak, substantially one with his genius. Augustine

79

wrote "confessions," while Dionysius employed symbols, not as a mere literary whim, but rather to translate his own vision of the world. Saint Thomas wrote no dialogues, he wrote commentaries. He wrote no confessions, he gave us a *summa*. Due to his upbringing in the scholastic "craft," he tended to expunge symbols, except for those which classroom use had conventionalized and thereby rendered neutral. All his writings were the direct or indirect outcome of his professional work as a teacher. This fact cannot be immaterial.

Within the bounds of his craft as a Schoolman, however, the writings of Saint Thomas are nevertheless diversified. It is important to recognize that they vary in technique in accordance with teaching methods themselves. One cannot read one of his commentaries on Aristotle in the same manner that one would read one of his commentaries on Scripture. His *Disputed Questions* contain resources far different, both in power and in quality, from those found in the exactly corresponding sections of the *Summa theologiae*. As a literary construction, any one of his *Quodlibeta* is disconcerting for the modern mind.

Let us then first examine the general procedures of exposition that were applied in the university teaching of the XIIIth century. With this as a starting point, we shall then take up the several types of works that Saint Thomas composed.

II. THE PROCEDURES OF EXPOSITION

The "style" of the Scholastics in its development as well as in its modes of expression can be reduced, as if to its simple elements, to three procedures. These followed progressively one upon the other and typify, moreover, both their historical genesis and their progress in technique. First came the *lectio* [reading]; from the reading was developed the *quaestio* [question]; from the question, the *disputatio* [disputation]; and in *summas*, the "article," somewhat as the residue of the disputed question, became the literary component.

1. The *lectio*

The entire medieval pedagogy was based on the reading of texts, and in the universities, scholasticism gave this type of work institutional form and enlarged upon it.

"One who aspires to wisdom should therefore apply himself to *reading, learning,* and *meditation,*" wrote John of Salisbury (1), while

---

1) "Qui ergo ad philosophiam aspirat, apprehendat *lectionem, doctrinam,* et *meditationem.*" *Metalogicon,* lib. I, c. 24; Webb ed., 53; *P.L.,* 199, 853D; McCarry ed., 65.

Hugh of Saint Victor observed: "There are two things in particular by which one is instructed for knowledge: namely, *reading* and *meditation*" (2). Whereas *meditatio* meant that by an assimilative process that was strictly personal one tended toward a grasp of the deeper nature of things not yet well known, *lectio* and *doctrina* were concerned with the handing over of a body of knowledge already discovered. Whereas *doctrina* stood for the complex of the means of instruction, by *lectio* was meant the process of acquiring science by means of the reading of texts. "*Reading* is the process of becoming informed in rules and precepts, from a study of written texts" (3). There was the *lectio* of the master, or the magistral reading *(lego librum illi);* the *lectio* of the pupil, or the discipular reading *(lego librum ab illo);* and the *lectio* that was done in private, or the personal reading *(lego librum)* (4). To teach meant to read, that is: to read in the technical sense. The professor "read" his text. The course that he gave was called a *lectio;* and he himself was referred to expressly as *lector* [reader]. When the teaching of Aristotle was put under a ban, the wording of the decree of prohibition forbade that his works be "read," that is, taught either publicly or in private, leaving open the question of their being studied by the individual on his own (5). The old monastic term *lectio,* as found in the 48th chapter of the Rule of Saint Benedict, thus came to new life in a cultural and academic meaning.

If the word reading came to have this renovation in meaning, and if there was such a broadening out of the thing it stood for—a broad-

---

2) "Due praecipue res sunt quibus quisque ad scientiam instruitur, videlicet *lectio et meditatio.*" *Didascalicon,* praef.; Buttimer ed., 2; *P.L.,* 176, 741A; Taylor ed., 44.

3) "Lectio est cum ex his quae scripta sunt, regulis et praeceptis informamur." *Ibid.,* lib. III, c. 7; Buttimer ed., 57; *P.L.,* 176, 771C; Taylor ed., 91.

4)*Ibid.:* "There are three kinds of *lectio:* that of the teacher, that of the learner, and that of the one who reads by himself. Thus we say: 'I am reading the book to him'; or 'I am reading the book from him'; or simply 'I am reading the book.'"—ABELARD designated the pupils of Alberic of Reims as "those who read from him." *Theologia christiana*; *P.L.,* 178, 1258D. In SAINT ANSELM we find: "I have heard that you are reading from Master Arnulf." *Epistolae,* lib. I, *epist.* 55; *P.L.,* 158, 1125; Schmitt ed., t. III, *epist.* 64, 180.

JOHN OF SALISBURY proposed calling the reading done by the master *praelectio,* and the personal reading *lectio.* [The word "reading" is equivocal. It may refer either to the activity of teaching and being taught, or to the occupation of studying written things by oneself. Consequently, the former, the intercommunication between teacher and learner, may be termed (to use Quintilian's word) the pre-reading *(prae-lectio);* the latter, or the scrutiny by the student, the "reading" *(lectio)* simply so-called.] *Metalogicon,* lib. I, c. 24; Webb ed., 53; *P.L.,* 199, 853D; McCarry ed., 67–68.

5) See *ChUP,* I, 70 n. 11: "Neither Aristotle's books on natural philosophy nor any commentaries thereon are to be read publicly or secretly at Paris; and this we enjoin under penalty of excommunication."

ening far beyond the learning potential derived from ordinary book reading—the reason lies in the recovery of the works of Antiquity and the prodigious success that they enjoyed. Men were anxious to explore these treasures, with the result that the latter became objects of study, that is, texts used in the teaching program of the day. Previously, in theology, the object of study was found in Scripture, the bearer of Revelation. The normal and in principle the necessary procedure for learning was to study the text itself of the Scriptures. Now, however, without any rule of religious belief compelling adhesion to their contents, other texts became the official matter in all the various fields of instruction. These the university enrolled, little by little, in the academic programs of study and required the book-dealers to place available copies of them at the student's disposal for a fixed sum (a).

In grammar, the *auctores* were Donatus whose *Ars Minor* and *Ars Major* presented in a single manual grammatical knowledge in two stages, and Priscian, whose *Institutiones* furnished the student with a basic text that was at once clear, solid, and abundant. In rhetoric, it was Cicero with his *De Inventione*, and the pseudo–Ciceronian *Rhetorica ad Herennium*, along with Quintilian and his *Institutio Oratoria*. In medicine, the texts were those of Galen and Constantine the African; in law, the various books of the *Corpus Juris*; and in philosophy, those of Porphyry and Boethius.

Gradually, texts began multiplying. After 1215, it soon became the general practice in theology to read the *Sentences* of Peter Lombard before the Scriptures. The future master in theology was required to have done a public reading of the *Sentences*, as in the case of Saint Thomas arriving at Paris, and having to exercise the office of "Bachelor of the Sentences" for a two-year period (1254–1256). In grammar, new texts set to verse supplanted those of Priscian: the *Doctrinale* of Alexander of Villedieu (1199), and the *Graecismus* of Evrard of Béthune (1212). Similarly in science, medicine, and other fields, recently discovered and translated books, like the *Canon* of Avicenna and the *De Animalibus* of Aristotle invaded the areas. In philosophy, it was all of Aristotle, and one can discern the various stages in the spread of his thought by the successive enrollment of his books on the program of studies. The entrance of his *De Anima* on the curriculum of the faculty of arts in 1252 marked the official breaking of the bar-

---

a) On the medieval bookdealer, at Paris for instance, see H. RASHDALL, *The Universities of the Middle Ages*, ed. F. M. Powicke and A. B. Emden, Oxford, 1936, I, 421–424. On everything concerning books in the Middle Ages, see especially J. W. THOMPSON, *The Medieval Library*, in *UCSLS*, 1939, and in particular Part IV: *Making and Care of Books in the Middle Ages;* ch. XVIII— *The Scriptorium*, 594–612; ch. XIX—*Library Administration and the Care of Books*, 613–629; ch. XX—*Paper, the Book Trade, and Book Prices*, 630–646; ch. XXI—*The Wanderings of Manuscripts*, 647–661.

rier that, with not too much efficacy however, had been set up against him for some forty years. We have the tax lists that were drawn up for the *stationarii* or book-dealers at Paris in 1275 (?) and 1303 (6) and at Bologna in 1289 (7). These lists give the names of the required textbooks for the various courses, along with the publications of professors then actually teaching. Thus, even down to the material details of the institution the regime which we have described took on concrete form. In it, thinking developed around an *auctoritas*, that is to say, around some text held to be the authoritative expression on the subject that it dealt with (a). This was scholasticism, the end-product of the discovery and re-birth of ancient learning.

As a consequence, we can practically measure the upsurge of work at the universities of the XIIIth century by noting the progress in both quantity and quality of the texts of the *auctores*. Yet, at the same time, one can foresee that these same texts, playing the important part that they did, were quickly to become a source of stagnation from the moment that the school people limited themselves to their pages as if they contained the ultimate in science. Instead of being the means to open the mind to a knowledge of objects, of realities, the tendency was to consider them themselves as the "objects" of learning. Thus, science in medicine meant to know, not the human body but the *Canon* of Avicenna. Knowledge in grammar was to know, not the actual living speech of men but Priscian. Philosophical knowledge meant to learn Aristotle, instead of trying to discover the laws that govern the phenomena of nature, and the causes that explain all being. Away with reality, if it is not found in our books! The commentator allowed himself to be taken in by his own game. Having lost little by little his power of discovery, he condemned in principle anyone so imprudent as to find anything in contradiction to his book. We know what degree of obtusion the medical doctors reached when confronted with the anatomical discoveries of the XVth century and how the philosophers at Padua, fanatical followers of the Stagirite, rose up in condemnation of the theories of the new physics. Scholasticism died under the annihilating load of its texts. These texts, riddled throughout with artificial exegesis, overburdened, tortured to meaninglessness, were drained of every drop of live-giving sap. In fact, the very first plank in the platform of the XVth century Renaissance was: "Back to sources," that is to say, back to the reading of the originals over and beyond the commentaries. Could there be any greater derision against the School, born of these same sources? Descartes, for

---

6) See *ChUP*, I, 644, n. 530; II, 107, n. 642.

7) See *I libri della bottega di Solimano stazionario dello studio bolognese* (July 30, 1289), list published in *ASI*, XLV (1910), 388–390.

a) See below, ch. IV.

instance, protested that he wanted to write "meditations," and no longer "questions" (8).

Before the decay set in, however, the *lectio,* in itself and later in the "questions" in which authentic scholasticism reached its triumph, had run a magnificent course. In the language of Varro who had handed down the practice of the ancient *grammatici* [grammarians] as interpreters of texts, the term *lectio* stood for nothing more than a modest exercise in reading. It prepared for the *emendatio,* the *enarratio,* and the *judicium,* all elements of an analytical commentary touching upon both form and content and issuing in an aesthetic judgment (9). In the Middle Ages, the *lectio* covered, both in surface and in depth, this whole field of study. As the academic techniques became better established, the *lectio* became more and more diversified—ranging from the simple verbal annotation that was inserted as a "gloss" between the lines *(glossa interlinearis)* or in the margins *(glossa marginalis)* of manuscripts, all the way up to the ample *expositio* [exposition] which was a uniform and continuous commentary. As early as the year 1215, the statutes of the University of Paris distinguished between two ways of reading Aristotle's texts: one read *ordinarie* [in the ordinary way], wherein a full exposition was given, or one read *cursorie* [in the cursory way], that is, in rapid style and not pushing beyond an understanding of the letter of the text (10).

---

8) *Réponses aux secondes objections,* in *Oeuvres de Descartes,* ed. C. Adam and P. Tannery, t. VII, Paris, 1904, 157: "What prompted me to write *meditations* rather than *disputations* or *questions,* as the philosophers do; or again, *theorems or problems,* in the manner of the geometricians . . . so as to bear witness in this way that I have written only for those willing to take pains to meditate seriously with me and to consider things with attention." [See *GBWW,* trans. G. S. HALDANE and G. R. T. ROSS, XXXI (1952), 129. Also published under the title: *The Philosophical Works of Descartes,* 2 vols., in *Dover,* T71 and T72 (1955).]

9) On this program of the ancient commentators, see H. I. MARROU, *Saint Augustin et la fin de la culture antique,* 2d ed. in *BEFAR,* CXLV (1949), 20–25. ["Since Varro, it had become classical to distinguish four phases in this study: the *lectio,* the *emendatio,* the *enarratio,* the *judicium.* The *lectio* was an expressive reading aloud, carrying within itself the practical teaching of diction, that element bound to be so useful to the future orator. . . . The *enarratio* was a commentary, what we mean nowadays when, in our 'explanations of texts,' we speak of both the literal commentary and the literary commentary. The *emendatio,* the διόρθωσις of the Greek grammarians, has no exact counterpart in our modern teaching; it comprised two exercises which we distinguish one from the other: textual criticism . . . and criticism of style. . . . The *judicium* was the crowning point of any study; it was a brief general review of everything that previous analysis had brought out, and it gave a final aesthetic judgment on the work that had been studied" (20–21).]—On the manner in which the work was carried out in the ancient commentaries, an already stylicised affair at Alexandria in the VIth century, see E. BRÉHIER, in *RDP,* 1942–43, 93–94.

10) "[The masters of arts] will read in the schools Aristotle's books on dialectics, both the old and the new, not in the *cursory,* but in the *ordinary*

Completely fitted out, the *lectio* unfolded in three layers of textual consideration: the *littera,* which was a simple explanation of the words and phrases of the text, according to the tenor of their immediate interconnection; second, the *sensus,* in which the meanings of the various elements in the passage were analyzed and reformulated in clear language; and third, the *sententia,* in which there was an endeavor to infer, beyond everything that exegesis had brought out, the depth of thought contained in the text and its true meaning. "What else," asked Robert of Melun, "is sought after in the reading of a text, if not its inner meaning which is called *sententia?*" (11). At each layer, the quality of the exegetical work depended on the precision and the insight of the commentator. Under its apparent limitations, the *lectio,* as we shall see (in chapter IV), exhibited an astonishing degree of plasticity. Taken as a whole, however, the method of reading tended to remain completely analytic. The text was mastered by a successive grasp of its elements rather than in its entirety, that is as a total organism. It is something of an embarrassment for us to see how Saint Thomas, following the fashion of his day, breaks down, divides, and subdivides an epistle of Saint Paul. Yet, over and beyond this parcelling of the text, he, more than the others, disengaged its general idea.

2. The birth of the *quaestio*

It is quite natural that, in any reading of a text, one should pause here and there before some obscure word, or some more difficult thought, which suddenly raises questions. Where the reading has been organized as a schoolroom exercise as was the medieval situation, these problems, which confer contrasts in a text as it unfolds, become

---

reading." *ChUP,* I, 78, n. 20. In the regulation for the English nation at the faculty of arts, in 1252, the *ordinary* and *cursory* readings were likewise distinguished: "[The future bachelor will have attended] two *ordinary* readings and at least one *cursory* reading of Aristotle's *Topics* and *Fallacies*; and if not the *cursory* reading, then at least three *ordinary* readings." *Ibid.,* 228, n. 201.

11) "Quid enim aliud in lectura quaeritur quam textus intelligentia, quae *sententia* nominatur." *Sententie,* praef., Martin ed., in *SSL,* XXI (1947), 11.— See HUGH OF SAINT VICTOR, *Didascalicon,* lib. III, c. 8; Buttimer ed., 58; *P.L.,* 176, 771D; Taylor ed., 92: "The exposition contains three things: the *littera* [letter], the *sensus* [obvious sense], and the *sententia* [deeper meaning]. The *littera* is the congruent ordering of the words, which is also called construction. The *sensus* is a certain easily-recognized and apparent meaning which the *littera* offers at first sight. The *sententia* is a deeper understanding which is not arrived at except by means of exposition or interpretation. With the preceding, this is the order of inquiry that should be followed: first, the *littera,* then the *sensus,* then the *sententia.* When this has been done, the exposition has reached the stage of completion."—See also JOHN OF SALISBURY, *Metalogicon,* lib. I, c. 24; Webb ed., 56; *P.L.,* 199, 855; McGarry ed., 67.—At the end of his commentary on the VIIth book of the *Ethics,* Saint Thomas concludes: "And thus the *sententia* of the seventh book is brought to a close."

the occasion for active research and more extensive elaboration. It is in this way that the medieval literary form of *quaestiones* came to emerge from the *lectio*. Early in the days of the Church, and apart from the running commentaries that were made on the Bible, there had already grown up a literature of *quaestiones et responsiones* [questions and answers] in which particular problems bordering upon or even overreaching the text were discussed and doctrinal research went beyond exegesis (12). The medieval *lectio*, in like manner, was to give rise to *quaestiones* that went beyond the mere explaining of the texts, the latter, however, still furnishing the substance with which they dealt. In these *quaestiones*, together with the resources of the ancient dialectic and later of demonstrative logic, came into play the great complex of problems instigated during the XIIIth century by the entrance of Aristotle and the new surge of inquisitiveness in theological matters. With the "questions," scholasticism reached the peak of its development. In them, it found the literary medium best answering its creative inspiration in philosophy as in theology.

At the level of the text, there were several sources out of which questions could develop. One could be the vagueness of some expression calling for more precision; another, the clashing of two interpretations; and still another, the opposition between two "authorities" giving contrary solutions on the same problem. The last-named situation extended beyond the immediate exegesis of the text. With a view to personally enlarging on a doctrine, two contradictory texts, or even two authors, were summoned into the discussion: ". . . some [various sayings of the Fathers], apparently at loggerheads with one another, giving rise to a question," as Abelard had expressed it (13). Yet, much ground was covered after the latter's *Sic et Non* had expressedly introduced dialectic to obtain this purpose. Due partly to the progressive demands of the mind and partly to the added refinement that was given to the tools of speculation, the stage of textual exegesis was decidedly left behind. In its place, the various doctrines proposed by the text were treated *in themselves*, and soon after, other new problems as they gradually emerged.

Following upon this first shift in the center-line of work, a generalization of the already developed technique came to be added. It became no longer a simple question of submitting to research those problems already under discussion or still open to debate. Even the points accepted by everybody and set forth in the most certain of

---

12) See G. BARDY, *La littérature patristique des* Quaestiones et responsiones *sur l'Ecriture sainte*, in *RB*, XLI (1932), 210–236, 341–369, 515–537; XLII (1933), 14–30, 211–229, 328–352. In this study, research is pursued as far as the IXth century.

13) ". . . aliqua [diversa patrum dicta] ex dissonantia quam habere videntur, quaestionem contrahentia." ABELARD, *Sic et Non,* prol.; *P.L.,* 178, 1349A.

terms were brought under scrutiny and subjected, by deliberate artifice, to the now usual processes of research. In brief, they were, literally speaking, "called into question," no longer because there was any
real doubt about their truth, but because a deeper understanding of
them was sought after. Theologians as well as philosophers asked the
question: Does God exist? Is the soul spiritual? Should a person honor
his parents? etc. Yet, of the question, only the form remained (14),
with the typical word *Utrum* [Whether] everywhere, and over and
over again employed.

Therein was a progress in technique of capital importance, out of
which scholasticism, both in its deep mental outlook and in its writing
procedures, came to be built up. An illustration of it may be seen in
the case of the young man who can be said to have begun leading a
life of the mind when, at the time of his intellectual puberty, he starts
"calling into question" (in the sense already mentioned) anything
that heretofore he had accepted in a purely passive manner. Western
reason, even in theology, had reached the state of adulthood. From
this point on, a professor was no longer an exegete alone, he was a
master who, to employ the word then in use, "determined" the questions. He did this no longer by bringing authorities into play—a
process that would only leave the mind empty despite its acceptance
in obedience and certitude—but rather by appeal to reasons that
would display to the mind the roots of things. In these very terms
Saint Thomas, in his famous fourth *Quodlibet* (a. 18), defined the
working status of the theologian, as of one whose task it is, once he
has taken possession of the datum of revelation, to build up into a
"science" the intelligibility of his faith (15).

---

14) This evolution in technique was quite exactly recognized as such by the
contemporary CLARENBALD OF ARRAS, a member of the school of Chartres and
the author of a commentary on the *De Trinitate* of Boethius, written after 1153.
Here is his diagnosis: "It seems necessary to recall just what a question is. . . .
When [Aristotle] wrote these words: *utrosque idem utrisque opinari,* he wanted
it understood that this kind of question referred to propositions that were certain,
as for example: Whether the pearl is a stone or not. Hence, in the same treatise
on the *Topics,* though in a different place (I, 3), he reminds us that a problem
can be made up out of every proposition. But these questions that are made up
from propositions that are certain, have nothing of a question but its form." *Der
Kommentar des Clarenbaldus von Arras zu Boethius* De Trinitate . . . hrsg.
von W. Jensen, in *BSHT,* VIII (1926), 34.

Judging by what his disciple, JOHN OF SALISBURY, says about the matter,
Alberic was the first master, in the field of dialectic, to make use of this generalized calling into question: "The first of these [Alberic], who was punctilious in
everything, found everywhere occasion for questioning, to the point that not even
a polished surface would be without a flaw, and, according to the saying, 'for
him, the bulrush would not be free of nodes,' for even there he pointed out what
had to be unknotted." *Metalogicon,* lib. II, c.10; Webb ed., 79; *P.L.,* 199,
876C; McGarry ed., 96.

15) SAINT THOMAS, *Quodl. IV,* a. 18: *Whether theological determinations
should be made by authority or by reason.* ". . . Then there is the magisterial

Of a generalized calling-into-question of this nature, such was the gravity, such equally the grandeur. Yet, such was also to be the risk, for, standing next to the technique would be the danger of dialectical formalism, due to come into play as soon as the question procedure would become an end in itself without a further thought given to real objects in and throughout the texts. If one should entertain any doubts about the extent of an operation of this sort, one need only review— from the invectives of Roger Bacon to the troubled entreaties of Pope Gregory IX (16)—the resistance—at times angry or stubborn, at times intelligent or obtuse, according to the writer's temperament—that it provoked in the field of theology, the field par excellence of authority.

3. The evolution of the question: the *disputatio*

It was in the nature of things that the question should detach itself, little by little, from the text from which it had originated, and that it should come to be set up in a form of its own, independent of the *lectio*. It is not our object here to follow the course of this evolution, the successive stages of which have been shown to be, in theology: Robert of Melun's *Quaestiones de divina pagina* (around 1145), Odo of Soisson's *Quaestiones* (around 1164), and Simon of Tournai's *Disputationes* (around 1201) (17). Suffice it to note that this achieving

type of disputation in the schools, whose goal is not the removal of error, but rather the instruction of the listeners so that they may be led to understand the truth that the master intends to bring out. In this latter case, recourse should be had to reasons that search to the root of the truth and show how the thing which is said to be true is actually so. Otherwise, if the master determines the question by appeal to bare authorities, the listener will have a certainty that the thing is so, but he will have acquired no science or understanding and will go away with an empty mind."

16) Among other texts in which ROGER BACON bewails the current taste for *questions* to the abandonment of the literal commentary on the texts, here is one from his *Compendium studii theologiae*: "Although the main business of the study of the theologians should be concerned with the sacred *text*, it should be known, as has been ample times proved in the prior part of this work, that nevertheless theologians for the past 50 years have been mainly preoccupied with *questions*, evidence of which any one can see in the number of treatises and *summas*, and burdens enough for horses, which many have produced, and not with the most sacred text of God. Wherefore, the theologians show more inclination to receive a treatise on questions rather than on the text. . . ." H. Rashdall ed., in *BSFS*, III (1911), 34. See also, *ibid.*, 25. Bacon speaks of fifty years before. This brings us back to the years 1225–1230, at the time when Gregory IX addressed two solemn bulls to the masters of Paris (one dated July 7, 1228, and the other April 13, 1231), in which he recalls the principles that must regulate the use of reason in theology. See *ChUP*, I, 114–115 n. 59; 136–138 n. 79. See also M.–D. CHENU, *La théologie comme science au XIIIe siècle*, 3d rev. ed., in *BibTh*, XXXIII (1957), 26–32.

17) See ROBERT OF MELUN, *Quaestiones de divina pagina*, Martin ed. in *SSL*, XIII (1932); ODO OF SOISSONS, *Quaestiones*, Pitra ed. in *ANSS*, II (1888); SIMON OF TOURNAI, *Disputationes*, J. Warichez ed., in *SSL*, XII (1932).—On the evolution of this literary genre, see R. M. MARTIN, *op. cit.*, introd., xxxiv–xlvi.

of literary independence was the outward sign that autonomy had also been reached in matters of doctrinal research and of scientific curiosity. Problems and their solution were no longer bound up with a text.

Another feature of this evolution needs to be expressly indicated. Two or more masters, regardless of whether they might be in agreement or disagreement, took a hand in the positing and resolving of questions. Here again, it was normal that, in the face of a problem, divergent views should be held. Yet, in the present case, this divergence was to be given an institutional form in a university exercise. Things so developed that apart from the *lectio,* which by the same token resumed its more simple exegetic character, special exercises were held during which one of the masters submitted, in the presence of the school body, some question of current interest to be discussed with his fellow-masters. Objections were raised, points discussed, retorts flung back, with the debate finally coming to an end with the master in charge giving his own conclusion or "determination" on the question. Picture the renewal in liveliness in sessions of this sort and what they did for competition in research! They produced the "disputed question" (18). One recalls here the famous incident in the career of Saint Thomas at the moment when the intellectual crisis, centered around the condemnation of Aristotelianism, had reached a peak of acuteness at the University of Paris. Brother John Peckham, master regent of the Friars Minor, rose up against Brother Thomas Aquinas, master regent of the Friar Preachers, and in the presence of all the masters and bachelors, sharply criticized "in pompous and inflated terms" the account he had just given of the Aristotelian theory of the unity of forms (19).

---

18) To be sure, all during the early Middle Ages, there had been "disputes" between masters who were the protagonists of diverging opinions. Lanfranc, for example, in the XIth century, as the chronicler tells us, emerged victorious in his dispute with Berengar. See GUITMUNDI *De corporis et sanguinis Christi veritate in Eucharistia libri tres,* lib. I; *P.L.,* 149, 1428B [See R. W. SOUTHERN, *Lanfranc of Bec and Berengar of Tours,* in *SMH,* 1948, 27–28]. It is a known fact that Abelard excelled in disputations and that he was one of the creators of the technique. In their time, however, disputes were not yet a part of an academic order of things set up in an organized university and with a definite apparatus and regularity. [A number of XIIth century works carry the word *disputatio* in their title. See R. W. HUNT, *The Disputation of Peter of Cornwall against Symon the Jew,* in *SMH,* 1948, 143–156.]

19) "The aforesaid witness said he heard from several Friar Preachers worthy of credence that once Brother Thomas was conducting a disputation in Paris, which was attended by Brother John of Pizano of the Order of Friars Minor, who later became Archbishop of Canterbury, and that however much the said Brother John, in his pompous and inflated terms [*verbis ampullosis et tumidis*], showed himself aggravating to the same Brother Thomas, not once did the latter himself cease to use the language of humility, but was always pleasant and humane in his answers." ASS, March 7, *Processus inquisitionis,* c. 9, n. 77, 712; Foster ed.,

It is difficult to say at what exact date this sort of exercise first appeared and how often it was held. One thing, however, is certain; in the middle of the XIIIth century, a master's responsibility at the faculty of theology included a threefold duty: *legere, disputare, praedicare* [to read, "to dispute," to preach]. In fact, when Saint Thomas assumed the duties of the masterate, the two types of teaching (leaving out the question of preaching) were expressly marked off from each other and set up in institutional form. It is doubtful, however, that the number of "disputations" was fixed, although the master was required to give his *lectio* every day.

Father Mandonnet describes the sort of event that the disputation had come to be at the faculty of theology.

> When a master disputed, all the morning lectures of the other masters and bachelors on the faculty were dispensed with. Only the master who was to conduct the dispute gave a short lecture, in order to allow time for the audience to arrive. Then the dispute began: and it took up a more or less considerable part of the morning. All the bachelors of the faculty as well as the students of the master who was disputing had to be present at the exercise. The other masters and students, it would appear, were left free to do so; but there is small doubt that they too showed up, in numbers that depended on the reputation of the master and on the topic that was being discussed. The clergy of Paris, the prelates and other Church dignitaries who happened to be at the capital at the time, were quite willing to attend these academic jousts that passionately absorbed the contemporary mind. A dispute was a tournament for the clergy.
>
> The question to come under debate was fixed in advance by the master who was in charge of the disputation. Both the disputation and the day on which it was to be held were announced in the other schools of the faculty. The matters argued by one and the same master might vary widely, because, under ordinary circumstances, a professor held only a small number of annual disputations. . . .
>
> The disputation was controlled by the master, but, strictly speaking, he was not the one who did the actual disputing. Rather, his bachelor assumed the task of replying, thus starting his apprenticeship in exercises of this sort. The objections usually represented different currents of thought, and were first formulated by the masters present, then by the bachelors, and finally, if the situation warranted it, by the students. The bachelor gave response to the arguments proposed, and, if need be, got help from the master. Such, in a summary way, were the main features of an ordinary dispute. They made up, however, only the first part of the exercise—though the principal and most lively part.

107–108. Compare this account with Peckham's own, and with the latter's variant interpretation of the episode, *Registrum Epistolarum fratris Johannis Peckham*, Vol. III, in *RBMAS*, LXXVII (1885), 866. [On Peckham's subsequent condemnation of Thomistic doctrines, see D. L. DOUIE, *Archbishop Pecham*, Oxford, 1952, 272–301, and D. A. CALLUS, *The Condemnation of St. Thomas at Oxford*, in *AqP*, V (1955), 17–35. See bibliographies therein.]

The objections, put forth and solved in the course of the disputation without any pre-arranged order, presented in the end a doctrinal matter that stood in quite a state of disorder, resembling, however, much less debris scattered over a battlefield, than half-worked materials laid out across a construction job. That is why, in addition to this first session of doctrinal elaboration, a second one was held. It was called the "magisterial determination."

On the first "reading" day, to use the language of the time, that is, on the first day when the master who had conducted the disputation was able to lecture (a Sunday, a feast day, or some other obstacle could prevent him from doing so on the day that followed his disputation), he went over, in his own school, the material over which the disputation had been held the day or a few days before. First, he co-ordinated, as far as the matter would allow, in logical order or sequence, the objections which had been opposed to his thesis, and cast them in definite form. These were followed by a few arguments in favor of the doctrinal position which he was going to propose. He then passed on to a more or less extended exposé of his own doctrine on the question under debate. This exposition furnished the core and essence of his determination. He wound up by replying to each objection that had been stated against the doctrine of his thesis.

This second act, following on the disputation [20], was known as the *determinatio* [determination], because the master determined, that is, gave an authoritative formulation of the doctrine that had to be held. To determine or define a doctrine was the right or privilege of those who held the title of master. A bachelor did not have the authority to perform such an act.

The acts of determination, set down in writing by the master or an auditor, make up the writings that we call the *Disputed Questions,* and the latter represent the final part of a disputation. A disputed question, then, is not a sort of recording or a stenographic account of the disputation itself, but rather, of the determination of the master. Through the disputed question [as we have it], however, we are able to recognize the objections being raised against the doctrine of the master, the bachelor, and, when necessary, the master himself, arguing for it in reply—and again, in some instances, certain particularities that showed up in some disputations and which have been preserved in the edited determination [21].

4. The *quaestio de quolibet*

A very original type of disputed question sprang forth and developed in the same style from within that literary genre, and we moderns have been even more trouble trying to get the right idea about it. Even if it is only in a very sketchy way, an examination of the physionomy of the disputation *de quolibet,* or quodlibetal disputation,

---

20) The double session was not, moreover, confined to quodlibetal disputations alone, but was also, it would seem, in operation in the case of ordinary disputed questions. See A. TEETAERT, *La littérature quodlibétique,* in ETL, XIV (1937), 75–105.

21) P. MANDONNET, *Chronologie des questions disputées de saint Thomas d'Aquin,* in RT, XXIII (1928), 267–269.

as it is called, will have its advantages, first because Saint Thomas was one of those who pioneered in its use, and again because, through this type of disputation, it becomes possible to complete the picture of the intense vitality animating the medieval university milieu, especially that of Paris, where it was brilliantly successful (22).

Twice a year, near Christmas and Easter, in the faculties of arts, law, medicine, but especially in the faculty of theology, the masters were free to hold a disputation in which the choosing of the subjects to be debated was left to the initiative of the members of the audience, who could raise any problem they liked. In the phrase of Humbert of Romans, it was a disputation "on anything at anyone's will" (23). The Medievals spoke of it as a "general" disputation. In it were raised the most diverse and ill-assorted questions, ranging from the highest speculations in metaphysics all the way down to the small problems of public or private everyday life. All this was left to the initiative of anyone in the audience. The multiplying of questions lacking all unity in subject and altogether unforeseeable, coming as they did from the audience, was enough to give rather a strange air to the session itself, and no less to its results which have been preserved in the master's "determination." This kind of session was a hard one to conduct, and many a master refused to risk himself at it, or felt satisfied when he had done so once in his career. This explains why we have so few large collections of *quodlibeta*.

The session began around the hour of Terce perhaps, or of Sext; in any case, quite early in the morning, since there was the risk that it would go on for a long time. In fact, what characterized it was the capricious and off-hand manner in which it unfolded, along with an ever-present uncertainty hovering over the proceedings. It was no doubt devoted to disputing and argumenting like so many others, but with this special feature that the master had lost the initiative in bringing up the matter for discussion which now rested with the members of the audience. In ordinary disputes, the master had announced beforehand the subjects everyone would be occupied with; he had had time to mull them over, and to prepare them. In the quodlibetal dispute, it was everyone's privilege to raise any kind of problem at all. Herein lay the great danger for the master who was host to the affair. The questions or objections could come from every direction, and it mattered not at all if they sprang from hostility, simple inquisitiveness, or cunning. One could question the master in all good faith, simply to know his opinion, but one could also try to have him

---

22) Complete information about the structure, evolution and characteristics of interest concerning this literary genre will be found in P. GLORIEUX, *La littérature quodlibétique de 1260 à 1320*, in *BibTh*, V (1925), introd., and even more in a second volume of his: *La littérature quodlibétique, ibid.*, XXI (1935), introd. See also his *Le Quodlibet et ses procédés rédactionnels*, in *DTP*, XLII (1939), 61–93, and *Où en est la question du Quodlibet?*, in *RMAL*, II (1946), 405–414.

23) ". . . de quolibet ad voluntatem cujuslibet. . . ." HUMBERT OF ROMANS, *Instructiones de officiis Ordinis*, c. 12, in *BHROVR*, II (1889), 260.

contradict himself, or oblige him to give his own views on burning subjects he would prefer never to touch upon. At one time, it would be some inquisitive stranger or some apprehensive worrier; at another, it was a jealous rival or a curious master attempting to put him in bad straits. In some instances, the problems were clearcut and interesting; in others, the questions were ambiguous and the master had great trouble in seeing their full import and understanding their real meaning. Some questioners would candidly confine themselves to a strictly intellectual level, while others nurtured some secret thought of diplomacy or of disparagement. . . . Anyone, therefore, willing to hold a general disputation must have a presence of mind quite out of the common, and a competency almost universal in its scope [24].

The interesting thing about these disputes was less the fullness of doctrinal exposition they gave occasion to than the incidental and current character of the questions and answers. Positions were adopted from one session to another—right at the heart of conflicts between doctrines and persons, right in the midst of the liveliness caused by the competing of different ideologies. A study of the cross-indications supplied by these conflicts and competition (the chronology of which is so precious for the historian) permits one to establish methodically the successive stages in the evolution of the problems and to grasp the immediate and precise reactions of authors. In Saint Thomas's day, these exercises were in the best state of balance they were ever to know, for soon, at least in their written form, they were to fall into lengthiness, yielding to amplification and subtleness, and no longer giving a true idea of the living reality which had formerly given rise to them.

5. The construction of an "article"

Within this perspective of the question and disputation we have to understand, in its construction and dynamic qualities, that unit which in scholastic works is still today called an *articulus* [article]. Through this unit, the Schoolmen drafted and developed their doctrines in their works comprehensive of a whole subject, such as, for example, their collections of disputed questions, or their *summas* (25). The *Summa theologiae* of Saint Thomas, for instance, is not made up of chapters, but of articles.

---

24) P. GLORIEUX, *La littérature quodlibétique*, in *BibTh*, XXI (1935), 10–11. Here is a significant text: "In the quodlibetal disputations, ten questions were proposed by my associates, because of the two which I had proposed myself. Out of the ten, five were concerned with the matters under dispute, and the other five on matters related in some way with them. . . . Likewise, the unrelated questions, which were brought up in the quodlibetal disputation by associates. . . ." *London ms.*, British Museum, King's Library, 10 C. VI, fol. 152.

25) See Z. ALSZEGHY, *Einteilung des Textes in mittelalterlichen Summen*, in *Greg*, XVII (1946), 46–58. The word *articulus* always indicated what was considered to be the elemental unit in every field and in every discipline ("What is

What is an "article"? (26) It is an account reducing to simple elements and expressing in schematic form for the benefit of the students all the work that was required to raise, discuss, and solve a question under dispute (a). First of all and properly speaking, it is a question. *Circa primum quaeritur . . .* [Concerning the first it is asked . . .]: such were the words that served to introduce an article, and here the word *quaeritur* [it is asked] must be taken in its technical sense. It is charged with the same impelling pressure towards research as was the ἀπορία [problem] in Aristotle (*Metaph.*, B, I, 995a24–b4), confirmation of which we find in the strong formulation of Boethius: "A question is a proposition carrying doubt" (27). Hence the vigorous sense of the scholastic *Utrum* with which, invariably and to the point of monotony, the Schoolmen opened each one of their articles (28).

From this starting point, the pro and con are brought into play, not with the intention of finding an immediate answer, but in order that, under the action of *dubitatio* [doubt], research be pushed to its limit. A satisfactory explanation will be given only on the condition that one continue the search to the discovery of what caused the doubt. Therein is the διαλέγεσθαι (*disputare*). It should be well understood that in stating the pro and con the arguments are not, at least where the technique is employed to perfection, simply lined up and juxtaposed one after another. On the contrary, they are interlocked with the purpose of leading the mind on to the knottiest part of the problem. *Sic proceditur* [In this manner does one proceed] means, we are going to reason, to discuss. In the language of the times, *arguere* [to argue], *argumentari* [to offer arguments], *objicere* [to set forth] are words all synonomous with the term *disputare*, so that *objicere* and *objectio* [setting forth] do not, in themselves and always, have the meaning that the word "objection" today denotes. *Objicere* is to *inducere rationes* [bring in reasons] in favor of the one or the other part; it is not to oppose a fact or an argument against a previously established thesis. If the latter were the case, things would be reversed insofar as

---

intended in the article is found in a fourfold discipline. . . ." ALEXANDER HALENSIS, *Summa*, III, q. 69, n. I, a. I, obj. ult., Venice ed., 295; Quaracchi ed., t. IV, vol. 2, n. 698, 1113, 5). It ranged from the simple announcing of a point to be debated during the course of a commentary on a text to the "article of faith" in theology.

26) See the scrupulous and scrupulously documented study of F. A. BLANCHE, *Le vocabulaire de l'argumentation et la structure de l'article dans les ouvrages de saint Thomas*, in *RSPT*, XIV (1925), 167–187.

a) See ch. IX, note 2.

27) "*Quaestio est dubitabilis propositio.*" BOETHIUS, *In Topica Ciceronis*, lib. I; *P.L.*, 64, 1048D.

28) See ARISTOTLE, *Metaph.*, X, 5, 1055b–1056a3, and SAINT THOMAS, *In X Metaph.*, lect. 7; Marietti ed., 488, n. 2060.

the dynamics of the dialectical process are concerned. Such a reversal, harmless in appearance, would destroy the cogency for inquiry which is pressing continuously from one end to the other the *pro* and *contra* proposed in the *quaestio,* and which leads the mind on to its highest working pitch. An objection, in the modern sense of the word, would be, in XIIIth century style, an *instantia,* an *obviatio,* words indicating resistance. The medieval "objection," on the contrary, was in reference to the open quest of a problem's intelligibility, *in-ducere rationes.* We insist on this very exact attitude which has been obliterated—annoyingly—by formalism in the case of some modern interpretations (29).

If we understand things in this way, we shall avoid misinterpreting the *Sed contra* [On the contrary]—as we see almost always done. The *Sed contra,* in itself, is the expression neither of the author's thesis nor of an argument borrowed from some authority as the foundation of his own position. In itself, the *sed contra* is the presentation of the alternate position, an expression of *rationes quae sunt ad oppositum* [the reasons which stand for the other position].

> The arguments in the second sequence are not proposed *against* those of the first series; they are given *in favor of* the second part of the alternative, and it is only *indirectly* that they are in opposition with those expressed in favor of the first part. The part in the article which is *directly* in opposition with the arguments rejected from the viewpoint of the thesis which the determination established, is the one which contains the answers that follow the body of the article, the *responsiones ad objecta,* that is, the answers to the *arguments* (in the sense already established) which diverge from the thesis, no matter if they be from the first or from the second series (30).

And the stage is set for the master to "answer." *Respondeo dicendum* [I answer that it must be said]: the answer will contain whatever must be stated in order that the doubt raised by the question be dispelled. Herein is the body of the article in which are expounded at least the principles from which the author would solve the problem if not always the organically structured doctrine he holds. The author's solution is called his *determinatio* of the question. Always the perspective is that of a disputation; and ever present in the background also, is the Aristotelian technique of διορίζειν [determining] and διορισμὸς [determination], working in depth.

The master's answer to those of the proposed arguments that, in one part (sometimes in both parts) of the alternative, do not agree with the position he has just stated are usually given in the form of a distinction, since rarely is the opposing position simply rejected. Rather the master marks off upon what share of truth this position

---

29) See A. BLANCHE, *op. cit.*, 177–179.
30) *Ibid.*, 180.

is founded. He distinguishes in it that aspect or that viewpoint which has been successfully grasped: *Haec ratio procedit de . . .* [This reason proceeds from . . .]. In a way, there is an effort to embody the truth that the opposing position contains within a wider framework which, far from casting it aside, underwrites its truthfulness. This valuable piece of observation will again turn up when we set out to define through what processes of construction Saint Thomas built up his works (a).

Such, then, is the inner meaning of those formulas whose fate it was to become stereotyped. In historical fact, they were actually brimming with life as they were used in a disputing of questions. This same life—the very life of a mind at work—they kept in the articles drawn up in the silence of a cell. For an article is a *quaestio*, not a *thesis*, the word that was to be used in the manuals of modern scholasticism. The change in terms is in itself a denunciation of the heinous reversal to which have been subjected the exalted pedagogical methods set up in the XIIth century universities: "active" methods, mindful to keep open, even under the dead-weight of school work, the curiosity of both the student and the master.

> Let us make no mistake about it. Concerning the medieval school, which was so impulsive and tumultuous in its reactions, we have come to draw up a most miserable picture, closely-copied from the modern manuals of XVIIth century scholasticism. Therein barrenness, far from existing to the benefit of an exacting technique, was simply the end-product of a rationalizing that was short-sighted in its views, lacking in intuition and power for synthesis, and stiffly collared by clerical or lay protectiveness, with the result that freedom in quest and ardor for progress paid the price for official favors. A distressingly equivocal state of affairs. . . . To read Abelard, Hugh of Saint Victor, Albert the Great, Saint Bonaventure, and Saint Thomas in a Wolfian atmosphere, is to misconstrue their thought to the point of no return. However deserving they may be, the *Disputationes metaphysicae* of Francis Suarez, from the standpoint of intellectual formation, have no more than their name in common with the *quaestiones disputatae* of the XIIIth century (31).

III. CLASSIFICATION OF THE WORKS OF SAINT THOMAS

The foregoing describes the dress and inspiration of the literary forms—we can now say, doctrinal forms—within which the works of Saint Thomas were composed, and within which they are to be classified. The forms employed in medieval teaching did not, in effect, develop all at the same time and along a single front. Rather their development took place according to the objects studied and as the

---

a) See chapter V.

31) G. PARÉ, A. BRUNET, P. TREMBLAY, *La renaissance du XIIe siècle. Les écoles et l'enseignement,* in *PIEM,* III (1933), 132.

texts, which served as the basic tool in teaching, were progressively exploited. In those cases in which the text selected for teaching purposes was a revealed one, it was normal that the understanding of it should take place on the level of exegesis, of the *lectio*. Only little by little did questions come to be knit out of it, and, through gradual amplification, to go beyond, and finally to gobble up textual reading. When the books of Aristotle were first circulated, they were the object of a simple commentary—at a time when, after fifty years of official reading, the text of Peter Lombard was already overloaded with questions. In like manner, in the production of Saint Thomas, we find works ranging, as the case goes, from the simple commentary all the way to the independent question.

Among the works that are no more than simple commentaries making up an *expositio*, we have, on the one hand, those dealing with Aristotle and Dionysius (a), and on the other, those related to Scripture (b). In the first case, the books of Aristotle were, in the time of Saint Thomas, still the object of a textual *lectio,* whereas in the second case, the evolution [from the *lectio* to the *quaestio*] had run its course. Consequently, with the *quaestio* having become a completely independent exercice at the faculty of theology, teaching of the Bible was divided between a course on the text of the Bible, the latter remaining the basic textbook, and the disputation of questions. Let us immediately observe, moreover, that these *expositiones* vary greatly in form, running the gamut between literal commenting and paraphrasing, between impersonal glossing and original elaborating.

On Peter Lombard's *Sentences*, the text of his teaching as a bachelor, and on the Boethian *De Trinitate* (c), Saint Thomas, like all his contemporaries, no longer limited himself to a simple *expositio*. He did go along with the text, of which he gave an analysis (*divisio textus*) and a summary literal explanation (*expositio textus*); but the latter are only remnants of the form they originally had. In reality his whole effort is directed to the study of questions whose great number and variety are wholly outside the text from which he started.

Then, we have both the ordinary and the quodlibetal questions that Saint Thomas disputed in his capacity of master (d).

The two *summas*, both the *Summa contra Gentiles* (e) and the *Summa theologiae* (f), especially the latter, are linked with the literary forms we have spoken about, but they were composed and built up free of Saint Thomas's official teaching and in reference to some

a) See chapter VI.
b) See chapter VII.
c) See chapter VIII.
d) See chapter IX.
e) See chapter X.
f) See chapter XI.

external circumstances or to certain scientific needs that the author himself will tell us about later.

Likewise, in the case of his works written for occasions, there is reference to historical or doctrinal contingencies. These works show great variety in content and form and were subsequently to be grouped together under the neutral title of *Opuscula* (g).

Finally, as we have already had the occasion to state, it was a master's duty, at the faculty of theology, to preach to his students, as well as to teach them. Saint Thomas has left us a number of sets of *collationes* [collations].

The foregoing grouping of his works according to the technique of their composition enables us to bring into focus the picture of the organic character, as well as of the historical conditions, of the Master's scientific activity. It is against these general contexts that we shall have to look into each one of his works. Yet before doing so, let us examine the working conditions and the resources all his works have in common: the language, the processes of documentation, the procedures of construction (h).

IV. RESEARCH SUGGESTIONS

Establish a list of the works that from one generation to another were progressively used as basic texts for teaching in the schools, especially during the XIIIth century. To do this, use either university records, or actual commentary-literature (for example, the commentaries on Dionysius in the mid-XIIIth century), or letters and private memoirs.

Prepare and document a glossary concerning the techniques of teaching starting with the *glossa* and continuing all the way up to the *sententia*. Bring out their psychological and sociological settings.

Follow the evolution of the *quaestio* in the various disciplines. In addition to the works already quoted, see:

—for biblical exegesis, the works of SPICQ, LOTTIN;
—for theology, the bibliography at the beginning of A. LANDGRAF'S *Quelques collections de* Quaestiones *de la seconde moitié du XIIe siècle,* in *RTAM,* VI (1934), 368–393;
—for the canonists, S. KUTTNER, *Repertorium der Kanonistik (1140–1234)* in *StT,* LXXI (1937), 243 ff., 423 ff., to be completed by *Zur neuesten Glossatorenforschung,* in *SDHJ,* VI (1940), 275–319;
—for the Romanists, E. GENZER, *Die justinianische Kodification und die Glossatoren,* in *Atti del Congr. Internat. di Diritto*

---

g) See chapter XII.
h) See chapters III, IV, V respectively.

romano, Bologna, t. I, 415 ff.; H. KANTOROWICZ, *The* Quaestiones disputatae *of the* Glossatores, in *RHD,* 1937–1938, and *Studies in the* Glossatores *of the Roman Law* . . . , Cambridge, 1938.

Analyze the first observations made about the meaning and on the methods to which the above-mentioned evolution gave rise, for example, the observation made by Clarenbald of Arras, quoted in note 14 of this chapter. Analyze also the suspicions and reactions which this development provoked among the textualists of every stamp, among the anti-dialecticians, among the anti-reason biblicists.

Analyze Robert of Melun's famous Preface at the beginning of his *Sententie,* Martin ed., in *SSL,* XXI (1947); his indictment against glosses and commentaries.

Mull over the methodological and scientific scope of the *quaestio,* especially in theology, starting from the historical spectacle of its much-discussed arrival on the scene. To put the word of God in *quaestiones* is to put it in question before human intelligence. Such is the vigorous root of a theology conceived and organized as a science. Therein lies the great life-work of Saint Thomas. The Medievals did not fall into the dichotomy between "problem" and "mystery"; through the *quaestio,* however, theology will, if we can put it that way, build itself up out of the expression of mysteries by way of problems.

The "commentary" (*lectio, expositio*) is really the basic literary genre during the Middle Ages, in philosophy as well as in the other disciplines. See E. BRÉHIER's suggestive reflexions on this way of expressing "the duration of a philosophic doctrine" (*La philosophie et son passé,* Paris, 1940, 21–44). Beyond the commentary, however, the development and the seduction of the *quaestio* really determined the balance and the inventiveness of the scholastic age. [See M.-D. CHENU, *La théologie au douzième siècle,* in *EPM,* XLV (1957), ch. XV; also *La théologie comme science au XIIIe siècle,* 3d ed., in *BibTh;* XXXIII (1957), ch. I.]

[In addition to the works referred to in the present chapter, the reader will find further bibliographical data on the various literary genres in chapters VI and ff. wherein the author deals with the works of Saint Thomas according to the classification he has just presented. Further to be consulted is I. T. ESCHMANN's *A Catalogue of Saint Thomas's Works* (*CSTW*) wherein is presented a new distribution of Saint Thomas's works, together with *Notes* on the text of each work (its nature, condition, chronology, editions, translations), and a *List of Books Used* which does not claim to be an exhaustive bibliography, but rather a complement to the notes.]

Chapter III

The Language and Vocabulary of Saint Thomas

I. THOUGHT AND LANGUAGE

Perhaps it will be thought that it is again going far afield to make entry into the thought of Saint Thomas by devoting so much attention to his language. Language is just a modest tool, and it would seem to be making some show of pedantry to attach that much importance to it. In fact, however, there are few philosophers or theologians who have incorporated the make of their minds in their vocabulary to the same degree as Saint Thomas, and as few whose accessibility consequently is found to be so organically consolidated with the literal understanding of their expressions.

In any case, it is a known fact that the textual apparatus with the help of which Saint Thomas outwardly expressed his thought is disconcerting for his modern reader. Even if the latter is experienced in Latin, it becomes disheartening for him to come to grips with a style where grammar lacks contrast, procedure is stereotyped, divisions are unending, where the output is all academic, dried out of any show of emotion, however sober, and in which the most refreshing biblical image is devitalized by allegory. As for the richness he feels is masked behind all this, he knows it cannot be reached without his coming into the technical information that alone could give body to each word and initiate him into the semantic sculpture of each concept. In brief, he is up against a prominent case wherein the lan-

100

guage used is "scholastic" in the fullest meaning of the term, and wherein this same language characterizes at once a thought, a method, and means of expression. It is important, therefore, that this case of "scholastic" language be defined on the very grounds of that language which thus equates both method and thought.

In order to give support to the analyses we are going to undertake, let us first recall, in a summary way, a few characteristic examples of his vocabulary. These examples will serve to shed some light on both the qualities of this vocabulary and what is required to understand it.

1) *Mens* [mind], *spiritus* [spirit], *anima* [soul]. We have here three words used to designate the mind that testify to the willingness with which, in the XIIIth, as well as in the XXth century, philosophers tried to understand its subtle nature. One notices immediately that, in this multiplying of words to name the mind, philosophical as well as Christian themes have been woven together. *Mens, spiritus, anima* translate respectively νοῦς, πνεῦμα, ψυχή, and the meaning, together with the development of each one of these Latin and Greek words, quickly reveals itself as very complex.

To start with, we have the properly Biblical theme in the Paulinian trilogy of σάρξ, [flesh], ψυχή [soul], and πνεῦμα [spirit]. This trilogy reflects, through a reference to the spirit of Christ, the whole mystery of the fall and of the redemption of mankind. It is a strictly religious perspective, which the Aristotelian philosopher in Saint Thomas leaves aside (see his commentaries on Aristotle), yet, this perspective is involved everywhere in his philosophy of man.

With the word νοῦς, we have Aristotle and the problems concerning the structure of the intellect, the agent intellect, the spiritual and personal nature of intelligence, its relationship to the other parts of the soul, the substance of the mind and the ἕξις [habit] of first principles, finally the definition of the soul. When Saint Thomas uses the word, all his Peripatetic background is involved, and it is not an easy thing to untangle in this use the dilemma of the soul and of the spirit, as we say in French. Yet, with the word νοῦς we have still another cosmos, that of Dionysius, with his emanation of beings and their hierarchical order, his "analogy" of names, his angels as prototypes of the νοῦς, his mystical power. In the Greco-Latin versions of the Middle Ages, Aristotle's νοῦς was translated by the word *intellectus*, while the νοῦς of Dionysius was rendered by the word *mens*. This Latin doublet of *intellectus* and *mens* for the one Greek word left intact, even to verbal resonance, the wide difference in meaning these words had in their respective parent ideologies. And Saint Thomas was aware of it. Furthermore, Augustine came on the scene—the originator of a *mens* that no longer had anything of the Oriental ontology of Dionysius and in which was expressed an intense perception of the internal workings of mental life. Here was yet another world within which the Latin Christians were to live and which, once engaged within theology, was to nourish lofty contemplation on the Trinity. Augustine's *mens* is the perfect specimen of that type of Augustinian vocabulary that resists attempts at abstractive analysis. Yet the latter was the working norm in the Aristotelian philosophy of Saint Thomas.

With the word πνεῦμα, we are at the extreme opposite of any religious connotation. In the vocabulary of the physiologists, πνεῦμα stood properly for animal life. Augustine used it in this sense, although not exclusively, and the Medievals followed his example. Under the name *spiritus*, they catalogued the phenomena that had to do jointly with body and mind. For instance, imagination, for the followers of Augustine (who were here translating Porphyry), is a *spiritus*, but the word is also used by them to designate breath in voice production and "animal spirits." Yet, at the other end of the line, *spiritus* attains to the meaning of *mens*—as already in Saint Paul: *spiritu mentis vestrae* (*Eph.*, IV, 23)—and designates, at the summit of *anima* bound up to body, that subtle and topmost part of the mind through which man can escape the limits of matter and ascend to God—the ever actual theme of the dialogue between *spiritus* and *anima*.

Anima, for the medieval philosopher, translated Aristotle's ψυχή. The word, therefore, stood for something common to both man and animal. *Anima* was the form of a body, and it was united to the latter as to a matter which it animated and outside of which it was unable to subsist. Yet, the word was so well accredited in the language of Latin Christianity that even the truest Aristotelians used it without reservation to designate the immortal soul of man, and this, to the exclusion of the word *spiritus* which was not used in the translations of Aristotle.

When Saint Thomas arrived on the scene, these words had reached the hub at which their meanings converged. This should be remembered, not only by the philologist interested in words, but also by the philosopher who attempts to understand them, since the philosophical compactness of these words is not measured according to the standards of a benevolent making of concordances. Read, for instance, the disputed question entitled *De mente* (*De ver.*, q. 10) (1).

---

1) And see how much a GARDEIL has contributed to the profound understanding of Saint Thomas by having recourse to those living springs which have their source in the Augustinian *mens*. Cf. A. GARDEIL, *La structure de l'âme et l'expérience mystique*, 2d ed., in BTheol, 1927; vol. I, 1st part: The *mens*, 3–350. Refer again to GARDEIL concerning *formatio*, the next example treated in our text: *ibid.*, L'âme "informe" selon saint Augustin, 155–204. [See also A. SILVA-TAROUCA, *La notion "formalis" selon saint Thomas d'Aquin et la formation de l'homme*, in APCIPM, 545–553.]

2) *Formatio* [information]. In this instance, we have a single word that picked up in its meaning the vital powers of two different doctrines and mental outlooks. The first of these was Aristotle's hylomorphic theory (μορφή, form) with all its contexts and applications (*forma* [form] operating on three levels, since it is solidary in its meaning with three different Greek words: μορφή used to signify the principle of being; εἶδος, the principle of knowledge; and φύσις, the principle of movement), and with the metaphysics it connotes within the Aristotelian theory of the four causes. In Saint Thomas, efficient and formal causality will support a doctrine of creation in which it is God's efficiency that ensures the proper being of existing things and their intelligibility. The whole of Thomism is in here.

Formatio, however, was no less strongly centered in its meaning upon the Platonically-inspired ontology and noetics of Saint Augustine. (In the latter, both ontology and noetics were included in the explicit synonymy of the words *forma, idea* [idea], *species* [species], *ratio* [reason].) *Formatio*, therefore, referred to the doctrine of participation of ideas—of ideas that in God are perfect in their being, eternal, and creative of things but which in things other than God suffer limitation and imperfection because of their ties with matter. Yet, these ideas explain the being and intelligibleness of these same things which are copies of them and are unable to reach their own perfection except through conversion to them in a contemplation that is both creative and "informing." The whole theory of illumination in Augustine's psychology proceeds along these lines. In his conception of rational nature, it is through grace, conceived as a light and a power, that *formatio* is brought about. Without "formative" grace, rational nature remains "formless," but through its presence it becomes in its "return" to God the image of Him. The Augustinian theme of *formatio* made its way through the entire medieval philosophical vocabulary. In Saint Thomas, despite the amending he gave to it with his Aristotelian background, its presence constantly animated his analyses and expressions. In Saint Bonaventure, however, a reader will find that *formatio* retained an accent that Augustine would more readily have recognized.

Let us add here that it was through the translators of the Aristotelico-Arabian works (Saint Thomas was the one who noted it), that the first operation of the mind, Aristotle's simple apprehension, came to be designated by the word *formatio* (or *informatio*). This is true at least in the case of Averroes, for in the Latin versions of Avicenna's works, Aristotle's τῶν ἀδιαιρέτων νόησις [intellection of indivisibles] was translated by the word *imaginatio* [imagination].

3) It is not only, however, the flexibility of these sensational terms that has to be perceived. One must also look into the more ordinary

terms in order to get a close hold on them in their exact historical and formal meaning. *Ars* [art] and *scientia* [science] were at times used synonomously, at other times they were opposed; *disciplina* [teaching], on the other hand, always retained the technical flavor that Boethius had injected into it. *Potentia* [capacity] and *virtus* [power] were delicately interwoven in their meaning. *Habitus* [habit], *sapientia* [wisdom] cannot be translated in French without loss, or even falsification of sense. *Probabile* [probable] has become an equivocal term ever since the XVIIIth century controversies. *Imaginatio* had another extension and comprehension than our contemporary psychologists give to it. *Intentio* [intention] was one of the trickiest words in epistemology, and only recently has it been rediscovered by a few of our modern philosophers, while *synderesis* [habit of first principles in the practical order] remains untranslated to this day. And one could go on and on with examples such as these.

II. MEDIEVAL LATIN

Saint Thomas did his thinking in Latin, but in a Latin foreign to the tongue of a Cicero or a Seneca and no less foreign to that of the Humanists who contended that they were bringing classical Latin back to life. His was the so-called "barbaric" Latin of the Middle Ages.

Even if it be only in a very summary way, it will not be useless to locate, at its proper place within the general development of post-classical Latin, the special kind that was called scholastic. The philologists—and this is a known fact—were precisely the ones who, in their intent to divide the history of the West into periods started from the principle of language evolution. They gave for the first time the name of *media aetas* [middle age] to that hollow and much-decried period that extends from the classical language of Antiquity to its revival among the XVth century Humanists. The philologists of our day no longer maintain such scornful disregard. Even before looking for aesthetic values in it, they try to discover the expressive qualities of that Latin tongue which was about the only vehicle of culture during the period extending from 400 to 1400 A.D. Quite evidently, with this Western millenium, we are not on what could be called a level surface, and to speak of linguistic continuity would be only equivocal. Yet, there are at least different phases that can be discerned in the development of medieval Latin; and to mark both the extension and quality of those zones wherein its vitality shows up, will enable one to see the literary tool of medieval thought gradually taking shape.

First, we have the period during which classical Latin disintegrated: a period extending over a length of three centuries and coinciding with the overrunning of Europe by the Barbarians. After the Vth century, with the disappearance, at least outside of Italy, of the schools run by the rhetors, the low Latin of the pre-Romanic koine became extremely poor in vocabulary and syntax and even in orthography. This was true both in the case of the language written by the literate, in which was displayed their narrow-minded conservatism, and in the case of the language spoken by the common people, which was riddled throughout with words of Germanic and Celtic origin. Out of the wreck, however, arose a few figures, men of whom it would be too much to say that they were geniuses, yet men to whom intelligence had not been denied. They contrived to transfer some of the riches of classical Antiquity into their own products of pen, which displayed some degree of digestible pedagogy. Boethius (+524), Cassiodorus (+about 570), Gregory the Great (+604), Isodorus of Sevilla (+636), the Venerable Bede (735) have justly been called the "founders" of the Middle Ages (a).

Boethius, "the last of the Romans" and "the first one to teach the barbaric speech" (as L.Valla has put it), besides writing his *Consolatio philosophiae* in an elegant Ciceronian style, translated and commented upon the logical works of Aristotle, thus building up a lexicographical capital through the use of which the first creative efforts of the XIIIth century were ensured. Cassiodorus, with his *Institutiones*, preserved and passed on the humanistic content of the seven arts. By religious design, Gregory the Great was opposed to classical culture, and he had no more the genius or linguistic mastery of an Augustine than the two others; nonetheless, he passed on, in a tongue that was balanced, penetrating, and understandable by both the uneducated as well as the learned, the moral conceptions that were to serve as matter for future generations to mull over. The candid compilations (*Etymologiae*) of Isodorus became an enduring encyclopedia and the source of ideologic vocabulary for five centuries, even after the XIIth century Renaissance had provoked a return to sources and after the works of Aristotle had been rediscovered. Finally, in Bede, whom Dante was to place at the side of Isodorus in heaven (b), there is proof of the extension to the new nations of the practice of correct Latin and of the cultivating of the liberal arts. By writing his biblical commentaries and his ecclesiastical history in the lay language of old, he sanctioned its use to express what was most real and original in Christian thought. However small a figure all of these 'founders' may have cut in the construction proper of the work of Saint Thomas, it is

---

a) The very title of E. K. RAND's book, 1st ed., Cambridge (Mass.), 1928; 2d ed., 1929; reprint, 1941; recently re-issued in *Dover*, T369 (1957).

b) See *The Divine Comedy of Dante Alighieri: Paradise*, X, 130–131, trans. by C. E. NORTON, in *GBWW*, XXI (1952), 121.

nonetheless a fact that they were ever present at the very roots of his language and thought; and this is something that one has to become accustomed to, if one does not wish to change the atmosphere of his life-work.

The aforementioned components of these three centuries can be formulated in the following way: early medieval Latin was a continuation not of the classical language but of that used by the authors of the low-Latin period. It was heavily influenced by the Latin of the Church, of the liturgy, of the vulgate Bible, and of the Fathers. It was constantly fed—either during the patristic period or especially at the time of Gregory of Tours and after him—with words and phrase constructions drawn from the Latin of the masses and of the vernacular. Such being the Latin used in the early Middle Ages, school work and scholastic speech were destined to be permanently stamped with definite traits, namely: a taste for compiling excerpts, which finally issued in a masterpiece of this sort of literature, the *Sentences* of Peter Lombard, the classic manual of medieval theology; the prevalence of grammar and its techniques over rhetoric and its adornments; the multiplying of glossaries, which proved themselves to be precious instruments in concept refining and served philosophy and theology with the supporting points they needed, even in times when speculation was at a weak point; the presence of the Church in education, even in the teaching of the seven liberal arts to beginners; and finally, already discernible at the summit of these arts, a cult for dialectics that showed up even in such byproducts as the pseudo-Augustinian *Categoriae*, or the pseudo-Boethian *Dialectica*. As a result, in reading through the religious works of the period one already feels very far from the language of Saint Augustine, even in those passages wherein his expressions have been borrowed. See, for example, the wording used in the councils of Toledo in 635, 688, and 693.

With the gulf widening between the spoken and written language, Latin would no doubt have suffered even greater alteration if the awakening that took place in the VIIIth century had not recaptured its better elements through a direct reading of the *auctores*. The Carolingian renaissance, centered mostly on grammar and literature, tended toward a return of Latin to its sources. As a result, grammar became more correct, syntax was discovered, ideas were logically fitted together, semantics enriched. In the field of literature, a large segment of the antique works was recovered, although, through lack of information and good taste, these works were not always evaluated in right hierarchical order. Statius, for instance, was placed on an even footing with Virgil and Martianus Capella with Quintilian. Only in part were the Medievals able to free themselves from this mortgage, but it is to those Carolingian copyists and their libraries that we owe the transmission of the classical works and of the Christian works as well. Theirs was a modest work of transcription, hardly raised in stature by their being pieced together in anthologies. A typical product of this kind is found in Walafrid Strabon's gloss, upon which one medieval generation after another was to enlarge and whose literary form even Saint Thomas was to preserve in his *Catena aurea.* Alcuin, Eginhard, Loup of Ferrieres were notable literary figures in their own right. Scotus Erigena, moreover, had the wide range of a great thinker, with the vocabulary and doctrine displayed in his writings still acting as a powerful ferment throughout the XIIIth century.

This cult of Antiquity developed in both language and style the practice of an imitation that was artlessly passive—and laden with the academic dullness which imitation involves. The recuperation itself of the ancient works suffered from this lack of creative power. Latin was no longer a "mother" tongue. It became erudite and artificial in character in the very measure that a lack of balance developed between a culture born for other times and the new-born surroundings in which the peoples of the West lived. Either there was no spoken language to correct deviations arising from artificial apprenticeship in a tongue no longer spoken, or the written language of the day was too far away from the traditional school tongue to act as a corrective. This is the reason medieval Latin was affected by an absence of movement, life, and spontaneity. This Latin, however, was not "dead," as would be the classical Latin that the Humanists later reproduced in a servile way; it continued to evolve, and with the plastic qualities inherent in it, it answered the needs of intellectual life (c).

It was to be the lot of the XIIth century to bring this Latin tongue to the height of its perfection and to make of it, over and beyond the elements that it borrowed, an admirable instrument for intellectual life, doctrinal culture, and religious expression. This time, the *auctores* of Antiquity gave birth to more and better than copies and imitations. If the *Organon* came back to life in Abelard, if Plato and Boethius were food for the scholars of Chartres, if the various treatises *De dilectione Dei* [On the Love of God], in matters spiritual, were praiseworthy counterparts of Ovid's *Ars amandi* [Art of Loving], if Saint Anselm revived the tradition of Augustine's psychology and his religious speculations as well, if John of Salisbury extolled the discovery of the *Topics* in terms worthy of a Quintilian, it was because Latin

---

c) ". . . it is essentially quite different from Humanistic Latin, which can really be called "dead" in its slavish imitation of antiquity, while Medieval Latin was capable of change and refashioned as the need occurred." K. STRECKER, *Introduction to Medieval Latin,* trans. and rev. R. B. PALMER, Berlin, 1957, 36.

was not a dead language and it still had the power of embodying within itself, so to speak, the thoughts, feelings, and desires of those who were using it (2).

True however, this flow of sap did not permeate all the tissues. Some entire zones, in the language itself let us understand, remained dull with the weight of imitation or artifice. No more did Christian of Troyes master his ancient sources than the poetic *Arts* revive Horace, William of Champeaux, Aristotle, or Peter Lombard, Augustine. The techniques for speculation invaded the field of dialectics, wherein lay the risk of replacing research with playful juggling. In the "battle of the seven arts," the literary minded were often beaten without thereby any benefit to thought. Nothing substantial was gained by sacrificing form. The drama of scholasticism had its beginning right here at the elementary level of language, and the various factors which we have just analysed enable us to foresee its misadventures.

III. SCHOLASTIC LATIN

The world spins on. Having abandoned the grounds of the language spoken by the masses, Latin, little by little, lost contact also with the field of everyday living. At the end of the XIIth century, at the same time that the urban middle class was coming of age and was turning as a matter of course toward the living languages for the conduct of its business, art, and ventures, the universities were also undergoing their initial organization. Latin there was pressed back into the literary forms of those disciplines that were cultivated in their environment: theoretical grammar, philosophy, theology, and law. The time had come when the living powers of the mind were no longer apportioned along homogeneous lines. As a result, if thinkers were still able

---

2) "How was it possible for the Latin language—a bookish, as it were, and written language; a language, on the one hand, perpetually surviving the wear and tear of its everyday use by the ancient peoples of the Roman Empire; a language, on the other hand, which was only an imported product in all of those countries which the Roman power had not subjugated, as with the Scots, the Anglo-Saxons, and the Hungarians—how [to repeat] was it possible for this language to serve as the vehicle of thought over a period of almost a thousand years? We have here a case, maybe unique, but certainly the most outstanding, in the history of the idioms employed by mankind. A language half-artificial, yet still animated with a last breath of life; a spark almost snuffed-out at the end of the Merovingian era, but later brought back to life through an effort so astonishing that it became, for man's intelligence and over a period of centuries, the only source of light capable, notwithstanding regional and personal variations, of casting rays for intimate intercommunication over the thoughts and feelings of those who almost all over Europe approached it: therein is an enigma extraordinarily interesting and persistent, which repeated itself in the history of its origins as well as of its spread and duration over the centuries." J. DE GHELLINCK, *L'essor de la littérature latine au XIIe siècle*, in *ML–SH*, V (1946), 311–312.

to hammer out from Latin a wonderful tool for their purposes of analysis and construction, this was only done in a narrow field of endeavor, over a period of hardly more than two generations in extent—happily favored by a number of geniuses, Albert the Great, Bonaventure, and Thomas Aquinas. "Scholastic" language, soon after, coiled up upon itself, deprived of life for a long time to come. The moment has come to determine the characteristics of this school language before going into the personal traits which it was to have in Saint Thomas (a).

We have used the words "scholastic language." The very name "scholastic" points here to the first of its characteristics; it was a school language. The stages in the history of medieval Latin have led us to this conclusion, and the evolution is amply confirmed by the facts. Work in the classroom was governed by pedagogical aims, with usefulness taking precedence over literary beauty, and effectiveness for instruction prevailing over the communication of emotions. In the classroom, work tended to be impersonal in character, not of course that this lessened the qualities of the master, but the latter were subordinated to the presentation of truth and of the resources of its object. Augustine's *Confessions* were not used as a teaching manual; the living qualities of his language would have been in the classroom the source of sense-falsification of the worst kind, both in words and in thought. In the XIIIth century, moreover, the universities, just about the only centers of culture of the time, made up a sort of linguistic community with its own formalistic ways of expressing things and its own ritual—the almost exclusive practice of oral teaching had determined all this. Hence, the resulting monotony in the system of verbal signs employed in presenting arguments, making up paragraphs, dividing questions, and analysing texts. Any variation would have sounded like an ill-timed piece of oratory. It was enough to use the word *Item* [Again] to pass from one idea to another, or the expression *videtur quod . . . non* [it would seem that . . . not] to introduce, in thousands of articles, what was held on the question in an opposing opinion.

Being a school language, Latin was by the same token a technical language, that is, one entirely controlled by the special requirements of research in a given course of study. It was also located on the same plane of abstraction that determined the field of this same course of study, since abstraction, according to the tenets of scholastic doctrine, was the principle through which were distinguished and classified the various sciences. Abstraction thereby controlled the laws of verbal sig-

---

a) ". . . there is no common universal Medieval Latin. It remains axiomatic that a philological study must be made of each author's language, style, and models." K. STRECKER, *op. cit.*, p. 38.

nification. In Augustine, who had a dislike for abstractions and distinctions, language was altogether fluid and responsive to the continuities, to the radiating action, and to the fringes of the intelligibleness of things rather than to the fine edges of concepts. Words were like sounds calling after one another, and they took pleasure [so to speak] in passing from one discipline to another. In vain Schoolmen sought to seize upon the sinews of the word *mens,* and as many as thirty-one different meanings have been counted for the word *sapientia* in Augustine. The medieval philosopher, on the contrary, sacrificed to scientific precision those ductile qualities that constant use preserves in words where concrete realities are expressed. The triumph of Aristotelian logic made this rule of precision a permanent one. The Schoolman never gave up trying to arrive at the proper meaning, at the "most proper" meaning of words, just as he persisted in establishing definitions. Examples abound in Saint Thomas. The Schoolman, moreover, took pleasure in concocting abstract words that expressly referred to the formal aspect through which things are such as they are. For instance, the word *substantia* [substance] gave birth to the word *subsistentia* [subsistence] (cf. *Ia Pars,* q. 29, a. 2), *proportio* [proportion] to *proportionalitas* [proportionality] (cf. *De ver.,* q. 3, a. 1, ad 7um), not to speak of *quidditas,* [quiddity], *haecceitas* [thisness], and even of *anitas* (b) and *unalitas* [singularness]. Granted that such formalizing was often pushed to the point of ridiculousness, one must nevertheless also grant that such subtleness was far from always being without bearing on expression and thought, as the two first examples [*subsistentia* and *proportionalitas*] testify. Need we recall that Cajetan praised Aquinas, and justly so, because "he always expressed himself in formal language": *Semper loquitur formaliter.*

From all this arose, in the Schoolman's use of Latin, repugnance to metaphorical language and, in general, to figures of thought and of speech, since these retain no consistency whatsoever when subjected to the most elementary abstraction. One must, however, distinguish periods and places. In the XIIth century, the various masters even in their didactic treatises preserved the benefit issuing from a creative imagination, and this gave great liveliness to their style, as may be witnessed from Saint Anselm to Richard of Saint Victor. At the heart of the XIIIth century, William of Auvergne wrote in an endless flow of words, while Bonaventure, in his *Itinerarium,* lit up, with some very sparkling images, the road he followed in his ascent to metaphysical

---

b) The word is quite untranslatable. It was invented, it seems, by Gerard of Cremona who was trying to translate from the Arabic the abstract term corresponding to Aristotle's *an sit* [Does a thing exist?]. See M. T. D'ALVERNY, ANNIYA-ANITAS, in *Mélanges E. Gilson* (EPM, extra ser., 1959), 59–91, especially, 69 ff.

heights, and he delighted in multiplying synonyms, adjectives, comparisons, and parallels. Yet, in its ambitious theory of scientific demonstration, in its tendency at putting everything in conceptual form, in its very temperament, flourishing Aristotelianism carried with it a lively aversion to the use of literary or poetic procedures in doctrinal speculation. Saint Thomas, as we shall see later, made his own the Stagirite's biting criticism of Plato's style, and the medieval Aristotelians considered the language used by the Platonists, including Dionysius and Augustine, as something impure, bound up with the famous theory of ideas. Scholasticism of the periods to follow was to be more and more afflicted with literary barrenness of this same type.

At this point, the case of theological speech is worthy of special consideration. Theology would not, it seems, adapt itself to a situation of this kind, since Holy Scripture, its feeding source, was all metaphor, parable, allegory, and example. Faith, also, the principle from which theology issued, implied mystery in its object and loving assent to it, both of which could not be enclosed within the boundaries of abstraction. Yet, if "sacred doctrine" was to harbor legitimately the possibility of being elaborated in a science, it had to accept, whether in systematic wholes or in a drafting of details, the particular techniques of human reason along with the means and even the style that science used to express itself. Having become a scholastic theology, sacred doctrine excluded from its literary genre pastoral exhortation, pious consideration, and mystical confiding. The *Summa* was not written and cannot be read like a sermon of Saint Bernard or a chapter from the *Imitation.* Cut away from anything subjective, from spiritual life in the concrete, the *Summa,* as we have seen, is related in form much more to the *Disputed Question,* which derives from Aristotle with his ideal of scientific knowledge and his technique of demonstration. In this way we can explain the severity with which Saint Thomas treated the use of the metaphor and the Platonic style (3). That severity, however, applied to them only inasmuch as they were inserted in a theology having scientific stature. Otherwise, Augustine himself would have been condemned, and with him any theology conceived as a wisdom crowning a spiritual experience. The austerity implied in this technical objectiveness did not, in a Thomas Aquinas, curtail the religious powers of his theology. Rather it served to give its style to a knowledge, which must have its place, and an eminent one, within the many-sided whole of the *intellectus fidei* (4). Among his peers,

---

3) "Whether Sacred Scripture should make use of metaphors?" *Ia Pars,* q. 1, a. 9. On the Platonic style, see below, 169–171.

4) Cf. E. GILSON, *Le christianisme et la tradition philosophique,* in RSPT, XXX (1941–42), 249–266. The latter shows in perfect manner how both the Platonic

an Anselm and a Bonaventure, Saint Thomas was the master beyond compare of sacred doctrine's scholastic tongue.

The third characteristic of scholastic Latin: the language of the Schoolmen was in good part the language derived from efforts at translation. In order to measure the strong and weak points of medieval Latin in the field of speculation, we have to go back to its initial indigence in the expression of philosophical ideas. Viewed from this angle, the Western Middle Ages exhibit one of the most astonishing phenomena in the history of languages (5). It had been long recognized that Latin lacked a capacity for expressing philosophical thought. Seneca complained about Romans being obliged to force the sense of words when they wanted to translate the concepts of Greek philosophy, noting, moreover, that even Plato's ὄν [being] had no corresponding word in Latin (6). The Latin word *ens* [being], was, in fact, a barbarism of a horrible sort. The new word *essentia* [essence] was far from pleasing. The same could be said of *qualitas* [quality] before Cicero, and of *specificus* [specific], *subjectum* [subject], *praedicatum* [predicate] before Boethius. Boethius precisely, the first of the barbarians, according to Valla, was to contribute actively in creating a Latin philosophical vocabulary, and the unassuming glossators of the early Middle Ages offer an object of fascinating interest in this enterprise of long duration. There were many weaknesses to be overcome: a lack of clarity in the noun's expressiveness due to the absence of an article, a sin of capital gravity for a tool of logic;

---

and the Aristotelian philosophies answer different needs in theology, and how, in the unity of the one and same sacred doctrine, they are the commanding factor in the building up of two different, but complementary, types of theology.

5) It is a long time ago that E. K. RAND asked that "the entire history of the Latin philosophical vocabulary from Cicero to St. Thomas Aquinas" be written. *Founders of the Middle Ages*, 313 in both ed. referred to above.

6) SENECA *ad Lucilium Epistulae morales*, ed. and trans. R. M. GUNMERE, in *LCL*, 2d ed., 1943; *Epist*. CXVII, 5, vol. III, 338: "Our authors are forced to twist words. . . ." On the Platonic "being", see *Epist*. LVIII. 7, vol. I, 390. See also QUINTILIAN, *De institutione oratoria*, X, I, 123–124 (H. E. BUTLER ed. and trans. in *LCL*, 1936, vol. IV, 71): "There remain to be dealt with the writers on philosophy. Of this category, Roman letters have produced but few who recommend themselves for their style". See A. PITTET, *Notes sur le vocabulaire philosophique de Sénèque*, in *REL*, 1934, 72–83; also the texts assembled by M. D. ROLAND–GOSSELIN, *Le "De ente et essentia" de S. Thomas*, in *BibTh*, VIII (1926), 9.

Saint Jerome referred to Cicero those who would reproach him the novelties of his vocabulary: "If, therefore, those who are used to reading the works of the wordly erudites, start making fun of us because of the novelty and lowliness of our language, let us refer them to the works of Cicero, which, as we previously noted, deal with philosophical questions, and let them see to what extent he was there forced by necessity to bring forth words of such portent that never the ear of a Latin had heard them; and this at a time when he was translating to our tongue from the Greek, which is a language close to ours." *Comm. in epist. ad Gal.*, 1, 12; *P.L.*, 26, 323 B. See E. K. RAND, *op. cit.*, 144, 313.

little shading in the verb's expressiveness, because the aspects implied in action could be rendered only through the use of prefixes; lack of philosophical depth in words otherwise powerfully realistic; a disturbing deviation from the concrete to the abstract, with a consequent disappearance of realistic original meanings; a brevity suited for juridical formulation, *imperatoria brevitas* [the imperial brevity], but unfit for clear-cut analysis and research; a syntax well-equipped, it is true, to provide a strong framework for sentences, and precision for analysis but whose handling the Medievals were unable to rediscover. Most of all, something had to be done to overcome that semantic indigence resulting from the very poverty of Latin philosophical culture, especially in the days of the later Empire, whose writers provided the Middle Ages with its immediate arsenal of literary works. Thus, one can observe that each leap forward in speculative thought during the Middle Ages came about through the influx of Latin translations from the Greek or the Arabic. The story of this influx consequently takes on a place of importance in the history of the foundations of philosophy and of theology. To confirm all this, one need only look into the story of the IXth, and of the XIIth and XIIIth century revivals, and again, to consider the fact that it was, not Plato, but Aristotle who was translated.

A language built upon translation is, to some extent, one that has not as yet come of age; one, consequently, that has not reached the stage of complete spontaneity and still relies on the original as its parent. Obviously, the expression *Intellectus agens* [agent intellect] had no buoyancy right from the start. The Schoolmen suffered from this handicap; yet, after what has just been said in the preceding paragraph, their creative powers also appear as all the more striking. As a matter of fact, a word is not necessarily weakened in the process of translation; translation can protect and give to a word richer meaning by its entrance into a foreign language. The period prior to 1230 was one during which the Medievals were intensely active at the labor of translation, proof of which one will readily find just by looking at the unbelievable number of Greco-Latin and Arabo-Latin versions of Aristotle's works (7). This provoked—even with the help of some of the most outlandish mistranslations and amusing mishaps —the arrival of a multiplicity of doublets, of a taste for variants and classification of concepts, and of etymological analyses (8). Between

---

7) See their number and variety as accounted for in the *Aristoteles latinus*, vol I of the *CPMA*, Rome, 1939.

8) *Intellectus-intelligentia* (see *Ia Pars*, q. 79, a. 10), *mens-spiritus*, *opinio-aestimatio-existimatio*, *conscientia-synderesis* (see *Ia Pars*, q. 79, a. 13), *imaginatio-phantasia*, *virtus-potentia*, etc. BOETHIUS, in his interpretation of the text on the universals in *Post. An.*, I, 22, 83a33, had translated: ". . . monstra enim sunt" [for, they are monstrosities] *(Post. An. Arist. Interpretatio*, lib. 1, c. 18;

1230 and 1260, the manuscripts of Aristotle were covered with glosses, which commentators jotted down above difficult words, synonyms the fate of which was to be sealed by the law of survival of the fittest (9). Technical meanings took shape through additions to current meanings. To the Roman word *cogitatio* [cogitation] twice were added meanings, that of Aristotle's *cogitativa* [cogitative power], and that of Augustine's *cogitatio* [thought]. *Prudentia* [prudence] was used to translate Aristotle's φρόνησις [prudence], but it meant something altogether different from Seneca's *prudentia* [prudence]. Upon *passio* [passion] were heaped the meanings which the Damascene and Aristotle respectively attached to it (see *De ver.*, q. 26, a. 3, ad 10um). *Potentia* in the Aristotelian sense no longer had anything in common with *potentia* as used by Cicero, and the same with *virtus* in the Dionysian sense and *virtus* in its original Roman meaning. The word *ratio*, already an equivocal term in the Latin of the Empire, became inflated with all the dynamic expressiveness of the Greek word λογός (a). The same can be said about *forma, idea,* and *species.* The words *generatio et corruptio* [generation and corruption] conveyed all of Aristotle's philosophy of nature, while *esse* [to be] and *essentia* became the support of a metaphysical edifice which would have astounded Cicero. Let the translator make a mistake, however, and utter

---

P.L., 64, 733 B). He had read τερατισματα γὰρ ἐστι [for, they are monstrosities] instead of τερετισματα [mere sounds]. And the Medievals fell in step with him. for instance: JOHN OF SALISBURY, *Metalogicon*, lib. 11, c. 20; Webb ed., 100; *P.L.*, 199, 878 C; McGarry ed., 121 [see the latter's note 349]; ALEXANDER NECKAM, *De naturis rerum*, c. CLXXIII; Wright ed., in *RBMAS*, XXXIV (1863), 291; and others.

In his theory on individuation by matter, Albert the Great held that in the corporeal substances there was a *hyliathis.* What is that? The Arabic text of the *De causis*, prop. 9, reads *koullyah*, which means "universality." Failing to understand this word, the translators disfigured it into different transcriptions, such as *hylachin, hyliathim*, words that made them think of ὅλη [whole]. See SAINT THOMAS, *In De causis*, prop. 9; Saffrey ed., 64 f. The same type of doublets, variant readings, and textual accidents occurred in the transmission of Dionysius. See FR. THÉRY's studies on the latter.

9) There is an example of this in the *British Museum ms.*, O. Roy., 12. G. 11, fol. 346r, on *De an.*, III, 3, 427b14–16: "Et hec [imaginatio] non fit sine sensu et intellectu, et sine hac non fit opinio" [And this (imagination) does not come about apart from sense and intellect, and without it, no opinion comes about]. The gloss reads: "Opinio, i.e. estimatio, vel secundum quosdam intellectus possiblis. Alia translatio: consilium" [Opinion, that is, the estimative power, or according to some, the possible intellect. Other translation: Counsel.—Compare this Latin translation with the original Greek (*Aristotle: On the Soul* . . . with an English trans. by W. S. HETT, in *LCL*, 1947, p. 156), the translation printed in the Marietti ed. of Saint Thomas's commentary: *In III De an*, lect 4, p. 153, and Saint Thomas's commentary itself: *ibid.*, 156, n. 632].

a) See the various meanings of the term in H. D. LIDDELL and R. SCOTT, *A Greek-English Lexicon*, 9th ed., Oxford, 1940 (reprinted, 1948), II, 1057–1059, and for Aristotle's use of it, H. BONITZ, *Index Aristotelicus*, in *AO*, V (1961), 433–437.

confusion followed. βούλησις [purpose] and Θέλησις [wish], for instance, were both rendered by the same word *voluntas* [will]. The Schoolmen, as a consequence, were left in a quandary, and some theologians were no longer able to measure the role of *voluntas* in the act of faith. The same thing happened over and over again in this continuous transfer of old words to new meanings. When we come upon Saint Thomas throwing a load of analyses upon a verbal sense-structure, let us not think that he is being artificially subtle, as we often do because we are ignorant in scholastic Latin. Let us rather acknowledge in it a beautiful eagerness in analyzing psychological and moral matters, a practice we appreciate in some French moralists. With the scholastics, translating was not a passive endeavor but the handling of an instrument alive with thoughts of the mind.

Right at the point just mentioned, the influence of the new layout of problems made itself felt, and first in line, the religious problems that played, in the renovation of Latin, a part of prime importance even in rational philosophy. It was not just a case in which a few hundred words were found to answer the needs of expression for Christian dogma and worship. It was rather a case in which a leaven permeated all human vocabulary and truly renewed it in spirit. Particularly worthy of notice was the contribution of XIIth century authors in this creation of a vocabulary. Perhaps there has been too little attention paid to the fact that, beneath the Aristotelian supply of new matter, the life-giving sap flowing from their efforts was permanently at work during the XIIIth century. From Richard of Saint Victor and William of Saint Thierry, so much expressive power flowed that it would be a mistake to limit it to the expression of their mystical thoughts. Let one also think about the internal transformation that the introduction of the properly Christian notion of *peccatum* [sin] brought about in moral analysis, the material elements of which had been borrowed from either Aristotle or Cicero (10). In this instance, it was Augustine's contribution which triumphed, and, even if weighted down with rhetoric, it gave life to the Latin capital inherited from the Ancients.

Almost the same should be said about the problems that were properly of a philosophical order. First posited by the Greeks and the Arabs, they were now being rethought by the philosophers of the West. Well- and little-known masters became overexcited in trying to fabricate new concepts. Albert the Great seems to have had the gift of an almost disorderly flow of words for an enterprise of this sort, while Roger Bacon, a better writer, displayed an astonishingly

---

10) See A. FESTUGIÈRE, *La notion de péché présentée par S. Thomas (Ia-IIae, q. 71) et sa relation avec la morale aristotélicienne*, in NS, V (1931), 332–341.

rich vocabulary. With the differentiating of the various disciplines, and because the latter came from different sources and were set in autonomous contexts, it became possible to draw up some very timely parallels between the technical words used in each one (11). Recourse to etymology, the classical procedure of the day, was a protective agent against verbal inflation. It forced the mind back to the incipient state in which a word embodies more closely the reality it expresses and in which it still enjoys its vivid expressiveness.

By this creative vividness, the language of the Schoolmen differs profoundly from that of the Humanists. The Latin of the latter did, to be sure, recover correctness in its morphology and syntax, along with its literary form and aesthetic resources. Yet, the Humanists achieved this through aristocratic imitation that, except in a few cases, cut their language off from life, even from the life of the mind. With them, grammar served only rhetoric. Humanistic Latin is a dead language. Scholastic Latin, on the other hand, remained a living language. More precisely, being isolated in the schoolroom and specialized in technique, as we have said, scholastic Latin was a language in a stage of survival. It served as the means and vehicle of a thought that went back to using a language of the past. By the very pressure of these needs, this language of the past became a currently-used, if not the commonly-spoken, language. Scholastic Latin was the living language of the university people.

When, in the course of the XVIth century, Vitoria and Melchior Cano tried to introduce into the School the language of the Humanists, they were right in criticizing the abstract and barbaric verbalism of their colleagues. Their attempt, however, could only be an unfruitful one, but as such it soon served to make all the more tangible the state of exile of scholasticism in the midst of a new world. Pico della Mirandola showed more insight when he went about extolling, against his Florentian friends, the *lingua parisiensis* [language of Paris], that is, the language of the Schoolmen. Yet, in his day, the latter had already reached a state of decay. "Perhaps our ears reject their language as coarse; reason, however accepts it as nearer to reality. Yet they, even if they were born among Latins, have had to invent a language and not speak Latin" (12).

---

11) For instance, where the grammarian talks of *impositio* [application of a word to a thing], the logician speaks of *intentio* [intended meaning]; in a noun, the grammarian distinguishes between its *substantia* [substance] and *qualitas* [quality], the logician between its *suppositio* [supposition] and *significatio* [signification].

12) PICO DELLA MIRANDOLA, 2d letter to Ermolao, June 5, 1485, *(Aureae Epistolae*, Epist. 4, vol. I, fol. 61 in *Omnia quae extant opera . . .* Venice, J. Scot, 1557). [On Pico, see A. J. FESTUGIÈRE, *Studia Mirandulana*, in *AHDLMA*, VII (1932), and the introduction to the edition and Italian translation of some of his works by E. GARIN, in *ENCPI*, I (1942), 3–99.]

IV. THE LANGUAGE OF SAINT THOMAS

Having thus determined the common traits of medieval scholastic Latin, it remains for us to observe through what elements Saint Thomas gave his own personal touch to this language, and especially, to its vocabulary.

"Saint Thomas always speaks in a formal way" (a). No better words could have been found to praise a Schoolman. The statement is Cajetan's. What does it mean? The philosophical resources of a language (and the theological ones as well, insofar as sacred doctrine is "scientific") may be broken down under two headings: (1) aptness at expressing abstract data and general ideas; (2) the capacity of voicing the deep and synthetic perceptions of the mind. Concerning the first, scholastic language, as we have already said, was an instrument of quality. Saint Thomas, by taste and method, excelled in the handling of this instrument. He expressly defined that the internal order of science and its capacity to illuminate came from its *formal* object, that is, from the particular type of intelligibleness (*ratio cognoscibilis*) that is set up through the process of detaching a common property of things considered from one particular viewpoint (13). This abstraction was the condition for the use of terms in their proper sense, for clarity of analysis, for distinctness in construction. Abstraction, as we know, was the key-process of the method Aristotle had developed from his psychological theories in which he held that man is a spirit substantially united to matter. The ever-increasing familiarity that Saint Thomas had with Aristotle served to reinforce the clearness, conciseness, and incisiveness that his language, like his mind, possessed by natural temperament. If, today, the word *subtilis* [subtle] is decried because of the inordinate "formalizing" of the Scotists and nominalists, that word, in medieval parlance, expressed these qualities of language and mind which we have just mentioned. While an Augustine endeavored to conjure up reality in expressions that would respect the latter's spiritual and verbal interlockings which he dared not disrupt, Saint Thomas, on the other hand, through distinctions, aimed at extracting the proper object of his study from anything that would contaminate it and at expressing it in the most precise terms possible. Later on, we shall come again upon this trait of his; let us note here its stylistic conditions.

Quite evidently, with this object in mind, Saint Thomas brushed aside any figures of speech and thought. Antithesis and alliteration were placed under ban; comparisons were strictly controlled; meta-

---

a) "Sanctus Thomas semper loquitur formaliter."

13) Hence the intensity of meaning and the frequent use of the expression *inquantum*, "inasmuch as," to single out the point of view according to which a word or a concept is valid.

phor and any other similar imagery reabsorbed. In the same degree as Saint Thomas held fast to the Aristotelian principle that anything which comes into the mind must needs have been channelled through sensible knowledge, he limited and excused almost the Dionysian method of symbols. Metaphor remained an infirmity. We have already remarked upon the severity with which he judged Plato's poetic language (14). It was not without satisfaction that he noted that this language had fallen into disuse among "moderns" (15). He, at any rate, cast it aside. In his works, it is true, a few metaphors are magnificently and prudently treated (16), yet these were metaphors which a venerable tradition had passed on and which he took up again only to illustrate a theoretical exposition rather than to use their

---

14) See *In I De an.*, lect. 8 (Marietti ed., 31, n. 107; Foster–Humphries ed., 107); *In I Phys.*, lect. 15 (Marietti ed., 68, n. 138; Kocourek ed., 75); *In I De coelo*, lect. 22 (Marietti ed., 109, n. 228); *In I Metaph.*, lect. 15 (Marietti ed., 68, n. 231; Rowan ed., 95).

15) "Dionysius frequently makes use of that style and way of speaking which was employed by the Platonists, but which is not used among the moderns." *In De div. nom.*, prooem.; Marietti ed., 1.

16) The metaphor of reason dawning in the shadow of intelligence, as formulated by Isaac Israeli. See *In II Sent.*, d. 3, q. 1, a. 6; d. 7, q. 1, a. 2; *In III Sent.*, d. 14, q. 1, a. 3, obj. 3 and ad 3um; *De ver.*, q. 8, a. 3, ad 3um; q. 24, a. 3; q. 26, a. 9, ad 3um; etc.

The metaphor of God, the infinite sphere whose center is everywhere and circumference nowhere (Hermes Trismegistus), mentioned in *De ver.*, q. 2, a. 3, obj. 11 and ad 11um; *Cont. Gent.*, III, c. 17; *In De div. nom.*, c. 7, lect. 1 [The text of the metaphor has been omitted from the Marietti ed. (262, n. 702) which gives it as a variant on LI. The Vivès ed. has it in vol. XXIX, 515 b].

The comparison between the diffusion of the sun's rays and the diffusion of God's creative action (a Platonic theme). See *In I Sent.*, d. 43, q. 2, a. 1, ad 1um: *De pot.*, q. 3, a. 15, ad 1um; *Ia Pars*, q. 19, a. 4, obj. 1 and ad 1um; q. 23, a. 4, obj. 1 and ad 1um; *In De div. nom.*, c. 4, lect. 1 (Marietti ed., 88, n. 271).

The comparison between the reflecting of things in a mirror and the reflecting of things in the mind of God (a comparison greatly amended). See *De ver.*, q. 12, a. 6 in its entirety.

The comparison between the artist thinking out the work he will produce and God the Creator. See *In I Sent.*, d. 38, q. 1, a. 3, ad 1um; and everywhere in Saint Thomas's works.

The comparison between water changed into wine and reason assumed by faith in theology. See *In De Trin.*, q. 2, a. 3, ad 5um.

The comparison between coursing or moving after something and reason's pursuit of understanding. See *De ver.*, q. 15, a. 1.

Nor is there a lack of succintly-recalled little scenes, as witness, taken from the same sources: the prudent doctor who allows a lesser illness to go on (*De ver.*, q. 25, a. 7, ad 5um), the woman who wins the hand of the king with her beauty (*ibid.*, q. 26, a. 6, at the end), the zitherist who gives free rein to the spontaneity of his fingers (*ibid.*, q. 26, a. 7, ad 3um), grace and freedom related to one another as a rider to his horse (borrowed from the Ps.–Augustine; *ibid.*, q. 24, a. 4, s.c.).

Refer to J. wébert, *L'image dans l'oeuvre de S. Thomas, et spécialement dans l'exposé doctrinal sur l'intelligence humaine*, in RT, XXXI (1926), 427–445.

original power. These metaphors had already become part of the intellectual field. In like manner, he reduced to rational factors what the mystics had to say about mystical experience and their amplified description of affective states, doing the same with the tropes and figures of Scripture. In a word, Saint Thomas scissored out anything resembling literary garb. His was a language of austere conciseness that takes a long time to become accustomed to, but then it makes one find some otherwise excellent writers to be intolerable praters. In soberness of this sort the *imperatoria brevitas* of Latin is reached, and many of the formulas chiseled out by Saint Thomas remain forever in philosophy itself.

Saint Thomas was thereby able to carry on his analysis of philosophical concepts with rigor and lucidity—collecting, classifying, building up meanings, ideologically and historically most diversified. For examples of the latter, see the way in which he proceeds for the word *natura* [nature] (a), the words *passio* (b), *habitus, sapientia,* and so forth. In these examples, he respected conjointly the internal evolution of words, including their misadventures, and the objective connections of their meanings as well.

On the other hand—and here we have the counterpart of Cajetan's *loquitur formaliter*—Saint Thomas did not ignore the fact that words are irreducibly supple in their meanings. He even formulated a philosophy of language proving how extremely relative he considered it to be. He looks for the *propria ratio nominis* [proper definition of a name] with great care, but this does not mean that he condemns the use of a word in its other meanings, or even in the meanings that have been added to the word or which remain very general. On the contrary, he recognizes that a vital unity holds these meanings together. For instance, after having rigorously defined the famous Platonic word idea, he goes on to say: "*Si ideam communiter appellamus*" [If we speak of the idea in its *common* sense . . .](*De ver.*, q. 3, a. 3, *in fine*). Again, when he says: "*Passio dicitur transumptive*" [We speak of passion by *transfer of sense* . . .], he is registering a customary usage, the master of true speech (*De ver.*, q. 26, a. 3). When he tries to explain how the word *pati* [to suffer] can be applied to the intellect, he turns for an explanation to the equivocity of the word (*De an.*, a. 6, ad 5um). When he attempts to define the deepest meaning of the word sacrament, he preserves its historical and sociological shifts in meaning during the course of the economy of salvation. In like manner, he remarks upon the different "connotations" of a noun or of an adjective, of the tenses of a verb, of the flexional ending of a word, all serving to protect the fringes of meaning which the essen-

---

a) See *IIIa Pars*, q. 2, a. 1; *Ia Pars.* q. 29, a.1, ad 4um; q. 115, a. 2.
b) See *Ia–IIae*, q. 22, a. 1; *De ver.*, q. 26, a. 3.

tial sense of a word centers around itself. He even accepted the usage of words in an equivocal meaning. After all, the lover of wisdom is primarily concerned, not with words, but with realities (c).

Words change in sense from one author to another: *memoria* [memory], for instance, in Aristotle and Augustine; *mens* in [Augustine and] Dionysius; *passio* in Aristotle and the Damascene; *cogitare* [cogitate] in Aristotle and Augustine, and so on. The criss-crossing of the sources that Saint Thomas consulted maintained permanently the relativism involved in these changes of meaning. In a manner, he molded himself on the tongue of his authors to the point where he gives the illusion that he is simply copying them, when, on the contrary, he is transferring them into his own thought (17). He did not believe that a term is so completely adequate in expressing a concept that any rival term should be eliminated. At times, he himself did not deny himself the privilege of using one word in place of another, or of successively using in the same sentence the same word in two different meanings (18). He feels the inadequacy of certain terms, and with the word *quodammodo* [in a way], he calls to his reader's attention the frailty of the most classical expressions. With a *quasi* [as it were], he avoided the loss of the benefit deriving from comparisons between concepts, otherwise inexact if considered in the abstract (19). More than in any other medieval author, the attributing of names and qualities to God provoked in him a rigorous filtering

---

c) See *In II Sent.*, d. 3, q. 1, a. 1, at the end; *Ia Pars*, q. 54, a. 4, ad 2um; also *In I Sent.*, d. 27, q. 2, a. 2, at the end.

17) By failing to see that Saint Thomas "is preserving Aristotle's language right where he is most decisively "outstepping his thought" (E. GILSON), there are some who speak about Saint Thomas's Aristotelianism in a clumsy way.

One will observe, moreover, that there are likewise groups of words which retain within a given treatise, a more or less autonomous meaning, while on the contrary they vary from one treatise to another. There exists, furthermore, a specific terminology for particular problems which should not be diluted into a common vocabulary, nor, on the other hand, made to bear heavily on generic meanings legitimately employed in other sectors.

18) For instance, in *IIIa Pars*, q. 76, a. 7: "For since Christ's mode of being in this sacrament [the Eucharist] is thoroughly *supernatural [supernaturalis]*, that mode of being is capable, in itself, of being seen by a *supernatural [supernaturali]* intelligence, namely: divine intelligence . . ." The first *supernaturalis* refers to the character of extraordinariness of a fact (this meaning of the word coming from classical Latin); the second *supernaturalis* describes any reality which surpasses the natural order (it comes from the Dionysian ὑπερφυής). See H. DE LUBAC, *Surnaturel. Etudes historiques,* in *ESJLF–Th,* VIII (1946), 3rd part: *Aux origines du mot "surnaturel".* There are likewise shifts of meaning as regards the word *videre* [to see] as used in the treatise on faith, for example: *IIa–IIae,* q. 1, a. 4, ad 2um; ad 3um; a. 5, ad 1um.

19) An outstanding case of this: the use of Aristotle's categories in the ontology of existence, something which is foreign to Aristotelianism. See E. GILSON, *L'être et l'essence,* in *PrC,* 1948, 74, 107–108, note. For an example of the use of *quasi:* ". . . communitas *quasi* unus homo" [. . . the whole community as one man]. *Ia–IIae,* q. 81, a. 1, corp. See other examples.

of his vocabulary. On the other hand, he showed how much words can be distended without their, on that account, falling into equivocation. Besides, he did not reject the use of metaphorical analogy, which is so abundant in the Scriptures and so fresh and enjoyable for one who has faith. Saint Thomas, it is true, did not have the Franciscan soul of Saint Bonaventure, but neither did he have the dried-out mind of the XVIIIth century Scholastics. In a nutshell, verbal clarity did not hide from him the mystery of things. With his *formaliter,* Cajetan gave us only one side of Saint Thomas (20).

It would be passionately interesting to examine and to draw the line around the creative powers of Saint Thomas in the field of language, after having done so around the creative powers of medieval Latin—a beautiful task still to be undertaken. To give a few samples: we believe that the phrase *potentia obedientialis* [obediential potency] is the perfect product resulting from the seemingly impossible transposition of the ancient word *potentia* to its use in the highest speculation on the relations that exist between created being and the transcendent creator. The word *instrumentum* [instrument] was, in a manner, rebuilt from within from data of Averroistic origin and used as the framework for analysis throughout the whole Christian economy of salvation. In the expression *appetitus inquisitivus* [inquiring appetite], we have a concentration of all the vigor as well as of the diverging orientations of Aristotle and John Damascene, used to define one of the cogs of human action considered in its deliberative phase. We could go on with examples of this sort.

There remains the style itself of Saint Thomas. His grammatical equipment suffered from the same weaknesses as medieval Latin, and especially scholastic Latin. His syntax, in particular, was a rudimentary one (21), although less so than that of Albert. From this point

---

20) In connection with Saint Thomas's theory on language, the following reflexions of J. LACHELIER which have precisely been quoted by A. LALANDE *(Vocabulaire technique et critique de la philosophie,* new ed., Paris, 1928, p. 505, at the word *Nature),* are pertinent: "The exclusive usage of a more precise word, specially reserved to one meaning, would tend to banish what there is that is really one, and at the same time that is profound and philosophical in that broad signification. Perhaps there should not even be that much distinguishing and specifying of meanings, and one should let the same word freely undergo evolution from one meaning to another, provided it be perceived that, between those meanings, there are relations of dependency and a fundamental identity. The words of a language are not tokens, and they themselves have a φύσις [nature]. They do not have a determined number of meanings, there is in them, as in everything that is living, infiniteness."

21) Examples of it: "Studium philosophiae *non est ad hoc quod* sciatur quid homines senserint . . ." [The study of philosophy is not done in order to know what men have thought. . . .]. *In I De coelo,* lect. 22; Marietti ed., 109, n. 228.

"Judicium intellectus non dependet a sensu *hoc modo quod* actus iste intellectus per organum sensibile exerceatur" [The judgement of the intellect is not

of view, much ground had been lost in the School since the days of Saint Anselm. Through his abundant use of adjectives, synonyms, repetitions, it was easier for Bonaventure to reveal his unctuousness, his humility, and his saintly ardor. In this also, the latter was closer to Augustine whose subjective style was quite evidently unsuited to fulfil the needs of the doctrinal enterprise of Saint Thomas. One cannot accumulate contrary gifts. To refuse to recognize, however, that in the most abstract passages of Saint Thomas there is hidden away great religious power would be to yield to the religious enfeeblement of a certain type of scholasticism. Granted that one is able to find in his works only four or five passages in which he gave way to a little show of emotion and two or three more where he displayed some amount of temper, it remains that the spiritual compactness of his words and texts is oftentimes discernible, at least by those who know how to see theology as his true *intellectus fidei* (22).

---

dependent upon sense in such a way that this act of the intellect must be exercised through a sense organ]. *De ver.*, q. 12, a. 3, ad 3um.

"Dicendum *quod hoc est* ex nobilitate hominis *quod* in generi humano possit inveniri tam digna perfectio . . ." [It should be said that it is by reason of man's nobleness that such worthwhile perfection can be found . . .]. *Ibid.*, ad 12um.

". . . causa *hujus quod* intelligitur unum in multis, non est ex parte intellectus, sed ex parte rei" [. . . the reason for understanding the one in the many arises, not from the intellect, but from the thing]. *De an.*, a. 3, ad 8um.

22) The following is one of those sentences in which "the rigid technicalness of language has more meaning, for one who knows how to understand it, than any stirring outburst of ardor" (L.–B. GEIGER, *La participation dans la philosophie de S. Thomas d'Aquin*, 2d ed., in *BibTh*, XXIII (1953), 102; creative action is what is being dealt with in the text): "The ultimate end is not the communication of goodness, but rather Divine goodness itself. It is from His love of this goodness that God wills it to be communicated. In fact, when He acts because of His goodness, it is not as if He were pursuing something that He does not have, but, as it were, willing to communicate what He has. For He does not act from desire for the end, but from love of the end." *De pot.*, q. 3, a. 15, ad 14um.

The same must be said of those texts on the identity in God of essence and existence, in which metaphysical analysis and religious feeling unite in feeding the expressing of that "sublimis veritas" [sublime truth] *(Cont. Gent.*, lib. I, c. 22). See, on this expression, the beautiful commentary of E. GILSON, *Le Thomisme*, ch. IV: *Haec sublimis veritas*, 5th ed., in *EPM*, I (1948), 120–136 [English trans. L. K. SHOOK: *The Christian Philosophy of St. Thomas Aquinas*, in *RHLL*, 1956, 84–95].

As regards the use of the term *viae* [ways], refer to J. MARITAIN's very well balanced spiritual sensitiveness expressed in the following: "May we be allowed to bring to notice what refined sensitiveness, what filial fear shows through in the very word *ways* employed by Saint Thomas. These ways are proofs, demonstrations. But when we are dealing with things that are proportionate with or connatural to our intelligence, demonstration, while submissive to its object, also, after a fashion, submits that object to our grasps, to the means of verification we have, and which measure it, delimit it, define it. . . . Perhaps the scholastics sometimes forget to what extent the words demonstration, science, proof have become weighted down with materiality in their usage by the moderns, ever

If, therefore, the study of the language of Saint Thomas is a task that one has to undertake, the reason for this is not some nostalgic reaction, or the need for linguistic catholicity in theology, or even less, some humanistic outworn taste for linguistics. Rather, the reason for it is philological exactingness itself which, with Saint Thomas, has all the more reason to be sought after, since in his case like in that of every master, his language is substantially one with his thought. His language, therefore, introduces us to the very depths of his thought (a).

V. RESEARCH SUGGESTIONS

Without engaging in historico–philological studies on the general evolution of Latin during the Middle Ages, one should not fail to consult the works of J. DE GHELLINCK which we have restated in résumé: *Littérature latine au moyen âge*, 2 vols. (up to Saint Anselm), in *BCSR*, LXXXV–LXXXVI (1939), and *L'essor de la littérature latine au XIIe siècle*, 2 vols. in *ML–SH*, IV (1946). [See also M. HUBERT, *Quelques aspects du latin philosophique aux XIIe et XIIIe siècles*, in *REL*, XXVII (1949), 211–233; C. MOHRMANN, *Le dualisme de la latinité médiévale*, in *REL*, XXIX (1952), 330–348; and especially K. STRECKER, *Introduction to Medieval Latin*, English trans. and rev. R. B. PALMER, Berlin, 1956, in which the reader will find most of the bibliography pertaining to the subject. See also M. HÉLIN, *A History of Medieval Latin Literature*, rev. ed. (of *Littérature d'Occident. —Histoire des lettres latines du moyen âge*, in *CLeb*, 4th ser., XL, 1943), trans. J. C. SNOW, New York, 1949; L. R. LIND, *Medieval Latin Studies. Their Nature and Possibilities*, in *UKP–HS*, XXVI (1941); F. A. WRIGHT and T. A. SINCLAIR, *A History of Later Latin Literature from the Middle of the Fourth to the End of the Seventeenth Century*, New York–London, 1931; and H. LECLERCQ's article, *Latin*, in *DACL*, VIII, 1 (1928), col. 1422–1528.] Let one apply oneself to perceiving the deep difference there is between the Latin of the Middle Ages and the Latin of post-Renaissance scholasticism.

To experience the ends, method and reaches of the medieval Latin speech, peruse the works of E. R. CURTIUS, and read especially his collection of studies: *Europäische Literatur und Lateinische Mittelalter*, 2d ed., Bern, 1954 [1st ed. trans. into English by W. R. TRASK,

---

since thought has turned above all to the domination of sensible nature. . . . They run the risk of not explaining sufficiently their own terminology." *Distinguer pour unir ou Les degrés du savoir*, 4th ed. rev. with additions, Paris, 1946, 445 [trans. under the supervision of G. B. PHELAN: *Distinguish to Unite or The Degrees of Knowledge*, New York, 1959, 225].

a) See A. DONDAINE's remarks on the study of the vocabulary of Saint Thomas, and the information it is likely to supply for the dating and authenticating of some of his works, in *Secrétaires de saint Thomas*, Rome, 1956, 218–220.

European Literature and the Latin Middle Ages, New York, 1953.]

The proper way to learn and master the language of Saint Thomas is not to take courses in Latin—any more that one takes courses in Greek under the pretext of studying Aristotle—but to pursue suitable semantic analyses on words, guiding oneself throughout on the evolution of doctrines and the influence of sources. The more the instruments for this type of work are lacking, the more this type of work reveals itself as urgent. The *Thomas–Lexicon* of L. SCHÜTZ, 2d ed., Paderborn, 1895 [photomechanically reproduced at New York in 1949 and at Stuttgart in 1958] is only a very material tabulation, as such. Many recent monographs, however, each in its own sector, can supply a basis and framework for the investigations we are speaking about. For instance, L.-B. GEIGER, *La participation dans la philosophie de S. Thomas d'Aquin*, 2d ed., in *BibTh*, XXIII (1953), supplies numerous notations that one could gather. R. J. DEFERRARI, I. BARRY, and I. MCGUINESS have completed their *A Lexicon of St. Thomas Aquinas* based on the *Summa theologica* and selected passages of his other works, Washington, 1948–1953. [DEFERRARI and BARRY have since published *A Complete Index of The Summa Theologica of St. Thomas Aquinas*, Washington, 1956, and DEFERRARI has brought out *A Latin-English Dictionary of St. Thomas Aquinas*, based on the *Summa theologica* and selected passages of his other works, Boston, 1960. Should be mentioned at this point the *Indices auctoritatum et rerum occurrentium in* Summa theologiae *et* Summa contra Gentiles . . . prepared by the editors of the Leonine commission, and published in Leonine ed., XVI (1948), an abridged manual edition of which, in 2 vols., was also brought out by the same editors the same year. For reviews of these *Indices*, see *BT*, VIII (1947–1953), 11–16, and 168, n. 133.]

At the end of its section on the medieval authors, and for each one of their texts, there is being prepared in the *Corpus philosophorum* of the University of Paris, a lexicon of philosophical terms which promises to be very precious.

Other suggested investigations, besides those we have had the occasion to point out in the course of the present chapter. Establish in Saint Thomas's terminology a list of terms which are representative of a great system of thought, and which were brought into use at a given moment through the coming into circulation of a translation; for example, the vocabulary of Dionysius and of his translators (see J. DURANTEL, *Saint Thomas et le Pseudo–Denys*, Paris, 1919; G. THÉRY, *Scot Erigène traducteur de Denys*, in *ALMA*, VI (1931), 185–278), and the vocabulary of Avicenna which left its particular mark on the *Commentary of the Sentences*. Examine cases of the crisscrossing of various concepts (referring, for examples, to J. WÉBERT,

Reflexio, in *Mélanges Mandonnet,* I *(BibTh,* XIII, 1930), 285–325; M.–D. CHENU, *Disciplina,* in *RSPT,* XXV (1936), 686–692; IDEM, *Imaginatio,* in *Miscellanea Mercati (StT,* CXXII, 1946), 593–602; L.–M. RÉGIS, *Analyse et synthèse* [Resolutio, Compositio] *dans l'oeuvre de saint Thomas,* in *SMM,* 303–330) [on the same, the latters *Epistemology,* in *CWS,* 1959, 438–465]. Draw up a collection of new words created by the languages commonly in use *(valore,* for instance, in Dante), and ferret out their absence from or their possible equivalents in the works written in the then-outdated Latin of the day.

Establish a lexicon of the words used in the psychological and moral analysis of the virtues, as the Aristotelian concepts poured into the Christian vocabulary; utilize O. LOTTIN, *Psychologie et morale aux XIIe et XIIIe siècles,* VI t. in VII vols., Gembloux–Louvain, 1942–1960.

In these investigations as in others, note that one can discern two contrary operations going on as early as the XIIth century: on the one hand, an effort at discerning, sharpening, and defining concepts; on the other hand, the use of patristic dossiers which continually bring to the fore ancient ambiguous terms, improper word usages, inaccurate comparisons, all of which were nonetheless rich in human and Christian experience.

Chapter IV

The Procedures of Documentation

If we were dealing with an author of recent times, it would really be of little interest, save perhaps to gather some limited bits of erudite information, to go about inquiring into the procedures through which this author gathered his materials. It is, of course, extremely profitable to follow up the genesis of a work, to learn about both its settings and sources and to locate it within its surrounding cultural contexts. Yet, in the present instance, it is something entirely different that we are dealing with, namely: the technical laws of a type of work which all of the Middle Ages, including Saint Thomas, rested upon the support of texts—it matters not in how personal and faithful a manner this was done—which were transmitted by way of school tradition and carried the weight of authority. We have already said that this constant recourse to *auctores* was undoubtedly the most characteristic element of scholasticism. It now remains for us to analyse the methods used in that recourse by the Schoolmen, and, unabashed, to examine sympathetically those methods as they were put to work, in order to understand them both in what they were and in the dialectics of the critique through which they were exploited.

I. THE PROCEDURE OF AUTHORITY IN THE MIDDLE AGES

Anyone who opens at random a medieval work and glances through its textual apparatus cannot but be struck immediately by the constant citing of authors to bear witness to any step taken by the writer. Expressions such as: *Ut dicit Augustinus . . .* [as Augustine says . . .] or *Unde dicitur apud Aristotelem . . .* [whence it is said in Aristotle . . .] indicate the beginning of a reasoning process and the ratification of conclusions. So much is this so that the modern editor of a medieval text finds himself at grips with the tedious and interminable task of having to identify the sources of the text he is editing. In just the first twelve questions of the *Summa Theologiae.* Saint Thomas refers to other authors 160 times: Aristotle 55 times, Augustine 44, Dionysius 25, the Latin Fathers 23, the Greek Fathers 4, and secular authors 9. In the whole sum of his works, citations of Dionysius occur 1,702 times. There is in all this a fact, literary as well as doctrinal, the reasons and full significance of which are hereinafter explained (a).

There are a number of dissimilar yet interlocking reasons explaining the medieval method of recourse to authors, a method further embedded through classroom routine.

To start with, there was the contingent fact that an age-long custom weighed in favor of it. The barbarian mind, during the course of its slow ascent to culture from the ruins of the Roman Empire, did not open up directly to the reading and understanding of the great works of the preceding centuries. The latter, whether from the pen of a Cicero in ancient matters, or of an Augustine in Christian matters, were located at a level that the Barbarians were unable to reach. Before they actually did so five centuries were needed, with the glamor of the Carolingian renaissance only a beautiful episode quickly buried by the Xth or "iron century." Save for a few exceptions, in every field men of that time were content to abide by an elementary teaching that fed on by-products and was far-removed from any kind of theoretical systematizing and aesthetic arranging—not to speak of the unwieldy burden of an artificial language. Anthologies of selected texts (*sententiae*), collections of spiritual prescriptions and of canonical decisions, compilations gradually organized into florilegia of authors or into records of doctrinal data were the authoritative means of transmitting an inheritance of some value. Yet they were also the factor through which the minds of these peoples became accustomed to the primitiveness of a literary genre in which phrases taken out of their context acquire a sort of juridical dignity having something imposing about it. All this became a background of mere material practice when outstanding personalities appeared on the scene and when antonomous scientific procedures imposed themselves. It is necessary, nevertheless, to measure the extent of its use and to recognize the formalistic ways in which it was employed. At any rate, so modest a literary genre did produce its masterpiece—an eminently representative one: the so-called but well-named *Liber Sententiarum* of Peter Lombard, composed at precisely the moment when the stage had been

a) See M. RIQUET, *Saint Thomas d'Aquin et les "auctoritates" en philosophie,* in *AP*, III (1925), [261]–[299].

set for a well-chosen and organized array of texts to make up a body of doctrine worthy of becoming a classic. This, in fact, the Lombard's work did. The same can be said of Gratian's work in matters of law.

There was a second component factor. During the Middle Ages, any initiating of work in the field of teaching, as well as the whole framework of culture, was organized by clerics. That civilization was born within the Church. Clerics had by no means tried to inveigle it, but it resulted from the existing material and moral conditions easily explainable by the times. Whether at the court of Charlemagne, the monastic schools of the early Middle Ages, the communal schools of the XIIth century, or the universities of the XIIIth, initiative and inspiration came from churchmen. Teaching was polarized by religious ends. Even more than that, whatever the various subjects it dealt with (the seven arts of the old *disciplina* [teaching regime]), teaching was set up and ratified under the influence of the spiritual power of a Christian conception of man and of the world. It was, therefore, normal that theology should be considered the supreme science, since it was the first and supreme object of interest to these men. Theology was the science of a book, of the book of books, the Bible. Theology was such by right. Since it was the science of God, it found in this book the word of God, the revelation of God. Theology was such in fact, since the teaching of it had settled, spontaneously and without a break, upon the text of this word of God, upon the collating of the texts of a tradition which interpreted it by congealing around it. Authority, the "authorities" were the rule abided by in theological work. Thus from theology, the first body of knowledge to have been made up into a whole, a type of pedagogy was compounded wherein, by force of habit, the mind followed the lead of theology in the other branches of teaching. All this came about without authority becoming in any way an authoritarianism in principle, which our moderns accuse it of having been.

On precisely this point, we have a third circumstance helping to explain the Medieval recourse to authority. This type of pedagogy blended in with the procedures and techniques of a civilization which the discovery of the ancient texts had put on the alert. Within a renaissance, as we have already stated, the forward progress of medieval man's thought was engineered, both as regards doctrinal substance and the successive stages through which it grew. Under circumstances of this sort, man's curiosity, in whatever unrestrained fashion it was to show up, found its channel of expression within the processes of imitation. From Donatus in grammar all the way up to Aristotle in metaphysics, cultural achievement came by the texts of authors considered as the masters of right thinking and of right expression. They were "authorities," and their texts were "authentic."

There was undoubtedly the risk that a reading of the *auctores* with an eye to the aesthetic values that their texts contained would be ousted by the formalism of the pedagogues. In like manner, a direct feeding upon the *originalia* of the Fathers would give way to a lazy transmitting of ready-made sentences. In philosophy, finally, the authority of Aristotle would be an excuse for the mind's not returning to the problems that the objects of reality permanently raise regardless of what part of truth may have been acquired about them. Yet, we repeat, this corrupted state of affairs of a later day did not compromise the initial state of interest to which recourse to the Ancients gave support.

One should not, in any event, end up giving a summary interpretation of this state of mind and judging it outright as if it were some product of an infantile and ceremonious passiveness. Alongside this recourse to the masters, the medieval mind was at work developing the processes of its thinking and pushing research far beyond the trajectory described by the original text. It went so far, indeed, that referring to authors soon came to mean no more than a conventional citing of them. Thus, we shall see that the innumerable texts of Augustine in the works of Saint Thomas must be classified as: references for the sake of authority, references for purely dialectical support, references for ornament. This literary procedure is perhaps annoying to the modern purist. Actually however, it was no more than an innocent practice, incidental to a highly valuable system of pedagogy. Precisely because the highly supple meaning of these *auctoritates* was ignored, this practice came to be made up into a frightening bogy. What, then, was the meaning, both in its actual use and in its almost unperceived evolution, of this word *auctoritas* when applied to a text?

When *auctoritas* and the corresponding term *authenticus* (1) first started being used in the vocabulary of the medieval language, these

---

1) Be their interpretation of objective root-meanings what it may, the medieval grammarians (the true witnesses in this instance) build etymology and semantics upon orthography. In his *Grecismus,* the manual used throughout the entire XIIIth century, EVRARD OF BÉTHUNE sums up in the following manner (c. 11) the data supplied in the glossary tradition:

Auctor ab augendo nomen trahit, ast ab agendo
Actor. Ab autentim, quod graecum est, nascitur *autor.*
[The word *auctor* takes it name from *augendo,* but the word *actor* comes from *agendo.* From *autentim,* which is Greek, arises *autor.*]

In his *Institutiones grammaticae,* V, 20, as a matter of fact, PRISCIAN had already resorted to αὐθέντης and HUGUCCIO (end of the XIIth century) tied *autor* in with αὐθέντης in the sense of: worthy of credence or of obedience, DANTE will be relying on the latter when stating that Aristotle is par excellence an *autor* (See *Il convivio,* tr. IV, c. 6 [in *Le opere di Dante Alighieri,* 4th ed., rev., P. Toynbee, Oxford, 1924, 302]).

SIMON OF TOURNAI, a master theologian of the last third of the XIIth century,

words carried within themselves a whole past of signification. In it, the subsequent variant senses are already discernible as implicitly determined. In it also, these variants are already impregnated with the outright and characteristically juridic meaning that the words originally had. An *auctor* among the Latins was, as a matter of fact, a person who took the initiative in an act. More properly, an *auctor* in common law was a person who transferred to another person, subject to liability of some sort, a right for which he could vouch. A seller, for instance, was in respect to a buyer an *auctor*. The guarantee itself was called an *auctoritas,* and a *secundus auctor* could in turn vouch for the *auctoritas,* inasmuch as he had one or the other of the various titles which could make him, in the low Latin term, *auctorabilis* [capable of guaranteeing]. This juridic connotation of the word *auctoritas* persisted throughout the Middle Ages, adding its weight to the usual sense of *auctoritas* meaning dignity, and thus strengthening the precise scope that its meaning was to have in theological language (2).

With the help of the superabounding documents and of the skilful classification provided by the *Thesaurus linguae latinae,* we can thus extract the lines of semantic development of the word *auctoritas.* Whether taken in its juridic meaning or in the wider sense of dignity, *auctoritas* originally signified that quality in virtue of which a man— whether magistrate, writer, witness, or priest—was worthy of credit, of consideration, of credence. By metonymy, the word designated secondly the person himself who possessed this quality. Soon after, by a transposition of meaning from the human subject to his outward act, the word came to designate the writing, the document in which the judgment or the decision of this human subject was expressed. This instrument was invested with authority, or what comes to the same, was considered authentic. This meaning, naturally, applied first

---

writes: "When the word "movement" is said of God, it does not predicate an 'action' [*actionem*], the word derived from 'acting' [*agendo*], but rather an 'authority' [*au(c)toritatem*] which is derived from 'authentic' [*authentico*]." *Summa,* in *Paris ms., Nat. lat. 3114 A,* fol. 11 d, and *14886,* fol. 8 d.

Thus, through an induration of spelling (still discernible notwithstanding confusions made by copyists), the various meanings of these words are divided up as follows. An ACTOR is the author of a work, in accordance with the meaning of *aliquid agere* [to do something], as precised above; an AUCTOR is one who, as a result of an official recognition, whether civil, scholastic, or ecclesiastic, sees his opinion, his thought, his doctrine accepted as authentic, to the point where they have to be acceded to with respect and accepted with docility. To the idea of origin is joined the idea of authority, of dignity. Thus, the word takes on the juridic coloring of the entire system of the vocabulary which, from Antiquity itself, had developed around the concept of *auctoritas.* To the word AUTOR (or AUTHOR) is explicitly linked *autenticus* (or *authenticus*).

See M.-D. CHENU, *Auctor, actor, autor,* in ALMA, IV (1927), 81–86.

2) See *TLL: Auctor, Auctoritas; DAGR: Auctor;* and, naturally, *GMIL,* I (1883), 466–468.

of all to official documents. The rescripts of the princes and later the letters of the Popes were *auctoritates*, and the Justinian Code as well as Pope Gregory will speak of the *authentica et originalia rescripta* [authentic and original rescripts] (3), opposing them to the *exempla* [copies]. Already, however, it may be seen that through a new metonymy, the text itself was directly called an *auctoritas*; no longer was it just qualified as having authority. The text itself which was called to witness was an authority.

This last meaning of the word circulated among the compilers of sentences, of *auctoritates* during the early Middle Ages. *Auctoritas Augustini, Gregorii* [the authority of Augustine, of Gregory] did not refer to the personal worth of Gregory or of Augustine; the expression meant a text written by Gregory or by Augustine (4).

Through this recalling of the meaning of the classical terminology, one sees that if the words *auctoritas* (and *auctor* itself) and *authenticus*, pointed, in their etymological sense, to the idea of origin and to that of authority (5), it was in fact this second sense that held the upper hand, at least in the stereotyped and technical formulas over which the juridic sense had more or less spread out. Legal recognition—in this case, ecclesiastical recognition—in the final analysis made a text authentic and officially gave it the right of abode in theological argumentation (6).

It was really this recognition that the medieval historians, jurists,

---

3) *Codex Justinianus*, lib. I, c. 23, n. 3, in *CJCiv*, II (1954), 76: ". . . the 'authentic' [*authentica*] and original rescripts themselves, signed in our own hand, not copies of them." GREGORIUS MAGNUS, *Registrum epistolarum*, lib. IX, epist. 46, in *P.L.*, 77, 978: "We will make them 'authentic' [*authenticas*]" (opposed to *exemplaria* [copies]). [The translators have been unable to find the latter quotation in the reference given by the author. The German ed. has replaced it by one from the letters of Leo the Great, *Epistola* 119, 4, in *P.L.*, 54, 1045 A. See M.-D. CHENU, *Das Werk des heiligen Thomas von Aquin*, trans. O. M. PESCH (*Die deutsche Thomas-Ausgabe*. 2. Erganzungsband), Heidelberg–Graz–Vienna–Cologne, 1960, 143, note 3.]

4) Here are a few examples: "The authorities testify it must be conceded that [original sin] is an offense" (PS-HUGH, *Quaestiones in epistola ad Romanos*, q. 104; *P.L.*, 175, 460 D). "The empyrean heaven one does not find asserted except by the authorities of Strabo and Bede, and also by that of Basil" (SAINT THOMAS, *Ia Pars*, q. 66, a. 3).

5) *Augeo*, to grow. The idea of growth develops in two forms: if one refers to the process of growth as it is beginning, to grow is *to bring out;* if one refers to its ending, to grow is *to complete, to accomplish*. The concrete word *auctor* (*author*) refers to the first case, the abstract word *auctoritas* to the second, in which perfect growth is made to be the model of something.

6) There was, in the XIIIth century, however, a definition of *auctoritas* as text in which there was no reference to an appeal to something extrinsic to the rational truth undergoing elaboration, but which simply treated the word as containing rational truth itself, perfectly discovered, and with only the slight difference that it had been transmitted from the past. "*Auctoritas* is nothing else than a truth of reason which has been discovered, and consigned in writing to be used by posterity." Albert the Great, who quotes this definition (in his

theologians, school teachers had in mind when they spoke, each according to the subject of his own inquiry, of their "authentic" sources (7). The philosophers also (meaning here, the pagans) will be considered "authorities" in their own subject matters (8).

---

prol. to the *Sentences*, in *AMOO*, XXV (1893), 11, and in *Sent.*, lib. III, d. 23, a. 19, obj. 4, in *AMOO*, XXVIII (1844), 440), attributes it to the "Commentator" of Dionysius (on the Divine Names), "John the Bishop," that is, John of Scythopolis, the author of scholia on the Areopagite, whom, in any case, he is unable to distinguish from John Scotus.

7) One has only to skim through the pages of MATTHEW OF PARIS to notice that this sense was in current use during the XIIIth century to either designate official documents or to qualify persons: ". . . in the presence of the most Christian King of the Franks and of many authentic *(authenticorum)* prelates" *(Historia Anglorum*, for the year 1247, Madden ed., in *RBMAS*, XLIV (1869), III, 26). And in French FROISSART spoke of "a notable and *authentic bourgeois*" *(Chroniques*, book III, ch. 4), while, in the *Roman de la Rose*, verse 16196, we find: "Si con Tulles le nous remembre, au livre de sa Retorique, Qui mout est, science *autentique*" [quoted from the E. Langlois ed., Paris, 1914–1924, 5 vols. See the English trans. by H. W. ROBBINS, *The Romance of the Rose*, New York, 1962, 345. See also G. PARÉ, *Les idées et les lettres au XIIIe siècle. Le Roman de la Rose*, Montréal, 1947, 15–18]. Among the jurists, the anthology of JUSTINIAN's *Novellae*, authenticated by Irnerius of Bologna, was given the name of *Authentica* [Ed. of the *Novellae*, in *CJCiv*, III (1954)].

Here are a few Saint Thomas texts confirming this sense of the word, and wherein are expressed the rating, the quality, the accreditation of a work, rather than, as in our modern languages, the genuineness of its origin. About the famous *Liber de causis*, he says: "Therefore, as regards this subject matter, [this book] is not authentic" *(In II Sent.*, d. 18, q. 2, a. 2, ad 1um), and about the *Liber de spiritu et anima*, a compilation that was a real condensation of the Augustinian themes and that was set up at every step as an "authority" against his Aristotelian novelties, Saint Thomas answers: "The *Liber de spiritu et anima* is not authentic, and is not thought to be of Augustine" *(De ver.*, q. 15, a. 1, ad 1um). Later on, he said about the same book: "That book is not of Augustine, nor is it very authentic" *(De spirit. creat.*, a. 3, ad 6um); "That book has no authority; what is written in it, therefore, can be spurned as easily as it is asserted" *(Ia Pars*, q. 77, a. 8, ad 1um). Saint Augustine is the "most authentic" doctor, says Saint Bonaventure: "And it is very absurd to say this [that Augustine was mistaken] about so great a father and the "most authentic" [*maxime authentico*] doctor among all the expositors of sacred Scripture" *(Quaestio disputata de scientia Christi*, q. 4, corp., in *BOO*, V (1891), 23).

8) There will even be composed a *Pharetra auctoritates et dicta doctorum philosophorum et poetarum continens* ["An arsenal containing the authorities and the sayings of the doctor philosophers, and of the poets"] (still being printed in the XVth century, at Nuremberg in 1474, and at Cologne in 1478; see HAIN, IV, 96, 12907 ff.). Abelard will produce side by side with the Fathers the statements of the unbelievers: ". . . we have brought in, as to rely on their authority, the statements of the unbelievers, just as those of the holy Fathers" *(Introductio in theologiam*, lib. II, 1; *P.L.*, 178, 1035 A). [*Introductio in theologiam* is a false title given to the work *Theologia scholarium*, which was a revision of the work *Theologia christiana*, itself a recast of the *Theologia summi boni*. See the word "Abaelard", in *LThK*, vol. 1.] Bacon, in order to denounce "the seven vices of theological studies," will gather together "the authentic testimonies of the philosophers used in theological matters" *(Metaphysica de viciis contractis in studio theologiae*, R. Steele ed., in *OHIRB*, I (1905), 1). Thus, also, Saint Thomas will gloss an "authority of Sallust" *(IIa–IIae*, q. 30, a. 3, ad 1um).

If such were the meaning, genesis, and use of the "authorities," and if such were the customs out of which grew the generalized use of them, then it appears that we cannot see in them the exact medieval equivalent of what we call, since the XVIth century, the argument of tradition, that is, the argument established through a consensus of witnesses unanimously testifying throughout the centuries in favor of a doctrine of faith. Here more often than not, in Saint Thomas as well as in his contemporaries, it is *one* author who is cited, *one* text that is brought to witness, without consideration of time and place and without any intention of establishing a dossier. Citing, furthermore, swings between a testifying to a matter of faith as such and a simple illustrating of a pre-elaborated thesis. In a usage of this sort, let us not go looking for a witness to what we today call "positive theology," except in sporadic cases and when the text explicitly deals with polemic matters. The medieval practice of the *auctoritas* is both a more extensive and a more summary one (9). For example, in the psychological analysis of the assent to faith which he builds up from Augustine's text: "To believe is to think with assent" (a), Saint Thomas develops what had been a lofty perception of his master. He does not try to prove a thesis with a collection of texts from the Fathers, which at any rate have no reason to be called in at this particular point. When he establishes that theology is a science (*Ia*, q. 1, a. 2), he quotes a beautiful text from Augustine. His demonstration of the thesis, however, both in its structure and in its conclusion, is wholly outside the thinking of Augustine for whom the very word science has another range of meaning. Saint Ambrose is called in to testify that charity is the form of virtues. (*IIa–IIae*, q. 23, a. 8), but he never considered the problem in these terms. The Dionysian axiom: *Bonum est diffusivum sui* [Goodness is self-diffusing], a classical authority if ever there was one, concentrates within itself a deep metaphysical intelligibility, and it need not provide itself with sufferance from other sources. Saint Thomas enumerates seven sacraments, seven gifts of the Holy Spirit, eight beatitudes, eleven passions, eight integral parts of the virtue of prudence (by combining the "authorities" of Plotinus-Macrobius, Cicero, and Aristotle; *IIa–IIae*, q. 48). Needless to say, the basic authorities invoked in each case are completely heterogene-

---

9) See J. DE GHELLINCK, *Patristique et argument de tradition au bas moyen àge*, in *Aus der Geisteswelt des Mittelalters* (BGPTM, Suppl. III, 1), 403–426. That is enough to set aside both untimely apologetics and ill-begotten criticism. Thus, we believe that both the praise and reserves offered by I. BACKES in his excellent monograph *Die Christologie des heiligen Thomas von Aquin und die griechischen Kirchenväter*, Paderborn, 1931, must be brought to the point. Only the consensus establishes the proof, he says (117); by all means, but that is not what is in question in the XIIIth century.

a) "Credere est cum assensu cogitare." *IIa–IIae*, q. 2, a. 1.

ous as regards their origin, their value, and their truth. Examples like these could be multiplied.

The medieval *auctoritas* is much more supple in its application than the modern argument based on tradition, and it is not required to fulfill the same scientific objective. Thus, one can discern, side by side with unmistakably positive references (which, to be sure, can be used in theological documentation), appeals to authority that are purely dialectical in character and other citations that are simply ornamental. The latter classification, proposed a number of years ago for the citations of Saint Augustine (and which *must* serve as the basis of a study of the mighty Augustinian-Thomistic problem) (10), can be extended to the citations of Dionysius, Gregory, Scripture, and even, all things being equal, of Aristotle. The same classification can also be improved upon through a concrete observing of how the "authorities" were handled. The texts referred to in the treatise on baptism, for instance, have been distributed into citations serving as sources of problems, as pure ornaments to the text, as sources of a doctrine, as proofs of a doctrine, as confirmations, as explanations, or as justifications of some assertion or another (11). This is enough to show how relative the citation procedure can be.

It was within this same context that, in order to meet the renewed and broadened problems raised by speculation, the practice began during the third quarter of the XIIth century of gathering and (a bit later of quoting side by side with the "authentic" sayings of the Fathers) the *sententiae modernorum magistrorum* [sentences of the modern masters]. Therein we have a new source of relativism. The

10) G. VON HERTLING, *Augustinuszitate bei Thomas von Aquin*, in *SBAW*, philos.–philol. Klasse, 1914, H. 4, 535–602. Hertling examines 250 quotations, 200 of which are taken from the *Summa*.

11) See G. GEENEN, *L'usage des* auctoritates *dans la doctrine du baptême chez saint Thomas d'Aquin*, in *ETL*, XV (1938), 278–329. Before him, I. BACKES, *op. cit.*, in his development of von Hertling's analysis, had observed that among the texts subjected to a dialectical interpretation, there were those discussed for themselves alone (for example, the θέλησις and βούλησις of John Damascene), those compared to other authorities, those whose explanation was attempted by recourse to their context (thus 15 passages of the same Damascene are reviewed, 83–105), and those interpreted through an appeal to a later ecclesiastical tradition (for instance, the Dionysian formula, taken over by John Damascene, on the "theandric operation" of Christ, 108–114).

It is a profitable exercise, and not for the sake of erudition only, to track a text-authority, starting from the public status of it, if one may put it that way (in the Gloss, in Gratian, or the Lombard, in a semi-official florilegium), all the way up to the utterance of it by its author. In it, one finds human reactions recorded alongside accidents of chance. An example is the development of eucharistic symbolism centering around the famous text on the *Corpus triforme* found in the *IIIa Pars*, q. 83, a. 5, ad 8um, of Saint Thomas. See H. DE LUBAC, *Corpus mysticum*, in *ESJLF–Th*, III (1944), 308 ff.

typical example of this new practice was the anthology known under the title of *Liber Pancrisis*: "Herewith begins the Pancrisis book, that is, the all-gold book, so qualified because herein are contained the golden sentences or questions of the saintly Fathers Augustine, Jerome, Ambrose, Gregory, Isodorus, Bede, and of the *modern masters* William, bishop of Chalons, Ivo, bishop of Chartres, Anselm and his brother Radulfus" (12). In his *Eulogium*, a repertory of texts concerned with the various explanations given about the Incarnation, John of Cornwall quoted *concurrently* from both sources "in order," in his words, "that the lighter armor of the Doctors of these times be a prelude to the mighty wedged-formations of the Saints" (c.3; *P.L.*, 199, 1053) (a), and after having brought in the *auctoritates sanctorum* [authorities of the saints] (ch. 2, *ibid.*, 1048–1050), he gave the pro and con *auctoritates magistrorum* [authorities of the masters] (ch. 3 and 4, *ibid.*, 1050–1056). Saint Thomas later wrote: "According to the exposition of the ancient saints, according also to the magisterial exposition, the sin against the Holy Spirit may be said to be . . ." (*De malo*, q. 3, a. 14, ad 2um) (b).

If the *magister* was vested with a quality of this kind, it was because he had officially received, at least from the start of the XIIth century, a canonical mission through the conferring upon him of the title of master or doctor. The license to teach after his examination for the masterate was for him the real ground of a right that he exercised when he "determined," that is, when he gave a doctrinal, one might say, a doctoral solution to a question that had been raised. The institutional development of the universities at the start of the XIIIth century cleared the way for the emergence of this right of determining and enlarged upon it. The lecturing bachelors, meanwhile, had absolutely no claim to it.

Not only the more eminent personalities among the masters, in virtue of the high degree of their learning, became accredited and won for themselves the assent of the theologians who came after them. The same became true also of the *magistri* in a body, as little by

---

12) "Incipit liber Pancrisis, id est totus aureus, quia hic auree continentur sentie vel questiones sanctorum patrum Augustini, Iheronimi, Ambrosii, Gregorii, Ysodori, Bede, et *modernorum magistrorum* Willelmi catalaunensis episcopi, Ivonis carnotensis episcopi, Anselmi et fratris ejus Radulfi." *Ms. 425 A* of the *Troyes Library*, fol. 95–148, and with a variant in the title, *ms. 19* of the *Avranches Library*.

a) ". . . ut fortissimis sanctorum cuneis, etiam doctorum hujus temporis levior armatura praeludatur."

b) "Secundum expositionem antiquorum sanctorum, et etiam secundum expositionem *magistralem*, peccatum in Spiritum Sanctum potest dici . . ." *De malo*, q. 3, a. 14, ad 2um.

little a relative unanimity was set up among them on a question under dispute or on a definition. Their opinion, often expressed under anonymous cover, then prevailed (13). It became the "accepted" opinion, without, however, its imposing itself as would an "authority." Thus, it became customary to speak of a *sententia magistralis* [magisterial sentence], a *definitio magistralis* [magisterial definition], a *glossa magistralis* [magisterial gloss], a *via magistralis* [magisterial way], and even—through a transition in application that was almost abusive of the word (14)—of an *auctoritas magistralis* [magisterial authority]. Thus a whole new field of possible references was developed to support the steps taken as work went along. They were given usually without any names affixed and, more often than not, reduced to the form of an expression of opinion rather than presented through the explicit quoting of a text. These references, at least in part, were those announced by the word *quidam* [some], which anonymously called to mind the controversies of the contemporary masters and located the latter at a level completely different from that of the ancient positions.

Thus, with these *dicta magistrorum* [sayings of the masters], we are little by little getting away from the *auctoritates*, since they were not accredited on a par with the *sancti* [saints]. While the *auctoritas* was, in a way, law in itself and had to be accepted, the *magistrale dictum* [magisterial dictum], on the contrary, had no constraining value and could be rejected without scruple. "This is a *magisterial* gloss and is of little worth" (a), Saint Thomas wrote, as he dropped the gloss of a certain master. When, with his customary benevolence, he found something acceptable in the texts of Hugh of Saint Victor on the contemplation of the first man, he, nevertheless, went to the pains of declaring: "Although the sayings of Hugh of Saint Victor are magisterial and do NOT have the cogent power of an authority, neverthe-

---

13) In this typical example Saint Thomas opposes to his contradictors producing the opinion of William of Auxerre, William of Paris, and Hugh of Saint Cher, the *communis sententia* of the Parisian masters: "Could they, moreover, if they were now alive, pass judgment against the *common position of the master regents at Paris,* who hold the contrary." *De forma abs.,* in *Opusc. theol.,* Marietti ed., I, 175 n. 683. This common opinion of the masters sometimes took on canonical vigor, as was the case for the 1241 condemnation ("the positions reproved by the masters"); for instance, concerning the creation of the bad angels: ". . . This opinion, therefore, has been reasonably reproved by the masters as erroneous." *Ia Pars,* q. 63, a. 5.

14) See SAINT THOMAS, *In I Sent.,* d. 19, q. 5, a. 1, at the end; "*The magistral* definition of truth: The true is the indivision of being and of that which is . . ." (the definition is Philip the Chancellor's who made it up from a text of Avicenna). *In IV Sent.,* d. 4, q. 1, a. 2, qa. 2, obj. 1: "It seems that this other *magistral* definition is not assigned to character correctly. It reads thus: Character is a distinction impressed by the eternal character. . . ."

a) "Haec glossa *magistralis* est et parum valet." *In I Tim.,* c. 5, lect. 2; Marietti ed., II, 249, n. 195.

less . . ." (b). Peter Lombard, the "master" par excellence, did not escape this dosage of approval and these restrictions—as witness the lists circulated throughout the Middle Ages that contained more and more of these propositions *in quibus non tenetur Magister* [in which the Master is not abided by] (15). Roger Bacon protested with acrimony against the credit shown to Alexander of Hales and Albert the Great who, simple "masters," were nevertheless adduced and quoted as "authorities" at the University of Paris (16).

Two other terms were also used for collective reference, and in them, as a matter of fact, may be witnessed the development of problems that took place as scholasticism progressed during the course of the XIIIth century. These collective names, the *antiqui* [ancients] and the *moderni* [moderns], refer us to two very different generations of the aforementioned *magistri* or *quidam*. Sometimes, under these words, the reference is to the Ancients—the Greeks in philosophy, the Fathers in theology—and they are opposed to the Moderns. In most cases, however, in the technical sense that these categories then take on, *moderni* refers to an immediately preceding or to an almost contemporaneous generation of masters, while *antiqui* refers to those of two or three generations before. This is something worthy to be noted by those who wish to follow up the genesis of problems. Thus, the *antiqui,* for Saint Thomas, are the generations of masters who were on the scene from the dawn of the University of Paris to the decade of 1220–1230 and on whom had fallen the task of drawing up a synthesis that the documentary efforts of Peter Lombard and the dialectics of Abelard had prepared. They quickly became obsolete,

b) "Quamvis dicta Hugonis a S. Victore *magistralia* sint, et robur auctoritatis NON habeant, tamen. . ." *IIa–IIae,* q. 5, a. 1, ad lum.

15) SAINT BONAVENTURE gives a list of eight of these propositions. See *In II Sent.,* d. 44, in *BOO,* II (1885), 1016. At the end of the XIVth century, Nicolas Eymeric will give a list of twenty-two. See the Quaracchi ed. of PETER LOMBARD's *Sentences,* I (1916), lx–lxi, lxxviii–lxxx.

16) "The common man believes that they [Alexander of Hales and Albert the Great] have come to know everything, and he gives to them his adherence as if to angels, for they are cited in the disputations and 'readings' as if they were 'authors' [*sicut auctores*]. And, the one who is still alive [Albert] is given at Paris the name of doctor, being cited as an 'author' [*sicut auctor*] in that studium, a thing that cannot be done without bringing confusion and destruction to wisdom." *Opus minus,* in *RBO,* 327. See also his *Opus tertium,* c. 9; *ibid.,* 31.

It was only at the end of the XIVth century, at the time of the dreadful conflict between the University of Paris and the Preachers (1387–1403), that the question was sharply raised of whether "Master" Thomas was finally to be treated as an "authority," as an "authentic" doctor. PETER OF AILLY then wrote a treatise in which the entire third part was devoted to rejecting the claims of the Preachers on this point. See M.-D. CHENU, *Maître Thomas est-il une "autorité"?,* in *RT,* XXX (1925), 187–194. [On early legislation concerning Saint Thomas, see M. BURBACH, *Early Dominican and Franciscan Legislation Regarding St. Thomas,* in *MSt,* IV (1942), 139–158.]

however, through the intellectual revolution brought about by Aristotelianism. One could identify the "moderns"—Robert Grosseteste, for instance—through their contacts with the new philosophy (17). These references are valuable since they enable one to restore to their concreteness problems that Saint Thomas presents in abstractly-formulated *status quaestionis* [states of the question].

Finally, to complete this inventory of the complex equipment at the disposal of the master in the documentary system and authoritative method then in vigor, there was the division through objects offered in the categories: *sancti, philosophi,* [saints, philosophers]. The *sancti* are the Fathers of the Church (the word *Patres,* [Fathers], in XIIIth century vocabulary, refers rather to the members of a council) whose testimony holds sway in religious matters. The *philosophi* are the non-Christian thinkers in whom reason finds masters worthy of being heard, even though they are excused, on the grounds of the autonomy of their science, from giving the last word on the destiny of man and on the whole conditioning of his existence. It happens that the word *theologi* [theologians] replaces the word *sancti* in that couplet, but in both cases, the vocabulary is itself revealing of the difference between their objects and their methods (18).

All this use of the *auctoritates* falls under the critical judgment of Saint Thomas in consequence of his formal distinction between knowledge by faith and knowledge by reason. If, he says, in the realm of revelation, the authority of the word of God is decisive because it is here a question of supra-rational truth, in the realm of science, authorities do not have the same quality, and their value is a "very weak" one. They lead one only to assent in belief and can only have

---

17) Saint Albert the Great, the most sensitized witness to the evolution of these two generations, was precisely the one to employ most frequently the *antiqui-moderni* classification. About the nature of dogmatic formulas, SAINT THOMAS writes (*IIa–IIae,* q. 1, a. 2): ". . . And that is why both opinions have been held among the 'ancients' [*apud antiquos*]," that is, William of Auxerre (1231) and Philip the Chancelor (+1236); and concerning the dispositive causality of the sacrament (*IIIa Pars,* q. 69, a. 6): "Some *ancients* have posited that grace and the virtues are not given to children in baptism, but that a character is impressed on them. . . ." See M.-D. CHENU, *Antiqui, moderni. Notes de lexicographie médiévale,* in RSPT, XVII (1928), 82–94.

18) To give a few examples: "[The operation] through which the simple quiddities of things are grasped . . . is called *formatio* by the philosophers [*philosophi*]" [see the Latin trans. of Averroes], whereas in Augustine *formatio* is the expression typifying the doctrine of Divine illumination (SAINT THOMAS, *In III Sent.,* d. 23, q. 2, a. 2, sol. 1). "To cogitate is an act of the cogitative power which is located in the sensitive part by the *philosophers*," whereas for Augustine it is the act of the mind (*In III Sent.,* d. 23, q. 2, a. 2, qa. 1, obj. 3). "The *philosophers* did not consider the virtues directing human action from the standpoint of their being ordered to God's providence . . ." (*In IV Sent.,* d. 14, q. 1, a. 1, qa. 3, ad 4um). See M.-D. CHENU, Les *"philosophes" dans la philosophie chrétienne médiévale,* in RSPT, XXVI (1937), 27–40.

dialectical scope in the debating of opinions (19). Even more than that, a pupil who, in his study of scientific theology, would limit himself to the exclusive acceptance of a solution as determined by the authorities would be left deprived of any actual understanding of the problem in question (20). The severeness of this diagnosis is in vivid contrast with the superabundant use that Saint Thomas makes of these *auctoritates*. This very disproportion, however, helps us to perceive both the state of mind and the literary habits he brings to his work.

II. THE TECHNICAL HANDLING OF AUTHORITIES

We are now in a position to understand the handling of this authoritative documentation, along with the rules that controlled it. There is more precision to these rules than it would seem at first sight, and although they are not always explicitly formulated, they reveal themselves to have been generally employed and decidedly effective in practice.

During three or four centuries, then, a modest understanding of problems had come about through the means of textual *defloratio* [defloration] (a). This picking of *flores* [flowers] from the works of the ancient writers had resulted in the compounding of anthologies of *sententiae,* from which originated Peter Lombard's *Liber Sententiarum.* The latter work in turn—without this taking anything away from other enterprises—became the driving force behind the development of medieval theology. Already, however, the discreteness in form and spirit that showed up in this master work was the outcome of a lively intervention on the part of keen-minded critics in handling *sententiae.* Through his *Sic et Non,* Abelard had brutally raised the

---

19) "The source arising from authority based on human reason [is] the weakest" *(Ia Pars,* q. 1, a. 8, ad 2um). "To prove by means of authority is not to prove demonstratively, but to form an opinion on a thing through faith . . ." *(Quodl. III,* a. 31, ad 1um). "When sacred doctrine utilizes philosophical writings, it does not admit of them because of the authority of those who wrote them, but rather because of that which they formally contain" *(In De trin.,* q. 2, a. 3, ad 8um). And in the same vein WILLIAM OF AUVERGNE: "Because I know the source arising from authority to be solely dialectic, and to produce faith only . . ." *(De an.,* c. 1). ALBERT THE GREAT: "In theology, the source arising from authority is inspired by the Spirit of truth . . .; in the other sciences, the source arising from authority is weak, weaker than the others" *(Summa theol.,* Ia Pars, q. 5, m. 2, in *AMOO,* XXXI (1895), 24 B).

20) ". . . Otherwise, if the master determines the question on the strength of bare authorities, the auditor, to be sure, will have a certainty that the thing is so, but he will have acquired no science or understanding and he will leave empty in mind." *Quodl. IV,* a. 18.

a) For examples of these florilegia, see *Florilegium morale Oxoniense. Ms. Bodl. 633.* Part I: *Flores philosophorum,* texte pub. et commenté par P. DELHAYE, in *AMN,* V (1955). Part II: *Flores auctorum.* Text first pub. with Introd. by C. H. TALBOT, in *AMN,* VI (1956).

problem of their interpretation, a problem that definitely had to be raised due to the serious deficiencies of these texts in which abounded imprecisions, inconsistencies, unilateral solutions, polemical assertions, all the drawbacks, in a word, pertaining to quotations plucked out of the historical, literary, and doctrinal contexts that gave them a meaning. Abelard fearlessly insisted upon the role that should be played by dialectics in solving the problem. Yet, from their being engaged in the use of dialectics, rules of interpretation asserted themselves, and XIIIth century teaching used them and amplified the scope of their activity. It will be sufficient for our own purpose to see that they were centered around the principle of *concordia auctoritatum* [the concordance of authorities], which was the governing rule in both theology and law (cf. Gratian's *Concordia discordantium canonum*). Therein we shall come upon both the method and principles Saint Thomas applied in his exegesis of the Fathers. The understanding of his works requires that we learn what they were both in themselves and in his day—guarding all the while against the false preoccupation of making of him a forerunner of the historical method (21).

1. "Most often it will be easy to bring most controversies to a solution, if the use of the same words in different meanings by different authors can be defended" (22). One recognizes here the famous text in which, in the Preface of the *Sic et Non,* is formulated the most fertile rule in the Abelardian method. This method systematically proclaimed that the philosophy of language should be applied to the interpretation of texts, with considerations on grammar, rhetoric, psychology, and pedagogy thrown in to shed light on the process. What we have here is the phenomenon of multi-signification studied in modern semantics. The entire art of scholastic interpretation starts from this principle, and Saint Thomas is a master in this art. The then currently-employed formula became: *Sed hoc multipliciter dicitur* . . . [But this is said in a multiple sense . . .]. Caught in between two texts contradicting one another, Peter Lombard wrote: "In order to

---

21) The following are, summarily recalled in their textual order (*Sic et Non,* prol; *P.L.* 178, 1339–1349), the considerations and rules that Abelard proposed in order to solve the discrepancies observable between authorities:

Use of the words in an unusual sense, or with different meanings;

Inauthenticity of the works, or corrupted state of the texts;

Passages wherein the author is simply recalling the opinions of others, or in which he is going along with the current ideas;

Passages wherein the author is speaking by manner of exhortation, advice, or dispensation;

Variance of word meanings according to different authors;

Prevalence of the best authority, if divergences are irreducible.

22) "Facilis plerumque controversiarum solutio reperietur, si eadem verba in diversis significationibus a diversis auctoribus posita defendere poterimus." *P.L.*, 178, 1344D.

get away from this apparent contradiction, we say that the word un-engendered is used by Jerome in one way, by Augustine in another . . ." (a). Examples such as this abound in medieval works. In the hands of Saint Thomas, the major terms that he uses in each one of his treatises undergo a treatment in which he distinguishes: *Communiter* `. . . proprie . . . propriissime dicitur* [It is commonly . . . properly . . . most properly said]. For a typical case, let us refer to his analysis of the concept of *imago* [image], which the Greeks apply to the Holy Spirit while the Latins refuse to do so: "But because it is presumptuous to go against the so-clearly expressed authorities of such great doctors, we can as a matter of fact say that . . ." (23).

2. In line with this rule of critical interpretation, the scholastics bring out the fact that, within the varying meanings that words undergo, the sense given to them in everyday use may be playing against their proper meaning. This is a delicate situation for the speculative thinker who is trying to express concepts in rigorous terms. As Abelard had formerly done, Saint Thomas states expressly that common usage must be given priority (24), even if it means sacrificing the exactness of a translation (25).

3. One of the laws that Saint Thomas applies most intelligently is the observing of the style of an author, his *modus loquendi* [way of speaking], which refers us to his grammar, his imagery, his manner of conceptualizing things, and to all that is included in the literary genre he employs. We know to what extent modern exegesis, Biblical as well as philosophical, has benefited from the resources supplied by the literary-genre theory. In however summary a way he may have done so, Saint Thomas did make good use of these resources, particularly in his interpretation of Dionysius and Augustine, whose Platonic style could not but strike the Aristotelian in him and be a source of

---

a) "Ut istam quae videtur repugnantiam de medio abigamus, dicimus quod Hieronymus aliter accipit nomen ingeniti, et aliter Augustinus." *Sent.*, lib. I, d. 13, c. 6.

23) "*Sed quia praesumptuosum est tantorum doctorum tam expressis auctoritatibus contraire, possumus quidem, dicere. . . .*" *Cont. err. Graec.*, c. 10, in *Opusc. theol.*, Marietti ed., I, 321 n. 1050. See also, concerning the application of the concept of movement to God, the distinctions made on the texts of Plato, Augustine, Dionysius, and on Scripture itself, *In De trin.*, q. 5, a. 4, ad 2um; or again, as regards the vocabulary concerning the Trinity, the relativism recognized as present in the concepts of Anselm, *De ver.*, q. 4, a. 2, ad 4um.

24) In *Ia Pars*, q. 29, a. 2, ad 1um, the *usus loquendi* [usage in speech] is said to prevail over the *propria significatio* [proper meaning].

25) Thus in the case of the words *hypostasis* [person] and *substantia* [substance] where the doctors were forced to establish in their vocabulary meanings that were contrary to these words, *veritas significationis* [true meaning], so as to bar out the equivocation arising from the meeting of Greek and Latin theories. *In I Sent.*, d. 23, q. 1, a. 1, ad 5um. See *Cont. err. Graec.*, prooem., in *Opusc. theol.*, Marietti ed., I, 315, n. 1029.

embarrassment, if we can put it that way, when he tried to adopt texts of this kind into the flow of his thought. For instance, he begins his *Commentary on the Divine Names* with an exposition on the difficulties of an exegesis of the Dionysian texts. The first of which comes from "the style and the way of speaking that the Platonists use, since the moderns are not accustomed to it" (26). Quite rightly, he sees in this "style" a consequence of the very manner in which the Platonic thinking is done (27). He likewise observes in the case of Augustine: "This way of speaking is the usual one with the Platonists whose doctrines Augustine was imbued with; having failed to take this into account, his words have been for some an occasion of falling into error" (28).

The case of Holy Scripture comes up at this point—with its metaphorical language, its literary genres, its semitisms. This case, however, has provoked a series of problems and a proliferation of methods, all of which should and will be studied by themselves in a later chapter dealing with Saint Thomas, the expositor of Scripture.

4. In some cases, Saint Thomas probes deeper into the style of an author, going so far as to disjoin the latter's expression from the thought expressed. For instance, he is inclined to interpret Aristotle's criticism of some of Plato's doctrines as bearing upon the latter's formulation of them rather than upon the underlying thought. "Aristotle, accordingly, is not objecting here against the *sense* conveyed by Plato, but against the *words* used by the Platonists, lest they lead someone into error" (29).

5. In other instances, on the contrary, it is the very thought of the authors—even of the sacred doctors—that is caught up in the web of historical relativism. Being, in fact, solidary with their sources, the *auctoritates* also partake in the latter's condition of contingency. When Augustine, disciple of Plato, sets about philosophizing, he thinks and speaks the same way Plato did. The Fathers are unanimous in their

---

26) ". . . stylo et modo loquendi quo utebantur platonici, quia apud modernis est inconsuetus." *In De div. nom.*, prooem.; Marietti ed., 1.

27) Saint Thomas judged this style to be inconvenient, since, he thought, the use of metaphors and of figures was unsuited to philosophical language. ". . . To say that the forms are the exemplars of sensible things . . . is not suitable, . . . because it is to make use of something approaching the metaphors which the poets introduce, a practice that does not behoove the philosopher. For, the philosopher should word his teaching from that which is proper to things. . . ." *In I Metaph.*, lect. 15; Marietti ed., 68, n. 231; Rowan ed., 95.

28) "Hic modus loquendi consuetus est apud Platonicos, quorum doctrinis imbutus fuit Augustinus; quod quidam non advertentes, ex verbis ejus sumpserunt occasionem errandi." *IIa–IIae*, q. 23, a. 2, ad lum.

29) "Secundum hoc Aristoteles non objicit hic contra *sensum* Platonis, sed contra Platonicorum *verba,* ne ab eis aliquis in errorem inducatur." *In III De coelo*, lect. 6; Marietti ed., 300, n. 584.

faith in the Scriptures, yet each comments upon it in different manner according to the philosophy in which he was reared. "They are not against one another, they diverge one from another" (a), but indeed, their case is a very delicate one.

> The expositors of Holy Scripture differed from one another according as they followed the different philosophers who taught them their philosophy. Basil, for instance, and Augustine, and many more of the saints follow the opinions of Plato in those philosophical matters that do not regard the faith. This is why they assert that the heavens partake of the nature of the four elements. Dionysius, on the other hand, follows Aristotle in almost everything, as becomes evident to anyone looking into his books . . . (30).

It sometimes happens that their disagreement is masked by the expediency of making them look like simple reporters of the opinions they are stating—another procedure of the Abelardian method. "In many of the doctrines that pertain to philosophy, Augustine makes use of the opinions of Plato, repeating them rather than asserting them as his own" (31). "The other saints have handed this down to us, not as if they were asserting it, but as using what they had learned in philosophy; what they say, therefore, has no more authority than the sayings of the philosophers whom they follow, except in this that they are exempt from any suspicion of infidelity" (32). In cases like these, it would undoubtedly be better, then, to confess their divergence, and Saint Thomas consents to it. "Should we want to reduce the opinions of different thinkers to agreement, a thing, however, which it is unnecessary to do, then it can be said that the authorities . . . are to be expounded . . ." (33).

---

a) "Non sunt adversi, sed diversi."

30) "Expositores sacrae Scripturae in hoc diversificati sunt secundum quod diversorum sectatores fuerunt, a quibus in philosophicis eruditi sunt. Basilius enim et Augustinus et plures sanctorum sequuntur in philosophicis quae ad fidem non spectant opiniones Platonis; et ideo ponunt caelum de natura quatuor elementorum. Dionysius autem fere ubique sequitur Aristotelem, ut patet diligenter inspicienti libros ejus. . . ." *In II Sent.*, d. 14, q. 1, a. 2, sol. (Soon after writing this, Saint Thomas, we know, modified his judgment on Dionysius [See below, ch. VI, 227–228].)

31) "In multis autem quae ad philosophiam pertinent, Augustinus utitur opinionibus Platonis, non asserendo, sed recitando." *Ia Pars*, q. 77, a. 5, ad 3um. See *De an.*, a. 21, ad 19um; *De malo*, q. 16, a. 1, ad 16um; and elsewhere.

32) "Alii sancti hoc tradiderunt, non quasi asserentes, sed sicut utentes his quae in philosophia didicerant; unde non sunt majoris auctoritatis quam dicta philosophorum quos sequuntur, nisi in hoc quod sunt ab omni infidelitatis suspicione separati." *In II Sent.*, d. 14, q. 1, a. 2, ad 1um.

33) "Si diversorum dicta ad convenientiam reducere volumus, quod tamen necessarium non est, potest dici quod auctoritates . . . exponendae sunt. . . ." *In II Sent.*, d. 2, q. 1, a. 3. See *Quodl. XII*, a. 26, ad 1um: "In other things which do not pertain to the faith, the expositors have made many a statement on their own; as regards the latter, consequently, they could make erroneous statements."

6. The following is a rule not quite so scabrous, based this time on the homogeneity of the thought of an author. When a text lends itself to ambiguity, it is the context (*circumstantia litterae*) that determines its meaning. "In that canon, we do not have an assertion, but rather a question, as may be understood from what surrounds the letter of the text" (34). "The words of the Philosopher are understood as applying to the intellect in act, in accordance with the context of what has been said before" (35). Not only the immediate context may supply this rule; outlying contexts can do the same, whether they are parallel passages (36), or contexts provided from within the same system of thought—the interpreting, for instance, of a text of the *De Anima* by recourse to some element contained in the *Metaphysics*.

7. Abelard had looked into those cases in which a critical examination of texts radically solves the problem of their disagreement. Their inauthenticity, or again the corrupt state in which they present themselves or are translated, brings about their dismissal. Saint Thomas makes use of this resource, and he shows an acuteness of perception that, as we shall see later, gives him the opportunity of purifying his Aristotelian, as well as his Augustinian, sources.

8. These rules and practices tend, with more or less effectiveness, to bring out what an author intends to express, and consequently the historical meaning of the text. There are cases, however, in which the expositor gives up this meaning; yet he is both unwilling and unable to put aside the *auctoritas* he is confronted with. What should be done in cases like these?

With this question, we are hitting upon one of the most curious and one of the most knowingly-used practices of the medieval method of textual treatment. The *auctoritates* have to be accepted, particularly in theological argumentation where they supply a traditional and decisive-in-itself support. Yet, these authorities display inadequacies, imprecisions, divergencies. They are, moreover, to be inserted within homogeneous thought constructions having their own systematic requirements. The solution, then, is to "interpret" them, *exponere*. "An authority," Alan de Lille writes in a pleasant vein, "has a wax nose, which means that it can be bent into taking on different

---

34) "Canon ille non loquitur assertive, sed inquisitive, ut ex circumstantia litterae haberi potest." *IIIa Pars.* q. 82, a. 8, ad 1um. See *De unit., int.,* c. 1, in *Opusc. philos.,* Marietti ed., 65 n. 179.

35) "Verba Philosophi intelliguntur de intellectu in actu, secundum contextum superiorum verborum." *De an.,* a. 5, ad 4um.

36) See *De unit. int.,* c. 1, in *Opusc. philos.,* Marietti ed., 66 n. 181: ". . . so that from the confronting of his words with one another may appear what it was that he held on the soul."

meanings" (37), and he concludes that, in theological work, the intervention of reason is a necessity. These men, imbued with "authorities," whose reason, however, enjoys fine health, know what it is all about. Knowingly and, one might say, as a matter of principle, they make every effort at treating the "authentic" texts in the aforesaid manner, smoothing out the roughness of their lines, refining the vocabulary used in them, rectifying the improper senses they contain, giving precision to the solutions they offer. All this is called *exponere reverenter* [to expound reverentially], a respectful act that in the actual practice of exegesis goes far beyond the well-wishing sympathy every author has a right to expect from his interpreter. *Exponere reverenter*: one should not entertain any illusions about the pious euphemism herein expressed. What it amounts to is an effective retouching of a text, or a noticeable redressing of it, or again a discreet deflecting of its meaning. No medieval thinker, moreover, is duped in the process. When Saint Thomas goes about transposing into his Aristotelian vocabulary the psychological descriptions of Augustine, he knows well that Augustine cannot, on account of this, be treated as if he were a Peripatetic (38).

Some moderns, we must admit, show less circumspection. They are sometimes taken in by the game when, not without precipitation, they find in this delicate method of textual concordance a oneness of meaning that the XIIIth century thinkers had not seen in it. Anyone is completely removed from their mental outlook, who holds, in their name and as being the only exact historical exegesis, an interpretation that they avowedly and intentionally place in the service of their own personal synthesis and, when the case warrants it, in the service of a truth of faith clumsily expressed here or there by this or that Father. The medieval theologians, at any rate, have good reasons—from the standpoint of their subject of study, as well as from that of method—for proceeding in this way (39). Yet, leaving aside their particular case, the same procedure is the rule commonly employed

---

37) "Auctoritas cereum habet nasum, id est, in diversum potest flecti sensum." *De fide catholica*, lib. I, c. 30; *P.L.*, 210, 333A.

38) "To think that Saint Thomas is not aware of his method as he draws the Fathers to his own sense, or that, for example, he does not understand the inner meaning of Augustine's thought, would be childish patter," Fr. MANDONNET writes in his *Siger de Brabant et l'Averroisme latin au XIIIe siècle*, 2d rev. ed., 1st Part, in *LPB*, VII (1911), 45, note.

39) We are here hitting upon both the theory according to which the theological sources are not unqualified as such and the observations which the historians make as regards the development of dogmas. Saint Thomas's statement which we shall quote further on could be illustrated by this or that reflexion of Duchesne concerning the betterment of dogmatic formulae which is necessary in the face of heresy.

in the faculty of arts by the glossators of Priscian or of Boethius (40). Most of all, it is the procedure followed by the jurists who are accustomed to treating texts in such a way as to extend, without losing the advantages ensuing from their venerability, their juridically stimulating power to other highly-developed social or administrative realities. This practice is one in which interpreting is tendentious. Yet, it is one the modern law masters recognize as being both expedient and legitimate from the standpoint of method, since this sort of casuistry belongs to the scientific methods applied in the elaboration of positive law (41). During the Middle Ages, as may be seen, the theologians and the jurists work along the same lines in their partially related disciplines.

Passing up the examples that could be picked from the innumerable instances in which, implicitly and *in actu exercito* [in actual practice], the theologians apply this method of "reverential exposition" to their authorities, let us give a few texts taken from the XIIIth century authors (42) in which, explicitly and *in actu signato* [with actually-

---

40) "As the glossators [of Priscian and others] explain their text, they are not trying to understand the thought of their author, but rather to teach the science itself which they supposed was contained within it. An *authentic* author, to speak the language of the day, could neither be mistaken, nor contradict himself, nor follow a defective plan, nor be in disagreement with another authentic author. In order to bring the letter of the text in line with what was considered the truth, recourse was had to exegetical artifices of the most far-fetched variety" (examples follow the passage just quoted). C. THUROT, *Extraits de divers manuscrits latins pour servir à l'histoire des doctrines grammaticales au moyen âge*, Paris, 1869, 103–104. The technical handling of authorities which we are describing shows, however, that the latter judgment of Thurot is too summary a one.

41) See G. RENARD, *La théorie des "leges mere poenales"*, Paris, 1929, 70: "It is through the procedure of tendentious interpretation that the American tribunals have gained the power of controlling the constitutional correctness of the law, and that our own Counsel of State has undertaken to imitate them; Saleilles did not believe it becoming to break away more openly from the authority of the law" (Preface to the work of J. CÉNY, *Méthodes d'interprétation et sources en droit privé*, 2d ed., Paris, 1919); and while GASTON MORIN proclaims this authority to be "decadent," he extols "the magnitude of the results obtained through the use of this method with its so cleverly camouflaged boldness. The jurists who used it appear to be politicians entertaining no scruple whatsoever in employing intellectual duplicity so as to conform to the necessity of living and progressing, without interfering with that sort of religious mysticism with which the common man enshrouded the law" (*La décadence de l'autorité de la loi*, in RMM, 1925, 269).

42) As regards the XIIth century, let us quote only Hugh of Saint Victor as witness to the *pia interpretatio* theory: "I know that some of the saintly Fathers . . . have left, concerning this enquiry, certain, as it were, contrary writings. . . . Myself, I believe these men of wisdom neither, in matters so obscure and doubtful . . . to have temerariously asserted what they did not know, nor, in that which they did assert, especially in that which they had shown so much diligence to prove, to have been able to be mistaken. I would be more inclined to believe that their effort at inquiry was sometimes expressed in the form of an assertion.

worded purpose], they express both the rule and the principle of this deferent treatment.

There are quite a few patristic texts in which the verb *generare* [to engender] is improperly employed when speaking of the divine essence. Faced with this problem, Alexander of Hales has this to say: "To all the authorities which apparently state that the word to engender is suitably applied to the [divine] essence, there is a common answer: it is that all of these authorities use improper and emphatic, that is, overstating, language, which should, therefore, be *interpreted*" (a).

In connection with this same terminology employed in Trinitarian theology, Saint Thomas remarks in the same way: "The holy Doctors have sometimes expressed more than the propriety of their statement allows. Statements of this kind, therefore, should not be extended but interpreted" (b). He makes a similar statement in connection with the Incarnation: "Statements of this sort are not to be extended as if their meaning were a proper one; rather, they are to be *piously interpreted* wherever they are used by the sacred Doctors" (c).

About the Christology of Saint Hilary, Albert the Great writes: "Some say that Hilary retracted these words, and, in my opinion, this solution is [would be?] the better one. Yet since I have not seen the book of his retraction, it is necessary therefore, to use force upon his words in three places . . ." (d). "To do violence" to the texts is the way we were tempted to translate *vim facere*. Bacon testifies that the procedure has become universal in the schools: "The catholic Doctors now (1267) installed in the more important places of study have publicly changed many of the sayings of the Saints, *piously interpreting* them with a thought to saving as much as possible of their

---

Those who would *interpret piously* (*pie interpretari*) such statements of the saints, neither fall into error through belief in falsehood, nor into conceit through reproval of truth." *De sacramentis*, lib. I, pars 1, c. 2; *P.L.*, 176, 187C [trans. into English under the title: *On the Sacraments of the Christian Faith*, by R. J. DEFERRARI, in *MAAP*, LVIII (1951), 8].

a) "Ad omnes auctoritates quae videntur dicere quod generare convenit essentiae, generalis est responsio: quod omnes illae sunt impropriae locutiones et emphaticae, id est expressivae; unde *exponendae* sunt." *Ia Pars*, q. 42, m. 3, a. 1, ad obj.; Quaracchi ed., I (1924), 427, n. 297, lines 15–19.

b) "Santi doctores *aliquando* expressius locuti sunt, quam proprietas locutionis patiatur. Unde hujusmodi locutiones non sunt extendendae, sed *exponendae.*" *Ia Pars*, q. 39, a. 5, ad 1um.

c) "Hujusmodi locutiones non sunt extendendae tanquam propriae, sed *pie sunt exponendae*, ubicumque a sacris doctoribus ponuntur." *IIIa Pars*, q. 4, a. 3, ad 1um.

d) "Quidam dicunt Hilarium haec verba retractasse; et haec est [esset?] meo judicio convenientior solutio. Sed quia librum retractationis ejus non vidimus, ideo oportet *vim facere* in verbis ejus in tribus locis. . . ." *In III Sent.*, d. 15, a. 10, in *AMOO*, XXVIII (1894), 287.

truth" (e). He speaks again of "correcting Aristotle through a *pious and reverential interpretation*" (43).

Now here is how Saint Thomas explains himself on this procedure and justifies it from the standpoint of theology. One can see that he and the others of his day knew what it was all about, at least in principle. One can see also to what extent one would be going astray in believing that they were lacking in perspicacity or laboring under illusions running counter to historical truth.

> The sayings of the saints are found to contain certain things that seem dubious to the moderns. In my estimation, this comes from a twofold reason. The first is that the errors arising about the faith furnished the holy doctors of the Church with the occasion of being more circumspect in their imparting of the matters of faith, so as to eliminate these errors that had arisen. This is clear from the fact that the holy doctors who wrote before the error of Arius did not use so explicit a language concerning the unity of divine essense as did the doctors who came afterwards. The same thing happened with other errors appearing in explicit language not only in different doctors but in one who is outstanding amongst them, Augustine. Hence, in the books that he published after the rise of the Pelagian heresy, he speaks more cautiously about the power of free choice than he did in his books published before the rise of the aforesaid heresy. In the latter, where he was defending freedom of choice against the Manicheans, he came out with certain statements that the Pelagians, the adversaries of divine grace, took up in defense of their own error. There is no cause for astonishment, therefore, if the modern doctors of the faith after the rise of various errors, speak about the doctrines of the faith with more caution and in, so to speak, better filed-down words. What they are trying to avoid is heresy of whatever kind it may be. Consequently, if, in the sayings of the ancient doctors, we find certain statements that are not worded with as much caution as is practiced by the moderns, these statements are not to be treated with contempt or cast aside; nor, however, are they to be extended in their use. They must, on the contrary, be *interpreted reverentially* (44).

---

e) "Doctores catholici in studiis solemnibus constituti nunc temporis [1267] in publicis multa mutaverunt, quae sancti dixerunt, *eos pie exponentes*, ut possunt, salva veritate." *Opus majus*, prima pars, c. 6; Bridges ed., 15.

43) ". . . corrigere Aristotelem *pia interpretatione et reverenda*." *Opus majus*, quoted by E. CHARLES, *Roger Bacon: sa vie, ses ouvrages, ses doctrines d'après des textes inédits*, Paris, 1861, 312.

44) "Quod autem aliqua in dictis Sanctorum inveniantur, quae modernis dubia esse videntur, ex duobus aestimo provenire. Primo quidem, quia errores circa fidem exorti occasionem dederunt sanctis Ecclesiae doctoribus ut ea quae sunt fidei, majori circumspectione traderent, ad eliminandos errores exortos; sicut patet quod sancti doctores qui fuerunt ante errorem Arii, non ita expresse locuti sunt de unitate divinae essentiae, sicut doctores sequentes; et simile de aliis contingit erroribus, quod non solum in diversis doctoribus, sed in uno egregio doctorum Augustino expresse apparet. Nam in suis libris quos post exortam Pelagianorum haeresim edidit, cautius locutus est de potestate liberi arbitrii quam in libris quos edidit ante praedictae heresis ortum, in quibus libertatem arbitrii contra Manichaeos defendens, aliqua protulit quae in sui defensionem erroris assumpserunt Pelagiani, divinae gratiae adversantes. Et ideo non est mirum, si moderni fidei

Father Mandonnet calls attention to this text of capital importance, and he comments upon it in the following words:

> Thus, Saint Thomas is not in the least ignorant as to the general fact that dogma undergoes development, nor as to the divergence of positions which we find amongst the Fathers and even within the doctrinal career of Augustine himself. This is, for Saint Thomas as it is for us, the historical viewpoint. Yet when he is acting as a philosopher or a theologian, he is not writing history; he is building up a system and doctrinal expositions whose aim is truth in itself. In line with this, when, along his way, he comes upon the opinions of the Fathers, he leads them round and reduces them to the meaning that he himself holds, by interpreting them in the sense that his own system and ideas have taken on. Instead of saying that the Fathers are more or less mistaken, or that he thinks along other lines, he expounds them *reverenter*, as he terms this manner of acting (45).

This peculiar technique, even more than the other rules spoken of above, brings us now to determining what were the meaning and scientific implications of this recourse to "authorities."

III. HISTORY OR DIALECTIC?

When Abelard composed his table of discording authorities, he developed his work in two successive approaches, the effectiveness of either stimulating the other. His first effort consisted in bringing these texts out into the open, following this up with rational proceedings aimed at working them out in detail. The more integral data-investigation was in the first approach, the more inciting this sincere probing proved to be for the second, calling for the vigorous force of dialectics to go to work—in contrast with a lazy submissiveness usual in textual perusal. Within these correlative approaches was contained the efficacious equilibrium destined to control the whole of theology's history. If every science, for it to profit in its systematic construction, requires a previous investigating of its datum, if again, for the benefit of the very momentum of its reasoning processes, every science renews itself inasmuch as it returns to an examining of this datum and experimenting upon it, in the same way, and *a fortiori*, theological science, that science of the gratuitous revelation of God, must be built up from a revealed datum. The more scrutinizing, the more taking stock, the more savoring of the texts theology does, the more avidly will it draw itself up to its understanding. Authorities and reasons are one in their dependency upon one another; documentation and specu-

---

doctores, post varios errores exortos, cautius et quasi elimatius loquuntur circa doctrinam fidei, ad omnem haeresim vitandam. Unde, si aliqua in dictis antiquorum doctorum inveniuntur quae cum tanta cautela non dicantur quanta a modernis servatur, non sunt contemnenda aut abjicienda; sed nec etiam ea extendere oportet, sed *exponere reverenter*." *Cont. err. Graec.*, prooem., in *Opusc. theol.*, Marietti ed., I, 315, n. 1029.

45) *Op. cit.*, 44–45, note.

lation interlace with one another in the oneness of *sacra doctrina.* Just because Abelard, from the examination he made of the authorities themselves, insisted upon a place being kept for the use of reasons, does not make him a rationalist, even if he did give in to some intemperate verbal blasting. The requirements of his method foreshadowed the elaborate XIIIth century scholasticism.

The fact remains, however, that Abelard's investigating of the authorities—a remarkable piece of text recording—shows a definite bent toward dialectics, the latter being called upon to insert reasoned unity into these so-easily ill-assorted texts. Will not the dialectical techniques weigh down somewhat the process of data registering, and will they not be conducive to textual telescoping? In the above-stated rules drawn from the *Sic et Non* and from the consciously applied practice of Saint Thomas, the role of historical criticism shows up in a fine light (46). Yet, rationalizing devices can be quick to take root, and not always with legitimate cause excepting perhaps for some extrinsic reason more expedient for systematizing purposes than for an exhaustive inquiring into the whole area of the revealed datum. How does Saint Thomas work out these two approaches?

First, comes the approach of Saint Thomas toward the requirements for gathering data. He is actively at pains to gather the documentation available to him in his day and to enlarge upon it. There is no question that this is the case where Scripture is concerned, which he comments upon *ex officio* every day (see chapter VII on Saint Thomas and the Scriptures). The same is true for his patristic texts and, in his philosophical readings, for basic philosophical texts. It is enough for our purpose to give here a few instances, referring the reader to the qualified monographs for detailed information on the subject.

In connection with the foregoing, two facts stand out massively. Twice in his career, Saint Thomas had the actual opportunity of handling and working upon dossiers of patristic "authorities." First, upon Urban IV's request (therefore between 1261 and 1264), he undertook an unbroken gloss on the four Gospels with texts that he picked out from the ancient Christian writings—from the XIVth century on, this gloss was called the *Catena aurea* (a). Secondly, upon the same Urban IV's proposal, he answered, through an interpretation of ambiguous texts, a patristic dossier of Greek texts that went against the dogmas of the Latins. This answer was entitled *Contra errores Graecorum* (b). These two works have been put to critical

---

46) "These pages of Abelard should be quoted in a history of critique."
L. SALTET, *Les Réordinations. Etude sur le sacrement de l'ordre,* Paris, 1907, 291.

a) See below, ch. VII, 248–249.
b) See below, ch. XII, 343–344.

examination many a time since the XVIIIth century, and again even recently (47). Today, the consensus is that these works were very well done and that the reservations made about them do not touch upon the critical principles judiciously expounded therein but rather upon certain results unavoidably linked up with the instrumentation and the procedures of the day. In them we find Saint Thomas attentive at identifying *auctores* and their works, at noting down explicit and anonymous references, revealing defective translations, extending the inquiry to new sources, and more especially, having recourse to the Oriental tradition. "I have had the expositions of the Greek Doctors translated into Latin" (a). These are so many traits (48) proving that he had a discriminating sense of the investigating that had to be done.

The extent of Saint Thomas's inquisitiveness is testified to, not only by the picturesque anecdote in which he told his students about his desire of having Chrysostom's homiliary at his disposal (49), but much more and right at the heart of his theology, by his Dionysian sense of God's transcendency, his Augustinian outlook on the primacy of beatitude, his Cyrillian theandricism, the realism of grace he took from the Greeks, his well-balanced Christology inspired by the Damascene. All these fine fruits had issued from the rich documentation furnished by the Greek Fathers and worked upon anew since the end of the XIIth century (50). The same is true in philosophy where his keenness of perception reveals itself in his obtaining Wil-

---

47) For the first episode of it, see B. DE RUBEIS, *De gestis et scriptis . . . S. Thomae Aquinatis dissertationes criticae et apologeticae*, Venice, 1750, reproduced in the Leonine ed. of Saint Thomas, I (1882), CII–CXII: Dissertatio V: *De expositione continua quae appellatur* Catena aurea. For the most recent one, see A. GARDEIL, *La documentation de S. Thomas*, in RT, XI (1903), 197–215; XII (1904), 206–211, 286–293, 582–592; XIII (1905), 194–197.

a) ". . . expositiones doctorum Graecorum in latinum feci transferri." *Catena aurea*, new Marietti ed., 1953, I, 429.

48) Read the prefaces to both the *Contra errores* and the *Catena*. The IVth book of the *Contra Gentiles* utilizes the acts of the Councils of Ephesus and Chalcedon, which until then the XIIIth century theologians had neglected and which Saint Thomas probably came upon at the Roman curia. In the *De unione Verbi incarnati* and the *IIIa Pars* are utilized the acts of the 2nd Council of Constantinople which Saint Thomas discovered.

49) As he was returning from Saint Denis and admiring the spectacle offered by the city of Paris, his students said to him: "That it would belong to you!" To which he replied: "To be truthful, I would prefer to possess Chrysostom on Matthew." See Bartholomew of Capua's testimony at the process of canonization, in ASS, VII (1865), March 7, c. 9, n. 78, p. 711B [Foster ed., 108–109].

50) See, for the Christological doctrines, the conclusions of I. BACKES, *Die Christologie des heiligen Thomas von Aquin und die griechischen Kirchenväter*, Paderborn, 1931; for the *Ia Pars*, G. BARDY, *Note sur les sources patristiques grecques de S. Thomas dans la 1ère Partie de la Somme théologique*, in RSPT, XII (1923), 493–502; for Dionysius, J. DURANTEL, *S. Thomas et le Pseudo-Denys*, Paris, 1919; etc.

liam of Moerbeke's assistance to penetrate the Greek commentators (Simplicius, Philoponus, Themistius), or to revise the translations of Aristotle himself, and again, in his using assiduously the commentaries of Averroes.

In respect to the authenticity of the works at his disposal, he rules out, among many others, the *De spiritu et anima*, a work that imposed upon the Augustinian heritage, and the *De causis*, another work that disorientated the Aristotelian system as a whole toward a neo-Platonic metapyhics. He recognizes that the latter writing attributed to Aristotle is in fact the *Elementatio theologica* of Proclus (51). As regards the correctness of the texts, he controls one version by another in the Dionysian as well as in the Aristotelian works. He inquires on different occasions about original Greek readings (52). He turns to the commentators to make the right choice from amongst variant readings. Thus, his work on Aristotle turns out to be, as we shall see, one of literal precision that surpasses, in exegetic quality itself, the commentaries of Averroes.

One must admit, there remain shortcomings whereby Saint Thomas is a master of his times, those times in which the compilation method in particular had finally overwhelmed—after being its fortunate result —the reading of what was called *originalia*, that is, the reading of the works themselves in their enlivening completeness (53). By taking them out of their context and through selections oftentimes open to question, the sentence-compilers had reduced the texts to stock phrases, preserving them as in herbariums. No longer were the sources looked into; refined dialectics had replaced invigorating reading, formulas had become conventionalized, words enhardened in their meaning. John Damascene is judged severely because of a word he uses (*Ia Pars*, q. 36, a. 2, ad 3um), when recourse to a neighboring text would have perfectly explained it. Bonaventure quotes Augustine's precious *De utilitate credendi* eleven times, but it is always the same text that is quoted (10 times), taken no doubt from a florilegium. In fact, three anthologies often prove to be the too-easy-to-reach immediate repertories: the Gloss, Peter Lombard, and Gratian. The Trinitarian and Christological concepts of the Greeks are sometimes ill-treated because their original meaning is not grasped

---

51) But, as all the other Medievals, he assigns the *Corpus dionysiacum* to a contemporary of the Apostles. On the pseudepigrapha in Saint Thomas's documentary sources, and, in general, on his knowledge of the patristic texts, see G. GEENEN, in the article *Thomas d'Aquin*, in DTC, XV (1946), col. 738–761, and S. *Thomas d'Aquin et ses sources pseudépigraphiques*, in ETL, XX (1943), 71–80.

52) Did Saint Thomas know Greek? This is an old controversy. See J. DURANTEL, *op. cit.*, 39–49.

53) See J. DE GHELLINCK, *Originale et originalia*, in ALMA, XVI (1939), 95 and 105.

(54). The advantages attendant upon John Damascene's analysis of the human act are lost because his translator has perverted the distinction, basic in it, between θέλησις and βούλησις (55), and a similar accident has blurred the traditional description of *acedia* (56). In philosophy, the formulas expressing the Dionysian metaphysics of participation lose their sinew when the Aristotelian distinction between the formal and efficient causes is introduced (a), while the stating of the Augustinian theory of illumination dissolves away when the theory of abstraction arrives on the scene. In the theology of the Incarnation, the texts of Saint Cyril have weighed on one side of the scale, without their always having been firmly established in themselves and in their context, while the formulas used in the Council of Constantinople (553) have commanded assent, without being given those shades of meaning which a qualified measuring of its "authorities" would have required. These are shortcomings that no one can deny and that have already been classified as such.

Passing on to the work Saint Thomas does in the field of interpretation, we note that he has the historical meaning of texts, obtained through an inquiry into the *intentio auctoris* [intention of the author] prevailing, in principle, over the exploitation of them through the use of dialectics. It is striking to see to what extent he is preoccupied with fixing this intention which he discovers by looking into the contexts, the parallel passages, the literary genres, the sources of thought, systems as a whole. Whether it is Augustine, Dionysius, Anselm, and more especially Aristotle, whom he is studying, Saint Thomas is wont to expressly summon in their *intentio* (57). This

---

54) See V. GRUMEL, S. *Thomas et la doctrine des Grecs sur la procession du Saint-Esprit*, in EchO, XXV (1926), 257–280, 2nd part.

55) See O. LOTTIN, *Psychologie et morale aux XIIe et XIIe siècles*, t. I, Louvain, 1942, 393–424: *La psychologie de l'acte humain chez S. Jean Damascène et les théologiens du XIIIe siècle occidental.*

56) See BT, V, (1937), 140–141, n. 188, concerning *Ia–IIae*, q. 35, a. 8.

a) On the whole question of participation, see L.-B. GEIGER, *La participation dans la philosophie de saint Thomas d'Aquin*, 2d ed., in BibTh, XIII (1953), and C. FABRO, *La nozione metafisica di participazione secondo S. Tommaso d'Aquino*, in StS, 1950; also, *Participation et causalité selon saint Thomas d'Aquin*, in CCM, II (1961).

57) "Dionysius's *intention* is to say that . . ; hence, instead of this, the other translation has it that . . ." (*De ver.*, q. 3, a. 1, ad 6um); "Anselm's *intention* is to say, as is clear to one who looks into his words, that . . ." (*ibid.*, ad 10um); "Although it is said, in the 3rd distinction of the first book of the *Sentences*, that . . ., this is not, however, in accordance with the *intention* of Augustine who expressly states in the XIVth book of the *De trinitate* . . ." (*Ia Pars*, q. 79, a. 7, ad 1um); "It is clear that this is against the *intention* of Aristotle, because, on the one hand, he uses the same manner of speaking when he is giving examples . . ., and because, on the other hand, he expressly states in the VIIth book of the *Physics* . . ." (*Ia–IIae*, q. 50, a. 1); "And this answer seems to be a suitable one in accordance with the *intention* of the work in which Chrysostom . . ." (*Quodl. III*, a. 17, ad 1um).

seems to be a trait characterizing him among his contemporaries. It must be admitted, however, that the method of "reverential exposition" so frequently and consciously used, as we have seen, implies some check to the *intentio* criterion, something like a means of escape from the avowed historical meaning. The two procedures do not always perform within the limits of their own competency.

This leads us to discerning the precise ends that control his reading of texts and authorize him in using these texts—over and beyond a pure and sole exegesis of them—within a doctrinal undertaking, whether this undertaking is an authentic tradition (that of the Church in theology) or whether it is a personal systematic whole. Therein the Abelardian dialectics resumes its role, beyond history. When, for instance, we read that Augustine, in a certain passage, is engaged in a controversy against the Manicheans and that this is the factor warping his thought, so far we have a case of historical exegesis. Again, when we read that Aristotle is referring to the theories of the first philosophers of nature and that, in his controversy, he is looking only at one side of the problem, this is good exegesis. When, however, concerning a certain word used by Augustine (for example, the role played by concupiscence in original sin), or concerning a certain statement made by Aristotle (for example, the pure act is non-provident), a distinction is brought in which these thinkers have not foreseen, more precision is undoubtedly being given to a truth, but the attainment of their genuine thought is being given up. Well then, Saint Thomas says (and here is the famous text whose meaning we should like to establish at the close of this chapter): "The study of philosophy is not done in order to know what men have thought, but rather to know how truth herself stands" (58). Taken absolutely, this text—in which is magnificently underlined, together with the unrestricted grandeur of truth, the spiritual freedom of one who attempts a conquest of it—would seem to flout both exegesis and history. It is easy, however, to see what it meant in the mind of Saint Thomas if one ponders the exegetical exactingness that he showed when, in philosophy, he carried out his Aristotelian enterprise, the way he reacted in favor of the literal sense in Scripture, the intense curiousness he manifested, in theology, concerning the revealed datum and the "authorities" in which it is expressed. He did all this, moreover, without prejudice against the mind's appetite for understanding whose rights he upholds against a certain type of positivism ("If a master determines a question on the strength of bare authorities, his

---

58) "Studium philosophiae non est ad hoc quod sciatur quid homines senserint, sed qualiter se habeat veritas rerum." *In I De coelo,* lect. 22; Marietti ed., 109, n. 228.

listener . . . will leave, empty in mind") (a). Aristotle and Augustine really live anew in Thomas Aquinas, but it is Thomas Aquinas who, via Aristotle and Augustine, adheres to timeless truth.

Such is, in principle, the way in which Saint Thomas has exegesis and pure thought, the datum and the constructed, correctly interlocking. If, in fact, his dialectical tools do at times prejudge about texts, it becomes a matter in which each case has to be examined according to circumstances. The inserting of speculation within the tissues of a text, in other words, the engaging of reason within an "authority" is always a delicate problem. This problem, however, we shall examine in the chapter that follows, in which it will be the first case studied within Saint Thomas's procedures of construction.

IV. RESEARCH SUGGESTIONS

One will never be too greatly convinced of the fact that these composition techniques are of interest for the literary and doctrinal understanding of the medieval texts. As we have seen, the exact point around which they revolve is very delicate to determine. The investigation of sources, frequently and fruitfully carried out nowadays, is only preliminary eruditeness to this activity of the mind. To one and all appertains the task of practicing the one and the other operation at every turn in the reading of Saint Thomas. The examples we have adduced are only an incentive to a broad practicing of this exercise.

Materials and methods concerning the first history of this procedure of learning are presented in an excellent manner by J. DE GHELLINCK, *Le mouvement théologique du XIIe siècle*, Paris, 1914; considerable additions in the 2d ed., in *ML-SH*, X (1948). [In addition to the various articles of Father Chenu already cited in this chapter, see his *La théologie au XIIe siècle*, in *EPM*, XLV (1957). See also, as regards Saint Thomas's handling of the Platonic *authorities*, R. J. HENLE, *Saint Thomas' Methodolgy in the Treatment of* positiones *with Particular Reference to* positiones platonicae, in *Greg*, XXXVI (1955), 391–409; and his *Saint Thomas and Platonism. A Study of the* Plato *and* Platonici *Texts in the Writings of Saint Thomas*, The Hague, 1956.]

---

a) ". . . si nudis auctoritatibus magister quaestionem determinet, auditor . . . vacuus abscedet." *Quodl. IV*, a. 18.

Chapter V

The Procedures of Construction

I. THOUGHT AND METHODS

When judging the caliber of a mind, one should not lessen the all important role played by the contents of its thinking. Quite obviously, its greatness is measured through the very truths which it grasps and expresses. It would be a mistake, however, to treat this truth-object of the mind outside the ways and means through which precisely it conquers these truths and builds them up within itself. Right within the capturing and the holding of truth, methods and objects are so solidary one upon the other that it becomes impossible to reach an understanding of a system of thought if this system is not expressly seen from within that inner light through which it has bit by bit been perceived, built up and unified in the mind. The surest way of understanding the truths proposed by a living mind is to follow the various steps it takes as it makes its way from its initial intuitions to its final constructions. In this sense, there is no Thomism outside the thought of Saint Thomas.

It, therefore, becomes necessary—setting aside any conventionalized form of interpreting the thought of Saint Thomas—to turn once again to its living sources and to penetrate into the very begetting of his system. This time, however, our quest will no longer be centered upon the material elements brought into play according to the uses and customs of the times. We must discover within the literary apparatus used in his day the inner initiatives of his mind as he set about implementing his initial perceptions and building up his understanding of objects. In this stage of our inquiry, we shall be looking into the inner life of Saint Thomas, at least into that rational part within which a system of thought is elaborated, especially if the author is a Schoolman. How then does Saint Thomas go about doing his work?

At this point, we shall examine only his personal works. His commentaries belong to a very well-defined literary genre from which construction proper is excluded; the latter will have to be studied for itself further on in this book. But we shall look into his personal works in their entirety, including those whole blocks of questions which unfortunately in practice have only too often been set aside because of the modern system of distributing subject-matter or due to a shift in the importance of problems. We are thinking, in particular, about many portions of the Second Part of the *Summa* having for us a twofold interest: methodological as well as doctrinal, since the analysis of moral matters is therein developed through means that differ considerably from the theoretical constructions of other treatises.

This is an observation of major import, inciting us to take note, in the present case as well as in many others, of the near indefinite diverseness of the procedures of analysing, reasoning, and dialectical research employed by Saint Thomas. Reducing the articles of a *Summa* to a schematic compass may be of some convenience in the hands of pedagogues; on the other hand, it ruins the mind's living suppleness and it masks the variety of methods which reason must inevitably employ. Counter to this sort of leveling, we shall take delight in observing this variety and suppleness that cannot be satisfactorily classified under the theoretical headings furnished by the rational operations of analysis and synthesis. Our task will be one of discovering and describing that variety and suppleness in the concrete and hardly-conscious performance of a living intellect, striving—*in actu exercito*—after understanding in its multiple objects.

II. DIALECTICAL EXEGESIS

Inserting a speculation within the tissues of a text is, we have said, one of the steps that characterizes scholastic thought. This step is a modest one; nevertheless, through it there is a progress from authority to reason, and through it, therefore, is marked off an already noticeable stage in the elaboration of a theology, or of a philosophy based upon the ancient masters. Let us take a close look into the various ways of applying the method, for many articles of the *Summas* or the *Disputed Questions* come under this literary genre, which is far-removed from formal syllogizing.

A first group of articles offers an interpretation of texts—philosophical, literary, scriptural, patristic—in which the content is broken down into rational categories mostly borrowed from the Aristotelian system.

In this process, we pass from an expression in experimental, intuitive, affective, or rhetorical terms to an intellectualistic formulation in which the intelligible elements that the former contains are brought out and organized, at the risk of reducing the emotive power or the helpful paradox present in the original text. When, for instance, Saint Paul declares that "virtue [power] is made perfect in infirmity" (*II Cor.*, XII, 9), Saint Thomas, in order to preserve the idea of rational power that he attributes to the notion of virtue, reduces this "infirmity" to the feebleness of the physical and sensitive powers alone, whether or not the impact and the mystical bearing of the Pauline formula lose their vigor in the process (*Ia–IIae*, q. 55, a. 3, ad 3um; *IIa–IIae*, q. 123, a. 1, ad 1um).

Many treatises in Saint Thomas begin in like manner. Therein, he avails himself of a traditional saying in which he recognizes as present one or the other of the following: the genus and specific difference of a definition (see the definition of the notion of person according to Boethius, *Ia Pars*, q. 29, a. 1); the four constituent causes of a reality (the definition of virtue according to Augustine, *Ia–IIae*, q. 55, a. 4); the proper qualifying of a psychological state (the notion of habit according to Aristotle, *Ia–IIae*, q. 49, a. 1); the material and formal aspects in a human act (the definition of sin according to Augustine, *Ia–IIae*, q. 71, a. 6); the integral expression of all the component elements of a thing (the definition of virtue according to Augustine, *De virt, in com.*, a. 2; the definition of scandal, *IIa–IIae*, q. 43, a. 1); a psychological analysis capable of supporting a definition (the definition of justice according to the jurists, *IIa–IIae*, q. 58, a. 1); a specific trait pertaining to a special virtue (the definition of fortitude according to Cicero, *IIa–IIae*, q. 123, a. 2), etc. (1).

It goes without saying that an elaboration of this kind overruns the limits of sheer exegesis. It implies, together with the use of pre-established categories, the contribution of a personal reflexion. It can even happen that, in certain cases, the original text is so far exceeded that its only remaining purpose is to furnish the material occasion for an extensive build-up. Within the following text of Saint Paul, for instance, "Faith is the substance of things to be hoped for, the evidence of things that appear not" (a), Saint Thomas locates the extremely complicated elements that make up the notion of faith, recognizing all the while that these elements are far from being formally expressed

---

1) It will be an opportune practice for every reader to look into the various cases that, in the course of this paragraph and of those that follow, will be brought up as examples.

a) "Fides est substantia rerum sperandarum, argumentum non apparentium." *Heb.*, XI, 1.

therein (*IIa–IIae,* q. 4, a. 1). Similarly, he finds in a word used by Augustine the specifying character of the assent of faith, by reference to the Aristotelian classification that he is using (*IIa–IIae,* q. 2, a. 1). Many times, to co-ordinate two rather different perspectives in the theology of the Incarnation, for instance, he exploits, far beyond its original meaning, the notion of instrument (ὄργανον) borrowed from the still rather summary observations of John Damascene on the subject, and he uses it to determine what causal role Christ-the-man plays in sacramental life(see in *IIIa Pars,* q. 64, a. 3, the remarkable article in which he declares the two conflicting opinions to be right). Elsewhere he throws completely off keel a classical notion—one adorned with all of Augustine's prestige at that—by inserting it within a different context. This he does with the notion of *ratio superior et inferior* in the philosophy of mind (*De ver.,* q. 15), and with the notion of concupiscence in the theology of original sin (*Ia–IIae,* q. 82). One would be mistaken in judging this practice to be only cases where recourse is had to dialectical expedients (for instance, when he says that original sin is concupiscence *materialiter* [materially speaking]). Such an interpretation would be to minimize the original vigor of a profound conceptual and organic transposition which the apparatus of dialectics is summoned to foster.

In the same manner, he brings out the value and, as it were, weaves within the fabric of rational analysis those descriptions given by the moralists who now and again spontaneously word them in a language expressing a rich experience, if not always an intent so subtle as he sees in them. Thus, Aristotle furnishes the essential circumstances present in any human act (*Ia–IIae,* q. 7, a. 3); John Damascene and Gregory of Nyssa, the varieties of sadness (*ibid.,* q. 35, a. 8), fear (q. 41, a. 4), anger (q. 46, a. 8); Plotinus (Macrobius), the ideal progressive development of the virtues (q. 61, a. 5); Cicero, the elements integral to fortitude (*IIa–IIae,* q. 128, a. 1); Saint Gregory, the "daughters" of the vices: vain glory (q. 132, a. 5), gluttony (q. 148, a. 6), lust (q. 153, a. 5), anger (q. 158, a. 7), and so forth. The same is done with the classification adopted in Christian tradition for the ten moral precepts, the seven gifts of the Holy Spirit, and the eight beatitudes. The three Scriptural narratives concerned with creation, the ancient law, and the life of Christ are, in a similar way, the source supplying whole blocks of questions and articles in the *Summa* (*Ia Pars,* q. 67–74; *Ia–IIae,* q. 105; *IIIa Pars,* q. 30–58), thus preserving in a theology of the most speculative kind a biblical content and atmosphere.

Likewise, we shall cull the passages in which Saint Thomas adopts from one of the ancient writers and makes his own a beautiful text,

packed with insight yet somewhat obscure because of its compactness, and subjects it along the very lines of its contents to an elaborate
amplification. It is a practice in the grand style. For an example see
the way in which he comments upon this text of Saint Hilary: *Esse
non est accidens Deo* [For God, to be is not an accident], in *In I
Sent.*, d. 8, exp. textus: *De pot.*, q. 5, a. 4, ad 3um; *Quodl. II*, a. 3;
Quodl. XII, a. 5.

It would be an easy thing to bring in a large number of examples
of these cases wherein exegesis is overstepped. Let us simply notice
the cases in which two texts divergent in source and climate are combined or brought together in reinforcement of one another within a
unique construction that evidently their original materials did not
forecast. Aristotle, for instance, and the Roman jurists co-operate in
the definition of justice (*IIa–IIae*, q. 58, a. 1); Boethius and Aristotle
reveal the two different aspects pertaining to happiness (*Ia–IIae*,
q. 3, a. 2, ad 2um); Ulpian and Isidorus of Seville are brought to
agreement in the definition of the laws of nations (*IIa–IIae*, q.
57, a. 3).

III. ANALYSES, DEFINITIONS, IMAGES

[1. Analyses]

Many articles thus founded upon the exegesis of a text develop
into psychological, moral, and metaphysical analyses very different in
type. Yet they are all done in such a manner as to reveal the concrete
unity of a reality beneath the mind's analytical endeavors. In their
descriptive part, with or without indication of the course being followed, these analyses unfold through the insertion of rational viewpoints with the help of which order, and therefore, intelligibleness, is
introduced within the phenomena undergoing study. Thus, in the
psychological treatises of the *Ia Pars*, an analysis is made of the vege-
tative faculties, followed by that of the external senses, the internal
senses (qu. 78), and then of the other powers. Thus especially, in the
IIa Pars, there is an analysis of the emotions and passions, followed
by one of the virtues and vices, according to their variety, and ranging
from the wider categories of prudence, justice, fortitude, and temperance, right down to the lesser categories to which the latter spread
out. Moderns would be surprised to see how attentive Saint Thomas
is at analysing the physiological and psychological effects of anger
(*Ia–IIae*, q. 48), and the tension felt by the contemplative as he
sways between delight and sadness (*IIa–IIae*, q. 35, a. 5); how attentive he is also at observing what makes the difference between
cruelty and brutality (*IIa–IIae*, q. 159, a. 2, based upon Seneca), what

the psychological elements are that make up contrition of the heart (*IIIa Pars*, q. 85), and so on.

This is the place to speak of those articles wherein the objective sought is to distinguish between the different species of anger (*Ia–IIae*, q. 46, a. 8), sadness (*Ia–IIae*, q. 35, a. 8), fear (*ibid.*, q. 41, a. 4), and the various effects of law (*ibid.*, q. 92, a. 2), and so forth. In these articles, it is not a purely inductive method based upon concrete observation that is brought into play, although a great number of sharply-observed points are therein gathered; we have, rather, an *a priori* analysis of the reactions which appetite is apt to undergo when faced with good and evil. It is from within this analysis that the treatise on passions finds its subject-matter distributed.

It is, however, especially in this context that justification is found for the partitioning of moral life's resources within the broad schema supplied by the distinction between the integral, subjective, and potential parts of the cardinal virtues. This schema is an abstract one, to be sure, or *artificialis* [artificial], to use the word employed without disparagement by the Medievals. Yet, it is a schema furnishing, within a much more supple framework than would at first appear, a spiritual and intelligible location for the various qualities of the soul, and, therefore, one already determining their meaning and their contexts. The key-article about this schema is the one in which its machinery is described and then applied to the virtue of prudence (*IIa–IIae*, q. 48, a. 1; for the virtue of fortitude, see *ibid.*, q. 128, a. 1; of temperance, *ibid.*, q. 148, a. 1). Concerning this partitioning of the virtues, it is important, for the sake of exegetical soundness, to take a good look at both its scientific quality and its delicate relativism; see, for instance, the other competing sources of classification in the case of the virtue of justice (*IIa–IIae*, q. 80, resp. ad obj.), or, in the case of religion, how the latter virtue is attentively encompassed within the bounds of justice, yet, to how great an extent it oversteps these bounds (*IIa–IIae*, q. 81, a. 5, and ff.; *In De trin.*, q. 3, a. 2).

It is not our task, however, to examine the contents of the latter treatises. Rather we must insist upon the method of analysis applied in them, one that is not without recalling to mind many a step characteristic of the phenomenological method. The detecting of structures in objects and the investigating of essences in things are therein managed by reference to a sort of *consensus* issuing from what is most objectively, most universally, most immediately, valuable in mankind's experience. One would be mistaken in seeking to oppose in them a psychology based upon observation as against one based on metaphysics, or to cast aside the former in the name of the latter. What we have here is an all-inclusive psychology, one refusing to set itself apart from moral science, and even from theology, since its goal is to shed light not only upon the nature but upon the concrete condition of man as well (2). In this instance again, Augustine and Christian experience step in to give the Aristotelian materials and method another dimension.

This concern for discerning the structure of the various components of spiritual deportment and for characterizing them from the standpoint of moral issues directs Saint Thomas in his insistent search to find out on what score each virtue is specifically a virtue: just how, for instance, *gnome*, or that ability to judge prudentially on the basis of the higher principles, notwithstanding the bypassing of the immediate rules, has the characters of virtue (*IIa–IIae*, q. 51, a. 4), or again just how magnanimity is a special virtue located within the field of fortitude (*ibid.*, q. 129, a. 4). The same concern shows up when he is determining why fear (*Ia–IIae*, q. 41, a. 2), anger (*ibid.*, q. 46, a. 1), or the like, are special passions. The same type of analysis and the same exactingness are found where the question of the "distinction" between sins is being studied (*ibid.*, q. 72. See the whole question).

This quest of the mind for insight into what specifically distinguishes the various objects is at the root of the choice explicitly made by Saint Thomas concerning the meaning that should be given to the classification of the cardinal virtues. This classification is not primarily dependent, as was thought by many at the time and by Saint Thomas himself in his *Sentences,* upon a consideration of the four general conditions whose presence is a requisite for an act to be virtuous. It is rather the express result of a distinguishing between four special matters within each of which an original type of virtue comes into being, within each of which is contained the formal ground of a rational good to be sought after (*Ia–IIae*, q. 61, a. 4). It is upon this principle that Saint Thomas builds up the key articles of all his treatises on the virtues wherein he subtly goes looking for—far over and above the pious "adaptations" with which the moralizing preachers are wont to be satisfied—the deeper reasons securing an intelligible and intelligent framework for human conduct. It, therefore, becomes imperative that the firm design meant for these articles be preserved in them and that it be well discerned what, in their drafting, represents their true content and what the "adaptations" (3)

---

2) We are making our own here the statements which E. BORNE makes in his review of M. SCHELER's *Le sens de la souffrance* [trans. from the German by P. KLOSSOWSKI, in *PhEs*, 1936]. See *RT*, XLIII (1937), 147.

3) This is the scornful word which ALBERT THE GREAT uses: "And all of these do not show what the number of the virtues is; they are rather "adaptations" [*adaptationes*], which can easily be disproved, moreover, by anyone who knows." *Summa de bono*, tr. 1, q. 4, a. 1; Col. ed., XXVIII (1951), 80, n. 119.

that Saint Thomas sometimes records in simple reverence to oratorical or school traditions. True, this practice raises a difficult problem. The spirituals, on the one hand, give in readily enough to an extolling of the all-inclusive value of humility, patience, poverty, and purity; on the other hand, the theologian in Saint Thomas has in mind the determining of the cardinal points from which is started, under the impulse of grace and aiming to serve it (see *Ia–IIae*, q. 61, a. 3, obj.), the build-up of a rational order. Consequently, the dynamics present in either analysis are different. It would seem that, in the latter, the "Christian" virtues are doomed to be consigned within the subdivisions of a classification. There is herein a neat problem, namely: to see how Gospel-inspired thinking can become food-stuff for a moral theology that aims at being scientific. This problem, however, we shall not go into. Our purpose was only to establish a characteristic type of article construction especially present in the *Summa*.

The expositions wherein the end-product of analysis is an inserting of an external or internal reality within one of the categories or predicaments are to be considered as belonging to the same line of procedure (4). As an example, because of its historical fortune and of its theological bearing, let us cite the case of grace defined as an accidental form appertaining to the genus of *quality*. The practice, however, is a classical one, applied in all fields, especially in that of the life of the mind. The first principles of this life, for instance, whether in the order of knowledge or in the order of action (*synderesis*), are presented as depending upon a *habitus* (*Ia Pars*, q. 79, a. 12); the same goes for the gifts of the Holy Spirit (*Ia–IIae*, q. 68, a. 3). Free choice, on the contrary, and what it involves, must be considered as sufficiently accounted for if viewed from the angle of a pure faculty, a *potentia* (*De ver.*, q. 24, a. 4; see in this article the very interesting way in which the debate with the opposing thesis is conducted); and so on. In another sector, we touch upon one of the most profound traits of Saint Thomas's method of thinking when we see him building up hope, the Christian virtue, from an analysis of hope, the passion, as his starting point (*De spe*, q. 1, a. 1). We understand, then, why Saint Thomas and his contemporaries so insist upon elaborating these categories. Today, the latter are no longer in use. No longer do they spontaneously offer themselves to our minds as having technical value and evocative power. Whatever our opinion about

---

4) This happens especially where the different kinds of qualities are involved. See ARISTOTLE, *Categories*, ch. 6 (H. P. Cooke ed., in *LCL*, 1938): *habitus et dispositio* [habit and disposition], *potentia et impotentia* [potency and impotency], *passio et patibilis qualitas* [alteration and alterableness], *forma et figura* [shape and figure]. ". . . all [the modes of quality] are reducible to these species, which is clear from the fact that it has not been possible thus far to discover any other species of it." *In IV Sent.*, d. 4, q. 1, a. 1.

them, they must be reinstated in accordance with the terms of the latter twofold resource, if many an analysis is not to be reduced to a mere dialectical schema and deprived of its living flesh. The Greek Aristotelians, the Arabic philosophers, the theologians of the West, all made the four species of quality an object of their study, and Saint Thomas who at first held there was only a difference in degree between a *habitus* and a *dispositio,* finally pronounced the two to be specifically different (*Ia–IIae,* q. 49, a. 2, ad 3um). When one perceives that the *habitus* theory is the factor governing the whole of his psychology of the virtues—whether intellectual, moral, or theological—and that in particular his ethics is one, not of casuistry and precepts, but of the "virtues" and of the interior life, then one can no longer be giving too much importance to the analysis of these categories (*De virt. in com.,* a. 1; *Ia–IIae,* q. 49 and ff.). Joking à la Molière about the difference between the form and the figure of a hat may serve to mark off the limits within which the procedure can be legitimately used, but it should not ruin the principle of it.

In however summary a way it will be done, we must underline the particular character of another type of analysis, one which develops around the perceiving of the transcendentals, irrespective of all the categories. The prototype of this sort of analysis is contained in the opening article of the disputed question *De veritate* (q. 1, a. 1), in which precisely, the transcendentals are tabulated, with being, considered as the object of a concept, furnishing the point of departure. A replica of this article is given at the beginning of the *De bono (De ver.,* q. 21), in which the "reducing" (a) of the other transcendentals to that of being is carried out in a manner differing entirely from the logical analysis employed in the case of univocal notions (5). It would be going beyond our purpose to undertake the study of the nature of metaphysical knowledge that is based upon analogy in both its method and its object. It must be asked of the reader of Saint Thomas, however, that he preserve attentively both the procedures and the atmosphere present in these and similar developments, constantly resisting the threat of a rationalistic interpretation of these procedures and respecting throughout that ontological mystery wherein the obscurity inherent in the notion of existence is preserved in the science of being. In them, there is, implicitly at least, one dimension more than found in the texts of Aristotle, which, never-

a) See below, 188–191.

5) Likewise, the theory of relation which, for Aristotle, remains within the predicamental framework, but which, for Saint Thomas and the Medievals, oversteps this framework and serves to define the transcendental notions: the true, the good. [See A. KREMPEL, *La doctrine de la relation chez Saint Thomas, Exposé systématique et historique,* Paris, 1952: *La relation parmi les transcendentaux,* 65–75].

theless, are the basis of these articles of Saint Thomas. The observing of this is a matter of capital importance, and a delicate one to handle as well, for it is of the order of the mind. Without yielding to the temptation—opposed by Saint Thomas—of reserving for this transcendental and immanent universe an extra faculty conceived of as freed from the procedures employed by *ratio* [reason], one must nevertheless discern that, within the knowledge of this field of intelligibility, some characteristics are specific to an appropriate conceptualization of it and that it has its own proper dynamic power. There is a logic of the analogous, a "dialectic" upon which the Platonic method has left its mark. The "degrees" of being, the "ways" to demonstrate and to know God or to discover his presence are not travelled upon as the routes of the philosophy of nature (6). As he closes that analysis of the metaphysical structure of concrete reality, wherein he is led on to pronouncing that in God essence and existence are identical, the metaphysician in Saint Thomas finds himself in the midst of a religious atmosphere, and none other than biblical expressions then find their way under his pen to express "that sublime truth!" (*Cont. Gent.*, I, c. 22). Who will bespeak the spiritual intensity conveyed, over and above the categories he uses as a philosopher and as a theologian, in this exclamation wherein he discreetly gives himself away (7)?

Likewise, the whole method of theology would have to be presented if we had to set about examining how Saint Thomas proceeds in establishing and analysing those human concepts that are transferred to the knowing of God and His ways of managing the eternal and the temporal. That examination would bring us from directly-revealed concepts such as those of generation, verb, mission, sacrament, to the metaphysical concepts of substance, person, cause, instrument, and the like. In this field, the *analogia entis* [analogy of being] does its work at the heart of an *analogia fidei* [analogy of faith] (a). Faith can put to her use all the techniques of reason, but she subjects the objects and tools of it to a purifying process such as meets the demands of the mystics. It is actually in a climate of mystery that these analyses unfold, and therein success is achieved through negation. The process is less conductive to illusion of knowledge than is

6) Read the chapters devoted to metaphysical knowledge in J. MARITAIN, *Distinguer pour unir ou Les degrés du savoir*, 4th ed., Paris, 1946, 399–484 [trans. under the supervision of G. B. PHELAN: *Distinguish to Unite or The Degrees of Knowledge*, New York, 1959, 202–244], and in L. B. GEIGER, *La participation dans la philosophie de S. Thomas d'Aquin*, in *BibTh*, XXIII (1953), 315 and ff.

7) Read E. GILSON's beautiful chapter entitled *Haec sublimis veritas*, in *Le Thomisme*, 4th ed., in *EPM*, I (1948), 120–136 [trans. L. K. SHOOK: *The Christian Philosophy of St. Thomas Aquinas*, in *RHLL*, 1956, 84–95].

a) See G. SÖHNGEN, *Analogia entis in Analogia fidei*, in *Barth–Festschrift* "Antwort," Zurich, 1956, 266–271.

the use of superlatives. "It is as to one completely unknown that it [the soul] is united", Saint Thomas writes, in the wake of Dionysius (b). True, in the language of Saint Thomas, the superlatives and the negations used by Dionysius lose the color they had in their Oriental rhetoric, but his treatment of the "Divine Names" is not reduced to one of human grammar because of it. Nothing would be more deceiving and nothing more intellectually perverse than to move among these theological texts, and not all the while maintain oneself under the secret communicative action of the word of God and as under the spell of contemplation. The rational structures of these texts can be the same; the light that promotes them has first placed our mind within another world (8).

[2. Definitions]

Any sort of analysis, whether it is the psychologist's inductively-conducted type of observation or the theologian's critique that ends up in negation, tends to being condensed in a definition. The building up of a definition is one of the traits of the scholastic method, and it is one of the perfect types of articles found in the *Summa* of Saint Thomas. We have here an operation of a major kind, the manifold procedures of which we must now examine. It would be a task not lacking in difficulty, nor again one undertaken without naïveté, if one were to attempt to apportion the processes that Saint Thomas so spontaneously applies within the compass of the some 300 processes of construction, critique, and verification that Aristotle's commentators have counted in his art of definition (9). We shall only propose a few reflexions likely to provide fuller benefit from the reading of Saint Thomas's texts, as well as a reflexive understanding of them.

Let us note first of all that in his "hunting down" of definitions, Saint Thomas brings into play a combination of suppleness in procedure and of tenacious concern for exactness. To present in its *debita forma* [due form] an otherwise already exact and precise

---

b) ". . . unitur [ille] ei sicut omnino ignoto." *Ia Pars*, q. 12, a. 13, obj. 1. See also, *ibid.*, ad 1um; q. 84, a. 5, obj. 1; *I–IIae*, q. 3, a. 8, obj. 1. For Dionysius, see *Theologia mystica*, c. 1, in *Dion*, I (1937), 578.

8) It is not sufficient, therefore, to study the theory which Saint Thomas proposed concerning the theological work that is accomplished under the light of faith. It is, moreover, indispensable to observe the manner in which he actually—*in actu exercito*—worked out the elaboration of theological concepts. Once again his practice goes beyond his theory. Without his contemplative life, his theology would be only "so much straw."

9) Such is the evaluation made by the author of the *Nova Explanatio Topicorum Aristotelis*, Venice, 1559, 2. Such too, that of s. MAURUS (+ 1687), *Paraphrasis*, I (*Aristotelis Opera omnia quae exstant brevi paraphrasi . . .*, Ehrle ed., Paris, 1885).

definition is to fashion a work stamped with truth. Here is one of the notable cases of that technicalness we have said to be one of the traits of scholastic thought (10). As an example, let us bring in the case of justice (*IIa–IIae*, q. 58, a. 1). While he accepts as his own the authorized definitions, the one handed down by the jurists, the other by Aristotle, Saint Thomas devotes all his efforts at rebuilding them so that they be correctly understood, *ut recte intelligantur*. He operates in the same way when he is defining virtue (*Ia–IIae*, q. 55, a. 4), faith (*IIa–IIae*, q. 4, a. 1), (the Dionysian) hierarchy (*In II Sent.*, d. 9, q. 1, a. 1), and so on. "Explanations," of course, are necessary; they do not replace a definition worded in correct form, and to establish one is to prove one's self not only a good professor, but a good philosopher.

This hunting down of a definition begins with an analysis of the very names of the realities that are to be defined. The artfulness that shows up in these nominal definitions is a surprising one—surprising in its effectiveness as well as in the sometimes ingenuous foundations upon which it rests. The analysing of the various meanings of a word makes use of a capital amassed from observation or tradition. The critical handling of this capital is already, under modest appearances, a noteworthy achievement of intelligence. The latter should not be reduced to what is to be found in an ordinary Larousse dictionary; oftentimes the die has already been cast when the meaning from which a reasoning process has begun is indicated. The two sources of these various word meanings are etymology and common usage. Even when he accepts, like everybody else in his day, the famous etymological meanings set forth by Isodorus, Saint Thomas sees and oftentimes expresses what an assortment of resources can be supplied by these linguistic sources for *denominatio* [denomination] and, therefore, definition. We are here in the field of "Wordlogic" (*Sprachlogik*), that typical discipline which stands at the point of juncture between grammar and logic and in which the XIIth and XIIIth century masters were schooled (11).

"*Intention*, as implied in the sound of the name itself, signifies *to tend to something else* . . ." (a). "The name *mind* has been taken from the word *to measure* . . ." (b). "Properly speaking, *conscience* is not

---

10) See above, ch. I, 59ff.

11) Besides the general work of c. thurot, *Notices et extraits de divers manuscrits latins pour servir à l'histoire des doctrines grammaticales au moyen âge*, Paris, 1868, see f. manthey, *Die Sprachphilosophie des heiligen Thomas von Aquin und ihre Anwendung auf Probleme der Theologie*, Paderborn, 1937.

a) "*Intentio*, sicut ipsum nomen sonat, significat *in aliud tendere* . . ." *Ia–IIae*, q. 12, a. 1.

b) "*Nomen mentis a mensurando* est sumptum . . ." *De ver.*, q. 10, a. 1.

a power, but an act; and this is clear both from the formal meaning of the name and also from those things which, in the common way of speaking, are attributed to conscience . . ." (c). "Free-will, if the force of the word is taken into account, denotes an act, but through the use that has been made of it in language, it has been drawn to mean that which is the principle of an act . . ." (d). Thus, the *proprietas vocabuli* [proper meaning of a word], that precious quality through which words convey intelligibility *(ratio nominis)*, is either limited, confirmed, or corrected by usage (12). Since usage reveals their intended signification this is a richer source for their being understood than their original meaning can be. "The etymology of a word differs from its meaning. For its etymology depends on what it is taken from for the purpose of signification, whereas its meaning depends on the thing to which it is applied for the purpose of signifying it. Now these things "sometimes differ" (a) *(IIa–IIae*, q. 92, a. 1, ad 2um; see *ibid.,* q. 57, a. 1, ad 1um, wherein it is said that "It is usual for words to be distorted from their original signification so as to mean something else") (b).

Without going into an account of the methods of *denominatio* employed and pointed out by Saint Thomas in his elaboration and critical appraisal of definitions (13), let us call attention to the important procedure wherein the uses of a word are classified and end up in a determination of the word's proper meaning. Thus, he arranges in orderly fashion the senses of the word *passio*, used in an extremely wide range of meanings in the various philosophies, and finally comes to the word's use *propriissime* [in its most proper sense], which defines the field of the various passions *(Ia Pars*, q. 79, a. 2; *Ia–IIae*, q. 22, a. 1; *De ver.,* q. 26, a.3). This procedure does not imply that the common meanings or the less proper meanings of a word are dis-

---

c) *"Conscientia,* proprie loquendo, non est potentia sed actus; et hoc patet tum ex ratione nominis, tum etiam ex his quae secundum communem usum loquendi conscientiae attribuuntur . . ." *Ia Pars,* q. 79, a. 13.

d) *"Liberum arbitrium,* si vis vocabuli attendatur, nominat actum; sed ex usu loquendi tractum est ut significet id quod est principium actus . . ." *De ver.,* q. 24, a. 4.

12) Even in the dogmatic formulae, the *usus loquentium* [the usual meaning of those using the word] with its practical requirements takes precedence over the *veritas significationis* [true meaning]. See *In I Sent.,* d. 23, q. 1, a. 1, ad 5um; *Ia Pars,* q. 36, a. 1.

a) ". . . aliud est etymologia nominis, et aliud est significatio nominis. Etymologia attenditur secundum id a quo imponitur nomen ad significandum; nominis vero significatio attenditur secundum id ad quod significandum nomen imponitur."

b) ". . . consuetum est quod nomina a sui prima impositione detorqueantur ad alia significanda."

13) A first classification of it is given in L. SCHÜTZ, *Thomas–Lexicon,* 2d ed., Paderborn, 1895 (photomechanically reproduced at New York, 1949, and at Stuttgart, 1958). See the word *Denominatio.*

carded as not belonging to the field of true knowledge; they also reveal a portion of the intelligibility in things.

In principle, there is only one definition of an object. This is the one wherein the defined object's essential properties, its quiddity, have been adequately expressed. An object, however, can be exactly, if not totally, defined either by one of its properties, or by one of its causes, or by one of its principles (14). De facto, Saint Thomas draws up his definitions by determining either a thing's proximate genus and specific difference—this is the perfect, but rarely achieved, type of definition—or its four causes (for example, his definition of virtue, *Ia–IIae*, q. 55, a. 4), or the elements that serve as a thing's principles (for example, his definition of faith, *IIa–IIae*, q. 4, a.1), or a thing's sole formal or final cause (see his gloss on Aristotle's famous text in which the definition of a house is given: *De an.*, I, 1, 403a30), or finally the properties from which one ascends to the essence of a thing as from an effect to its cause (for example, any passage wherein he defines the soul) (15).

In all these cases, one should, for the benefit of doctrinal insight itself, closely examine the steps that are taken one after another as the methods for discovering and verifying definitions are being applied. Among them, the method of division stands out in the opinion of Saint Thomas (16) as being the most adapted one (for instance, amongst the various acts of assent, the case of the act of faith in *IIa–IIae*, q. 2, a. 1). In Saint Thomas, however, as in Aristotle himself, one will note that there is a wide margin—one of relativism and of vital flexibility—between his theory concerning the laws of definition and his actual application of them (17).

[3. Images]

Let us add to this compass of the methods of analysis, and contrasting with the techniques of definition, the use made of comparisons and metaphors. It is a pretty well known fact that, except for a few slight differences, following in the pattern set by Aristotle's principles, and probably because his genius was related to that of the Stagirite, Saint Thomas considers imaginative procedures as very

---

14) "Since, in certain definitions, some principles are posited, and not the others, hence it happens that definitions of one and the same thing vary." *In III Sent.*, d. 23, q. 2, a. 1, ad 8um (written about the multiple definitions of faith).

15) Thus, Saint Thomas is imitating Aristotle in his endeavor to define the soul and to justify his procedure (see *De an.*, I, 1, 402b16 ff.; Hett ed., in *LCL*, 1946, 12), although the method is not always decisive and does not teach how to discern the genus and the difference.

16) ". . . the method best suited for discovering definitions is the one done through divisions." *In III Phys.*, lect. 1; Marietti ed., 140, n. 279.

17) See M.–D. ROLAND–GOSSELIN, *Les méthodes de la définition d'après Aristote,*

in *RSPT*, VI (1912), 236–252, 661–675.

inferior resources where the philosopher's work is concerned (18). This is why he criticizes the method and the style of Plato who is always expressing himself in figures and symbols (19); why, also, he underscores the difficulty one meets in interpreting the texts of Dionysius who makes use of the Platonic method and style (20). Even if he had not made reference to these imposing personages, however, he undoubtedly would still be tempted to consider the use of images as nothing more than an artifice giving the appearance of truth and as conducive to illusion. In point of fact, it does not seem that Saint Thomas was blessed with an imagination endowed with the quality of creativeness for this type of figurative expression; in his works one finds nothing that would reflect the outside world in which he lived. His temperament was in keeping with the principle upon which he founded his censure of the imaginative process. In contrast with a Bonaventure, for instance, he is, within the School, the master whose genius is the most divested of literary trappings. His power is elsewhere—let us not hide its limitations; it resides in that utter soberness and unemotional objectivity sought by the pure light of intelligence. It is in this manner that a diamond is cut. No doubt if looked for, an original image could be found coming forth from his pen (21). In the majority of cases, however, it is from the sources of his thought, especially the religious ones, that he borrows comparisons and metaphors, analogies and symbols. Would it be possible, indeed, for a theologian to break away completely from the evangelical style? The reader of Augustine and of Dionysius cannot, for sure, empty their wondrous images of the true spiritual riches they contain and which it is perhaps impossible to conceptualize. As a result, it is the method of image treatment that then takes on interest, and, one could say, the stripping of them rather than their splendor.

---

18) He quotes without contradicting it—locating it all the while front to the metaphorical language of revelation—the following statement of Aristotle: "Proceeding by means of various resemblances and figures is proper to poetic, the weakest among all the methods of learning." *Ia Pars*, q. 1, a. 9, obj. 1.

19) "Plato's method of teaching was a poor one, for he proposed everything in figures and by the aid of symbols, having words mean something else than what they themselves convey, as when he called the soul a circle." *In I De an.*, lect. 8; Marietti ed., 31, n. 107; Foster–Humphries ed., 107.

20) "In the afore-mentioned books, difficulty arises from a number of sources; and first from the fact that most often he uses the style and manner of speaking that was employed by the Platonists, which style is unusual among the moderns." *In De div. nom.*, prooem.; Marietti ed., 1.

21) Should the following texts be interpreted as expressing original images? *Ia–IIae*, q. 63, a. 1: ". . . as when iron is made bright by being polished"; *Ia Pars*, q. 55, a. 3, ad 3um (written about the particular kinds of prudence which are limited to their objects): ". . . that prudence which is in the lion, leading to acts of magnanimity, and that which is in the fox, leading to acts of wariness." See other similar texts.

Here are some of the classical images Saint Thomas employs:

the image of movement and rest as figures of *ratio* and *intellectus* (*De ver.*, q. 15, a. 1; *Ia Pars*, q. 79, a. 8), or in an abbreviated form, the pursuing of a course portraying the work accomplished by the mind in its searching out of causes (this image is from Isaac of Stella);

the image of the point and the line, the latter as virtually contained in the point, or again that of light as containing the colors; both images as figures of the relationship that exists between divine essence and created beings (*De ver.*, q. 2, a. 4; *Ia Pars*, q. 14, a. 6; in the ad 4um of the *De veritate* article, there is an extensive critique made about the comparison founded on colors);

the image of circular movement as a figure of contemplation (we have here the famous Dionysian image; see *IIa–IIae*, q. 180, a. 6);

the image of seeing as in a mirror, used in the analysis of the intellectual knowledge of the singular as present in the phantasm and founded upon the continuity that exists between intelligence and imagination;

the image of the sun and its rays, a Dionysian image par excellence, illustrating and supporting the notion of participation (*In II Sent.*, prol.), but also calling for a rigorous distinguishing as to the way this image can be used (*In I Sent.*, d. 43, q. 2, a. 1, ad 1um; *In De div. nom.*, c. 4, lect. 1; *De pot.*, q. 3, a. 15, ad 1um; *Ia Pars*, q. 19, a. 4, ad 1um; etc);

the image of art and the artist, a comparison so often utilized to support the analysis of divine action (*Ia Pars*, q. 44, a. 3; and many other passages).

Then there is that whole train of images picturing love, utilized, for instance, in attempting to seize the mystery of the Holy Spirit. In each and every one, an effort, oftentimes an exacting effort, is made at purifying the image, with the result that the latter becomes the victim of the very office it is called upon to render.

The image most frequently recurring, because the most spontaneously arising, is the analogy of light used in describing intelligence. The latter is οἷον τὸ φῶς [like a light], to use the words of Aristotle (22). There is nothing original in this image if one considers it in its primitive state for it represents an inheritance that men of all civilizations have drawn from. The manner, however, in which philosophers avail themselves of its resources varies in the extreme. Aristotle, Augustine, Dionysius, Avicenna discover these resources each according to the horizon of his own insight, while the Christian

---

22) ARISTOTLE, *De an.*, III, 5, 430a16; Hett. ed., in *LCL*, 1946, 170.

Middle Ages increase their action twofold in the case of the "light" of faith (23). Things are carried to the point at which this image finally becomes entirely conceptualized, with the result that, henceforth in philosophic parlance, the word itself refers directly to that which was compared to it. The word no longer implies a metaphor; *de plano* [outright], it designates the mind (24). Such a devoiding of the figurative power of words is the normal and accepted outcome of Saint Thomas's philosophical style (25).

In theology, however, certain analogies, even after having undergone the process of intellectualization, play an inspirational and constructional role, broad in its importance. For example, the image of the sacrament conceived of as a remedy, a Christian theme if ever there was one, was, during the XIIth century, and is, in effect, the factor directing a whole way of conceiving the economy of the sacraments. It is of great importance to see in what manner Saint Thomas deals with it. His thought is to reduce the concepts issuing from it and the images branching out from it to a more comprehensive view of the sacramental order, without, on this account weakening the evangelical inspiration of the image in the process. The image of ransom, which is biblical in its origin, but with juridic elements appearing in its framework, undergoes in the same manner an extremely penetrating critical analysis.

It has been justly observed that an attentive examination of the images employed by Saint Thomas would open the way to a genuine deeper penetration into the understanding of his thought. This is an indication, therefore, that these images should be reinvestigated, imagined anew, in line with the outlook customary to the medieval mind; that they should be followed up in their refined, suppled, interknit forms; that they should be freed from elements alien to what they would convey; that they be dematerialized. It is the pursuing of ideas through conceptual discourse that is always occurring anew, even when one would think one had finally reached the intuition of a thing over and beyond the glimmer of the image employed (26).

---

23) One can obtain a first idea of the flourishing of this image's uses by going over L. SCHÜTZ's classification of them, in his *Thomas–Lexicon* referred to above (note 13), at the words *lumen, lux.*

24) "If, then, the word 'light' is taken in the sense that was first given to it, its meaning when applied to spiritual objects is a metaphorical one, but if it is taken, as in the common usage, to extend to any kind of manifesting, then its application to spiritual objects is a proper one." *Ia Pars,* q. 67, a. 1.

25) Examples of such metaphor intellectualizing are not lacking, for instance: *reflexio* [reflexion], *continuatio* [continuation], *reditio* [coming back], *circulatio* [circulation], and so on.

26) See the suggestive notes of J. WÉBERT, *L'image dans l'oeuvre de S. Thomas et spécialement dans l'exposé doctrinal sur l'intelligence humaine,* in RT, XXXI (1926), 427–445.

IV. DISTINCTIONS

There would seem to be no reason for treating the technique of distinctions apart from that of analysis, since distinguishing is the tool usually utilized whenever analysis, in any of its forms, is undertaken. However, even if the *distinguo* [I distinguish] is a normal procedure employed by reason and a condition for the mind's achieving precision, it is nevertheless a fact that this procedure is justly considered a characteristic trait of scholasticism. In point of fact, in Saint Thomas as well as in the thinkers of the entire School, the practice of distinguishing is a constant one. There are articles that are expressly built on an *Uno modo . . . Alio modo . . .* [This can be considered in two ways: in one way . . .; in another way . . .]. Objections are answered in such a manner that the full significance of the solution offered in the body of the article is almost always weighed through a distinction. Finally, within the very tissues of the reasoning processes, one finds terms and propositions narrowed down in their meaning by means of distinctions.

Let us abandon to their fate the excesses of the low Scholastics who replaced by formalism even the soundest form of analysis. It remains that, exploited as it was within an art of thinking, the art of distinguishing is revealing of a philosophy, or to put it in a better way, is revealing of a well-defined philosophic turn of mind. One can become aware of this by lining up a comparison between this method and Augustine's. With the latter, things are not primarily distinct from one another; they are linked up in an intricate system of relationships, interlocks, analogies, and even of symbols. They are, like sounds, calling one after another. Unity, rather than distinction, is the factor governing them. When sought after to excess, the distinguishing procedure would end up dislocating reality. Augustine's is a philosophy of participation wherein attention is focused on beings in their "degrees" rather than in their autonomy, in the exemplary reasons according to which they are fashioned rather than in the internal causes that explain them.

Scholastic logic, on the other hand, is one concerned with the determining and the identifying of things. Its main work is to arrive at a definition prepared or established through the apparatus of distinctions. To experience the difference, one need only examine the treatment that the Augustine-styled texts undergo in Saint Thomas's exegesis of them. Thought is decanted and a scientific quality is achieved, but to the detriment of the spiritual and even literary *aura* that expanded their immediate signification. It is with this in mind and putting all of one's acumen, and respect as well, to the task that one should read anew those *Disputed Questions* that are so Augustinian in their substance: the *De mente (De ver.,* q. 10), the *De magistro* (q. 11), the *De superiori et inferiori ratione* (q. 15) (27). It is not just a question of precise but inadequate formulations given to a thought still remaining primitive in its very richness—as some scholastics, not without disdain for Augustine, sometimes appear to assert. It is, without doubt, a question of a mental attitude that has built up its own methods of analyzing reality. Abelard was the first master to be aware of this, and with his *Sic et Non,* he remained the protagonist in the art of distinguishing. With the re-appearance of Aristotle, this art was provided with all the resources needed to make it a lofty science of the mind. The French word *subtilité* [subtlety] has acquired—and blame the low scholastics for it—a meaning ringing of the pejorative, but in the language of the Medievals, the word *subtilis* [subtle] referred to a neat quality of the mind.

Subtilis. This epithet traditionally describes Duns Scotus. This fact gives us the opportunity of measuring just how far-reaching distinctions can be within a medieval system of thought. If Scotus is subtle, it is no doubt because, in connection with the philosophical and theological techniques used during the Middle Ages, he was the author of the *distinctio formalis a parte rei* [formal distinction existing in things] and thus became the patron of the *formalizantes* [formalizers], that is, of those thinkers who discern, within the unity of a concrete reality, a number of *formalitates* [formalities], really distinct from one another and objectively existent. De facto, the system of Scotus can be said to rest upon, together with his theory of the univocity of being, his famous formal distinction. When the Thomists rejected it, maintaining that there were only those distinctions which Saint Thomas had known (the real distinction and the distinction of reason), they revealed the importance that a type of analysis and of abstraction assumes in the structuring of psychology and metaphysics.

The scope of a distinction will also be measured by observing its repercussions in the elaboration and the balance of a system. While, for instance, Aristotle's paramount distinction between substance and accidents dominates his philosophy, Saint Thomas by going deeper into the matter with his distinction between essence and existence

---

27) The same should be done with the texts in which Saint Thomas subjects to distinctions Augustine's stamped-in-metal statements; for instance, Augustine's *omnis virtus est amor* [all virtue is love], in *Ia–IIae,* q. 56, a. 3, ad 1um, or again, his *Deus est bonum omnis boni* [God is the good of all good], in *De ver.,* q. 21, a. 4, ad 3um.

By examining, moreover, how Augustine united a dialectics of purification, *exercitatio animi* [exercizing of the mind] with dialectics as a method of creative work (see H.-I. MARROU, *S. Augustin et la fin de la culture antique,* 2d ed., in *BEFAR,* CXLV (1949), 308–327), one will be in a better position to grasp the characteristics of the dialectics used by Saint Thomas.

has modified not only the categorial scheme but the very soul of metaphysics as well. In psychology, the Aristotelian distinction between what is more knowable *in itself* and what is more knowable *for us*—developed by Saint Thomas through his analysis of the *modus intelligendi* [mode of knowing] proper to man within the hierarchy of spiritual beings—becomes the ordering principle of his noetics, and beyond this, the factor explaining the very possibility of a supernatural order.

Similarly, with the help of a correct distinction, Saint Thomas gives another twist to a problem or gently ruins an adverse position. The center-line of Augustine's theology of concupiscence undergoes a complete shift of position when a distinction is brought in whereby it is given a "material", and not a "formal" role in original sin (*Ia–IIae*, q. 82, a. 3). In another instance, Saint Thomas holds that the soul of man knows all things in the *rationes aeternae* [eternal reasons], but in the sense that they are the principle of knowledge and not the object known. As a result, it is Aristotle and all his experimentalism that come on the scene replacing Augustine and his Platonism (*Ia Pars*, q. 84, a. 5).

Let us bring this section to a close by making a few observations on this art of distinguishing.

The XIIIth century masters rather rarely avail themselves of those distinctions that can be drawn from the broad categories of logic, for example: *per se . . . per accidens* [in itself . . . by accident], *materialiter . . . formaliter* [materially speaking . . . formally speaking], *in genere . . . in specie* [generically . . . specifically], and others of the same kind. These distinctions, if used as passkeys, would be no more than the clichés of a pure formalism. Albert the Great oftentimes gives vent to his anger against those who, in explaining the realities of nature, would rely on the commonplaces of logic rather than on their proper causes (28). One should, therefore, look for the physical and psychological realism that is the basis upon which distinctions are founded and through which the conditions of a sound and effective use of them are guaranteed. Picking at random an illustration from a reading of Saint Thomas, we can mention those texts wherein he analyses the limits of one's consciousness regarding one's possession of charity (this he does when he is answering, in the form of dis-

---

28) "Extraneous we call those reasons that come from common principles and which, found in many, are proper to none, such as are logical reasons" (*In IV Phys.*, tr. 3, c. 1, in *AMOO*, III (1890), 305). "They made no other investigation about things except a logical one. . . . For my part, I abhor such conclusions based on logic in the sciences that deal with things" (*In I Metaph.*, tr. 1, c. 2, in *AMOO*, VI (1890), 6b; in Col. ed., XVI, 1 (1960), 5a).

tinctions, the objections which open article 10 of *De ver.*, q. 10. Note, however, the dialectical character of the distinction brought forth in the 8th answer, wherein it is just a question of unraveling a pun). In the Third Part of the *Summa* (q. 64, a. 3), there is offered an admirable piece of textual architexture wherein the most realistic spirituality spontaneously issues from the distinctions brought forth in the analysis of the Christological character of the sacramental regime.

Under penalty of grave misinterpretation, distinctions must be examined and maintained within the perspective and the context in which they were worked out. Even more care must be taken not to allocate them within a sort of classification wherein bracketing becomes all the more worthless as its use is multiplied. Subdistinctions are rare, and they are valuable only inasmuch as the original distinction has already hit upon the formal elements of the reality undergoing scrutiny. The necessity of all this is linked with the most rigorous laws that govern the mind as it goes about doing its work of definition and division.

One should likewise maintain distinctions in the authentic state they had when they were first proferred. The partitioning of concepts under the threefold heading of univocal, equivocal, analogous, is not without some weakening of the original analysis wherein a distinction was made between two categories: the univocal and the equivocal, with a further discerning between equivocity *a casu* [by chance] and ἀναλόγως [by analogy]. Classifying the types of Christian contemplation as being either intellectual (as in theology), or acquired (as in meditation), or infused (as in the passive states issuing from the gifts of the Holy Spirit), is to make use of distinctions that are clumsy and alien to the language and thought of Saint Thomas.

In any case, the exegete should not succumb to the temptation of dwelling upon the distinction which he is analyzing, as if this distinction represented his own or his author's final effort. Rather should he re-unite its divided elements in order to recover, in its concrete unity, the reality that a necessary, valid, but temporary, abstraction has broken up. The benefit of clearness begotten of this abstraction will be decisively attained only inasmuch as a return is made to this synthetic unity. "Distinguish to unite" (29).

---

29) It is well known that this is the title which J. MARITAIN, to express his way of thinking, placed at the head of one of his works, *Les degrés du savoir,* 4th ed., Paris, 1946 [trans. under the title: *Distinguish to Unite or The Degrees of Knowledge,* under the supervision of G. B. PHELAN, New York, 1959].

V. THE DISCURSIVE ACTIVITIES OF REASON

[1. Proofs]

Cursus causae in causatum [the progress of a cause toward its effect]: this phrase coined by the Xth century Jewish philosopher, Isaac Israeli, is taken over by Saint Thomas. Through the metaphor it contains, he expresses, as does the author of it, the movement taking place within an intelligence that is incarnate in matter and is, therefore, at one with time and space. Reason is the name of this type of intelligence compelled to act by means of a *dis-cursus* [dis-course] (30). Every one of the operations we have just analysed, from the operation of simple description to that of perfect definition, is accomplished and can be accomplished only by means of this "course" from one intelligible to another. Any attempt at observing how, in Saint Thomas, the discursive understanding of things actually works would be an enterprise without end. Moreover, attempting a rigorous classification—even if done by recourse to Aristotle—of the various forms of this discursive procedure would be an artificial undertaking. Once again, therefore, while remaining within the bounds of discretion as far as uncovering theoretical schemas in Saint Thomas's style of thought is concerned, our task will be one of noticing its extreme mobility, which shows up everywhere from the dialectical question right up to the demonstration of science.

". . . from the dialectical question right up to the demonstration of science. . . ." Ponder each one of the extremes herein expressed: the one, at the very beginning of mind's awakening to a problem where her approach to it is by means of a first *sic et non;* the other, at the end of mind's acquiring her weighty and definite certainties. Between these extremes, the field is vast, with an abundance of forms of expression showing up in it. All of them generate inferences that lead the mind on from one position to another; all combine in different ways (31), συλ–λογοι, in which the syllogism, whether dialectical or scientific, furnishes the most organic type. It would be of little interest, however, to limit ourselves to a sort of formal analysis of Saint Thomas's reasoning processes, ranging from the enthymeme or

---

30) "*Reason* designates a certain 'dis-course,' by means of which the human soul attains to or arrives at an object to be known by going from one known object to another. Hence, ISAAC, in his book *On definitions*, states that reasoning is the progress of a cause to its effect." *De ver.,* q. 15, a. 1. See *In De trin.,* q. 6, a. 1, corp., ad 1am q., Decker ed., 206: "It is proper to reason . . . to discourse from one to another."

31) "For it is proper to reason to branch out on many objects, and to gather therefrom one single piece of knowledge." *In De trin.,* q. 6, a. 1, corp., ad 3am q.; Decker ed., 211.

abbreviated syllogism to the sorites or to the dilemma (32). Rather, we wish to look into the intellectual tonality present in these procedures and thus obtain experience in perceiving the ultimate coherence that exists between the truth of established conclusions and the fulness of the mind that produces them. To repeat, the articles of the *Summa* are not just so many little inert blocks, they are the expression of a thinking mind gradually bringing out the intelligibleness that springs out of things (a).

This course of the mind from one intelligible object to another covers more or less ground. It may be a simple matter of unfolding a concept and making it more explicit, but it may also be a matter reaching as far as demonstration itself, wherein from two pre-known truths a third effectually follows. The latter, indeed, is the creative operation of that knowledge called science, in which mind discovers the necessary connections present in the nature of things and obtains a total explanation of their properties. It can be foreseen that so lofty an ideal, in which Greek rationalism in its entirety has been inserted, will not be realized in each article of the *Summa*. Neither the objects call for it, nor does the life of the mind have the need of it. Even in those articles where the deductive form of reasoning is preserved—and this does not happen so very frequently—we are far from having in each instance a syllogism that deals with a necessary object and is productive of science. Let us not conceive the steps taken by Saint Thomas as if they were all shaped on the prototype found in the *Analytics;* let us rather see in them an application of all those resources described in Aristotle's *Topics* as being an art of invention and of discussion. That author was right who recently vindicated the role played by *opinion* in Aristotle's epistemology (33). The probabilism of the casuists, moreover, should not be allowed to cast discredit upon "probable" knowledge, one that shows up so valuable in the ordinary course of thinking, and the only one conceivable in certain vast domains of thought.

The first effort to be made, therefore, must be one of discerning within the uniformity of reasoning structures—and guarding against the temptation of putting everything in the same boat—the proper understanding and certitude procured by this or that piece of reasoning. This discerning, quite evidently, must take into account the two great types of demonstration: demonstration *propter quid* [by cause]

---

32) We would, however, be very tempted to observe how, in practice, Saint Thomas deals with those "straight, circular, oblique" movements that the Christian neo-Platonists had recognized as present in the life of the mind, after the fashion, as it were, of these movements of place. See *IIa–IIae*, q. 180, a. 6. Saint Thomas was not solely a practitioner of the *Topics* and *Analytics*.

a) See above, 93–96.

33) See L.–M. RÉGIS, *L'opinion selon Aristote*, in *PIEM*, V (1935).

and demonstration *quia* [by effect]. The demonstration of the immortality of man's soul has neither the same structure, nor the same tonality, nor, in the end, the same evidence as does the demonstration of the union in one substance of soul and body. (The proof of this lies in the fact that the two demonstrations face in opposite directions when they are placed in relation with the dynamics of the pristine Aristotelianism, which furnishes to the second its governing principles while it places a hindrance upon the first.) The dialectics of beatitude (*Cont. Gent.*, III, c. 25–48 and *Ia–IIae*, q. 2, a. 1–8) unfolds from starting points and with overtones differing greatly from the physical foundations and the speculative steps from which the five proofs of God's existence take their departure. The analysis of transcendentals such as true (*De ver.*, q. 1, a. 1) or of good (*ibid.*, q. 21, a 1) cannot be broken down to the form of a correct syllogism.

It is no less important to examine what lies beneath and supports the premisses—especially the major premiss. It oftentimes happens that the intelligible content in them is derived from adopted, yet hardly explicit, positions, and also at times simply from axioms (see below, 186–188). The intellectualistic theses concerning beatitude (*Ia–IIae*, q. 3, a. 4), or about the nature of the act of *imperium* [command] (*ibid.*, q. 17, a. 1), are backed up with formal demonstrations. Yet underlying them is implied a certain conception of mind, a certain understanding of human conduct, from which the major premiss in these demonstrations receives its depth of meaning but which supporters of the voluntaristic position are unable to penetrate. He who does not willingly ponder these underlying resources condemns himself to perceiving in these proofs only their carcass, not their inner light.

If it is true that demonstration draws its entire forcefulness from the discovering of a "proper cause" through "proper principles" (*I Post Anal.*, 2, 71b9–11), then it follows that the reader should devote his efforts to unearthing in the texts the manner in which this discovering is achieved. Rarely is this ideal schema of demonstration realized. More often than not, the apparatus used in demonstrating extends through a number of arguments drawn up through recourse to the various aspects of the objects involved, and unfolding either in a simple sequence of them or in a manner meant to achieve their convergence. When such is the case, one should ascertain, through an exact determination of the principles from which they start, what value the individual arguments have and how they are brought to mesh together. The bounty of examples to be culled testifies to the complexness of even the smallest problem.

Serviceable in achieving the aforementioned discerning are the multifarious arguments brought forward to establish a proof, which one should not forego using by comparing them, either in parallel works, or in their immediate contexts. Thus for the proof of the unicity of God: the most simple exposition of it is given in question 11, a. 3 of the *Ia Pars*, but various, even complicated, forms of it are presented in the first book of the *Summa contra Gentiles*, in chapter 42. In the *De ente et essentia*, the real distinction between essence and existence is demonstrated through proofs initiating from different elements, and in some instances, through secondary channels of thought. One should neither give up when only one argument is given nor take delight in a compilation of arguments. In any case, one should respect the formal value of arguments even if it is only a relative one. A Saint Augustine, or, in Saint Thomas's day, a Bonaventure, readily goes into reasoning arrangements that are disconcerting, into arguments that are parasitic, using literary forms that are completely different, with each one having its own value and its own role. No one of them should be interpreted as compromising the other, for the very spirit of their authors and users would then be affected. Let us foster within ourselves apprehension lest the genius of such thinkers be levelled off through academic treatment.

Among the various types of demonstration an altogether original place must be allowed for those wherein internal structuring is peculiar to a certain metaphysical way of proceeding, such as in the proving of the existence of a perfect being through an inequality in the degrees of being. A dialectic of this sort, which stands at the summit of a metaphysics of participation, can no doubt find expression in the form of a syllogism. In reality, mind is here performing in a more simple and concentrated way, for here we are touching upon that point at which man's intelligence is formally functioning as a properly transcendent nature, no longer as simply a reasoning intellect (34).

This brings us to evoking, as opposed to the type of demonstration wherein a step-by-step advance through an intelligible field is recorded, those syllogisms that are purely expository in character. These, in reality, are much more "displayings" of an intelligibility that is already there. In them, progression is marked, not so much in the order of a perception of the steps that are taken, even if some amount of

---

34) See the observation and the analyses of L.-B. GEIGER, *La participation dans la philosophie de S. Thomas d'Aquin*, 2d ed., in *BibTh*, XXIII (1953), 353–355. On 355, the author adds: "Furthermore, this manner of proceeding is peculiar from another aspect, inasmuch as it is a point of departure which never reaches the point of fulfillment. It has always to be begun anew, and it is never so truly what it should be than when it creates in us the conviction both of its necessity and of its inevitable imperfection. It is a setting out on a journey which on this earth will never attain to repose in full possession." This could not be stated better, nor can one insist too much on the character of this work which reason carries on *within* the "mystery."

pleasure is shown in the displaying of them, as in the order of a becoming aware of a reality that was present right from the beginning. In these instances, Saint Thomas is proceeding in the manner of the Platonic-type thinkers, of a Plotinus, an Augustine. Aristotle is no longer his master in logic.

The questions that are inspired by a formal *sic et non* are not always brought to a solution through demonstrations. Due to the most diversified of reasons the first of which is that the objects undergoing study do not require a demonstration, more often than not arguments and their conclusions remain within the limits of the probable (in the Aristotelian sense of the word). The latter is a vast, a variegated domain in which, seemingly, the mind should feel ill at ease, but in which, in reality, the mind proves her true keenness and her finest balance. Let us grant that we have a sign of this in the case of Saint Thomas (35), of Saint Thomas the theologian especially. If, in fact, there is a knowledge in which objects do not always require a demonstration, it is really that of theology in which the objects of the entire Christian economy are subject to the pleasure of the Divine will and not governed by some internal necessity. As a matter of fact, each treatise: on Christ, on the supernatural in man, on the sacraments, begins, in each phase of its development, with a so-called argument "by the appropriate." This sort of argument does perhaps mold itself upon the syllogism, but it would be very naive to go along with its syllogistic form without measuring both the compactness and the type of intelligibility of which this argument admits (36). As regards the mystery of God Himself, Whom no contingence touches upon, then

35) As a matter of fact, his conduct in things intellectual is only the putting in practice of the most explicit principles of his methodology, starting with the famous Boethian axiom he comments upon: "It appertains to the educated man to attempt obtaining a belief on each thing in accordance with what it is" (*In De trin.*, lect. 2 and q. 6; and passim). And let us not forget his comments on the relativism implied in everyone's personal quest of truth: *In II Metaph.*, lect. 5 (Marietti ed., 93, n. 334; Rowan ed., 135), on ARISTOTLE, *Ibid.*, II, 3, 995a8–12 (H. Tredennick ed., vol. I, in *LCL*, 1933, 94).

36) As a consequence, one must preserve, in the intelligible categories serving to build it up and presented, in syllogisms, as the major premiss of arguments, the irreducibly original character of the Christian fact (the Christological, the anthropological, the sacramental fact). See M. J. CONGAR, article *Theologie*, in *DTC*, XV, 1 (1946), col. 354–355, 391–392.

Likewise, one must not be satisfied with unfolding what is implied in a definition; one should rather bring together, in readiness and willingness of mind, the data that Christian thought has transmitted and meditated upon. The latter are the regulative factors at work beneath the dialectical apparatus. Saint Thomas, for instance, does not "deduce" the concrete conditions of the divine missions from a definition of them (*Ia Pars*, q. 43, a. 3). See the "Technical Indications" supplied by H. DONDAINE, in his trans. of *Somme théologique. La Trinité*, Revue des Jeunes ed., 2d ed., Paris–Tournai–Rome, 1950, II, 432.

it is the very transcendency of the object itself—over and beyond the relationships implied in the facts of creation and redemption—that strikes our intelligence with absolute impotency and forces it to build, within faith, nothing more than arguments by the appropriate: ". . . a reason is introduced, not as furnishing a sufficient proof of a principle, but as confirming an already established principle, by showing the congruity of its results . . ." (a).

It is impossible to reduce to the Aristotelian categories and criteria these "arguments by the appropriate" used by the medieval masters (Aristotle would not have treated them without contempt). The two broad classes in the field of opinion are the contingence of objects and faith in authority—not to speak of the role of δόξα [opinion] in passing a judgment of existence on material beings. These classes, by the intervening of the revealed transcendent object, have in each case, right within their deeper spiritual reaches, been rent asunder far too much not to be strained over and beyond the limits of their original competency. The very soil of these two processes of argumentation is different. Notwithstanding their similar underlying techniques, therefore, their sap rises and their fruits ripen within an altogether different climate of intelligibility. The "necessary reason" for the fact of the Incarnation, to use the words of Saint Anselm (b), develops human resonances that set off, for understanding both the nature of man and the mystery of his destiny, illuminating powers having more value than the surest geometrical patterns conceived by the mind. Let us perceive with satisfaction to what depth (and not to what virtuosity) Saint Thomas penetrates in discovering, ordering, dressing up these internal suitabilities which he unfolds concerning all of the episodes of the Christian economy. Indeed, therein is a fruit of that true contemplation implied at the very roots of theological science. Anyone scamping all this and pursuing in subtle distinctions what is rational in the mysteries, would be proceeding in a direction opposed to true theology as well as to the real work accomplished by Saint Thomas in his thinking.

Suitabilities do not thereby become less rational. How delicately balanced everything comes out! There are seven sacraments. This is the fact, one to which the searching theologians have just recently been awakened and that the Lateran Council of 1215 has explicitly formulated into a dogma. Now, this fact is a datum in the raw, one that a traditional positivistic theology would be content to record, for there is so little "reason" to put down at seven the number of symbols

---

a) ". . . inducitur ratio, non quae sufficienter probet radicem, sed quae radici jam positae ostendat congruere consequentes effectus." *Ia Pars*, q. 32, a. 1, ad 2um.

b) See above, ch. I, 61, note b.

that efficaciously produce grace—unless one dawdle in treating seven as a sacred number. Yet reasons there are! In the course of a man's life and in the building up of a Christian community, there are seven constitutional (if we may so speak) circumstances in which the grace of Christ must take hold of a man in order to divinize him in those points upon which his life hinges (read *IIIa Pars*, q. 65, a. 1). And to measure the intelligibility present in the argument brought forward by Saint Thomas, compare it with that other suitability which his predecessors, Albert and Bonaventure, and the others since Hugh of Saint Victor, abide by, seeing in the seven sacraments the seven cures for the seven characteristic sins. In their case, the sacramental economy is one of reparation, while for Saint Thomas it is over and beyond reparation, a framework designed to promote divine life within the make-up of man as a person and as a member of the community. His is a theological intuition ranging afar, and with consequential effects extending to the least *ad 3um* in his treatise on the sacraments.

Another example may be taken, this time not from the cycle to which the fact of Incarnation belongs but from the cycle of the mystery of God's nature wherein eternal necessity prevails. God thinks Himself in the production of a word; God engenders a son; God is not outside the metaphysical laws of love; and so forth. These are universal laws of the mind brought in these cases to the supreme degree of their effectiveness, thus rendering for us the mystery of divine life not only acceptable but harmonious, not only harmonious but intelligible and organic. Richard of Saint Victor had reveled in harmonies of this sort, and Anselm had said of them that they were "necessary" (37). Thomas, more master of himself as he pushed further into the scope of concepts, reduced them to "manifestations"; in his words: *Congruunt rationes* [There are appropriate reasons]. Therein lies a type of "proof" differing entirely from demonstration, not a demonstration shorn of its value through the application of it to mystery. The mind remains in disproportion with mystery, but once mystery is posited many an inferred particular comes to the fore (here, for instance: To think is to bring forth a word) revealing itself verified in a matchless prototype when applied to God in his Trinity. Anyone having failed to perceive this has never been in communion with the grand theological realization of Saint Thomas and of his like.

In an entirely different order, there is no necessary link in the "demonstration" that over and beyond the virtues and within the economy of grace in us there are gifts that are granted us. Even more than this, the revealed datum furnishes us with only meager bits of information that would start the mind searching on the subject. Yet,

---

37) See RICHARD OF SAINT VICTOR, *De Trinitate*, prol.; *P.L.* 196, 890 A–D, and for SAINT ANSELM, *Monologion*, Schmitt ed., I (1946).

these meager beginnings are picked up through an observing of the dynamics present in all mental life, something that Aristotle had already brought to notice. Working from so powerful an analogy, the mind builds within the unity of spiritual life two specifically different types of habits and activities, namely: the virtues and the gifts (*Ia– IIae*, q. 68, a. 1).

It is not only in theology, however, that "arguments by the appropriate" are set to work. The knowledge of the universe and of man does not deem unsuitable recourse to these resources of understanding. These range from purely imagined, poetic, almost verbal, suitabilities right up to others so well in harmony with objects that reason allows herself to be led on to a cordial adherence to them. They should be pondered in fairness of mind. When Saint Thomas is establishing the existence of free choice, he does not proceed to do so through psychological analyzing or metaphysical reflecting on the nature of the mind; or to put it in a better way, he simply prepares the way for such modes of argumentation by presenting a comprehensive view of the world and the hierarchy of beings within it. The order of the universe calls for the presence of a category of beings that are gifted, at the summit of a series of increasingly worthy activities, with the capacity of acting by themselves by means of an internal judgment which they pass on their actions (*De ver.*, q. 24, a. 1). With the help of this procedure Saint Thomas oftentimes locates man and defines his condition as one of a nature composed of mind and matter, which lies at the point of juncture where two worlds meet (38).

The most typical case of this proof taken *ex ordine universi* [from the order of the universe] is the one that he brings forward in demonstrating his thesis that angels are specifically different from one another. When it is a question of individuals in a species, there is no essential order between them, a fact explained through the shortcomings of the inferior being which, metaphysically speaking, cannot be entered into an order. Yet if we go higher up in the scale of beings, a clear-cut order must prevail as we come closer to the principle of the universe. The angels, therefore, are species co-ordinated with

---

38) This analogy remains at times completely extraneous, as, for example, when he rests his thesis concerning the unicity of the power of free choice on the parallel between man-the-microcosm and the macrocosm (See *De ver.*, q. 24, a. 5, s.c.). It is quite often that the microcosm–macrocosm parallel influences the mental outlook of the Medievals: "The order of the parts in the microcosm or smaller world corresponds to the order of the parts in the larger world. But just as we see that, in the nature of the human body, above the heart which is warm and partakes of the nature of fire, there is posited the brain which is cold and partakes of the nature of water, so too in the larger world, above the sun and other warming bodies, there will have to be posited an aqueous nature." SAINT BONAVENTURE, *In II Sent.*, d. 14, pars 1, a. 1, q. 1, in BOO, II (1885), 336.

one another according as their being is more or less perfect, and no longer by some accidental element that they would share (*De spirit. creat.*, a. 8, *secunda ratio*). If one were to weigh this argumentation by strictly logical standards alone, one would find it loaded with gratuitous assertions; yet, through its being located within a Weltanschauung, it obtains scope and suggestive power.

Of greater interest for us and for the whole of theology is the famed "demonstration" according to which a supernatural order must of necessity exist if man is to achieve complete happiness. Prior to entering upon an analytical exegesis of it, one should measure the breadth of that metaphysical vision which Saint Thomas invites us to share with him (a). It is that of a well-ordered universe wherein every nature can attain to its own perfection only inasmuch as it is linked up with the nature immediately above it, and not through its internal powers alone (*IIa–IIae*, q. 2, a. 3). The laws governing this perfecting subalternation define both the gratuity and the coherence of the supernatural order, its appropriateness, as we say today.

Whether the procedure employed be one based upon analogy or upon an harmonious envisioning of the universe, arguments of this sort achieve value insomuch as they reveal over and beyond the external suitabilities first recognized in the beings under consideration their internal coherent structure. It is as far as this that one must push the inquiry into them, if a correct reading of the texts is to ensue. These arguments are then seen as leading to a true understanding of reality. In the end, and at least in principle, they would attain to the quality of a demonstration and to the good results deriving from the latter. For instance, when the (contingent) fact of creation and the (supercontingent) fact of Incarnation are placed within the setting of the Dionysian theme of participation, it becomes apparent that they are the offspring of supreme Good's riches. Thus again, if humanity be considered as a unique individual of whom we are the members, it then becomes logical that original sin should be transmitted to all of us (*Ia–IIae*, q. 81, a. 1). At recurring intervals, theologians are lured into the perilous situation wherein mystery is emptied of its mysteriousness. An attractive temptation indeed, wherein theological reasoning attains to its glory, and to its limits as well. Unfortunate the theologian who has not experienced it!

Should the use of the terms: *Necesse est* . . . [It is necessary that . . .], *Oportet* . . . [One must . . .], *Evidens ratio* . . . [An evident reason . . .], be considered as an indication of the thrust Saint Thomas assigns to these arguments? More often than not, he uses the adjective *conveniens* [appropriate], the meaning of which he oftentimes had

---

a) See J. H. WRIGHT, *The Order of the Universe in the Theology of St. Thomas Aquinas*, in AnGreg, LXXXIX (1957).

the occasion to define (See *Ia Pars,* q. 32, a. 1, as regards the cycle of the mystery of God, and *IIIa Pars.* q. 1, a. 2, as regards the cycle of the Incarnation). Here and there, however, the words *necesse* or *oportet* pass into his phrasing, but it is not necessary that the meaning of these expressions be pressed. The School was always haunted by Anselm's *necessariae rationes,* but the masters, like Anselm, upheld these bold conceptions and necessary relationships only within the realm of mystery wherein faith had led them.

2. Axioms

An argument's comprehensiveness in intellectual content has its source in the major premiss, or at least in the principle to which the argument refers as it goes on unfolding. If this is true, then emphasis must be laid upon those pieces of reasoning that are entirely regulated by and encompassed within propositions expressing a category of judgments that are very general in character, not demonstrable in final analysis, accepted for their intrinsic clearness, and expressed in abstract and imperative formulae giving an inkling of both the vast reaches to which they extend and their worth for the mind's understanding of things. *Supremum infimi attingit infimum supremi* [The highest in a lower order attains to the lowest in a higher order]; *Primum in unoquoque genere est causa omnium illius generis* [The first in any one order is the cause of all the others in the same order]; *In quolibet genere id quod maxime dicitur est principium aliorum* [In any given order, that which is said to be supreme is the principle of the others in the same order]; *Quidquid recipitur ad modum recipientis recipitur* [Whatever is received, is received after the fashion of the recipient]; *Ordo agentium respondet ordini finium* [Ordering in agents corresponds to ordering in ends]; and so on. What we have here are axioms (*dignitates* in the Latin translation of the Greek word; *communes animi conceptiones* [common conceptions of the mind] in the language of Boethius). They are the support and soul of many major texts of Saint Thomas and of many of his broad systematic perspectives.

These propositions, dressed in atomic formulations, run the gamut between the peremptory theorem, which is at one with the internal coherence of a system of thought, and the commonplace statement, more closely knit in words than scientifically effective. *Quidquid recipitur ad modum recipientis recipitur.* In neo-Platonic thought, this axiom was a fundamental law in the theory of participation employed to explain cosmic coming-into-being (See *In De causis,* prop. 12: *Causa est in causato per causati modum* [a cause is in the caused object after the fashion of the caused object]; see also *In De div. nom.,* c. 5, lect. 1). The same axiom, however, can also be a vague common sense statement applicable to any kind of recipient. The handling of an axiom is a delicate thing, therefore; all the more delicate that the precise meaning of it must be set forth, not as in the manner of a term being defined, but as in the case of a judgment. The meaning of a term is established by reference to other terms with the help of which it can be defined and thereafter singled out as having a given meaning, taking into account the part convention plays in any vocabulary. A proposition, on the other hand, expresses an act of judging wherein the mind commits herself. Her committing herself may be necessary only hypothetically. It is necessary that this or that proposition be accepted if this or that demonstration is to be carried out (this is the modern meaning of the word axiom, or again the case in scholastic arguing *ex suppositione* [from hypothesis]). This commitment can be an unqualified one, however, even if the proposition is not subject to demonstration. In this case, the commitment arises from a complex of perceptions controlling a systematic whole. Many of our medieval axioms have an evidently neo-Platonic coloring and origin; it is within the perspective of the system—the Dionysian system, for example—that they normally operate (39). To be sure, use of them can be made outside the system, but to avoid ambiguity the reasons for their being presented as imperative must be given and the points upon which their imperativeness has bearing, determined. Saint Thomas explains the genesis and dynamism of the hierarchy that exists in the powers of the soul through a recourse to the neo-Platonic axioms pertaining to the doctrine of emanation and to the theory of contact between hierarchical orders (*In I Sent.*, d. 3, q. 4, a. 3; *Ia Pars*, q. 77, a. 7; q. 78, a. 2). The Aristotelian principle: *Ab uno primo et simplici non procedit nisi unum* [From a prime and simple unit only a unit proceeds] (*Phys.*, VIII, 6) is made to regulate the dialectics of the one and the many in the explanation of the creative emanative process, but this is not without its ambiguous feature (*De pot.*, q. 7, a. 1, obj. 1; q. 3, a. 4, c.; q. 3, a. 6, ad 22um) (40). *Ars imitatur naturam*

---

39) In the XIIth century, one of theology's first efforts at building itself up into a science—through the use of the axiomatic procedure precisely—developed in a neo-Platonic atmosphere. See ALAN OF LILLE (+ 1203) and his *Regulae de sacra theologia* (P.L., 210, 621–684), and NICHOLAS OF AMIENS and his *Ars catholicae fidei* (P.L., 210, 595–618). [More recent research has restored the authorship of the latter treatise to Alan of Lille. See the conclusions of C. BALIC, *De auctore operis quod "Ars fidei catholicae" inscribitur*, in *Mélanges J. de Ghellinck*, II (ML–SH, XIV, 1951), 793–814.]

40) Fr. GEIGER rightly draws attention to Saint Thomas's use of principles borrowed from other systems that, on the other hand, he considers to be erroneous as a whole. Even more than that, Saint Thomas does not always go to the pains of rectifying those ambiguous principles each time he invokes them. See *La participation dans la philosophie de S. Thomas d'Aquin*, 2d ed., in *BibTh*, XXIII (1953), 163, note. A number of the Platonic-type principles and axioms are examined in the latter work.

[Art imitates nature]. Herein is expressed a generalized and con-verted-into-a-principle induction. It is a most valuable one. Yet, to use it as an axiom in defining the duties of a prince (*De reg. princ.*, I, 12) is not equal to a recourse to the specific principles deriving from an analysis of moral and political matters (*IIa–IIae*, q. 47, a. 10–12).

Only with great discrimination, therefore, should one turn to those lists of axioms that were rife during the period of lower scholasticism and are still today in schoolbook indices. Mindful of this, however, one will never be too appreciative of their value for understanding things. Wherever Saint Thomas begins an article with one of them, the practice should be to meditate upon them intensely.

3. "Re-solutions"

We must locate, within the same Platonic zone, another type of discursive activity, one contrary to demonstration. A demonstration unfolds from within a *deductio* [deduction], wherein a predicate is drawn by way of analysis from a containing subject, since that predi-cate is part of the subject. One may, in a contrary manner, start from the contents of a subject and go back to their necessary prerequisites, to the conditions that make them intelligible. In this case, the process is one of *reductio* [re-duction], wherein is revealed something com-pletely different from what is implied in deduction. It is, in the strict technical sense, a *resolutio* [re-solution] through which thought, in actual possession of a complex of objects, re-possesses what makes them one and is led on even to the contemplation of being (41).

We had occasion in speaking about metaphysical analysis (a) to underscore the originality and exacting demands of a mental operation of that sort. We come across it anew in the present context from an-other angle, and we deem it indispensable to lay stress upon the way it operates and is structured. Saint Thomas, it is true, did not leave us a description of its modes of operation as he did in the case of syllogis-

---

41) The following is the main text in which Saint Thomas defines that opera-tion: "It is clear, therefore, that rational consideration ends in intellectual con-sideration by way of reduction, inasmuch as from the many things it considers, reason brings together a single simple truth. . . . Sometimes, reason proceeds from one thing to that which is other in reality, as when it demonstrates through extrinsic causes or effects. . . . Sometimes, however, the progression is from one thing to that which is other according to reason, as when the progression is made from intrinsic causes: by composition, indeed, when one proceeds from the most universal forms to the more particular objects, or by reduction, when the contrary process takes place, and this because the universal is the simpler. Now, that which is most universal is that which is common to all things, and therefore the ultimate term in this kind of reduction is the consideration of being, and of objects that belong to being as such." *In De trin.*, q. 6, a. 1, c., ad 3am q.; Decker ed., 211–212.

a) See above, 164–166.

tic deduction; but he did make use of it, knowing clearly all the while what made it original (42).

The major instance of it found in his works is the case of the transcendentals, with "re-duction" leading us to the notion of them and furnishing the proper tool for their analysis. Take, for example, what the transcendentals the true and the good mutually imply. The good implies the true. As an end, it is a form and, therefore, a knowable reality having its truth in the category of true objects. The true, on the other hand, implies the good; and de facto, as term of the operation of the mind, the true is, for the mind, a good (See *De malo*, q. 6, a. 1; *De ver.*, q. 21, a. 1).

Light is shed upon the dialectics of human action through the same process of a "re-solution" to the depths of man's will. The will seeks out the immediate end of its acts by virtue of the effectiveness of a supreme end, with the result that the particular goods it pursues take on their value from within this all-encompassing willing that leads us to happiness through their acquisition. The least action performed in pursuit of some particular good is laden—in its intelligibleness and in its realization—with the very will urging us on to the pursuit of the absolute. Therein is found the measure of its moral tonality. The pleasure deriving from the love of a particular good—condemned by the Jansenists as a *cupiditas* [coveting] because they think of it as rendering asunder the love of the universal good—encounters its legitimacy, its forcefulness, its pureness, through this "re-duction" from within, through this striving for depth over and beyond its concrete realization. The entire beginning of the *Ia–IIae* (q. 1 and 2) is a pointed illustration of this method (43).

The most remarkable application of "re-ductive" analysis is the one found in the five "ways" through which Saint Thomas proves the existence of God. Starting from a "metaphysical fact," either the fact of coming-into-being, or of the ordering in agents, or of contingency, or the others, he goes back to its necessary prerequisites and finally to pure Being. The entire dialectics of essence and existence—the two distinct from one another in created being, whence arises the latter's ontological deficiency; one with the other in God Who is *Ipsum Esse* [Being Itself]—unravels according to the technique and within the

---

42) G. RABEAU has rightly insisted upon the role of "re-solution", in his work entitled: Species. Verbum. *L'activité intellectuelle élémentaire selon S. Thomas d'Aquin*, in *BibTh*, XXII (1938), 173–179. On page 214, he writes: "Through the analysis of the structure of the *species* and through the process of *reduction*, Thomism disposes of a method of discovery and of proof which is more simple than that of reasoning through the syllogism. It possesses the principle and method of a reflexive metaphysics, and Saint Thomas is fully aware of it."

43) See the reflexions of A. FOREST, *Consentement et création*, in *PhEs*, 1943, 140–183, which we are here making our own.

atmosphere of *resolutio*. We see, then, to how great an extent the God of Aristotle and the God of Saint Thomas differ from one another as regards both the technical approach to them and the degree of their spiritualness. This is due to the fact that the Aristotelian proof, concluding to the existence of a prime mover, ontologically segregated from all the rest, differs from the Thomistic way which leads on to *Ipsum Esse subsistens* [subsistent Being Itself] Whom the existence of things, by the very fact of their deficiency, reveals as present. A religious act, which should never be masked behind a rational construct, is implied within the latter intellectualistic *resolutio*. Therein, dialectics and contemplation maintain an association graced by mutual fondness within a very exalted experience.

History—the history of Greek thought, but the history of Western thought as well—reveals to what extent the bearing of the *resolutio* or *reductio* method is bound up with a system disapproved of by Saint Thomas. It was the ingenuously and violently neo-Platonic Scotus Erigena who had put the word *resolutio* into circulation, to designate an operation of the mind just as essential as the three other operations of dividing, defining, and demonstrating (44). Saint Thomas criticized the generalized usage Ibn Gebirol made of the *via resolutoria* [re-solving method] (45). Before him, Albert the Great had denounced, as being at the origin of David of Dinant's pantheistic errors, the method of "re-solutions" to the absolute and simple One (46). Once more, we observe that systems cannot monopolize the treasures they exploit, nor even their methods. *Resolutio*, the soul and technique of the return to God, or if one prefers, of the quest for the absolute, is not bound up with the dialectics of the Ideas. It is the very method of transcendental reflecting, even in a realistic philosophy wherein the sense of the concrete supports the loftiest contemplation, for it is the method whereby transcendentals become knowable

---

44) "[Dialectic] is known to have twice two main parts that are necessary in the solving of any question. It pleased the Greeks to name them διαιρετική, ὁριστική, ἀποδεικτική, ἀναλυτική, and in Latin we may call them *divisoriam* [the divisive], *definitivam* [the defining], *demonstrativam* [the demonstrative], *resolutivam* [the resolving parts]. Of these, in fact, the first separates the one into many by division, the second gathers the one from the many by definition, the third uncovers the hidden by means of the manifest in demonstration, the fourth reduces the composite into the simple by separation." JOHN SCOTUS ERIGENA, *De praedestinatione Dei*, I, 1; P.L., 122, 358 A. See M. CAPPUYNS, *Jean Scot Erigène: sa vie, son oeuvre, sa pensée*, in *UCL*, ser. II (1933), 305–306.

45) See *De subst. separ.*, c. 5 (Lescoe ed., 56, n. 19, and his trans., 35): "[Avicebron] . . . proceeded by way of a certain reductive method, investigating the compositions of things. . . ."

46) ALBERT THE GREAT, *Summa theologiae*, IIa Pars. tr. 12, q. 72, m. 4, a. 2, obj. 9, in *AMOO*, XXXIII (1895), 43: "In all reductions, matters are such that one arrives at that which is most simple, which is not further reduced, and within which the things reduced do not differ one from the other."

within a world of becoming and of time. This is not Plotinus, it is not Aristotle, even when they are right there on the scene. It is Saint Thomas in one of the most personal pieces of his methodology.

4. Refutations

We cannot end the description of the various types of discursive activity found in Saint Thomas without drawing attention to a final element included in his work. It is secondary, since it is instigated by external factors, yet its presence is nonetheless revealing of the bent of his mind. What reactions are registered in his text when controversy arises through opposition from his associates? How does he conduct a discussion and undertake a refutation? If one takes into account the fact that there is a congenital connection between scholastic thought and the *Sic et Non* method, a sector dealing with the latter questions then takes on great importance (47).

The reading of Saint Thomas's works confirms the testimony concerning his temperament that, his contemporaries tell us, was made up of great self-possession, mental and moral serenity, a somewhat heavy calmness in social contacts, and to crown it all, a freedom of spirit embedded in contemplation. All his life, from his first day to his last, Saint Thomas fought a relentless battle: either, in the unfolding of the general undertaking of his life, to constitute a science of theology with the help of all the resources of Greek thought; or in the various episodes connected with: the entrance of Aristotle upon the scene (in particular, when, with Siger of Brabant, the crisis was reaching its most extreme point), the development of theology (the "three opinions" on Incarnation, the question of the structure of the sacraments, etc.), the evolution of institutions (in particular, the new forms of religious life and of the apostolate). All this battling cannot but have constantly made its mark upon his work. Yet, his work nevertheless remains free, in content and in form. If we were studying the works of Saint Thomas the polemicist, we would have to look closely into both the episodes and the undertaking just mentioned. Our purpose, however, is only to bring out the traits that characterize his mental performance under circumstances of this sort.

---

47) This observation is expressedly made by Saint Thomas: "Now, it is expedient for him who wants to come into the knowledge of some truth, to know the doubt-causing difficulties that are raised against that truth, because the solving of problems that one doubts about is a coming into truth, as is stated in *Metaph.*, III, c. 1 [995a29–33; H. Tredennick ed., in *LCL*, 1933, 96]. And therefore, in order to learn what the truth is, there is great value in seeing into the reasons of contrary opinions." *In I De coelo*, lect. 22; Marietti ed., 108, n. 223. See *De per. vit. sp.*, c. 26, in *Opusc. theol.*, Marietti ed., II, 153, n. 764: "For there is no better way of unfolding truth and confounding error than by throwing up resistance against the contradictors."

Without giving the lie to what we have said, let us first record a few heated utterances coming here and there from his pen. They thrust us briskly right at the heart of the January 1256 controversy, which almost turned into an open battle, since it was under the protection of the royal archers that the college of Saint James was able to go on with its university teaching. Saint Thomas writes of his opponents: "It is not enough for them to feed on their own iniquity or to bring hurt to their neighbors; but once they have come to hate something, they have to defame it all over the world and inseminate their blasphemies everywhere" (48). The same kind of bitterness reappears in 1269–1270 against the *pestifera doctrina* [plague-bearing doctrine] (49) of those who would ruin, together with his Order, the Gospel movement whose truth and accrediting he was establishing. Well-known is the expression he uttered against Averroes who was compromising Aristotle: he, the par excellence Commentator, was *potius depravator* [rather, a depraver] (50). One could, furthermore, make up a list of opinions, held on various subjects, described by him as "frivolous," "ridiculous."

The fore-going having been recorded—with some amount of humanly-motivated pleasure—the fact remains that, in Saint Thomas, contact with an opponent takes on the aspect as of a dialogue wherein the thought of the other, far from being barred from the search in progress, is made a part of it. This happens, in the case of the Ancients, of the "authorities," no doubt due, as we have seen (a), to the pre-decided course of interpreting them benevolently, which is what "reverential exposition" implies. There is more to it than that, however. In the case of the contemporary William of Auxerre, Albert the Great, Bonaventure, and others, he tries, in his own mind, to be sensitive to the reasons for their holding their opinion, examines the grounds upon which they based it, and marks off the boundaries within which it works, leaving us with a precious distinction in the bargain. The opponent is thus enabled to have his say in the dialogue, since he sees that the share of truth he had perceived, is adopted, since also he finds it inserted within a more ample synthesis wherein

---

48) "Non enim sufficit eis iniquitatem propriam devorare, vel proximos laedere; sed quod semel oderunt, per totum orbem conantur infamere, et ubique blasphemias seminare." JEROME's *Gloss*, quoted by Saint Thomas, *Cont. imp. Dei cult.*, prooem., in *Opusc. theol.*, Marietti ed., II, 6 b, n. 3 (written in 1257).

49) See his *Contra pestiferam doctrinam retrahentium homines a religionis ingressu* (written in 1270), in *Opusc. theol.*, Marietti ed., I, 159 ff.

50) ". . . to err with Averroes, who was not so much a Peripatetic as a depraver of the Peripatetic philosophy." *De unit. int.*, c. 2, in *Opusc. philos.*, Marietti ed., 76, n. 214; Keeler ed., 38, n. 59.

a) See above, 144–149.

it is properly balanced (51). "Brother Thomas," as his biographer Tocco declares, "refutes an opponent as one would instruct a disciple" (52). He does it through that interior enlightening which he himself describes in Augustinian terms in his *De magistro*. Things are really so. Consider, for example, those grandly-dealt-with questions in the *De veritate*: the one on ideas in which the Dionysian themes are introduced (q. 3); the other on mental life wherein Augustinian inwardness is dealt with to its own satisfaction (q. 10); still another on the immanence of the transcendentals in which one is made to benefit from the efforts of the Platonists (q. 21, a. 5); and so many others, within the interplay of discussion, in which, in one way or another, opposing opinions are given their fair share. "Hence both sides of the question were truthfully held in Ancient opinions, and both have a share of truth" (written about the human structuring of faith, *IIa–IIae*, q. 1, a. 2) (a). Most often, these words of an article: *Per hoc patet responsio ad objecta* [By this, the answer to the arguments is clear], are more than a simple recording of reflexions bordering on the question; they introduce within the body of the thesis those elements judged to be true in the opposing thesis. "The arguments for both sides of the question contain a share of truth" (b) (*IIIa Pars*, q. 64, a. 3, about the role played by the humanity of Christ; in the article, the contribution of Greek theology is taken in and given structure).

Note that there is no mental laxness passing into such a procedure. Statements are clear; argumentation is close. As elsewhere, the same rigid compactness is present. Truth, in the charity of his mind, is the factor ruling over the hardest kind of charity to exercise (53).

VI. GENETICAL AND HISTORICAL ACCOUNTING

Saint Thomas's entering into the thought system of another is not with him, as we were just saying, a matter of easy-going benevolence. On the contrary, he is working in a positive way at reaching the under-

---

51) "The first thing to do, if one wishes to destroy an opinion of some kind, is to become master of it a little more than those who best uphold it" (VALÉRY). Saint Thomas says: "One should love both, namely: those whose opinion we follow, and those whose opinion we repudiate, because the one and the other have been at pains to seek out truth, and have helped us in that quest." *In XII Metaph.*, lect. 9; Marietti ed., 599, n. 2566; Rowan ed., II, 901.

52) ". . . sic arguebat adversarium quasi doceret discipulum." WILLIAM OF TOCCO, *Vita S. Thomae Aquinatis*, c. 26; Prummer ed., in *FVTA*, II (1924), 100.

a) "Et ideo utrumque vere opinatum fuit apud antiquos, et secundum aliquid utrumque est verum."

b) ". . . utraque enim pars objectionum secundum aliquid vera est."

53) See P. GLORIEUX, *Un maître polémiste: Thomas d'Aquin*, in *MSR*, V (1948), 158–174.

standing of this thought. We have proof of it, in a more extensive field, in those passages wherein he posits, develops, and solves a problem by examining its historical genesis throughout the flow of solutions offered by successive philosophers up to his day. There are, in fact, a number of articles or disputed questions that offer themselves as a dynamic account of the stages that man went through in his quest for solutions, not as a static piece of research on an object. What we have in mind are not the passages in which *status quaestionis* are often established through the enumeration of opinions, but rather the texts wherein it is intended to arrive at the internal intelligibleness of systems—even if they are judged to be erroneous—by means of an understanding of problems and of their evolution. The following are the most remarkable instances of this sort of procedure.

The two main points wherein Christian thought drew up lines of firm resistance against the philosophy of Aristotle were the creation of the world and the spirituality of the soul. Within the treatment of the latter Saint Thomas discovers the context in which the Stagirite engages problems, making clear the limitations of it, yet accepting at the same time the true values it contains. "[Aristotle] did not proceed from that consideration whereby the origin of the universe is understood as coming from God, but from that consideration whereby an agent is thought to begin acting through movement, which is something that pertains to a particular cause and not to the universal one. And on account of that, to prove the eternity of the world, he draws his arguments from movement and from the prime mover's immovability" (54). "Aristotle proceeded to a study of the intellect from the starting point of its resemblance to sense" (55).

Observations on Plato and successive Platonic systems are presented along a similar pattern. In their case, however, pressure develops in an opposite direction. The desire is to preserve, over and beyond the condemning of the system as a whole, the admirable truths that inspired Augustine's doctrine and furnished Christian thought with the metaphysical dimensions of his noetic system. The text in *De spirit. creat.*, a. 10, ad 8um, is a famous one; one should bring out its framework and measure the depth of meaning revealed in its developments and intuitions. In another passage, Augustine's entire dialectics of the moral issue is qualified, with its limitations, in these words occasioned

---

54) "Non processit [Aristoteles] ex consideratione illa qua intelligitur exitus universi esse a Deo, sed ex illa consideratione qua ponitur aliquod agens incipere operari per motum; quod est particularis causae, et non universalis. Et propter hoc ex motu et immobilitate primi motoris, rationes suas sumit ad mundi aeternitatem ostendendam." *De pot.*, q. 3, a. 17.

55) "Aristotles processit ad considerandum de intellectu per similitudinem sensus." *De spirit. creat.*, a. 9.

[by a citation from Augustine]: "Augustine, in this passage, is speaking of human nature, not as it is considered in its natural being, but as it is ordered to beatitude" (56).

Broader in perspective and perfect in their discerning are the texts in which Saint Thomas describes the stages of development of Greek thought, especially as regards the metaphysics of being which he pushes all the way up to the demand for a creator (see *De pot.*, q. 3, a. 5; q. 3, a. 17; *De spirit. creat.*, a. 5). He writes in the *Summa*: "The ancient philosophers gradually, and, as it were, step by step, came into the knowledge of truth" (a).

The errors in the metaphysics of forms and qualities are explained away by the various temptations that the mind encounters in the illusions of language and imagination (*De virt. in com.*, a. 11). The seduction exercised by spiritualistic pantheism is not without deep psychological motivation (*Cont. Gent.*, I, c. 26). Augustine invented the expressions: "matutinal knowledge" and "vesperal knowledge" in order to subtract time from the Biblical narrative on creation (*De ver.*, q. 8, a. 16) (57). The developments that the efforts of the heretics marked off and occasioned, introduce, likewise, in *Cont. Gent.*, I, chapters 28–39, the dogmatic notion of hypostatic union.

Saint Thomas, in brief, perspicaciously puts to work Aristotle's principle of methodology: "He who considers things in their first growth and origin . . . will obtain the clearest view of them" (58). The principle is a valid one in mental life as well as in the nature of things.

---

56) "Augustinus loquitur de natura humana non secundum quod consideratur in esse naturali, sed secundum quod ordinatur ad beatitudinem." *De spirit. creat.*, a. 8, ad 1um. See what E. GILSON says today: "It is a capital fact for the understanding of Augustinianism that wisdom, the object of philosophy, should always have been, in his mind, at one with beatitude." *Introduction à l'étude de saint Augustin*, in *EPM*, XI (1943), 1 [trans. L. E. M. LYNCH: *The Christian Philosophy of Saint Augustine*, New York, 1960].

a) ". . . antiqui philosophi paulatim et quasi pedetentim intraverunt in cognitionem veritatis. . . ." *Ia Pars*, q. 44, a. 2.

57) A. MANSION rightly observes: "Whether the question be one of opinions touching upon psychology, physics or physiology, Saint Thomas is always particular about locating within the whole of their systems the particular views which the Greek philosophers set forward on this or that point of detail. His historical exegesis thus takes on a characteristic of much greater comprehensiveness than Alexander's; his interpretation is not less historical, perhaps it is more so, but it hereby becomes more philosophical, since it goes back to the principles which brought the thinkers of Antiquity to the conclusions the exact meaning of which is being sought after". *Le commentaire de S. Thomas sur le De sensu et sensato d'Aristote*, in *Mélanges Mandonnet*, I (*BibTh*, XIII, 1930), 98. The best modern interpreters of Augustine recognize this historico-philosophical perspicaciousness in Saint Thomas's exegesis. See E. GILSON, *La philosophie de saint Bonaventure*, 3d ed., in *EPM*, IV (1953), 345 (his comment on *De ver.*, q. 11, a. 1).

58) *Politics*, I, 2, 1252a 24–26; H. Rackham ed., in *LCL*, 1932, 4.

It does not mean that Saint Thomas is proceeding, in cases such as the foregoing, in the manner of the pure historian, treating philosophies as if they were events. He is a philosopher. Yet, his sensitiveness to mental coherence, to the laws of research, to the internal dialectics of concepts, to the relativeness of systems, provides him with one of historical sense's finest qualities; one which Albert the Great, even though he was more curious and erudite, possessed nonetheless to a much lesser degree.

VII. *INTELLECTUS ET RATIO*

"Intellect is the beginning and the end of reason" (a). As we reach the end of these unending, yet always incomplete, analyses, we find it difficult to overcome a feeling of deception. After having accumulated trait upon trait to such a great extent, we know for certain that we have not made our way into the living suppleness of Saint Thomas's mind. The more we bring out, in its diverseness, the internal performing of his reason at work, the more we feel compelled, in order to seize upon it correctly, to push beyond it, right into the intuitions from which it arises and obtains justification. Maritain writes: ". . . it is essential to Thomism that it require whatever has to do with its construction and 'machinery' to be rigorously subordinated to the immanent activity and the vital movement of intellection; it is not a system, an artifact [*artefactum*]; it is a spiritual organism. Its inner connections are vital ties where each part exists by the existence of the whole. The principal parts are not initial parts but, rather, dominant parts or central parts, each one of which is already, virtually, the whole" (59). The same is undoubtedly true of every great thought, but in the case of Saint Thomas the didactic apparatus masks, to a greater degree than in others, the presence of his spirit. One must pursue, therefore, by dint of slow and tenacious maturing, the broadranging intellectual views he has working within his constructions and avoid abiding by the anatomical structures he used, howsoever exact the latter may be. All his theses in anthropology, for instance, are controlled, over and beyond demonstration of any kind, by two or three master perceptions on man's condition. There is all the more reason for doing the same in the areas of theology, wherein communion with mystery encompasses every effort at conceptualization, with organic options taken, after prolonged contemplation, on the

---

a) "Intellectus est rationis principium et terminus." *In III Sent.*, d. 35, q. 1, a. 3, sol. 2.

59) J. MARITAIN, *Distinguer pour unir ou Les degrés du savoir*, 4th ed., Paris, 1946, xv [trans. under the supervision of G. B. PHELAN: *Distinguish to Unite or The Degrees of Knowledge*, New York, 1959, xiii].

unity of the word Incarnate, on the absoluteness of grace, on the realism of the sacraments, etc.

In order, on some points of cardinal importance, to avoid a reduction of the system's internal pressure to a *sic et non* dialectic—an otherwise precious expression of this pressure—the hidden coherence present in a twofold intuition must needs be attained. Such is the case, right at the heart of the problem of creation, with the intuition of the sovereign independence of God and that of the metaphysical value of reality; or again, in the conception of human nature, as regards the harmonizing of mind's freedom with its being enmeshed within the universe. It is over and beyond reason and its reasoning that intelligence's understanding takes place (60).

From this fact proceed both the determinism and relativeness of the system in Saint Thomas and his doctrine. Determinism of the system: all parts entering in the construction are dependent upon one another; no concept obtains its full meaning except by reference to the whole. The commentator, the good commentator, excels at discovering these connections. Even more than that, he may at times, led on by the necessity in concepts, seem to be pushing further into the logic of the system than did his master—a redoubtable undertaking! On the other hand, we are not dealing here with a closed universe, if, precisely, understanding remains in submission to spirit, to that spirit which, even in the constructing of the system, has revived it with elements beyond their foreseeable potential in universes foreign to it. Thus we have seen the Aristotelian Saint Thomas adopting the neo-Platonic *resolutio,* or feeding upon the great Augustinian themes pertaining to interior illumination (just as today we see a certain philosophy combining the Cartesian mathematization of the world with the Hegelian dialectics of history). In Trinitarian theology, he adopts Augustine's points of departure and basic concepts, all the way down to, and including, the theory minimizing appropriations; yet, as in the contemplation of the Greeks, he sees the eternal processions as the principle whence creatures proceed. He is not yielding to concordism, to be sure, nor to eclecticism, for his thought stays firm, as it remains one; but even in his faithfulness to Aristotle, his vision was focused beyond Aristotle, just as his faith looked down upon the best theologies, theologies ever inadequate compared to the revealed datum. At times, he is the very one who reveals these transfers from a system to his own. "Thought," Maritain continues in the text quoted above, "makes no personal choice among the elements of the real; it is infinitely open to all of them." Perhaps one could look, here and there

---

60) "That which is supreme in our knowledge is not reason, but rather intellect which is the source of reason." *Cont. Gent.,* I, c. 57.

by way of counter-proof, for the "seams" that remain after the spirit has moved on. I am thinking, for instance, about certain details in the text of the famous question *De ideis,* in which a creature's individual relations to God must respect the metaphysics of the One.

It is precisely by its spirit that a philosophy, or a theology (61), is timeless and permanent while the systematic elements in it are one with sources and historical contexts: those mediating agents needed, all the while, to reach, transmit, and preserve that spirit (62). Time is not alien to thought, therefore, and the temptation to define the essence of Thomism through formulae independent of the works and contingencies within which it has expressed itself, runs the risks involved in any abstraction. Spirit and realization are made to be one when, in reality, they are two. To guard against the peril of this abstracting, one's effort should tend to the concrete perceiving of mind's performance in the most modest of its incarnations and the most accidental of its associations:

> . . . a condensing, within the mind of a genius, of an enormous amount of duration, which as it pushes farther back into the past, keeps ramifying and spacing out almost without end, but which, in the creating of a work, is collected together, unified, and then projected in the manifold richness of the works that pour forth from it. This inner duration, which condenses so much of the past, is quite different from the outer time of its expression. . . . As Mr. Bergson has suggested, if Plato had been born in another time, his thought would have been the same, though he would have written not a line of what he has written. . . . This inner duration [of a philosophy, of a theology] is the future that every doctrine carries within itself, and forecasts, and covets; this future, for example, is all the revivals of Platonism [of Thomism] which make it possible to say that the history of Platonism [of Thomism] is not yet over. These revivals are never fresh starts; they are themselves creative; they reproduce the same doctrine, but in a new atmosphere; and in the progress and the repeated attempts they make, they tend to give effectiveness to that operation which no historian has a right to formulate in the abstract, namely: the separation of the essential from the accidental, through which the fecundity of the Platonic [Thomistic] message is brought to light.
>
> We cannot think out a great doctrine such as Plato's, or Descarte's [or Saint Thomas's], in its depth, without having the feeling that, in

61) In theology, this is so simply by the [Holy] *spirit,* the word of God in Scripture.

62) At this point, we are making our own the developments of MR. E. BRÉHIER on *La Philosophie et son passé* [Philosophy and Its Past], Paris, 1940, 40–43, permitting ourselves to borrow even his expression, and to apply in Thomism and to the study of Saint Thomas, what he has observed in all the great philosophical doctrines, in Platonism for instance.

it, something is coming to an end and something is coming to a start; without seeing that a doctrine of this kind endeavors to step outside the bounds of duration and almost to eliminate time. Failure in this effort shows itself when, on the one hand, a doctrine comes to grief in a closed system that enbalms it like a corpse ever to remain unmoved; when, on the other hand, a doctrine's actuality and opportuneness make it one with the hour fleeting by. The success of it is seen in a doctrine's power of expansion which is not the result of a tradition holding it down, but of a rebirth and revival withstanding moral, social, and economic change (63).

---

63) If we are not proposing any work notes at the end of this chapter, the reason is that the entire chapter—one already overloaded—is an invitation to carry out analyses and exercises on all the trails that have been opened.

Part Two
Works of Saint Thomas

Chapter VI

The Commentaries on Aristotle and Dionysius

I. THE BACKGROUND

Perhaps we are no longer sufficiently surprised at seeing what a prominent place the commentaries on the works of Aristotle occupied in the teaching of Saint Thomas. Yet, such teaching, carried on over a period of years, poses a real problem in the case of a professor of theology who was working within the framework of and according to a university regime expressly reserving these secular—so long suspected, moreover—texts to the faculty of arts. What is most piquant in the matter is that, of the various commentaries on Aristotle left to us from the XIIIth century, those written by the masters of arts were not the ones that played an important role and enjoyed a happy destiny, but rather those written by the masters of theology, more especially those of Albert the Great and Thomas Aquinas. This fact is undoubtedly not the result of chance (1).

To find the institutional framework within which these two philosophical enterprises developed, then, we must turn to the particular legislation on school matters that was enforced in the Order of Preachers. In both cases, circumstances played a role in bringing out this framework in bold relief. Within a university regime such as was then in vigor, however, the framework, in itself, is very significant since Dominican legislation on the teaching of philosophy ran counter to this very regime. Today, we can hardly any longer imagine an initiative of this kind.

---

1) One should nonetheless examine the literary and doctrinal development of these commentaries, as they supply the context of Saint Thomas's work in this field. See the Research Suggestions below, 230.

When Albert the Great arrived at the University of Paris around 1240 after some ten years of teaching in Germany, the situation, juridically speaking, had not changed. The Dominican Constitutions of 1228 stipulating that the religious must devote all their energies to the study of Scripture and theology, and busy themselves only on occasion with the secular sciences (understand here: the liberal arts over which philosophy, for the past twenty years, had become preponderant) were still in force. Yet, even at that moment, a provision stipulated that, under control of the major authorities, a few qualified religious might devote themselves to their study (2). This legalized exception to the rule was a remarkable one already, considering the Church's general legislation, the canon of which, still in vigor, had been supplied by Gratian (3). At that very moment, moreover, to counteract the pressure of a vivid attraction for philosophical studies and the secular "novelties" of the "sons of the Greeks," Gregory IX, in a bull, solemn in tone and content, had just reminded the masters of the faculty of theology, that they had to be faithful to their evangelical object (July, 1228) (4).

The same tension came to the fore among the Preachers. Resistance to secular studies and the asserting of the latter's purely propaedeutic role bear witness by the very fact of their formulation to the existence of pressure exerted by certain opposing minds. At this moment, amid these counter-tendencies, Albert the Great took a stand, we know with what degree of vigor (5). At the same time, it became the usual thing to institute schools of arts in the convents. Grammar and dialectic became the propaedeutics of formation, but with the philosophical enlarging noted above (6). A regime of this sort was unheard

---

2) "[The brothers] will not study in the books of the gentiles or of the philosophers, granted that they may look into them momentarily. They will not learn the secular sciences, nor the so-called liberal arts, unless the Master of the Order or the General Chapter decides otherwise by sometimes granting a dispensation to a few." *Constitutions* of 1228, Denifle ed., in *ALKGMA*, II (1886), 222. HUMBERT OF ROMANS, who by reason of his authority as well as of his judgment was quite qualified to speak on the subject, wrote—thirty years later, however: "Let there be a relaxing of the bonds as regards the study of subjects of this kind." *Expositio regulae beati Augustini*, n. CXLIV, in *BHROVR*, I (1888), 435.

3) *Decretum Magistri Gratiani*, d. XXXVII, pars prima, in *CJC*, I (1922), c. 135: "But the question is: Is it necessary that they [the clerics] be versed in the secular letters?"

4) See *ChUP*, I, 114–116.

5) See above, ch. I, 42–43.

6) One can recognize the broadening out that took place about 1240 by looking over the division of subjects and the frameworks of teaching in the examination manual made known through a discovery of Mgr Grabmann and analysed by J. VAN STEENBERGHEN, *Siger de Brabant*, t. II, in *LPB*, XIII (1942), 415–420 [The manual is also utilized by J. ISAAC, in his study: *Le Peri Hermeneias en Occident de Boèce à Saint Thomas. Histoire littéraire d'un traité d'Aristote*, in

of and anomalous, one entirely private in any case, since until then it was imperative that religious, even more than clerics, fix themselves outside such scientific and cultural preoccupations. Thus, while Albert the Great, officially titular in a chair, taught Scripture and the *Sentences* at the faculty of theology, at the same time *ex professo* but without a university mandate he taught philosophy in the convent of Saint James, with the works of Aristotle as his text. We have seen what kind of reactions Aristotle's entrance on the scene provoked (a); let it be here observed what kind of juridic situation it created and implied in university regulations.

Twenty years later, at the time when Aristotle had conquered his right of abode in the Christian world, the schools of liberal arts and of philosophy achieved definite stability among the Preachers. Wherever a convent was founded with a "lector," a teaching program was organized. By dint of specialization requirements, the convents parceled out the work. In one, a school of grammar and dialectic was opened, in another, a school of logic, elsewhere a school of philosophy of nature, or even a school of ethics. It goes without saying that the university colleges (*studia generalia*) organized a complete curriculum of philosophical disciplines, the recognized basis of which was the "reading" of Aristotle's texts (7). Thus, the Order was actively contributing to the drawing up of school texts to be used in the various faculties since, in other fields also, it had undertaken for theology, under Hugh of Saint-Cher's direction, a correction of the Bible and with Raymond of Penyafort, a reorganization of the *Corpus juris*, the text studied in the law schools.

Within the framework of this now-terminated evolution, Saint Thomas, during the years 1261–72, depending on place and circumstance, undertook his successive commentaries upon the *Analytics*, the shorter and longer books of the *Physics*, the *Metaphysics*, and the *Ethics* (8).

BibTh, XXIX (1953), 70–74]. See also the *De ortu et divisione philosophiae* of KILWARDBY, who was master of arts around 1240. [On the treatise mentioned here, see D. E. SHARP, *The De ortu scientiarum of Robert Kilwardby*, in *NS*, VIII (1934), 1–30.]

a) See above, ch. I, 34ff.

7) Saint Thomas himself, then the young regent of Saint James College at Paris, together with Albert, regent at Cologne [and Peter of Tarentasia; see Foster ed., 143, note 23], was a member of the commission of studies that in 1259 at the General Chapter of Valenciennes made up a vigorous code of the Order's academic regime and decreed that each province would henceforth have a school of liberal arts, with philosophy heading the list of subjects to be taught. See *Acta Capitulorum generalium*, Reichert ed., vol. I, in *MOFPH*, III (1898), 99–100.

8) M. GRABMANN treated the subject of this chapter some time ago in *Die Aristoteleskommentare des heiligen Thomas von Aquin*, in *MAG*, I (1926), 266–313.

II. THE INTENTION OF SAINT THOMAS

What are the circumstances, doctrinally speaking, when Saint Thomas began his commentaries? The first battle had been won by Albert the Great. Within the field of his conquest, however, a more definite and more serious problem had arisen. Aristotle, the master of thought, concealed riches of an equivocal nature. It was quickly discovered that, in the course of history, his principles had proliferated systems far different in tenor, starting with the materialism of Alexander of Aphrodisias, the "exegete" par excellence as the Greeks named him, all the way up to Avicenna, who, for his part, transubstantiated Aristotelianism into a neo-Platonic sort of mysticism. Right at that moment, Averroes, the last one to enter into circulation, was seducing minds with an exegesis of high quality, which was all the more useful that it applied itself very closely to the so greatly-riddled-with-difficulty text of Aristotle. He arrived as the "commentator" par excellence. Right at the height of the Averroistic crisis—between the 1256 incident (Albert's *De unitate intellectus*) and the 1270 and 1277 condemnations (Siger of Barbant)—the teaching of Saint Thomas on the works of Aristotle entered the record. Clearly, those contexts gave the meaning of what he intended to do. This intention, in turn, governed, in whole and in detail, the exegesis he offered in his commentaries. We must keep this constantly in mind, just as he did.

What is this intention? Or to formulate the question with more precision: outside his personal works wherein he accepts for his own the positions of Aristotle or rises up in battle against them, does Saint Thomas use his commentary as a tool for controversy to the benefit of his own system, and thereby bring forth a tendentious work, or does he restrict himself to the purely objective efforts of the exegete? Looking at the heat with which Albert the Great answers this question on his own, we can measure both the exact importance of the problem and the bitterness of the criticism that was directed against those who contended they were "reading" the Philosopher's texts objectively (9).

---

9) "The *Book on Animals* is now finished, and with it the end of the entire work on the books of natural philosophy has been reached. In this work, I have applied a method such as would allow me to expose, to the best of my ability, the sayings of the Peripatetics; nor can one discover in it what I myself hold in natural philosophy. But should one have a doubt, let him compare what is said in my books with the sayings of the Philosophers. Then, he can either take me to task or approve me, saying that I have been an interpreter and expositor of their science. If, however, he takes me to task without having read and compared, then it becomes clear that his taking me to task comes from either hate or ignorance—and I care little whether I am taken to task by such men." ALBERT THE GREAT, *De animalibus*, lib. XXVI, in *AMOO*, XII (1891), 582. See his *De somno et vigilia*, lib. III, tr. I, c. 12, in *AMOO*, IX (1890), 195. De facto, whether through a lack of discipline due to his temperament or as a result of his

A preliminary fact must be noted. It is true, not only of Saint Thomas alone, but of every medieval university commentator, whose line of work it sets. The commentary—this is the opportune place for us to recall it (a)—is the basic literary genre in the cultural renaissance of the XIIIth century, to the point where scholasticism can be partly defined by it. Work is done on texts considered authoritative in their field, even if it is common to treat them according to interpretations of the most personal kind. Thus, the commentator proceeds along a crest lined up between two objectives: he prizes his text, and he wants to penetrate its inner meaning; but his intent is not as of the erudite who contentedly goes about the historical reconstruction of an obsolete system. His purpose is to find in his text a witness to truth. This witness may be more or less perspicacious, more or less limited, but it will be suited to the purpose of forward progress in search of truth. This is the pedagogical purpose intended in the *lectio*. There is a subtle balance achieved here that, today, we find disrupted as a result of the distinctions that have been made among the literary forms. With the Medievals, attention is paid to the letter of the text, to be sure, but to the *intentio auctoris* as well. Against an ill-disposed critic, Saint Thomas will uphold his right to respect the tenor of texts without one's faith passing judgement on them beforehand: "And I fail to see how the words of the Philosopher are exposed has something to do with the doctrine of faith" (10). In addition to this, however, by bringing the procedure of reverential exegesis into play (see chapter IV), the principles and the first steps toward truth included in the text will be brought, so to speak, to their ripening. Whence Cajetan's saying: "Very often, [Saint Thomas] glosses Aristotle as Philosopher, not Aristotle as such; and this, in favor of truth" (11). Thus, counter to the practice of the modern exegete who abstains from taking as his own the thought of his author and who does not have to say so if he does not accept it, the medieval commentator implicitly makes the contents of the text his own, and if he does not

---

being prompted by his evident sympathy for the Peripatetics, Albert did not, as he was pursuing his work in detail, remain within the bounds of what he had intended in principle.

a) See above, ch. II.

10) "Nec video quid pertineat ad doctrinam fidei qualiter Philosophi verba exponantur." *Resp. de art. XLII*, a. 33; Marietti ed., *Opusc. theol.*, I, 217. Side by side with this reflexion, let us place those of Siger of Brabant which perhaps coincide materially with it, but which in reality reveal another spirit: "In this passage, therefore, the intention of Aristotle, even though it is contrary to truth, is not to be concealed"; one must look for "the intention of the philosophers rather than for truth." Quoted by M. GRABMANN, *Methoden und Hilfsmittel des Aristotelesstudiums im Mittelalter*, in *SBAW*, V (1939), 37.

11) "Pluries glossat [S. Thomas] Aristotelem ut Philosophum, non ut Aristotelem; et hoc in favorem veritatis." CAJETAN, *In IIa–IIae*, q. 172, a. 4, ad 4um.

accept it, he says so explicitly whereas he is presumed to make it his own, if he says nothing.

How, de facto, in Saint Thomas, is balance achieved between the determining of Aristotle's thought and the expanding of it, and even the correcting of it, which the search for objective truth calls for?

1. Concern for the literal meaning.

Let us place concern for literal meaning as topmost in the intentions of Saint Thomas. The circumstances we were just evoking invited such an attitude; they even imposed it since recourse to the text had to be the means of deciding between the interpretations of it. Counter to the paraphrastic procedure employed by Albert, Saint Thomas was, we shall see, thoroughly preoccupied with the literal sense and committed himself to an exegesis of the text, part after part, almost word after word. It is noticeable, furthermore, how often he declares expressly that his purpose is to bring out the *intentio auctoris*, which is the deep criterion for attaining the *littera*. In order to arrive at it, he appeals to contexts: the immediate context, the general ones, or the more-delicate-to-handle context of the system's implications. Examples abound, and it is a valuable exercise to examine how the procedure is worked out in them, even if one does not agree with their conclusions (12).

A good way to detect in what measure the exegesis of Saint Thomas remains self-governing is to compare his commentaries with his personal works and to note the difference between them in their doctrinal elaborations upon the same texts. For instance, in the *Analytics (In I Post. An.,* c. 13, lect. 25), the theory of science is treated in its proper Aristotelian style, while in the *Summa* (and the other parallel works), the same theory is stretched to the point of strain, as regards both the spirit of the theory and its technical schemas, by being applied to theological knowledge, one far-removed in genus from all the other sciences (13). Another example: on the questions of the transcendency of contemplation and of the man-centered moral

---

12) Plainly, this preoccupation becomes the more expressly declared as his polemic is pushed further on. "But before going into the words of Aristotle that are found in the third book *On the Soul,* let us dwell even more on his words of the second book, so that by comparing his words with one another it may become evident what he really did hold about the soul." *De unit. int.,* c. 1; Marietti ed., 66, n. 181. "Because, however, on the strength of some words that follow, Averroes has decided that Aristotle intended to say that . . ., therefore, the words that follow must be considered with even more diligence." *Ibid.,* 67, n. 185, "This manner of exposing, however, does not seem to be in accordance with Aristotle's intention." *In I Perih.,* lect. 8; Marietti ed., 40, n. 102; Oesterle ed., 68.

13) It is by effecting a dislocation of the theory of the subalternation of sciences, which is a very carefully done up technical component of the Aristotelian

virtues of the active life, the difference is quite perceptible—and quite meaningful—between the commentary on the *Ethics* and the *Summa theologiae* (14).

To give one more example where observation will produce good results: comparing in style and content the commentaries on Aristotle with those on Dionysius, one will perceive that, in these commentaries, the originals have been respected, not only in the proper interpretation to be given of them, but in their own atmosphere, mentality, and vocabulary.

2. A deliberately sympathetic approach.

This sympathy is fully sincere as well as candid. We said it before, sympathy is the rule in the medieval commentary. History, with its aim at objectiveness (or presumed objectiveness), and doctrine are not disjoined through that abstracting method characteristic of the later study of the ancient texts. There is no concealing that such an approach is a delicate one to handle, but at least it gives the text a sort of freshness and productiveness that the archeologically minded interpreters will have to sacrifice deliberately. In the present case where the reader is the theologian Saint Thomas, the Stagirite's works are read through Christian eyes. He entertains no illusion about certain parts of the system; nevertheless his presumptions are in their favor.

3. Hence we see Saint Thomas . . . keeping problems open, and the system along with them.

A system of thought remains open to every reality, therefore, to every truth, in the very measure that it proceeds from a great mind. Aware that intelligibles are unlimited in their amplitude which exceeds the grasp it has of them and even more the construction it gives them, a system produced by a great mind does not hem itself in within itself. It refuses also to surrender to its own limitations. As a result, its history, even its homogeneous history, is one of proliferation. One can observe it expressing itself in the most profoundly varying forms, even to the limits of faithfulness, and sheltering thinkers extremely different in temperament. The system of Saint Thomas, "Thomism," is a good example of a system of this kind. The system of Aristotle is another one. The latter, one of the most organic

---

epistemology, that theologians are able to transfer the notion of "science" into theological knowledge. See M.-D. CHENU, *La théologie comme science au XIIIe siècle*, 3d rev. ed., in *BibTh*, XXXIII (1957), 71–92.

14) In analysing this fine example, refer to E. GILSON's reflexions in *Dante et la philosophie*, in *EPM*, XXVIII (1939), 135–138 [trans. into English by D. MOORE: *Dante the Philosopher*, New York, 1949. The work is also available in *TB/1089*, under the title: *Dante and Philosophy*].

and most firmly designed, remains open nonetheless to many different interpretations, whether in some of its explicit parts as in the case of the agent intellect, or in its possible prolongations under the impact of unheard of problems as in the question of the world's creation. To repeat, an attitude of this sort is a delicate one to handle because the boundaries between authenticity and betrayal may be unknowingly crossed. Yet, it is a delicate one in the very measure that it is a spiritual one. Authenticity is more of the order of the spirit than of the letter, although letter and spirit are no more separable than body and soul. His deliberately sympathetic approach as well as his greatness of intelligence furnished Saint Thomas with resources making possible an interpretation in which his faithfulness and freedom combined to favor his sensitiveness to the homogeneous progress of Aristotle's system.

Technical procedures reveal the inner tension of an orientated development of this sort which overruns here and there the limits of historical exegesis. The typical case of it is undoubtedly the problem of the creation of the world. This problem is plainly outside Aristotle's immediate perspective. Yet, attendant upon his analysis of coming-into-being and its metaphysical conditions, there is a possibility for his analysis to reach greater depths. At these depths it can outdo itself, provided one pushes it beyond the contingency of the modes of being to the radical contingency of the very existence of beings (but how much farther this new intuition leads!). ". . . others there are who arose to the consideration of being, as being . . ." (a). Saint Thomas credits Aristotle with knowing the universal cause of things—not with knowing the creative cause of the existence of substances. Even this however, we know, is refused to Aristotle by Bonaventure and the Augustinians who are more sensitive to the difference between the Greek and Christian thoughts and the modern exegetes, strictly historians, back them up. Let us add that, in connection with this problem, there arises the whole question of the difference between Aristotle's prime mover and the Christian's personal God. On this point, however, the exegesis of Saint Thomas remains extremely reserved (15).

In order for us to measure whether in each case of piecemeal

---

a) "Ulterius aliqui erexerunt se ad considerandum ens in quantum est ens . .". *Ia Pars*, q. 44, a. 2.

15) See an excellent stating of the problem in E. GILSON, *L'esprit de la philosophie médiévale*, 2d ed., in *EPM*, XXXIII (1944), 63–84 [English translation of the first edition by A. H. C. DOWNES, *The Spirit of Mediaeval Philosophy*, New York, 1940, 64–83 and notes, 435–443]; also, R. JOLIVET's comprehensive study: *Aristote et la notion de création*, in *RSPT*, XIX (1930), 5–50, 209–236, re-edited in *Essai sur les rapports entre la pensée grecque et la pensée chrétienne*, new ed., in *BHP*, 1955, 1–84.

exegesis there is continuity or discontinuity between Saint Thomas and Aristotle, we should, applying skill, gather the indications which Saint Thomas himself furnishes. Thus, when he is commenting upon the demonstration that "matter in itself is neither corrupted nor generated" (a), he adds, ". . . but by this it is not excluded that it begin to be by creation" (b). In an extreme case, the commentator, blocked by his text, will go so far as to say: "Aristotle speaks here by way of inquiry" (c). That, to be sure, is the limit of fidelity. Again, he will excuse the shortcomings of the Philosopher by having recourse to the latter's respect for the proper and limited objects of a discipline. For instance, to solve the problems of the soul as separate from the body is outside the field of the philosopher of nature (d). Again, he asserts that Aristotle is arguing either *ad hominem* or *ad positionem* [in rebuttal] to explain the shallowness and objective ineffectiveness of his arguments (16).

4. . . . fathoming the depths of principles rather than drawing rigid conclusions.

This is the homogeneous and true way to keep a system open. As a matter of fact, it is beyond the ever narrow formulae and hardened deductions that one reaches the insights contained within the inner principles of a system. As a result, a litteralness that one might find annoying or obscure is either removed or relieved. The most obvious feature of this procedure can be noted when Saint Thomas is explaining the limitations and shortcomings of Aristotle through the limitations of the questions he raised. The genesis of his thought is made to explain its obscurities and its exclusions, and it is therefore possible to reabsorb them without betraying their author's intention. Once again the classical case is the problem of creation and of the eternity of the world. Everyone knows the reflexion that Saint Thomas makes: "[Aristotle] did not proceed from that consideration through which one understands that the universe came forth from God, but from that consideration by which it is postulated that an agent starts operating through movement, which is appropriate to a particular

---

a) ". . . materia secundum se neque corrumpitur neque generatur." *In I Phys.*, lect. 15; Marietti ed., 69, n. 139; Kocourek ed., 75.

b) "Sed ex hoc non excluditur quin per creationem in esse procedat." *Ibid.*

c) "Aristoteles loquitur inquirendo . . ." *De unit. int.*, c. 1; Marietti ed., 71, n. 199. [In the editions, the text reads: "loquitur sicut inquirens."]

d) *Ibid.;* Marietti ed., 72, n. 200.

16) "Although the arguments of Aristotle seem to have little force, they are nonetheless effective, for they are given in rebuttal." *In I De an.*, lect. 6; Marietti ed., 24, n. 74; Foster-Humphries ed., 91. "In the preceding book, he [Aristotle] proceeded dialectically . . . ; here he starts to proceed demonstratively. . . ." *In IV Metaph.*, lect. 1; Marietti ed., 150, n. 529; Rowan ed., I, 216.

cause and not to the universal cause" (a). Likewise, as regards the interpretation of the theory about intelligence, it is simultaneously true that the exegesis according to which there exists only one unique spiritual intellect is nearer to the opinion of the Stagirite and that, nevertheless, the solution of Saint Thomas according to which each person has his own intellect is inspired by the principles of Aristotelian metaphysics and psychology.

An exegetic operation of this kind is not without drawbacks. In fact, at times, it leads to a disjoining of the principles from the conclusions Aristotle draws from them. Thereby one risks proposing an Aristotelianism that does not dare to go to the full extent of its conclusions. Augustinians and Averroists will not fail to reproach Saint Thomas for presenting an Averroism ashamed of itself. (17).

5. . . . introducing elaborations and inserting distinctions.

This is another means of loosening up the literalness of the text. When Saint Thomas is elaborating his theory about the knowledge of concrete singulars (*In III De an.*, lect. 8), he rests it, not without reason, on the text upon which he is commenting (Aristotle, *De an.*, III, 429b10–20). Yet his elaboration, howsoever homogeneous it may be, goes beyond the text. Distinctions reach even further. More often than not they involve the introduction of structures which exceed simple commentary. Cases abound. For instance, there is the distinction brought in to preserve the transcendence of the intellect whose operation needs a body "not as its instrument, but only as providing its object" (a). Likewise, another distinction is provided to introduce divine providence into chance and contingency: "In the passage Aristotle is speaking of contingent events which happen in time as related to particular causes, as may be seen by his example" (b). Furthermore, a distinction is brought in to ensure for

---

a) "Non enim processit [Aristoteles] ex consideratione illa qua intelligitur exitus universi esse a Deo, sed ex illa consideratione qua ponitur aliquod agens incipere operari per motum; quod est particularis causae, et non universalis." *De pot.*, q. 3, a. 17, c.

17) "By dint of emphasis on what he was borrowing from Aristotle and only discrete hinting at what he was adding to him, by even giving the impression at times that he was borrowing that itself which he was adding, Saint Thomas was making it difficult for himself to show that in his own thought Aristotle's principles were not bound with the consequences ensuing from them in Aristotle." E. GILSON, *L'esprit de la philosophie médiévale*, 2d ed., in *EPM*, XXXIII (1944), 78, note 2 [English translation of the first edition by A. H. C. DOWNES, *The Spirit of Mediaeval Philosophy*, New York, 1940, 441, note 12].

a) ". . . non sicut instrumento, sed sicut objecto tantum." *In I De an.*, lect. 2; Marietti ed., 7, n. 19; Foster-Humphries ed., 55.

b) "Aristoteles hic loquitur de contingentibus quae hic fiunt, in ordine ad causas particulares, sicut per ejus exemplum apparet." *In VI Metaph.*, lect. 3; Marietti ed., 308, n. 1216; Rowan ed., II, 477.

divine science the characteristic of the supreme and architectonic science and to refuse the same for political science (*In I Eth.*, lect. 2; Marietti ed., 8, n. 28 and 31). And so on.

6. . . . Finally [weighing and rejecting seemingly unwarranted exegeses].

Like any other exegete, for the benefit of his own exegesis but also for the benefit of his own thought, Saint Thomas discusses the merits and refutes such exegeses as he judges unjustified. Thus, during the Averroistic crisis, he directed his effort toward combatting the interpretation of the Arabian philosopher, which a group of masters of arts at Paris were then adopting and extolling (18). This does not mean that once he has expressed his opposition, and expressed it with intensity, he does not appreciate "the Commentator" at his true value. At any rate, he often leans upon other commentators to reject or redress this or that interpretation. Thus he adopts as regards the primacy of substance (*In XII Metaph.*, 1, 1069 a 19, lect. 1; Marietti ed., 567, n. 2417) the positions of Themistius, while at the same time taking into account the criticism of Averroes (19).

In this way Thomas Aquinas the commentator proceeds. In this way, the medieval commentators proceed—except to the point of genius, whose intellectual clarity is linked with honesty of a special kind.

> . . . it is true to say that it is not as historians that they are interested in Greek philosophy. The Aristotle of history carries with him his failures as well as his successes; he is less made up of the truths his principles could support than of the truths that he saw in his principles. History, then, takes him in all his greatness but also with his limitations. The same is also true of Plato. What the philosophers of the Middle Ages ask of them is, on the contrary, all and only what makes them true; and where they are not yet wholly true, how they can become so. This is a delicate, sometimes subtle, elaboration in which, however, Saint Bonaventure, Saint Thomas, and Duns Scotus always show the greatest steadiness. There is nothing artificial in their method since they never force principles with a violence which would risk destroying them. Rather, they extend them or prolong them as far

18) "This answer [of Averroes] goes against both what Aristotle intended and truth." *In VIII Phys.*, lect. 21; Marietti ed., 614, n. 1149. "And the argument which he [Averroes] adduces is quite ridiculous." *In II Metaph.*, lect. 1; Marietti ed., 82, n. 286; Rowan ed., I, 119. Reflexions such as these are abundant.

19) See A. FESTUGIÈRE, *Notes sur les sources de saint Thomas au livre XII des Métaphysiques,* in *RSPT*, XVIII (1929), 282–290.

as necessary to have them say everything that they can say and make them yield the totality of their truth. The age of the commentators, as some are pleased to call it, was above all an age of philosopher-commentators. They are not to be blamed, therefore, if they unceasingly have the name of Aristotle at the tip of their tongues and constantly have him say what he himself did not say. They never played the historian; they wanted to be philosophers, and, unless we demand, God forbid, that philosophy be peopled exclusively with historians of philosophy, history itself has nothing for which to reproach them (20).

It would be to falsify, however, by going to the other extreme, the correct equilibrium of this literary genre—and, therefore, the intention of Saint Thomas—to seek in the commentaries his personal thought and to build a Thomism whose theology would be in his *Summa* and his philosophy in his commentaries on Aristotle. Some have tried to do this, and some have even proposed this as a judicious pedagogical program. This partitioning, however, reverts to the detriment of these two thus ill-assorted segments. It is very difficult, to be sure, to elaborate a Thomistic "philosophy" from the works of Saint Thomas and from their concrete implications. But it is to pervert the components of the problem to state it in these terms right from the beginning. It would also be a misunderstanding of the historical and doctrinal relations between Aristotle and his commentator Saint Thomas (a).

III. THE TOOLS

After having studied the spirit of the commentary, we can now analyze the tools at its disposal, which cannot be a matter of indifference to that spirit. In fact, one must rid oneself of the illusion evinced by a first glance at the commentaries of Saint Thomas. His text, uniform and almost without references, could lead one to believe that it was poured out in full stream, with attention paid to only the statements of the Philosopher. In point of fact, however, when Saint

---

20) E. GILSON, *L'esprit de la philosophie médiévale*, 2d ed., in *EPM*, XXXIII (1944), 401–402 [English translation of the first edition by A. H. C. DOWNES, *The Spirit of Mediaeval Philosophy*, New York, 1940, 424–425].

a) See the recent book *Aristote et Saint Thomas d'Aquin. Journées d'études internationales*, in *CCM*, 1957, containing a number of communications the aim of which was to determine "the nature and the limits of the influence exercised by Aristotle's philosophy upon that of Saint Thomas" (6). See in particular the studies of D. A. CALLUS, *Les sources de saint Thomas. Etat de la question*, 93–174; L.-B. GEIGER, *Saint Thomas et la métaphysique d'Aristote*, 175–220; E. VON IVANKA, *Aristotelische und Thomistische Seelenlehre*, 221–228; A. THIRY, *Saint Thomas et la morale d'Aristote*, 229–258. About the study of H. V. JAFFA, *Thomism and Aristotelianism. A Study of the Commentary by Thomas Aquinas on the Nicomachean Ethics*, Chicago, 1952, see R. A. GAUTHIER's review in *BT*, IX (1954–56), 157–159.

Thomas was at work, his table was littered with reference works. Quite evidently, then, it is important to restore within the texture of his commentary the resources he was thus exploiting.

The chore of writing a commentary is very complex. Technical equipment differs according to the works commented upon, according to the progress and the hazards of the successive Aristotelian expansions we have spoken about, and again, in a more modest way, according to the places and the milieux in which our commentator found himself. Thus, Averroes is the permanent substrate of his commentary on the *Metaphysics,* while in the *De sensu et sensato* Alexander of Aphrodisias is just about the only one used. Saint Thomas is in constant dependence upon Themistius for his commentary upon the first book *De Anima,* but apparently much less so in the second and third books. Simplicius will be at his disposal only little by little, thanks to the translations of William of Moerbeke. In his *Perhermenias* he quotes many Greek commentators, but in reality, he has contact with them through Boethius (b). When he was expounding the *Ethics,* he had before his eyes both the Greek commentators translated by Grosseteste and the very *Notulae* of the translator himself. Because Moerbeke had just translated the *Politics,* Saint Thomas, together with Albert the Great, is the first among the Latins to comment upon this work. Recent research has thus made it possible to observe more closely, in the intensive development of Latin Aristotelianism during the XIIIth century, the resources and the procedures in the work of Saint Thomas. We cannot review here all their elements. We can only show, through several instances, their importance for an adequate reading of the commentaries.

In effect, Saint Thomas was preoccupied with obtaining good texts of the Philosopher as well as of the latter's ancient Greek or Arabic commentators. To his Aristotelian undertaking we can transpose the attitude he explicitly manifests for the ancient Christian writers: the moving desire of uncovering works still unknown and of having recourse to the most correct translations (21). As a matter of fact, his biographer tells us that it was upon his intervention that his confrere William of Moerbeke (+1286)—highly competent in Greek studies for his day and involved in cultural exchange with the learned contemporary devotees of the Greek sciences—undertook to translate or to revise the texts of Aristotle, "a new translation containing with greater clarity the truth of Aristotle's statements," and also the transla-

---

b) Recent research has brought out the fact that it was also through Ammonius that Saint Thomas presented the opinions of some of the Greek commentators on matters dealt with in the *Perihermeneias.* See the works of G. VERBEKE and of J. ISAAC referred to below, at the end of note 22.

21) See above, ch. I, 48.

tion of many Greek commentators (22). Therein is recorded a meaningful episode of that intellectual eagerness which moved the Christian world as it discovered Hellenism.

> In fact, it cannot be through a fortuitous circumstance that William of Moerbeke, the new translator of Aristotle, and Thomas Aquinas, the new commentator, find themselves together at the papal court, at the time they were carrying out their twofold work. Urban IV, who had brought them together at the very time that he renewed the former prohibition against the teaching of the Stagirite's books (1263), had manifestly commissioned their work (23).

The text of Aristotle will concern us first. Saint Thomas neither effectively knew nor handled the Greek original, although there are allusions that presuppose his having occasional encounters with the Greek, or his receiving information from someone well versed (24). Let us note, however, that through and throughout the Latin versions which he uses, Saint Thomas was put in contact with different traditions of the Greek text. Thus, for the *Ethics*, the translation of Grosseteste provides him with a tradition today represented by *Parisinus 1854*, while the Moerbeke revision refers him to a tradition dependent upon manuscripts such as *Marcianus 213* and *Riccard 46* (25).

To get an idea of the swarm of readings used, originating from the

---

22) "[Thomas] also wrote on natural and moral philosophy, and on metaphysics. He saw to it that a new translation of these books be done which would embody more clearly the truth of Aristotle's statements [*nova translatio quae sententiae Aristotelis contineret clarius veritatem*]." WILLIAM OF TOCCO, *Vita S. Thomae Aquinatis*, in *ASS*, March, I, 663 B [The text quoted is also found in *FVTA*, II (1912), c. 17, 88]. "Brother William of Brabant, [Archbishop] of Corinth, translated from Greek into Latin at Brother Thomas's request all the books on natural and moral philosophy." *Stams Catalogue* (1312), Denifle-Ehrle ed., in *ALKGMA*, II (1886), 226. On the activity of William of Moerbeke, see P. MANDONNET, *Siger de Brabant et l'Averroisme latin au XIIIe siècle*, 2d rev. ed. Part I, in *LPB*, VII (1911), 39–41; M. DE WULF, *Histoire de la philosophie médiévale*, 6th ed., vol. II, Louvain-Paris, 1936, 44–56. [English trans. of the 6th French ed., by E. C. MESSENGER, *History of Mediaeval Philosophy*, 3d ed., 2 vols., New York-London, 1952.—See also G. VERBEKE, *Thémistius. Commentaire sur le traité de l'âme d'Aristote, traduction de Guillaume de Moerbeke*, in *CLCAG*, I (1957), LXII–LXXXI, and by the same, *Ammonius. Commentaire sur le* Peri Hermeneias *d'Aristote, traduction de Guillaume de Moerbeke*, in *CLCAG*, II (1961), LXVII–XCIII. The reader will find therein the pertinent bibliography on the subject. Refer also to J. ISAAC, *Le* Peri Hermeneias *en Occident de Boèce à Saint Thomas. Histoire littéraire d'un traité d'Aristote*, in *BibTh*, XXIX (1953), 104–105, 158–171.]

23) P. MANDONNET, *loc. cit.*, 39.

24) We have already mentioned the controversy on the degree of Saint Thomas's knowledge of Greek. His was a rather limited one, to tell the truth. See J. DURANTEL, *Saint Thomas et le Pseudo-Denys*, Paris, 1919, 39–49.

25) See E. FRANCESCHINI, *S. Tommaso e l'Etica nicomachea*, in *RFNS*, XXVIII (1936), 313–328.

different versions, one can look at the conclusions at which Father Pelster arrived at the end of his analysis of the *litterae* [readings] quoted in the commentary on the *Metaphysics* (26).

From book I to the first lessons of book IV, the *media* version is, in principle, the text commented upon, at least in this sense that it is the *media* which furnishes most of the lemmas. It also happens, however, that the division of the text is indicated by means of the *vetus* version. On the other hand, the *vetus* is clearly favored in the course of the commentary: its variants are explicitly preferred (the other reading is better, is clearer—*alia littera melius, planius habet*); its readings are reproduced in Saint Thomas' paraphrasing; it even happens that *alia littera* refers to the *media* which is thus relegated to a second place. Some traces of the *Moerbecana* version are also found.—Starting at book IV, lesson 6, the *media* takes over first place. *Vetus*, then, has no more than an accessory role and disappears almost immediately after book IV, lesson 7. In the meantime, more and more traces of *Moerbecana* are identified. This state of affairs lasts as far as the end of book V. After having many times preferred the *Moerbecana* reading to the *media*, Saint Thomas seems to have definitely made his choice in favor of the version of his Belgian confrere. From then on, it is the *Moerbecana* which is the basis for his commentary, while *media* is reduced to an auxiliary role. Starting with book VI, citations from the *media* are, as a matter of fact, exceptional. Throughout the whole treatise, moreover, allusions to the *arabica* version are found, and also, to the still unknown Greco-Latin texts, which we have already pointed out.

As regards the exegesis of the *Ethics*, we are now in a position to discern the role played by the Moerbeke revision done upon the previous version of Grosseteste. In fact, as we have seen, a manuscript tradition of the Moerbeke Greco-Latin version is clearly discernible (27).

---

26) F. PELSTER, *Die Uebersetzungen der aristotelischen Metaphysik in den Werken des heiligen Thomas von Aquin*, in *Greg*, XVI (1935), 325–348, 531–561; XVII (1936), 377–406. The summing up which follows in our text is borrowed from D. SALMAN's review of the work being done on the subject at the time he wrote *Versions latines et commentaires d'Aristote*, in *BT*, V (1937–1939), 95–107. [The quotation is from 105–106.]

27) See E. FRANCESCHINI, *La revisione moerbekiana della* Translatio Lincolniensis *dell'Etica Nicomachea*, in *RFNS*, XXX (1938), 150–162; A. DONDAINE, Review of the current works on the subject, in *BT*, VI (1940–42), 90–94. One can evidently not trust the Latin vulgate of Aristotle's texts supplied in the modern editions of Saint Thomas's commentaries. This vulgate is a compound of texts and it is corrupt; Saint Thomas, moreover, did not use it as he worked out his commentaries. [The author restricted himself in the above section to examples on two only of Aristotle's works translated into Latin. For an idea of the vast amount of work being done on the Latin Aristotle, one should consult the sections of the *BT* dealing with the literature on the problem. For an example on one of the Latin texts of Aristotle, see L. MINIO-PALUELLO, *Le texte du "De anima" d'Aristote. La tradition latine avant 1500*, in *AAr*, 217–243. The editing of the various versions of Aristotle's Latin text is under way. They are being included in

With respect to the so greatly varied utilization of the ancient commentators, the problem is an even more extensive one. There are three ways for us to analyze this problem. First, we can observe the role played by one of the commentators throughout the works of Saint Thomas. Second, we can try to discern in one of the commentaries of Saint Thomas how he handles the resources provided by the various commentators: the Greek, the Arabic, or even the Latin (Albert the Great). Finally, on a point of doctrine, we can record the discussions engaged in by the various interpreters and from which he builds up his own exegesis.

To give an example of the first case: the paraphrase of Themistius on the *De Anima* was translated only in 1267. Saint Thomas used it immediately at Paris, at the crest of the Averroistic crisis, for a course whose transcription by Reginald of Piperno forms the text of book I. As a result, in the text now in circulation, the two other books, derived from previous teaching, do not reveal that Saint Thomas had a direct knowledge of Themistius, while the first book is full of him (28).

For the second case, an example is furnished by the *Commentary on the Metaphysics* that Saint Thomas worked at over a long period (29). It gives a constant, if not a manifest account of the various elaborations of the Ancients. Consequently, each chapter should be closely looked into in order that the controversies and options present in it be detected (30).

As an example of the third case, record what happens in the medieval commentators, after the arrival of Averroes, to Aristotle's theory on time. Through this study, one detects the evolution that Saint Thomas undergoes, which is stabilized in his *Commentary on*

the *CPMA* decided upon in 1930 by the Union académique internationale. Under the title of *Aristoteles latinus*, a number of volumes have been published: *Description of the codices*, 3 vols.: Pars prior, Rome, 1939; Pars posterior, Cambridge (England), 1955; Supplementa altera, Paris-Bruges, 1961;—*Categoriae vel Praedicamenta*, vol. I, 1–5, Bruges-Paris, 1961;—*Analytica priora*, vol. III, 1–4, Bruges-Paris, 1962;—*Analytica posteriora*, vol. IV, 2–3, Bruges-Paris, 1953–1954;—*De mundo*, vol. XI, 1–2, Rome, 1951;—*Politica* (libri I–II, 11), vol. XXIX, 1, Bruges-Paris, 1961;—*De arte poetica*, vol. XXXIII, Bruges-Paris, 1953. On the *Aristoteles latinus*, see A. MANSION, *Les prémices de l'*Aristoteles latinus, in *RPL*, XLIV (1946), 104–129, and *Le progrès de l'*Aristoteles latinus, *ibid.*, LIV (1956), 90–111.]

28) See M. DE CORTE, *Thémistius et saint Thomas*, in *AHDLMA*, VII (1933), 47–83; D. SALMAN, in *BT*, III (1930–1933), 1014–1020. G. VERBEKE opposes this position. See *Les sources et la chronologie du commentaire de S. Thomas au De anima d'Aristote*, in *RPL*, LXV (1947), 314–348 [and his *Thémistius. Commentaire sur le traité de l'âme d'Aristote*, in *CLCAG*, I (1957), IX–XXXVIII.]

29) See A. MANSION, *Pour l'histoire du commentaire de S. Thomas sur la Métaphysique*, in *RNSP*, XXVI (1925), 274–295.

30) We have already referred to A. FESTUGIÈRE's provocative *Notes sur les sources du commentaire de saint Thomas au livre XII des Métaphysiques*, in *RSPT*, XVIII (1929), 282–290, 657–663.

the Physics. As a result, the dating of this work must be retarded to about 1268 (31). In instances of the present type, however, an analysis of the commentaries debouches into the history of doctrines.

As these equally fruitful and exciting researches are pursued, it will be opportune to take notice of the exegetical lacunae that Saint Thomas and his contemporaries have to contend with because of their lack of available historical knowledge about Aristotle's works: texts in a state of corruption (32); sections of the *corpus* still unknown (judging from the manner in which Saint Thomas complains about it, one can guess what he desired and wanted); finally, lack of awareness of the inner genesis of the Philosopher's *corpus* and of the concrete conditions of its composition (33).

31) See A. MANSION, *La théorie aristotélicienne du temps chez les péripatéticiens médiévaux, Averroès, Albert le Grand, Thomas d'Aquin,* in *RNSP,* XXXVI (1934), 275–307. [Also I.TH. ESCHMANN, *CSTW,* 404, and the references given by him.] For another example, examine the influence which the *De coelo* of SIMPLICIUS, translated in 1271, had on the last works of Saint Thomas.

32) For example, the text of the *translatio media* of *Metaph,* IV, 4, 1005b35–1006a5 (on the first principles) is so obscure that Saint Thomas in his commentary has reversed the problem (see lect. 6; Marietti ed., n. 606); yet, without having been able to read the doctrine in the passage, he has nonetheless understood it. See E. GILSON, *Réalisme thomiste et critique de la connaissance,* Paris, 1939, 201.

In *In VII Eth.,* lect. 11; Marietti ed., 393, n. 1470, due to the translation he is using in which he finds: "*Iste* enim architecton ad quem respicientes . . . ," Saint Thomas reads that "pleasure is the architectonic end," whereas the word *iste* [of Aristotle's text] refers to the political philosopher. The doctrine Saint Thomas exposes is nonetheless one of good Aristotelianism; see *Ia–IIae,* q. 34, a. 4, s.c.

In *Metaph.,* VI, 1, 1026a14, Saint Thomas reads ἀχώριστα as furthermore occurs in the manuscripts. The true reading is a very hard one to determine, and today some propose to read χώριστα. [On this point, see V. DÉCARIE, *La physique porte-t-elle sur des "non-séparés"?,* in *RSPT,* XXXVIII (1954), 466–468, and *L'objet de la métaphysique selon Aristote,* in *PIEM,* XVI (1961), 117–118, note 3.] The choice of Saint Thomas on this point determines his conception of the ordering of the physical disciplines. See A. FESTUGIÈRE, *La place du "De anima" dans le système aristotélicien d'après S. Thomas,* in *AHDLMA,* VI (1931), 26, note 2.

33) For example, unawareness as to the wavering and the development of Aristotle's doctrine on truth and error, from the *Perihermeneias* to the Vth book of the *Metaphysics.*

Saint Thomas believed the works of Aristotle had been drafted as organic and finished wholes. "It is moreover ridiculous to say that Aristotle renews his examination of the subject from the beginning, as if he had left something out, as the Commentator imagines. There was ample opportunity for Aristotle to correct his book, and to supply at the right place what had been left out, if he wanted to avoid proceeding inordinately." *In VIII Phys.,* lect. 1; Marietti ed., 500, n. 966. The authors of that day could not imagine what has been revealed to us in our day by the researches of W. JAEGER, *Aristoteles. Grundlegung einer Geschichte seiner Entwicklung,* Berlin, 1923 [trans. with the author's corrections and additions by R. ROBINSON, *Aristotle. Fundamentals of the History of his Development,* Oxford, 1934], of F. NUYENS, *L'évolution de la psychologie d'Aristote,* trans. from the Dutch and ed. in *ATE,* VI (1948), of A. MANSION, and of others.

IV. THE TECHNIQUE OF THE COMMENTARY

As one follows the long effort of the medieval peripatetics relentlessly working at their texts, one is led to presume that they found them as difficult as do Moderns, be they translators or exegetes. M. Grabmann has described with very fruitful results the literature wherein are recorded the efforts, methods, and means employed during the XIIth and XIIIth centuries (a). It is within the context of this work that we have to locate Saint Thomas and his technical efforts whose elements may be described as follows:

Saint Thomas brings his whole effort to bear upon a minute and closely literal analysis. Tradition supplied him with two types of interpretation: the paraphrase and the piecemeal literal commentary. We have already seen that circumstances as well as his temperament moved him to make use of the second method, which he pushed to even a word for word commentary, whereas Albert had paraphrased successive paragraphs and transformed his exegesis into questions and investigations (34). At times, it is true, Saint Thomas brings in doctrinal digressions. When he does so, however, one feels that his digressing oversteps the text under the pressure of the controversies that the Stagirite's positions impose on his contemporaries and on his own tenets as a Christian. His concern for the letter of the text places him akin to Averroes in technique. The latter's commentary was, in fact, the prototype of the literal commentary and the precise reason he was accepted, as both the need for and the difficulty of a close exegesis of the Philosopher's very compact text became apparent. A few attempts at literalness of this kind may be found among the Latins. They were produced in the faculty of arts. They have little import, however, and do not manage to reduce the originality of Saint Thomas (35).

Parcelling of the text is one of the first results issuing from the

---

a) See above, note 8.

34) This manner of paraphrasing was described by his bibliographer as one "per modum *scripti*" [in the manner of a *writing*] (*Stams Tabula*, Denifle-Ehrle ed., in *ALKGMA*, II (1886), 236), as opposed to one "per modum *commenti*" [in the manner of a *commentary*]. As a matter of fact, when Albert gave his second teaching on the *Posterior Analytics* and on the *Ethics,* this time he used the commentary method. See G. MEERSSEMAN, *Introductio in opera B. Alberti*, Bruges, 1931, 4.

35) This originality had been noticed by his contemporaries. TOLOMEO OF LUCCA, in his *Historia ecclesiastica nova*, c. 24, in *RIS*, XI (1727), col. 751, writes: ". . . he wrote out a commentary of . . . unique and new in its way of imparting." See P. MANDONNET, *Des écrits authentiques de saint Thomas d'Aquin*, 2d rev. ed., Fribourg, 1910, 60 [Foster ed., 131]. Later on, as we saw above (ch. II), interpretation in the form of *quaestiones*, as practiced from the XIVth century onwards, led to an abandoning of literal exegesis. Hence the reaction of the Renaissance Aristotelians. See A. RENAUDET, *Préréforme et Humanisme à Paris pendant les premières guerres d'Italie (1494–1517)*, in *BIFF*, 1st ser., IV (1916) [2d ed., 1953], 281, 424.

literal method. The commentator proceeds to divide and subdivide his text, all the while seeking to discover in it a perfectly co-ordinated logical plan (36). Today we feel that an attempt to find this kind of logical coherence in a text approaches the point of artifice. It does not take into account the fact that something may have been spontaneously added and that the text may contain some amount of meandering. In Aristotle, we know, the text is far from always having been "composed". The fact becomes particularly perceptible when we try to establish the general outline of one of his works, of the *Metaphysics* for instance, which its author did not in the least compose to form an organically integrated unity (see the plan proposed by Saint Thomas, whereas, among others, book V is an independent summary of metaphysical concepts). The method has less drawbacks where the commentator, working on the detail of the text, is devoting his main effort to a minute exegesis of it (37).

Turning now to the treatment of textual detail, we observe to how great a degree the analysis of words and concepts is pushed, with the terms *idest* [that is] and *scilicet* [namely] used to present basically equivalent meanings, or at times to prepare the way for ideological options. A close notice of them should be taken, for they are not simple verbal glossings.

References to contexts—the immediate context, the more general one, or the system as a whole—are the rule adhered to when litigious or obscure points come up. No doubt that the estimation and the handling of these contexts reveal, over and beyond philological speculation of any kind, the commentator's mental acumen. The so minute parcelling we were speaking about has its counterpart here in the commentator's feeling for the implicit coherence of doctrines. He is led thereby to a rediscovery of the intuitions through which his author achieved the unity of his thought. A. Mansion's observation about the commentary of Saint Thomas on the *De sensu* can be extended to the whole of his work:

> Whether the question be one of opinions touching upon psychology, physics, or physiology, Saint Thomas is always particular about locating within the whole of their systems the particular views which the

---

36) An idea of the procedure can be gathered through the use of the outlines which the recent editors of many of the commentaries, R. CATHALA and A. PIROTTA [R. M. SPIAZZI, MAGGIOLO, and others], have placed before each section of the text. See any one of the recent Marietti editions of the commentaries. The reader must extract these outlines if he wishes to make his way through the series of subdivisions.

37) As regards the classification of the treatises in their relation to one another, Saint Thomas managed to have his preoccupation for doctrinal and pedagogical systematization prevail over Aristotle's views, as is seen, for the works on natural philosophy, in his commentary on the *De sensu et sensato*. See A. FESTUGIÈRE, *La place du "De anima" dans le système aristotélicien de S. Thomas*, in *AHDLMA*, VI (1931), 25–47.

Greek philosophers set forward on this or that point of detail. His historical exegesis thus takes on a characteristic of much greater comprehensiveness than Alexander's. His interpretation is not less historical, perhaps it is more so, but it hereby becomes more philosophical since it goes back to the principles that brought the thinkers of Antiquity to the conclusions the exact meaning of which is being sought after (38).

A mindfulness for synthesis of this sort compensates to a large degree for the ignorance of the Medievals about the genesis of Aristotle's system and about Greek thought's circumstantial history. To be sure, Saint Thomas was not an historian. Yet counter to Albert who was an easy prey to concordism, he discerns vividly the inner movement, the spiritual autonomy, and the progress of currents of thought. Within the limits we have distinctly marked out, one could, without paradox, make a study on Saint Thomas, historian of philosophy (39).

V. THE WORKS SAINT THOMAS COMMENTED UPON

Whereas Albert the Great, with his encyclopedic curiosity and the zeal with which he undertook to reveal Aristotle to the Latins, tackled the whole of the then-known *corpus* of the Philosopher, including the latter's physiological treatises *De Animalibus* which furnished the matter for one of his most brilliant commentaries, Saint Thomas applied himself to the more directly philosophical works. Within this field, however, his commenting took him from the psycho-physiological *Minor Works* to the *Politics*, and from the works on logic to the *Meteorologica*. The list of these commentaries has long been established on the basis of the catalogs that determined at a very early date the authentic works in this field. Some editions, however, followed the Stams catalogue (40), accepting the three commentaries on the

---

38) A. MANSION, *Le commentaire de S. Thomas sur le* De sensu et sensato *d'Aristote*, in *Mélanges Mandonnet*, I (*BibTh*, XIII, 1930), 98.

N.B.—Whereas in his referring from one treatise to another Albert the Great refers the reader to his own commentaries, Saint Thomas in most cases refers to Aristotle's text. The reference remains a vague one (*alibi*) [elsewhere] when he refers to his own works.

39) TH. DEMAN gives a good example of this kind of study on one of the delicate problems of Greek philosophy in his article: *Remarques critiques de saint Thomas sur Aristote interprète de Platon*, in *RSPT*, XXX (1941), 133–148.

40) See the Denifle-Ehrle ed. of it in *ALKGMA*, II (1888), 237, or P. MANDONNET, *Des écrits authentiques de S. Thomas d'Aquin*, 2d rev. ed., Fribourg, 1910, 92, who reveals the imperfections of this catalogue. In it, the *De somno et vigilia* alone is mentioned, but the two other treatises, very short ones, are no doubt understood as going with it [Latin ed. *In De somno et vigilia*: Parma, XX, 214–228; Vivès, XXIV, 293–310.—*In De somniis*: Parma, XX, 229–238; Vivès, XXIV, 311–323.—*In De divinatione per somnium*: Parma, XX, 239–244; Vivès, XXIV, 325–331].

De somno et vigilia, the *De somniis,* and the *De divinatione per somnium.* Today there is agreement to reject their authenticity. As a result, we have the following commentaries (in parentheses is an indication of the terminal point of the unfinished ones) (a):

In libros Perihermeneias (as far as book II, chapter 2 inclusively)
In libros Posteriorum Analyticorum

a) Latin ed. and English trans.—*In libros Perihermeneias expositio*: Parma, XVIII, 1–83; Vivès, XXII, 1–102; Leonine, I, 5–128; Marietti, 1955 (Leonine text). English trans. J. T. OESTERLE, *Aristotle: On Interpretation. Commentary by St. Thomas and Cajetan,* in *MPTT,* XI (1962).—*In libros posteriorum Analyticorum expositio*: Parma, XVIII, 84–225; Vivès, XXII, 103–291; Leonine, I, 129–403; Marietti, 1955 (Leonine text). English trans. P. CONWAY, *Saint Thomas Aquinas. Exposition of the Posterior Analytics of Aristotle* (mimeographed ed.), Quebec, 1956.—*In octo libros Physicorum expositio:* Parma, XVIII, 226–538; Vivès, XXII, 292–709; Leonine II; Marietti, 1954 (Leonine text). English trans. of book I by R. A. KOCOUREK, *An Introduction to the Philosophy of Nature,* St. Paul, Minn., 1948; trans. of book III, lect. 1–5 by J. A. MC WILLIAMS, *Physics and Philosophy. A Study of Saint Thomas's Commentary on the Eight Books of Aristotle's Physics,* in *CUA-PS,* II (1945).—*In libros De caelo et mundo expositio:* Parma, XIX, 1–207; Vivès, XXIII, 1–266; Leonine, III, 1–257; Marietti, 1952 (Leonine text).—*In libros De generatione et corruptione expositio:* Parma, XIX, 208–299; Vivès, XXIII, 267–386; Leonine, III, 261–322; Marietti, 1952 (Leonine text).—*In libros Meteorologicorum expositio:* Parma XIX, 300–441; Vivès, XXIII, 387–571; Leonine, III, 325–421; Marietti, 1952 (Leonine text). English trans. of book I, lect. 8–10 by L. THORNDIKE, *Latin Treatises on Comets between 1238 and 1368.* Chicago, 1950, 77–86.—*In libros De anima expositio:* Parma, XX, 1–144; Vivès, XXIV, 1–195; Marietti, 4th ed., 1959. English trans. by K. FOSTER and S. HUMPHRIES with an Introduction by I. THOMAS, *Aristotle's De anima in the Version of William of Moerbeke and the Commentary of St. Thomas Aquinas,* in *RMPS,* 2d printing, 1954; trans. of book I, lect. 1–2, book II, lect. 1–13, 24, book III, lect. 1–13 by R. A. KOCOUREK, *The Commentary of Saint Thomas Aquinas on Aristotle's Treatise on the Soul,* St. Paul, Minn., 1946. —*In librum De sensu et sensato expositio:* Parma, XX, 145–196; Vivès, XXIV, 197–267; Marietti, 1949.—*In librum De memoria et reminiscentia expositio:* Parma, XX, 197–214; Vivès, XXIV, 269–292; Marietti, 1949.—*In duodecim libros Metaphysicorum expositio:* Parma, XX, 245–654; Vivès, XXIV, 333–649; XXV, 1–229; Marietti, 1950. English trans. J. P. ROWAN, *St. Thomas Aquinas. Commentary on the Metaphysics of Aristotle,* 2 vols., in *LLCT,* 1961.— *In decem libros Ethicorum expositio:* Parma, XXI, 1–363; Vivès, XXV, 231–614; XXVI, 1–88; Marietti, 1949. English trans. of books VIII and IX by P. CONWAY, *St. Thomas Aquinas. On Aristotle's Love and Friendship (Ethics, Books VIII–IX),* Providence, 1951.—*In libros Politicorum expositio:* Parma, XXI, 364–716; Vivès, XXVI, 89–513; Marietti, 1959.—To gather an idea of the condition of the vulgate text of the commentaries of Saint Thomas—or for that matter, of any one of his texts not yet critically worked out by the Leonine editors—the reader is referred to the article by C. MARTIN, *The Vulgate Text of Aquinas's Commentary on Aristotle's Politics,* in *DSt,* V (1952), 35–64. From this case as from others that could be adduced (see below, ch. VIII, 247, note b), one sees why critical editions such as those being brought out by the Leonine editors are a necessity. On the Leonine edition itself, see G. M. GRECH, *The Leonine Edition of the Works of St. Thomas Aquinas, Its Origin, Method and Published Works,* in *FAS,* 218–258.—Concerning all of the commentaries mentioned here, and the other works of Saint Thomas studied later in this book, the reader should consult I. T. ESCHMANN's important *CSTW.* On the commentaries on Aristotle, see 400–405.

In VIII libros Physicorum

In III libros de Caelo et Mundo (as far as book III, chapter 8; finished by Peter of Auvergne)

In II libros de Generatione et Corruptione (as far as book I, chapter 17; finished by Thomas of Sutton?)

In IV libros Meteorologicorum (as far as book II, chapter 10)

In III libros de Anima

In librum de Sensu et Sensato

In librum de Memoria et Reminiscentia

In XII libros Metaphysicorum

In X libros Ethicorum

In libros Politicorum (as far as book III, chapter 6; finished by Peter of Auvergne).

In order to locate the enterprise of Saint Thomas within the Aristotelian crisis, as well as to note the insertion of controversial issues into the detailed commenting of the texts, it is helpful to fix the date of composition of the commentaries. The consensus is to defer the composition of them as a whole to the second part of the career of Saint Thomas, at the end of his first sojourn in Italy and during his second sojourn at Paris. It is difficult, however, to arrive at precisions on either the relative chronology of the various treatises or the dating of each one. It has been possible, nevertheless, to establish a few points of reference, the most interesting of which are as follows (41):

—the use made of Simplicius (his *Categories* translated in 1266, his *De caelo* in 1271), with the result that various sections of the *Metaphysics* and of the *De caelo* have been dated;

—the doctrinal evolution of Saint Thomas on the problem of the eternity of the world with the result that the *Physics* are dated after 1268, while the *Ia Pars* comes before (in 1266);

—the commentary on the *Politics* left unfinished as Saint Thomas was approaching the end of his career at Paris, where Peter of Auvergne, who carried on the work, was his pupil only after 1268.

Let us mention finally the commentary on the famous *Liber de causis* composed in the same style and under the same circum-

---

41) Father Mandonnet attempted a chronological distribution of the commentaries according to the indications Tolomeo of Lucca supplies in his catalogue of Saint Thomas's works (The catalogue was edited and presented in his *Des écrits authentiques de S. Thomas d'Aquin*, 2d rev. ed., Fribourg, 1910, 55–63). The data furnished by Tolomeo, however, are unreliable [See Foster ed., 141, n. 8 and 13; 142, n. 16; 144, n. 25]. See A. MANSION, *Le commentaire de S. Thomas sur le De sensu*, in *Mélanges Mandonnet*, I (*BibTh*, XIII, 1930), 84–88; also *Date de quelques commentaires de saint Thomas sur Aristote* (De interpretatione, De anima, Metaphysica), in *SMM*, 271–287 [Also *CSTW*, 400–405 and the reviews of the work being done on the commentaries, in the *BT*].

stances (a). The work was part of the Aristotelian *corpus* then in circulation (see the manuscripts). Through his sensitiveness to the Platonism of the work, Saint Thomas was the one to make its origin known with the help of William of Moerbeke's translation of the Στοιχείωσις Θεολογική [*Elementatio theologica*] of Proclus (42). The importance of this work is not thereby diminished, however, either as regards XIIIth century Aristotelianism or as regards its place among the commentaries of Saint Thomas. The commentary remains one of great interest from both standpoints.

The commentary on Boethius' minor work, entitled *De hebdomadibus,* a work less far-reaching in scope, also belongs to the same literary genre (a). This *De hebdomadibus* is, on the whole, a Platonic treatise on participation: "How can substances, by the fact that they are, be good, when they are not substantial goods?" (b). Boethius answers this question for one of his disciples, John the Deacon, who had questioned his master on certain difficulties he had run into while reading a work called *De hebdomadibus,* which we no longer have today. Hence the medieval title given to Boethius' answer, which thus obtained a position in XIIIth century university teaching (43).

---

a) Latin ed.—*In librum De causis expositio:* Parma, XXI, 717–760; Vivès, XXVI, 514–570; Marietti, 1955; especially the critical ed., prepared by H. D. SAFFREY, in *TPF*, IV/V (1954), in the introduction of which the reader will find extensive data on the historical, doctrinal, and critical aspects of the work. See *CSTW*, 407.

42) The *Liber De causis* is a work of Arabic origin. The substance of it, however, is borrowed from the treatise of Proclus. Saint Thomas himself states the problem concerning it in the following words: "And in Greek, as a matter of fact, one finds a book done up in this manner. It is the work of the Platonist Proclus. It contains CCXI propositions, and is entitled *Elementatio Theologica.* Now, the present book called *De causis* by the Latins is also found in Arabic. One notices that the Latin of it is a translation from the Arabic, and that it is absolutely not found in Greek. It would seem, therefore, that it represents an excerpting from the said book of Proclus done by one of the Arabic philosophers, considering especially that everything it contains is present in the other in a much fuller and detailed fashion." *In lib. de causis,* prooem.; Saffrey ed., 3. See H. BÉDORET, *L'auteur et le traducteur du* Liber de causis, in *RNSP*, XLI (1938), 521–533; M. GRABMANN, *Die Proklosübersetzungen des Wilhelm von Moerbeke* . . . in *MAG*, II (1936), 413–423.

a) Latin ed.—Parma, XVII, 339–348; Vivès, XXVIII, 469–481; *Uecelli*, 255–274; Marietti, in *Opusc. theol.,* II, 391–408. See *CSTW*, 406.

b) ". . . modum quo substantiae in eo quod sunt, bonae sunt, cum non sint substantialia bona. . . ." *In De hebdom.,* lect. 1, textus Boetii; Marietti ed., of the *Opusc. theol.,* II, 392.

43) In the title *De hebdomadibus,* one must read neither the meaning of *conceptiones* [conceptions] as did Gilbert of la Porrée, nor that of *editiones* [editions] as did Saint Thomas, but rather a reference, no doubt, to the division of the original work, in which the chapters or the questions must have been grouped by series of seven in accordance with a procedure of which Boethius was not the creator. See U. DEGLI INNOCENTI, *Nota al* De Hebdomadibus *di Boezio,* in *DTP*, XLII (1939), 397–399. C. FABRO, *La nozione metafisica di*

VI. THE COMMENTARIES ON DIONYSIUS

After Aristotle, Dionysius: another world. Yet, Saint Thomas proceeds into it with the same ease as in that of Aristotle, except as regards procedures of textual attire. If Saint Thomas, in his courses on the texts, had done nothing else than to work as an historian after the modern fashion, this fact alone would be witness, no further one needed, to the broad and objective suppleness of his mind in respecting texts so different in their make-up. We have seen, however, that the medieval commentator is one who believes in his text. When he is penetrating it, he does so in a hearty adherence to it. Under these circumstances, let Saint Thomas comment upon Dionysius on a par with Aristotle—if not as extensively, at least as attentively—and we become alerted to the genesis of his thought and to the dimensions of his system (44).

Let it be added that this commenting is, also, the fruit of a teaching that was done after the same type and within the same framework as that upon Aristotle, although it is hard to say in what measure the practice of commenting on Dionysius established itself at the faculty of theology during the XIIIth century. Saint Thomas, we know, had followed at Paris as well as at Cologne the courses of his master Albert, who was then busy at his running commentary on the works of Dionysius (45). It is an annoying shortcoming, therefore, and one laden with consequences that modern Thomists, who are assiduous readers of the commentaries on Aristotle, should open the commentaries on Dionysius only for a few occasional references. Let us censure once more this unbalanced state of affairs affecting, over and beyond the understanding of Saint Thomas, the whole of theology called modern. At the University of Paris, the name Dionysius stood as a text for teaching, a source of thought, and a master in matters Christian.

---

partecipazione secondo S. Tomaso, 2d ed., in *StS,* 1950, 24–35, and L.-B. GEIGER, *La participation dans la philosophie de S. Thomas d'Aquin,* 2d ed., in *BibTh,* XXIII (1953), 36–73, have revealed the significance of this commentary of Saint Thomas. [See also FABRO's *Participation et causalité selon S. Thomas d'Aquin,* in *CCM,* II (1961), 268–280.]

44) Saint Thomas quotes Dionysius frequently. More than 1700 quotations have been counted. [Latin ed.—*In librum Beati Dionysii de divinis nominibus expositio:* Parma, XV, 258–405; Vivès, XXIX, 374–580; Marietti, 1950. See *CSTW,* 406–407.]

45) We have, probably in the handwriting of Saint Thomas, the *reportatio* [lecture transcript] of the *Commentary on Dionysius* which Albert taught at Paris around 1247 and at Cologne after 1248. The manuscript containing the *Commentary on the Celestial Hierarchy* is marked with the word *petiae* [parts] which testifies to the work's official recording with the University bookdealer. See G. THÉRY, *L'autographe de S. Thomas conservé à la Biblioteca Nazionale de Naples,* in *AFP,* I (1931), 15–86. See below, note 56. [On the *pecia,* see above, ch. I, note 2.]

Dionysius, then, was an "authority" as a text for teaching as well as through his being accredited as a Christian writer. Moreover, he had the aureola of being thought at that time to have been a disciple of Saint Paul. His works were a particularly active ferment in the revival brought about by the reading of the Oriental Fathers in the XIIth century, and they enjoyed very broad diffusion as a result of their multiplied translations (46). It would seem that this penetration of Oriental neo-Platonism unbalanced a few theologians for a while, or rather certain currents of thought in which the Dionysian theories fed a type of syncretism that the Western theologians had not foreseen (47). From the XIIth century, however, the exegesis of the Victorines had brought in what was required to tone down both texts and thought. The result was that when Saint Thomas began his public commentary on Dionysius, he did so without its involving the sort of exegetical conflicts that Aristotle provoked. Consequently, if the interest he took in the Dionysian *corpus* was not a novelty, on the other hand, it was due to give a powerful expression to a doctrinal and university tradition destined to become one of the components of the medieval mentality. It also seems that, from the standpoint of the living substance of his theology conceived as a science of God, he found in Dionysius an outstanding ingredient. A literal commentary on his texts would, in his opinion, give an adequate preparation for a later personal elaboration. Such are the motives and intentions of Saint Thomas in his Dionysian commentaries.

It would seem, on the strength of a few external resemblances, that Saint Thomas thought for a time that Dionysius, whose symbolism promotes the value of the sensible as regards the life of the mind, approximated the views of Aristotle (48). Very soon, however, he perceived that the Dionysian contemplation of the sensible world had nothing to do with the Philosopher's almost sensualistic experimen-

---

46) Recent researches (Théry) have revealed both this multiplication and diffusion. The undertakings of Thomas Gallus (1238–1244) and of Robert Grosseteste (around 1240–1243)—enterprises furthermore bonded by the friendship and the spiritual culture of the two men (see D. CALLUS, *The Date of Grosseteste's Translations and Commentaries on Ps.-Dionysius and the Nicomachean Ethics,* in *RTAM,* XIV (1947), 186–210)—bear witness to the inquisitiveness aroused by Dionysius in the pre-Albert the Great and Thomas Aquinas generation. [See furthermore D. CALLUS, *Robert Grosseteste as Scholar,* in *RGSB,* 55–61, and H. F. DONDAINE, *Le corpus dionysien de l'Université de Paris au XIII siècle,* Rome, 1953.]

47) Witness to this syncretism and lack of balance are the incidents provoked around 1200 by the revival of Erigenism (Amaury of Bène), and again, later on, as the University of Paris was in full development, the syllabus of ten propositions condemned in 1241. See M.-D. CHENU, *Le dernier avatar de la théologie orientale en Occident au XIIIe siècle,* in *Mélanges A. Pelzer (UL-RTHP,* 3d ser., XXVI, 1947), 159–181.

48) "Almost everywhere Dionysius follows Aristotle, as appears evident to one inspecting his books with care." *In II Sent.,* d. 14, q. 1, a. 2.

talism, and he recognized that Dionysius lived in another universe (49). This is not the place to look into the way Saint Thomas built his own system starting from masters that were so far apart. From the standpoint of his literal commentary, however, we must note the internal resistance he experienced, to the point of expressing it bluntly (a thing he rarely does), as regards the style, the way of thinking, in brief the mentality of the Areopagite—a man for whom symbolism is the key to the understanding of the universe, and therefore the privileged form of thought (50). We have had occasion to quote these reflexions made by Saint Thomas. In the present instance, they become of prime importance to define as one of deep-reaching transposition of style—literary and mental style—the effort at analysis he pursued as a commentator. No doubt that we have here, at least at this level, the essential trait and, therefore, the key to this commentary, namely: to reduce to homogeneous mental categories the mystico-metaphysical attire of the Oriental doctor (51). On this point Saint

---

49) ". . . very often, he uses the style and the way of speaking which was in use among the Platonists, but which is uncommon among the moderns". *In De div. nom.*, prooem.; Marietti ed., 1. "Dionysius who in many things was a follower of the Platonic tenets. . . ." *De malo*, q. 16, a. 1, ad 3um.

50) "The Blessed Dionysius uses an obscure style in all of his books". *In De div. nom.*, prooem.; Marietti ed., 1. "If however Dionysius is here speaking according to his own opinion, then one must say that he is speaking in a metaphorical sense." *Ibid.*, c. 4, lect. 19; Marietti ed., 197, n. 540. One must, moreover, distinguish between metaphorical language proper and the expressing procedures issuing in all Platonisms from the theory of Ideas. Saint Thomas is very accurate in his uncovering of this origin of the Dionysian vocabulary. See *ibid.*, prooem.; Marietti ed., 1–2.

To the elements which raise difficulties for him in the language of Dionysius, he adds a curious mixture of conciseness ("he often implies these [reasons] in a few and even in one word") and of abundance ("he often practices a certain multipleness of words which, superfluous though they appear, are discovered to contain great depth in what they assert, if one looks into them with care." *Ibid.*). Of Aristotle, on the contrary, he said: "Using an admirable conciseness." *In I Perih.*, lect. 7; Marietti ed., 35, n. 84; Oesterle ed., 61, n. 2.

51) It goes without saying that this conceptual reducing implies some shifting and outstepping of the Dionysian thought. Herein as in the case of Aristotle, by declaring himself in agreement with Dionysius, Saint Thomas is sometimes consciously drawing him to his own meaning, as for example when he has the metaphysics of the good concurring with the metaphysics of being. MR. GILSON quotes very opportunely the following text in which Saint Thomas notes the Platonic primacy of good over the Christian primacy of being (*L'esprit de la philosophie médiévale*, 2d ed., in *EPM*, XXXIII (1944), 94, note 5 [The text does not occur in the English trans. of the 1st ed. by A. H. C. DOWNES, *The Spirit of Mediaeval Philosophy*, New York, 1940]): "According to the Platonists, the prime cause is in fact above being inasmuch as the essence of goodness and of oneness, which the prime cause is, surpasses separate being itself, as was stated above; according to truth, however, the prime cause is above being inasmuch as it is infinite being itself." *In De causis*, lect. 6; Saffrey ed., 47.

To give a characteristic case of this kind of exegesis which proceeds through a simple reversal of words, on a famous text lying at the very heart of the Dionysian method: About the knowledge we can have of God, Dionysius says (*De div.*

Thomas is to be located within the tradition opened up by Maxim the Confessor who was to make Dionysius intelligible to the Western world. Maxim, Aristotelian in technique, but Dionysian in spiritual orientation, had been and remained the tutor of all the commentators on Dionysius. Likewise, the lifework of Saint Thomas must be located within history, since it gives the true and ample measure of his enterprise.

From the standpoint of equipment, the translations Saint Thomas the commentator used are perhaps of greater importance in the case of Dionysius than in the case of Aristotle. They have, to a greater extent, in the access they give to the original text, their own means of creating vocabulary (this expression must be taken in its fullest sense) and of psychological perception. It is in this way that one should measure the role played by Scotus Erigena whose efforts were a source of fermentation in the Western world over a period of centuries (52). Saint Thomas made use of the versions then available to him, all of which depended on that of Scotus (53) because Hilduin's (IXth century) had had no diffusion. It would be useless— and at any rate almost impossible—to look for the part each one played in the work of Saint Thomas. As a matter of fact, he faces a henceforth aggregate whole made up of versions, scholia, interlinear or marginal glosses, résumés (*extracta*), commentaries (*expositiones*), all of which overspread one another and compose an extremely compact context of interpretation. This context has to be reconstructed in order to encamp the commentary of Saint Thomas on its own grounds. Let us recall briefly the elements making up this context.

The two master versions are those of Scotus Erigena, the *vetus translatio* [the old translation], and of John the Saracene (around 1167). The latter, which Albert the Great had already chosen as the better one (54), is basically the one used by Saint Thomas. Maxim's scholia, as a medium of a common inheritance, feed directly or in-

---

nom., c. 7, in *Dion*, I (1937), 403–404): ". . . we rise [to God] by removing from Him all else, by attributing to Him all else in an eminent degree, by making of Him the cause of all else"; Saint Thomas, however, restates these three operations in an inverted order: "[Dionysius] says that from creatures we arrive at God in three ways, namely: by way of causality, of removal, of eminence" (*In I Sent.*, d. 3, div. textus). De facto, the entire Dionysian doctrine is thus reversed. See E. GILSON, *Le thomisme*, 5th ed., in *EPM*, I (1944), 201 [English trans. L. K. SHOOK, *The Christian Philosophy of Saint Thomas Aquinas*, New York, 1956, 140.].

52) On this fermentation of vocabulary, see G. THÉRY, *Scot Erigène traducteur de Denys*, in *ALMA*, VI (1931), 94.

53) About Erigena, SAINT THOMAS says: "One of the first to study the books of Dionysius . . . ; and this was John Scotus who was the first to comment on the books of Dionysius." *In Hebr.*, c. 1, lect. 1; Marietti ed., 355, n. 86.

54) "We intend to expound from the translation of John the Saracene because it is a better one." *In De div. nom.*, prol. (*Munich ms. Clm. 6909*, fol. 111 r).

directly the work being done, as we have seen (55). Hugh of Saint Victor's commentary on the celestial hierarchy was in circulation and its author quoted with the accreditation of a *commentator*. It is not known whether Saint Thomas was acquainted with the works, versions or expositions of Thomas Gallus and of Grosseteste. But it is a sure thing that from the time of his formative years he learned to read the works of Dionysius by means of the direct oral teaching of his master, Albert the Great. It is even probable that we possess a copy of his master's commentary written in Saint Thomas's own hand (56).

VII. RESEARCH SUGGESTIONS

1. With the help of recent discoveries, attempt first of all an inventory of the commentary literature that was done on Aristotle during the second third of the XIIIth century, by the masters of the Faculty of arts especially. The most remarkable one, to start with, is Roger Bacon's who was then at the Faculty of arts, at Paris, around 1245. It was recently edited by R. STEELE and F. DELORME, in *OHIRB*, VII–XIII (1926–1935). We believe that the commentary of Albert the Great who, for his part, was at the Faculty of theology, was undertaken during the same period. Examine this problem (having recourse to Bacon's texts themselves, to the works on the chronology of Albert, examining van Steenberghen's differing opinion expressed in his *Siger de Brabant*, vol. II, in *LPB*, XIII (1942), wherein, moreover,

---

55) In his works, Saint Thomas quotes Maxim's commentary only eleven times, but the latter's influence on him cannot be limited to these explicit references. The *Scholia*, we know, restate the contents of the notes of John of Scythopolis (around 520) and carry on his Christian integrating of the Areopagite's tenets.

56) The problem hinges on a manuscript preserved in the National Library of Naples. In a first part made up of *petiae* [parts], it contains the *Commentary on the Celestial Hierarchy*, and in the second part made up of fascicles, the commentaries on the three other treatises. See G. THÉRY, *L'autographe de S. Thomas conservé à la Biblioteca Nazionale de Naples*, in *AFP*, I (1931), 15–86; M. GRABMANN, *Die Autographe von Werken des heiligen Thomas von Aquin*, in *HJ*, LX (1940), 514–537. [See the references on the *pecia* in ch. I, note 2.]

PETER OF PRUSSIA was the one who recorded the tradition according to which, as a student, Saint Thomas followed the courses of Albert on Dionysius. "As the astonishingly silent Brother Thomas was eagerly intent at prayer and study, the reason of his coming, Master Albert started his 'reading' of the book on the Divine names" (*Vita B. Alberti Magni* [written and edited by PETER OF PRUSSIA; reedited with the minor work *De adhaerendo Deo*, Antwerp, 1621], c. VII, 102. See c. XLII). Indications are that the *Celestial Hierarchy* was commented upon at Paris before 1248, the others at Cologne, between 1248 and 1252.

Vat. Greek ms. 370 contains the works of Dionysius with Latin interlinear glosses borrowed from Scotus Erigena's translation. The oldest catalogs state this manuscript had belonged to "Brother Thomas"; hence the identification: Thomas Aquinas. See G. THÉRY, *Le manuscrit Vat. grec 370 et saint Thomas d'Aquin*, in *AHDLMA*, VI (1931), 5–23.

will be found, together with the pertinent bibliography, a report of researches on the question, 420–446). Seize this opportunity to make a comparison between the works of the two men. Assemble whatever information there is on the commentaries of Shyreswood, Peter of Spain, Grosseteste, Kilwardby, Adam of Buckfield, and others, observing all the while, of course, the stages in the course of which Aristotle's texts were brought into circulation. See the works of Grabmann, Pelster, Lottin, Franceschini, Callus, and of others, and the periodic reviewing of them by A. Dondaine [and others] in the *Bulletin thomiste*.

2. Gather together and analyse the texts testifying to an opposition or to an express reserve concerning Aristotle's teachings: official texts (read attentively the bulls of Gregory IX), sermons, the *pietism* of the *Vitae fratrum* (1256), etc. Observe Albert's violent retorts.

Follow the evolution of the Dominican Order's school legislation. Look into the texts of Humbert of Romans, one who was qualified to speak up. See c. douais, *Essai sur l'organisation des études dans l'Ordre des Frères Prêcheurs*, Paris, 1884.

3. Assemble from one or another of the commentaries the reflexions and observations that illustrate and give precision to what has been noted in the course of the present chapter. Do the same as regards the techniques that were applied.

4. Undertake the study of one of the commentaries in the historical and technical perspective of the ancient Greek or Arabian commentators whose works Saint Thomas was familiar with, so as to penetrate within the latter's own elaboration. Consult the works we have cited. So far, the small number of general works published on the question are only mediocre in value; thus the work of r. laubenthal, *Das Verhältnis des heiligen Thomas von Aquin zu den Arabern in seinem Physikkommentar*, Würzburg, 1933. [See, however, the work done recently in this field by g. verbeke, quoted above, note 28.]

5. Compare Saint Thomas's interpretation with the "historical" exegesis of the moderns. As regards the treatise *On the Soul*, rodier [*Aristote. Traité de l'âme*, traduit et annoté, Paris, 1900] did not give the Medievals much attention, but mansion does it fruitfully in the case of the *Physics* [*Introduction à la Physique aristotélicienne*, 2d ed., in *ATE*, 1946]. With this object in view, see those of the doctrinal monographs in which this comparison is worked out expressly, for example, those of r. jolivet on the notion of creation [*Essai sur les rapports entre la pensée grecque et la pensée chrétienne*, in *BHP*, 1931] and of m. de corte on the theories about the soul [*Thémistius et saint Thomas d'Aquin. Contribution à l'étude des sources et de la chronologie du Commentaire de saint Thomas sur le* De anima, in

AHDLMA, VII (1932), 47–83. See also the works of VERBEKE referred to above, note 22], etc.

6. As regards Dionysins, the work of J. DURANTEL, *Saint Thomas et le Pseudo-Denys*, Paris, 1919, furnishes a basic starting point; it should, however, be made over—with the research done by G. THÉRY over the past 25 years serving as a point of departure. Also A. FEDER, *Des Aquinaten Kommentar zu Ps.-Dionysius De divinis nominibus. Ein Beitrag zur Arbeitsmethode des heiligen Thomas*, in Sch, 1926, 321–351 [and the works referred to above, note 46].

It would be of prime interest to finish the work started here and there on Albert the Great, commentator of Dionysius.

Chapter VII

The Commentaries on the Bible

Many times thus far we have had the opportunity to observe that in XIIIth century theological teaching the Bible was the basic book. It served not only as the prime treasury of the authorities to be used in presenting an assortment of proofs for the arguments undergoing elaboration but as the directly exploited matter itself of that sacred science which theology is—the science of God which takes its departure from the word of God. The master who taught was, literally speaking, and as his official name indicated, a *magister in sacra pagina* (1).

Here, then, is the fact: Saint Thomas, master in theology, took the text iself of the Old and the New Testament as the subject matter of his official course. What we have to find out is under what conditions and with what results he did so, because this fact is one of major importance. It is true that in the history of Thomism the *Summa theologiae* has monopolized everyone's attention and commentaries; but therein precisely lies a grave problem, and to understand and solve it, the first condition is to avoid obliterating the fact that the *Summa* is embedded in an evangelical soil. By no means is this the result of some sort of devotion aiming to retain piousness within its rational systematization, but because therein is provided the law itself of its genesis. In the XIIIth century, the university institution produced disputed questions and *summas* only within the framework

1) See J. DE GHELLINCK, *"Pagina" et "Sacra pagina". Histoire d'un mot et transformation de l'objet primitivement désigné*, in *Mélanges Auguste Pelzer* (*UL–RTHP*, 3d ser., XXVI, 1947), 23–59.

233

of scriptural teaching. In this pedagogical framework, theology found an apt expression of the law that rules over it since theology can become a science only inasmuch as it remains in communion with the word of God that has first to be heard for itself. A tree cut from its roots dies, even if it remains standing.

I. EVANGELISM: THE BASIS

Consequently, before entering upon any kind of analytical examination of Saint Thomas's scriptural work, this is the moment to reconstruct that evangelical atmosphere we have previously evoked (a) and to determine, on documentary and spiritual evidence, the components of it, the very ones Saint Thomas labored on as he "read" Scripture.

During the half-century that preceded the upsurge of the School— to mark off a chronological reference of some kind, let us say during the period between the IIIrd (1179) and the IVth Lateran Councils (1215)—one of the immediately evident characteristics of Christendom at work is the sprouting of interest in the Gospel and the intense curiosity about Scripture that then take hold of the Christian conscience, affecting the plain faithful as well as the professional master. What we have here, in effect, is not only nor primarily the technical effort of a few theologians but rather the stirring up of the Christian soul that becomes sacred-text-intoxicated and Gospel-illumined under the pressure of manifold causes wherein the Spirit is truthfully immerged. From Peter Valdès to Saint Francis, from the *Umigliati* to the Friar Preachers, the movement has shaken up every generation of the end of the XIIth century and of the beginning of the XIIIth. The bristling richness of these movements, their effectiveness, the variety of their content and destiny are known, and any judgement to be passed on them calls for many circumlocutions and insights (2). Yet, the common denominator and the undeniable value of all of them show up more and more as they return to the Gospel that becomes either the directly-sought-after object of knowledge or the fermenting agent in the renewal of institutions. Saint Francis and the Minors, Saint Dominic and the Preachers are the ripe fruits of this fertileness. The difference in their spiritual as well as in their institutional temperaments underscores the transcendency and the poly-

---

a) See chapter I, 44–50.

2) The following "sentence," which had originated in the surroundings of the school of Laon, was in circulation during the XIIth century: "If anyone does not mingle in due proportion Scripture with common sense, the more subtly he reads into it, the madder he is." Quoted by B. SMALLEY, *The Study of the Bible in the Middle Ages*, 2d rev. ed., Oxford, 1952, 68, note 1.

valency of the evangelical ferment which is at work in individuals and communities. Evidence of it is present in even the disequilibrium of those movements that succeeded in the wrong direction. In counteraction against the obsolete institutions and the pharisaic aristocracies, all these "poor" engage in imitation of the Apostles, in itinerant preaching, in teaching of the masses on a witness bearing basis, in ingenuous confraternizing, and in a taste for literal evangelism. The pristine community, as described in the *Acts of the Apostles,* comes to new life in this century of the revolutionary Communes and of the corporate confraternities. A solution will be found for the very difficult passing from evangelical witnessing on a personal basis to the institutionalized form of it in Christendom. Counter to prevalent conservative tendencies and with the tenacious support of Innocent III, "Orders" completely new in structure will stabilize the success of the evangelical movement. The preaching of the word of God, until then in the throes of an insurmountable crisis (3), was freed from its bonds.

It is with this context in mind that one must measure and characterize the technical enlargements and the popular adaptations of the texts of Scripture that were designed for the use of this keenly eager people. Its elites henceforth fill the schools now established outside the traditional cloister which cannot cope with them in either body or spirit. The "scholars," the true scholars, are no longer the monks.

The headings under which the various activities on the Bible can be classified are known: a considerable multiplying of complete or partial copies of the sacred text; translations of it in the vernacular—how greatly deserving they were considering the times—that make it accessible to the nonpossessing the clerical trade-mark; a breaking up of the text into pericopes rendering the manipulation of it possible; practical arrangements of it so as to render its use by the people effective. And if, as always happens, this evangelical wine tends to go to work outside the Church institution, the heretical perverting of it provokes in the faithful a redoubling of inquisitiveness so long as narrow protectionistic tendencies do not channel these efforts into by-products. How well we know what the episodes of that Scripture-based controversy were, and the literature to which it gave rise, running all the way up to and including expositions on tactic and method.

In thus beclad contexts do the renewed techniques for the study of Scripture as pursued in the *magistri in sacra pagina* between 1179

---

3) See R. LADNER, *La pitié de la prédication au tournant du XIIe siècle,* in P. MANDONNET, *Saint Dominique. L'idée, l'homme et l'oeuvre,* Paris, 1937, t. II, ch. 1.

and 1215, offer themselves to us. Miss B. Smalley has brought to light, more than anyone else thus far, the breadth, quality, methods, and promoters of this renovation (4).

Some time ago, in his *Geschichte der scholastischen Methode*, Mgr. Grabmann grouped, in a most provocative manner, under the title of "Biblico-moral School," the three great *magistri in sacra pagina*: Peter Comestor (+ around 1169), Peter the Chanter (+ 1197), and Stephen Langton (who ended his teaching in 1206) (5). He located them in the perspective of the "scholastic method," that is to say, in the perspective of book-of-sentence and *summa* building, opposing them, therefore, to the dialectically inclined theorizers. In order to understand more deeply their role, however, we must furthermore locate them in the perspective of the scriptural work that underlies and expresses the evangelical effervescence of the generations of their day. B. Smalley's erudite prospecting comes, moreover, as a pressing invitation to do so. It would seem that the combined activity of the three masters was a factor of major preeminence, and I, for one, feel some pangs of remorse for having long treated with indifference, beneath the crushing grandeur of the giant theologians of the XIIIth century, these modest plowers of the scriptural soil—the Comestor in particular—upon which precisely those giants trod.

The first indication we have of the evolution then in progress is an external and institutional one, but a far-reaching one. Those being taught the Bible are no longer monks who feed their private life through pious reflexion upon it, they are rather secular clerics engaged in an active program of apostolic conquest. The audience is no longer one of *claustrales* [cloistered people], but of *scholares*, let us translate, of "students," with the unescapable intellectualistic connotation the word has. Disinterested contemplation pays the price for it, since it recedes under the pressure of school procedures, including examination competition, and even the professor's temptation to charge for his lessons. Scripture is the textbook, and to help understand it, instrumentation, methods, grammars, are developed and put to use. The pious suaveness and the literary savoriness so characterstic in the expositions of the Victorines and of a Saint Bernard are made to disappear through the introduction of the *reportatio* [lecture transcript]

---

4) B. SMALLEY, *The Study of the Bible in the Middle Ages*, 2d rev. ed., Oxford, 1952. [A number of studies have since appeared which deal with medieval exegesis in its various aspects. The student should consult in particular: H. DE LUBAC, *Exégèse médiévale. Les quatre sens de l'Ecriture*, 3 vols. (another forthcoming), in *ESJLF–Th*, XLI–XLII (1959–1961), in which he will also find most of the recent bibliography on the subject].

5) See vol. II, Freiburg im Breisgau, 1911, 476 and ff.

technique (a), which is destined to become more extensively used and to be commercialized. Comestor will excuse himself for his *stylus rudis* [unpolished style] (6). Spiritual interpretation itself, which is so difficult to reduce into school formulae due to the role allegory plays in it, conforms to the new requisites. A whole literature of *Distinctiones*, a very curious literary genre destined to flourish over a period of a half-century, establishes a sort of dictionary of the meanings of Scripture. With it, we are far removed from the mystical pliancy with which Saint Bernard comments upon the *Canticle* (7). The *magister in sacra pagina* has taken the place of the abbot, and his exegetical concern replaces monastic paternalism. It is no longer a *collatio* he offers, it is a *lectio*. And he is proud of it. Robert of Courson will say: "He who reads Sacred Scripture publicly, has undertaken a road to perfection superior to that of the Clairvaux monk" (8).

This direct allusion to the Cistercian monk must not make us forget that Citeaux was the herald of Christendom during the XIIth century. It does, however, oblige us to fall in step with a time during which apostolic zeal, pastoral concern, and popular earnestness, read the sacred text in the light of a prevalence of action over contemplation. It has been brought to notice that a number of these *magistri* became great bishops or active reformers. They are the very ones to declare that even though contemplation, by dint of right, is eminent in its essence, the life of him who unites action with contemplation obtains even more excellence (9). The pressure brought to bear by the Christian people gives this principle its context and dynamic force, even if ambition comes to soil its beautiful apostolic service.

Thus, the scientific study of Scripture is undertaken with a view to founding pastoral teaching upon the professor's teaching. Here, as a matter of fact, is the way in which the functions of the *magister*—closely linked functions, but due to become more and more differentiated ones—are marked off from one another: *legere* or to explain

---

a) On this technique, see G. MÜLLER, La *"Reportatio"*, in *Sal*, XXI (1959), 647–659.

6) PETRUS COMESTOR, *Historia scholastica*, prol.; *P.L.*, 198, 1054.

7) This, in fact, is, we believe, the origin and the context of this literary genre from among the various forms of biblical treasuries. On this kind of literature, see besides B. SMALLEY, *op. cit.*, 246 ff., G. LACOMBE, *La vie et les oeuvres de Prévostin*, in *BibTh*, XI (1927), 117–125; C. SPICQ, *Esquisse d'une historie de l'exégèse latine au moyen âge*, in *BibTh*, XXVI (1944), 175–176 [and M.–D. CHENU, *La théologie au XIIe siècle*, in *EPM*, XLV (1957), 196–200].

8) "Qui legit publice sacram scripturam, iter majoris perfectionis arripuit quam aliquis clarevallensis." ROBERT OF COURSON, *Summa*, in *Paris ms., Bibl. nat. lat.* 14524, fol. 74r (quoted by CH. DICKSON, *Le cardinal Robert de Courson*, in *AHDLMA*, IX (1934), 73).

9) B. SMALLEY, *op. cit.*, 249 ff., cites to this effect Robert Pullus, Peter Comestor, Gerald of Wales, and Stephen Langton.

the text, *disputare* or to solve by discussion the questions it raises, *praedicare* or to preach it to the faithful. At the beginning of his *Verbum abbreviatum*, Peter the Chanter marks off their connexion and unfolding in this very manner (10). We have not yet reached, of course, those specialized literary forms to which the development of XIIIth century university life will give rise. From this very moment, however, one can foresee their coming, as Peter the Chanter maintains there is a connexion between the school "lesson" and the pastoral "predication."

In his famous *Didascalicon*, Hugh of Saint Victor had recently furnished the organic principle of a study of Scripture to be done along these lines. Our three masters, the Comestor at the head of the list, bring the Victorine's program into existence: the general plan of it, its method, and the practical advice it contains. Success is achieved, but at the price of the program's involvement in school entanglements in which the Victorine tradition loses its humanistic nature and grace. But at least the principle is consecrated of the primacy of the literal meaning among the multiformed constructions of biblical exegesis: "The basis and principle of sacred teaching is *history*, from which, like honey from the honeycomb, the truth of allegory is extracted" (11). The particular influence exercised by Andrew of Saint Victor (+1175) enters the record here. Parting with the homiletic tone and with theoretic discussions, he attaches himself to a direct and literal interpretation of the text, thus following in the footsteps of Saint Jerome whom he claims as his patron (12).

This is where we have to locate the work of Peter Comestor, that *Historia scholastica* whose role in XIIIth century culture will com-

---

10) PETRUS COMESTOR, *Verbum abbreviatum*, c. 1; *P.L.*, 205, 20: "The usual way of studying Scripture is threefold: reading, disputation, preaching. . . . Reading is, as it were, the foundation and substrate of those following it, for through it the other two procedures are prepared for. Disputation is, as it were, the wall in this practice and building, since nothing is fully understood nor faithfully preached, unless it is first chewed by the tooth of disputation. Preaching, on the other hand, to which the previous are subservient, is, as it were, the roof protecting the faithful from the heat of vices and their agitations." [The words *Verbum abbreviatum* used by Comestor as the title of his work were a current expression to designate Christ. See H. DE LUBAC, *Verbum abbreviatum*, in *op. cit.*, III, 181–197.].

11) ". . . fundamentum autem et principium doctrinae sacrae historia est, de qua quasi mel de favo, veritas allegoriae exprimitur." HUGH OF SAINT VICTOR, *Didascalicon. De studio legendi*, lib. VI, c. 3; Buttimer ed., 116; *P.L.*, 176, 801 C; Taylor ed., 138. [See H. DE LUBAC's chapter on Hugh of Saint Victor, in *op. cit.*, III, 288–359.]

12) Investigations are making more and more evident the influence of Andrew of Saint Victor on the masters of the first half of the XIIIth century, and in particular on Hugh of Saint Cher, the great leader of the works undertaken upon Scripture among the Preachers at Saint James. [See B. SMALLEY, *Andrew's Influence*, in *op. cit.*, 173–185.]

plement that of Peter Lombard's *Sentences*. The title it bears is significant for two reasons. First, the work will see and present Scripture as a "history," not as a pretext for disharmonized reflexions or for speculative researches; second, this history will be explained to students in a school with the required techniques applied in the process. The content of the medieval word *historia* must not, of course, be blown up into a modern meaning. "Historical method" is not what is in question here, and Saint Jerome is not dethroning Saint Augustine, even if the writer is a disciple of Andrew of Saint Victor. Within his own medieval contexts, however, Peter Comestor knows that he is attempting a revelation of "sacred history." His explicit intention can be stated as follows. Faced with the increasing discontinuity of glosses, he will aim to rediscover the *veritas historiae* [truth of history]. In order to achieve this and leaving to the more competent the vast "ocean of the mysteries," he will follow the small stream running from the cosmography of Moses to the ascension of Christ. When needed and in line with the flow of time, he will have recourse to the pagan peoples' histories, the coinciding events of which are not devoid of interest (13).

A historical view of this kind on humanity's religious destiny, howsoever modest the actual description of it may be, encamps itself therefore: on the one hand, in front of the *Gloss*, the classical inheritance whose collecting the XIIth century is completing, upon which the XIIIth century will sustain itself, but whose forward progress is achieved, however, through a juxtaposition of witnesses that end up pulverizing the biblical "narrative"; on the other hand, in front of the Lombard's *Sentences,* which represent the definitive instauration of systematic organization and dialectical elaboration within the revealed datum. These works and these methods must not be opposed to one another, even if in fact they harbor tendencies liable to engage in conflict (14). The legend according to which Comestor and the Lombard were brothers in the flesh is a symbol full of truth. On the other hand, the part played by Comestor's *Historia* and the meaning of it within the combination of these three enterprises has no doubt

---

13) ". . . starting then from the cosmography of Moses, I have followed the rivulet of history as far as the Ascension of the Savior, leaving to the more competent the ocean of the mysteries. . . . Borrowing also from the history of the nations, I have inserted a number of deeds, according to times, taking example from the rivulet which fills whatever it may find along its bed, and yet does not cease to flow by." *Historia scholastica*, prol.; *P.L.*, 198, 1054.

14) Tendencies and conflicts that disunited the partisans and adversaries (biblicists) of the *quaestiones*. SAINT BONAVENTURE will still be alluding to "the new theologians [who] often shy away from Sacred Scripture itself as from something precarious and lacking in order; as from a sort of dark forest." *Breviloquium*, Prol., 6, 5, in *BOO*, V (1891), 208. See M.–D. CHENU, *La théologie comme science au XIIIe siècle*, in *BibTh*, XXXIII (1957), ch. I.

been reduced. Yet, his influence both on persons and on the teaching regime was considerable, persisting right into the midst of the XIIIth century (15). He was truly part of the scriptural soil of theology, or, if one prefers, he was one of the tools daily used in the plowing of that soil. Some have considered that, as regards the reading of the biblical text, the use of this history, which certain universities (Oxford) imposed as a regulation, was a sign of decay (16). Yes and no! The answer is surely no, however, inasmuch as the *Historia* was the means suited to making the development of the economy of salvation understood, and that it was thus an opportune counterweight to the increasing prestige enjoyed by the *quaestiones* wherein another type of textual understanding was set to work. As a matter of fact, the Bible, as we know, was to remain the basic text used at Paris in the master of theology's courses. Nothing more meaningful, at the institutional level, could result from the evangelical reawakening that had taken place during earlier years.

Quite plainly, the university college of Saint James in which Saint Thomas finds himself, first as a student, then as a young professor of the Bible, is one of the milieux where sensitiveness to the effects and demands of this evangelical reawakening is most pronounced. Saint James is a spiritual milieu, an apostolic milieu; it is furthermore an intellectual milieu, with spiritual fervor and apostolic zeal having therein knowingly built up methods of work blending with appropriate techniques. In order to serve an open-minded and intense intellectual life, there was need of the resources of a community workshop able to assume the considerable tasks required to fit out the Bible with an equipment that would be at once scientific and practical. We cannot support it on explicit documents, but it appears that, during the two decades prior to the arrival of Saint Thomas, a team had, with effective relentlessness, pursued work at Saint James and elsewhere within the latter's radius of influence under the direction of Hugh of Saint Cher who first was regent of the college (1230–1235), then provincial, and soon after cardinal (1244). The foregoing may be presumed from the results of it that have come down to us and by means of which we are able to restore not only the technical resources that were accumulated but the spiritual climate permeating them as well.

15) In addition to B. SMALLEY's chapter, *op. cit.*, 196 ff., see PETER COMESTOR, *De sacramentis*, ed. R.–M. MARTIN, in *SSL*, XVII (1937), Introd., i–xxviii.

16) See A. KLEINHANS, *Der Studiengang der Professoren der Heiligen Schrift im 13. und 14. Jahrhundert*, in *Bibl*, XIV (1933), 381–399.

First in line was the task of establishing a text of the sacred books, expunged of the increasing corruption which, to an even greater degree than to common teaching, ran foul to scientific work of any kind. Therefrom emerged the *Correctoria*, undertaken, then redone and recast, by recourse to the original texts and with the collaboration of a converted Jew for the collation of the Hebrew text. The second task was the turning out of a "word" concordance designed as a means to a literal and organic exploitation of texts amid contexts and in agreement with parallel passages. It was the first of its kind to face the [so-called] "real" concordances that block off, prematurely and oftentimes artificially, analysis on not fully abstracted notions with the result that a fresh and evenly-conducted study of the texts themselves vanishes away. Progress here was far-reaching. To these undertakings, let us add the attempts—somewhat marginally done, and almost completely thwarted by the distrust of the conservatives— at translations in the vernacular that were intended for the use of the new lay elite (17). In intent as well as in realization, these enter- prises had great breadth, far surpassing the personal achievement of Hugh of Saint Cher who, for his part, composed a commentary of all of Scripture, the fruit of his own teaching. *Postillae* [postills] was the term then used for commentaries such as his. They make up the intermediary stage between XIIth century work on the Bible and the type of university commentary which Saint Thomas will compose (a).

Thus at the start of the XIIIth century, the renewal of theology centered within a sort of tension that was spiritual and pedagogical all at once. The tension was between, on the one hand, that return to Scripture with its inborn and untransferable value, its stirring power within faith, its appetite for things religious, and on the other hand, that speculative elaborating which was to find in the discovery

---

17) Among the evangelicals, Durandus of Huesca, who was leader of the "Catholic Poor," seems to have pursued this undertaking (A. Dondaine).

a) On postills and postillators, see B. SMALLEY, *The Study of the Bible in the Middle Ages*, 264–281. On the coining of the word "postill" to translate the Latin *postilla*, the latter writes: "Before considering their character, we must pause at the unfamiliar name. *Postilla* perhaps derives from 'post illa verba' (DuCange, *Glossarium med. et inf. lat.*, VI (1886), 434). It may perhaps refer to the fact that the comment was written out as a continuous gloss, interposed between the *loci* of the text. From about the time that Hugh's postills were circulated, the word came to designate all commentaries of this kind. The word *glosa* or *glosula* is no longer applied to continuous, but is restricted to marginal and interlinear glosses. An abridgement of the *Gloss* is called a *glosarium* (B. Smalley, 'Some more exegetical works of Simon of Hinton', *Rech. Théol. anc. méd.*, XV (1948), 104(5). The words *expositio* and *lectura* are also used; but the precise shade of difference between these two terms and *postilla* has not yet been satisfactorily worked out; so it will be simpler to adopt the name 'postill' for commentaries emanating from the schools" (270).

of Greek philosophy not only instrumentation of an admirable kind but a conception of nature, man, and reason. The role of reason will grow in theology's epistemological effectiveness and ontological quality; it is the reawakening to the Gospel, however, that comes first in theology's development. The spiritual is the element first commanding the intellectual. The intellectual element will thereafter protect the spiritual. It is no chance happening if the XIIIth century leaders of the theological enterprise are recruited from among the sons of the evangelicals of the beginning of the century—the Minors and the Preachers—and not in the old corporations. It may be that the balancing of objects, ends, and methods will be a delicate thing to achieve and that the engagement of reason will at times compromise the unadulterable freedom of the word of God. Yet, in historical and in objective fact, the Gospel was the leaven that raised the dough of all intelligence's requirements and resources. The *magistri in sacra pagina* will give birth to the *magistri in theologia*. It will be up to the latter to remain true to their birth.

II. *MAGISTER IN SACRA PAGINA*

In what way had the biblical reawakening come to be registered within the university teaching regime at Paris when Saint Thomas arrived there as a young professor in 1252? Spiritual reawakenings, as a matter of fact, whatever the difficulties they may encounter, end up being expressed in regulations and in pedagogical methods. This applied especially in the case of Paris at the time its young university was mustering everyone's enthusiasms and embodying the hopes of all. In and outside of France, XIIIth century university regulations will, *de facto*, bear explicit trace of the *modus parisiensis* [the manner of Paris], of that Parisian status of Bible teaching which Christendom will little by little adopt.

A first biblical cycle extended over the young theologian's first two years of study during the course of which the Bible was "read" (understand always as above, was taught) *secundum modum parisiensem* [after the manner of Paris], *cursorie*. The professor upon whom this teaching rested, the *baccalaureus biblicus*, was called the *cursor biblicus* [cursory reader of the Bible]. After two more years devoted to the reading of the Lombard's *Sentences*, a second biblical cycle itself was the personal teaching responsibility of the "master." In this case, the master applied himself to a minute and prolonged exegesis of the one or the other of the books of Scripture.

Thus, it was experience that had led the theologians of Paris to divide into three progressive and diversified stages a teaching which up till then had gelled around the text of the Bible. The proliferation of *quaestiones* (see ch. II) had little by little disjointed the commentary, as the *Book of Sentences* after conquering its place in the pedagogical regime tended, especially since around 1200, to have the work done in the *quaestiones* centered upon itself. Competition of a sort between the upsurge of speculation in these *quaestiones* and the return to the biblical source had ended in a balanced state of affairs wherein the role of the bachelor of the Bible took on a meaning. He taught the whole of Scripture cursorily *(cursorie)*, pinning himself down without any digressing or raising of questions to the text alone *(textualiter)*, upon which he rapidly shed light by means of the currently accepted glosses (18). Plainly, it was a summarily done initiation; however, many a cleric today could envy it as a basis for his theology. To teach the Bible *biblice* [biblically], as it was said, was the Parisian manner. It was the manner of young Brother Thomas. The Order of Preachers, furthermore, had set itself both to the task of this biblical teaching in its various *studia* and, in rhythm with the Order's growth, to increasing rapidly the number of professors capable of performing the task satisfactorily.

Except for his recently discovered and published inaugural course on the dignity of Scripture and on the distribution of books in it (19), we evidently possess nothing of this teaching of Saint Thomas which, by definition, had only a minimum of originality. Consequently, the texts we do have are of the teaching he gave as a master starting in 1256.

Saint Thomas's written work *in sacra pagina* must certainly have extended over the whole of his teaching career since commenting on the Bible was the prime task of the master in theology. It is, nevertheless, difficult to locate the various parts of it chronologically and to distribute these parts in their proportion to the rhythm of university life, a thing it would be important to know in order for us to measure the place this teaching held in the whole of the work and preoccupations of a master, in our case, of Saint Thomas. At first sight,

---

18) SAINT THOMAS, in fact, defines the role of the bachelor of the Bible when he writes: "To run through [the text] is to come to the end of it by running the course of it rapidly . . . without dubitation coming in to impede." *In Isaiam*, prooem.

19) It, as well as the address he gave upon receiving his masterate in theology (March–April, 1256), was published by F. SALVATORE, *Duo sermoni inediti di S. Tommaso*, Roma, 1912. It was reprinted in the Lethielleux ed. of the *Opuscula omnia*, t. IV [and more recently in the Marietti ed., of the *Opusc. theol.*, vol. I, wherein the two sermons are edited under the title of: *Principia Fratris Thomae: (1) Principium Fratris Thomae de commendatione et partitione Sacrae Scripturae* (433–439); (2) *Breve principium Fratris Thomae de commendatione Sacrae Scripturae* (441–443)].

it is rather disconcerting to find the university regulations completely indeterminate as regards the regular scheduling and the frequency of professors' courses and disputations. It seems that once they had been titulared, professors were left to decide of their own free will. On the strength of verisimilar inferences, Father Mandonnet supposes that when Saint Thomas was in Paris he gave two weekly courses on Scripture, whereas at Naples where technical exercises were on a smaller scale in a university still in its youth, he probably lectured daily. The chronological hypotheses supporting this distribution lead us to no firm conclusion. There are only a number of reference-points by means of which the critics, on external and internal evidence, are able to determine the date of this or that commentary (a).

As regards the portion of books commented upon, it is presumed with some probability of truth that, over a school year and according to his own choice, the master alternatively commented upon one book of the Old Testament and one of the New. In point of fact, in accordance with an old custom governed by the doctrinal or spiritual benefit to be reaped from the various books of Scripture, current teaching clung most usually, for the Old Testament, to commentaries on *Genesis*, one or another book of the Prophets, the *Psalms*, the *Canticle of Canticles*, and the *Book of Job*, which was recommended by the fact that Saint Gregory had done on it a commentary that became a classic; for the New Testament, to commentaries on the *Gospels according to Saint Matthew* and *Saint John*, the *Epistles of Saint Paul*, and the *Apocalypse*.

The probability is that the commentary-courses of Saint Thomas were not all redacted, nor all published. Even more than that, despite various efforts at identification, we no longer have the *Commentary on the Canticle of Canticles*, which the best catalogs tell us he composed. Of the remaining works, some he composed directly (*expositiones*); of the others, we have only lecture transcripts (*lecturae*). Here is the list of them with some very brief notations (b).

---

a) See his series of articles entitled *Chronologie des écrits scripturaires de saint Thomas d'Aquin*, in *RT*, XXIII (1928), 27–45, 116–155, 211–245; XXIV (1929), 53–69, 132–145, 489–519. See the criticism directed against his methods by P. GLORIEUX, *Essai sur les Commentaires scripturaires de saint Thomas et leur chronologie*, in *RTAM*, XVII (1950), 237–266.

b) Latin ed. and English trans. (in the order of their listing): *Expositio in Isaiam prophetam:* Parma, XIV, 427–576; Vivès, XVIII, 688–821; XIX, 1–65; Uccelli, 1–243.—*Expositio in Jeremiam prophetam:* Parma, XIV, 577–677; Vivès, XIX, 66–198.—*Expositio in Threnos Jeremiae prophetae:* Parma, XIV, 678–685; Vivès, XIX, 199–225.—*In Psalmos Davidis lectura:* Parma, XIV, 148–353; Vivès, XVIII, 228–556; Uccelli, *Psalms* 52–54, 241–254.—*Expositio in Job ad litteram:* Parma, XIV, 1–147; Vivès, XVIII, 1–227; critical Leonine ed. prepared by the Canadian section of the Leonine Commission due to be released in 1964.— *Super Evangelium S. Matthaei lectura:* Parma, X, 1–278; Vivès, XIX, 226–668;

THE COMMENTARY ON ISAIAH (*expositio*).—We have, in part (chapters 34–39), the autograph manuscript of Saint Thomas (today *Vatican Lat. Ms. 9850*, fol. 105–114), which Ucelli used in his two editions (1847, 1880). All other manuscripts depend on the transcription that Jacobinus of Asti made on the autograph at Naples between 1274 and 1278. This leads us to believe, despite Mandonnet's very strong arguments, that this commentary would only date from the end of the life of Saint Thomas, during his second sojourn in Italy perhaps (c). Jacobinus of Asti further inserted 126 *collationes*—plans, after a fashion, for short talks, introduced by the formula: *Nota super illo verbo* [Note on this saying]. They have passed into the text of the modern editions, making up the eleventh part of the work. These schemas of preachable matter are probably not of Saint Thomas, but of Jacobinus, the transcriber (20).

THE COMMENTARY ON JEREMIAH AND THE LAMENTA-TIONS (*expositiones*).—The commentary on the prophecies is unfinished, which leads one to believe (Mandonnet) that it was interrupted by Saint Thomas's unexpected coming to Paris in November 1268.

THE *COMMENTARY ON THE PSALMS*, at least on the first 54 *Psalms* (*lectura* transcribed by Reginald of Piperno).—"Whereas each book of canonical Scripture deals with a special matter, this book deals with the general [matter] of all theology. . . . The Psalter is more frequently used in the Church because it contains all Scripture"

5th Marietti ed., rev., 1951.—*Super Evangelium S. Joannis lectura:* Parma, X, 279–645; Vivès, XIX, 669–842; XX, 1–376; 5th Marietti ed., rev., 1952.—*Expositio in S. Pauli Apostoli epistolas:* Parma, XIII; Vivès, XX and XXI; 8th Marietti ed., rev., 2 vols., 1953.—*Expositio continua (Catena aurea) in quatuor Evangelia:* Parma, XI and XII; Vivès, XVI and XVII; new Marietti ed., 2 vols., 1953. English trans.: *Catena aurea. Commentary on the four Gospels* collected out of the Works of the Fathers by St. Thomas Aquinas, trans. by J. D. DALGAIRNS, M. PATTISON, and T. D. RYDER, prefaced by M. PATTISON, 4 vols., Oxford–London, 1841–1845.

On the works of this section, see I. T. ESCHMANN, *CSTW*, 393–399, who quotes in particular Pattison's highly-appreciative judgement of the *Catena aurea*, 397. See also F. STEGMÜLLER, *Repertorium biblicum medii aevi*, t. V: *Commentaria*, auctores R–Z, Madrid, 1955, 322–353.

c) Recent research on this commentary would indicate, however, a much earlier date, "the beginning of Saint Thomas's teaching," writes L.-J. BATAILLON, in his review (*BT*, X, 80, n. 144) of R. GUINDON, L'Expositio in Isaiam *est-elle une oeuvre de Thomas d'Aquin "bachelier biblique"?* (in *RTAM*, XXI (1954), 312–321). See also the latter's *Béatitude et théologie morale chez saint Thomas d'Aquin*, Ottawa, 1956, 149–157.

20) See J. DESTREZ, *Etudes critiques sur les oeuvres de saint Thomas d'Aquin d'après la tradition manuscrite: Le commentaire de saint Thomas d'Aquin sur Isaïe d'après la tradition manuscrite*, in *BibTh*, XVII (1933), 161–224.

(a). Thus Saint Thomas speaks in his Prologue. *De facto,* the *Psalms* are, as regards the Old Testament, the object most frequently chosen by the *magistri in sacra pagina* for their commentaries, and it is normal that they should have occupied a place of prime importance in the formation of clerics since they make up the most extensive matter of their liturgical office.

THE *COMMENTARY ON THE BOOK OF JOB* (*expositio*).—Concerning this commentary, Saint Thomas declares expressly that he will limit himself to the literal sense of the text, whereas the universal custom was to dwell extensively upon the spiritual senses, especially in the case of the Old Testament (21). His reason for this, our commentator tells us, is that Pope Gregory has sufficiently elaborated upon the "mysteries" of this book (22). To this may be added another motive. Saint Thomas was then devoting the better part of his activity to his struggle against the Averroistic doctrines that had made inroads into the faculty of arts (a). They involved a negation of Providence, and by denying the soul's personal survival, they also made distributive justice impossible. The presence of evil in the world brought to these problems, as always, an air of woefulness and urgency. The text of the *Book of Job* furnished Saint Thomas with one of the richest scriptural bases for the elaboration of these difficult Christian doctrines. Whence this commentary is particularly firm being much less than others carved up into subtle divisions.

As regards the New Testament, we have a *lectura* on the *GOSPEL ACCORDING TO SAINT MATTHEW.*—The transcript of it was done by Peter of Andria (chapters 1–15), and by a secular student who was then in Paris following the courses of Saint Thomas (chapters 15–28). *Lectura . . . quae defectiva est* [A lecture transcript . . . which is defective], says the official catalog. Understand not that it is

a) 'Cum singuli libri canonicae Scripturae speciales materias habeant, hic liber generalem [materiam] habet totius theologiae . . . Magis frequentatur Psalterium in Eccelsia, quia continet totam Scripturam."

21) Roland of Cremona, the first Dominican master at the University of Paris (1229), was, it seems, the first one to return to a literal interpretation of this book. See A. DONDAINE, *Un commentaire scripturaire de Roland de Crémone,* in *AFP,* XI (1941), 109–137.

22) BERNARD GUI says about this commentary: ". . . none of the doctors has attempted to supply a literal exposition of it such as he did." Catalog of the works of Saint Thomas in the *Legenda,* ed. MANDONNET, *Des écrits authentiques de saint Thomas d'Aquin,* 2d rev. ed., Fribourg, 1910, 69.

a) The author is here following the chronology of Mandonnet and Glorieux which would place the writing of this commentary between 1269 and 1272 (see their works referred to above, 244, note a). ESCHMANN, in *CSTW,* 393–394, believes Tolomeo of Lucca's definite chronology for this work, "the times of Urban, IV, i.e. 1261/4" seems to be "confirmed by the circumstantial evidence of the work itself," suggesting "a date close to 1260."

incomplete, but rather that it is defective in the quality of its transcript (b). The redaction of it is relatively summarily done, and solutions of difficulties, not very elaborate (23).

THE *COMMENTARY ON SAINT JOHN* (*lectura*).—As against the case with the previous commentary, an excellent transcript of the present one was done by Reginald of Piperno; . . . *quam recollegit idem frater Raynaldus, sed correxit eam frater Thomas* [". . . a transcript which was done by the same Brother Reginald, which Brother Thomas however corrected"]. The official catalog adds: . . . *qua non invenitur melior* [". . . than which no better one is found"]. Posterity has ratified this judgment. A final notation in Reginald's transcript, referring to the friendship of Adenulphus of Anagni, provost of Saint-Omer, bids us to place the composition of the work during the second sojourn of Saint Thomas at Paris (1269–1272) (24).

---

b) Recent studies have changed to a considerable extent the commonly held opinions on the text and date of this transcript. B.-G. GUYOT, reviewing (*BT*, XI, 1, 11–14) H. V. SHOONER, *La* Lectura in Matthaeum *de saint Thomas (Deux fragments inédits et la* Reportatio *de Pierre d'Andria)(Ang*, XXXIII (1956), 121–142), writes: "In brief, in the present state of our knowledge, we can say that the teaching of Saint Thomas in his commentary on the Gospel of Saint Matthew has come down to us in two ways: 1) by means of a continuous transcript, partly unedited until now, of I, 22 to the end of ch. 12; 2) by means of an agglomerate of many texts: Peter of Andria's transcript, from the beginning (or at least from I, 22) to 5, 10 (Marietti edition, n. 443); an arrangement of texts taken from Peter of Scala's commentary, from 5, 11 (444) to 6, 8 (582); the transcript of Leger of Besançon, from 6, 9 (583) to 6, 13 (602); Peter of Scala anew, from 6, 16 (603), to 6, 18 (610); finally, Leger of Besançon to the end.

"Concerning the date, the common opinion until now was that Saint Thomas had commented upon Saint Matthew at the start of his career, during his first Parisian sojourn of 1256–1259 (cf. for example, MGR GLORIEUX [*Essai sur les Commentaires scripturaires de saint Thomas et leur chronologie*], RTAM, 17 (1950), 246–249, and GUINDON [*Le De Sermone Domini in monte de saint Augustin dans l'oeuvre de saint Thomas*], RUO, 28 (1958), 84* [See also his *Béatitude et théologie morale chez saint Thomas d'Aquin*, Ottawa, 1956, 149–157]).

"Serious indications make it necessary to retard this work to 1263 at the earliest (cf. the article [*The Quotations of Aristotle's Politica in St. Thomas's Lectura super Matthaeum*, in MSt, 18 (1956), 232–240] of Father Eschmann, noted in *Bull. thom.*, t. X, n. 269, and reviewed by Father Shooner) . . . one point is established with certainty: the *Lectura super Matthaeum* dates at the earliest from the beginning of the first sojourn in Italy" (12–13).

23) One must no doubt connect with the time of writing of this commentary the anecdote related by Bartholomew of Capua at the canonization proceedings, according to which Saint Thomas, upon returning to Paris from Saint Denys and surveying the beauty of the city, exclaimed: "To be truthful, I should wish much more for Chrysostom on Matthew" [*In veritate plus vellem Chrysostomum super Matthaeum*]. ASS, VII, March 7, ch. 9, n. 78, 711 A; also in *FTVA*, IV, 376; Foster ed., 109.

24) On the authority of the unique and defective manuscript of the official catalog it was long thought that Saint Thomas had composed an additional *Expositio super quatuor evangelia ad litteram* [Exposition on the four Gospels

THE *COMMENTARY ON THE EPISTLES OF SAINT PAUL.*—
The case of this commentary is more complex and more important all
the while, not only because the text of it alone represents a third of all
the exegetical writings of Saint Thomas but especially because it deals
with the book of Scripture that, by its subject matter, is the most
propitious to theological exegesis. Twice Saint Thomas commented
upon the Epistles, a first time from one end of them to the other,
leaving to Reginald the task of writing out the text, then, a second
time during his last sojourn at Naples no doubt, where he took them
up again and wrote out his exposition himself. But death interrupted
his work after chapter 10 of the *First Epistle to the Corinthians.* His
faithful Reginald, putting order in the writings of his master, took the
missing part of it from his own previous transcript to thus complete
the work of Saint Thomas. It is in this state that the commentary has
come down to us (25).

The work commonly called *CATENA AUREA,* the exact title of
which is, in Saint Thomas' own words, *Expositio continua,* must quite
plainly be treated separately. Nicolas of Trevet describes the work
perfectly when he says: "He glossed the four Gospels by means of a
continuous exposition taken from the sayings of the saints" (26). The
title *Catena aurea,* moreover, is employed in manuscripts as early as
the XIVth century, and is aptly appropriated to this concatenation of
patristic texts cleverly coordinated into a running commentary. In the
present case, it was no longer the school regime that led Saint Thomas
to undertake his work but rather the politico-religious circumstances
pertaining to the secular conflict between the Greeks and the Latins.
Urban IV, who had formerly been patriarch of Jerusalem and who was
no less attentive to theological problems than to the military conflicts between the East and the West, had asked (around 1263)
Thomas Aquinas to do both: a theological criticism of an anthology

---

according to their letter] that remained undiscovered. By means of a shrewd
correction of the text, FATHER SYNAVE has shown the indication to be unfounded.
See *Le commentaire de saint Thomas sur les quatre évangiles d'après le catalogue
officiel,* in *Mélanges thomistes (BibTh,* III, 1934), 109–122.

25) For the commentary on *I Cor.,* VII, 14 to X included, the text of Peter of
Tarentasia was introduced within the texture of Saint Thomas's commentary as
the result of an accident in the editing of it. For this section, therefore, we do
not have the text of Saint Thomas. [According to H.-D. SIMONIN, *Les écrits de
Pierre de Tarentaise,* in *BIQ-SD,* 163–355, the text of our editions for this section
is a complete recast of Peter of Tarentasia's text. The traditional authorship of
Nicolas of Gorran for this second edition can be retained until new evidence
disproves it. See 226–230.]

26) "Quatuor evangelia continuata expositione de dictis sanctorum glossavit."
Catalogue of Saint Thomas's works published by MANDONNET, *Des écrits authentiques de saint Thomas d'Aquin,* 2d rev. ed., Fribourg, 1910, 48.

of Greek texts recently arrived from the East, and a commentary, a "gloss," on the Gospel wherein the Greek writers would testify side by side with the Latin authorities. The first of these works was the famous opusculum *Contra errores Graecorum* (see below, chapter XII); the second makes up our *Catena aurea.* Urban died (October, 1264) before Saint Thomas had finished the second work he had requested; he had received only the gloss on Saint Matthew. Saint Thomas finished his commentary upon the three other Gospels and dedicated it to Cardinal Hannibald, his former pupil and very dear friend. See the dedications. It is especially in the second part of his commentary that he had time to supply himself with Greek writings, translated and carefully controlled beforehand, as far as this could be done at the time. He writes in his dedication to Hannibald: "That this commentary may be more complete and have more continuity, I have had many works of the Greek doctors translated into Latin, and I have added extracts of them to the commentaries of the Latins, being careful to place the names of the authors before their testimonies" (a). We have had occasion to observe the importance these steps and care took on, even amid partial failures (b). Let us note at present, at the level of scriptural studies, which always have a link with the reading of the Fathers, the value of this recourse to the Oriental interpreters, one that is indispensable for the Christian good health of the Latin West.

III. SCHOLASTIC EXEGESIS

Accustomed as we are now to a technical exegesis wherein both the Christian and the profane texts are treated according to the very searching norms of verbal objectivity, we are no longer sensitive enough to that first great effort made in the Western world that caused Bible reading of a pastoral type to evolve into a scientific discipline. Yet, this effort becomes manifest when one passes from the *sermones* of Saint Bernard to the *expositiones* of the XIIIth century university scholars. It would be incongruent to oppose these two types of commentary and therefrom to prefer the one as opposed to the other; but, failing to examine closely the procedures and the structures of these two literary genres would be, to as great an extent, to shut off one's understanding of the one as opposed to the other, and especially of the second one. As a matter of fact, the differentiation of the latter genres is the first trait of the steps that were progressively

---

a) ". . . Et ut magis integra et continua praedicta sanctorum expositio redderetur, quasdam expositiones Doctorum graecorum in latinum feci transferri, ex quibus plura expositionibus latinorum Doctorum interserui, auctorum nominibus praenotatis." New Marietti ed., 1953, I, 429.

b) See chapter IV, 150–152.

taken as Christian thought at work developed and its teaching organized from a paraphrasing in pastoral form to an exegesis of "scholastic" type. This means an exegesis wherein an objective analysis of the text by means of appropriate techniques, no longer the spiritual edification of auditors, was the objective aimed at in school pursuit. An evangelism that would fail to give rise to a pursuit of this sort and to accept its results open-heartedly would be evangelism of an unbalanced kind.

1. The first step that this objective exegesis takes is to treat the text, not by reference to the reader's own interests, difficulties, or enthusiasms, even if they are inspired by his faith, but rather according to the internal order governing the development of the text and the arrangement of its parts. As a result, the text from the beginning of it to the end is divided and subdivided, first into broad portions, and then pericope after pericope, sentence after sentence. Whereas traditional glossing latched upon one or another difficult word as one drifted through the text, it is now a matter of seeking to grasp textual wholes, to determine trains of thought by means of a logical analysis pushed to the point of minuteness, regardless of the suppleness most certainly present in the narrative. In the XIIIth century just as came to be done in the XXth, technique is borrowed from the secular disciplines, from the masters of arts especially who put it to use in the reading of their texts, as Roger Bacon observes, not unreproachfully (27). Technique, it would seem, becomes fixed with Hugh of Saint Cher. Albert the Great, Bonaventure, Thomas Aquinas make a constant use of it. One can foresee its merits in the precision it imposes on exegesis and doctrine as regards both details and wholes. Yet one can also foresee its shortcomings. Not only does the insertion of rationalization within the text block off spontaneously-arising pious comments; it opens the door, moreover, to an artificial subtlety that empties all texts of any literary and psychological mobility, particularly where the texts are historical narratives (the Gospel) or writings in the form of epistles (Saint Paul). A measure of the advantages and disadvantages of this rationalization will be had by reading, for instance, what arrangement is adopted at the start of the commentary of the Sermon upon the Mount (*Matthew,* V); it ranges from the Gospel's broad divisions all the way down to the incidentals found

---

27) Roger Bacon, on the "sins" of theology: "The things done in the text, especially in the reading and preaching of it, are principally three, namely: *divisions* into various sections, such as are done by the artists, violent *concordances,* such as are used by the law-men, and *rythmic consonances,* in the style of the grammarians. Of these three things does the main method used by the craftsmen in scriptural exposition consist. And even though they have their usefulness, they have nonetheless been extracted from philosophy." *Opus minus,* in *RBO,* 323.

in the first verse (28); or again, the ordering that is proposed for the thought contained in the Prologue of *Saint John*; or heading the *Epistles* of Saint Paul, the very organically made up plan within which the fourteen epistles of the Apostle come to insert themselves—a plan that is extremely penetrating in its discerning of their doctrinal homogeneity, but one also that is an expedient insofar as it treats writings of an occasional nature after the fashion of a work of Aristotle.

2. The first result ensuing from this procedure is a setting of the interpreter within a closely-knit exegesis of the text's words and statements, counter to the paraphrase's facileness. He is compelled, in a manner of speaking, to stick constantly to the letter, to extract its immediate meaning, in order to arrive at a grasp of the thought. This, furthermore, is the progression Hugh of Saint Victor had formerly described expressly for the explanation of a text. According to him, there was the *littera,* that is, the words and their connected sequence, (*constructio* and *continuatio*), then the *sensus,* or the obvious meaning, and finally the *sententia,* the understanding in depth supplied by the perfect *expositio* (29). The entire technique of the ancient grammarians here weighs on the procedure, just as it had formerly done in the case of Augustine (30). Its atomizing in many an instance steps out of bounds, ending up in a more literal than literary interpretation. Servius explaining Virgil is a case in point. This procedure

---

28) "Herein, the Lord proposes his doctrine, which is divided into three parts. In the first part is posited Christ's doctrine, in the second is posited the power of that doctrine, in the third, the end to which it leads—the second part in chapter XIII, the third, in chapter XVII. The first part is divided into three: in the second, the ministers of the doctrine receive instruction, in the third, the adversaries are confounded—the second part in chapter X, the third in chapter XI. The first part is divided into two: in the first, the doctrine of Christ is proposed, in the second, it is confirmed by miracles, in chapter VIII. The first in two: in the first part, is prefixed something as a title to the doctrine, in the second, the doctrine itself is explained, starting with the words: 'Blessed are the poor in spirit.' Concerning the first, he does three things: first, he describes the place where the doctrine was proposed, second, the auditors of the doctrine, third, he posits his method of teaching—the second starting with the words: '. . . and when he was set down . . . ,' the third, with the words: 'And opening his mouth,' He says, therefore. . . .' *In Matt.,* V, 11; 5th Marietti ed., 64, n. 396.

29) HUGH OF SAINT VICTOR, *Didascalicon. De studio legendi,* lib. III, c. 8; Buttimer ed., 58; *P.L.* 176, 771D; Taylor ed., 92; "The exposition contains three things: the *littera* [letter], the *sensus* [obvious sense], and the *sententia* [deeper meaning]. The *littera* is the congruent ordering of the words, which is also called construction. The *sensus* is a certain easily-recognized and apparent meaning which the *littera* offers at first sight. The *sententia* is a deeper understanding which is not arrived at except by means of exposition or interpretation. With the preceding, this is the order of inquiry that should be followed: first, the *littera,* then the *sensus,* then the *sententia.* When this has been done, the exposition has reached the stage of completion." See above, chapter II.

30) See H.-I. MARROU, *Saint Augustin et la fin de la culture antique,* 2d ed., in *BEFAR,* CXLV bis (1949), 424–427.

actually translates the adherence to the letter of the text implied in any fresh reading of Scripture, which everybody admits is a characteristic trait of the commentary of Saint Thomas. If applied to the episodes of a narrative, it is easy for the procedure to slide into abstract conceptualism (for example, in the treatment of images like *civitas* [city], *fundamentum* [foundation], and the like), but when the case is one of doctrinal stating, it procures a sound and fruitful understanding opening the way to biblical theology.

3. The XIIIth century medieval master yields to the latter preoccupation of reason. He tends to define the words and concepts, to classify them within categories. If he comes upon the word *oblatio*, he analyses the four conditions required for an offering (31); the word *timor*, he recalls to mind the different species of fear (32); the particle *per*, he observes that this preposition denotes indirect causality (33); and so on. He presents and analyses a work by means of the four causes: efficient, material, formal, and final. This Saint Albert and Saint Bonaventure frequently do; this Saint Thomas does at the beginning of the Paulinian corpus, of the *Epistle to the Ephesians*, of the *Book of Jeremiah*.

4. Another step, and here we are at the peak of this scholastic exegesis. The quest is for reasons, the reasons for things, for events, for words, for steps taken. Always it is supposed that the evangelist or the prophet had reasons in mind. *Et ponit duas rationes* [And he posits two reasons] is the short clause by means of which the commentator frequently uncovers the logical connections of a narrative. The *Book of Job* purports to show *per probabiles rationes* [by means of probable reasons] that Providence governs human affairs. Why does Christ entering Jerusalem go to the Temple? Two "reasons" lead him there (34). Why does he manifest himself? There are two reasons (35). And so on.

This quest for reasons reaches the point where the text is exegetically built up according to reasoning procedures. In one instance, the text is said to contain the minor proposition of an argument (36); in another, the text is a proof taken "as from the field of division" (37). The text of *Romans* VIII: 5–6 is said to imply two syllogisms, the

---

31) See *In Matt.*, V, 23; 5th Marietti ed., 78, n. 498.

32) See *In Joan.*, XV, 15; 5th Marietti ed., 380, n. 2015.

33) See *ibid.*, I, 3; 5th Marietti ed., 16, n. 76.

34) See *In Matt.*, XXI, 12; 5th Marietti ed., 262, n. 1696.

35) See *ibid.*, XXIV, 27; 5th Marietti ed., 302, n. 1953.

36) See *In Joan.*, VI, 7; 5th Marietti ed., 184, n. 977: "Herein he posits the minor proposition."

37) See *ibid.*, III, 18; 5th Marietti ed., 93, n. 484: "Herein he proves what he had said, as from the field of division."

premisses of which are extracted (38). Rigidness is foreseeable in an exegesis of this sort, which a modern would render more flexible by an insertion of some degree of psychological relativism into it. Yet, one can also see the vigor of its demands.

5. Arrived at this point, the medieval master passes spontaneously from the *expositio* to the *quaestio*. We have seen how in the history of medieval teaching a passage from the *lectio* to the *quaestio* was little by little accomplished (a). In the XIIIth century, the differentiation of these genres had reached the stage of completion, with the disputed questions unquestionably having become school exercises different from the commentary on the text. The latter, however, as a result of the pressure its rational analysis brings to bear, involves anew the emergence of short *quaestiones* that, to be sure, are linked to the text, yet enter nonetheless into theological elaborating. *Hic oritur quaestio* [The question arises here]; *Hic est duplex quaestio* [There is here a twofold question]; *Potest aliquis quaerere* [One may ask]; *Hic oritur dubitatio* [A doubt arises here]. Even where a formula is not employed, exegesis often develops along the lines of doctrinal research, argumentation, arguing from suitabilities, and, lengthily at times, refuting errors.

Thus, imperceptibly, the passage is accomplished from exegesis to theology and to its *modus ratiocinativus* [ratiocinative mode], as happens in the commentary on *John* III: 34: ". . . God doth not give the Spirit by measure"; on *John* V: 20: ". . . the Father loveth the Son"; on *John* X: 17: "Therefore doth the Father love me: because I lay down my life . . ."; on *Romans* V: 3, concerning the transmission of original sin. In many cases, the procedure is pushed to the limit, as in the cases where we meet with the structure of an article of the *Summa*, objections, *sed contra*, answer, distinctions. The *magister in sacra pagina* begets the *magister in theologia*, exegesis, scholasticism.

IV. THEOLOGICAL EXEGESIS

On first impulse, we were going to entitle this paragraph: From the "spiritual" exegesis to the scholastic exegesis, so as to account for the transition from the allegorical commentary that was practiced until then (and in high dosage even at the heart of the XIIth cen-

---

38) See *In Rom.*, VIII, 5–6, lect. III; 8th Marietti ed., 112, n. 616–617: "And [Paul] brings in two syllogisms . . . First, he posits the minor proposition of the first syllogism . . . Second, he posits the minor proposition of the second syllogism . . . Third, he posits the major proposition of the first syllogism. . . ." HONORIUS OF AUTUN had previously said: "Syllogisms are hidden in Sacred Scripture just like fish in deep water; and just as a fish is withdrawn from water to be used by man, so a syllogism is said to be extracted from Scripture for its usefulness." *Expositio in psalmos selectos*, on *Psalm I*; *P.L.*, 172, 279 C.

a) See above, chapter II.

tury) to the university commentary of Saint Thomas. After reflexion, however, we believe the contemplated formula inadequate to cover the data of the problem and that, beforehand, it passes judgement summarily on the delicate solution it requires, one which is linked to the increasing diversification of literary genres—and therefore of methods—taking place within the whole of Scripture-based theological knowledge.

If we read over without sophistication the commentaries whose scholastic aspect we have just examined, we became very sensitive to the fact that symbolic interpretations are regularly interposited, thus doubling up the rational analysis of the text. This is done in varying degrees, to be sure, yet enough to be noticed, not only as regards the texts of the Old Testament which, by definition, are figure-laden, but even in the commentary on Saint Matthew which expressly purports to be "historical" in its relating of the evangelical events. *Mystice considerandum est quod* [According to the mystical sense, it should be considered that]; . . . *aliquid mystice hic praetenditur* [. . . something is proferred here in the mystical sense]; *Quantum autem ad mysterium, per Joseph signantur praedicatores* [As for the mystic meaning, by Joseph are indicated the preachers]; *Per istam occisionem significatur* [By this slaying is signified]. These specimens occur within the space of three pages (b). What, in the thought and teaching of Saint Thomas, does this spiritual (allegorical, moralizing, eschatological) level of the commentary represent? Is this super-positing of senses knowingly included within the structure of Scripture as a whole, *de necessitate sacrae Scripturae* [necessarily belonging to Sacred Scripture] *(Quodl. VII, a. 15, obj. 5)*, or is it a passive survival of the pristine symbolism of the Fathers? And in the case of Saint Thomas precisely, does his theory about the senses of Scripture have an adequate control over his own practice of them, in a teaching regime blocked off by custom and by the rather slow-moving train of pedagogy's evolutions? It is known that, for him, without prejudice to the typological sense of Scripture, the literal sense alone has value and can be used in theological argumentation (see *Ia Pars*, q. 1, a. 10, ad 1um). Under these circumstances, where should one locate in the edifice of theology the quasi-permanent figurative value of Scripture that remains in the commentary even after it has taken on the scholastic garb?

A first observation about this manner of acting. With it, we find that the Medievals are fully in line with the practice of the Fathers for whom spiritual interpreting is made part of the tissue of their reading of the Bible. De facto, it is probably never of his own that

---

b) See *In Matt.*, c. II; 5th Marietti ed., 31–33, n. 200, 201, 213, 224, on *Matthew*, II, 11, 13–14, 16.

Saint Thomas proposes a mystical sense. The latter is borrowed either expressly from Saint Augustine, Saint John Chrysostom, Saint Gregory, or anonomously from the florilegia and glosses that the XIIth century reinforced with repertories of allegories (39). It must be noted, however, that the transfer of these spiritual senses into the teaching regime of the schools involves some degree of hardening as a result of the objectifying of values which originally were substantially one with ritual and figurative wholes, initiation to the mysteries, faith at work in a catechesis, or at least (as in the case of the monastic *lectio divina*) the climate of a spiritual community in actual pursuit of vital understanding. By setting outside these indigenous contexts for teaching purposes, allegorization loses flexibility in regard to image creation and poetic-analogy invention.

Allegorization does not on account of that become in the minds of the XIIIth century masters a simple matter of illustration, one external to Scripture and to *doctrina sacra* which issues from it. It remains part of the biblical capital, involving for the theologian not only a dogmatic or a conceptualized para-dogmatic datum but a way of seeing and thinking, a mentality, perspectives, a sort of sensibility whose privileged field of expression lies in the liturgy. Therefore, the plus-value of meaning present here is internal to biblical reading. It is, to take over the expression of Saint Thomas, *de necessitate sacrae Scripturae.*

At this point, we must bring in a distinction not included in the practice of Saint Thomas. It is, however, in line with his theory on method and lies at the point of juncture of the literal and figurative senses.

Typology develops at two levels. At the first level, it is a matter of a general figuring, essentially included in the economy of the Judeo-Christian revelation. The stages of this economy's development —from the old to the new alliance, then from the new alliance in the Church to the consummation of the kingdom in heaven—are accomplished not only through both a historical preparation and a prefiguration that expresses itself precisely by means of resemblances, of types, on the basis of the unity of this economy. Plus-value in meaning is, therefore, realized through the medium of symbols. Not only was Abraham the father of believers historically speaking, he

---

39) Two broad categories of treasuries spread (and hardened) the patristic inheritance: the *Allegoriae in Sacram Scripturam*, the most famous of which were RICHARD OF SAINT VICTOR's *Allegoriae*, annexed as a "spiritual" doublet to PETER COMESTOR's *Historia scholastica*, and the *Distinctiones*, dictionaries of the Bible's symbolic values. These dictionaries no longer followed the historical sequence of the books of the Bible, but rather the alphabetical order of words having typological value, as in that of ALAN OF LILLE, *Liber in distinctionibus dictionum theologalium*; *P.L.*, 210, 685–1012. [See above, note 7].

remains the type for believers of all times. Jerusalem, historically the city of the Israelitic people, symbolizes in turn the Church, city of God; the soul, abode of the Spirit; the Heavenly City; and so on. Thus, of itself, a scriptural theology implies a symbolic theology (40). The eschatological dimension in it expands exegesis even further, beyond doctrinal allegory and moral tropology. The theory on the four meanings whose classical formulation is quoted and used by Saint Thomas is known (41). Now, these meanings are not only classifications of the text's interpretation, they refer to distinct disciplines having their own particular methods which make up something of a pedagogy of scriptural teaching (42).

Among the medieval biblicists, as among the ancient catechizers, however, this organic figuring, the very expression of an economy realized in time, extended gradually to the details of narratives, events, and texts. There came about a crossing over from the figurative state of the Israelitic people to the events and doings of its history so as to find in each one of them a figure, a "spiritual sense." This was done all the more that those events, doings, and sayings were definitely things of the past and out-of-date, no longer of any interest to the Christian (43). The allegorizing procedure deported the true values of old into interminable excesses. ". . . all these things happened to them in figure" (a). Everything was a sign, even numbers

---

40) This symbolic theology is inscribed, as a matter of fact, in the university (or pre-university) statute of teaching. See the letter of GUY OF BAZOCHES (around 1180) dealing with the Isle of the City, center of the schools of Paris: "This fountain of salutary doctrine exudes abundance, and, giving rise from its bosom as if to three most limpid rivers so as to irrigate the prairies of the mind, it divides into three parts the spiritual understanding of the sacred page: the historical, the allegorical, and the moral" (*ChUP*, I, 56, n. 54).

41) Littera *gesta docet, quid credas* allegoria,
   Moralis *quid agas, quo tendas* anagogia.
   [The letter teaches *what was done*, allegory, *what to think*,
   The moral sense, *what to do*, anagoge, *what to pursue*.]

See H. DE LUBAC, *Sur un vieux distique: la doctrine du "quadruple sens"*, in *MFC*, 347–366. [See especially the latter's *Exégèse médiévale. Les quatre sens de l'Ecriture*, quoted above, note 4, all of volume II.]

42) See C. SPICQ, *Esquisse d'une histoire de l'exégèse latine au moyen âge*, in *BibTh*, XXVI (1944), 99. Hugh of Saint Victor was the doctor of that constructing of methods.

43) Witness to this crossing over from general to particular is the following recording of it by SAINT THOMAS: "The Jewish people was chosen by God that Christ might be born from it. As a result, it was necessary that the entire state of that people be prophetic and figurative. . . . And this is why even the judicial precepts given to this people were more figurative than the judicial precepts given to other peoples, just as the wars and deeds of this people are also expounded in the mystical sense, but not the wars and deeds of the Assyrians or the Romans, even though the latter were far more outstanding in the eyes of men." *Ia–IIae*, q. 104, a. 2, ad 2um.

a) "Omnia in figura contingebant illis." *I Cor.* X: 11.

and names (44). The smallest resemblance, the least parallel in words was exploited symbolically, regardless of any psychological or prophetic continuity. The *moralisatio* [moralizing methods] turned textual contents that had no typological value outside their historical context into lessons on practical living. Entire books were submitted to this kind of treatment, with Saint Gregory's *Moralia in Job* their prototype constantly imitated during the Middle Ages. When in turn Saint Thomas commented upon the book of Job, he deemed the *moralisatio* to have reached sufficient proportions. He proposed that the literal sense alone be adhered to (a). His reaction was a significant one, for it brought out the fact that theology was putting up a safety-catch against the multiplying of figures and allegories without criterion or limits. It remains that, *de facto*, Saint Thomas did practice on his own, in his running interpretation of the texts, that classical type of interpretation wherein utilization of the Bible for spiritual purposes oversteps the explanation of the word of God.

We shall not linger on the history of this spiritual exegesis, nor on the discriminations it calls for (45). Let us observe, however, that following in the footsteps of the Fathers, the Medievals, in their exegetical treatment of the permanent values of biblical typology, make it one piece with the exploitation of these values by means of the procedures and the categories they inherited from the Hellenistic culture. In the pagan authors, in Philo and Origen as a matter of fact, a literary genre had developed for the purpose of interpreting texts (Homer, Virgil, and others) beyond their literal meaning. This devel-

---

44) The procedure had been laid down as a principle by SAINT AUGUSTINE: "Anything in the Divine word that cannot be referred in the proper sense to the integrity of morals or to the truth of faith, you will know that it is figurative." *De doctrina christiana*, III, 10; *P.L.*, 34, 71. And SAINT JEROME: "All individual names have their own secret meaning; there are, in fact, as many mysteries as there are words." *Tractatus sive homiliae in Psalmos quattuordecim*, Morin ed., in *AM*, III, part III (1903), 33.

a) "We intend . . . insofar as we shall be able to, and confident in Divine help, to expose in a compendious manner, according to the literal sense, this so-called book of the Blessed Job, for Blessed Pope Gregory has opened its mysteries to us in so subtle and discreet a way, that it seems nothing further can be added." Prol.

45) Of these discriminations, Saint Thomas lays down the principle in the famous text in which he no longer gives, as a basis for the spiritual sense, the *words* (the signification meant by the human author), but rather the *realities* (governed by God, and becoming therein significative in turn). See *Ia Pars*, q. 1, a. 10. The doctrine was fundamentally a classical one, but unceasingly overstepped. Saint Thomas gives it an organic and clearcut formulation. [On the spiritual sense in Saint Thomas, see M.-D. MAILHIOT, *La pensée de saint Thomas sur le sens spirituel*, in *RT*, LIX (1959), 613–663.]

To be noted, also, his vigorous reaction against the tendency of allegorizing everything, in which the Old Testament was emptied of any ritual value, and reduced to the sole role of a "figure." See *Ia–IIae*, q. 102, a. 2.

opment took place by means of a doubling wherein the body of a narrative, a myth, a mystery was in fact broken up, supposedly in favor of their "spirit" which had become heterogeneous to their letter. The Christians (and Philo himself) maintained the original historical datum, to be sure; yet, they accepted, especially at Alexandria, the methods of their contemporaries. Through Ambrose, Augustine, Gregory, these methods, laden down with an allegorizing intellectualism, penetrated the medieval West's exegesis. Thus it came about that in medieval exegesis allegorizing made a single block out of the Christian transfiguration of history and a moral transposition wherein the biblical narratives were made symbols of the just man's interior life.

What we have detected in the foregoing necessary investigations— necessary as regards what truly happened in Bible interpretation as well as for an intelligent reading of the commentaries of Saint Thomas —does not ruin that type of exegesis the XIIIth century university masters practiced. Quite willingly would we give it the name of *theological* exegesis. Our intention thereby would be to characterize the lot of methods that aimed to seize in its historical and suprahistorical entirety the biblical content of an economy which had been inscribed, to be sure, in a letter dependent on the rules of human writing, yet which overstepped, through and within its realization, the successive elements entering its history. Among the elements internally linked up within this lot, prefiguring, so faith has it, plays an important pedagogical and doctrinal role because an exegesis that would "build up" (46) its datum in its entirety, that would organize the word of God, owes it to itself to integrate those resemblances and those symbolisms that are charged with religious value, as bear witness the liturgy, catechesis, homiletics, and the monastic *collatio*.

Yet, this very enumeration of the native "grounds" of the *lectio divina*, from Saint Augustine to Saint Benedict and Saint Bernard, enables us to foresee that the transfer of it into a university regime that was de-pastoralized, if we dare use the word, will end up in a literary genre lacking in homogeneity in the measure that theological *explanation (rationes* et *quaestiones)* will occupy the ground next to, and soon, above typological *signification*. There will be a passing from the *lectio divina* to *doctrina sacra* wherein various functions will gradually take on their legitimate specification. While remaining in continuity with Scripture, theological "science" will acquire its own technical autonomy in relation to exegesis, to the *lectio*. The content of the very words *doctrina sacra* will become ambiguous, preserving,

---

46) See HUGH OF SAINT VICTOR, *Didascalicon*, lib. VI, c. 4; Buttimer ed., 118; *P.L.*, 176, 802 B; Taylor ed., 140: ". . . for it [Scripture] too has a *structure*."

meanwhile, the very precious advantage of maintaining continuity between the *pagina sacra* and *theologia-scientia*. From the literary and doctrinal standpoints, the commentaries on Scripture of Saint Thomas stand at this point—today left behind—in the history of pedagogy. Therein they illustrate Hugh of Saint Victor's beautiful saying: "The cathedral of the doctor is Sacred Scripture" (47).

V. BIBLICAL THEOLOGY

Even though we are passing from the commentaries on Scripture of Saint Thomas to those of his works in which theology is systematized, we must mark, at least summarily, what place the master in theology's attitude towards the Bible will have within his ulterior undertaking of building a science. The fruit of his "theological" exegesis, in the sense stated above, will be, right at the heart of his science, a biblical theology. That is to say, whole sections of doctrinally elaborated biblical matter and of sacred history will be inserted within his very systematization, making the latter a *doctrina sacra*. We shall have to account for this phenomenon when the study of the *Summa theologiae* is pursued, but right now is the time to cast light on what connections it implies concerning method.

Roughly speaking, the *Summa* contains three sections wherein there is a direct elaboration of Holy Scripture: of *Genesis*, in the treatise on creation *(Ia Pars, q. 65–74)*, of the books on the Law, in the treatise on ancient Law *(Ia–IIae, q. 98–105)*, finally of the Gospels, in the treatise on the life of Christ *(IIIa Pars, q. 27–59)*. These three sections the speculative trend of modern theology will gradually eliminate, or push aside to a preliminary, and no longer integrant, zone of study. Whatever one's opinion about this evolution wherein the normal diversification of the functions of theology pays the price in unfortunate spiritual breaches, the fact is that the equilibrium of a medieval *summa*—of Saint Thomas's *Summa*—implies, through the blessed action which a basic biblical pedagogy has on the master in theology, the permanency of a massive dose of direct scriptural elaboration, let us use the words, of biblical theology. The fact is all the more meaningful in that it represents an express novelty if compared with the distribution of matters in the classical commentary on the *Sentences* in which the biblical datum, whether the Old Testament (*Genesis*, the Law) or the New (the life of Christ in the Gospels), was left outside the *quaestiones* ever since Peter Lombard.

In the present case, we are plainly passing beyond exegesis and the commentary. The scriptural datum is organized around doctrinal

---

47) "Cathedra doctoris sacra Scriptura est." HUGH OF SAINT VICTOR, *Miscellanea*, I, 75; *P.L.*, 177, 510 C.

categories that overstep the original letter. Thus, in the treatise on creation, the narrations of *Genesis* are organized around the two works of *distinctio* [distinction] and *ornatus* [adornment] (48). In the treatise on the ancient Law, the theological edifice is built up around three elements that are rich in spiritual and scientific insights: the [*praecepta*] *moralia* [moral precepts], *caeremonialia* [ceremonial precepts], *judicialia* [judicial precepts], however informally and accidentally they may occur in the text that is referred to (*Deut.*, VI, 1) (a). The treatise on the life of Christ enlists the evangelical narrative in a rational, a "scholastic," analysis similar to the one we observed in the commentaries, and wherein suitabilities, value-laden examples, and so forth, are brought in. In all these cases, but especially in the treatise on ancient Law that is figurative by definition, letter and facts are sifted out to the benefit of a comprehensive view offering a homogeneous and intelligent expression of the divine economy, its aims, the carrying out of it, and its stages. Therein, as in the commentaries, allegorization and the *rationes figurales* [figurative reasons] weigh down on details to the detriment of the letter and of history. In a better way than in the commentaries, however, a discerning is made of the general values that, over and beyond history, reveal the prefigurations that are an integral part of a theology of God's people, of a theology of history. It is a *doctrina sacra*.

VI. RESEARCH SUGGESTIONS

1. If it is true that the intellectual equilibrium of the Christian world is founded upon the interaction of its pastoral of the Gospel and of its teaching of theology, then the XIIIth century enterprises on Scripture must be read and judged in the light of the evangelical reawakening of the end of the XIIth century. Consequently, recourse must be had both to the history of the movements of reform (see H. GRUNDMANN, *Religiöse Bewegungen im Mittelalter*, Berlin, 1935; P. MANDONNET, *Saint Dominique. L'idée, l'homme et l'oeuvre;* 2 vols., Paris, 1957; see Research Suggestions to chapter I) and to the works on the evolution of biblical studies in the monastic, the urban, and, subsequently, the university schools (see in particular, B. SMALLEY, *The study of the Bible in the Middle Ages*, 2d rev. ed., Oxford, 1952).

On the development of exegetical methods in general, and on Saint Thomas's positions in particular, see the indispensable repertory of

---

48) In this word, the old Platonic theme handed down by the school of Chartres underlies the biblical use that is made of it. See E. GILSON, *La cosmogonie de Bernardus Silvestris*, in *AHDLMA*, III (1928), 7.

a) See M.-D. CHENU, *La théologie de la loi ancienne selon saint Thomas*, in *RT*, LXI (1961), 485–497.

C. SPICQ, *Esquisse d'une histoire de l'exégèse latine au moyen âge,* in *BibTh,* XXVI (1944), with all the pertinent bibliography given therein on this matter. [Also his *Saint Thomas exégète,* in *DTC, XV,* 1 (1946), col. 694–738, and F. STEGMÜLLER, *Repertorium biblicum medii aevi,* Madrid, 1955, which lists the medieval commentaries on the Bible and gives the essential bibliography.] Concerning the works undertaken on the Bible amongst the Preachers, the article published long ago by P. MANDONNET, in *DB,* II (1899), col. 1463–1482: *Dominicains [Travaux des) sur les saintes Ecritures,* still fixes the essential points.

The articles of P. MANDONNET, *Chronologie des écrits scripturaires de saint Thomas d'Aquin,* in *RT,* XXXIII (1928), 27–45, 116–155, 211–245; XXXIV (1929), 53–69, 132–145, 489–519, supply abundant data and suggestions which, one would not, going by their title, expect to find in them; on the other hand, the chronological arrangements therein proposed remain hypothetical. [See above, 244.].

2. So as to observe with effective results the "scholastic" procedures of Saint Thomas's exegesis, compare, on a given text, an homily of one of the Fathers, a sermon of Saint Bernard, an allegory of Richard of Saint Victor, a postill of Hugh of Saint Cher, a commentary of Saint Albert, a commentary of Saint Thomas, and the exegesis done by one of our contemporaries. Make use of the frameworks and of the examples supplied by C. SPICQ, *Esquisse d'une histoire de l'exégèse latine au moyen âge,* ch. VI: literal exegesis, dialectical exegesis, theological exegesis, verbal exegesis, scientific exegesis, the rules of hermeneutics.

Analyse closely two or three illustrative specimens of Saint Thomas, for example, his commentary on the Prologue of Saint John or the organic presentation of the Epistles of Saint Paul as a whole.

3. So as to grasp the principles and especially the practice of an exegesis within which the "spiritual" sense is integrated, study, upon the patristic background, the formation of symbolic theology during the XIIth century, especially in Hugh of Saint Victor. See G. PARÉ, A. BRUNET, P. TREMBLAY, *La Renaissance du XIIe siècle. Les écoles et l'enseignement,* in *PIEM,* III (1933), ch. V on the teaching of Scripture: *The theorizers on exegesis before Hugh,* 213–218; *The teaching of Scripture according to the "Didascalicon,"* 218–229; *Techniques and methods,* 229–239.

Concerning the doctrine which is at the root of that type of hermeneutics, see J. GRIBOMONT, *Le lien des deux Testaments selon la théologie de saint Thomas,* in *ETL,* XXII (1946), 70–89. On the divisions of typology, see H. DE LUBAC, *Sur un vieux distique: la doctrine du quadruple sens,* in *MFC,* 347–366.

Observe how symbolism tends to eat its way into the literal and historical meanings that support it. [See M.–D. CHENU, *La théologue au XIIe siècle,* in *EPM,* XLV (1957), ch. VIII: *La théologie symbolique,* 191–209.] Gather and classify a number of "mystical" interpretations, then note the procedures and quality of the arguments that rest on them. Analyse this procedure in fields other than the theology of Saint Thomas, for instance, in Gratian (see G. LE BRAS, *Les Ecritures dans le Décret de Gratien,* in *ZSK,* XXVII (1938), 47–80), in the chroniclers and biographers, in collections of sermons (see E. GILSON, *Note pour l'explication de quelques raisonnements scripturaires au moyen âge,* in *RHF,* II (1925), 350–360), in the liturgists (see E. DE MOREAU, *Les explications allégoriques des cérémonies de la messe au moyen âge,* in *NRT,* 1921, 100–143), in the image-carvers and the sculptors (see the works of E. MÂLE).

4. In order to observe the passage from an exegesis of the Bible to a construction upon its text, in order also to observe how theology feeds upon Scripture, read those questions of the *Summa* dealing with the life of Christ, which are always left out nowadays in current teaching. See I. M. VOSTÉ, *Exegesis Novi Testamenti et sancti Thomae Summa theologica,* in *Ang,* XXIV (1947), 3–19. In particular, bring out what type of argumentation is used in articles such as:"Whether it was becoming that Christ should lead an austere life in this world?", "Whether Christ should have led a life of poverty in this world?", *IIIa Pars,* q. 40, a. 2 and 3; or again in the article "Whether Christ ought to have suffered on the Cross?", *Ibid.,* q. 46, a. 4, whose symbolic (patristic) theme a miserable intellectualistically-obsessed commentator has reduced to having the value of a demontration, as if this could be possible. Compare on the same text an exegetical commentary and a theological elaboration; for example, on Saint Paul's definition of faith, compare *In Hebr.,* XI, 1 and *IIa–IIae,* q. 4, a. 1; or, on an allegory, *In I Cor.* IX, 9 (which quotes *Deut.* XXV, 25) and *Ia–IIae,* q. 102, a. 6, ad 8um.

Put together the admirable ritual theology of the Old Testament which is proposed in *Ia–IIae,* q. 102. Extract the Old Testament's political and social theories from the presentation of them in *Ia–IIae,* q. 105.

More generally, determine what influence the study of Scripture had on the theology of Saint Thomas. See J. VAN DER PLOEG, *The Place of Holy Scripture in the Theology of St. Thomas,* in *Thom,* X (1947), 398–422 [answered by G. GEENEN, *The Place of Tradition in the Theology of Saint Thomas,* in *Thom,* XV (1952), 110–135; see the latter's *Saint Thomas et les Pères,* in *DTC,* XV, 1 (1946), col. 738–761); also R. GUINDON, *Le caractère évangélique de la morale de Saint*

Thomas d'Aquin, in *RUO,* XXV (1955), 145*–167*, and the section bearing the same name in his *Béatitude et théologie morale chez saint Thomas d'Aquin,* 323–333]. Determine, for instance, the influence his study of the Epistle to the Hebrews, and behind it, of the Old Testament, had on his theology of the priesthood (*IIIa Pars,* q. 22; q. 63–64); how he treated, within an intellectualistic theology, the texts fostering the primacy of love (*Cant.,* VIII, 7; *I Cor.,* XIII, 13; *Rom.,* XIII, 10; *Matt.,* XXII, 40); how the evangelical theme of the beatitudes feeds a theological speculation (see M.–D. ROLAND-GOSSELIN, *Le sermon sur la montagne et la théologie thomiste,* in *RSPT,* XVII (1928), 201–234 [R. GUINDON, *Béatitude . . .,* 297–303]).

Chapter VIII

The Commentaries on Peter Lombard and on Boethius

I. THE PRESTIGE OF THE MASTER OF THE SENTENCES

A young professor of theology at the University of Paris began his personal efforts and made his choices in doctrine and methodology through a commentary upon the *IV Libri Sententiarum* (a). Indeed, the two years that he had previously been obliged to devote to a "cursory reading" of the Bible, however meaningful they may have been as regards the medieval regime of theological knowledge, could play only a limited role in the determining of his choices. Thus, after the years 1252–1254 during which he had just fulfilled the tasks of the *baccalaureus biblicus* [Bachelor of the Bible], Brother Thomas was to comment on Peter Lombard, who, for many decades previous, had been given the name of "Master of the Sentences," a name bespeaking his prestige and reserved to him in the university institution (1).

---

a) Latin ed.: Parma, VI–VIII; Vivès, VII–XI; Mandonnet ed. of books I and II, 2 vols., Paris, 1929; Moos ed. of books III and IV (as far as d. XXII inclusively), 2 vols., Paris, 1933 and 1947.

1) On Peter Lombard and his role, see J. DE GHELLINCK's article, *Pierre Lombard*, in DTC, XII, 2 (1935), col. 1941–2019 [and P. DELHAYE, *Pierre Lombard: sa vie, ses oeuvres, sa morale*, in CAG, 1961].

On the literary genre of the *Sentences*, see P. GLORIEUX's article, *Sentences (Commentaires sur les)*, in DTC, XIV, 2 (1941), col. 1860–1884; F. STEGMÜLLER's Introduction to the *Repertorium commentariorum in Sententias Petri Lombardi*, Würzburg, 1947 [supplemented by V. DOUCET, in AFH, XLVII (1954), 88–170; 400–427].

His, in fact, was a unique destiny for a theologian in the history of Christian thought. One century after its publication (around 1152), the work of Peter Lombard had become the official *textus* [text] of the bachelor's teaching at the University of Paris. From this starting point, it gradually extended over a period of three centuries to all universities of Christendom. The institutionalization of it did not come about, and it was normal that it should not come about, without resistance since immediate contact with the word of God is an ever present requisite in theology, even at the stage during which it equips itself with rational instrumentation.

That requisite had made itself known as the work of reason took on importance in teaching. At the beginning of the XIIIth century, indeed, one can measure that increasing importance through the very stages of the pedagogical accrediting of the *Book of Sentences*, howsoever discreet a use it may have made of dialectics. From the last third of the XIIth century, certain masters, such as the Lombard's impassioned disciple Peter of Poitiers (professor for 38 years at the school of Notre-Dame-de-Paris, +1205), were already using it as a textbook, and the plan of its treatises, even when their speculative or practical lacunae were recognized, was rather generally adopted. Once the opposition of Joachim of Fiore and of the followers of Gilbert of la Porrée had been broken by the explicit approbation of the Lateran Council of 1215 ("We believe and profess with Peter Lombard") (a), its accrediting asserted itself. Around 1230, one might say, the *Book of Sentences* had become the official text at the moment when the teaching of theology was split into two stages, with the master, titular of a chair, "reading" Scripture, while his young collaborator, the bachelor, took the four books of the *Sentences* as his text, whence his title, *baccalaureus sententiarius* [Bachelor of the Sentences]. In 1254, this arrangement was the basis of all University regulations (2).

To about the same decade of 1230 we are referred not only by the general protests against the invasion into theology of rational tech-

---

a) "Nos . . . credimus et confitemur cum Petro Lombardo . . ." *Denz,* n. 432, 201.

2) Each Dominican student received, together with the Bible and PETER COMESTOR's *Historia scholastica,* a copy of the *Sentences.* [See the text in *Die Constitutionen des Predigerordens in der Redaction Raimunds von Penafort,* ed. H. DENIFLE, in *ALKGMA,* V (1889), 563. Raymond of Penyafort's edition of the Dominican Constitutions was also edited from *British Mus. ms. 23935* by G. R. GALBRAITH as Appendix I in his *The Constitutions of the Dominican Order 1216 to 1360,* in *PUMHS,* XLIV (1925). The information given above is therein found on page 251. See also the quotation of the relevant part of the text in A. FRANKLIN, *Les anciennes bibliothèques de Paris,* Paris, 1867, I, 193]. The College of the Sorbonne received as a gift fifty copies of the *Sentences* before the middle of the XIVth century (See L. DELISLE, *Cabinet des manuscrits,* Paris, 1881, III, 23–25, list of 1338).

niques but also precisely by the violent diatribe of Roger Bacon against the prestige enjoyed by the Bachelor of the Sentences (3). In fact, the prestige progressively given him was the normal consequence of theology's being constituted as an organized science, which was done on the de facto narrow basis, as we shall see, of the work of the Lombard (4).

Such was the role of the Master of the Sentences in the development of theology, and foremost in that of the theology of Saint Thomas. That role was to be underlined, with a view, precisely, to reducing it, through the decision the latter took later on to build a *summa* freed from the framework and the constraints imposed by the *Sentences*—in particular from that constraint which ran counter to the *ordo disciplinae* [order of teaching], the *librorum expositio* [exposition on books] (Prologue to the *Summa theologiae*). Framework, partitioning of subject matter, building-up of treatises were, in fact, the first constraining elements to operate against the ever fresh initiatives of scientific elaboration. As a consequence, a theologian was making a decisive choice when he classified the contents of revelation according to synthetic categories (*res et signa, frui et uti*: the Lombard following Augustine) or, on the contrary, when he followed the order of a historical economy (Hugh of Saint Victor), or again when he partitioned his object into four great sections wherein a supernatural conception of man would be divided into two parts: the one connected with creation (*Sent.*, lib. II, d. 24 f.), the other, rather artificially, with the virtues of Christ (*Ibid.*, lib. III, d. 23 f.).

To take the contents of these *IV Libri* as the basic datum for a theological science, even in cases where their limits would be over-

---

3) "The fourth sin [of the study of theology] is the preferring of a certain magistral *summa*, namely: the *Book of Sentences*, to the text of the faculty of theology. In fact, in it consists the entire glory of the theologians, and on it also, everyone does work enough to burden a horse. And after one has 'read' the book, he already presumes to obtain the masterate in theology, even though he does not understand the thirtieth part of its text. And the bachelor who 'reads' the text [of Scripture] makes way, at Paris and everywhere else, for the 'reader' of the *Sentences* who is honored and preferred in everything. For, at Paris, the 'reader' of the *Sentences* obtains the principal hour of 'reading' according to his own choice; among the religious, he also has his *socius* and his own room. The 'reader' of the Bible, however, is wanting in all this, and begs for an hour to 'read,' at the good pleasure of the 'reader' of the *Sentences*. Elsewhere, the latter holds disputations and is considered a master, while the 'reader' of the scriptural text cannot even dispute, as was the case this year at Bologna and in many other places, all of which is absurd . . ." ROGER BACON, *Opus minus*, in *RBO*, 328–329 (See above, ch. II, note 16).

4) In this perspective, the title of the work: "*Libri sententiarum*", must be correctly understood. The evolution in the meaning of the word *sententia*, which, from the recording of an opinion in a florilegium, came to signify the doctrinal and authorized solution of an opinion, reveals the work of theology making its way to rational matureness. See G. PARÉ, A. BRUNET, P. TREMBLAY, *La renaissance du XIIe siècle. Les écoles et l'enseignement*, in *PIEM*, III (1933), 267–274.

stepped, was—if we analyse the matter more profoundly—an under-taking grave in consequence. One reaped the benefits, but also the limitations, of a well-ordered, selected, digested, wisely assimilated patristic inheritance in which the personal inquisitiveness of the Ancients, reduced to a common denominator, was held in a precious but rather prosaic balance. At any rate, through this facileness and clarity there resulted an inclination to neglect or to reabsorb what-ever new contributions might be added. Then again, the problems that the elaboration of this datum posed were controlled by the spiritual and technical perspectives of the XIIth century. In utilizing them copiously, the Lombard integrated within the common property of Western theology the investigations and the positions of Hugh of Saint Victor, of the *Summa Sententiarum,* and of Abelard. Any com-mentator on the *Sentences* was in advance committed to these per-spectives. Finally, it all was permeated with Augustinian vigor and organized into the categories of Augustine—of an Augustine whose stimulating metaphysical purviews and religious experiences would at any rate have to be toned down for the use of good students (5). Peter Lombard, to be sure, did not presume on his own genius, as he reproached others for having done (Book I, d. 9, c. 3; Book III, d. 5, c. 1; d. 9; etc.), and he preserved the moderation he preached ("mak-ing use of a temperate mean between the two") (a). But on account of this, he sanctioned the most successful advances and furnished for the future an area of work wherein the freest initiatives would be able to operate, rendering the soil from which they grew more and more neutralized (6). Thus, when Saint Thomas arrived on the scene, the teaching of the *Sentences,* as we shall see, had already largely gone far beyond the *expositio* of the text.

Until he was promoted to the masterate in 1256, Saint Thomas taught the *Sentences* for two years at the college of Saint James in the chair of visiting professors, while Elie Brunet was regent of studies. We have every reason to believe that the redaction and the

---

5) See F. CAVALLERA, *Saint Augustin et le Livre des Sentences de Pierre Lom-bard,* in AP, VII (1930), [438–451].

a) ". . . temperato inter utrumque moderamine utentes." Prol.

6) "Essentially impersonal, except for the choice of materials, the stating of well-ordered questions, and the judicious weighing of solutions, all of which are really worthy of praise, the work presents itself, from the literary point of view, as a résumé shorn of life and of enthusiasm, and, moreover, with hardly a philo-sophical view, but also as a well-ordered, reasonably complete, proportioned, résumé of everything that is then being discussed in the schools and which must be used as the basis of teaching. . . . Colorless and gaunt, the *Quattuor libri Sententiarum* lent themselves excellently on each particular question to an exposi-tion of original views by means of an appropriate commentary, and one can see that original commentaries did not fail to avail themselves of that liberty." J. DE GHELLINCK, *L'essor de la littérature latine au XIIe siècle,* in ML-SH, IV (1946), 72–73.

publication of his work followed immediately upon his oral teaching. As early as 1256, at the age of 30, Saint Thomas had already presented to his contemporaries a general exposé of his entire thought on all theological subjects then under discussion. Then also, his biographer tells us, he outclassed his colleagues and captivated his listeners (7).

By means of a detailed account of Tolomeo of Lucca, who had been a student of Saint Thomas at Naples, it seems certain that Saint Thomas conceived the project of recasting his commentary on the Lombard, once he had reached the height of his activities some ten years later. Tolomeo asserts that the first book was actually written, that he saw a copy of it, but that even in his day this copy had been lost (8). We are reduced to conjectures in the face of that ambiguous text (9). On the other hand, it would not be without interest were we

---

7) "Having been made a bachelor, when he began to pour out through his 'reading' that which, in his taciturn temperament, he had mulled over in silence, God infused in him so much science, and so much doctrine was poured on his lips from the Divine source, that he was seen to surpass everyone, even the masters, and, by the clarity of his teaching, to move more than the others the students to the love of science." WILLIAM OF TOCCO, *Vita S. Thomae Aquinatis*, c. 14; Prummer ed., in *FVST*, II (1924), 81; in *ASS*, VII (1865), 661 B, n. 15.

This pious evocation must not disguise the conjunctures, in which, during the years 1252–1256, Saint Thomas was pursuing his teaching, writing his work, and receiving his title of master in theology. At the time, the most violent of conflicts was then raging between the Preachers (together with the Minors) and the University, with, spear-heading the attack, William of Saint Amour whose *De periculis novissimorum temporum* was diffused in 1255–1256. Saint Thomas's refutation of the latter work, his *Contra impugnantes Dei cultum* which he wrote after the condemnation of October 1256, was published at the end of 1256. A truce that came about in March-April of 1256 created favorable circumstances for Saint Thomas's being admitted to the licentiate and giving the usual discourse (*principium*). [On this conflict, see D. L. DOUIE, *The Conflict between the Seculars and the Mendicants at the University of Paris in the Thirteenth Century*, in *AqP*, XXIII (1954). See also below, ch. XII, 340–343].

8) "[Thomas] also wrote, at the time he was at Rome (of this, we have spoken above) and when he was already a master, on the first book of the *Sentences*, which writing I saw at Lucca, but which, withdrawn since then, I have never seen again." TOLOMEO OF LUCCA, *Historia ecclesiastica nova*, lib. XXII, c. XV, in *RIS*, XI (1727), col. 1172. See P. MANDONNET, *Des écrits authentiques de S. Thomas d'Aquin*, 2d rev. ed., Fribourg, 1910, 63 and 146, and Foster ed., 139.

9) Father MANDONNET (*loc. cit.*, 146) supposes with extreme likelihood that, because of the constraining limitations which the outdated framework of the Lombard imposed upon him, Saint Thomas gave up work on a new commentary, and undertook on his own a methodic exposition of theology, the outcome of which was the *Summa theologiae*.

The hypothesis proposed by A. HAYEN (*S. Thomas a-t-il édité deux fois son Commentaire sur le livre des Sentences*, in *RTAM*, IX (1937), 219–236), according to which the current text we have in the manuscripts and editions would be, not the first one which he composed in 1254–1256, but rather the one which he wrote when he was at Rome and a master, makes the text of Tolomeo even more ambiguous, and runs into unsolvable objections. See A. DONDAINE's review, in *BT*, VI (1940), 100–108. [The question was raised anew by P. VANIER,

to discover the relevant places where Saint Thomas may have corrected the first redaction of his course from the beginning of its circulation. We know, in effect, through his extant autographs (in the present case, through the autograph of the third book of the *Sentences*) (10) that he corrected, deleted, recast his text. It is possible that, after the work had been put in circulation, he continued this work upon a manuscript that may have served as a second prototype (11). It would seem, moreover, that certain elements incorporated in our standard editions today, just as they were in most of the manuscripts, were introduced later during the life of Saint Thomas to give the answer to controversies then current (12).

II. BEYOND THE LOMBARD

In the text that we have quoted, Roger Bacon rose up in rebellion against the increasing prestige of the Bachelor of the Sentences and also against the overflow of *quaestiones* and their intellectualistic seduction from which this disorder originated (13). An overflow, surely, literally speaking, in this sense that the "texts" for teaching were over-reached by questions that were no longer related to the true meaning of the datum (in an *expositio*), but rather ended up

---

Théologie trinitaire chez S. Thomas d'Aquin. Evolution du concept d'action notionnelle, in *PIEM*, XIII (1953), who suggested that the current text could be a partially revised one (see 124). Here again, serious difficulties have been raised against the hypothesis. See J. HAMER's review of the work, in *BT*, IX (1954–56), 596–601, wherein the reader will also find, on page 596, a list of other reviews of the work.]

10) This autograph is preserved in *Vatican Latin ms. 9851*.

11) On this autograph and the divergences between the text it contains and that of our editions, see G. ROSSI, *L'autografo di S. Tommaso del Commento al III libro delle Sentenze*, in *DTP*, XXXV (1932), 532–585 [reprint in *MCA*, XII (1932)].

12) This would be the case for *In I Sent.*, d. 2, a. 3, which would be the text of a disputation on the divine attributes held at Rome, in 1265 or 1266, the occasion of it furnished by the controversy that had arisen concerning the *Commentary of the Sentences* of PETER OF TARENTASIA. See A. DONDAINE, *S. Thomas a-t-il disputé à Rome la question des "attributs divins"?* in *BT*, III (1933), *Notes et communications*, 171–182; also *S. Thomas et la dispute des attributs divins. Authenticité et origine*, in *AFP*, VIII (1938), 253–262.

There is that other case to be examined, that of *In I Sent.*, prol., a. 3, sol. 2, concerning the structure of theological science. See M.-D. CHENU, *La théologie comme science au XIIIe siècle*, 3d rev. ed., in *BibTh.*, XXXIII (1957), 76–78.

13) "Likewise, it is impossible for the text of God to be known because of the abusive use that is made of the *Books of Sentences*. For, the questions that should have been raised on the text in the exposition of it, as is done in every faculty, are now separated from the text. . . . As a result, those who 'read' the text do not give an exposition of it, because they are not raising questions that are appropriate and necessary for the understanding of it." ROGER BACON, *Opus minus*, in *RBO*, 329.

having their own independent life. As a result, the pristine datum was made obsolete.

The *Sentences* of the Lombard were themselves subjected to this immoderate handling. In a half-century, they passed from a regime of glossing to one of questions increasingly posited, treated, and organized outside the original text (14). During the period from the glossator Peter of Poitiers (he taught from 1167 to 1205) up to Alexander of Hales (he did his commentaries around 1230), who set approximately the golden age of the Lombard—I mean by that the period during which his work, notwithstanding surrounding oppositions, represented an active source of inspiration and design for theological teaching—the commentary evolved into that form which we see stylized in Saint Thomas and of which Alexander of Hales, as the chronicler tells us, was one of the first practitioners (15).

The arrangement in the commentary of Saint Thomas gives us, then, the following picture: whole series of questions ordered more or less according to their number in articles and lesser questions and framed by a *divisio textus* [division of the text] and an *expositio textus* [exposition of the text], which were the more and more neglected vestiges of the old literal commentary (16).

We have reached, therefore, a point beyond the Lombard. The *Hic quaeritur* by which the Lombard himself had introduced the questions in his *Sentences* had been the starting-point, it is true, of the aforementioned type of speculative elaboration. Their number multiplied to such a degree, however, brings us, theologically speaking, to another literary and doctrinal genre. Bacon, for all his conservatism, had foresight.

We have reached a point beyond the Lombard even as regards plan and framework. The broad sections are, to be sure, materially preserved. The basic categories—*res-signa, uti-frui*—however, are sub-

---

14) On this evolution from the gloss to questions in the literature concerned with the Lombard, see the works of A. LANDGRAF and of Dom LOTTIN periodically reviewed in the *BTAM*. For a general view of that literary genre made up by the commentaries on the *Sentences* and on its destiny, see P. GLORIEUX's article, *Sentences*, in *DTC*, XIV, 2 (1941), col. 1880–1884.

15) "Died at Paris the noble cleric, master Alexander of Hales, 'reader' of the sacred page, who was the first among the Minors to hold a chair of theology, which he did most honorably, and who left behind him *a skillful way of 'reading' invented by him, as concerns the scholastic divisions and meanings of the letter of the text*. For, before him, the letter was not pressed, nor its meaning elicited." *Chronicon de Lanercost* for the year 1245, ed. J. STEVENSON in *Bannatyne Club*, LXVIII, Edinburgh, 1839, 53. The chronicler's praise meets the criticism of Bacon who denounces (in the *Opus minus* referred to above) Alexander as the first one responsible. See the current research being done by PELSTER and DOUCET on the *Sentences* and the *Summa* of Alexander of Hales.

16) Instead of the *expositio textus*, Saint Bonaventure proposes *dubia circa litteram* [doubts concerning the letter], which offer considerable doctrinal interest.

merged and rather superficially exploited (17). In each "distinction" (18), new problems give rise to blocks of questions that, one feels, are closely ordered by recent discussions, techniques, and vocabulary. Hence to understand these questions, it is necessary to refer no longer to the Lombard or to his contemporaries of Saint Victor or of Chartres, but rather to the immediately preceding *magistri*, whom Albert the Great has already classified, for a period extending over two or three generations, into the *antiqui* (those who have taught around 1200, but also William of Auxerre and Philip the Chancelor whose activity has extended over the years 1220–1235) and the *moderni* (Grosseteste is thus described) (19), and who often appear in the description of opinions presented by Saint Thomas under the anonymous title of *quidam.*

The documentary contributions feeding such a speculative effort are of two kinds. First, there are contributions arising from a renewed investigation of the ancient Christian authors, in particular of the East, who ever since the last third of the XIIth century had broadened the working basis of theology. Second, there is the decisive contribution made by philosophical material which furnishes an instrumentation much more perfect than the XIIth century dialectics and which especially, changes the points upon which theology focuses its attention. No longer is it only a question of means of organization and of a method of elaboration; it is rather a question, in the very domain of the objects of theological science, of an ideological material, of a rational view of the world, of man, and of the mind, all these involving not only methods but also the term and content of thinking (20). No

---

17) On the Lombard's plan and the principles of his division, which he applies loosely, see J. DE GHELLINCK's article, *Pierre Lombard,* in *DTC,* XII, 2 (1935), col. 1980–1981. In *In I Sent.,* d. 2, div. textus, however, Saint Thomas brings out the fruitfulness of these categories for an organization of the theological datum.

18) The division in "distinctions" of the *Quattuor libri* originated with the commentators. The author had divided his work into *capitula* [chapters].

19) See M.–D. CHENU, *Antiqui, moderni. Notes de lexicographie médiévale,* in *RSPT,* XVII (1928), 82–94.

20) See M.–J. CONGAR's article, *Théologie,* in *DTC,* XV, I (1946), col. 374–377.

Among the major cases of that surpassing of the Lombard (and of the transformation of theology), let us choose, as an example, one of the least noticed, that of the introduction of an ethics based upon a science of man, that of Aristotle. Commenting upon d. 33 of the third book, Saint Thomas brings up and solves 41 questions (for two pages of text to be commented upon). This is the first treatise of moral theology to have been developed. Odo of Rigaud had proposed only 5 questions, Albert 4, Bonaventure 6. As early as 1256, once the narrow framework of the Lombard had been broken, we have a first outline of the *IIa Pars* of the *Summa.* There is a fact at the root of this, it is the entrance on the scene of Aristotle's *Ethics* (Saint Thomas has just transcribed Albert's course on it at Cologne, in 1248–1252). As a commentator of the *Sentences* (before 1248), Albert had quoted the *Ethics* about a dozen times, Bonaventure quotes it 3 times, Saint Thomas refers to it 125 times.

doubt herein lies the distinction by means of which, with Aristotle's third entrance, as it has been called, the *moderni*, of whom we were speaking, step out of the category of the *antiqui* (21). For a work of this kind, the book of the Lombard is evidently nothing other than, and will no longer furnish anything except, an entirely external occasion maintained by university regulations. It will be a kind of purely formal framework, which the XIVth century nominalists, not unlike the XIIIth century classic masters, Albert the Great, Bonaventure, or Thomas Aquinas, will fill out as they please.

III. SAINT THOMAS'S FIRST WORK AND THE EVOLUTION OF HIS THOUGHT

It is not, however, within the historical framework supplied by contemporary commentators on the *Sentences* that Saint Thomas's commentary is principally interesting, it is within the perspective of the theological life of Saint Thomas himself. In it, we have his first organic construction, ten years before he undertook the *Summa theologiae*. This situation provides us with a wonderful advantage for entering into the internal elaborating of his thought at work, which will be made known, meanwhile, in the *Disputed Questions*, the *Commentaries on Scripture*, and the *Commentaries on Aristotle*. The *Commentary on the Sentences* will not be for us a reference work wherein we may find a few formulae and arguments to season the reading of the *Summa theologiae*. Likewise, shall be avoided the ready temptation of harmonizing the *loca parallela* [parallel passages] so that therein the *Sentences* and the *Summa* will overspread one another in mutual neutralization. Even less shall we fall back upon the *Sentences*, as has sometimes been done (22), where the texts of the *Summa* are eliptical and too concise. This would be to proceed contrary to history and doctrine. In each one of these works, on the contrary, their original framework, particular context, own responses, own ways of proceeding, nuances, and conclusions will be examined. The purpose will not, of course, be to contrast them for the sake of contrast but to take part in the genesis of each one of the elements that make up the synthesis of Saint Thomas.

It will be quickly discovered that, from his very first extensive work, Saint Thomas had established his basic positions and that his master intuitions already held sway. Yet, satisfaction will also be

---

21) It was at that time that the category of *philosophi,* as sources of thought, and as opposed to the *sancti,* obtained stability. See M.-J. CHENU, *Les "phi-losophes" dans la philosophie chrétienne médiévale,* in *RSPT,* XXVI (1937), 27–40.

22) As, for instance, even in recent controversies, for the theory on the causality of the sacraments.

found in observing the progress, at times in quality, at times in technique, that the *Disputed Questions* and then the organic purviews of the *Summa* have provided for his genial mind. Besides, the first generation of his disciples perceived, in a rather material way it is true, that there were differences between the two works, and they composed *concordantiae* [concordances] one of which bears the significant title: "Articles in which Brother Thomas expresses himself better in the *Summa* than in the *Writing* [*on the Sentences*]" (23). In fact —and this observation is an important one for the history of Thomism —during two centuries, the *Commentary on the Sentences* remained the rule for the interpretation of Saint Thomas, since the professor, who was bound to the text of the Lombard by the university regulations, spontaneously referred to the *Sentences* and limited himself to a consultation of the *Summa*. Thus proceeded the first great commentator on Saint Thomas, Capreolus (+1444). Today, the resources of the historical method, for the sake of doctrine and not just from a taste for erudition, have decided the interpreters of Saint Thomas to follow step by step the operations of his thinking, even where his conclusions are identical. Thus we join in the reflexion of Saint Thomas himself who was clearly conscious of the conditions of the progress of thought in the individual as well as in humanity (24). Besides, is this not the reason that in the *Summa* he had reorganized from top to bottom the work he had first done during his youth?

The first attitude resulting from the curiosity aroused in us by Saint Thomas *junior* is one of attention to the contexts upon which the *Commentary on the Sentences* depends, we would almost be tempted to say, one of attention to the permanent dialogue that he therein carries on with his contemporaries, with Albert, his master, in particular, and with Bonaventure, his colleague in the neighboring college of the Minors. There is a certain article in the treatise on the sacraments wherein the nine objections from which the status of the problem is determined are the nine arguments of the exposition of Bonaventure. How great a gain there is in restoring in this way the concrete issues of a dialogue that are more easily perceived in an apprentice theologian! It has been noted that, from the IVth book of the *Commentary*

---

23) "Articuli in quibus frater Thomas melius dicit in *Summa* quam in *Scripto* [*Sententiarum*]." See P. MANDONNET, *Premiers travaux de polémique thomiste*, 2d article: *Les* Concordantiae, in *RSPT*, VII (1913), 245–262. [An edition of these articles done from a group of 12 manuscripts has been published with an introduction to them by R. A. GAUTHIER, *Les "Articuli in quibus frater Thomas melius in Summa quam in Scriptis"*, in *RTAM*, XIX (1952), 271–326.]

24) "For if, as time goes on, one devotes his efforts to the finding of truth, he is helped by time in the finding of it, both *in the case of the single individual who will see later what he had not seen*, and also in the case of diverse individuals, as when one looks into some truths discovered by his predecessors, and adds to them." *In I Eth.*, lect. 11; Marietti ed., 36, n. 133.

onward, Saint Thomas frees himself from a number of the favorite themes of his master, Albert, who was more attached to the neo-Platonic elements and Dionysian categories.

Making this a point of departure, and before proceeding to any comparison of the opinions stated in the *Commentary* with those stated in the *Summa,* one should make efforts at discovering each newly-added *Utrum* that, in every treatise, reveals the fresh advances made in the *Summa* and the emergence therein of heretofore un-formulated problems. The subject-distribution of both works should be compared closely. Especially in a *summa* the ordering of questions reveals the direction in which research will unfold and the manner in which solutions will balance one another. For example, on the question of the complex of elements that enter in the sinner's conversion and penance, a question so often subjected to close inspection in the psychological analyses and the doctrinal considerations collected and treated in the wake of distinction 17 of the IVth book of the Lombard's *Sentences,* the *Summa* considers separately those elements that are relative to the sinner's justification and rebirth, developing them through the Aristotelian schema of the coming-into-being of forms (in the treatise on grace in the *Ia–IIae*), whereas the *Sentences* considers the role played by the sacraments in this conversion within its concrete and historical economy, by reference to justification through Christ and to the sacred institution of his Church (in the *IIIa Pars*). To give another example: in the *Summa,* original sin is stripped, so to speak, of the historical contexts it has in *Genesis* and is located, outside any narrative about creation (no longer in the *Ia Pars* therefore, but rather in the *IIa Pars*), at an essentially doctrinal and moral level wherein it will be defined as a "sin of nature"; in the second book of the *Sentences,* however, Saint Thomas had left original sin inserted within the history of man's origins: creation (d. 16–20), the fall of first man (d. 21–29), the transmission of first man's sin to his descendants (here is original sin, d. 30–33), finally, original sin's influence on actual sins (d. 34–54). A detemporalizing such as is present in the *Summa* is not without consequence.

The application of this method will allow for greater penetration in discovering the pressure exercised by certain notions henceforth to be the pole of attraction of mind's effort. Whereas, in the *Sentences,* the theology of the Trinity is built around the concept of filiation, in the *Summa,* a shift takes place with work now centering upon the notion of word. In the *Sentences,* Saint Thomas seeks to understand the divine missions and the supernatural presence of the Trinity within the soul by aligining these missions with the properties of the one or the other person who is sent; he is thus exploiting the Dionysian schema of creative procession. In the *Summa,* however, in accordance with the riches he reaps from Augustine's analyses, he brings to the fore the original relationship of subject to known and loved object in a mind capable of knowing and loving God (25). In the treatise on the sacraments, especially in that on the Eucharist, developments point with insistence to a theology building on the notion of sign.

The causes explaining the evolution typified by these examples will be found to be, in part, the author's more extensive accession to the biblical, patristic, and philosophical datum which a broader investigation of the sources of his thought has procured him. One is permitted to suppose that the direct reading of Augustine's *De praedestinatione sanctorum* is at the origin of the remodeling of his doctrine on preparation to grace (26). The Dionysian inspiration of the treatise on God in the *Sentences* sheds light, by way of contrast, upon the construction of the same treatise in the *Summa* (27), while the Victorine conception of the sacraments as remedies (present in the *Sentences*) is overstepped [in the *Summa*] by means of a Dionysian-styled analogy borrowed from the relationship between the corporeal and the spiritual (28). The proof of the distinction between essence and existence that was first established within an Avicennian context, such as we find in William of Auvergne, is given, from the *Contra Gentiles* onward, its best formulation in a reversed order (29). The psychological analysis of the human act benefits from the contributions of John Damascene and of Nemesius, and, at the same time, from the analyses contained in the *Ethics* that have been commented upon in the meanwhile (30). Beyond the meritorious causality of Christ, a better knowledge of Greek theology leads him to an understanding of His causality as an instrument. Furthermore, Averroes is made to share in the

---

25) The balance between the Dionysian ontological perspective and the Augustinian psychological perspective is one of great importance. It is the factor controlling the diverging interpretations of Fr. Gardeil and Dom Chambat. See H. DONDAINE, *Bulletin de théologie: La Trinité*, in RSPT, XXXI (1947), 433–437.

26) See H. BOUILLARD, *Conversion et grâce chez S. Thomas d'Aquin. Etude historique*, in ESJLF–Th, I (1944), 108–122. DOMINIC OF SOTO had already observed. "After having, in the second book of the *Sentences*, followed the common opinion, asserting on the one hand that . . . on the other hand that . . . Saint Thomas, after having later on meditated more profoundly on the sacred sayings and on the sentences of the Fathers, and foremost on those of Augustine, retracted both." *De natura et gratia libri tres ad synodum Tridentinam*, II, 3.

27) See T. DELVIGNE, *L'inspiration propre du traité de Dieu dans le Commentaire des Sentences de saint Thomas*, in BT, III (1932): *Notes et communications*, 119°–122°. In it, likewise, has been observed the strong influence of the Greek Fathers of Platonic inspiration. See F. P. SLADEK, *Gott und Welt nach dem Sentenzenkommentar des heiligen Thomas von Aquin*, Würzburg, 1941.

28) See A. M. ROGUET, *Les sacrements*, in the French trans. of *La Somme théologique*, Paris, 1945: *Renseignements techniques*, 262–265.

29) It is a known fact that Saint Thomas, the Sentence-commentator, remained under the influence of Avicenna's prestige then at its zenith.

30) See DOM LOTTIN, *Psychologie et morale aux XIIe et XIIIe siècles*, t. I, Louvain, 1942, 415–424.

elaboration of this notion of instrument within a philosophy of the causal.

Finally and above all, and howsoever delicate an operation it may be, understanding the progressive spiritualness of the inspirations of Saint Thomas will supply the measure of his *Summa's* newness. Protracted meditation on his texts, and even more on the internal bindings of his thought, will bring about such an understanding—an understanding located at the level of *sapientia* [wisdom], beyond that of *scientia* [science]. Only at this level may the most refined of theological speculation resolve itself into the purest evangelical perception.

After that, and at that level only, will it be of interest and worth the trouble to look into the passages containing the diverging positions which interpreters have recorded and the first lists of which are furnished in the XIVth century *Concordantiae*. One of the latter, although not authentic, has been published in the Vivès edition of the *Opera omnia*, and it may be used for the purpose (31). Yet, to say it over again, these divergences have bearing as such only upon particular points, which explains why the common and simple practice is permissible of supporting the texts of the *Sentences* and of the *Summa* one upon the other. The listed divergences, however, invite us to read, within the movement that is proper to each, these two works of the Angelic Doctor.

IV. THE COMMENTARY ON THE *DE TRINITATE* OF BOETHIUS

This is the place to mention a work of Saint Thomas [called the *Commentary on the* De Trinitate *of Boethius*] (a) that is usually cataloged within the neutral category of *Opuscula*. It belongs, in fact, to the same literary genre as the commentary on the Lombard. In it, questions have submerged direct reading of the text, the two

---

31) That concordance begins with the words: *Pertransibunt plurimi.* See Vivès ed., XXVIII, 560. It is probably the work of Thomas of Sutton.

In some instances, Saint Thomas himself has noted his change of opinion, but quite plainly one cannot be content with such notations that are of an entirely occasional character.

a) Latin ed.: Parma, XVII, 349–396; Vivès, XXVIII, 482–550; Marietti, in *Opusc. theol.*, II, 315–319; Uccelli, 277–357; critical text by B. Decker, Leiden, 1955; Questions V and VI edited from the autograph *Vat. Lat. 9850*, by P. Wyser, Fribourg–Louvain, 1948.

English trans.: *The Trinity and the Unity of the Intellect*, by R. E. BRENNAN, St. Louis, 1946.—*On Searching into God. An Exposition of the "De Trinitate" of Boethius*, q. 2: *On the Making Manifest of the Divine Knowledge*, foreword, trans., and notes by V. WHITE, Oxford, 1947.—*The Division and Methods of the Sciences. Questions V and VI of his Commentary on the* De Trinitate *of Boethius*, trans. with introd. and notes by A. MAURER, 2d rev. ed., Toronto, 1958.

still subsisting elements of which are an *expositio* and a *divisio textus*. In the present case, they have both been placed before the questions.

As in the case of the commentary on the Lombard, the text on Boethius is the redaction of a course actually taught by Saint Thomas. Some have tried to see in it the text of "*disputed* questions" in the proper sense of the word (32). We believe that, in accordance with the evolution of the literary forms that we have described (a), and as in the case of the text on the Lombard, it is a commentary, an *expositio* that was distended into questions. The consensus is to date this teaching in 1256 at the start of Saint Thomas's career at Paris (33). There is agreement also in openly acknowledging the precocious mastery of a theologian who was thus able from his earlier years to define the laws and method of his science, a capacity that is normally the epistemological attribute of elders. It is not surprising, then, that today when the constituent elements of theology are again put in question this opusculum has, during some past fifteen years, aroused theologians to a major show of interest. Its importance, as a matter of fact, cannot be too highly stressed (34).

That a text of Boethius could serve as a text for teaching at the University of Paris in the XIIIth century is no cause for surprise. One has only to think of the prestige enjoyed by the "first of the scholastics," Boethius the logician, who had been the vehicling agent of Aristotle's *Organon* during the preceding centuries, but Boethius the philosopher and theologian also, who had fed Platonic themes to the XIIth century school of Chartres, and whose *Opuscula sacra* contained the elements needed to support a theological knowledge in the

---

32) See P. SYNAVE, *La révélation des vérités divines naturelles d'après S. Thomas*, in *Mélanges Mandonnet*, I (*BibTh*, XIII, 1930), 359–361.

a) See above, ch. II.

33) Besides SYNAVE, *loc. cit.*, who ingeniously places that teaching between Easter and July of the 1256 school year, see M.–D. CHENU, *La date du commentaire de S. Thomas sur le* De Trinitate, in *RSPT*, XXX (1941), 432–444. The commentary remained uncompleted.

It is in the course of Saint Thomas's dictating of the text of this commentary that BERNARD GUI, his biographer, places the episode of the lighted candle. Completely absorbed in the meditation of his subject, he left the candle burning in his fingers without being aware of it, until the candle became consumed. See *Vita S. Thomae Aquinatis*, Prümmer ed., in *FVST*, III (1911), c. XXVIII, 194; Foster ed., 47.

34) For example, the list of articles of the second question is as follows: "Whether it is permissible to treat of things Divine through an investigation of them?" "Whether there can be a science of things Divine that are subject to faith?" "Whether it is permissible to make use of philosophical reasons in the science of faith having God as its object?" "Whether things Divine may be expressed under the veil of new and obscure words?"

Questions 5 and 6 entitled: *De divisione scientiae speculativae* [on the division of speculative science] are of prime importance for the philosopher.

process of being built. The *De Trinitate* is the first of these *Opuscula* (35). It seems, however, that the initiative of Saint Thomas to comment upon it remained all his own, because we have no testimony as to its having been set down in a general regulation of the faculty of theology (36).

As regards its contents, suffice it to say here that even more than in the case of the commentary on the Lombard its positing of problems and of doctrine greatly overreach the basic text of Boethius. From the VIth century text, we pass to the XIIIth century commentary in which the questions dealt with reveal perhaps the topmost point reached by XIIIth century's critical reflexion upon itself.

V. RESEARCH SUGGESTIONS

1. In order to locate the role of the Lombard in the development of theology, weigh the resistance which the introduction of his work encountered. See J. DE GHELLINCK, *op. cit.* [264, note 1]. Read among others, and going into their detail, the texts of Bacon, a few extracts of which we have quoted.

2. As much to measure the breadth and the multiplication of the new problems, as to obtain, in that jumble of divisions, a general view of each one of the treatises of the commentary of Saint Thomas, it will be fruitful to utilize the plan established by P. PHILIPPE, *Plan des Sentences de Pierre Lombard d'après S. Thomas*, in BT, 1932: *Notes et communications*, 131–154.

3. A classic type of research, though often not worked out far enough, is to compare on this or that question the commentaries of Albert, Bonaventure, and Thomas. For an example, see A. STEVAUX, *La doctrine de la charité dans les commentaires des Sentences de S. Albert, S. Bonaventure, S. Thomas*, in ETL, XXIV (1948), 59–97. It goes without saying that, since all the commentators were bound by the same framework, it becomes an easy matter to foresee just where in their commentaries will be found this or that doctrine that one

---

35) On this Boethian opuscule, its polemical contexts, the doctrinal importance of it, see V. SCHURR, *Die Trinitätslehre des Boethius im Lichte der skytischen Kontroversen*, Paderborn, 1935. The famous "theopaschite" controversy is thus found to be at the origin, not only of Greek scholasticism (Leontius of Byzantium), but also, through Boethius, of Latin scholasticism.

36) Let us recall that we still possess, in *Vatican Lat. ms. 9850*, fol. 90r–104v, the autograph of a section of the work (q. 1, a. 2 as far as q. 2, a. 4) which is to be completed by a section of the autograph preserved in *Rome ms. Casanate 3997*, fol. 11 (q. 5, a. 1, ad 1um, as far as a. 2, s.c.). See M. GRABMANN, *Die Autographe von Werken des heiligen Thomas*, in HJ, XXXIII (1940), 523–526. The text of the current editions is very bad. FR. WYSER recently published questions 5 and 6 from *Vat. Lat. ms. 9850*, in DTF, XXV (1947), 437–485, and XXVI (1948), 74–98 published in book form in 1948 [See above, editions of the work, 276, note a].

wishes to study. Works of a general character such as that of J. HINZ, *Verhältnis des Sentenzenkommentars von Thomas von Aquin zu dem Alberts des Grossen,* Würzburg, 1936, are evidently insufficient.

4. Establish the state of affairs as regards the difference of positions held by Saint Thomas in the *Sentences* and in the *Summa.* For the more important of them, seek out their causes, and even the controversies that gave them their context. For instance, after having been willing to speak of a *verbum essentiale* [essential word] in *In I Sent.,* d. 27, q. 2, a. 2, he will have nothing but a *verbum notionale* [personal word] in *Ia Pars,* q. 34, a. 1 [See B. LONERGAN, *The Concept of* Verbum *in the Writings of St. Thomas Aquinas,* in *TSt,* VII (1946), 349–392; VIII (1947), 35–79, 404–444; X (1949), 3–40, 359–393. Also, P. VANIER, *Théologie trinitaire chez saint Thomas d'Aquin. Evolution du concept d'action notionnelle,* in *PIEM,* XIII (1953)]. One of his opponents, Roger Marston, relates the circumstances of the lively incident that controversy raised during the holding of a disputed question (See his *De emanatione aeterna,* q. VI, in Fr. ROGERI MARSTON *Quaestiones disputatae* (*BFSMA,* VII, 1932), 116–117: "I myself was present at Paris, and I heard with the ears of my body . . .")*.* One may refer, for a few examples and reflexions, to J. DE GUIBERT, *Les doublets de saint Thomas. Leur étude méthodique, quelques réflexions, quelques exemples,* Paris, 1926.

5. As regards the commentary on the *De Trinitate* of BOETHIUS, one will find, together with all the documentation required on the work, a rich analysis of its methodological content in M. GRABMANN, *Die theologische Erkenntnis- und Einleitungslehre und die philosophische Wissenschaftstheorie des heiligen Thomas von Aquin auf Grund seiner Schrift* In Boethium de Trinitate. *Im Zusammenhang der Scholastik des 13. und beginnenden 14. Jahrhunderts dargestellt,* in *ThSt,* IV (1947). On q. 5, a. 3 of the work, see L. B. GEIGER, *Abstraction et séparation d'après saint Thomas (In de Trinitate, q. 5, a. 3),* in *RSPT,* XXXI (1947), 3–40 [reprinted in *Philosophie et spiritualité,* pref. by E. GILSON, Paris, 1963, I, 87–124.—See also, on questions 5 and 6, the studies of P. WYSER, his introduction to the edition of these questions (see above, 276, note a), and *Die wissenschaftstheoretischen Quästionen 5 u. 6* In Boethium de Trinitate *des heiligen Thomas von Aquin,* in *DTF,* XXV (1947), 437–485; XVI (1948), 74–98].

Chapter IX

The Disputed Questions

I. THE ORDINARY DISPUTATIONS

With the *Quaestiones disputatae* which Saint Thomas held while his career as a master was in full swing, we are dealing with the finished product of scholastic thought (both philosophical and theological), as well as with the richest accomplishment of his personal genius. The disputed question was, as we have seen (a), the fruit that had ripened out of the evolution of the intellectual technique of the School. For the theologian, it was the most daring peak reached by the activity of reason at work within faith which, to build itself up, allowed itself "to put in question" its very datum. "When we are unable to give an explanation, let us offer faith alone, not a disputation," it was said a century before in the school of Laon (1). With the disputed question, we attain the opposite position in which the *reddere rationem* [to give an explanation] was precisely done within a *disputatio*.

When Saint Thomas rose to the chair of Saint James in 1256, the disputed question had shortly before reached its own proper consistency outside the basic course on the Bible. We can no doubt presume, however, that with Saint Thomas it achieved within the organization of teaching, a stability and a frequency that it had not previously known. Until then, the master "disputed" from time to time, and probably according to his own preference. [The University regulations made no provisions for, nor did they impose any rules concerning the frequency of these exercises. It appears that the

---

a) See ch. II.
1) "Cum autem nequeamus reddere rationem, solam credulitatem, non disputationem exhibeamus." ANSELM OF LAON, *Sententiae divinae paginae*, Bliemetzrieder ed., in *BGPTM*, XVIII (1919), 9.

masters held two disputations a year at the most. From the start, Thomas decided to hold his own disputations at a regular rhythm, but it is difficult to determine exactly their frequency, which varied according to place and circumstances. As regards his teaching activity at Paris, however, we can set their number at one a month at the least. The first series that we have in redacted form, the 29 questions *De veritate*, belong to the first three years of his teaching at Paris, in 1256-1259. They are proof of an intense activity, if one keeps in mind their literary genre wherein the final redaction as well as the actual public discussion of them demanded a considerable effort. (To these 29, must be added a number of isolated questions and of quodlibetal disputations. See below.) The disputations held by Saint Thomas mark off in so impressively masterful a fashion the entire field of current conflicts that it is possible to follow in them the unfolding of controversies and the taking of positions. We possess the text of 63 disputations (2) distributed under the seven following titles: *De veritate, De potentia, De malo, De spiritualibus creaturis, De anima, De virtutibus, De unione Verbi incarnati* (a).

---

2) By counting these 63 disputations as questions, we are departing from the generally adopted opinion which followed the work done by P. Mandonnet, and according to which each "article" was considered the unit of work resulting from each individual session. Thus, MANDONNET counted 253 disputations in the *De veritate* and a total of 510. See his *Chronologie des questions disputées de S. Thomas*, in *RT*, XXIII (1918), 266-287, 341-371, and especially 271.

The academic calendar did not permit such over-abundance, nor can the brevity of an article have required the extensive ceremonial of a session frequently attended by the colleagues of the disputing master, and during which all other lectures were cancelled. If we accept the number of 63 disputations, we obtain a better idea of life at the university and of the work of Saint Thomas, as well as of the editorial make-up of his text.

It is clear, of course, that the counting of the disputations as representing the questions such as we have them today can be correct only "in principle." A question like the first one in the sequence of the *De veritate* could not possibly have resulted from a single session. Thus, evidence, to some extent, is still lacking. For a solution, we should perhaps turn to a second and later redaction, in which the determination had been carefully worked over anew and in more detail with a view to publication. See for all this A. DONDAINE, *Secrétaires de saint Thomas*, Appendix I: *De l'étendue de la question disputée*, Rome, 1956, 209-216.

a) Latin ed. and English trans.—*De veritate:* Parma, IX, 5-458; Vivès, XIV, 315-640; 8th Marietti ed., revised, 1953, I, 1-569; critical Leonine ed. in preparation. English trans.: *Truth* trans. from the definitive [?] Leonine text, in *LLCT:* vol. I, q. I-IX, by R. W. MULLIGAN, 1952; vol. II, q. X-XX, by J. V. McGLYNN, 1953; vol. III, q. XXI-XXIX, by R. W. SCHMIDT, 1954. Question I has been translated, with Introd., by R. McKEON, *Selections from Medieval Philosophers*, in *TMSL*, A-12 (1958), II, 149-234. Question X was partially trans. by M. H. MAYER, *The Philosophy of Teaching of St. Thomas Aquinas*, Milwaukee, [1929]. —*De potentia Dei:* Parma, VIII, 1-218; Vivès, XIII, 1-319; Marietti, II, 7-276. English trans.: *On the Power of God*, literally trans. by the English Dominicans (trans. by L. SHAPCOTE), 3 vols., London, 1932-34.—*De malo:* Parma, VIII, 219-424; Vivès, XIII, 320-618; Marietti, II, 445-699. English trans. of q. VI: *On Free Choice*, by A. C. PEGIS, New York, n. d.—*De spiritualibus creaturis:*

It is impossible to determine what was, year by year, the sequence in these disputed questions. It is possible, however, to shed light upon the stages of their redaction (3). It is established, as we have said, that the questions classified under the title *De veritate* cover the three years of Saint Thomas's first teaching at Paris (4) (a).]. For the other groups of disputations, there are reference-points that permit a sure and already useful division of them. The 10 questions of the *De potentia* are to be placed during the second sojourn in Italy (1259–1268); the 16 questions of the *De malo*, at least for the majority of them, were, it seems, held and, in any case, put together and edited at Paris (1269–1272), as well as the question *De anima*, the questions *De virtutibus (De virtutibus in communi, De virtutibus cardinalibus, De spe, De caritate, De correctione fraterna)*, and probably the question *De unione Verbi incarnati*. There is more uncertainty, on the question of place and date, for the disputation *De spiritualibus creaturis* (5).

Parma, VIII, 425–464; Vivès, XIV, 1–61; Marietti, II, 367–415; critical ed. by L. W. KEELER, in *PUGTD*, ser. ph., XIII (1946). English trans.: *On Spiritual Creatures*, by M. C. FITZPATRICK and J. J. WELLMUTH, with Introd., in *MPTT*, V (1942).—*De anima*: Parma, VIII, 465–532; Vivès, XIV, 61–160; Marietti, II, 281–362. English trans.: *The Soul*, by J. P. ROWAN, St. Louis, 1949.—*De virtutibus* (including *De virtutibus in communi, De virtutibus cardinalibus, De spe, De caritate, De correctione fraterna)*: Parma, VIII, 545–638; Vivès, XIV, 178–314; Marietti, II, 707–828. English trans. of *De virtutibus in communi: On Virtues (in generali)*, by J. P. REID, Providence, 1951.—*De unione Verbi incarnati*: Parma, VIII, 533–544; Vivès, XIV, 161–178; Marietti, II, 421–435.—For the other isolated and occasional disputations, see below, note 5. On all the preceding, see *CSTW*, 388–391.

3) See P. MANDONNET, *Chronologie des Questions disputées de S. Thomas*, in *RT*, XXIII (1918), 266–287, 341–371. For later research, see P. GLORIEUX, *Les Questions disputées de S. Thomas et leur suite chronologique*, in *RTAM*, IV (1932), 5–33, and the periodical reviews of the *Bulletin thomiste*. [For the latest stating of the question, see ESCHMANN, *CSTW*, 390–391, with bibliography.]

4) If one rejects Mandonnet's hypothesis as above, then one must also drop any attempt at trying to date exactly, almost to the week, the sequence of the *De veritate* articles, such as was done by P. SYNAVE, in *La révélation des vérités divines naturelles d'après S. Thomas*, § 3: *La date respective de quelques écrits de saint Thomas*, in *Mélanges Mandonnet*, I *(BibTh*, XIII (1930), 353–365.

a) This bracketed passage, together with notes 2, 4 and 7 of the present chapter, differs from the text of the French edition. It represents a change of position which the author requested be drawn from the German edition: *Die Werk des heiligen Thomas von Aquin*, trans. by O. M. PESCH, Heidelberg–Graz–Vienna–Cologne, 1960, 317–319. The translators are grateful to the German publishers for permission to reproduce the change.

5) [On this question of chronology, ESCHMANN, *loc. cit.*, concludes that there is certainty only for the *De veritate*, the *De potentia*, and the *De virtutibus*. For the others, the problem "remains open to research and discussion."] It is an undeniable fact that Saint Thomas also held a number of isolated and occasional disputations. A disputation *De sensibus sacrae scripturae* was held at Paris in 1256; another *De opere manuali religiosorum*, probably in 1257, occurred within the controversies on the religious state against William of Saint Amour; the one and the other were put in circulation with *Quodlibet VII*, wherein they occupy articles 14–18. A disputation *De pueris in religione admittendis*, held in 1271

Each disputation formed a consistent unity. The master, however, took on problems of an homogeneous character, not according to the systematic plan of a treatise, to be sure, but in a succession in which the subjects were ideologically bound together. Thus, Alexander of Hales had disputed *De peccato, De passionbus,* and so forth. And it would seem that the work of Albert the Great, which was organized and published in the form of the *Summa de creaturis,* was the outcome of series of disputed questions. The titles chosen by Saint Thomas give us to understand that the grouping of questions was done around a general idea running throughout the entire field of theology and of philosophy, rather than from within a determinate object; thus, for the titles *De veritate, De bono* (since questions 21 and following of the *De veritate* are bound up with the notion of good), *De potentia, De malo.* Should one push further and seek within each series a generating idea doctrinally governing the management of it, as some have tried to discover in the *De potentia?* (6) We believe that this would be taking a rather artificial step, one determined from hindsight. It is preferable to allow for the play, within the series, and without failing to recognize their leading thread, of the incidence of the current controversies and problems to which the author was devoting his attention under the cover of the general line of his researches. More than that, it seems that this or that series was made up only *post factum* [afterwards] through an assemblage within which isolated disputations were entered. This is probably what happened in the case of the *De anima* (7). Question VI of the *De malo,* the very long and unique disputation on free

during the second episode of the controversies on the religious state, is edited at the end of *Quodlibet IV,* a. 23–24.

It is equally certain that the disputation on the divine attributes, held at Rome in 1265–1266, has been integrated in *In I Sent.,* d. 2, a. 3; see above, 269, note 12. It is very probable that one or another element of the series *De anima* issued from a disputation of occasional character.

In our day, it has been proposed to annex two other disputations to the traditional inheritance. A question *De beatitudine* has been presented and edited by Fr. MANDONNET (see his article referred to above, and the Lethielleux edition of the *Quaestiones disputatae,* Paris, 1926). Its authenticity, however, cannot be retained. See A. DONDAINE, *Le problème de l'attribution du "tractatus de beatitudine",* in *BT,* III (1932), *Notes et communications,* 109–118. A question *De immortalitate animae,* ed. by E. Gomez, in *BToE,* III (1935), would seem to offer better signs of authenticity. See A. DONDAINE, *BT,* V (1937), 61–63, 217–219. [See also A. FRIES, *Thomas und die Quaestio De immortalitate animae,* in *DTF,* XXXI (1953), 18–52, and A. DONDAINE, *Secrétaires de saint Thomas,* Rome, 1956, 86–88, who, on the basis of his study of *Vat. Lat. ms. 781,* concludes: "The attribution of the disputation to the Angelic Doctor is almost certain."]

6) See M. BOUYGES, *L'idée génératrice du* De potentia *de saint Thomas,* in *RDP,* XXXVIII (1931), 113–131, 246–268.

7) It is possible that the question *De veritate* was placed only *post factum* at the head of the series bearing the same name. See A. DONDAINE, *Secrétaires de saint Thomas,* Rome, 1956, 86.

choice that is rather strangely inserted between a question on original sin and another on venial sin, seems sure enough to have been motivated by the doctrinal conflict in which Saint Thomas found himself engaged during the years 1270–1271. An attentive exegesis should endeavor to keep united, so as to reap the fruits of their crisscrossing, the author's personal steps and intentions, and the objects of study summoned forth by conjunctures having a doctrinal character.

Therein, without doubt, and by definition, lie the prime characteristics and the prime interest of these works of Saint Thomas. We are dealing with elaborations that were conducted with the animation, if not always of a controversy, at least, of an active and continuous dialogue with definite colleagues. The latter were often of fine stature, and all were equally involved in the problems that gave design to the forefront of research at the time. The redaction of these elaborations, however objective and serene it may be in general, has preserved for us, in the objections and answers copiously enveloping the master's determination, those elements that were placed in opposition to one another in those dialogues. To treat such texts as if they were the results of classroom exercises would be to render them stale. That famous question VI of the *De malo* on free choice, for example, bears the vivid marks of the conflicts provoked at Paris by the Averroistic-Aristotelianism of Siger of Brabant (8).

One accounts in this way for the amplitude taken on by each question wherein are accumulated opposing presentations and argumentations of a problem, far beyond the theoretical stating of it. Thence also, in the body of the article, the air of a synthesis which the position of the master seems to take on. More often than not, Saint Thomas takes over the problem from its general presuppositions, sketches the broad historical stages of it, and marks off its links with the other sectors of research. As a result, the genetic lines of thought and the architectural designing of doctrine shed light upon one another in a very fine manner. He was right, that old Venetian commentator of the XVIIth century who, after dedicating himself without end to the study of Saint Thomas, declared he had drawn more profit in his old age from the expositions offered by the *Disputed Questions* than from all the rest of his works (9).

---

8) In addition to the answers to the 24 objections, see in the very body of the article: "Some have posited that the will of man is moved of necessity . . . and yet they did not pose that the will undergoes coaction. . . . This opinion, however, is heretical. . . . Some men, however, were led to positing opinions of the present kind, partly no doubt through unruliness, and partly through certain sophistic reasons. . . ."

9) SANTÈS MARIALÈS, O. P., *Amplissimum artium scientiarumque omnium Amphiteatrum, hoc est, De rebus universis celeberrimae Quaestiones disputatae,* Bologna, 1658.

That richness shows up when one compares, in their parallel passages, the *Disputed Questions* and the *Summa theologiae,* the latter implying, in consequence of its literary genre, an extreme conciseness in the exposition of history and doctrine. The great theme of participation of *Ia Pars,* q. 6, a. 3 takes on historical perspective and speculative fullness only in *De veritate,* q. 21, a. 5. Whatever its length, the article of *Ia–IIae,* q. 52, a. 1 on the growth of habits must receive further enlightenment from *De virtutibus,* a. 11. The same must be said on the question of plurality in God, *De potentia,* q. 9, a. 7, in relation to *Ia Pars,* q. 30, a. 3. And so forth.

Some historians, very judiciously inspired by this parallelism, have come to think that, throughout the sequence of questions that were disputed from 1266 onwards, the intention of Saint Thomas was to feed the *Summa theologiae,* the composition of which he had already undertaken. All the while he was seizing the problems of the day as they came along, Saint Thomas, according to these historians, was pushing forward with his disputations in accordance with the needs of the plan of the *Summa.* As a consequence, the main elements of the *Summa* would expressly depend upon the *Questions* as upon their grounds of elaboration (10).

II. THE DISPUTATIONS "DE QUOLIBET"

We have already brought out (in chapter II on literary forms) what the genesis, management, and procedures of redaction were of that particular kind of "disputation" called the *quaestio de quolibet:* a session in which the multiplicity and heterogeneity of the questions raised and the unforeseeable form the participation of those present took, gave these disputations a very original and extraordinarily animated air. We have also said that, through his twelve *Quodlibeta,* Saint Thomas is to be inscribed in the brief period within which this literary genre preserved a spontaneousness that was without artifice and that he was one of the originators of it. Father Mandonnet even describes Saint Thomas as the "creator of the quodlibetal disputation"

10) See A. BIRKENMAJER, *Uber die Reihenfolge und die Entstehungszeit der* Quaestiones disputatae *des heiligen Thomas,* in *PJ,* 1921, 31–49; P. GLORIEUX, *Les Questions disputées de S. Thomas et leur suite chronologique,* in *RTAM,* IV (1932), 31–33 (end of the article). The following table is borrowed from these pages:

The parallel of *De anima*	is found in *Ia Pars,*	q. 75–87
— *De virtutibus,* a. 1 and 5	— *Ia–IIae,*	q. 55–69
— *De virtutibus,* a. 2–15	— *IIa–IIae,*	q. 17–33
— *De malo,* 1 and 16	— *Ia Pars,*	q. 48–64
— *De malo,* 2–7	— *Ia–IIae,*	q. 71–89
— *De malo,* 7–15	— *IIa–IIae,*	q. 35–153
— *De unione Verbi Incarnati*	— *IIIa Pars*	

(11). We dare not accept this description literally, and we believe that before him the genre had significant antecedents (12). Only with the brilliance of certain defenses and the proof of their technical value, however, did that type of disputation become fixed within the university institution. The consistency of that literary genre was due to the success of the *Quodlibeta* held by Saint Thomas during his first years as a master at Paris in 1256–1259, when he was struggling against Gerard of Abbeville (a). It was to degenerate rapidly in any case, as will bear witness, even before the end of the century, the interminable *Quodlibeta* of Godfrey of Fontaines and of Thomas of Sutton. In the meantime, it will have given us one of the essential parts of the life-work of Saint Thomas.

A first series, then, *Quodlibeta* VII to XI, was held at Paris, at Christmas and at Easter of the years 1256–1259. A second series, held in an order the inverse of the one presented in our editions, came later. *Quodlibeta* I through VI are to be dated from the second sojourn at Paris, 1269–1272. What we have of *Quodlibet* XII is the lecture transcript, done up more summarily than a personal redaction, and even incompleted, of an otherwise authentic disputation held at Paris, probably at Christmas 1270 (b). Saint Thomas did not, it will be noted, hold any quodlibetal disputations in Italy. The probability is that there, as at Oxford (13), neither the existing regulations nor the conditions of the teaching and of the taught personnel were conducive to the introduction of such University of Paris innovations (14).

The original interest of the *Quodlibeta* may be illustrated by the famous episode of the very lively dispute that took place between

---

11) P. MANDONNET, S. *Thomas créateur de la dispute quodlibétique,* in *RSPT,* XV (1926), 477–506; XVI (1927), 5–38.

12) See P. GLORIEUX, *Aux origines du Quodlibet,* in *DTP,* XXXVIII (1935), 502–522.

a) See ch. XII, 340–343.

b) Latin editions: Parma, IX, 459–663; Vivès, XV, 357–611; new Marietti ed., 1953. See *CSTW,* 392–393.

13) It was probably Peckham who, arriving from Paris around 1271, introduced the *Quodlibet* at Oxford.

14) The two basic studies on the *Quodlibeta* of Saint Thomas are those of J. A. DESTREZ, *Les disputes quodlibétiques de S. Thomas d'après la tradition manuscrite,* in *Mélanges thomistes (BibTh,* III, 1934), 49–108, and of P. MANDONNET, *loc. cit.* The latter study is extremely precious, notwithstanding the reservation made above.

For the latest on chronological problems, see: P. GLORIEUX, *Les Quodlibets VII–XI de saint Thomas d'Aquin,* in *RTAM,* XIII (1946), 282–303; F. PELSTER, *Literarhistorische Probleme der Quodlibeta des heiligen Thomas von Aquin. Eine kritische Übersicht,* in *Greg,* XXVIII (1947), 78–100; XXIX (1948), 62–87. The doubt raised by P. GLORIEUX, *Le plus beau quodlibet de S. Thomas (IX) est-il de lui?,* in *MSR,* III (1946), 235–268, is not founded. See J. ISAAC, *Le quodlibet 9 est bien de S. Thomas,* in *AHDLMA,* XVI (1947–48), 145–186.

John Peckham and Saint Thomas on one of the main theses of Aristotle's science of man. The episode, related in very different terms by Peckham and by witnesses, friends of Saint Thomas, refers no doubt to *Quodlibet III,* a. 4, held at Easter in 1270 (15).

---

15) See the account and texts of the episode in P. MANDONNET, *Siger de Brabant et l'Averroisme latin au XIIIe siècle,* 2d rev. ed., Part I, in *LPB,* VII (1911), 99–100. [Also A. WALZ, *Saint Thomas d'Aquin.* Adaptation française par P. NOVARINA, in *PM,* V (1962), 155–156; BARTHOLOMEW OF CAPUA's testimony at the canonization enquiry, in Foster ed., 107–108; and above, ch. II, note 19.]

The same *Quodlibet III* provoked a short memoir wherein Saint Thomas was denounced by Nicholas of Lisieux, one of his adversaries. See P. GLORIEUX, *Une offensive de Nicolas de Lisieux contre S. Thomas d'Aquin,* in *BLE,* 1938, 121–129 (with publication of the text). [Also A. WALZ, *ibid.,* 152–155.]

Chapter X

The *Summa Contra Gentiles*

With the *Summa contra Gentiles* (a) we come to the works the composition of which does not depend upon effective teaching. This is not to say that its make-up and style escape the "scholastic" form. We find in it the same procedures, the same conciseness, the same language, although the thought is developed outside the framework of the type of argumentation found in questions and in articles. But, in this instance, the work was determined by a personal initiative, destined to serve ends the author himself had chosen, together with the methods implied by these ends. The problem is, therefore, to discover these ends and methods in order to enter into the perspective of the author. Who are these "gentiles" against whom Saint Thomas writes? To what readers does he address himself against them? For the sake of what cause and of what object? The significance of these three connected problems is apparent if one observes that they control

a) Latin ed.: Parma, V; Vivès, XII; Leonine, XIII–XV. The Leonine text has also been reprinted in manual form by the Leonine editors themselves, Rome, 1934. The Marietti editors have brought out books II and III of the same text in 2 vols., 1961, and the French translators have also reprinted the same entire text in: SAINT THOMAS D'AQUIN, *Contra Gentiles*. Livre premier: Introd. de A. GAUTHIER; trad. R. BERNIER et M. CORVEZ, Paris, 1961. Livre deuxième: trad. M. CORVEZ (ch. I–XLVIII), et L.–J. MOREAU, Paris, 1954. Livre troisième: trad. M. J. GERLAUD, Paris, 1950. Livre quatrième: trad. R. BERNIER et F. KEROUANTON, Paris, 1957.

English trans.: *The* Summa contra Gentiles *of Saint Thomas Aquinas* literally trans. by the English Dominican Fathers from the latest Leonine ed. (trans. L. SHAPCOTE), 5 vols., London-New York, 1923–29.—*On the Truth of the Catholic Faith. Summa Contra Gentiles*, newly trans. with introd. and notes: Book I, by A. C. PEGIS, in *ImB*, D26 (1955); Book II, by J. F. ANDERSON, in *ImB*, D27 (1956); Book III, by V. J. BOURKE, 2 vols., in *ImB*, D28A and D28B (1956); Book IV by C. J. O'NEIL, in *ImB*, D29 (1957).—Book III, ch. 1–113, has also been published in English by A. C. PEGIS, *The Basic Writings of St. Thomas Aquinas*, vol. II, New York, 1945.

the very nature of the work. It has been considered, in turn, as a philosophical *summa,* as an apologetical *summa,* as a theological treatise. What, in fact, is it? Must this work be read as an undertaking of rational research, or as an elaboration initiated by faith? The avowals of the author given in the form of a preface, as well as the various steps taken in the unfolding of his plan, will help us to give a reply, as a matter of fact, a rather complex one.

I. THE "GENTILES" IN THE XIIIth CENTURY

According to a long tradition, Saint Thomas composed his work at the request of Raymond of Penyafort, that Catalan Dominican, former Master-General of the Preachers, who, haunted by the presence of the Moors on Spanish soil and by the new hope of converting Islam, had asked his young confrere to equip the missionaries with the necessary intellectual arms. This tradition rests on the testimony of a certain Peter Marsilio, another Catalan Dominican, who in his history of James I of Aragon, reports the fact and its purposes (1). This testimony is worthy of credit, because Marsilio finished his *De gestis Jacobi I* in 1313, whereas Raymond of Penyafort, whose brilliant role, both in public life and among the Dominicans, entailed the memory of these deeds, had died only around 1275 (2).

We would, therefrom, seem to be enlightened on those to whom the work was destined, as well as on the *Gentiles,* its intended adversaries. Actually, this testimony raises more problems than it resolves, as we are going to see. Yet, the main information it gives at least imparts a decisive enlightenment. The *Contra Gentiles* is to be located within the very state of affairs of Christendom, as it confronted Islam in the middle of the XIIIth century. Of this situation, Saint Thomas will be an outstanding witness. His work straightway takes on vital importance, which subsequent utilizations should not becloud. Rarely has a doctrine been more "historical."

---

1) "Desiring ardently, also, that the unbelievers be converted, he [Saint Raymond] asked the outstanding doctor of the sacred page and master in theology, Brother Thomas of Aquino, of the same Order, who, after Brother Albert the philosopher, was considered the greatest amongst all the clerics of this world, to compose a work against the errors of the unbelievers, by which both the shadows of darkness would be lifted, and the doctrine of true light would be presented to those unwilling to believe. This master did what the humble request of so great a father required, and he composed the *summa* against the Gentiles, as its title goes, a work believed to be unequalled in that field." *De gestis Jacobi I regis Aragonum,* quoted by F. DIAGO, *Vita S. Raymundi de Pennaforti Ordinis Praedicatorum per fratrem Petrum Marsilii ejusdem Ordinis olim conscripta et nunc primum per fr. Franciscum Diagum in lucem edita,* Barcelona, 1601.

2) Peter Marsilio, counselor to and historiographer of James II of Aragon, lived at the convent of Barcelona. His notice on Raymond of Penyafort contains elements that are peculiar to him.

Marsilio's hagiographic anecdote must, in fact, be given body and context. When Saint Thomas began the layout of his *Summa* in the course of the year 1258, the attention of Christian thinkers had just been put on the alert through their discerning of profound ambiguities in Aristotelianism. Even those who publicly declared that they wished to introduce it into the Christian world, as Albert the Great had been doing for more than 15 years, experienced what great problems its interpretation was posing, especially now that the complete Aristotelian *corpus* had been inscribed among the textbooks of the University (1255). The reading of several interpreters, more exactly of the Arab philosophers, began to make public the latent ambiguities in the *corpus*. Averroes in particular, who twenty years earlier was still being treated innocently as a "very noble philosopher, master of thought" (William of Auvergne) (3), was disquieting in proportion as his work was becoming known. Without yet feeling the seduction that was to set in motion, with Siger of Brabant ten years later, the violent crisis of "Latin Averroism," one felt both the quality and the danger of his work, already, at least, as regarded certain positions on the nature and destiny of man. Such is the context of the episode that publicly will point to the irruption of this problem. In 1256, Alexander IV took advantage of the presence at the Pontifical court at Anagni of Albert the Great, just then at the height of his reputation, to ask him just what should be the reaction and the line of Christian thought in the face of the Averroistic teaching on the unity of the intellect, a thesis putting into question the personal survival of man. Albert had then composed his *De unitate intellectus contra Averroistas*. It was not a positive Averroistic teaching that Albert attacked, as it became necessary to do ten years later, but the first understanding of Averroism, and more generally of Arabic thought, which had become alarming by the very success of Aristotle (4).

Thus it was on two fronts that Christendom had henceforth to confront Islam. Geographically, on the missionary level, the relaxing of the hold on Spain of the Moors favored the freedom of movement of Christians and made possible a crusade that would no longer be merely warlike but rather doctrinal in an apologetic dialogue. Intellectually, at the level of an Arabic civilization which conveyed the assets of Greek science and philosophy, menace and attraction simultaneously operated at the same pace as this Arabic literature was being discovered and translated. Thus, during the fifties, the XIIIth

---

3) WILLIAM OF AUVERGNE, *De universo*, Rouen, 1674, I, 651b: ". . . who are to be followed and imitated as the leaders of philosophy."

4) See D. SALMAN, *Albert le Grand et l'averroïsme latin*, in RSPT, XXIV (1935), 38–64.

century witnessed the grand strategy of Christendom undergoing modification, with the missionary movement and the crisis of high culture meeting in the same context of problems. The *Summa Contra Gentiles* is to be located at this meeting place. On the one hand, the missionary movement was evolving at this time toward a new type, because Islam was revealing itself no longer as a violent military menace alone but as a civilization that was superiorly rich. The entrance of Aristotle, on the other hand, was opening to Christians, thanks to Islam, a scientific vision of the universe outside the religious imagery of the Bible. This problem facing Christendom was a knot, unique in its kind, and Saint Thomas found himself right in the midst of it. One would be wrong in opposing the information coming from the missionary milieux to that coming from the contemporary intellectual milieux.

Who then were these *Gentiles?* Who were the ones for whom this *Summa* was intended that were at grips with these gentiles? Candidly, Marsilio directs us to the missionaries who were penetrating into Islam. At first glance, however, one realizes that the *Summa* is much more than a missionary manual, even one braced up to encounter the elite. As much by the breadth of its object as by the technique of its argumentation, it evokes the Parisian milieu and calls for a clientele of the university type. It is not, therefore, without some nearness to truth, that some, using only indirectly the hagiographic information provided by Marsilio, have endeavored to implant the *Summa* squarely in the University of Paris where the errors of the "Gentiles" —understand here, of the Arabic philosophers—had irrupted and seduced a few minds. The Averroistic agitation leading to the reaction of 1270 and to the long syllabus of 1277 would have started, in fact, as early as the fifties. The theses of this Averroism both contemporary and Parisian are what the *Contra Gentiles* would envisage and refute (5).

It does not seem necessary to push that far the interpretation of the historical situation. At Paris, in 1258, as at Rome in 1256, it was still bad foreign books that were being refuted. The real Latin crisis of Averroism was in its stage of preparation, but it had not yet begun. Consequently, the *Summa contra Gentiles* does not have Averroes especially in view; it is rather a whole lot of *errantes* [erring], pagans, Moslems, Jews, heretics, who are examined and censured (6). But, granting this chronological nuance about the stages of the Averroistic

---

5) See M. M. GORCE, *La lutte "contra Gentiles" à Paris*, in *Mélanges Mandonnet*, I (*BibTh*, XIII, 1930), 223–243, recast, as regards the problem which interests us here, in *L'essor de la pensée au moyen âge*, Paris, 1933, 242–247.

6) See D. SALMAN, *Sur la lutte "contra Gentiles" de S. Thomas*, in *DTP*, XL (1937), 488–509.

penetration, it is clear that the work goes far beyond the missionary manual that Marsilio's anecdote would have made one suppose. It offers itself as a defense of the entire body of Christian thought, confronted with the scientific Greco-Arabic conception of the universe, henceforth revealed to the West. The *Summa* is an apologetic theology: *Liber de veritate catholicae fidei contra errores infidelium*, as many manuscripts entitle it.

These views are confirmed when one takes into consideration the long period of years over which the composition of the work extends and the other circumstances which it encounters. Begun at Paris in 1258, it was only half completed when Saint Thomas left France during the summer of 1259 to go to teach in Italy (1). Yet work on it continued until after 1263. Not only the references of the IVth book to the translations of Greek works that could be known only at that time impose this judgment upon us, but the comparison with the *Contra errores Graecorum,* composed in 1263, obliges us to conclude that this minor work was written before the IVth book of the *Contra Gentiles* (8). This is a new perspective in which we see Saint Thomas, engaged, in answer to Urban IV's desire, in the controversies with the schismatic Christians of the East, utilizing in his *Summa* the documents that those controversies had put into circulation and attempting to ripen his thinking on the Trinity, the Incarnation, and the Sacraments.

II. THEOLOGICAL METHOD

In this light, the Prologue and the chapters on methodology wherein, several times, Saint Thomas reveals his intentions to us with insistence take on high relief. Without going into a detailed analysis of them here, let us fix the general movement they contain, and with this movement, the meaning of the work.

This is a theological work. That it makes use of the range of the rational arguments that can be utilized in a discussion with non-Christians, and therefore, that it expressly entails arguments accept-

---

7) It is a known fact that an entire lot of manuscripts (the pA tradition) contains the text only as far as book III, ch. 45, which would indicate decisively what part of the text had been put into circulation at Paris when Saint Thomas left the city. [On the questions of chronology and destination of the work, see ESCHMANN, *CSTW,* 387–388. The latest on all subjects dealt with in this chapter, however, will be found discussed extensively by A. GAUTHIER, in his Historical Introduction to the French ed. of *Contra Gentiles,* Paris, 1961, I, 7–123. The reader should not fail to have recourse to the latter study wherein wide information is given on this *Summa's* autograph, manuscript tradition, Leonine edition, place and date of composition, and on its author's intent and plan of composition.]

8) See H. DONDAINE, *Le* Contra errores Graecorum *de S. Thomas et le IVe livre* Contra Gentiles, in *RSPT,* XXX (1941), 156–162.

able to reason alone, does not contradict this general character. It matters only that theology be allowed the totality of its functions. "And so, moved by Divine piety, I have assumed confidence to embark upon the task of the wise man, even though this may exceed my powers, the object of my intent being to make known, in my own small way, the truth that the catholic faith professes, by setting aside the errors that are opposed to it" (a). To speak in the technical vocabulary of the time, Saint Thomas is assuming the office of "sage," of the sage, that architect of mental life, who considers the supreme causes, the Truth, source of all truth (see book I, ch. 1). This is what the pagan Aristotle had already declared himself to be; this *a fortiori* is what a Christian is who has received the communication of the word of God. The allusion to philosophical wisdom, far from intending to present philosophical wisdom alone as if its sole forces were going to be used, introduces theological wisdom.

It is true that the three first books (God, creation, the moral life) have as their object truths accessible to reason. But one cannot argue from that to make it a philosophical *summa* and reserve the Christian subject matter and the theological method to the IVth book. Actually, these rational truths are always presented as being part of the deposit of faith, and as having to be demonstrated and defended as such: "But there are some truths [about God] which even natural reason is able to attain" (b). "There existing, therefore, a twofold truth concerning what is understandable about God, . . . it is fitting that both of these truths be proposed to man for belief on Divine say-so" (c). "This, then, being the manner of proceeding which we intend to follow, our first effort will be to make known the truth *which faith professes and reason investigates*" (d).

The order followed in the three first books is a theological one. Saint Thomas notes it expressly: "Hence it is, also, that the one and the other teaching do not proceed in the same order. For in the teaching of philosophy, which considers creatures in themselves and leads us from them to the knowledge of God, the first consideration is that about creatures, the last, about God. But in the teaching of faith, which does not consider creatures except in their relation to God, the consideration of God comes first, and afterwards, the considera-

---

a) "Assumpta igitur ex divina pietate fiducia sapientis officium prosequendi, quamvis proprias vires excedat, propositum nostrae intentionis est veritatem *quam fides catholica profitetur,* pro nostro modulo manifestare, errores eliminando contrarios." *Cont. Gent.,* I, c. 2.

b) "Quaedam vero sunt ad quae etiam ratio naturalis pertingere potest." *Ibid.,* I, c. 3.

c) "Duplici igitur veritate divinorum intelligibilium existente . . . utraque convenienter divinitus homini credenda proponitur." *Ibid.,* I, c. 4.

d) "Modo ergo proposito procedere intendentes, primum nitemur ad manifestationem illius veritatis *quam fides profitetur et ratio investigat.*" *Ibid.,* I, c. 9.

tion of creatures. And thus, the doctrine of faith is more perfect, as being more like the knowledge possessed by God who, in knowing Himself, sees into the other things. And so, in accordance with this order, after what has been said in book I about God in Himself, there remains to continue with the things that come from Him" (9).

In this perspective, what sort of makes us hesitate in our modern way of thinking is the serene fullness with which, concerning the most hidden truths of the faith, the "suitabilities" (as we say today) of the divine mysteries are presented. Beyond the non-repugnance established against the pagan or heretical deniers ("solving the arguments of adversaries") (a), arises a harmonious coherence which, to be sure, does not found the faith since the latter is always inaccessible and freely-given, but which makes faith a friend of reason, in "verisimilitudes" *(veras similitudines)* (book I, ch. 8). However weak they may be, they are delectable. The most imperfect and weak knowledge of the supreme realities ("a modest and dialectical solution") (b) is higher and more worthy than the perfect knowledge of inferior things: ". . . the auditor experiences intense joy" (c). ". . . to be able to consider something of the loftiest realities, even if this consideration be only of the modest and weak variety, is conducive to the greatest joy" (d). We are well beyond what is today called apologetics with its external [motives of] credibility.

Such insistence on faith to mystery does not violate its mysteriousness, but rather causes it to be revered. Saint Thomas makes his own the very beautiful text of Saint Hilary: "Undertake in faith, move ahead, be persistent. You will not reach the end, I know, but I shall congratulate myself on your progress. For, he who pursues the infinite in piety of mind, will always become more proficient as he goes onwards, even if, as will happen, his efforts do not always succeed. But do not betake yourself into that mystery, do not plunge yourself into the arcanum of that unending nativity, presuming to comprehend the sum total of intelligence; understand, rather, that those things

---

9) "Exinde etiam est quod non eodem ordine utraque doctrina procedit. Nam in doctrina philosophiae, quae creaturas secundum se considerat et ex eis in Dei cognitionem perducit, prima est consideratio de creaturis et ultima de Deo. In doctrina vero fidei, quae creaturas non nisi in ordine ad Deum considerat, primo est consideratio Dei et postmodum creaturarum. Et sic est perfectior, utpote Dei cognitioni similior, qui seipsum cognoscens alia intuetur. Unde secundum hunc ordinem, post ea quae de Deo in se primo libro sunt dicta, de his quae ab ipso sunt restat prosequendum." *Ibid.,* II, c. 4. We are summing up the arguments of M. D. ROLAND-GOSSELIN in his note at the beginning of his article *Béatitude et désir naturel d'après S. Thomas d'Aquin,* in RSPT, XVIII (1929), 193–194.

a) ". . . solvere rationes adversariorum." *Ibid.,* I, c. 9.
b) ". . . parva et topica solutio." *Ibid.,* I, c. 5.
c) ". . . contingit auditori ut sit vehemens gaudium ejus." *Ibid.,* I, c. 5.
d) ". . . de rebus altissimis, etiam parva et debili consideratione, aliquid posse inspicere jucundissiumum est." *Ibid.,* I, c. 8.

are incomprehensible" (e). Let us take this text as a personal confidence of Saint Thomas, and let us see in his *Summa contra Gentiles,* without minimizing its dual missionary and doctrinal apostolic merger, a work of contemplation of truth.

III. RESEARCH SUGGESTIONS

1. Islam and Christendom. The following study topics will shed light on the subject: the new conjunctures leading the Christians to establishing language schools in view of a dialogue with the Moslems, instead of arming knights for war; the Mendicants becoming the leaders of the new type of missionary, with, among the Preachers, the outstanding names, those of Raymond of Penyafort, of course, called "the father of the (converted) Saracens," Humbert of Romans, Andrew of Longjumeau, Ivo the Briton, Raymond Marti; the arduous beginnings of a "studium arabicum" [studium for the study of the Arabic language]; between 1250 and 1260 precisely, the recommendation of the [Dominican] provincial chapter of Tarragona in 1256 (see *AOP,* 1898, 417), and Humbert of Roman's encyclical letter, at the general chapter of 1256; Raymond of Penyafort's letter to the master general to give an account on the opening of the "studium arabicum," after the general chapter of Valenciennes in 1259; and so on. See the works of B. ALTANER, in particular *Die fremdsprachliche Ausbildung der Dominikanermissionare während des 13. und 14. Jahrhunderts,* in *ZMR,* XXXIII (1933), 233–241.

2. Analyse closely and co-ordinate (without looking for the vocabulary and thought precisions that the modern controversies on reason and faith have brought about) the methodological texts contained in the first chapters of books I and II of the *Summa contra Gentiles.* On the plan and inspiration of the work, besides the good dissertation of B. DE RUBEIS which has been reproduced at the beginning of some modern editions of the work (in Marietti's, for example), see M. BOUYGES, *Le plan du* Contra Gentiles *de S. Thomas,* in *Etudes sur saint Thomas (1225–1925)* (*AP,* III, 2, 1925), 176–197; N. BALTHASAR and A. SIMONET, *Le plan de la* Somme contre les Gentils *de S. Thomas,* in *RNS,* XXXII (1930), 183–210. Compare the plan of the *Summa contra Gentiles* with that of the *Summa theologiae,* noting, for instance, that in the former an autonomous treatise *De Deo uno* [God as

---

e) "Haec credendo incipe, procurre, persiste: etsi non perventurum sciam, gratulabor tamen profecturum. Qui enim pie infinita prosequitur, etsi non contingat aliquando, semper tamen proficiet prodeundo. Sed ne te inferas in illud secretum, et arcano interminabilis nativitatis non te immergas, summam intelligentiae comprehendere praesumens: sed intellige incomprehensibilia esse." SAINT HILARY, *De Trinitate,* lib. II, 10, 11; *P.L.,* 10, 58–59. This quotation by Saint Thomas (*Ibid.,* I, c. 8) is ordered and worded somewhat differently from Hilary's own text as given by the *P.L.* editors.

One] has been built up, and the revealed mysteries transferred to the IVth book. [See, in addition, the Introd. of A. GAUTHIER to the French ed. and trans. of the *Summa contra Gentiles*, Paris, 1961, I, 100–120.]

3. Analyse, meditate upon, illustrate that rule which is given so as to proceed appropriately and effiaciously against error (book I, ch. 2), namely: to engage in dialogue with the adversary, marking off, for that purpose, some common ground, one ever more reduced and weak, if necessary, so long as it is common. This is the method that was implied in the new missionary attitude, which no longer thought in terms of a "crusade" but of a coming together, and consequently sought to equip itself with solid doctrine, erudition, and knowledge of errors (a difficult thing to do) rather than with arms.

4. The recent controversy on the natural desire of knowing God (implying consequently the problem of the relationship between reason and the supernatural order), during the years 1925–1930, has brought up anew the question of the interpretation to be given of chapters 50 and ff. of book III, and thereby, of the methodological orientation of the work, wherein these chapters occupy a place of capital importance from this standpoint. See, with the bibliography and precisions given, M.-D. ROLAND-GOSSELIN, *Béatitude et désir naturel d'après S. Thomas d'Aquin*, in RSPT, XVIII (1929), 193–222. [See in addition P. K. BASTABLE, *Desire for God. Does Man Aspire Naturally to the Beatific Vision? An Analysis of this Question and of its History*, London-Dublin, 1947; W. R. O'CONNOR, *The Eternal Quest*, New York, 1947, and his *The Natural Desire for God*, in AqLec, 1948; V. CAUCHY, *Désir naturel et béatitude chez saint Thomas*, in PPC, 1958, with the bibliography, 121–124; and A. GAUTHIER, *loc. cit.*]

Chapter XI
The *Summa Theologiae*

"Because the Doctor of catholic truth must teach not only the advanced student, but to him devolves, moreover, the task of instructing beginners . . . we intend, in the present work, to impart the matters that pertain to the Christian religion in such a way as may befit the instruction of beginners" (a). The praise directed toward the *Summa*

a) "Quia catholicae veritatis doctor non solum provectos debet instruere, sed ad eum pertinet etiam incipientes erudire, . . . propositum nostrae intentionis in hoc opere est, ea quae ad Christianam religionem pertinent eo modo tradere secundum quod congruit ad eruditionem incipientium." *Summa theologiae*, prol.

Latin ed.: Parma, I–IV; Vivès, I–VI; Leonine, IV–XII (see G. M. GRECH, *The Leonine Edition of the Works of St. Thomas Aquinas . . .*, in FAS, 244–246); Marietti, 3 vols., 1952–1956 (Leonine text); Ottawa, 5 vols., 1941–1945, rev. ed., 1953 (Piana text with the more important Leonine corrections; highly praised for its notes); Pauline, in 1 vol., 1962 (Leonine text with the notes of the Ottawa ed.).

English trans.: *Summa theologica* literally trans. by the Fathers of the English Dominican Province (trans. L. SHAPCOTE), 22 vols., 2d ed., London–New York, 1912–1936; re-edited in a first complete American ed., 3 vols., New York, 1945; reedited in a rev. ed., (by D. J. SULLIVAN) in GBWW, XIX (1952) containing *Ia Pars* and *Ia–IIae*, q. 1–48, and in XX (1952) containing *I–IIae*, q. 49–114, *IIa–IIae*, q. 1–46, 179–189, *IIIa Pars* and *Suppl.* The same original English ed. was used by A. C. PEGIS in his *The Basic Writings of St. Thomas Aquinas*, 2 vols., New York, 1945, for the reprint of *Ia Pars*, *Ia–IIae*, q. 6–21, 49–114, *IIa–IIae*, q. 1–7, which he revised and annotated; selecting from *The Basic Writings*, PEGIS has edited anew a number of questions and articles, prefacing them with an Introd. in his *Introduction to Saint Thomas Aquinas*, in MLWBB, 259 (1945). Trans. of *Ia Pars*, q. 75–88 by J. F. ANDERSON, *St. Thomas Aquinas. Treatise on Man*, Englewood Cliffs, 1962. Not a translation, W. FARRELL's *A Companion to the Summa*, 4 vols., New York, 1939–1942, is, in the author's own words, "an easy guide-book to St. Thomas' greatest work" for the ordinary catholic and the layman having no professional or theological knowledge (vol. II, vii). In the same vein: A. BERNARD, *Présentation de la Somme théologique*, Avignon, 1954, in which the author, addressing himself to any "reader of good will," tries to present "the doctrine of the *Summa* in as exact and substantially complete a manner as possible." See 7–8.

theologiae throughout the centuries, the technical difficulties one encounters in it, the power of the synthesis it contains should not mask the original purpose for which it was written, as expressed in the above opening words of the work. By the author's own avowal, it was dedicated to the instruction of beginners in theology. The *Disputed Questions* were the book suited to masters, the *Summa* is the book of the pupil.

There is perhaps in this intent some of that illusion which is common to professors as regards the capacities of their students—even university students. The fact remains it is a *summa* that Saint Thomas intended, not a manual (*compendium*), the pedagogical effectiveness of which always falls short of requirements in theology. The *summa* is the fruit that ripened out of the loftiest teaching in the medieval university.

I. WHAT IS A *SUMMA?*

The history of the word will help us arrive at a definition of the kind of work it was. In the school language of the XIIth century that created the name, *summa* first stood for a brief, synthetic, and complete collection of "sentences" in which one aimed at presenting the truths of Christian doctrine (or of any body of doctrine). The famous collection long attributed to Hugh of Saint Victor and surely one of the first models of this kind of work, was called precisely a *Summa sententiarum* (early in the second third of the XIIth century). No longer a simple compilation of the testimonies of the Fathers and of the ancient writers, it was rather an organized and elaborate assemblage of materials, although it still remained very close to the texts that it coordinated. When Honorius of Autun wrote a résumé of Christian history, he called it a *summa*: "It has deliberately been named *Summa totius*, since the series of events contained in the whole of Scripture appears in it in a summed-up way" (b). Abelard had said of the Apostle's Creed that it contains the essential truths of faith, *summam fidei* (c). In his *Introductio ad theologiam*, moreover, he organized his materials around three things which to him appeared as the three elements that make up the essentials of salvation: "Three things, as I see it, make up the sum (*summa*) of man's salvation: faith, charity, and sacrament" (d). "What else is a *summa*," asks Rob-

---

b) "Et ideo *Summam totius* placuit vocitari, cum in ea series totius scripturae videatur summatim notari." *Summa totius de omnimoda historia; P.L.,* 172, 189 A.

c) *Expositio symboli quod dicitur Apostolorum; P.L.,* 178, 619.

d) "Tria sunt, ut arbitror, in quibus humanae salutis *summa* consistit: fides videlicet, caritas et sacramentum." *Introductio ad theologiam,* lib. I, c. 1; *P.L.,* 178, 981 C. [See above, ch. IV, note 8.]

ert of Melun, "if not a concise gathering together . . . ? It is, in fact, a summary of particular data" (e). In this sense, *summa* designates properly—over and beyond the older *Sententiae* and *Florilegia*—the principal works of the XIIth century.

As time went on, the work of the theologians went ahead. Professional teaching first in the schools later in the universities became increasingly independent of pastoral, spiritual, and moral preoccupations. A favorable situation was thus created to bring about the systematization of theology and to bolster the effort being made at conceptualizing its object. In the process of becoming a science—even if only in a relative sense—theology strove to organize its object and objects, and hence to build them up from broad architectonic principles borrowed from the rational structures of mind working under the light of faith. Thus the word *summa* was being charged with new potential, or rather, the synthetic aspect became prevalent in its meaning. As a result, in the XIIIth century and making allowance for unavoidable fluctuations in an evolution of this kind (1), the word *summa* designates a literary work undertaken with a threefold purpose: first, to expound, in concise and abridged manner, the whole of a given scientific field of knowledge (this is the original meaning of *summa*); second, to organize, beyond piecemeal analysis, the objects of this field of knowledge in a synthetic way; finally, to realize this aim so that the product be adapted for teaching students. *Ordo disciplinae* [order of teaching]: in this phrase, one of good full-bodied Latin, will be expressed in an excellent way the intellectual values of an undertaking at once encyclopedic, synthetic, and in line with good teaching requirements. Examples abound in every field of endeavor (2). The *Summa* of Saint Thomas, in the field of theology, was and remains one of the most masterful realizations.

e) "Quid enim *summa* est, nonnisi singulorum brevis comprehensio . . . Siquidem *summa* est singulorum compendiosa collectio." *Sententie*, Martin ed., in *SSL*, XXI (1947), 3.

1) Making allowance also for differences in objects. It is obvious, for example, that the *Summae poenitentiae* (moral and casuistic treatises written in view of the receiving of the sacraments)—now in their golden period as a consequence of the Lateran council, with the Mendicants the masters in the composition of them—could not tend to the synthetic organisation of which we are speaking. [See P. MICHAUD–QUANTIN, *Sommes de casuistique et manuels de confession au moyen âge*, in *AMN*, XIII (1962).]

2) For instance, the *Summa philosophiae* formerly attributed to Grosseteste, in which, furthermore, the expression *summarum confectores* [makers of *summas*] is used (Tr. I, c. 11; Baur ed., in *BGPM*, IX (1912), 285); the *Summa juris* of HENRY OF SEGUSIA (+ 1271); the *Summa de virtutibus* of WILLIAM PÉRAUD (+ 1271). Should be added here those admirable smaller *summas*, Saint Bonaventure's *Breviloquium* and Saint Thomas's *Compendium theologiae*, in which were included the same far-above-manual-literature values.

The actual circumstances surrounding the writing of the *Summa* confirm the purpose sought after in a XIIIth century *summa*. Historians seem to be very near the truth in interpreting a statement of Tolomeo of Lucca, the biographer of Saint Thomas, as meaning that he gave up writing and actually-started second commentary on the *Sentences* and undertook a fresh work that would satisfy the demands of his mind (3). In any event, in his brief prologue, he himself censures the gaps, or at least the limitations in current teaching. Herein, the multiplying of questions and arguments, repetitions, needless digressions, clutter up the mind and produce aversion for study. Herein, moreover—and this is a more serious shortcoming—the framework itself of the teaching system, whether the commentaries on the basic texts or the disputed questions, blocks out the highest demands of mind, which can express the full understanding of its object only if given free constructive rein. "Things it is necessary to know are not imparted according to an *order of learning*, but rather according as the order of exposition in books demands [the *lectio*], or according as the occasion for disputation arises [the *quaestiones*]" (a). Whether in the *lectio* on Scripture—the course par excellence of

---

3) See above, ch. VIII, note 8. The *Summa*, as we know, was started in 1267. The stages of its composition can be discerned either by comparing it, from the standpoint of doctrinal development, with the parallel passages of the other works, or by using the new sources of information that have come to light. It was never finished. When Saint Thomas died (in 1274), redaction had reached *IIIa Pars*, q. 90, in the treatise on penance. It was quite likely Reginald of Piperno, Saint Thomas's companion, who completed it *(Supplementum)* through recourse to the *Commentary on the Sentences*—without exhibiting, need we add, the genius of his master. See P. MANDONNET, *Des écrits authentiques de S. Thomas*, 2d rev. ed., Fribourg, 1910, 153; also the prefaces to tomes XI (viii, xiv and ff.) and XII (xviii and ff.) of the Leonine edition, Rome, 1906. For the latest researches and precisions, see P. GLORIEUX, *Pour la chronologie de la Somme*, in *MSR*, II (1945), 59–98 [and a summing up of the question in ESCHMANN, *CSTW*, 386–388].

a) ". . . ea quae sunt necessaria . . . ad sciendum non traduntur secundum *ordinem disciplinae*, sed secundum quod requirebat librorum expositio, vel secundum quod se praebebat occasio disputandi." Prol. to the *Summa*. [For a commentary of the Prologue, see TH.-A. AUDET, *Approches historiques de la* Summa theologiae, in *Etudes d'histoire littéraire et doctrinale (PIEM, XVII, 1962)*, 7–14. Father Chenu's interpretation of the plan of the *Summa* as developed hereafter has given "the occasion to many of reflecting on the problem raised [in its pages, namely]: that of a study of the *Summa* from the standpoint of historical, literary, and doctrinal critique." This quotation is from the latest study on the subject, G. LAFONT's *Structures et méthode dans la Somme théologique de saint Thomas d'Aquin*, in *TET*, XII (1961), 16. In his Introduction (15–34), the author presents in addition to Chenu's position, those of A. HAYEN, *Saint Thomas d'Aquin et la vie de l'Eglise*, in *EP*, VI (1952), and of E. PERSSON, *Le plan de la Somme et le rapport "Ratio-Revelatio"*, in *RPL*, LVI (1958), 545–572; he groups, moreover, the problems raised by these studies (28 and ff.) before elaborating his own position which, although differing in its conclusions from that of Father Chenu, the latter acknowledges to be "in communion of method and inspiration" with his own. See M.-D. CHENU, *La théologie de la loi ancienne selon saint*

the master in theology—or in the *quaestiones disputatae*—the latter's most brilliant public activity as a master—it was impossible evidently to construct in the proper sense of the word a science of theology. The *lector* was bound to his text, the *disputator* to the contingent circumstances of controversy. In both cases, there was that lack of freedom within which it is possible for the mind to promote its key intuitions and to embody them in adequate systematic arrangements. Saint Thomas uses the words: *ordo disciplinae.* In point of fact, the construction of such an order is required by the very object of science. The latter does not surrender itself to the mind apart from that hidden order without which the most exact formulae would be, scientifically speaking, shapeless and impenetrable matter.

In order, therefore, to understand the *Summa theologiae* as well as the purpose of its author, it is important to perceive the *ordo disciplinae* that is worked out in it—not only the logical plan of the work, with its divisions and subdivisions, but also that inner flow of movement giving life to the structure after having created it. This movement, in fact, reveals, together with the scientific reasons that govern the whole arrangement, the intellectual options by means of which it was decided, here and there, to lay stress on this or that part, or to locate it just there. Was it, for example, through the simple material mechanics of a classification that in this *Summa* the treatise on grace ending the *Ia–IIae* was placed—to the great astonishment of some—before the treatise on Christ which opens the *IIIa Pars?* No! In doing this, Saint Thomas had in mind a definite purpose whose range cannot be too highly stressed. The plan of his *Summa* opens the way to his mind.

II. SACRED HISTORY AND THE *ORDO DISCIPLINAE*

In every realm of learning, the objects of science display a sort of resistance to mind's efforts at systematizing their content. In theology, the datum that faith proposes to man's intelligence turns up immersed, quite evidently, in conditions that are not only unfavorable for an organization of it in conceptual form but even irreducibly resistant to an adequate systematization of it. The word of God, revealed in a text and at the same time God's inner word, has perfect oneness only in the thought of God Himself. In theology, the need of a system is as much indicative of the weakness of man's mind as it is revealing of its power as it works on the datum of faith. The building of *summas* in the XIIIth century is a pointed illustration of the magnitude of the

---

Thomas, in *RT,* LXI (1961), 497, note. For his opinion on Hayen's position, see *BT,* VIII (1947–1953), 771–772, n. 1346, and on Persson's, *BT,* X (1957–1959), 470, n. 1100. Fr. HAYEN later published: *La structure de la Somme théologique et Jésus,* in *ScE,* XII (1960), 59–82.]

problem there is to transform a sacred history into an organized science (4). The master interpreter of Holy Scripture, *magister in sacra pagina,* becomes a *magister in theologia* (5). In this process, reason achieves, within the realm of faith, a decisive success. The factors of this triumph must be investigated in the case of Saint Thomas. This will be to understand the plan of his *Summa.*

For centuries, even the most advanced efforts at understanding the Bible had been limited to an immediate contact with the sacred text and with the unfolding of the historical events it relates. The need of simplifying and classifying had instigated, in actual productions, no more than a number of Creeds, Catechisms, and Florilegia. During the early Middle Ages, even in the schools, the prototype of literary production were interpretations of the *Hexaemeron,* that is, doctrinal commentaries on the opening chapters of *Genesis.* In the XIIth century, the magistral work of Hugh of Saint Victor, so powerful already in its structure, was characterized by the historical order it adopted in the division of its books and chapters. "The first book carries the unfolding of the narrative from the beginning of the world to the Incarnation of the Word. The second book proceeds in order from the Incarnation of the Word to the end and consummation of all things" (6). The economy of salvation centered wholly on the Incarnation: such is the very plot around which "the narrative unfolds," *narrationis series.* Hugh's work is "built up" and carried through within "sacred history."

During the same period, it is true, in the *Summa sententiarum,* in Abelard especially, we observe some entirely new experiments in which the historical order is completely abandoned and all the elements and events that form the economy of salvation reduced to "scientific" categories suited to classifying them in the light of general notions and synthetic principles. That brings us to the aim Saint Thomas himself was trying to achieve as he strove to discover an *ordo disciplinae* for his *Summa.*

Since the days of Abelard and of the Lombard in fact, the notion of science, nourished by all the resources of the new Aristotle, had been

4) Of this resistance, and of the tension which it provoked between exegetes and theologians, SAINT BONAVENTURE, at the very beginning of his *Breviloquim* to be exact, bears witness very provocatively against those "new theologians [who] often shy away from Sacred Scripture itself as from something precarious and lacking in order; as from a sort of dark forest." Prol., 6, 5, in *BOO,* V (1891), 208.

5) See above, ch. VII.

6) "Primus liber a principio mundi usque ad incarnationem Verbi narrationis seriem deducit. Secundus liber ab incarnatione Verbi usque ad finem et consummationem omnium ordine procedit." *De sacramentis,* prol.; *P.L.,* 176, 173 [trans. into English: *On the Sacraments of the Christian Faith,* by R. J. DEFERRARI, in *MAAP,* LVIII (1951)].

penetratingly worked out, and its technical demands were now better understood and applied. Science was organized knowledge. In the search after the causes of things, the elaboration of the data of experience and thought took place within a series of analyses and syntheses, through the combining, dividing, and co-ordinating of abstract ideas. Through the breadth and depth of these concepts, a basis was supplied for the establishment of an order in which the intelligibility of natures found its proper place within logical classifications. Such, in the fewest words, was to be henceforth the schema of any knowledge that would lay claim to the title of science. Now, at the very moment when, by means of the magnificent Aristotelian inheritance, the notion of science was taking on such vigor in method and meaningfulness, the masters of the first half of the XIIIth century were faced with the problem of applying this notion of science in their theological efforts. Is sacred doctrine a science? Can the study of the economy of salvation, can the doctrinal interpretation of the biblical narrative in which this economy is unfolded, take on the shape and structure required by science, without the nature of sacred history being altered?

One sees immediately the amount of resistance any attempt at putting a historical narrative into "scientific" form can encounter. As such, a historical narrative has a series of contingent events as its proper object. These events result from the free will of God and of man. They are, therefore, unconditioned both in their existence and successive appearance, and they are irreducible to a sequence of necessary causes as well as to deductive concatenation. If there is a discipline that the Aristotelian classification of the sciences excludes from its orbit, surely it is history! Will, then, the mystery of Christ, the very substance of this sacred history, be withdrawn from the context of those historical contingencies that surrounded it as it was being temporally prepared and realized—"the story of the temporal dispensation of Divine Providence", in the words of Saint Augustine (7)? In a nutshell, how was one to arrange the elements of the revealed datum within a speculative order expressing their authentic intelligibleness, without removing them from their original economy?

Abelard, it is true, had classified all the truths of faith according to a plan that was not without doctrinal and pedagogical value. *Fides, caritas, sacramentum* are, as a matter of fact, the elements that sum up the content of Revelation: the mysteries (the Trinity, Incarnation, creation, original sin), Christian life (charity, the virtues, the com-

---

7) *De vera religione*, c. 7; *P.L.*, 34, 128: "At the source of this religion which is to be embraced lies the story and foretelling of the temporal dispensation of Divine Providence [*historia et prophetica dispensationis temporalis divinae Providentiae*], aiming at the salvation of the human race which is in need of reformation and reparation for eternal life."

mandments), the sacraments—today we would speak of dogmatic, moral and sacramental theology (8). Plainly, however, such an order definitely eliminated all trace of historical unfolding, and if the dialectical temperament of Abelard was content to accept such an impoverishment, it does not seem that the benefit reaped from such an elimination amounts to more than giving a practical classification, and indeed one introduced somewhat from the outside. Hugh of Saint Victor's arrangement wherein the unfolding of sacred history was respected had just as much value. Without falling prey to the rather arbitrary abstraction of Abelard, Saint Thomas inserted within that history an *ordo disciplinae* that really brought out its intelligible content. By what artistic device was he able to achieve this?

Beyond the scientific world of Aristotle, Saint Thomas appeals to the Platonic theme of emanation and return. Since theology is the science of God, all things will be studied in their relation to God, whether in their production or in their final end, in their *exitus et reditus* [going-out from and coming-back to]. What a splendid source of intelligibility! Now, every thing, every being, every action, every destiny will be located, known, judged, in terms of the highest causality wherein the reason of their being will be fully revealed under the light of God itself. This is more than science, it is wisdom. This wonderful neo-Platonic theme—Christian or pagan does not matter right now—though in continuity with the epistemology of the Greek philosophers, develops the latter's potential beyond the horizon it had reached in order to explain the becoming of created being. It is the schema of a universal order in which all natures will be located, within an analytical array according to genus and species but in which, moreover, mind's understanding reaches to the root common to every nature.

Yet this neo-Platonic schema is also responsive to history, that sacred history whose opening page is precisely a description of the emanation of the world, whose whole course is an account of God's governing of His creatures, whose outcome is decided by the way men behave in their desire for happiness as they return to God. Upon this circuit, one can locate the facts and deeds recorded in sacred history—with all the contingency (herein is the trademark of Christian neo-Platonism) that their dependency on the free will of God and of man implies.

Such is the plan of the *Summa theologiae*, such the movement which it translates: *Ia Pars*—emanation from God-the principle; *IIa Pars*—return to God-the end; and because, *de facto*, by God's free and

8) ABELARD, *Theologia*, lib. I, c. 1; *P.L.*, 178, 981. One knows how rigourously characteristic this plan is of the whole Abelardian school.

utterly gratuitous design (sacred history reveals this to us) this return
is effected through Christ-the man-God, a *IIIa Pars* will study the
"Christian" conditions of this return. Plainly, in this third part more
than elsewhere in the *Summa,* history will dominate, because here it
yields a "revelation," in the strong sense of the word. Herein also,
mind's speculation will hit upon its true value by moulding itself upon
the sweet contingencies of divine love. Here is the text in which Saint
Thomas announces his plan: "Because the chief aim of sacred doctrine
is to impart the knowledge of God, not only as He is in Himself, but
also as He is the beginning of things and their end, and especially of
rational creature . . ., in our endeavor to expound this doctrine, we
shall treat: first of God; secondly of the movement of rational creature to God; thirdly of Christ Who, as man, is our way of tending to
God" (a). Then, at the beginning of the second part: ". . . now that we
have treated of the exemplar, that is, of God, and of those things
which came forth from the power of God in accordance with His will,
it remains for us to treat of His image, that is, of man, inasmuch as
he too is the principle of his actions, as having free-will and control
of his actions "(b). God, the "exemplar"—man, the "image": the very
vocabulary Saint Thomas uses discloses in pointed detail the neo-
Platonic theme he is working from (9).

Even in his commentary on the *Sentences,* when as a young professor he was just starting his teaching, Saint Thomas had explicitly proposed an identical organization of the science of theology. And if as
a commentator, he had respectfully adhered to the plan of the Master
of the *Sentences,* yet, one is free to see, in the discreet personal statement he makes, the first manifestation of a masterful view destined to

---

a) "Quia igitur principalis intentio hujus sacrae doctrinae est Dei cognitionem
tradere, et non solum secundum quod in se est, sed etiam secundum quod est
principium rerum et finis earum, et specialiter rationalis creaturae . . . ad hujus
doctrinae expositionem intendentes, primo tractabimus de Deo; secundo, de motu
rationalis creaturae in Deum; tertio, de Christo qui, secundum quod homo, via
est nobis tendendi in Deum." *Ia Pars,* q. 2, prol.

b) ". . . postquam praedictum est de exemplari, scilicet de Deo et de his quae
processerunt ex divina potestate secundum ejus voluntatem, restat ut consideremus
de ejus imagine, id est de homine secundum quod et ipse est suorum operum
principium, quasi liberum arbitrium habens." Prol. to the *IIa Pars.*

9) See JOHN OF SAINT THOMAS, *Cursus theologicus in Summam D. Thomae,*
Introd., Paris, 1883, I, 191: "Therefore, as may be seen from the prologue of
the second question of Part I, Saint Thomas divides the entire teaching of his
Summa theologiae according to the threefold consideration of the causality of
God, that is to say, of God as the effecting principle, of God as the beatifying
end, of God as the repairing savior. And thus, proceeding from God as he is
Himself and in His being, proceeding through God as He effects, and finalizes,
and saves, there is a return to God to be enjoyed in Himself through the ultimate
glory of the resurrection, *which is evidently to complete the golden circuit of
theology, which the divine Summa of Saint Thomas follows out.*"

be the ruling factor of his later work. "Since," he says, "sacred doctrine intends to deal with divine things, since also a thing is understood to be divine inasmuch as it is related to God as its principle or its end . . ., this doctrine will consider things as coming forth from God as from their principle, and as being brought back to God as to their end. Hence, in the first part, he [the Master of the *Sentences*] determines about divine things in their *proceeding* from their principle, in the second, in their *returning* to their end . . ." (a).

Exitus et reditus. The Christian neo-Platonists are plainly the thinkers who can supply Saint Thomas with expression and support for this vast theme, and, *de facto,* the Dionysian tradition, so full of life in his day, does just this. In this tradition, the theme preserves an ontological and cosmological meaningfulness that, in Augustine, is somewhat masked behind his psychological and moral views on man. *Exitus et reditus*—progression and conversion: this two-sided law of production, to be sure, no longer connotes the very specific contexture it had in a Plotinus where it was bound up with a whole philosophical system. The theme is now no more than a rather vague schema for envisioning the universe, a commonplace jointly shared within the mental outlook of Western Christendom; one, moreover, that the demands of orthodoxy have helped to extricate from its original context of emanationism. On this point, in fact, it had stood in need of being purged from the cosmic determinism and the idealistic dialectics which, in Greek philosophy, were made to characterize the rhythm of any production but were radically opposed to the Christian economy of creation and salvation, an economy based completely on God's free will. Thus is broken asunder what appears to be a paradox—that of inserting and expounding a sacred history within a representation of the universe which, more than any other one, right at its source, rules out all history.

This summary schema, an extremely impoverished one philosophically speaking, is nonetheless exploited by Saint Thomas to the full degree of its potential. It will not be, for him, a handy framework upon which he will be able to arrange as he pleases the vast subject matter of sacred doctrine, but rather an order for science, injecting intelligibility into the heart of the revealed datum (10). This, in fact,

---

a) "Cum enim sacrae doctrinae intentio sit circa divina, divinum autem sumitur secundum relationem ad Deum vel ut principium vel ut finem . . . consideratio hujus doctrinae erit de rebus secundum quod exeunt a Deo ut a principio, et secundum quod referuntur in ipsum ut in finem. Unde in prima parte determinat de rebus divinis secundum *exitum* a principio, in secunda secundum *reditum* in finem." *In I Sent.,* d. 2, div. textus.

10) Herein lies, *de facto,* the effectiveness of the Platonic theme, and it was in this sense that, as early as the IXth century, John Scotus Erigena had used

is precisely the very distinctive type of intelligibility that the theologian is looking for, and by which his science, in part, breaks with the
epistemology of the Greeks. The theologian strives to discover and
elaborate reasons ("necessary" reasons as Saint Anselm calls them) (a)
within a series of contingent facts. The whole edifice of demonstrations and theological conclusions which he builds, rests on a datum,
whose appropriateness but in no way its necessity, the human mind
can discover. Hence, at the beginning of each treatise—on creation,
the hierarchy of beings, the Incarnation, the Redemption, the Church,
the sacraments, and others—his first step is to establish the appropriateness of these "facts." Now, there is a hidden relationship between
this particular type of intelligibility, which the argument by the appropriate—scoffed at to such an extent in the Aristotelian epistemology, yet so essential in theological epistemology—begets for the
theologian and the schema of emanation and return whose rhythm of
unfolding is governed by God's free decree at decisive moments.
Within this relationship, sacred history and *ordo disciplinae* unite in
harmony under the jurisdiction of faith which leads both of them to
the absoluteness of God, wherein it furnishes them with their definite
intelligible consistency. The plan of the *Summa* is truly a theological
plan, that is, a plan in which God's science is formally and spiritually
the principle of man's science, supplying the latter at once with its
object, its light, and its character of necessity.

Furthermore—and we have here another advantage—this plan, of
its own impact, leads theological science beyond the historical economy considered in it to the divine reasons that govern such an
economy. Indeed, the object of theology is properly and primarily not
the economy by which man is the recipient of faith and of grace
through Christ but rather it is God in His very reality. All that He
has brought to pass in the course of history, all that He has done by
way of creation and re-creation, to use the words of Hugh of Saint
Victor who had remained faithful to Scripture's *series narrationis*, is

---

it in his organisation of theology. See M. CAPPUYNS, *Jean Scot Erigène: sa vie,
son oeuvre, sa pensée*, in UCL, ser. II, XXVI (1933), 302 and ff. P. VIGNAUX
offers these excellent reflexions: "In locating man within a cosmic setting, John
Scotus was touching upon a question that was essential for medieval thought.
As Mr. Bréhier remarks, 'the Christian image and the neo-Platonic image of the
universe have a sort of rhythm in common,' procession and return; but Christian
thinking offers 'a series of events, each one of which has free initiative at its
source: creation and the fall, redemption and the happy life to come'; with its
dual-timed analysis of things, the *De divisione* introduces this irreversible chain
of events, this *history*." *La pensée au moyen âge*, in CAC, 207 (1938), 18 [rev.
and reedited: *Philosophie au moyen âge*, in CAC, 323 (1958). The rev. text
of the quotation is on 20–21. The latter ed. was translated by E. C. HALL, *Philosophy in the Middle Ages. An Introduction*, in MerB, M81 (1959)].

a) See ch. I, 61, note b.

formally treated and judged *sub ratione Dei* [under the formality of God]. "All things are treated in sacred doctrine under the formality of God: either because they are God Himself, or because they have an order to God as their principle and end" (b). Thus, the Incarnation itself finds its final explanation in the bounteous overflowing of the goodness of God (See *IIIa Pars,* q. 1). Herein, surely, is intelligibility in the highest degree, exceeding all historical categories and making theology a wisdom. Now, as we have seen, the proper characteristic of the order chosen by Saint Thomas for his *Summa* is precisely that it builds upon the relation to God *ut ad principium et finem: exitus et reditus.* Let us read once more the text from the beginning of the *Sentences:* ". . . this doctrine will consider things as coming forth from God as from their principle, and as being brought back to God as to their end. Hence, in a first part . . ." etc. (c). Once rid of its emanatistic implications, the neo-Platonic schema expresses *of itself* the basic reference to God by which every being, every event, every nature, becomes an object of theology. "The study of creatures devolves to the theologian and the philosopher, but not in the same way. *Philosophers* consider them as they are in their proper natures, so their inquiry is bent on a knowledge of the proper causes and properties of things. The *theologian,* by contrast, looks at creatures as they have come forth from their first principle, and as they return to their end, which is God. Hence, the knowledge of the theologian is rightly called divine wisdom, because it considers the highest cause of all, which is God" (d). The plan of the *Summa theologiae,* and its divisions, derive from the very nature of the object of theology. No other plan can be more adequate.

Finally, a theology that has reached this stature remains a religious kind of knowledge, even in its most rational organization. Each one of its elements, by its location within theology, is referred, from within, to God and to the word of God. Its unity is not guaranteed by philosophical categories coming from without, which would reduce it

---

b) "Omnia autem pertractantur in sacra doctrina sub ratione Dei, vel quia sunt ipse Deus, vel quia habent ordinem ad Deum, ut ad principium et finem." *Ia Pars,* q. 1, a. 7. [For a further commentary on the organisation of the *Summa* "sub ratione Dei," see TH.–A. AUDET, *loc. cit.,* 14–29.]

c) ". . . consideratio hujus doctrinae erit de rebus secundum quod exeunt a Deo ut a principio, et secundum quod referuntur in ipsum ut in finem. Unde in prima parte . . . ." *In I Sent.,* d. 2, div. textus.

d) "Creaturarum consideratio pertinet ad theologos et ad philosophos, sed diversimode. *Philosophi* enim considerant creaturas secundum quod in propria natura consistunt; unde proprias causas et passiones rerum inquirunt. Sed *theologus* considerat creaturas secundum quod a primo principio exierunt, et in finem ultimum ordinantur qui Deus est; unde recte divina sapientia nominatur, quia altissimam causam considerat, quae Dens est." *In II Sent.,* prol.

to a sort of sacred metaphysics seasoned with allusions to the spiritual and with pious corollaries (11). The oneness of theology is really the oneness of the mystery at its heart. How often, in the interpretation of the *IIa Pars* in particular, I was shocked by the rigid and systematic way in which the Aristotelian structures present in the text were commented upon in detail, while the sap of evangelical and patristic spirituality supplying life to these otherwise dead branches was ignored or glossed over. To be sure, the Aristotelian structures in the theology of the *Summa* are not accidental to it, any more than the Platonic categories impregnating the theology of Augustine, of Dionysius, and of Gregory of Nyssa are accidental to their theology. Yet, the effort at systematizing theology, even if it tells against itself, must, at any cost, respect the strange logic of the Kingdom of God wherein God's designs are expressed in the obscurity of mystery (and in the story of the failures of the Kingdom) as well as in the suitabilities of their realization (and in the story of the successes achieved by the Church He established). Theology remains a *doctrina sacra*. It returns always to the Gospel, to the word of God, because it is fulfilled in the thought of God.

To dispel the impression of triteness that the use of the neo-Platonic schema might still leave in one's mind, to bring out, moreover, the distinctive effectiveness of the plan of Saint Thomas, it would be enough to compare it with the other attempts that were made in his age. The organic power of his plan shows up quickly when it is set side by side with the plan of Abelard—*fides, caritas, sacramentum*—which was built up from the material contents of sacred doctrine, rather than in the light of a general inner purview. As regards the ordering of materials found in the *Sentences* of Peter Lombard and generally accepted at the time, it has the advantage of putting to work the broad Augustinian categories of *res et signa, uti et frui* [things and signs, use and enjoy] (12), wherein are expressed a noetic and a conception of man especially helpful in explaining the soul's

---

11) Thus, whatever benefits one may reap from it in metaphysics, the work of A. REGINALD, *D. Thomae tria principia cum suis consequentiis* (Toulouse, 1670, re-edited in Paris, 1878), in which the theology of Saint Thomas is reduced to three principles (Being is transcendent; God alone is pure act; Absolute beings are specified by themselves, relative beings, by reference to others), is the best example of this sort of deformation.

12) "[Sacred doctrine] can be divided in another way, if one follows the intention of the Master, since, in a first part, his determination is of things, in a second, of signs—and that in the fourth [book]. Again, there is a division of the first part into three: in the first part, the determination is of the enjoyable, in the second part, of the useful—that in the second book—in the third part, of that which orders the useful to the enjoyable . . . and that in the third book." *In I Sent.,* d. 2, div. textus.

spiritual itinerary. Still, this order cannot have the objective breadth and the speculative reaches that the plan of Saint Thomas offers, because these Augustinian categories are centered on the psychology of man, not on the work of God as such.

Turning now to the *Summa* itself, let us see how, *de facto,* Saint Thomas develops his general idea in the main parts of its architecture.

III. THE CONSTRUCTION OF THE *SUMMA*

When an architect decides to give existence to a conception of his, he develops in his mind the order he will give to his monument. His creative inventiveness busies itself at finding out how he will manage masses, harmonize functions, apportion the segments of the whole, unify parts. He thinks out a synthetic whole that is called the "design" of an architect. What is this "design" that Saint Thomas thought out for the architecture of his *Summa*?

Two traits give this work its general physionomy, and both are immediately dependent upon the principle of emanation and return: 1) in the *Summa,* emanation and return unfold in two sections closely knit together in the unity of two reverse movements; the *Ia Pars* and the *IIa Pars* are related to one another as are *exitus* and *reditus.*

2) in the *Summa,* Incarnation, which is the center of the economy, enters into the circuit of emanation and return only as a means willed by God; it is dealt with in a *IIIa Pars* which, judging in the abstract, would seem to play the role of no more than a part added to the whole as an afterthought.

To start with the first trait: Examining the mass of contingent data that make up the plot of the economy willed by divine Providence, "the story of the temporal dispensation of Divine Providence" (13), we are impressed at seeing how they are ranged along the two segments of the circuit that takes its rise in the bosom of God and directs everything back to Him. Herein is an ontological order which supplies a wonderful setting for an order of learning. With the help of some amount of skilful disposing and apportioning of the facts related in sacred history (we are thinking about the events related in *Genesis,* for example, that are distributed in the treatise on first man in the *Ia Pars* and in the treatise on original sin in the *IIa Pars*), this order also furnishes favorable ground for scientific analysis and for the positing of theological problems.

More attention, however, must be given to the emanation-return

13) SAINT AUGUSTINE, *loc. cit.*

cycle itself seen in its entirety, as to an adequate principle of intelligibility, rather than to the systematic locating of data within it. All of Greek reason, that of Aristotle and that of Plotinus, is herein adopted within Christian soil, not indeed as an object, nor as a light; the matter, and especially the sap, of theological science's fine fruits remain intimately Christian. Greek reason is adopted as a tool, a simple tool, yet, an authentically qualified tool because of the coherence of nature and grace.

Emanation-return are intelligibility in fullness. All creatures, and particularly human creatures, all events, and particularly human events, are framed between two causes—the efficient cause, God-Creator-and-Conserver (*Ia Pars*), and the final cause, God-Beatifier-and-Glorified (*IIa Pars*)—as between the two supreme reasons giving them meaning and value before the mind. There is even more than that: the production of beings, their "procession," ending up in stable realities, in natures, is the very reason of their return; it is the ontological basis of the resources and steps of this return. Produced being, once the movement by means of which it was given being is completed, is *by its own nature* bound by an inverse movement, by a "conversion", to the principle of its production (14). These two movements are not disparate movements that one could study apart from one another in two different treatments of them, in two different treatises of a theological system. They are a circuit that is unique, its unity and intelligibleness based on natures whose end and form correspond with one another as designed by an efficiently causing intelligence. In other words: theology is a science eminently one. Dogmatic and moral theology are not two parts, lined up side by side, the one speculative, the other practical, the two linked together here and there by a few cross references. They are the two faces of a selfsame reality, wherein the categories, speculative and practical, far from setting them apart, simply furnish the lasting advantage of marking their technical differences. The acts of man (and through them the whole cosmos which they order and develop) are perceived as the "steps" by which human nature, on its return journey, realizes its end—its beatitude and perfection all in one. The practical knowledge of these human acts and of the laws that regulate them is a most intimate part of the knowledge of human nature itself as designed and predestined

---

14) "In the coming of creatures from the first principle, there is a circling or gyration, as it were, since all things return as to their end to that from which they came as from their principle." *In I Sent.*, d. 14, q. 2, a. 2. See E. BRÉHIER, *Le néoplatonisme*, in *La tradition philosophique et la pensée française*, Paris, 1922, 44: "There still remains to ask why and how this procession comes to a stop . . ., why, in a word, there are stable beings. The reason is that produced being, once it is separated from its principle by the movement that brought it into being, re-attaches itself anew to its principle by means of an inverse movement, the movement of return, which is a conversion."

by God. Thus the science of the theologian reproduces the very science of God, perfectly one because God "by one and the same science, knows what He is and what He does" (15).

This fullness of intelligibility leads us actually to the realm of the divine ideas, the real spiritual and scientific home of theology. It simultaneously combines a rational explanation of things, which is drawn precisely from their natures, with a religious explanation since these natures in themselves and in their destiny are the realization of a divine idea. The neo-Platonists of old had already endeavored to identify the principle of the rational explanation of things with the principle of the religious life (16), but pantheism had compromised their attempt. Saint Thomas, without sacrificing anything of the transcendent personality of God, principle and end of all things, will extract all the advantages and all the truth present in the doctrine of emanation and return.

This doctrine, in fact, is both the principle of the architecture of the *Summa* and the unqualified reason for the oneness of theological science, which the Moderns with their dissociation of "dogma" and "moral" have annoyingly jeopardized. Moral theology is not a catalog of precepts whose application is regulated by innumerable cases of conscience; neither is it the description of a mystical flight outside the bounds of our faculties. Moral theology is a science, a practical science, but nonetheless a science (a). A spiritual organism is its subject matter. This organism exists in us as a nature. This nature is a principle of our "return" to God, and of the whole complement of virtues which this return requires. And the marvel of our salvation is that grace, divine life injected in our souls, will perform in us as a nature and be the real and permanent principle of our effective "return" to God Whom we twice participate (17). The image is in communion with

---

15) ". . . eadem scientia se cognoscit et ea quae facit." *Ia Pars,* q. 1, a. 4.
16) See E. BRÉHIER, *loc. cit.,* 40.

a) See *Ia Pars,* q. 1, a. 4, and the following in a. 5, c.: ". . . this *science* [sacred doctrine] being speculative under one aspect, and practical under another, it transcends all other *sciences,* speculative and practical. . . . Of the practical *sciences,* that one is higher in dignity which is ordained to a more final end. . . . Now the end of this doctrine in its practical reaches is eternal happiness to which as to an ultimate end all the other ends of the practical *sciences* are ordained." In addition to considering that moral *theology* is a science, Saint Thomas also holds that moral *philosophy* has its own proper place among the philosophical sciences and ascribes it its own particular subject matter. See the recent article first written in French by CH. MURIN, *De l'être moral dans l'oeuvre de saint Thomas,* in *Etudes d'histoire littéraire et doctrinale* (PIEM, XVII, 1962), 175–237, translated and first published in English under the title: *Inquiry into the Nature of Moral Being in the Works of St. Thomas Aquinas,* in SS, II (1961), 97–167.

17) As a result, the treatise on grace will not be placed in "dogma" with the explanation that "moral" is not concerned with it.

This epistemological position of the *IIa Pars* does not rule out casuistic knowl-

its exemplar: ". . . man is said to be made after the image of God. . . .
Having spoken of the exemplar, that is to say, of God [in the *Ia Pars*]
. . . there remains to consider His image, that is to say, man [in the
IIa Pars] . . ." (a).

Truly, the plan of the *Summa*, *Ia* and *IIa Pars*, is a means of access
to its spirit. Divisions in treatises or the like, howsoever useful they
may be pedagogically speaking, must not obscure this plan's irreplace-
able and definitive intelligibility.

The same schema of "return"—and we are now in a position to see
that it is much more than a schema—is the ordering principle of the
IIIa Pars and the key to the understanding of it. Christ the Mediator
is the craftsman of this return; He is the "way." "Because our Savior,
the Lord Jesus Christ . . . has shown that He Himself is the way of
truth for us . . . in order to complete all of theology's business, it is
necessary, after having considered the final end of human life and the
virtues and vices, that we follow this up with a consideration about
Him Who is the Savior of all . . ." (b).

This was not the first attempt in theology to locate the fact of the
Incarnation and the role of Christ within a general economy of salvation. It seems, in fact, that when the Platonic schema is used by a
Christian theologian, it normally leads him to propose Christ as the
way by means of which the return process is achieved. Scotus Erigena
had sketched out—clumsily, yet magnificently—a theology of salvation
along these lines (18). With Saint Thomas, the choice of the Platonic
system is seen as yielding the full effects of its potential.

---

edge, either as a knowledge of the singular or as a dialectic of the probable;
on the contrary, it supplies it with a foundation, and has it serving a specific
function to its own ends (". . . every practical science reaches its stage of completeness in a consideration of the particular." *Ia–IIae*, q. 6, prol.). The casuists
were the ones—and equally, at the other end of the line, the spirituals—who
eliminated the scientific aspect from moral knowledge. See the introduction on
method of J. M. RAMÍREZ, in his *De hominis beatitudine tractatus theologicus*,
in *BTE*, VIII (1942).

a) ". . . homo factus ad imaginem Dei dicitur . . . postquam praedictum est de
exemplari, scilicet de Deo . . . restat ut consideremus de ejus imagine, idest de
homine . . ." Prol. to the *IIa Pars*.

b) "Quia Salvator noster Dominus Jesus Christus . . . viam veritatis nobis in
seipso demonstravit . . . necesse est ut ad consummationem totius theologici
negotii, post considerationem ultimi finis humanae vitae et virtutum et vitiorum,
de ipso omnium Salvatore . . . nostra consideratio subsequatur." Prol. to the
IIIa Pars.

18) See his *De divisione naturae*, 5, 24; *P.L.*, 122, 912 a–b:
"*Master.* Do you acknowledge, therefore, that the Word of God, in Whom
and by Whom and for Whom all things were made according to His divinity,
came down to dwell in the midst of caused being according to His humanity?
"*Pupil.* I acknowledge it most firmly.
"*Master.* And why did He come down?

One of the objections most often raised against the plan of the *Summa* by certain modern theologians and spiritual writers, is that this plan presents a fully developed theology before Christ appears on the scene. Redemptive Incarnation appears to have been added *post factum* to the whole, as if the real story of salvation were an unforeseeable contingency superimposing itself on a system of abstract metaphysics dealing with God, grace, and the virtues. Humanity is encountered in the *Summa,* not primarily as the mystical body of Christ, but as part of a cosmology. Objections are raised in particular —and with some emotion—against the treatise on grace wherein nothing is said about *Christian* grace, against a treatise on charity in which the Revealer of God's love is not named, against a theory of contemplation in which no provision is made for the Eucharist, the sacrament of union. In other words, there are no more than allusions and incidental references made to the whole Christian economy in the *Ia* and *IIa Pars.*

This objection brings us face to face with a key position of Saint Thomas who is simply working out this position in his plan in accordance with the teaching aims of his *Summa.* Let there be no surprise, consequently, if he is found to be breaking away intentionally from the other theological systems.

It is true that the tract on grace makes no reference to the unique Mediator, that the tract on charity fails to mention Saint Paul's "unique foundation" [*I Cor.,* III, 11], that in the theory of contemplation, He Who alone reveals the Father is not named. The Incarnation is, however, in point of fact, a contingent event, and it enters in the *exitus-reditus* cycle only as an absolutely gratuitous work of God's absolutely free will. The predestination of Christ is *de facto* capital, yet it does not have its place by dint of right in the economy of this cycle. It is impossible to locate it *a priori* in a dialectical list of divine decrees.

In the foregoing, one recognizes the famous controversy between the Thomistic and Scotistic schools over the motive of the Incarnation and the absolute primacy of Christ (19). Dwelling upon it at this stage would serve no good purpose. We are simply noting that the doctrine of Saint Thomas is already recorded and revealed in the very plan of his *Summa.* From this plan, everything else follows. Grace is

"*Pupil.* Tell me, I pray thee.

"*Master.* For no other reason, in my opinion, than to save through His humanity the effects of those causes which, from all eternity and without any possible change, he possesses according to His divinity, and to call back these effects to their causes, so that, in their causes, by an ineffable embrace, as it were, the effects would be saved just as the causes also are." On this assimilation of *reversio* [reversion] to a *deificatio* [deification], see M. CAPPUYNS, *loc. cit.,* 360–381.

19) See H. M. FERET's reflections on method: *Creati in Christo Jesu,* in *RSPT,* XXX (1930), 96–132.

studied in itself as a sharing in the life of God, and the adjective *Christian* is not added to it. This is because grace, as such, has its own nature, its own structure, its own laws, beyond the temporal conditions of its realization; in due course, filial adoption in Christ will follow. Charity is defined as a friendship with God; this is something worthy of consideration in itself, without anything being taken away from Christ's prayer for his disciples in Saint John [*John*, XVII]. The vision of God is realized only through and in Christ. Yet an analysis of what the knowledge of God requires and actually is, must be made before one looks into the concrete mode of its realization howsoever precious this mode may be. Redemptive Incarnation is the very substance of the Christian economy; yet the basic source of its intelligibleness is its characteristic of being a means. To see it thus inserted within the ontological framework of grace is not to minimize its marvelous unfolding in time.

On the strength of this, then, should we not admit that the attempt to join in a single science a speculation on God and a sacred history is a vain one? Not at all, unless the science of theology is reduced to pure deduction and hardly any attention is paid to the contingencies of God's free will. The transition from the *IIa* to the *IIIa Pars* is a passage from the order of the necessary to the order of the historical, from an account of structures to the actual story of God's gifts (20). In point of fact, Christian doctrine supplies a check to neo-Platonic teaching with its rigid theory of "procession," and the plan of Saint Thomas shows clearly that he is in complete control of the Platonic schema at the very moment when he is using it. The Word made flesh of the Christian is not the creating Logos of Plotinic emanationism. The former is the object of a history, while Plotinus rejected time as something contaminating and the freedom of God as an unintelligible imperfection. Theology achieves a paradoxical success when it unites, amid sensitiveness to God's transcendency, a science of the necessary and respect for the contingencies of a love which is eternally free. The *IIIa Pars* of the *Summa* is the story of that success.

One more item should be observed: how the various "events" that make up the economy of salvation are inserted in the plot of theological science wherein rational connections furnish the framework for the succession of events, and oftentimes supplant them. The crossing over from the historical to the scientific is not achieved with-

---

20) Yet this transition comes about without breach in the equilibrium of the *Summa,* for Christ does not become the *object* of theology, as implied in Hugh of Saint Victor who had remained true to the historical order. On the other hand, influenced by deism, a whole school of modern theologians fell into the opposite excess by setting forth a theodicy in which the God of Abraham and the history contained in the Bible and the Gospel were made to vanish from the scene.

out some shifts in the scale of values. This brings out the fact that no system can be commensurate with reality. The theologian must, as a result, compensate for the loss by actually returning to the datum of Scripture. "Biblical theology," as we say today, is the answer to this high function. Now, there is, in the *Summa*, a biblical theology, which the writers of handbooks and commentaries have treated by the method of preterition. No doubt elements in it are now outdated by the advances made in historical exegesis. No doubt also the development of new methods has introduced progressive autonomy in fields of research that were formerly homogeneous. The principle of a biblical zone throughout the *Summa* remains, however, and in any case, one cannot delete its place and meaning without throwing the whole edifice out of equilibrium. For example, attention must be given, among many others, to the three elaborate blocks of questions in which Saint Thomas develops what Scripture says about the six days of creation (*Ia Pars*, q. 67–74), the old law (*Ia–IIae*, q. 98–106), the life and the mysteries of Christ (*IIIa Pars*, q. 27–59) (a). The archaic elements of the exegesis employed must not nullify the fact that the Bible is present in a theology. What quantities of light and realities modern Thomistic theology lost when it failed to retain the elaborate, *religious* consideration of the cosmos and of the terrestrial creatures placed at man's disposal, the historical and prophetic perspective of the Old Testament, the Gospel itself now abandoned to the exegetes and to the spiritual writers! There are other examples: the beatitudes in the texts of the Synoptics, the fruits of the Spirit in Saint Paul, the precepts of the Decalogue, the enumeration of the charisms, and so on.

Quite evidently, this collocation of revealed data by reason provokes shifts that have their inconveniences, historically and religiously speaking. Ancient law, the "Law" par excellence, is quite logically located after the treatise on law in general. Hence, the historical role of the Old Law is reduced, to a certain extent, to a set of abstract categories (21). Saint Thomas is forced, as a result, to analyse the texts of Saint Paul on the Old Law without elaborating on their dynamic meaning, when in the Apostle they are entirely related to Christ the Redeemer.

The theological study of man had developed, before Saint Thomas, through an examination of the actual states of mankind in time: man's pristine state as he came forth from the hands of God, his state after his original sin, finally, his state after he was restored by

---

a) See above, ch. VII, 259–260.

21) We say "to a certain extent," for the theme of preparation for the coming of Christ which is set forth in q. 98, a. 1–3, remains important throughout all of questions 98–103.

the grace of Christ. We know how strongly attached Saint Augustine had remained to the examination of these historical *states* of man and how little concerned he was about exploring the theoretical condition of a human nature. The plan of the *Summa* will allow Saint Thomas to achieve coherence—a very delicate one indeed—between the two viewpoints. It will make possible a science of human nature as such that will not bring detriment to the analysis of man's historical states but will further, on the contrary, a correct estimation of what they imply. That a system requires a science of human nature is not open to question. If Augustine with his personal perspectives could do without one, its having been set aside weighs heavily on modern Augustinian theologians who would systematize him. But—and this is the counterproof—the realistic climate of Augustine's doctrine that we have evoked should caution us to avoid the blunder of that kind of commenting wherein one would fail to examine very closely Saint Thomas's integral acceptance of Augustine's Christian man under pretext of being faithful to the more Aristotelian theoretical analysis of human nature.

Theologians following Saint Bonaventure or Scotus have attempted several times to write Bonaventurian or Scotistic *summas* after the form and the plan of the *Summa* of Saint Thomas (22). Their attempts reveal candid enthusiasm, and the disciples of Saint Thomas are sensitive to it as to a friendly witness of the prestige of the "Common Doctor." All things considered, these attempts have more value than a breaking down of the *Summa* in modern categories and treatises wherein its spirit can no longer dwell. After what we have said, however, it is clear that neither type of operation can be done without danger. To be sure, the development of theology imposes, has in fact imposed, changes that have to be made, for it is necessary to incorporate within an ever-receptive synthesis those results that issue from ever-at-work faith and the Spirit. Yet, for an authentic exegesis of the *Summa* and for the latter's very capacity of assimilation, it is extremely important that the intelligibility included in its plan be first penetrated.

In final analysis, a theologian is not judged to be such through a *summa* he may have written. However powerful the latter may be in doctrinal reaches and in pedagogical effectiveness, it remains wholly subject to the light and the object of the faith that builds it (23).

---

22) On three Scotist *summas* done in this style, see F. DELORME, *La somme théologique du P. Eutrope Gagnon (+1673)*, in *FF*, 1930, 33. On similar Bonaventurian *summas*, see H. FELDER, in *EF*, 1931, 30–31.

23) This, in fact, was really the position the medieval writers of *summas* held, both at the institutional level and as a matter of personal conviction: "In the

Witness that Augustine did not write a *summa*. Yet, a faith mistress of herself can produce no work of greater beauty than a *summa*, and Christendom can ill do without one in its universe. "Believe that you may understand" (a). Saint Thomas is judged to be the master theologian and doctor of the Church through his *Summa*, his masterpiece. At its own level, it is the fullness of the Gospel.

IV. RESEARCH SUGGESTIONS

1. In order to test what a *summa* stands for as the literary form characterizing a system of thought and a particular age, recall the other forms of philosophical and religious thinking that appeared in the course of history: the Socratic *Dialogues* of Plato, the *Confessions* of Saint Augustine, the *Meditations* of Descartes, the *Pensées* of Pascal, the *Treatises* of the XVIIIth and XIXth centuries, the *Journals* of Maine de Biran and of Gabriel Marcel. Each genre requires its own procedures in carrying out research and setting forth intelligibility. Differences in expression are no more than the outcome of even deeper differences in mental outlook.

Summas and the XIIIth century. Note that the appearance of *summas* is consistent with the other phenomena of the civilization of the times, as for example, in the works of art wherein the trend of evolution tends to themes in which the realization of a whole is attempted, for instance at Bourges, the mystery of the Church; at Chartres, Christ, the Saviour of creation; and so on. As for the cliché on *summas* and cathedrals, setting aside the commonplace in it, develop the theme by reading, for instance, H. FOCILLON, *Art d'Occident*, Paris, 1947, in which the author arrives at truly philosophical views on medieval architecture by examining what relation there is between ideas and [architectural] forms in the oneness of the medieval art of thinking.

2. Let us point out two "introductions" to the study of the *Summa*, those of A. LEGENDRE, *Introduction à l'étude de la Somme théologique de S. Thomas d'Aquin*, Paris, 1923, and M. GRABMANN, *Einführung in die Summa theologiae des heiligen Thomas von Aquin*, 2d ed., Freiburg, 1928 [translated into English under the title *Introduction to the Theological Summa of Saint Thomas*, by J. S. ZYBURA, Saint Louis-

---

XIIth century, and during the two centuries that followed . . . in all the schools of theology . . . the first and essential duty of the master directing the school was to read and interpret the text of Holy Scripture. . . . Thus, even when the master, either in person or through a bachelor, added a lesson of theology to his lesson on Scripture, the study and understanding of the Bible remained an end, and theology a means." P. MANDONNET, *Chronologie des écrits scripturaires de saint Thomas*, in *RT*, XI (1928), 35.

a) "Crede ut intelligas."

London, 1930]. In the first one, which is still useful although no longer
to the point and lacking in body, a series of chapters will be found
on the relationship of the *Summa* to the Bible, to Church tradition,
to reason and the philosophers, and to immediate theological contexts as well as a number of reflexions on the aim, the plan, and the
method of the *Summa*. The second one is more technical and dis-
plays more erudition. It locates the *Summa* within the evolution of
the literary genre of *summas*, indicates its ulterior destiny, offers a
commentary of the Prologue in which Saint Thomas develops the
aim and methods of his work, and finally describes both the systematic
and the historical method of interpretation from which a full understanding of it will ensue. *De facto,* it is the whole lot of works dealing with the evolution of theology and the formation of *summas* in
the medieval university that really introduces us within the *Summa*
of Saint Thomas.

In several synoptic tables, the *Summa* is presented in its articulated
framework (the latest by G. PARIS, *Synopsis totius Summae theologiae
S. Thomae,* 3 vols., Napoli, 1950); when the latter was first published
in 1931, it was the sixth one to come out in a half-century, which
would lead one to presume that such tables have their usefulness.
[To these, add still another: *An Outline of the* Summa theologiae,
prepared by G. Q. FRIEL, Providence, 1950.] The student, however,
will find great profit in establishing on his own the plan of the *Summa,*
whether of the whole or of a section of it, bringing all the while his
effort to bear on the discovery, beneath divisions and subdivisions, of
the internal unfolding of problems, the sources from which they
spring, and the manner in which they are brought up. A comparison
with the arrangements arrived at in other *summas* (those of Alexander of Hales, Albert the Great, Bonaventure's *Breviloquium,* and
others) will, from this standpoint, provide useful light. The *Isagoge*
[Introduction] that JOHN OF SAINT THOMAS edited at the beginning
of his *Cursus theologicus* (translated, adapted, and completed by
M. B. LAVAUD, Paris, 1928) does not go beyond a formal explaining
of connexions, but it is very penetrating in its analyses. See also
A. PORTMANN, *Das System der theologischen Summa des heiligen
Thomas von Aquin,* 2d ed., Luzern, 1903.

The *Summa contra Gentiles* and the *Summa theologiae,* whether
as wholes or in their parallel parts, should also be compared. See
C. SUERMONDT, *Tabulae schematicae cum introductione de principiis
et compositione comparatis Summae theologicae et Summae contra
Gentiles sancti Thomae,* Torino, 1943. And the same should be done
with the *Compendium theologiae,* which is more closely related to
the *Contra Gentiles.*

Quite evidently, systematic expositions of Thomism (Sertillanges, De Wulf, Manser, in philosophy, and in theology, Scheeben, Diekamp, Garrigou–Lagrange, and others) are very fruitful. It must be recognized, however, that they involve some degree of personal reconstruction, required, to be sure, by the development of philosophy and of theology, but inevitably masking the steps taken by Saint Thomas and the original order he inserted in his works. The latter observation is particularly true in the case of those expositions wherein a "philosophy" is extracted from the Thomistic "theological" synthesis. See the just reflexions with which E. GILSON opens *The Christian Philosophy of Saint Thomas Aquinas,* New York, 1956, Introd. [translation by L. K. SHOOK of the 5th French ed. of *Le Thomisme. Introduction à la philosophie de saint Thomas d'Aquin,* in *EPM,* I (1948)].

3. Impressed by the reality of the Incarnation, theologians have attempted at varying intervals to center their work upon the mystery of Christ rather than upon the mystery of God. Hugh of Saint Victor was the first to formulate this position and to adopt it in a structured theology. For a modern version of it, see E. MERSCH, *La théologie du corps mystique,* Bruxelles–Paris, 1944, which one will furthermore notice to be in line with a re-awakening to the Gospel tending in the same direction. Test, therefrom, the scientific and spiritual reaches of the plan of the *Summa,* and of its location of Christology in the *IIIa Pars.* Note, on the other hand, that, without of course denying the presence of Christological elements in the *IIa Pars,* we do not agree with the scruples and apologetics of A. VAN KOOL, *Christus' plaats in S. Thomas moraal-systeem,* in *BB,* I (1947). [The author would no doubt profer a statement in the same vein about H. SCHILLEBEECKX's position according to which the *Summa* would be of *mainly* Christological inspiration (expounded in the Introduction (1–18) of his *De sacramentale heilseconomie. Theologische bezinning op S. Thomas' sacramentenleer in het licht van de traditie en van de hedendaagse sacramentsproblematiek,* Antwerp, 1952). If the latter is right in absolutely refusing to consider the *IIIa Pars* as a simple "appendix to the synthesis which would be substantially finished with the last question of the *IIa Pars,*" on the other hand, "it remains that the subject-matter of theology and the formal object of faith and of the virtues, is God, while 'things pertaining to the humanity of Christ and to the sacraments of the Church, or to any creatures whatsoever, come under faith inasmuch as by them we are ordained to God, and we assent to them moreover on the strength of Divine Truth' *(IIa–IIae,* q. 1, a. 1, ad 1)." A. PATFOORT, in *BT,* VIII (1947–1953), 1161–1162, n. 2198.]

4. Within the perspective the main lines of which we have determinded, the student should turn his attention to observing the original-

ity and the reaches of the articulations of the *Summa*. To give a few
instances:

—the explicit division into two independent treatises dealing with,
respectively, God as One and God as Trinity. However trite their division may appear, it is nonetheless the result of a characteristic choice
made by Latin theology, involving moreover a spiritual journeying
to the God of revelation;

—laden with metaphysics that it may be, the treatise on God as One
has as its object, not the God of the *Physics,* but the God of *Genesis,*
the God of Abraham, of Isaac, and of Jacob, Who will send us Christ.
This religious character should be jealously safeguarded, and pains
taken not to reduce the treatise to one of "deistic" theodicy. See A. R.
MOTTE, *Théodicée et théologie chez S. Thomas,* in *RSPT,* XXVI
(1937), 5–26; E. GILSON, *Haec sublimis veritas,* ch. IV of *The Christian
Philosophy of Saint Thomas Aquinas,* 84–95 [referred to above];

—the question dealing with the "missions" of the Divine Persons (*Ia
Pars,* q. 43) supplying the articulation between the treatise on God
and the theology of being as created and returning to God, between
the life of God and History. Without it being particular to Saint
Thomas, this question is nevertheless a very characteristic one, and
it supplies in excellent manner a framework for a scriptural and
patristic datum;

—the views of *Genesis* on creatures and on the link of man to the
universe, integrated within the plan of the *Ia Pars*—so badly impoverished in the modern treatises *De Deo creante*—which reveals
the constant interplay in it of those views on man and universe;

—the narrative of *Genesis* on first man and his fall, put to work in
three distinct units: *Ia Pars,* q. 94–102: man's pristine state; *Ia–IIae,*
q. 81–83: original sin as the cause of other sins; *IIa–IIae,* q. 163–165:
the sin of first man in itself;

—the locating of the treatise on religion under the moral heading of
justice, with this position being the deciding factor that gives rise to
a special form of spirituality;

—the place given to prophecy in the very broad sense which this word
has in the medieval vocabulary (*IIa–IIae,* q. 171–174);

—the treatise on the states of life (*IIa–IIae,* q. 183–189) wherein
spiritual life is placed in relation with one's social function.

As we were suggesting, there is a whole "biblical theology" (in the
sense stated above, ch. VII) included in the *Summa*. It would be a
worthy and delightful undertaking to go about extracting it, independently of Saint Thomas's commentaries on Scripture, from the
standpoint of the support it supplies to the *Summa's* organized presentation of theological knowledge. The fact can be illustrated and

confirmed by observing how this or that classic commentator, Cajetan for instance, drops entire sections of the *Summa* because they do not supply him with a matter he might conceptualize and systematize. And how great a number of glossators ignore the Sermon on the Mount!

Note that, in the scientific organization of the *Summa,* not every trait can be credited to Saint Thomas's personal design and constructiveness, for it does happen that this or that dossier on Scripture is located at one place or another as a result of the influence of the academic customs of the times and of routine arrangements practiced in the School. An examination of this fact should be made; it would serve to inject worthwhile relief within the monotonous outward appearance of the classification of questions and articles.

Another subject to be examined: how the legitimate and fruit bearing emergence of a new treatise within organized theology (for example, the treatise on the Church) has preserved, strengthened, or thrown off balance the perspective of the *Summa* and the order of values of its plan.

5. As regards the location of this work in the doctrinal life of Saint Thomas, let one always remember that his systematic *Summa* is implanted in and fed with a continuous study of Scripture (not only as a result of his personal devotion, but in accordance with the very institutional aspect of theology), and that its most perfect rational structures are never an end, but a means to arrive at a better knowledge of the Word of God. Therein precisely lies the greatness of any system of theology, as well as its relative character. This does not discredit Saint Thomas's *Summa,* nor scholasticism with its speculative characteristic; rather, it justifies them and locates them within the various activities and products of faith. On this spiritual equilibrium of *doctrina sacra* in the *Summa,* see M. GRABMANN, *Das Immerdauernde in der theologischen Methode des heiligen Thomas,* in *Klerusblatt* (Eichstätt), 1942, 374–377; TH. DEMAN, *Le thomisme comme cadre de pensée,* in *Apôtres d'aujourd'hui,* Paris [1942], 31–50.

Chapter XII

The Opuscules

I. IN GENERAL

Besides his major works, which depended more or less directly upon his university teaching, Saint Thomas left a certain number of less extensive writings the composition of which is connected with occasional circumstances: controversies, consultations, private interventions —all linked, furthermore, with the great problems of the times. Their doctrinal aim is, therefore, ordered by the occasion that provoked them. This is their limitation, but it is also their real source of interest, especially for those who want to keep Saint Thomas's intellectual life in its concrete range. One will know Saint Thomas better by seeing him take part in a controversy, reply to the consultation of a professor and to the requests of a friend or of a Pope, defend a calumniated confrere, sustain the theological and institutional truth of the new apostolic forms, interest himself in the moral problems raised by economic evolution. It is not, moreover, indifferent that he wrote his *Compendium theologiae* expressly for his secretary and friend, Reginald of Piperno.

Very early the disciples of Saint Thomas had the preoccupation of gathering together these minor writings, as bear witness the collections preserved in the manuscripts and printed thereafter in editions as early as the end of the XVth century. Even before the canonization of Saint Thomas (1323), the principal catalog of his works, which Father Mandonnet attributes to Reginald of Piperno and which he calls "official," gave at the top of the list a series of 25 works already then called *opuscula* (1). This series was later to be completed with

---

1) "All the aforementioned are called opuscules." See P. MANDONNET, *Des écrits authentiques de saint Thomas d'Aquin*, 2d rev. ed., Fribourg, 1910, 30. [About the class of works traditionally termed *Opuscula*, see the pertinent re-

authentic works, but it was also contaminated by illegitimate additions. Let us turn over to qualified historians these problems of critique (2). We can present here only a few of the more notable opuscules, each one of which, to be sure, would deserve a particular introduction regarding the circumstances of its redaction as well as its historical and its doctrinal scope. Several of them provide us with elements of information and of thought that the major works had no occasion to present. Here and there also, some expressions, some formulae that are particularly well struck have deserved to pass to posterity even outside of their context (3).

Here is the list of these opuscules, enumerated according to a rather empirical ordering, beginning with those that are of a philosophical character (4). The last ones in the enumeration,

---

marks of I. T. ESCHMANN, in *CSTW*, 381–382, who has abandoned the word, and proposed a new classification based on the literary genre of the works involved. The translators had no choice but to keep the word used in the text they were rendering. The English word "opuscule" has been used throughout, rather than "minor work."]

2) See P. MANDONNET's Introd. to his edition of *Opuscula omnia*, I, Paris, 1927, i–liii (The same study appeared in *RT*, XXXII (1927), 121–157), and M. GRABMANN, *Die Werke des heiligen Thomas von Aquin. Eine literarhistorische Untersuchung und Einführung*, 3d ed., considerably enlarged, in *BGPM*, XXII, 1/2 (1949). For the monographs on particular subjects, considerable in number over the past thirty years, refer to the *BT*. The new edition being prepared (t. I: *Opuscula philosophica* already published at Paris, 1949) by FR. PERRIER offers, together with an extremely improved text, brief notations on each opuscule.

The history of the *Opuscula* collection was done by B. KRUITWAGEN, *S. Thomae de Aquino Summa opusculorum anno circiter 1485 edita, vulgati Opusculorum princeps*, in *BibTh*, IV (1924).

3) This phrase, for example: "No one of the philosophers before the advent of Christ was able, putting all his effort to the task, to know as much about God . . . as a little old woman knows, after the advent of Christ, through her faith." *In symb. Apost.*, prol.; Marietti ed. of the *Opusc. theol.*, II, 193, n. 862. And again, this reflexion in which Saint Thomas expresses his freedom as regards his interpreting of Aristotle: "And I fail to see how the words of the Philosopher are exposited as having anything to do with the doctrine of faith." *Resp. de art.* XLII, a. 33; *ibid.*, I, 217, n. 806.

The theme of the "vetula," which seems to translate one of the deep-rooted feelings of Saint Thomas, recurs in a sermon that he gave in the presence of the University body as the Averroistic crisis was at its peak: "A little old woman of today knows more about things concerning the faith than all the philosophers of old." *Sermo in tertia dominica post festum Apostolorum Petri et Pauli*, Vivès ed., XXXII, 676 A (quoted and commented upon by P. MANDONNET, *Siger de Brabant et l'Averroisme latin au XIIIe siècle*, 2d rev. ed., Part I, in *LPB*, VII (1911), 109).

4) We have left out the commentaries (on Boethius and Dionysius) which, in modern editions, have been included among the *Opuscula*, and recently again in the Lethielleux edition [by Mandonnet], Paris, 1927. [It is most certainly through an oversight that the author has omitted the *De substantiis separatis* the authenticity of which raises no question. The latter opuscule has been re-integrated into his list.]

The editors have all adopted a different order and numbering of the *Opuscula*. A concordance of them has been worked out by H. D. SIMONIN, *Tabulae Opuscu-*

apocryphal according to Mandonnet, are pointed out as accepted by M. Grabmann:

De Principiis naturae [*ad fratrem Sylvestrum.—On the Principles of Nature, to Brother Sylvester.*—Latin ed.: Parma XVI, 338–342; Vivès, XXVII, 480–486; Marietti, *Opusc. philos.,* 1954, 119–128; Perrier, 2–17; J. J. Pauson ed., Introd. and Critical Text, in *TPF,* II (1950). English trans.: R. J. HENLE and V. J. BOURKE, with the Latin text, St. Louis, 1947; R. A. KOCOUREK, *An Introduction to the Philosophy of Nature,* St. Paul (Minn.), 1948.—See *CSTW,* 411].

De ente et essentia [*On Being and Essence*—Latin ed.: Parma, XVI, 350–357; Vivès, XXVII, 468–479; Marietti, *ibid.,* 5–18; Perrier, 24–50; C. Boyer ed., with Introd. and Notes, in *PUGTD,* ser. ph., V (1946); M.-D. ROLAND-GOSSELIN, *Le "De ente et essentia" de S. Thomas d'Aquin. Texte établi d'après les manuscrits parisiens. Introduction, Notes et Études historiques,* in *BibTh,* VIII (1948). English trans.: C. C. REIDL, in *SMCPT,* 1934; A. A. MAURER, with Introd. and Notes, Toronto, 1949; A. H. BACHHUBER, trans. arranged in sense-lines, St. Louis, 1957 (mimeographed).—See *CSTW,* 411].

De occultis operationibus naturae [*ad quendam militem ultramontanum.— On the Hidden Operations of Nature, to a Knight from beyond the Mountains.*—Latin ed.: Parma, XVI, 355–357; Vivès, XXVII, 504–507; Marietti, *ibid.,* 159–162; Perrier, 202–210.—English trans.: J. B. MCALLISTER, *The Letter of Saint Thomas Aquinas* De occultis . . ., in *CUA-PS,* XLII (1939), 20–30.—See *CSTW,* 423].

De mixtione elementorum (5). [*On the Combining of the Elements.*—Latin ed.: Parma, XVI, 353–354; Vivès, XXVII, 502–503; Marietti, *ibid.,* 155–156; Perrier, 18–22. English trans.: V. R. LARKIN, *On the Combining* . . ., trans. and annotated, in *Isis,* LI (1960), 67–72.—See *CSTW,* 420].

De motu cordis [*ad Magistrum Philippum.—On the Movement of the Heart, to Master Philip.*—Latin ed.: Parma, XVI, 358–360; Vivès, XXVII, 508–511; Marietti, *ibid.,* 165–168; Perrier, 62–69. English trans.: V. R. LARKIN, *Thomas Aquinas: On the Heart,* in *JHM,* XV (1960), 22–30.—See *CSTW,* 419].

De unitate intellectus [*contra Averroistas.—On the Unity of the Intellect, against the Averroists.*—Latin ed.: Parma, XVI, 208–224; Vivès, XXVII, 311–335; Marietti, *ibid.,* 63–90; Perrier, 70–120; L. W. Keeler, critical ed. with Introd., in *PUGTD,* ser. ph. XII (1946). English trans.: R. E. BRENNAN, *The Unicity of the Intellect,* St. Louis, 1946.— See *CSTW,* 409].

---

lorum D. Thomae, printed as a supplement in *RT,* XXXV (1930), 8 pages. It is important to always refer to the opuscules by their title, and not by a number alone. [For the reader's convenience, bibliographical data on Latin and English editions have been incorporated into the text, rather than presented in the footnotes as hereinbefore.]

5) [This authentic opuscule was used by a compiler to complete lect. 24 of *In I De gen.* (Marietti ed., Appendix I, 533 B, middle of the column, and all of page 534), the authentic part of this commentary ending with lect. 17 (See Leonine ed., Introd. to the *In De gen.,* III (1886), xxi–xxiv). ESCHMANN writes that the opuscule "almost would seem to be an elaboration" of *Quodl. I,* a. 6, ad 3um. See *CSTW,* 420.]

De aeternitate mundi [*contra murmurantes.—On the Eternity of the World, against the Grumblers.*—Latin ed.: Parma, XVI, 318–320; Vivès, XXVII, 450–453; Marietti, *ibid.*, 105–108; Perrier, 52–61; W. J. Dwyer ed., with critical Introd., Louvain, 1937.—See *CSTW*, 409–410].

[*De substantiis separatis, seu de angelorum natura, ad fratrem Reginaldum, socium suum carissimum.—On Separate Substances, or About the Nature of Angels, to Brother Reginald, his very dear associate.*—Latin ed.: Parma, XVI, 183–207; Vivès, XXVII, 273–310; Marietti, *ibid.*, 21–58; Perrier, 122–201; F. J. LESCOE ed., *Sancti Thomae Aquinatis Tractatus de substantiis separatis.* A newly-established Latin text based on 12 medieval manuscripts, with Introd. and Notes, West Hartford, 1962. English trans. of the same text: *Treatise on Separate Substances,* by the same F. J. LESCOE, West Hartford, 1959.—See *CSTW*, 412].

De regno (De regimine principum) [*ad regem Cypri.—On Kingship (On the government of Princes) to the King of Cyprus.*—Latin ed.: Parma, XVI, 225–291; Vivès, XXVII, 336–412; Marietti, *ibid.*, 257–358; Perrier, 220–426. English trans.: *On Kingship to the King of Cyprus,* by G. B. PHELAN (under the title *On the Governance of Rulers,* in *SMCPT*, 1935), rev. with Introd. and Notes by I. TH. ESCHMANN, Toronto, 1949.—See *CSTW*, 412–415].

De regimine Judaeorum [*ad Ducissam Brabantiae.—On the Government of the Jews, to the Duchess of Brabant.*—Latin ed.: Parma, XVI, 292–294; Vivès, XXVII, 413–416; Marietti, *ibid.*, 249–252; Perrier (*De regimine subditorum*), 212–219.—See *CSTW*, 422].

Compendium theologiae [*ad fratrem Reginaldum socium suum carissimum.—A Compendium of Theology, to Brother Reginald, his very dear associate.*—Latin ed.: Parma, XVI, 1–85; Vivès, XXVII, 1–127; Marietti, *Opusc. theol.*, I, 13–138. English trans.: by L. LYNCH, New York, 1947; also by C. VOLLERT, St. Louis, 1947; Part I, tr. 2, by R. J. DUNN, in *SMCPT*, 1934.—See *CSTW*, 411–412].

Declaratio XXXVI quaestionum ad lectorem Venetum [*Responsio ad lectorem Venetum de articulis XXXVI.—An Answer to the "Reader" at Venice, on XXXVI Articles.*—Latin ed.: Parma, XVI, 169–174; Vivès, XXVII, 256–263; J. Destrez ed., in *Mélanges Mandonnet,* I (*BibTh,* XIII, 1930), 156–161 (text of Letter A), and 162–172 (text of Letter B); Marietti reproduces the two letters, *ibid.*, I, 193–197 and 199–207. Parma and Vivès give only letter B.—See *CSTW*, 420–421, and below, 333ff.].

Declaratio XLII quaestionum ad magistrum Ordinis [*Responsio ad fratrem Joannem Vercellensem, Generalem Magistrum Ordinis Praedicatorum, de articulis XLII.—An Answer to Brother John of Vercelli, Master General of the Order of Preachers, on XLII Articles.*—Latin ed.: Parma, XVI, 163–168; Vivès, XXVII, 248–255; Marietti, *ibid.*, I, 211–218.—See *CSTW*, 416].

Declaratio CVIII dubiorum [*Responsio ad fratrem Joannem Vercellensem, Generalem Magistrum Ordinis Praedicatorum, de articulis CVIII ex opere Petri de Tarentasia.—An Answer to Brother John of Vercelli, Master General of the Order of Preachers, on CVIII Articles extracted from the Work of Peter of Tarentasia.*—Latin ed.: Parma, XVI, 152–162; Vivès, XXVII, 230–247; Marietti, *ibid.*, I, 223–240.—See *CSTW*, 415–416].

Declaratio VI quaestionum ad lectorem Bisuntinum [*Responsio ad lectorem Bisuntinum de articulis VI.—An Answer to the "Reader" at Besançon, on VI Articles.*—Latin ed.: Parma, XVI, 175–176; Vivès, XXVII, 264–265; Marietti, *ibid.*, I, 243–244.—See *CSTW*, 421].

Contra impugnantes Dei cultum et religionem.— [*Against those who attack the Cult and the Religion of God.*—Latin ed.: Parma, XV, 1–75; Vivès, XXIX, 1–116; Marietti, *ibid.*, II, 5–110. English trans.: J. PROCTER, *An Apology for the Religious Orders*, with Introd., London, 1902, 43–373.—See *CSTW*, 407–408.]

De perfectione vitae spiritualis.—[*On the Perfection of the Spiritual Life.*—Latin ed.: Parma, XV, 76–102; Vivès, XXIX, 117–156; Marietti, *ibid.*, II, 115–153. English trans.: J. PROCTER, *The Religious State, the Episcopate, the Priestly Office*, with Prefatory Notice, London, 1902; reprint, Westminster (Md.), 1950.—See *CSTW*, 408–409].

Contra doctrinam retrahentium a religione [*Contra pestiferam doctrinam retrahentium pueros a religionis ingressu.*—*Against the Pestiferous Doctrine of Those Who Would Divert Children from Entering into Religion.*—Latin ed.: Parma, XV, 103–125; Vivès, XXIX, 157–190; Marietti, *ibid.*, II, 159–190. English trans.: J. PROCTER, *An Apology for the Religious Orders*, with Introd., London, 1902, 377–483.—See *CSTW*, 409].

Contra errores Graecorum [*ad Urbanum IV Pontificem Maximum.*—*Against the Errors of the Greeks, to Urban IV, Sovereign Pontiff.*—Latin ed.: Parma, XV, 239–258; Vivès, XXIX, 344–373; Uccelli, 441–486; Marietti, *ibid.*, I, 315–346; P. Glorieux ed., with Notes, References, and Related Documents, in *MCS*, 1957.—See *CSTW*, 415].

De articulis fidei et sacramentis ecclesiae [*ad archiepiscopum Panormitanum.*—*On the Articles of the Faith and the Sacraments of the Church to the Archbishop of Palermo.*—Latin ed.: Parma, XVI, 115–122; Vivès, XXVII, 171–182; Marietti, *ibid.*, I, 141–151. English trans.: Tr. II on the sacraments, by J. B. COLLINS, *Catechetical Instructions of St. Thomas Aquinas*, New York, 1953, 119–131.—See *CSTW*, 417–418].

De rationibus fidei [*contra Saracenos, Graecos et Armenos, ad Cantorem Antiochiae.*—*On the Reasons for the faith against the Saracens, the Greeks, and the Armenians, to the Cantor of Antioch.*—Latin ed.: Parma, XVI, 86–96; Vivès, XXVII, 128–143; Uccelli, 489–508; Marietti, *ibid.*, I, 253–268. English trans. of ch. V: *Why did God the Son Become Man*, by H. NASH, in *LS*, VII (1952), 245–247.—See *CSTW*, 419].

Responsio super materia venditionis [*De emptione et venditione ad tempus.*—*On Temporary Buying and Selling.*—Latin ed.: Parma, XVII, 336–337; Vivès, XXVIII, 465–466; A. O'RAHILLY, *Notes on St. Thomas, III—St. Thomas on Credit*, in *IER*, LXIV (1928), 159–168; Marietti, *ibid.*, I, 185–186. English trans.: O'RAHILLY, *ibid.*—See *CSTW*, 421].

Responsio ad Bernardum abbatem Cassinensem.—[*An Answer to Bernard, Abbot of Monte Cassino.*—Latin ed.: Vivès, XXXII, 834–835; Marietti, *ibid.*, I, 249–250.—See *CSTW*, 418].

De forma absolutionis paenitentiae sacramentalis [*De forma absolutionis, ad Generalem Magistrum Ordinis.*—*On the Form of Absolution, to the Master General of the Order.*—Latin ed.: Parma, XVI, 295–299; Vivès, XXVII, 417–423; P. CASTAGNOLI, *L'Opuscolo "De forma absolutionis" di San Tommaso d'Aquino. Introduzione e Testo critico*, in *DTP*,

XXXVI (1933), 360–416 (Offprint: in *MCA*, XIII, 1933); Marietti, *ibid.*, I, 173–180 (reprint of Castagnoli's critical text).—See *CSTW*, 417].

De sortibus [*ad Dominum Jacobum de . . . (?)* .—*On Sortilege to Sir James . . . (?)* .—Latin ed.: Parma, XVI, 310–316; Vivès, XXVII, 439–448; Marietti, *ibid.*, I, 159–167.—See *CSTW*, 422–423].

In quibus potest homo licite uti judicio astrorum [*De judiciis astrorum, ad quendam militem ultramontanum.*—*On Judgments by the Stars, to a Knight from beyond the Alps.*—Latin ed.: Parma, XVI, 317; Vivès, XXVII, 449; Marietti, *ibid.*, I, 155.—See *CSTW*, 423].

Expositio super primam decretalem. Expositio super secundam decretalem [*Expositio super primam decretalem "De fide catholica et sancta Trinitate" et super secundam "Damnamus autem."*—*An Exposition on the First Decretal "On Catholic Faith and the Holy Trinity" and on the Second "We condemn however."*—Latin ed.: Parma, XVI, 300–306 and 307–309; Vivès, XXVII, 424–433 and 434–438; Marietti, *ibid.*, I, 417–426 and 427–431.—See *CSTW*, 418–419].

Collationes de Credo in Deum [*Devotissima expositio super symbolum apostolorum.*—*An Exposition Most Devout on the Apostle's Creed.*—Latin ed.: Parma, XVI, 135–151; Vivès, XXVII, 203–229; Marietti, *ibid.*, II, 193–217. English trans.: J. B. COLLINS, *Catechetical Instructions of Saint Thomas Aquinas*, New York, 1953, 3–66. L. SHAPCOTE, *The Three Greatest Prayers: Commentaries on the Our Father, the Hail Mary, and the Apostle's Creed*, with Introd. by T. GILBY, Westminster (Md.), 1956, 39–89.—See *CSTW*, 425–426].

Collations de Pater noster [*Expositio devotissima orationis dominicae.*—*An Exposition Most Debout on the Lord's Prayer.*—Latin ed.: Parma, XVI, 123–132; Vivès, XXVII, 183–198; Marietti, *ibid.*, II, 221–235. English trans.: J. B. COLLINS, *ibid.*, 135–170; W. K. FIRMINGER, with Introd. and Notes, London, 1927; L. SHAPCOTE, *ibid.*, 1–29.—See *CSTW*, 425–426].

Collationes de Ave Maria [*Devotissima expositio super salutatione angelica.* —*An Exposition Most Devout on the Angelic Salutation.*—Latin ed.: Parma, XVI, 133–134; Vivès, XXVII, 199–202; J. F. ROSSI, *S. Thomae Aquinatis Expositio Salutationis Angelicae. Introductio et textus*, in *DTP*, XXXIV (1931), 445–479 (Offprint: *MCA*, XI, 1931); Marietti, *ibid.*, II, 239–241. English trans.; L. SHAPCOTE, *ibid.*, 30–38; J. B. COLLINS, *ibid.*, 173–180; L. EVERY, *Explanation of the Hail Mary*, in *Dom.* XXXIX (1954), 31–38.—See *CSTW*, 426].

Collationes de decem praeceptis [*De duobus praeceptis caritatis et decem legis praeceptis.*—*On the Two Precepts of Charity, and On the Ten Precepts of the Law.*—Latin ed.: Parma, XVI, 97–114: Vivès, XXVII, 144–170; Marietti, *ibid.*, II, 245–271. English trans.: L. SHAPCOTE, *The Commandments of God; Conferences on the Two Precepts of Charity and the Ten Commandments*, with Introd. by T. Gilby, London, 1937.—J. B. COLLINS, *ibid.*, 69–116.—See *CSTW*, 425–426].

Officium corporis Christi [*Officium de festo Corporis Christi, ad mandatum Urbani Papae IV.*—*Office of the Feast of the Body of Christ, on the Mandate of Pope Urban IV.*—Latin ed.: Parma, XV, 233–238; Vivès, XXIX, 335–343; Marietti, *ibid.*, II, 275–281.—See *CSTW*, 424].

Sermo de festo corporis Christi [*Sermo de Eucharistia in Coena Domini, in consistorio coram Papa Urbano et Cardinalibus.*—*Sermon on the*

The Opuscules

Eucharist Preached on Holy Thursday in the Presence of Pope Urban and of the Cardinals.—Latin ed.: Parma, XXIV, 230–231; Vivès, XXXII, 680–682.—See *CSTW*, 427, n. 83].

Duo principia de commendatione sacrae scripturae [*De commendatione et partitione sacrae scripturae; De commendatione sacrae scripturae.*— *Two Inaugural Sermons on the Commendation of Sacred Scripture: On the Commendation and Division of Sacred Scripture; On the Commendation of Sacred Scripture.*—Latin ed.: F. SALVATORE, *Due sermoni inediti di S. Tommaso d'Aquino*, Rome, 1912; Marietti, *ibid.*, I, 435– 439 and 443.—See *CSTW*, 428, n. 87; also above, ch. VII, 243] (a).

De secreto [*On Secrecy.*—Latin ed.: Parma, XXIV, 235–236; Vivès, XXXII, 816–818; Marietti, *ibid.*, I, 447–448.—See *CSTW*, 417].

De propositionibus modalibus (very probable).—[*On Modal Propositions.*— Latin ed.: Parma, XVI, 388–389; Vivès, XXVII, 549–550; Perrier, 461–464; Marietti, in *Opusc. philos.*, 243–245; I. M. BOCHENSKI, *De modalibus opusculum et doctrina*, in *Ang*, XVII (1940), 180–218 (Offprint: Rome, 1945).—See *CSTW*, 410–411.]

De fallaciis (very probable).—[*ad quosdam nobiles artistas.*—*On Fallacies, to Some Faculty of Arts Noblemen.*—Latin ed.: Parma, XVI, 377– 387; Vivès, XXVII, 533–548; Perrier, 430–460; Marietti, *ibid.*, 225– 240.—See *CSTW*, 410.]

Epistola de modo studendi (probable).—[*Letter on How to Study.*—Latin ed.: Parma, XVII, 338; Vivès, XXVIII, 467; Marietti, in *Opusc. theol.*, I, 451. English trans.: V. WHITE, *How to Study. De modo studendi.* Latin text with transl. and exposition. 6th ed., London, 1956.—See *CSTW*, 421.]

Piae preces (probable).—[*Devout Prayers.*—Latin ed.; Parma, XXIV, 241–244; Vivès, XXXII, 819–823; Marietti, *ibid.*, 285–289.—See *CSTW*, 424–425.]

De differentia verbi divini et humani (Grabmann) (6).—[*On the difference Between the Divine and the Human Word.*—Latin ed.: Parma, XVI, 177–178; Vivès, XXVII, 266–267; Perrier, 587–590; Marietti, in *Opusc. philos.*, 101–102.—See *CSTW*, 430.]

De demonstratione (Grabmann).—[*On Demonstration.*—Latin ed.: Parma, XVI, 375–376; Vivès, XXVII, 531–532; Perrier, 465–467; Marietti, *ibid.*, 221–222.—See *CSTW*, 430.]

De instantibus (Grabmann).—[*On the Instant.*—Latin ed.: Parma, XVI, 361–366; Vivès, XXVII, 512–519; Perrier, 591–605; Marietti, *ibid.*, 111–118.—See *CSTW*, 428–430.]

De natura verbi intellectus (Grabmann).—[*On the Nature of the Intellect's Word.*—Latin ed.: Parma, XVI, 179–182; Vivès, XXVII, 268– 272; Perrier, 578–586; Marietti, *ibid.*, 93–97.—See *CSTW*, 428–430.]

---

a) There is, in addition to those mentioned above, a long list of sermons attributed to Saint Thomas, and edited in Parma, XV, 126–232 and Vivès, XXIX, 191–334. A great amount of work remains to be done concerning their authenticity and critical editing. For a state of the question at this time, see I. T. ESCHMANN, *CSTW*, 425–428. For an English version of a number of them, see C. J. CALLAN, *Sermon Matter from St. Thomas Aquinas on the Epistles and Gospels of the Sundays and Feast Days*, St. Louis-London, 1950.

6) This opuscule [Marietti ed. of the *Opusc. philos.*, 101–102] is a simple extract taken from the prologue of the commentary on the Gospel of Saint John [Marietti ed., 7–9, nn. 24–29].

De principio individuationis (Grabmann).—[*On the Principle of Individua-tion.*—Latin ed.: Parma, XVI, 328–329; Vivès, XXVII, 465–467; Per-rier, 573–577; Marietti, *ibid.*, 149–151.—See *CSTW*, 428–430.]

De natura generis (Grabmann).—[*On the Nature of Genus.*—Latin ed.: Parma, XVII, 8–26; Vivès, XXVIII, 5–30; Perrier, 495–545; Marietti, *ibid.*, 177–204.—See *CSTW*, 428–430.]

De natura accidentis (Grabmann).—[*On the Nature of Accident.*—Latin ed.: Parma, XVII, 5–7; Vivès, XXVIII, 1–4; Perrier, 489–494; Marietti, *ibid.*, 171–174.—See *CSTW*, 428–430.]

De natura materiae (Grabmann).—[*On the Nature of Matter.*—Latin ed.: Parma, XVI, 343–352; Vivès, XXVII, 487–501; Perrier, 546–572; Marietti, *ibid.*, 131–145; J. M. WYSS, *De natura materiae Attributed to St. Thomas Aquinas.* Introd. and Text according to the tradition of the manuscripts, in *TPF*, III (1953).—See *CSTW*, 428–430.]

De quattuor oppositis (Grabmann).—[*On the Four Opposites.*—Latin ed.: Parma, XVI, 367–374; Vivès, XXVII, 520–530; Perrier, 468–488; Marietti, *ibid.*, 207–217.—See *CSTW*, 428–430 (a)].

II. THE *DE ENTE ET ESSENTIA*

The *De ente et essentia* is the most famous of the opuscules and no doubt the only one effectively studied. This is because it presents something of a breviary on the metaphysics of being. Whether for the understanding of the thought of Saint Thomas, or for its elabora-tion in the service of problems periodically restudied in the course of history on the great theme of existence, these brief and concise pages offer precious resources. In fact, the work still provokes editions and commentaries, both of historians as well as of philosophers.

It is probably (7) the first writing to have come from the pen of Saint Thomas. He drafted it while still a young professor teaching the *Sentences* (1254–1256), and probably even before he began his com-mentary upon the IInd book. He dedicated it *ad fratres socios* [to his friar associates], probably his companions who, having come to Saint James for advanced studies, were following his teaching and had asked him to supply them with an analysis of the fundamental notions of philosophy, the novelty of which had taken them unawares. Perhaps Saint Thomas took this occasion to provide himself with more precision in his own philosophical vocabulary, because the treatise contains a number of definitions and explanations of terms. These details immediately encamp the work at the level of history and of doctrine.

Rarely, as a matter of fact, has the evolution of the language of metaphysics and of the concepts underlying it been swept around in such a crisscrossing of mentalities, intuitions, logical analyses, and

---

a) See the Research Suggestions below, 345.

7) The *De Principiis naturae* may have been written before, but during the same period.

suddenly-appearing historical contributions. The problem was one of determining what, in any reality, in particular in material substances, are the characteristics of essence, and then within these diverse realities (whether substantial or accidental) what, in relation to essence, the logical concepts of genus, species, and difference with the help of which we build a definition whose object precisely is essence signify. As a result, the maze of issues clings to the problems of individuation and of existence, together rebellious to definition which is universal. Material substances, beginning with the more knowable, cannot be defined outside of matter (Aristotle), which is essential to them, yet which individualizes them (Avicenna), unless primacy is given to form (Averroes). Immaterial substances, in order to be varied, must be composed, and it becomes necessary to introduce into their essence a certain spiritual matter that is without quantity (Latin theology, Avicebron), or to transpose, at the price of another distortion of words, the classical composition of *quo est* and *quod est* (Boethius) into a real composition of essence and existence. Aristotle's system seems closed to this introduction of contingency within the being of the universe; but, under the pressure of his belief in a creating God, Avicenna imposes it, to the point where existence and essence are no more than juxtaposed. Albert the Great, after William of Auvergne, enters into this path of a real composition of the creature, above and beyond hylomorphic dualism, but his position is influenced by the equivocations of the current vocabulary as well as by the variations of research. Saint Thomas fixes vocabulary and positions of problems. Against the positions of the neo-Platonists, he defends, as a good Aristotelian, the existence of "acts" that are without matter. The immateriality of the spiritual substances (against Avicebron), without this being the object of his opuscule, thus becomes the pivotal point of his elaboration and the immediate preoccupation in the sifting of the Arabic philosophies.

Saint Thomas brings equilibrium to his epistemology in conformity with that metaphysical analysis. He analyses, in the sense of Aristotle's rational empiricism, the relationship of our logical concepts to the various essences. Genus, species, differences, are universal attributes, and it is intelligence that makes the universal (Averroes), but the universality of ideas does not impose the unicity of the intellect (against Averroes). Each man has his own intelligence. Universality is based upon the resemblance of essence, conceived by an individual mind, to the essence realized or capable of being realized in multiple individual subjects. An intellectualism of this sort is not, as regards classification and definition, without limit or relativism. Of spiritual substances, we know neither the genus, not the difference, nor the proper accidents; of material substances, we ignore the essential differences and can name them only by their effects, that is, by means of their accidental differences. Accidents themselves are not always manifest in their proper principles, and then we name them only by their effects (a). The later works of Saint Thomas will fill out, by means of psychological analyses, the statements that are here concentrated around the laws of definition.

If we have brought to notice the sources and currents that are at work underneath the text of the *De ente et essentia*, it is not from an exaggerated taste for erudition; it is because they allow us to demarcate the intrinsic position of Saint Thomas, who, from the very start of his teaching career, revealed himself only—having left us no revelations about himself—in an objective dialogue with his colleagues (b).

III. THE *COMPENDIUM THEOLOGIAE*

The *Compendium Theologiae* offers itself to us as a summary abridgment of Christian doctrine. It is organized around the three master virtues: faith, hope, and charity. In point of fact, it was interrupted at the beginning of the treatise on hope, and 245 chapters out of 255 are devoted to the contents of faith according to the train of thought of the Creed.

It is not only by its extent that the *Compendium,* the broadest of the opuscules in dimension and in object, has aroused interest, but also by its chronological position. Presenting a number of the dogmatic problems of theology, it furnishes constant reference-points for a comparison with the *Summa theologiae* and thus affords the opportunity of following the successive steps, if not the variants, in the thinking of Saint Thomas. Father Mandonnet placed the redaction of it at the end of the life of Saint Thomas, probably because it was not completed. It is certain that, despite this indication, the *Compendium* must be placed before the composition of the *Summa,* probably around 1265–67 at Rome when Reginald of Piperno, to whom it was dedicated, had been for some time fulfilling the functions of secretary to the Master. It is therefore under these conditions that one should use the parallel passages of this opuscule, not so much, to be sure, concerning its details, which are summary in such an abridgment, as for the general construction and the—so important— arrangement of problems and arguments (8). From this standpoint it was fitting to present it here.

a) See ch. 5; Roland-Gosselin ed., 40; Marietti ed. of the *Opusc. philos.*, 15, n. 31.
b) See the Research Suggestions below, 346.
8) Note, in particular, that Saint Thomas had the *Summa contra Gentiles* under his eyes when he wrote out his *Compendium.* See A. R. MOTTE, *Un chapitre inauthentique* [I, 5] *dans le* Compendium *de S. Thomas,* in RT, XLV (1939),

IV. FIVE DOCTRINAL CONSULTATIONS

Thanks to the perspicacity of J. Destrez and of Father Mandonnet (9), the dossier of a controversy has been reconstructed. Relatively large, the controversy centered around cosmogonic themes that had developed in the Dominican philosophical and theological schools of Lombardy. Under the title *Declarationes* of 36 and 42 questions (a), two opuscules have preserved for us, outside its context, the main documents about it. A professor of the Convent of Venice, a certain Brother Bassiano from Lodi, had sent to Saint Thomas, then in Paris, a series of questions which in his surroundings were being discussed no doubt in a rather lively manner, since at that same time John of Vercelli, Master-General of the Friar Preachers then visiting Lombardy, was independently gathering a list of 42 propositions of the same calibre, many of them expressed in the same formulation as those of the lector at Venice. In the meantime moreover, the latter had addressed to Saint Thomas another consultation complementary to the first. The episode must be placed about the month of March, 1271, since Saint Thomas replied to the Master-General by return courrier on April 2 (Holy Thursday), every other duty then coming to a stop. The affair was to have its conclusion at the General Chapter of Montpellier (Pentecost, 1271), further enlarged, it seems, by the intervention of Kilwardby who was present at the Chapter (as were Albert the Great and Peter of Tarentasia) by reason of his being Provincial of England. He produced a long memoir on the same 42 questions asked of Saint Thomas by John of Vercelli (10). Thus, we have five documents by means of which the train of the intellectual life of the times is revealed:

a first redaction of the reply to the lector of Venice;
a second redaction, more organic, to the same;

749–753. [On the question of the dating of the *Compendium*, see R. GUINDON, *Béatitude et théologie morale chez saint Thomas d'Aquin. Origines-Interprétation*, Ottawa, 1956, 144 ff., and *A propos de la chronologie du* Compendium theologiae *de saint Thomas d'Aquin*, in *RUO*, XXVI (1926), 193*–214*. See *BT*, X (1957–1959), 77–78.]

9) See J. DESTREZ, *La lettre de S. Thomas d'Aquin dite lettre au lecteur de Venise, d'après la tradition manuscrite*, in *Mélanges Mandonnet*, I (*BibTh*, XIII, 1930), 103–189, and P. MANDONNET's review of this article in *BT*, III (1930), 129–139.

a) See the complete titles above, 326.

10) See M.-D. CHENU, *Les réponses de S. Thomas et de Kilwardby à la consultation de Jean de Verceil (1271)*, in *Mélanges Mandonnet*, I (*BibTh*, XIII, 1930), 191–222. [A recent discovery has brought to light the fact that Albert the Great was also consulted in this affair. See D. A. CALLUS, *Une oeuvre récemment découverte de S. Albert le Grand: De XLIII problematibus ad Magistrum Ordinis (1271)*, in *RSPT*, XLIV (1960), 243–261. A. WEISHEIPL has edited the text in *MSt*, XXII (1960), 303–354.]

some *"articuli iterum remissi"* [articles sent back a second time] (11);
the reply of Saint Thomas to John of Vercelli;
the memoir of Robert Kilwardby (12).

The controversy revolved (for some thirty questions) around the problem of the role of the heavenly bodies in the ordering of the world, at the point of juncture of the speculations of the physicists and of a certain Christian theology on the angels, which was then bound up with the theories on cosmogony. We find ourselves, therefore, facing a rather disconcerting mixture of theological views, metaphysical principles, scientific theories, celestial physics, even astrology that resulted here and there in bizarre oddities and childish questions (q. 37, 38 or 36, 37 in the editions). We have here a characteristic panorama of the inquisitiveness shown by the run of clerics in the schools. Under this apparatus, however, it is very explicitly a question of a "system of the world," as Duhem put it. Seeing the great divergences between two celebrities of the time, Thomas Aquinas and Kilwardby, one measures the swirl of the currents of thought through which Christendom was passing—a thought excited by the mechanical theories of Aristotle and of his Arabic interpreters, caught up between a lively inquisitiveness in experimental subjects and a purer type of metaphysical research, swaying between an ever seductive concordism and the freedom of faith in the face of scientific theories.

It will be observed that Kilwardby, who seems, moreover, to have let fly a few sharp words against Thomas Aquinas, treats at length of the problems in themselves within a celestial mechanical theory already quite "modern" (13), while Saint Thomas, in accordance with the directives of the one consulting him, contents himself with determining the theses from a Christian point of view. With insistence, in his long prologue and in the course of his examination, he proclaims the independence of faith, and therefore, with the freedom of one who knows, the necessary discretion a theologian should maintain in the domains of philosophy and physics. "And I fail to see how the

---

11) These are 8 articles discovered by Uccelli in a Parisian manuscript in which they were given the said title. They were edited in Vivès, XXXII (1879), 832–833. They do not represent the articles sent by the consultants, but rather the answers of Saint Thomas to the second group of questions (five on the Eucharist) sent from Venice. They are, consequently, a part of the second writing addressed to the lector of Venice, from which they were extracted and transcribed under the said title. See J. DESTREZ, *loc. cit.*

12) The memoir was partially edited by M.-D. CHENU, *loc. cit.*, 193–211.

13) See M.-D. CHENU, *Aux origines de la "science moderne,"* in RSPT, XXIX (1940), 206–217.

Philosopher's words are exposed has something to do with faith" (a).
Were it only for remarks such as these, the dossier of the Lombardian
controversy would be worthy of interest, but it clarifies besides the
conception that Saint Thomas had of the universe and of the
hierarchic implication of its various orders and causalities.

A similar consultation has provided us with another *Declaratio*. The
same John of Vercelli, Master-General of the Preachers, had received
(between 1264 and 1267) a long syllabus of 108 propositions, extracted from the *Commentary on the Sentences* of Peter of Tarentasia,
then Master of the College of Saint James at Paris, and reputedly
worthy of condemnation by his denouncer. John of Vercelli sent them
to Saint Thomas so that he might give his opinion and judgment (14).
The propositions cover the doctrinal grounds of the first book of the
Sentences (90 texts) and the first three distinctions of the second
book (18 texts). Saint Thomas is severe for the denouncer, certain
of whose incriminations go as far as calumny. Certain formulae of
Peter of Tarentasia would call for precisions and distinctions, but a
minimum of good will would give them an acceptable meaning. Here
is another witness of the backwash of a doctrinal evolution that provoked manifestations of bad humor, but also of the serenity of Saint
Thomas who therein gives us a lesson in the sympathetic understanding of truth.

It seems that the controversy was not without a sequence. It remains
uncertain whether Peter of Tarentasia recast the text of his work. *De
facto*, it was that text which was officially adopted by the bookdealers
of the University of Paris (15). In any case, he did not suffer from
this attack, since he was to become Provincial of France, Archbishop
of Lyons, Cardinal, and finally Pope in 1276. However, it was after
this controversy that Saint Thomas, censured through Peter of Tarentasia, held, about 1266 in Rome, the important disputed question on
the divine attributes (the entire problem of our knowledge of God)
that was to be inserted in his *Commentary on the Sentences (I Sent.,
d. 2, q. 1, a. 3) (16)*.

---

a) "Nec video quid pertineat ad doctrinam fidei, qualiter Philosophi verba
exponantur." *Resp. de art. XLII*, a. 33; Marietti ed. of the *Opusc. theol.*, I, 217,
n. 806.

14) See P. MANDONNET, *Des écrits authentiques de saint Thomas d'Aquin*, 2d
rev. ed., Fribourg, 1910, 123–127.

15) DOM LOTTIN has presented alluring arguments in favor of a revision. See
Pierre de Tarentaise a-t-il remanié son commentaire sur les Sentences? in *RTAM*,
II (1930), 420–433. Their value has been considerably reduced, however, by
H. D. SIMONIN's observations. See *Les écrits de Pierre de Tarentaise*, in *BIQ-SD*,
1943, 196–206.

16) See A. DONDAINE, *S. Thomas et la dispute des attributs divins (In I Sent.,
d. 2, q. 1, a. 3). Authenticité et origine*, in *AFP*, VIII (1938), 253–262.

Since we are on the subject of the *Declarationes,* let us mention his reply to the consultation of a certain good Brother Gerard, from Besançon. The latter had posed to his famous confrere six questions of a shallow naïveté (all except the last). Saint Thomas answers these questions with patience, but not without severity against too much complacency inspired by a misplaced piousness. ". . . this is spurned with the same facility as it is said" (a).

V. THE *DE REGNO (DE REGIMINE PRINCIPUM)*

The very pronounced interest recently shown in the history of the political doctrines of the Middle Ages, has drawn attention to the opuscule called *De regno* (or *De regimine principum*), thanks to which Saint Thomas holds a high place in the rich medieval litterature "Concerning the Government of Princes." Numerous translations bear witness to this renewal of interest (17).

The occasion that led Saint Thomas to compose his work determined also the orientation of it, if not in its substance at least in the insistence of certain statements that, in a complex and contingent doctrine such as political philosophy, sometimes noticeably shifts the equilibrium and the accent of a work. It is necessary to note this in order not to be surprised at the variants observed between the thought expressed in this treatise, although one written *ex professo,* and the elements of political theory contained in his other works which the dedication to a reigning sovereign did not instigate.

The opuscule was addressed, as a matter of fact, in 1266, to the King of Cyprus, Hugh II, who was then placed in delicate circumstances.

We are poorly informed about the political situation in this country in 1266. We know, on the one hand, that, in 1233, in order to juridically legalize a revolt against their head lord, the Cypriotes adopted the legislation of the Kingdom of Jerusalem. But this legislation obliged the princes never to take any measure without the authorization of the liegemen. It was in the interest of the liegemen to refuse any public service, and the state dissolved. We know, on the other hand, that in 1286, the kings of Cyprus had succeeded in establishing an absolute monarchy which was very beneficial. It is difficult to know what the situation was, in 1266, but it seems that the island was then in a complete state of anarchy and that a rein-

a) ". . . eadem facilitate contemnitur qua dicitur." *Resp. de art. VI,* q. 5; Marietti ed. of the *Opusc. theol.,* I, 244, n. 939.

17) Let us bring to notice, in particular C. ROGUET's French trans., *Saint Thomas d'Aquin. Du gouvernement royal,* pref. by C. JOURNET, new ed. [greatly rev.], Paris, 1931; G. PHELAN's English trans., with an excellent introd. by I. T. ESCHMANN, Toronto, 1949; A. MEOZZI's Italian trans., together with his long historico-doctrinal introd., Lauciano, 1924; the old XIVth Castilian trans., re-edited by F. GETINO, Valencia, 1931; L. VAN ACKER's Portuguese trans., Sâo Paulo, 1937.

forcement of the royal authority appeared indispensable. In 1264, in fact, Urban IV had written to Hugh of Lusignan, regent of Cyprus (and overseer for Hugh II, to whom the *De regimine* was going to be dedicated two years later), to invite him, in the interest of the public good, to arrest a certain excommunicated knight and to chastise the Greeks, in spite of the opposition of the liegemen and in spite of his oath to observe the Jerusalem constitution.

If, in 1266, the liegemen appeared in Cyprus as championing anarchy and the king as the only possible defender of the public order, one can explain why, in the *De regimine principum,* Saint Thomas did not express his preference for a mixed government and recommended a pure monarchy (18).

Saint Thomas announces that he will feed his exposition on three sources: Christian doctrine, philosophical thought, and the experience of history.

It is certain that the opuscule was not brought to completion by its author. Tolomeo of Lucca, a disciple and admirer of Saint Thomas, finished it beginning with book II, chapter 5. But Tolomeo, engaged in theocratic speculations and doctrinal contexts that were different, gave to this second part of the work an inspiration and conclusion altogether different from the master's, particularly on the relationship between the temporal power and the spiritual regulation of it (19). It has even been supposed, on the basis of a few indications, that the authentic part of the work underwent some manipulation by the one who continued the work (20).

VI. THE *DE UNITATE INTELLECTUS.* THE *DE AETERNITATE MUNDI*

Here we have Saint Thomas the controversialist. All his works, to be sure, certainly involve controversial elements that were embedded in the very course of his teaching. Yet, concerning the most animated controversies that arose, direct interventions, in another style, imposed themselves.

Two treatises were instigated by the major crisis in Aristotelianism, provoked by the pressure of the Averroistic interpretation. The seriousness and the episodes of it are known. These two opuscules are situated at the paroxysm of the conflict which, at the University of Paris, was intensified by the intervention of Siger of Brabant and his followers. The *De unitate intellectus* (1270) attacks one of the

---

18) We are here quoting a résumé, done by the author himself, of a paper M. GRANDCLAUDE presented at the "Journées d'histoire du droit," at Paris, in 1929, *Les particularités du* De regimine principum *de S. Thomas,* in *RHD*, 1929, 665–666.

19) See J. RIVIÈRE's article, *Lucques (Barthélémy de),* in *DTC,* IX (1926), col. 1062–1067.

20) See M. BROWNE, *An sit authenticum opusculum S. Thomae "De regimine principum",* in *Ang,* III (1926), 300–303. C. ROGUET, *op. cit.,* argues this point.

major theses, and the most ruinous from the Christian standpoint, of Averroism, that one which denied the personal character of man's mind. The retort of Saint Thomas is "the pivotal point of the Averroistic controversy in the XIIIth century" (van Steenberghen). But it is evident that it can be read intelligently only if replaced within the succession of the other writings and interventions of Saint Thomas, particularly the disputed questions *De spiritualibus creaturis* and *De anima* (1268–1269), and of course, in the context of the writings of his adversaries, within also the perspective of the impending condemnation of December, 1270. The appeal of Giles of Lessines to Albert the Great and the reply of the old master, the quodlibetal disputations, the university sermon given by Saint Thomas in a surprisingly violent oratorical tone (probably in July, 1270) (21), reveal the heatedness of the conflict.

Taking account of the doctrinal evolution of Siger of Brabant who was tossed from a provocative Averroism to a more objective Aristotelianism, it should be noted that the *De unitate intellectus* of Saint Thomas is undoubtedly not a reply to the *De anima intellectiva* of Siger, as Father Mandonnet had thought, but that, on the contrary, Siger's *De anima* is an answer to the intervention of Saint Thomas (22).

The De *aeternitate mundi* (1270 or 1271) faced adversaries of an opposite kind, the so-called Augustinian theologians. The latter were attached, as were the Fathers, to the doctrine of a creation in time in which, as against the pagan philosophers (23), they saw the decisive

21) One should not fail to read that sermon, published in Vivès, XXXII (1879), 676. P. Mandonnet quotes it and comments upon it, in *Siger de Brabant et l'Averroisme latin au XIIIe siècle*, 2d rev. ed., Part I, in *LPB*, VII (1911), 109.

22) See J. VAN STEENBERGEN, *Les oeuvres et la doctrine de Siger de Brabant*, Brussels, 1938, summarized in *Siger de Brabant*, t. II: *Siger dans l'histoire de l'aristotélisme*, in *LPB*, XIII (1942), 552–560. [IDEM, *Aristotle in the West. The Origins of Latin Aristotelianism*, trans. from the French by L. JOHNSTON, Louvain 1955, 198–235. The role played by Boethius of Dacia in the Averroistic crisis is becoming clearer as new research goes on. See IDEM, *Nouvelles recherches sur Siger de Brabant et son école*, in *RPL*, LIV (1956), 130–147, and G. SAJÓ, *Boèce de Dacie et les commentaires anonymes inédits de Munich sur la physique et sur la génération attribués à Siger de Brabant*, in *AHDLMA*, XXV (1958), 21–58; see also the latter's *Un traité récemment découvert de Boèce de Dacie "De aeternitate mundi". Texte inédit avec une introduction critique*, Budapest, 1954; A. MAURER's *Boetius of Dacia and the Double Truth*, in *MSt*, XVII (1955), 233–239; and E. GILSON's *Boèce de Dacie et la double vérité*, in *AHDLMA*, XXII (1955), 81–99.]

23) SAINT BONAVENTURE has given an admirable formulation—from his point of view—of the coherence there is in the chain of Aristotelico-Averroistic errors, of which the eternity of the world is a cog. See *Collationes in Hexamaeron*, coll. 6, in *BOO*, V (1891), 360–361. Aristotle's thesis is presented in SIGER'S *De aeternitate mundi* (See P. MANDONNET, *Siger de Brabant et l'Averroisme*

and necessary criterion of a Christian conception of the universe and of a faith in a provident God. Right here we reach the most advanced point of Saint Thomas's metaphysical analysis in which he empties the relation of creature to Creator, not only "of all imagery, but of all "historical" connotation. Time and movement, to be sure, render the state of the creature tangible, but contingency is inscribed within the creature in a much deeper way than these temporal instabilities. The fundamental problem is not that of the phenomena of nature; it is that of being (24). The condemnation of 1270 was to bring out the indissoluble bonds which the conservative theologians claimed to establish among these damnable propositions: the world is eternal, God knows nothing outside of Himself, God does not know singulars, human actions are not subject to divine providence (25). They, to be sure, were reaching the fundamental theories of the Averroistic interpretation of Aristotle; but in their condemning minds, they were also reaching Aristotle, not only in his explicit conclusions, but in the very soul of his system.

It is on this point that Saint Thomas stood up against those *murmurantes* [grumblers] (this is the "rider" added to the title in certain manuscripts), not that he might give his allegiance to Aristotle as to the master of thought in the manner of the Averroists, but in order to preserve at the same time the absoluteness of the faith and freedom of research, given this problem of the possibility of a creation *ab aeterno*. But the integralistic attitude of his adversaries refused a distinction of any kind, one which was certainly called for by the ambiguity in Aristotle's position. Supported by the masters of the faculty of arts, Saint Thomas was compromised by them. "Because of the gravity of the interests involved . . . the polemic of Saint Thomas takes on a character of violence which is not found in his theological disputations, except perhaps in the writings intended for the defense of the rights of the religious against the attacks of William of Saint Amour and of his followers" (26). Now, let us read the *De unitate intellectus* and the *De aeternitate mundi*.

On this matter of Saint Thomas the polemicist: it is certain that the voluntarily impersonal character of these expositions masks the liveliness of his imperturbable mind. It is not just a matter for us to collect the heated utterances that, here and there both in his public

---

latin au XIIe siècle, 2d rev. ed., Part II, in *LPB*, VI (1908), 131–142, and W. J. Dwyer, *L'opuscule de Siger de Brabant "De aeternitate mundi." Introduction critique et texte*, Louvain, 1937), and in the *De necessitate et contingentia causarum* (See P. MANDONNET, *ibid.*, 111–128).

24) See A. D. SERTILLANGES, *L'idée de création et ses retentissements en philosophie*, Paris, 1945, ch. I and II.

25) See *ChUP*, I, 486–487, n. 432.

26) P. MANDONNET, *op. cit.*, Part I, in *LPB*, VII (1911), 108.

addresses and in his academic writings, bring us closer to the humanness of the Angelic Doctor; it is a matter of discovering the fundamental attitude that reveals itself in this animation, wherein the manner of positing the problem of the highest truths renders one receptive to any thought, to even an adverse thought, without weakening the mind.

In any case, the treatise of Saint Thomas as well as that of Siger, an adversary of his own stature, remain, over and beyond their antiquated details, two fine specimens of the inheritance of Christian philosophy, "perhaps the best and the most complete expression of what the philosophical mind of the thirteenth century has produced" (27) (a).

VII. THE DEFENSE OF THE NEW RELIGIOUS LIFE

The same heated utterances, the same breadth of doctrine, occur in three other opuscules giving us another example in another domain in which the personal life and vocation of Saint Thomas were involved.

If the essential elements of Christian doctrine were put in question by the discovery of Greek thought, the institutional framework of the Church was also subjected to grave problems posed by the evolution of the human society in which the Church was implanted. We have brought to attention what degree of effervescence had been provoked in Christendom by the evangelical upsurge of which Saint Francis and Saint Dominic, after Peter Valdo and a few others, had been the heralds (b). This spiritual upsurge that the strange forebodings of Joachim of Fiore and economic circumstances had favored—at the two extremes of the aspirations of the times—had ended up in a profound recasting of the apostolic framework of the established Church and brought about the foundation of new forms of religious life that created new methods of Christian perfection and of being present to the world. The Mendicant Orders offered, as opposed to the old *ordo monasticus* [monastic order], profound innovation that showed up from one end to the other of the Christian way of life (and not only in juridical variants were they seasoned with the customary jealousies). The lively reaction of the "conservatives" could not help making itself known, bearing witness by the same token to the efficacy of the new religious state as much at the level of thought as of institutions. Therein lies the proportion of the controversies—nauseating ones in the bargain—which unfolded at the time.

As regards Saint Thomas, the controversies came about in two stages: during the first, around 1256, the very existence of the new

---

27) P. MANDONNET, *ibid.* 175.
a) See the Research Suggestions below, 346–347.
b) See ch. I, 44ff. and ch. VII, 234ff.

religious state was in question; during the second, around 1270, two more particular problems came up: that of the respective perfection of pastors and religious, whose relationship was modified in its structure by the new form of apostolate; and that of the place of the evangelical counsels in relation to the common precepts.

It was William of Saint Amour, master at the University of Paris, who launched the attack "against the perils of the new times" (28), understand here, those new apostles whom apocalyptic statements portended. He was thus giving voice to the opposition that the secular members of the teaching body had been carrying on for a few years (1253–1256) against the incorporation of these religious into the college of the University masters. The problem had its immediacy and, to be sure, its importance. The perspicacious William, going more deeply, however, transferred it to the question of the very status of these new religious in Christendom. And this is the way that Saint Thomas understood the situation (29). In final analysis, beneath the rivalries of the two bodies and the conflict of their interests lay a paradoxical phenomenon, one which is periodical in the Church, and upsetting in former days as well as today, for the established frameworks: the more the new teams are freed, spiritually and evangelically speaking, the more they become involved in the world, in its economy, in its culture, in its aspirations and in its institutional forms, whether university or other.

If William of Saint Amour placed his attack under the sign of the Apocalypse, it was because it was good strategy to merge the cause of the Mendicants with that of the recently condemned disciples of Joachim of Fiore, who announced, together with the advent of the

---

28) One recognizes in these words the title of his work: *De periculis novissimorum temporum* (1255), which was recast and re-edited a number of times. The third edition of it was the one condemned, and published among his works at Constance in 1632. It was probably the text of the fifth edition that Saint Thomas refuted.

29) "But now the same kind of perverse men, by means of cunning advice, direct their attention to the religious especially . . ., intent on adding certain things which will completely destroy their state of life, and render it too oppressive and contemptible. . . ." *Cont. imp. Dei cult.*, prooem.; Marietti ed. of the *Opusc. theol.*, II, 6, n. 3. We know what kind of counterpart these attacks by the secular clerics gave rise to in popular literature: the Romance of the Rose, the "Roman de Renart," Rutebeuf ["Rutebeuf's serious work as a satirist probably dates from about 1260. His chief topics are the iniquities of the friars, and the defence of the secular clergy of the university of Paris against their encroachments. . . . He was a redoubtable champion of the university of Paris in its quarrel with the religious orders, and he boldly defended Guillaume de Saint-Amour when he was driven into exile. The libels, indecent songs and rhymes condemned by the pope to be burnt together with the *Périls des derniers temps* attributed to Saint-Amour, were probably the work of Rutebeuf". *Encyclopaedia Britannica*, XIX (1947), 770–771, at the word "Rutebeuf"]. Only under the protection of the royal archers was Florent of Hesdin able to begin his lectures at Saint James in September, 1255.

"eternal Gospel," the coming of new apostles. *De facto,* these Mendicants sometimes applied to themselves the predictions of Joachim concerning the new age and its extraordinary graces in the progressive course of history.

The *Contra impugnantes Dei cultum et religionem* was the answer given by Saint Thomas who thus presented a common front with and at the same time as the Franciscan, Thomas of York. He follows his adversary and refutes him step by step, a procedure which is not without some degree of lengthy fastidiousness.

The intervention of the Roman Church, we know, almost immediately solved the conflict, not only in point of fact by its confirming of the new Orders, but also in point of doctrine (the condemnation of the *De periculis,* October, 1256). This confirms from hindsight that the conflict was one involving doctrinal perspective.

The conflict was to resume on the more specialized grounds of spiritual doctrine, in the course of the years 1269–1272, during the second sojourn of Saint Thomas at Paris. This time, it was Gerard of Abbeville, a forceful theologian and a rich collector of books, who led the attack that was furthermore bound up with the publication of the voluminous *Collectiones catholicae scripturae* of his elder and master, William of Saint Amour (1266–1267). The same theses, the same arguments, were illustrated with accusations against the "false preachers." This time, Saint Thomas answered them (November, 1269) not through a point by point reply but through an organic treatise dealing with Christian perfection and the state of perfection, the role of poverty, the legitimacy of vows, the relative perfection of the various states of man—clerics and laymen, seculars and regulars, bishops and pastors, all of whom were obligated and called, according to their various states, to the same perfection of charity.

A retort by Gerard provoked a new edition, containing an important complement, of this *De perfectione vitae spiritualis,* the most important and the best constructed document of the whole debate.

In the midst of the disputations, both ordinary and quodlibetal, that crisscrossed at the time, in the midst of the theses and the lists of errors being denounced back and forth, there emerged the question of the vows and of their lawfulness, in connection with the entrance of children into religious life. Saint Thomas answered the question in a *Quodlibet* (III, a. 11–14). He furthermore composed at the end of the 1269–70 school year an opuscule entitled *Contra pestiferam doctrinam retrahentium homines a religionis ingressu,* wherein he restates once again, in connection with this case, his doctrine on the state of perfection and the evangelical counsels. This abundant literature came to a serene conclusion in the articles which the *Summa Theologiae* devoted to the states of life *(II–IIae,* q. 182–189) (a).

VIII. THE *CONTRA ERRORES GRAECORUM*

Another internal problem, itself linked to the general policy of the Church and of the States, was a source of worry to Christendom. Like a sore on its side, the schism had dissolved its unity, the token of its evangelical truth. The painful happenings of the crusades, and in particular, the lamentable taking of Constantinople in 1204, had brought to the raw point the division between Rome and Constantinople, between the West and the East. The prevailing circumstances, however, seemed favorable. The emperor, Michael Paleologus, had returned victorious to Constantinople (1261). Menaced at the same time by the Moslems and by the intrigues of the former Latin emperor who was fomenting his revenge through an anti-Greek crusade, he was negotiating with the Pope for the purpose of coming to a religious agreement. Urban IV, then reigning, and former patriarch of Jerusalem, was paying active attention to the possibilities that offered themselves. Without neglecting political action, however, counter to Emperor Michael, he aimed at prompting work on doctrine at the same time. Consequently, he requested of Brother Thomas Aquinas, then in Italy, a twofold undertaking: a theological critique of an anti-Greek anthology of texts recently arrived from the East and a commentary on the Gospel in which would be entered, side by side with the Latin authorities, the testimonies of the Oriental writers. Saint Thomas was unable to complete before the Pope's death (October, 1264) the second of these works, which was to become the *Catena aurea* (see above, chapter VII), but the first one was published immediately (1263) (b).

It was a matter of examining a *Libellus de fide Trinitatis* extracted from a more extensive work of which the *Libellus* was the main section and in which were assembled patristic and conciliar texts on the dogmatic and ritual problems controverted between the Greeks and the Latins (c). This compilation, perhaps done by Nicholas of Durazzo, Bishop of Cotrone, and already in circulation around 1256 (Saint Thomas had already used it in his commentary on the *Sen-*

---

a) See the Research Suggestions below, 347.

b) On the usefulness of this writing for questions of chronology, see P. GLORIEUX, *Autour du* Contra errores Graecorum. *Suggestions chronologiques,* in *AAr,* 1955, 497–512.

c) See the text in Uccelli, 377–440, and in Marietti, *Opusc. theol.,* I, 347–412.

tences) seems to have weighed upon the current negotiations (30). Saint Thomas was given the task of clearing up its contents. In his introduction, he presents far-reaching rules of interpretation that bear the mark of a lofty intellectual honesty as well as a historical sense of the development of dogma and of the great relativism that formulas and words have from one language to another.

The *Contra Errores Graecorum* took its place in a copious series of writings of that kind, which multiplied during the course of the XIIIth century as much through the frequency of relations and voyages between Rome and Constantinople as through the evangelical obsession of the new apostles, so sensitive to the fraternal unity of Christians. (a).

IX. SAINT THOMAS THE POET

A versified short work of Saint Thomas, the sequence entitled *Lauda Sion,* commonly presents him to us under this somewhat exaggerated designation. The sequence is a part of the text of the Office of the Blessed Sacrament, composed at Urban IV's request at the time of the establishment in the Church of the liturgical feast that consecrated the then completed evolution of the devotion to the eucharistic body of Christ (1264). This Office is classified and edited among the opuscules, together with the eucharistic hymns *Pange lingua, Sacris Solemniis, Verbum supernum* (b).

The value of these items is to be judged according to three criteria: the rhythmic procedures of the Latin poetry of the Middle Ages, liturgical conventions, and what has been called "conceptual poetry" because of the intellectual content of the phrases used in devotional and liturgical expression. Within these forms it was possible to pass elements of lyricism that were supported by the traditional symbolic forms.

To these items is justly added, although with an ultimate reservation about its authenticity, the *Adoro te,* "one of those harmonious and genial compositions at once rich and simple which, more than many books, have served to form Catholic piety" (Dom Wilmart). This little morsel is part of the literature brought forth by the new ceremony of the showing or elevation of the Host after the consecration (c). It is

---

30) See R. LOENERTZ, *Autour du traité de Fr. Barthélémy de Constantinople contre les Grecs,* in *AFP,* VI (1936), 361–371.

a) See the Research Suggestions, 347–348.

b) See above, 328.

c) See V. L. KENNEDY, *The Moment of Consecration and the Elevation of the Host,* in *MSt,* VI (1944), 121–150, and *The Date of the Parisian Decree on the Elevation of the Host, ibid.,* VIII (1946), 87–96.

a popular and private prayer, different in meter from the Office of the Blessed Sacrament and less solemn than the latter, but of extreme originality (d).

X. RESEARCH SUGGESTIONS

1. ON THE OPUSCULES IN GENERAL.—Concerning them, it is of import to be attentive to the problems of critique and of authenticity. The *Summa totius logicae* (Parma, XVII, 54–117, and Vivès, XXVIII, 85–158), for instance, which is not only apocryphal, but permeated throughout with nominalist conceptualism, has annoyingly fed the logic of John of Saint Thomas, and of many other Thomists in his wake. [The *BT* devotes a section, in each of its volumes, to these problems. To keep up with the work being done everywhere on questions of authenticity, chronology, etc., the reader will find in the section entitled: "Etudes critiques" a critical appraisal of almost everything being worked out in the field. On the opuscules, in particular, see, for instance, the studies of G. F. ROSSI, *Gli Opuscoli di S. Tommaso d'Aquino. Criteri per conoscerne l'autenticità*, in *DTP*, LVI (1953), 211–236, 362–390 (see *BT*, IX (1954–1956), 92–94, n. 123); *Antiche e nuove edizioni degli opuscoli di San Tommaso d'Aquino e il problema della loro autenticità*, in *DTP*, LVIII (1955), 3–73 (*BT*, X (1957–59), 83–85, n. 148).]

The apocrypha are not for this reason devoid of either doctrinal or historical interest. A number of them are in whole or in part works of Albert the Great. The commentary on the *Sentences* described as "ad Hannibaldum" is the work of Annibald of Annibaldi, who was a master at Paris in 1261–1262, and very closely acquainted with Saint Thomas. Many of the apocrypha contain parts that were borrowed from the authentic works. See the studies of A. GALEA and I. WILD, summarized and completed by P. MANDONNET, *Des écrits authentiques de S. Thomas d'Aquin*, 2d rev. ed., Fribourg, 1910, 146–156; M. GRABMANN, *Die Werke des heiligen Thomas von Aquin. Eine literarhistorische Untersuchung und Einfürung*, 3d ed., in *BGPM*, XII, 1/2 (1949), at the end of ch. IV. [Also I. T. ESCHMANN, *CSTW*, with his sober and up-to-date (to 1956) account on the problems of chronology and authenticity.]. Following the example set in the old editions of the *Opera omnia*, it was, therefore, an opportune decision that was taken by the editor of the *Opuscula omnia* [P. Mandonnet] of the Lethielleux edition, Paris, 1927, to reproduce the apocrypha in the Vth volume of it.

---

d) See the Research Suggestions below, 348.

2. ON THE *De ente et essentia.*—For the study of this opuscule, the edition of M.-D. ROLAND-GOSSELIN, *Le "De ente et essentia" de S. Thomas d'Aquin,* in *BibTh,* VIII (1948), is a valuable instrument. Accompanying the text are abundant historical and doctrinal notations, together with two monographs on the evolution of the problems of individuation and on the real distinction between essence and being.

Other practical editions also containing notes are those of L. BAUR, 2d ed., in *OpTex,* ser. schol., I (1933), and of C. BOYER, in *PUGTD,* V (1946). To the German translation (with Latin text) by R. ALLERS, *Thomas von Aquin Ueber das Sein und das Wesen,* Vienna, 1936, are added two long appendices, noteworthy as regards both doctrine and contexts.

Among the classic commentators, Cajetan, with his customary subtle depth of vision, holds first rank [the last reedition of his commentary was prepared by M.-H. Laurent, *In De ente et essentia S. Thomae Aquinatis commentaria,* Torino, Marietti, 1934]. M. GRABMANN has set up a catalogue of the ancient and modern commentators, *De commentariis in opusculum S. Thomae Aq. De ente et essentia,* in *APAR,* V (1938), 7–20.

The "existentialist" controversy has provoked and fed renewed meditation of the texts of this opuscule. See J. MARITAIN, *Court traité de l'existence et de l'existant,* Paris, 1947 [trans. into English by L. GALANTIÈRE and G. B. PHELAN: *Existence and the Existent,* in *ImB,* D45 (1957)]; E. GILSON, *L'être et l'essence,* in *PrC,* 1948. There is a doctrinal analysis of pertinent vocabulary in L. DE RAEYMAKER, *De zin van het woord esse bij den h. Thomas,* TVP, 1946, 407–434.

3. ON THE *De unitate intellectus* AND THE *De aeternitate mundi.*—We bring to the reader's attention the correctly established newly-edited text of the *De unitate intellectus,* done by L. W. KEELER and published in *PUGTD,* ser. ph., XII (1946), and also B. NARDI's translation, together with his long and excellently done commentary, *Trattato sull'unità dell'intelletto contro gli averroisti,* in *CSTF,* 1938.

These opuscules supply an occasion for establishing the traits which characterize Saint Thomas as a polemicist. The interest here is not only a biographical or psychological one, but one especially helpful in determining what, in his way of thinking, are the ways and means that promote a *collective* search for truth. We refer the reader to the notations already pointed out above concerning refutations (ch. V, 191–193), and concerning his religious polemical writings (ch. XII, 340–343). The reader may then collate those texts in which Saint Thomas explicitly justifies the procedures adopted in his polemics, texts such as the following: "If, therefore, one wishes to write anew against what has just been said, this will be most acceptable to me. For there is no better way of unfolding truth and of confounding error than by throwing up resistance against the contradictors" (e). "Just as in lawsuits, no one can pass judgment unless the arguments for both sides have been heard, so in the matter of hearing out the case of philosophy, one will necessarily be in a better position to judge, if all of the disputing opponents, as it were, are heard" (f). See also Saint Thomas's answer to his querist wanting to know "Whether the religious should show tolerance to those attacking them" (g). To the lively things he has to say against Averroes and the philosophers (see his texts gathered together by M. GRABMANN, in *MAG*, I (1926), 294–295), one can set up as a counterpart this reflexion expressing emotion-packed admiration: "This shows enough what intense anguish they suffered in their brilliant minds from this situation" (h). And from the latter reflexion, the reader may pass on to those perspectives on the social conditions of the begetting of science and of its progress in time, through the texts that have been assembled by P. MANDONNET in *Siger de Brabant et l'averroisme latin au XIIIe siècle*, Part I, in *LPB*, VII (1911), 145–148.

4. ON THE DEFENSE OF THE NEW RELIGIOUS LIFE.—The opuscules of Saint Thomas dealing with this topic are presented by P. GLORIEUX in four monographs wherein they are placed in their polemical context and their doctrinal content is brought out. Concerning the first episode of the conflict, see his *Le "Contra impugnantes" de saint Thomas, ses sources, son plan*, in *Mélanges Mandonnet*, I (*BibTh*, XIII, 1930), 51–81. For the conflict's second episode, see *Pour qu'on lise le "De perfectione vitae spiritualis,"* in *VSp*, Suppl., XXIII (1930), [97]–[126]; *Les polémiques "contra Geraldinos,"* in *RTAM*, VI (1934), 5–41; *"Contra Geraldinos," l'enchaînement des polémiques*, Ibid., VII (1935), 129–155. The reader will find therein the appropriate bibliography related with the controversy as a whole. [For a more recent account on the question, see D. L. DOUIE, *The Conflict between the Seculars and the Mendicants at the University of Paris in the Thirteenth Century*, in *AqP*, XXII (1954)]

5. ON THE *Contra errores Graecorum*.—The *Libellus de fide*, preserved in *Vat. Lat. ms.* 808, was published by A. UCCELLI, in *S. Thomae Aquinatis In Isaiam prophetam . . . expositiones*, Rome, 1880, 377–

---

e) "Si quis igitur contra haec rescribere voluit, mihi acceptissimum erit. Nullo enim modo melius quam resistentibus contradicendo, aperitur veritas et falsitas confutatur." *De per. vit. sp.*, c. 26; Marietti ed. of the *Opusc. theol.*, II, 153, n. 734.

f) "Sicut autem in judiciis nullus potest judicare nisi audiat rationes utriusque partis, ita necesse est eum, qui debet audire philosophiam, melius se habere in judicando si audierit omnes rationes quasi adversariorum dubitantium." *In III Metaph.*, lect. 1; Marietti ed., 97, n. 342; Rowan ed., I, 142. The entire text of this lesson should be read.

g) "Utrum religiosi debeant tolerare suos impugnatores?" *Quodl. V*, a. 26.

h) "In quo satis apparet quantam angustiam patiebantur hinc inde eorum praeclara ingenia." *Cont. Gent.*, III, c. 48, at the end.

443. See s. MERKLE, *Ant. Uccelli und Thomas Contra errores Graeco-rum*, in *RQ*, 1927, 209–239 (this article to be given exactness by that of R. LOENERTZ, quoted in note 30 of this chapter).

In his *Die fälschungen in dem Tractat des Thomas von Aquin gegen die Grieschen*, in *ABAW*, 3. Klasse, XVIII, 3 (1889), 675–742, F. H. REUSCH has raised problems as regards the documentation used by Saint Thomas. In ch. IV above, we had occasion to define the elements involved in this problem on the basis of the literature of those times considered as a whole, with the means of transmission it had at its disposal and its procedures of interpretation.

On the immediate context of Rome's dealings with the Orient, see V. LAURENT, *Le pape Alexandre IV (1254–1261) et l'empire de Nicée*, in *EchO*, XXXVIII (1935), 25–55.

6. ON SAINT THOMAS THE POET.—On the elements that were used in the composing of the Office of the Blessed Sacrament, and on the texts and the variants of the latter, the tradition of which is still obscure, the reader is referred to the excellent research done by Dom C. LAM-BOT, *L'Office de la Fête-Dieu. Aperçu nouveau sur ses origines*, in *RB*, LIV (1942), 61–123, who does not question Saint Thomas's authorship, which was at a time the object of lively controversies.

On Saint Thomas's part in medieval Latin poetry as a whole, see F. J. RABY, *A History of Christian-Latin Poetry from the Beginnings to the Close of the Middle Ages*, ch. XII, 3: *Thomas Aquinas and the Poetry of the Eucharist*, Oxford, 1927, 402–411, and W. J. ONG, *Wit and Mystery: A Revaluation in Medieval Latin Hymnody*, in *Spec*, XXII (1947), 310 ff. (takes in from Adam of Saint Victor to Saint Thomas, and ties in hymnody with the mysteries and the psychological aspect of faith).

On the poetic resources of Saint Thomas, see, amongst so many others, C. VERSCHAEVE, *Thomas von Aquino. De Dichter*, in *Onze Jeugd*, 1924, 70–114. There is an analysis of his poetic items in O. HUF, *De Sacraments hymnen van den H. Thomas (Liturgische Studien*, IV), Maestricht, 1924.

On the *Adoro te*, see A. WILMART, *La tradition littéraire et textuelle de l'Adoro te devote*, in *RTAM*, I (1929), 21–40, 146–176, reprinted in *Auteurs spirituels et textes dévots au moyen âge latin*, Paris, 1932, 361–414 (The article contains notations on the *Preces* attributed to Saint Thomas).

Abbreviations and Sigla

I. LATIN AND MODERN LANGUAGE WORDS

a.	*articulus*	article	
bd.		band	
bde.		bände	
Bibl.	*Bibliotheca*	Bibliothèque	
c.	*caput*		
ch.		chapter	chapître
col.	*columna*	column	colonne
coll.	*collatio*		
corp.	*corpus*		
d.	*distinctio*	distinction	
div. textus	*divisio textus*	division of the text	
ed.	*editio*	edition	
	edidit	edited	édité
exp. textus	*expositio textus*	exposition of the text	
f. ff.		following	
h.		heft	
hrsg.		herausgegeben	
ibid.	*ibidem*		
id.	*idem*		
introd.	*introductio*	introduction	
lat.	*latinus-a-um*	Latin (e)	
lect.	*lectio*		
lib.	*liber*		
loc. cit.	*loco citato*		
m.	*membrum*		
ms.	*manuscriptum*	manuscript	manuscrit
n.	*numerus*	number	numero
nat.		national (e)	
obi.	*objectio*	objection	

349

op. cit.	*opus citatum*		
opusc.	*opusculum*	opuscule	
p. pp.	*pagina-ae*	page (s)	
philos.	*philosophicus-a-um*	philosophic(al)	philosophique
praef.	*praefatio*		
pref.		preface	préface
prol.	*prologus*	prologue	
prooem.	*prooemium*		
prop.	*propositio*	proposition	
p.s.	*post scriptum*	postscript	postscriptum
pub.	publicatus-a-um	published	publié
q.	*quaestio*	question	
qa.	*quaestiuncula*		
resp. ad obj.	*responsio ad objecta*		
rev.		revision	
		revised	revu (e)
s.c.	*sed contra*		
sect.	*sectio*	section	
ser.	*series*	series	série
ser. ph.	*series philosophica*	philosophical series	série philosophique
ser. th.	*series theologica*	theological series	série théologique
sol.	*solutio*	solution	
sq.	*sequens*		
sqq.	*sequentia*		
suppl.	*supplementum*	supplement	supplément
t.	*tomus*	tome	
theol.	*theologicus-a-um*	theologic (al)	théologique
tr.	*tractatus*	tract	
trad.			traduction
trans.		translation	
		translated	
vol. vols.	*volumen*	volume (s)	

II. EDITIONS, COLLECTIONS, PERIODICALS

AA	*L'amour de l'art.* Paris, 1920 . . .
AApap	*Ann Arbor Paperbacks.* Ann Arbor (Mich.).
AAr	*Autour d'Aristote.* Recueil d'études de philosophie ancienne et médiévale offert à Monseigneur Mansion. Louvain, 1955.
AB	*Van Nostrand Anvil Books.* Under the General Editorship of L. L. Snyder. Toronto, 1955 . . .

ABAW	*Abhandlungen der Bayerischen Akademie der Wissenschaften.* Munich, 1835 . . .
AFH	*Archivum Franciscanum historicum.* Quaracchi, 1908 . . .
AFP	*Archivum Fratrum Praedicatorum.* Institutum historicum Fratrum Praedicatorum. Rome, 1931 . . .
AHDLMA	*Archives d'histoire doctrinale et littéraire du moyen âge.* Paris, 1926 . . .
ALKGMA	*Archiv für Literatur- und Kirchengeschichte des Mittelalters.* Hrsg. von H. Denifle und F. Ehrle. 7 Bde. (Berlin)-Freiburg in Breisgau, 1885–1900.
ALMA	*Archivum latinitatis medii aevi.* Consociatarum Academiarum auspiciis conditum (Union académique internationale. Bulletin du Cange).(Paris)-Brussels, 1924 . . .
AM	*Anecdota Maredsolana seu Monumenta ecclesiasticae antiquitatis.* Ex mss. codicibus nunc primum ed. aut denuo illustrata studio D. Germain Morin. IV vols. Maredsous-Oxford, 1893–1932.
AMN	*Analecta mediaevalia Namurcensia.* Louvain-Lille, 1950 . . .
AMOO	*Alberti Magni Opera omnia.* Cura ac labore A. Borgnet. XXXVIII vols. Paris, 1890–1899.
Ang	*Angelicum.* Periodicum trimestre facultatum et Institutorum Pontifici Athenaei "Angelicum". Rome, 1924 . . .
AnGreg	*Analecta Gregoriana.* Cura Pontificiae Universitatis Gregorianae ed., Rome, 1930 . . .
AO	*Aristotelis opera.* Ex recensione I. Bekkeri ed. Academia regia Borussica. Accedunt *Fragmenta, Scholia, Index Aristotelicus.* Ed. altera: addendis instruxit, fragmentorum collectionem retractavit O. Gigon. V vols. Berlin, 1960–1961.
AnP	*Analecta Praemonstratensia.* Commissio historica Ordinis Praemonstratensis. Averboden Abbey, 1924 . . .
ANSS	*Analecta novissima Spicilegii Solesmensis.* Altera continuatio. II vols. Tusculum, 1885–1888.
AOP	*Analecta Sacri Ordinis Fratrum Praedicatorum.* Rome, 1892 . . .
AP	*Archives de philosophie.* Paris, 1923 . . .
APAR	*Acta Pontificiae Academiae Romanae S. Thomae Aquinatis et religionis Christianae.* Nova ser. Turin-Rome, 1934 . . .

APCIPM   *Actes du premier Congrès international de philosophie médiévale*. Louvain-Bruxelles, 28 août-4 septembre 1958. Louvain-Paris, 1960.

AqL   *The Aquinas Lectures*. Marquette University Press. Milwaukee, 1937 . . .

AqP   *The Aquinas Papers*. The Aquinas Society of London, London, 1946 . . .

ASI   *Archivio storico Italiano*, Florence, 1842 . . .

ASS   *Acta sanctorum* . . . Digessit, notis illustravit J. Bollandus. Ed. novissima contulit G. Henschenius. Paris, 1863–1867.

ATE   *Aristote: traductions et études*. Collection pub. par l'Institut supérieur de philosophie de l'Université de Louvain. Louvain, 1912 . . .

BB   *Bijdragen Bibliothek*. Roermond, 1947 . . .

BCSR   *Bibliothèque catholique des sciences religieuses*. Paris, 1928 . . .

BEFAR   *Bibliothèque des Écoles françaises d'Athènes et de Rome*. Pub. sous les auspices du Ministère de l'éducation nationale. Paris, 1877 . . .

BEHE   *Bibliothèque de l'École pratique des Hautes Études*. Pub. sous les auspices du Ministère de l'instruction publique. *Sciences historiques et philologiques*. Paris, 1869 . . .

BESP   *Bibliographische Einführungen in das Studium der Philosophie*. Hrsg. von I. M. J. Bochenski, Bern, 1948 . . .

BFSMA   *Bibliotheca Franciscana scholastica medii aevi*. Quaracchi, 1903 . . .

BGPTM (BGPM)   *Beiträge zur Geschichte der Philosophie und Theologie des Mittelalters. Texte und Untersuchungen.* Vols. I–XXVI. Munich, 1891–1927.— *Beiträge zur Geschichte der Philosophie des Mittelalters. Texte und Untersuchungen.* Vol. XXVII . . . Munich, 1928 . . .

BHP   *Bibliothèque d'histoire de la philosophie*. Paris, 1926 . . .

BHROVR   *Beati Humberti de Romanis Opera de vita regulari*. Ed. J. J. Berthier. II vols. Rome, 1888–1889.

Bibl   *Biblica*. Commentarii ed. a Pontificio Instituto Biblico. Rome, 1920 . . .

BibTh   *Bibliothèque thomiste*. Directeur: P. Mandonnet, vols. I–XXIV; M.-D. Chenu, vol. XXV . . . (Le Saulchoir)-Paris, 1921 . . .

BIFF — *Bibliothèque de l'Institut français de Florence (Université de Grenoble).* 1st ser.: *Collection d'études et de documents d'histoire et de philologie.* Paris, 1910 . . .

BIQ–SD — *Beatus Innocentius V. Studia et Documenta.* Rome, 1943.

BLE — *Bulletin de littérature ecclésiastique.* Institut catholique de Toulouse, Toulouse, 1889 . . .

BolS — *Bollingen Series.* Pantheon Books. New York, 1943 . . .

BOO — DOCTORIS SERAPHICI S. BONAVENTURAE *Opera omnia.* Ed. studio et cura PP. Collegii a S. Bonaventura. X vols. Quaracchi, 1882–1901.

Bridges ed. — *The 'Opus majus' of Roger Bacon.* Ed. with Introd. and Analytical Table by J. H. Bridges. II vols. Oxford, 1897.

BSFS — *British Society of Franciscan Studies.* Oxford-London, 1908 . . .

BSHT — *Breslauer Studien zur historischen Theologie.* Breslau, 1922 . . .

BT — *Bulletin thomiste.* Organe de la Société thomiste. Le Saulchoir, 1924 . . .

BTAM — *Bulletin de théologie ancienne et médiévale.* Abbaye du Mont César. Louvain, 1929 . . .

BTE — *Biblioteca de Teologos Españoles.* Dirigida por los Dominicos de las Provincias de España. Vols. I–IX, Salamanca, 1931–1942. Vol. X . . . (Consejo superior de investigaciones cientificas). Madrid, 1943 . . .

BTheol — *Bibliothèque théologique.* Paris, (Gabalda), 1907 . . .

BToE — *Biblioteca de tomistas españoles.* Madrid, 1923 . . .

Buttimer ed. — *Hugonis de Sancto Victore Didascalicon: De Studio Legendi.* A Critical Text by C. H. Buttimer. *CUA-SMRL,* X (1939).

CAC — *Collection Armand Colin.* Section philosophie. Paris, 1921 . . .

CAG — *Conférences Albert-le-Grand.* Institut d'études médiévales, Université de Montréal, Montréal-Paris, 1947 . . .

CCM — *Chaire Cardinal Mercier.* Louvain-Paris, 1952 . . .

ChUP	*Chartularium Universitatis Parisiensis.* Sub auspiciis consilii generalis facultatum Parisiensium ex diversis bibliothecis tabulariisque collegit et cum authenticis chartis contulit H. Denifle . . . auxiliante A. Chatelain. Vols. I–IV. Paris, 1889–1897.
CJC	*Corpus juris canonici.* Ed. secunda post A. L. Richteri curas . . . recognivit et adnotatione critica instruxit A. Friedberg. II vols. Leipzig, 1922.
CJCiv	*Corpus juris civilis.* 15th stereotyped ed. by P. Krueger, T. Mommsen, R. Schoell, G. Kroll. III vols. Berlin, 1928–1954.
CLCAG	*Corpus latinorum commentariorum in Aristotelem Graecorum.* Pub. par l'Institut supérieur de philosophie sous la direction de G. Verbeke. Centre de Wulf-Mansion. Louvain-Paris, 1957 . . .
CLeb	*Collection Lebègue.* Office de publicité. Brussels, 1941 . . .
Clio	*Clio. Introduction aux études historiques.* Paris, 1938 . . .
Col. ed.	*Alberti Magni Opera omnia.* Ad fidem codicum manuscriptorum edenda, apparatu critico notis prolegomenis indicibus instruenda curavit Institutum Alberti Magni Coloniense, B. Geyer praeside. Monasterii Westfalorum, 1951 . . .
CPMA	*Corpus philosophorum Medii Aevi.* Academiarum consociatarum auspiciis et consilio ed. (Union académique internationale). XXXIII vols. planned. 1939 . . .
CSTF	*Collana scolastica di testi filosofici.* Diretta da G. Gentile. Florence.
CSTW	A *Catalogue of St. Thomas's Work,* by I. T. ESCHMANN. Pub. as an Appendix in E. GILSON, *The Christian Philosophy of Saint Thomas Aquinas.* New York, 1956, 379–439.
CUA-PS	*The Catholic University of America. Philosophical Studies.* Washington, 1895 . . .
CUA-SMRL	*The Catholic University of America. Studies in Medieval and Renaissance Latin Language and Literature.* Washington, 1933 . . .
CWS	*Christian Wisdom Series.* New York, 1951 . . .
DACL	*Dictionnaire d'archéologie chrétienne et de liturgie.* Pub. par F. Cabrol et H. Leclercq, vols. I–XIV, 1, 1907–1939; par H. I. Marrou, vol. XIV, 2 . . . 1948 . . . Paris.

DAGR   *Dictionnaire des antiquités grecques et romaines.* Sous la direction de C. Daremberg et E. Saglio. V t. in IX vols. Paris, 1877–1910.

DB   *Dictionnaire de la Bible* . . . Pub. par F. Vigouroux avec le concours d'un grand nombre de collaborateurs. Paris, 1895–1912.

Decker ed.   SANCTI THOMAE DE AQUINO *Expositio super librum Boethii de Trinitate.* Ad fidem codicis autographi nec non ceterorum codicum manu scriptorum recensuit B. Decker. *STGM,* IV (1955).

Denz   H. DENZINGER, *Enchiridion symbolorum definitionum et declarationum de rebus fidei et morum.* 31st ed. by C. Rahner. Barcelona-Freiburg im Breisgau-Rome, 1960.

Dion   *Dionysiaca.* Recueil donnant l'ensemble des traductions latines des ouvrages attribués au Denys de l'Aréopage et synopse marquant la valeur de citations . . . II vols. Paris-Bruges, 1937.

Dom   *Dominicana. A Quarterly of Popular Theology.* Dominican House of Studies, Washington, 1900 . . .

Dover   *Dover Publications.* New York.

DSt   *Dominican Studies. A Quarterly Review of Theology and Philosophy.* Blackfriars Publications. Oxford, 1948–1954.

DTC   *Dictionnaire de théologie catholique* . . . Commencé sous la direction de A. Vacant et E. Mangenot, continué sous celle de E. Amann, avec le concours d'un grand nombre de collaborateurs. XV vols. Paris, 1909–1950.

DTF   *Divus Thomas. Jahrbuch für Philosophie und spekulative Theologie.* 3rd ser. Fribourg (Switzerland), 1923–1953. Pub. since 1954 under the title of *Freiburger Zeitschrift für Philosophie und Theologie.*

DTP   *Divus Thomas Commentarium de philosophia et theologia.* Piacenza, 1880 . . .

EB   *Etudes bibliques.* Collection pub. par l'Ecole biblique de Jérusalem. Paris, 1903 . . .

EchO   *Echos d'Orient.* Paris, 1897 . . .

EF   *Etudes franciscaines.* Pub. par des religieux de l'Ordre des Frères Mineurs Capucins. Paris, 1899 . . .

EH   *Economie et humanisme.* Centre d'études des complexes sociaux. Marseille, 1942 . . .

ENCPI   *Edizione nazionale dei classici del pensiero Italiano.* Promessa dal R. Istituto di studi filosofici. Florence, 1942 . . .

EP   *Essais philosophiques.* Louvain-Paris, 1946 . . .

EPM   *Etudes de philosophie médiévale.* Directeur: E. Gilson. Paris, 1920 . . .

ESJLF-Th   *Etudes.* Pub. sous la direction de la Faculté de théologie S. J. de Lyon-Fourvières. *Théologie.* Paris, 1944 . . .

EstF   *Estudios filosoficos.* Las Caldas de Besaya, 1952 . . .

ETL   *Ephemerides theologicae Lovanienses. Theologia dogmatica—Theologia moralis—Jus canonicum.* Universitas catholica lovaniensis. Louvain-Bruges, 1924 . . .

EvH   *L'évolution de l'humanité.* Synthèse collective dirigée par H. Berr (in *Bibliothèque de synthèse historique*). Paris, 1920 . . .

FAS   *From an Abundant Spring.* The Walter Farrell Memorial Volume of *The Thomist.* Ed. by the Staff of *The Thomist.* New York, 1952.

FF   *La France franciscaine. Mélanges d'archéologie, d'histoire et de littérature.* Lille, 1912 . . .

FM   *Histoire de l'Eglise depuis les origines jusqu'à nos jours.* Fondée par A. Fliche et V. Martin. Paris, 1935 . . .

Foster ed.   K. FOSTER, *The Life of Saint Thomas. Biographical Documents.* Trans. and ed. with an Introd. London-Baltimore, 1959.

Foster-Humphries ed.   *Aristotle's De anima in the Version of William of Moerbeke and the Commentary of St. Thomas Aquinas.* Trans. by K. FOSTER and S. HUMPHRIES, with an Introd. by I. THOMAS. *RMPS,* 1951.

FVTA   *Fontes vitae S. Thomae Aquinatis.* Notis historicis et criticis illustrati. Fasc. I–III, curis et labore D. Prümmer, O.P., Toulouse, 1912–1928; fasc. IV–VI, cura et labore M.-H. Laurent, O.P., Saint-Maximin, 1929–1934.

GBWW   *Great Books of the Western World.* R. M. Hutchins, editor in chief. Chicago-London-Toronto, (copyright 1952).

GCO   *Giraldi Cambrensis Opera.* Ed. by J. S. Brewer. VIII vols. *RBMAS,* XXI (1861–1891).

GMIL   *Glossarium mediae et infimae latinitatis.* Conditum a C. Du Cange . . . Digessit G. A. L. Henschel . . . Ed. nova . . . a L. Favre. V vols. Niort, 1883–1886.

Greg   *Gregorianum. Rivista trimestrale di studi teologici et filosofici.* Rome, 1920 . . .

GSB   *Great Seal Books.* A Division of the Cornell University Press. Ithaca, N. Y., 1955 . . .

Hain   L. HAIN, *Repertorium bibliographicum* . . ., IV vols. Milan, 1948; *Supplement* . . ., two parts in 3 t., by W. A. COPINGER, Milan, 1950; *Appendices ad Hainii-Copingeri* . . ., 6 fasc., Indices, Supplementum, in II vols., by D. Reichling, Milan, 1953.

HGMA   *Histoire du moyen âge.* T. I–X (in *Histoire générale.* Fondée par. G. Glotz). Paris, 1939–1946.

HJ   *Historisches Jahrbuch der Görres-Gesellschaft.* Cologne, 1880 ff.; Munich, 1950 . . .

HLF   *Histoire littéraire de la France* . . . Ouvrage commencé par des religieux bénédictins de la Congrégation de S. Maur, continué par des membres de l'Institut. Vols. I–XXXVIII . . . Paris, 1865–1949 . . .

IER   *Irish Ecclesiastical Record. A Monthly Journal* . . . Dublin, 1864 . . .

IHA   *Islam d'hier et d'aujourd'hui.* Collection pub. sous la direction de E. Lévi-Provençal. Paris, 1948. . .

IHP-DH   *Institutum historicum FF. Praedicatorum. Dissertationes historicae.* (Paris)-Rome, 1931 . . .

ImB   *Image Books.* New York, 1954 . . .

InPat   *Instrumenta patristica.* St. Peter's Abbey. Steenbrugge, 1959 . . .

Isis   *Isis. International Review Devoted to the History of Science and Civilization.* Bruges, 1913 . . .

JHM   *Journal of the History of Medicine and Allied Sciences.* Yale University, Department of the History of Science and Medicine. New Haven, 1946 . . .

Keeler ed.   SANCTI THOMAE AQUINATIS *Tractatus de unitate intellectus contra Averroistas.* Ed. critica. Ed. L. W. Keeler. *PUGTD,* ser. ph., XII (1946).

KHS   *Kerkhistorische Studien behoorende bij het Nederlandscharchief voor Kerkgeschiedenis.* The Hague, 1941 . . .

Kocourek ed.

R. A. KOCOUREK, *An Introduction to the Philosophy of Nature.* St. Paul, Minn., 1948.

KR

The Kenyon Review. New York, 1939 . . .

LCL

The Loeb Classical Library. Greek and Latin Authors. Cambridge (Mass.)-London, 1913 . . .

LPB

Les philosophes belges. Textes et études. Collection pub. par l'Institut supérieur de philosophie de l'Université de Louvain. Louvain, 1901 . . .

Leonine ed.

SANCTI THOMAE AQUINATIS DOCTORIS ANGELICI *Opera omnia.* Jussu impensaque Leonis XIII ed. XVI vols. pub. (with Indices) . . . Rome, 1882 . . .

Lescoe ed.

SANCTI THOMAE AQUINATIS *Tractatus de substantiis separatis.* A newly-established text based on 12 mediaeval manuscripts, with Introd. and Notes, by F. J. Lescoe. West Hartford, 1962. English trans. of the same text by the same. West Hartford, 1959.

LLCT

Library of Living Catholic Thought. Chicago, 1952 . . .

LS

The Life of the Spirit. A Blackfriars Review. Blackfriars Publications. London, 1946 . . .

LThK

Lexicon für Theologie und Kirche. New ed. Freiburg im Breisgau, 1957 . . .

MA

Miscellanea Agostiniana. Testi e Studi. Pub. a cura dell' ordine eremitano di S. Agostino nel XV centenario dalla morte del santo dottore. Rome, 1930–1931.

MAAP

The Mediaeval Academy of America Publications. Cambridge (Mass.), 1928 . . .

MAG

Mittelalterliches Geistesleben. Abhandlungen zur Geschichte der Scholastik und Mystik. III vols. Munich, 1926–1956.

Marietti (or Marietti ed.)

DIVI THOMAE AQUINATIS DOCTORIS ANGELICI (Various Works . . . by Various Editors). Pub. by the Casa Marietti. Turin-Rome.

Martin ed.

Oeuvres de Robert de Melun. III t. in IV vols., in *SSL,* 1932–1952.

MB

Mélanges bénédictins. Pub. à l'occasion du XIVe centenaire de la mort de saint Benoît par les moines de l'Abbaye de Saint-Jérôme de Rome. Saint Wandrille Abbey, 1947.

McGarry ed.	*The Metalogicon of John of Salisbury. A Twelfth-Century Defense of the Verbal and Logical Arts of the Trivium.* Trans. with an Introd. and Notes by D. D. McGarry. Berkeley and Los Angeles, 1955.
MCA	*Monografie del Collegio Alberoni.* Publicazione diretta dal Professori del Collegio di Piazenza. Piacenza, 1922 . . .
MCS	*Monumenta Christiana selecta.* Paris, 1957 . . .
MerB	*Meridian Books.* New York.
MFC	*Mélanges offerts au R. P. F. Cavallera à l'occasion de la quarantième année de son professorat à l'Institut catholique.* Toulouse, 1948.
MGM-SS	*Monumenta Germaniae Historica.* Ed. Societas aperiendis fontibus rerum Germanicarum medii aevi. *Scriptores.* Vols. I–XXXII. Hanover-(Leipzig), 1826–1934.
MHP	*Miscellanea historiae pontificiae.* Ed. a Facultate historiae ecclesiasticae in Pont. Universitate Gregoriana. Rome, 1939 . . .
ML-SH	*Museum Lessianum.* Sous la direction des PP. S.J. de Louvain. *Section historique.* Paris-Brussels, 1940 . . .
ML-SP	*Museum Lessianum.* Sous la direction des PP. S. J. de Louvain. *Section philosophique.* Paris-Brussels, 1921 . . .
MLull	*Miscellanea Lulliana.* Majorca, 1954.
MLWBB	*The Modern Library of the World's Best Books.* New York.
MOFPH	*Monumenta Ordinis Fratrum Praedicatorum historica.* Rome-Stuttgart, 1896 . . .
MPTT	*Mediaeval Philosophical Texts in Translation.* Marquette University Press. Milwaukee, 1942 . . .
MS	*The Modern Schoolman. A Quaterly Journal of Philosophy.* Saint Louis University, The College of Philosophy and Letters and the Department of Philosophy. Saint Louis, 1925 . . .
MSR	*Mélanges de science religieuse.* Pub. par un groupe de professeurs des Facultés catholiques de Lille. Lille, 1944 . . .
MSt	*Mediaeval Studies.* Pontifical Institute of Mediaeval Studies. (New York-London)-Toronto, 1939 . . .

MTPFCL	*Mémoires et travaux.* Pub. par des professeurs des Facultés catholiques de Lille. Lille, 1905 . . .
Muséon	*Le Muséon. Revue internationale.* Pub. par la Société des lettres et des sciences. Louvain, 1882 . . .
NRT	*Nouvelle revue théologique.* Pub. tous les mois sous la direction de quelques professeurs du Collège philosophique et théologique S. J. Saint Albert à Louvain. Tournai-Louvain-Paris, 1869 . . .
NS	*The New Scholasticism. A Quarterly Review of Philosophy.* Journal of the American Philosophical Association, 1927 . . .
Oesterle ed.	Aristotle: *On Interpretation. Commentary by* st. thomas *and* cajetan (*Peri Hermeneias*). Trans. from the Latin with an Introd. by j. t. oesterle. *MPTT*, XI (1962).
OHIRB	*Opera hactenus inedita Rogeri Baconi.* Ed. R. Steele. Oxford, [1905?] . . .
OpTex	*Opuscula et textus historiam Ecclesiae ejusque vitam atque doctrinam illustrantia.* Ser. scholastica ed. curantibus M. Grabmann et F. Pelster. Münster, 1926 . . .
Ottawa ed.	s. thomae de aquino *Summa theologiae.* Cura et studio Instituti Studiorum Medievalium Ottaviensis ad textum S. Pii Pp. V jussu confectum recognita. V vols. Ottawa, 1941–1945; rev. ed., 1953.
PanB	*Pantheon Books.* New York.
Parma ed.	sancti thomae aquinatis doctoris angelici *Opera omnia.* Ad fidem optimarum editionum accurate recognita. XXV vols. Parma, 1852–1873. Photographically reproduced, New York, 1948–49.
Pauline ed.	sancti thomae de aquino *Summa theologiae.* Paulinae ed. Alba-Rome, 1962.
PB	*Penguin Books.* Harmondsworth-Baltimore.
PBA	*Proceedings of the British Academy.* London, 1903 . . .
PEC	*Peuples et civilisations. Histoire générale.* Pub. sous la direction de L. Halphen et P. Sagnac. Paris, 1926 . . .
Perrier (or Perrier ed.)	*Opuscula omnia necnon Opera minora.* Ad fidem codicum restituit ac ed. J. Perrier. T. I. Paris, 1949.
PFLUS	*Publications de la Faculté des lettres de l'Université de Strasbourg.* Paris, 1921 . . .

PhEs	*Philosophie de l'esprit.* Collection dirigée par L. Lavelle et R. Le Senne. Paris, 1934 . . .
PJ	*Philosophisches Jahrbuch der Görres Gesellschaft.* Fulda, 1888–1952; Munich, 1953 . . .
PIEM	*Publications de l'Institut d'études médiévales.* Vols. I–X, Paris-Ottawa, 1932–1941; vols. XI . . ., Paris-Montreal, 1950 . . .
P.L.	*Patrologiae cursus completus. Series prima in qua prodeunt Patres, Doctores Scriptoresque Ecclesiae Latinae.* Vols. I–CCXXI. Paris, Migne, 1844–1864. Ed. altera, 1866 ff. Supplementum, 1958 ff.
PM	*Philosophes médiévaux. Collection de textes et d'études.* Pub. par l'Institut supérieur de philosophie de l'Université de Louvain. Centre de Wulf-Mansion. Louvain-Paris, 1948 . . .
PPC	*Philosophie et problèmes contemporains.* Montreal-Paris, 1944 . . .
PrC	*Problèmes et controverses.* Paris, 1948 . . .
PUGTD	*Pontificia Universitas Gregoriana. Textus et documenta.* In usum exercitationum et praelectionum academicarum. Ser. ph. . . . Ser. th. . . . Rome, 1932 . . .
PUMHS	*Publications of the University of Manchester.* Historical Ser. Manchester, 1904 . . .
Quaracchi (or Quaracchi ed.)	Editions of various (mainly) Franciscan authors. Prepared by the Fathers of St. Bonaventure College. Ad Claras Aquas (Quaracchi), near Florence.
RAM	*Revue d'ascétique et de mystique.* Toulouse, 1920 . . .
RBMAS	*Rerum Britannicarum medii aevi scriptores,* or *Chronicles and Memorials of Great Britain and Ireland during the Middle Ages.* Pub. by the authority of Her Majesty's treasury, under the direction of the Master of the Rolls. London-Oxford-Cambridge, 1857 . . .
RBO	FR. ROGERI BACON *Opera quaedam hactenus inedita.* Vol. I. Ed. J. S. Brewer. *RBMAS,* XV (1859).
RBPH	*Revue belge de philologie et d'histoire.* Recueil trimestriel pub. par la Société pour le progrès des études philologiques et historiques avec le concours de la fondation universitaire et du ministère de l'instruction publique. Brussels, 1922 . . .

RCSS	*Records of Civilization. Sources and Studies.* Ed. under the Auspices of the Department of History, Columbia University. New York, 1915 . . .
RDP	*Revue de philosophie.* Paraissant tous les deux mois. Paris, 1900 . . .
REF	*Revista española de teologia.* Consejo Superior de Investigaciones Cientificas. Madrid, 1941 . . .
REL	*Revue des études latines.* Pub. par la Société des études latines. Paris, 1923 . . .
RFNS	*Rivista di filosofia neoscolastica.* Pub. a cura della Facolta di filosofia dell'Università cattolica del Sacro Cuore. Milan, 1909 . . .
RGSB	*Robert Grossetete Scholar and Bishop.* Essays in Commemoration of the Seventh Centenary of his Death. Ed. by D. A. Callus, with an Introd. by Sir M. Powicke. Oxford, 1955.
RHD	*Revue d'histoire du droit.* Sous la direction d'A.S. de Blécourt (et autres). Haarlem, 1920 . . .
RHE	*Revue d'histoire ecclésiastique.* Université catholique de Louvain. Louvain, 1900 . . .
RHF	*Revue d'histoire franciscaine.* Paris, 1924 . . .
RHLL	*The Random House Lifetime Library.* New York.
RIS	*Rerum Italicarum scriptores.* Raccolta degli storici Italiani del 500–1500 Ordinata da L. A. Muratori. XXVIII vols. Milan 1723–1751. Nuova ed. riveduta, ampliata e corr. XXXIV vols. in course of publication. Città di Castello, 1900 . . .
RMAL	*Revue du moyen âge latin. Etudes-textes-chronique-bibliographie.* Lyon, 1945 . . .
RMM	*Revue de métaphysique et de morale.* Paris, 1893 . . .
RMPS	*Rare Masterpieces of Philosophy and Science.* Ed. W. Stark. London-New Haven, 1949 . . .
RNSP	*Revue néoscolastique de philosophie.* Pub. par la Société philosophique de Louvain. Vols. I–XLIII. Louvain, 1894–1945. Continued since under the title: *Revue philosophique de Louvain.*
Rowan ed.	ST. THOMAS AQUINAS. *Commentary on the Metaphysics of Aristotle.* Trans. J. P. Rowan. II vols., in *LLCT,* 1961.
RPL	*Revue philosophique de Louvain.* Fondée en 1894 sous le titre de *Revue néo-scolatique* (Vols. I–XLIII. Louvain, 1894–1945). Vols. XLIV . . . Louvain, 1946 . . .

RQ	*Römische Quartalschrift für christliche Altertumskunde und Kirchengeschichte.* Freiburg im Breisgau, 1887 . . .
RSPT	*Revue des sciences philosophiques et théologiques.* Paris, 1907 . . .
RT	*Revue thomiste.* Paris, 1893 . . .
RTAM	*Recherches de théologie ancienne et médiévale.* Abbaye du Mont César. Louvain, 1929 . . .
RUO	*Revue de l'Université d'Ottawa.* Pub. tous les trois mois par les Oblats de Marie-Immaculée de l'Université d'Ottawa. Ottawa, 1926 . . .
Saffrey ed.	H. D. SAFFREY, *Sancti Thomae de Aquino super librum de causis expositio.* TPF., IV–V (1954).
Sal	*Salesianum. Theologia, Jus canonicum, Philosophia et Paedagogia.* Rome, 1939 . . .
SB	*Spicilegium Beccense.* Congrès international du IXe centenaire de l'arrivée d'Anselme au Bec. Paris-Le Bec-Hellouin, 1959.
SBAW	*Sitzungsberichte der Bayerischen Akademie der Wissenschaften.* Munich, 1894 . . .
ScE	*Sciences ecclésiastiques.* Revue théologique et philosophique paraissant trois fois par année. Les facultés de théologie et de philosophie S. J. à Montréal. Bruges, 1948. . .
Sch	*Scholastik. Vierteljahresschrift für Theologie und Philosophie.* Freiburg im Breisgau, 1926 . . .
Schmitt ed.	S. ANSELMI CANTUARIENSIS ARCHIEPSCOPI *Opera omnia.* Ad fidem codicum recensuit F. S. Schmitt. VI vols. Edinburgh, 1946–1951.
Script	*Scriptorium. International Review of Manuscript Studies.* Antwerp-Amsterdam-Brussels-Paris, 1946 . . .
STHJ	*Studia et documenta historiae et juris.* Pontificium Institutum utriusque juris. Rome, 1935 . . .
SMCPT	*St. Michael's College Philosophical Texts. A Series of Translations.* Toronto, 1934 . . .
SMH	*Studies in Medieval History Presented to F. M. Powicke.* Ed. R. W. Hunt, W. A. Pantin, R. W. Southern. Oxford, 1948.
SMM	*Studia mediaevalia in honorem A. R.P. R.M. Martin, O.P.* Bruges, 1948.
Sophia	*Sophia. Rivista internazionale di fonti e studi di storia della filosofia.* Palermo, 1933 . . .

Spec	*Speculum. A Journal of Mediaeval Studies.* The Mediaeval Academy of America. Cambridge (Mass.), 1926. . .
SS	*Slovak Studies.* Slovak Institute. Rome, 1961 . . .
SSL	*Spicilegium sacrum Lovaniense. Etudes et documents.* Université catholique et Collèges O.P. et S. J. de Louvain. Louvain-Paris, 1922 . . .
StA	*Studia Anselmiana philosophica theologica.* Ed. a professoribus Instituti pontificii S. Anselmi de Urbe. Rome, 1933 . . .
STGM	*Studien und Texte zur Geistesgeschichte des Mittelalters.* Hrsg. von J. Koch. Leiden, 1950 . . .
StS	*Studi superiori.* Società editrice internazionale. Turin-Milan-Genoa-Parma-Rome-Catania, 1926.
StT	*Studi e testi.* Pub. per cura degli scrittori della biblioteca Vaticana e degli archivisti dell'archivio segreto. Vatican City, 1900 . . .
Taylor ed.	*The Didascalicon of Hugh of St. Victor. A Medieval Guide to the Arts.* Trans. from the Latin with an Introd. and Notes by J. Taylor. *RCSS,* LXIV (1961).
TB	*Torchbooks.* Library size paperbacks. New York.
TBS	*Transactions of the Bibliographical Society.* Vols. I–XV, 1893–1920; Suppl.: vols. I–XIX, 1926–1959. London.
TCHS	*The Century Historical Series.* New York-London.
TET	*Textes et études théologiques.* Bruges, 1954 . . .
Thom	*The Thomist. A Speculative Quaterly Review.* Ed. Dominican Fathers. New York, 1939 . . .
ThSt	*Thomistische Studien. Schriftenreihe des "Divus Thomas".* Fribourg (Switz.), 1943 . . .
TLL	*Thesaurus linguae latinae.* Ed. auctoritate et consilio academiarum quinque germanicarum . . . Leipzig, 1900 . . .
TMSL	*The Modern Student's Library.* New York.
TPF	*Textus philosophici Friburgenses.* Ser. moderatur I. M. Bochenski. Fribourg-Louvain, 1948 . . .
Trad	*Traditio. Studies in Ancient and Medieval History, Thought and Religion.* New York, 1943 . . .
TSHME	*Texts and Studies in the History of Mediaeval Education.* Ed. A. L. Gabriel and J. N. Garvin. The Mediaeval Institute, University of Notre Dame. Notre Dame, 1953 . . .

TSt	*Theological Studies.* Pub. by Theological Studies Inc., for the Theological Faculties of the Society of Jesus in the United States. (Woodstock)-New York, 1940 . . .
TVP	*Tijdschrift voor Philosophie.* Louvain, 1939 . . .
UBM	*Universitatis Bononiensis Monumenta.* Istituto per la storia dell'Università di Bologna. Bologna, 1932 . . .
Uccelli (or Uccelli ed.)	S. THOMAE AQUINATIS DOCTORIS ANGELICI *In Isaiam prophetam, in tres Psalmos David, in Boetium de Hebdomadibus et de Trinitate expositiones.* Accedit ANONYMI *Liber de fide Trinitatis* a S. Thoma examinatus in opusculo *Contra errores Graecorum,* una cum ipso opusculo et altero *Contra Graecos, Armenos et Saracenos.* Omnia quae supersunt ex autographis, cetera vero ex optimis codicibus et editionibus. Cura et studio P. A. Uccellii. Rome, 1880.
UCL	*Universitas catholica Lovaniensis. Dissertationes ad gradum magistri in Facultate theologica consequendum conscriptae.* Louvain-Paris, 1841 . . .
UCSLS	*University of Chicago Studies in Library Science.* Graduate Library School. Chicago, 1933 . . .
UKP-HS	*University of Kansas Publications. Humanistic Studies.* Lawrence, 1912 . . .
UL-RTHP	*Université de Louvain. Recueil de travaux d'histoire et de philologie.* 3rd ser. Louvain, 1940 . . .
VInt	*La vie intellectuelle. Revue mensuelle.* Juvisy, 1928–1936; Paris, 1937–1956.
Vischer ed.	BERENGARII TURONENSIS *De sacra coena adversus Lanfrancum.* Ed. A. F. et F. T. Vischer, in *Berengarii Turonensis quae supersunt tam edita quam inedita.* Typis expressa moderante A. Neandro. Berlin, 1834., T. I.
Vivès (or Vivès ed.)	DOCTORIS ANGELICI DIVI THOMAE AQUINATIS *Opera omnia.* Ed. S. E. Fretté et P. Maré. XXXIV vols. Paris, L. Vivès, 1871–1882. Reprinted 1889–1890.
VSp	*La vie spirituelle. Ascétique et mystique.* Paris, 1919 . . .
Webb ed.	JOANNIS SARESBERIENSIS EPISCOPI CARNOTENSIS *Metalogicon libri III.* Recognivit et prolegomenis, apparatu critico, commentario, indicibus instruxit C. C. I. WEBB. Oxford, 1929.

XTh   *Xenia Thomistica. Divo Thomae Doctori communi Ecclesiae occasione VI centenarii ab ejus canonizatione oblata.* Ed. P. Szabo. III vols. Rome, 1925.

ZMR   *Zeitschrift für Missionswissenschaft und Religionswissenschaft.* Internationale Institute für Missionswissenschaftliche Forschungen. Münster, 1911 . . .

ZSK   *Zeitschrift des Savigny-Stiftung für Rechtsgeschichte. Kanonistische abteilung.* Weimar, 1911.

III. WORKS OF SAINT THOMAS QUOTED
OR REFERRED TO (a)

In Perih.—In Libros Perihermeneias expositio: 215, 219, 223.
I, lect. 7, n. 84: 228—lect. 8, n. 102: 208.

In Post. An.—In libros posteriorum Analyticorum expositio: 205, 223.
I, lect. 25: 208.

In Phys. (b)—*In octo libros Physicorum expositio:* 205, 218, 223, 224.
I, lect. 15, n. 138: 118—n. 139: 211–III, lect. 1, n. 279; 169—
VIII, lect. 1, n. 966: 219—lect. 21, n. 1149: 213.

In De coelo—In libros De coelo et mundo expositio: 223, 224.
I, lect. 22, n. 223: 191—n. 228: 28, 118, 121, 154—III, lect. 26,
n. 584: 142.

In De gen.—In libros De generatione et corruptione expositio: 223,
224.
I, lect. 24: 325.

In De an.—In libros De anima expositio: 215, 218, 223, 224.
I, lect. 2, n. 19: 212—lect. 6, n. 74: 211—lect. 8, n. 107: 118, 170—
III, lect. 4, n. 632: 114—lect. 8: 212.

In Metaph.—In duodecim libros Metaphysicorum expositio: 205, 215,
217–219, 223, 224.
I, lect. 15, n. 231: 118, 142—II, lect. 1, n. 286: 213—lect. 5, n. 334:
181—III, lect. 1, n. 342: 347—IV, lect. 1, n. 529: 211—lect. 6,

---

a) In the present list, the works of Saint Thomas quoted or referred to appear in their order of treatment from chapter VI onward: the Commentaries on Aristotle and Dionysius, on Scripture, on the Sentences and Boethius, the Disputed Questions, the *Summa contra Gentiles*, the *Summa theologiae*, and the Opuscules. The complete works of Aquinas within these literary genres is found in the successive chapters where they are dealt with.

b) Not included in the list of editions and translations of Saint Thomas's commentaries on the works of Aristotle on page 223, note a, is the following English edition which became available to the translators only after the present work was at the printer's: *Commentary on Aristotle's Physics* by st. thomas aquinas, trans. r. j. blackwell, r. j. spath, and w. e. thirlkel, with introd. by v. j. bourke, London, 1963.

n. 606: 219—VI, lect. 3, n. 1216: 212—X, lect. 7, n. 2060: 94—
XII, lect. 9, n. 2566: 193.

In Eth.—In decem libros Ethicorum expositio: 205, 219, 215–217, 223,
224, 275.
I, lect. 2, n. 28, 31: 213—lect. 11, n. 133: 273—VII, lect. 11, n.
1470: 219—VII, *in fine:* 85—XII, lect. 1, n. 2417: 213.

In De causis—In librum De Causis expositio: 224, 225.
prop. 9: 114—prop. 12: 186—lect. 6: 224.

In De hebdom.—In librum Boetii De hebdomadibus expositio: 225.
lect. 1, textus Boetii: 225.

*In De div. nom.—In librum Beati Dionysii de divinis nominibus expo-
sitio:* 97, 226–230.
prooem., n. 1: 118, 142, 170, 228—c. 4, lect. 1: 171—lect. 1, n. 271:
118—lect. 19, n. 540: 228—c. 5, lect. 1: 186—c. 7, lect. 1, n. 702:
118.

In Isaiam—Expositio in Isaiam prophetam: 244, 245.
prooem.: 243.

In Psalmos—In Psalmos Davidis lectura: 244, 245.
prooem.: 246.

In Job—Expositio in Job ad litteram: 244, 246, 252, 257.
prooem.: 257.

In Matt.—Super Evangelium S. Matthaei lectura: 244, 246.
II, 3, n. 200, 201: 254—4, n. 213, 224: 254—V, 11, n. 396: 251—23,
n. 498: 252—XXI, 12, n. 1696: 252—XXIV, 27, n. 1953: 252.

In Joan.—Super Evangelium S. Joannis lectura: 245, 247, 251.
prol. n. 24–29: 329—I, 3, n. 76: 252—III, 18, n. 484: 252—34:
253—V, 20: 253—VI, 7, n. 977: 252—X, 17: 253—XV, 15, n.
2015: 252.

*Catena aurea—Expositio continua (Catena aurea) in quatuor Evan-
gelia:* 150, 151, 245, 248, 343.
Epist. dedic. ad Hannib. (Marietti, I, 429): 249.

In Rom.—Expositio in S. Pauli epistolas: ad Romanos.
V, 3: 253—VIII, 5–6, n. 616–617: 253.

In Cor.—Expositio in S. Pauli epistolas: I ad Corinthios.
IX, 9: 262.

In Tim.—Expositio in S. Pauli epistolas: I ad Timotheum.
c. 5, lect. 2, n. 195: 136.

In Hebr.—Expositio in S. Pauli epistolas: ad Hebraeos.
c. 1, lect. 1, n. 86: 229—c. 11, lect. 1: 262.

In Sent.—Scriptum super libros Sententiarum: 97, 162, 264–276, 270, 300.

I, prol., a. 3, sol. 2: 269—d. 2, div. textus: 271, 306, 308, 309—q. 1, a. 3: 335—a. 3: 269, 283—d. 3, div. textus: 229—q. 4, a. 3: 187—d. 8, exp. textus: 160—d. 14, q. 2, a. 2: 311—d. 19, q. 5, a. 1: 136—d. 23, q. 1, a. 1, ad 5um: 141, 168—d. 27, q. 2, a. 2: 120, 279—d. 38, q. 1, a. 3, ad 1um: 118—d. 43, q. 2, a. 1, ad 1um: 118, 171.

II, prol.: 171, 308—d. 2, q. 1, a. 3: 143—d. 3, q. 1, a. 1: 120—a. 6: 118—d. 7, q. 1, a. 2: 118—d. 9, q. 1, a. 1: 167—d. 14, q. 1, a. 2: 143, 227—ad 1um: 143—d. 16-20: 274—d. 18, q. 2, a. 2, ad 1um: 132—d. 21-29: 274—d. 30-33: 274—d. 34-54: 274.

III, d. 14, q. 1, a. 3, obj. 3 and ad 3um: 118—d. 23, q. 2, a. 1, ad 3um: 169—a. 2, sol. 1: 138—qa. 1, obj. 3: 138—d. 33: 271—d. 35, q. 1, a. 3, sol. 2: 196.

IV: 273—d. 4, q. 1, a. 1: 163—a. 2, qa. 2, obj. 1: 136—d. 14, q. 1, qa. 3, ad 4um: 138—d. 17: 274.

In De trin.—Super librum Boethii De trinitate expositio: 97, 276–278.

q. 1, a. 2 to q. 2, a. 4: 279—q. 2: 277—a. 3, ad 5um: 118—ad 8um: 139—q. 3, a. 2: 161—lect. 2: 181—q. 5 and 6: 276–279—q. 5, a. 1, ad 6um to a. 2, s.c.: 278—q. 5, a. 3: 279—a. 4, ad 2um: 141—q. 6: 181—q. 6, a. 1, c. ad 1am q.: 177—ad 3am q.: 177, 188.

De ver.—De veritate: 54, 281–283.

q. 1, a. 1: 164, 179—q. 2, a. 3, obj. 11 and ad 11um: 118—a. 4: 171—ad 4um: 171—q. 3 *(De ideis):* 193, 198—a. 1, ad 6um: 153—ad 7um: 110—ad 10um: 153—a. 3, *in fine:* 119—q. 4, a. 2, ad 4um: 141—q. 8, a. 3, ad 3um: 118—a. 16: 195—q. 10 *(De mente):* 102, 173, 193—a. 1: 167—a. 10: 176—q. 11 *(De magistro):* 174, 193—q. 12, a. 3, ad 3um and ad 12um: 122—a. 6: 118—q. 15 *(De superiori et inferiori ratione):* 159, 174—a. 1: 118, 171, 177—ad 1um: 132—q. 21 *(De bono):* 164, 179, 283—a. 1: 179, 189—a. 4, ad 3um: 174—a. 5: 193, 285—q. 24, a. 1: 184—a. 3: 118—a. 4: 163, 168—s.c.: 118—a. 5, s.c.: 184—q. 25, a. 7, ad 5um: 118—q. 26, a. 3: 119, 168—ad 10um: 114—a. 6, *in fine:* 118—a. 7, ad 3um: 118—a. 9, ad 3um: 118.

De pot.—De potentia Dei: 75, 281–283.

q. 3, a. 4, c.: 187—a. 5: 195—a. 6, ad 22um: 187—a. 15, ad 1um: 118, 187—ad 14um: 122—a. 17: 194, 195, 212—q. 5, a. 4, ad 3um: 160—q. 7, a. 1, obj. 1: 187—q. 9, a. 7: 285.

De malo—De malo: 281–283.

q. 1: 285—q. 2-7: 285—q. 3, a. 14, ad 2um: 135—q. 6, a. un.: 189, 284—q. 7-15: 285—q. 16: 285—a. 1, ad 3um: 228—ad 16um: 143.

De spirit. creat.—De spiritualibus creaturis: 281–282, 338.
   a. 3, ad 6um: 132—a. 5: 195—a. 8, 2a ratio: 185—ad 1um: 77,
   195—a. 9: 194—a. 10, ad 8um: 194.

De an.—De anima: 281–283, 285, 338.
   a. 3, ad 8um: 122—a. 5, ad 4um: 144—a. 6, ad 5um: 119—a. 21,
   ad 19um: 143.

De virt. in com.—De virtutibus in communi: 281–282.
   a. 1: 164, 285—a. 2: 158—a. 2–15: 285—a. 5: 285—a. 11: 195,
   285.

De spe—De spe: 282.
   a. 1: 163.

Quodl.—Quodlibetum: 80, 97, 285–287.
   I–VI: 286—I, a. 6: 325—II, a. 3: 160—III, a. 4: 287—III, a. 11–
   14: 342—a. 17, ad 1um: 153—a. 31, ad 1um: 139—IV, a. 18:
   87, 139, 155—a. 23–24: 283—V, a. 26: 347—VII–XI: 286—a. 14–
   18: 282—VII, a. 15, obj. 5: 254—XII: 286—a. 5: 160—a. 26, ad
   1um: 143.

*Cont. gent.—Summa contra gentiles (Liber de veritate catholicae fidei
   contra errores infidelium:* 292): 21, 38, 49, 54, 97, 151, 157, 275,
   288–296.
   I and II: 295—I–III: 293—I, c. 1: 293—c. 2: 293, 296—
   c. 3: 293—c. 4: 293—c. 5: 294—c. 8: 294–295—c. 9: 293, 294—
   c. 22: 122, 124, 165—c. 26: 195—c. 28–39: 195—c. 42: 180—
   c. 57: 197—II, c. 4: 294—III, c. 17: 118—c. 25–48: 179—c. 48,
   in fine: 347—c. 50 ff.: 296—IV: 292, 293, 296.

Summa—Summa theologiae: 29, 63, 68, 80, 93, 97, 124, 127, 157, 178,
   208, 209, 233, 259, 268, 271–276, 279, 285, 295, 297–322, 332.
Prol.: 266, 297, 300.
Ia Pars—Prima Pars: 55, 151, 160, 224, 274, 304, 310, 311, 313, 321.
   q. 1, a. 2: 133—a. 4: 312—a. 5: 312—a. 8, ad 2um: 139—a. 9:
   111—obj. 1: 170—a. 10: 257—ad 1um: 254—q. 2, prol.: 305—
   q. 6, a. 3: 285—q. 11, a. 3: 180—q. 12, a. 13, obj. 1 and ad 1um:
   166—q. 14, a. 6: 171—q. 19, a. 4, obj. 1: 118—ad 1um: 118, 171—
   q. 23, a. 4, obj. 1 and ad 1um: 118—q. 29, a. 1: 158—ad 4um:
   119—a. 2: 110—ad 1um: 141—q. 30, a. 3: 285—q. 32, a. 1: 186—
   ad 2um: 182—q. 34, a. 1: 279—q. 36, a. 1: 168—a. 2, ad 3um:
   152—q. 39, a. 5, ad 1um: 147—q. 43, a. 3: 181—q. 44, a. 3: 171—
   q. 44, a. 2: 195, 210—q. 48–64: 285—q. 54, a. 4, ad 2um: 120—
   q. 55, a. 3, ad 3um: 190—q. 63, a. 5: 136—q. 65–74: 159, 259, 316
   —q. 66, a. 3: 131—q. 67, a. 1: 172—q. 75–87: 285—q. 77, a. 5,
   ad 3um: 143—a. 7: 187—a. 8, ad 1um: 132—q. 78: 160—a. 2:
   187—q. 79, a. 2: 168—a. 7, ad 1um: 153—a. 8: 171—a. 10: 113—

a. 12: 163—a. 13: 113, 168—q. 84, a. 5: 175—obj. 1: 166—q. 94–102: 321—q. 115, a. 2: 119.

IIa Pars—Secunda Pars: 157, 160, 274, 304, 309–313, 315, 320.
  Ia–IIae—Prima pars secundae partis: 274, 301. prol.: 305, 313—q. 1 and 2: 189—q. 2, a. 1–8: 179—q. 3, a. 2, ad 2um: 160—a. 4: 179—a. 8, obj. 1: 166—q. 4, a. 1: 167—q. 7, a. 3: 159—q. 6, prol.: 313—q. 12, a. 1: 167—q. 17, a. 1: 179—q. 22, a. 1: 119, 168—q. 34, a. 4, s.c.: 219—q. 35, a. 8: 153, 159, 161—q. 41, a. 2: 162—a. 4: 159, 161—q. 46, a. 1: 162—a. 8: 159, 161—q. 48: 160—q. 49ff.: 164—q. 49, a. 1: 158—a. 2, ad 3um: 164—q. 50, a. 1: 153—q. 52, a. 1: 285—q. 55–69: 285—q. 55, a. 3, ad 3um: 158—a. 4: 158, 167, 169—q. 56, a. 3, ad 1um: 174—q. 57, a. 1, ad 1um: 168—q. 61, a. 3, obj.: 163—a. 4: 162—a. 5: 159—q. 63, a. 1: 170—q. 68, a. 1: 184—q. 71: 115—a. 6: 158—q. 68, a. 3: 163—q. 71–89: 285—q. 72: 162—q. 81–83: 321—q. 81, a. 1: 185—q. 82: 159—a. 3: 175—q. 92, a. 1, ad 2um: 168—a. 2: 161—q. 98–103: 316—q. 98–105: 259—q. 98–106: 316—q. 98, a. 1–3: 316—q. 102: 262—a. 2: 257—a. 6, ad 8um: 262—q. 104, a. 2, ad 2um: 256—q. 105: 159.

IIa–IIae—Secunda pars secundae partis: 50, 56, 157.
  q. 1, a. 1, ad 1um: 320—a. 2: 138, 193—a. 4, ad 2um and 3um: 120—a. 5, ad 1um: 120—q. 2, a. 1: 133, 159, 169—a. 3: 185—q. 4, a. 1: 159, 169, 262—q. 5, a. 1, ad 1um: 137—q. 17–33: 285—q. 23, a. 2, ad 1um: 142—a. 8: 133—q. 35–153: 285—q. 35, a. 5: 160—q. 43, a. 1: 158—q. 47, a. 10–12: 188—q. 48: 133—a. 1: 161—q. 51, a. 4: 162—q. 57, a. 3: 160—q. 58, a. 1: 158, 160, 167—q. 80, resp. ad obj.: 161—q. 81, a. 5ff.: 161—q. 123, a. 1, ad 1um: 158—a. 2: 158—q. 128, a. 1: 159, 161—q. 129, a. 4: 162—q. 132, a 5: 159—q. 148, a. 1: 161—a. 6: 159—q. 153, a. 5: 159—q. 158, a. 7: 159—q. 159, a. 2: 160—q. 163–165: 321—q. 171–174: 321—q. 180, a. 6: 171, 178—q. 182–189: 343—q. 183–189: 321.

IIIa Pars—Tertia pars: 151, 274, 285, 301, 304, 310, 313, 315, 320.
  prol.: 313—q. 1: 308—a. 2: 186—a. 7: 308—q. 2, a. 1: 119—q. 4, a. 3, ad 1um: 147—q. 22: 263—q. 27–59: 259, 316—q. 30–58: 159—q. 40, a. 2 and 3: 262—q. 46, a. 4: 262—q. 63: 263—q. 64: 263—a. 3: 159, 176, 193—q. 65, a. 1: 183—q. 69, a. 6: 138—q. 76, a. 7: 120—q. 82, a. 8, ad 1um: 144—q. 83, a. 5, ad 8um: 134—q. 85: 161—q. 90: 300.

De ente—De ente et essentia: 180, 330–332, 346.
  c. 5, n. 31: 332.

De subst. separ.—De substantiis separatis: 324.
  c. 5, n. 19: 190.

Resp. de art. XLII—Responsio ad fratrem Joannem . . . de articulis XLII: 326, 333–335.

    a. 33, n. 806: 207, 324, 335.

Resp. de art. VI—Responsio ad lectorem Bisuntinum de articulis VI: 327, 336.

    q. 5, n. 939: 336.

De reg. princ.—De regimine principum ad regem Cypri: 326, 336–337.

    I, 12: 188.

De unit. int.—De unitate intellectus contra Averroistas: 325, 337–338, 346, 347.

    c. 1, n. 179: 144—n. 181: 144, 208—n. 185: 208—n. 199: 211— n. 200: 211—c. 2, n. 214: 39, 192.

Cont. imp. Dei cult.—Contra impugnantes Dei cultum: 268, 327, 340– 342, 347.

    prooem., n. 3: 192, 341.

De per. vit. sp.—De perfectione vitae spiritualis: 327, 342, 347.

    c. 26, n. 734: 347—n. 764: 191.

Cont. err. Graec.—Contra errores Graecorum ad Urbanum IV Pontificem maximum: 150, 292, 327, 343–344, 347, 348.

    prooem., n. 1029: 141, 149—c. 10, n. 1050: 141.

In symb. Apost.—Devotissima expositio super symbolum apostolorum: 328.

    prol., n. 862: 324.

Technical Words and Expressions (c)

I. Latin

ab aeterno: 339.
acedia: 153.
actio: 130.
actor: 129, 130.
ad hominem: 211; —*ad positionem:* 211.
adaptationes: 162.
aestimatio: 113.
(agens), see *ordo agentium . . . ;* —*intellectus agens.*
allegoria: 256.
an sit: 110.
anagogia: 256.
analogia entis: 165; —*analogia fidei:* 165.
anima: 101, 102.
anitas: 110.
antiqui: 137, 138, 271, 272.
appetitus inquisitivus: 121.
arguere: 94.
argumentari: 94.
ars: 104; —*ars sermocinalis:* 62; —*ars imitatur naturam:* 187.
artefactum: 196.
artes dictaminis: 31; —*artes reales:* 62.
articulus: 93; —*articuli iterum remissi:* 334.
artificialis: 161.
auctor, auctores: 65, 82, 83, 126, 129–131, 137, 151.
auctorabilis: 130, 137.
auctoritas, auctoritates: 20, 83, 127, 129–136, 138, 139, 142, 144; —*auctoritas magistralis:* 136. —*auctoritas magistrorum:* 135. —*auctoritas sanctorum:* 135. —*auctoritatum concordantia:* 140.

auditus fidei: 69.
aura: 173.
aut(h)enticus: 129–132.
autentim: 129.
aut(h)or: 129–131.

baccalaureus biblicus: 242, 264. —*baccalaureus sententiarius:* 265.
biblice: 243.

capitula: 271.
capitulatio: 47, 52.
caritas, see *fides, caritas, sacramentum.*
causa essendi: 56; —*causa est in causato per modum causati:* 186; —*cursus causae in causatum:* 177; —see also *primum in . . .*
circulatio: 172.
circumstantia litterae, see *littera.*
civitas: 252.
claustrales: 236.
cogitare: 120.
cogitatio: 114.
cogitativa: 114.
collatio: 98, 237, 245, 258.
commentator: 230.
compendium: 298.
compositio: 125.
conceptiones: 225; —*communes animi conceptiones:* 186.
concordantiae: 273.
conscientia: 113.
consensus: 161.
constructio: 251.
continuatio: 172, 251.
contra, see *pro et contra;* —*sed contra.*
conveniens: 185.

c) Latin and Greek technical words and expressions are translated either on the first page on which they appear or on the page where explanations about them are given.

II. Greek

Proper Names of Persons

377